A HISTORY
OF
EARLY AMERICAN MAGAZINES

A HISTORY
of
EARLY AMERICAN MAGAZINES
1741-1789

by

LYON N. RICHARDSON

1966
OCTAGON BOOKS, INC.
New York

Reprinted by
special arrangement with Lyon N. Richardson

OCTAGON BOOKS, INC.
175 FIFTH AVENUE
NEW YORK, N.Y. 10010

LIBRARY OF CONGRESS CATALOG CARD NUMBER: 66-28376

Printed in U.S.A. by
NOBLE OFFSET PRINTERS, INC.
NEW YORK 3, N. Y.

TO
NORMAN GOFF RICHARDSON
ELLA LYON RICHARDSON
AND
HELEN HARTMAN RICHARDSON
IN TESTIMONY OF THEIR SEVERAL QUALITIES IN
THIS WORK

CONTENTS

PREFACE

In 1927, when work on this book began, little scholarly attention had been paid to magazines in America. Isaiah Thomas, in *The History of Printing in America* (1810 and 1874) had treated of a long period of publishing with invaluable reminiscent intimacy, but his comments on magazines had been brief; Albert H. Smyth, in *The Philadelphia Magazines and their Contributors 1741-1850* (1892), had called more particular attention to a limited field; Algernon Tassin, in *The Magazine in America* (1916) had written a popular and interesting summary in a small book which served its purpose well, though the author turned quickly to the nineteenth century for the larger game. Other scattered slight accounts and references lay in volumes engaged in their several diverse subjects. Frank Luther Mott was engaged in the first careful undertaking in the nature of a survey, and his estimable labors have since (1930) in part appeared in *A History of American Magazines 1741-1850.* But he accorded the eighteenth century limited and minor attention.

The present book has been written from a somewhat different point of view. The years 1741-1789—from the time the first two magazines appeared through the year of Washington's election to the Presidency—have been chosen as a restricted period for a much more elaborate and detailed study of the magazines published during those years than others attempted in previous surveys. The contents of the thirty-seven periodicals I have included for study, the incidents in the lives of the men involved with respect to their publications, the general circumstances of publishing, and the literary and historical trends of the period have been my special interests. A study of manuscripts, newspapers, and complete files and annotated copies of the magazines has served to throw further light on these subjects than is contained in existing surveys or in the many books which have treated of matters briefly crossing the field of early American magazines. In this quest I have found the libraries in New York, Boston, Philadelphia, Worcester, New Haven, and Washington the most serviceable for the project, but

I am also indebted for courtesies extended while I was working in Cambridge, Providence, Hartford, Newark, and Princeton. For library loans from collections in Iowa, Wisconsin, and Illinois I am also grateful.

In general, the term *magazine*, as its name implies, was used to designate a general miscellany or repository of instruction and amusement. It was also used commonly in the eighteenth century as a title for books which were collections of information on various subjects, such as *The Young Man's Magazine: Containing the Substance of Moral Philosophy and Divinity, Selected from the Works of the Most Eminent for Wisdom, Learning, and Virtue, among the Ancients and Moderns* (Philadelphia, 1786) and *The Young Misses Magazine. Containing Dialogues between a Governess and Several Young Ladies her Scholars* (Philadelphia, 1787). I have excluded publications of this latter kind, restricting the list to issues printed periodically. I have not, however, limited the magazines to general miscellanies, nor to stitched or stapled pamphlets issued regularly. The connotative implications of the terms *pamphlet, periodical, magazine, journal, review,* and *newspaper* are fairly distinctive and may be defined. But specific periodicals are often less easy to classify. My purpose, moreover, has been to present an adequate history of the general field, and I have on occasion expanded the bounds beyond those encompassed within rigid definition when such a measure seemed appropriate to the general theme of the book. For various reasons, explained in the text, I have therefore included *The Independent Reflector* (with its cohorts, *The Occasional Reverberator* and *John Englishman*), an essay-periodical; *The Instructor*, a true though most diminutive miscellany; *The Penny Post*, a unique diminutive newspaper, but in some respects not unlike *The Instructor, The North-Carolina Magazine: or, Universal Intelligencer, The New-Haven Gazette, and the Connecticut Magazine, The Worcester Magazine*, and the *Courier de Boston*, periodicals which, though pamphlets or newspapers in the basic sense of the words, were printed on pages of less than folio size and were published as essay-journal-magazines or newspaper-magazines.

I am happy to recall associations which this work has fostered. To Professor Ralph Leslie Rusk, of Columbia University, I am greatly indebted for his careful inspection of the manuscript and

many suggestions and criticisms. To Professor Ashley H. Thorn-
dike, Professor Emery E. Neff, Professor Evarts B. Greene, Pro-
fessor Dixon R. Fox, and Professor Frederick W. J. Heuser, of
Columbia University; Dean Elbert J. Benton, Professor Finley M.
K. Foster, Dean W. D. Trautman, Professor James H. Hanford,
Professor Frederick H. H. Adler, and Dr. Oscar F. Ellis, of
Western Reserve University, and Dr. Homer F. Barnes, of the
Kamehameha Schools, Honolulu, I am grateful for comments on
parts of the text. I have incurred also a large debt to many
librarians, and it is a pleasure to express my appreciation to
Messrs. J. B. Elliott, L. Nelson Nichols, Victor Hugo Paltsits,
and W. R. Leech, of the New York Public Library; Mr.
Clarence S. Brigham and Mrs. Mary Robinson, of the American
Antiquarian Society; Mr. George F. Strong, Mrs. Mary Cutting
Smith, Mrs. Marguerite Carver, and Miss Estelle Hudson, of Hatch
Library, Western Reserve University; Mr. J. H. Tuttle and Mrs.
Clara P. Shephardson, of the Massachusetts Historical Society;
Mr. George S. Godard, of the Connecticut State Library; Mr.
Albert C. Bates, of the Connecticut Historical Society; Mr. A. J.
Wall, of the New York Historical Society; Miss Isadore Gilbert
Mudge, of the Columbia University Library; Miss Anne S. Pratt,
of the Yale University Library; Mr. V. Valta Parma, of the
Library of Congress; Mr. Bunford Samuel, of the Library Com-
pany of Philadelphia; Mr. Lawrence C. Wroth, of the John
Carter Brown Library; Mr. George F. Baker, of the New York
Society Library; Mrs. Elizabeth Maxwell Sullivan, of the Western
Reserve Historical Society; and Mr. Harry Givens, of the His-
torical Society of Pennsylvania.

Finally, I wish to express my appreciation to my wife for her
sympathetic and unfailing assistance, especially in the preparation
of a working index of several thousand titles of articles in the
magazines of the period.

L. N. R.

Western Reserve University, August, 1931.

INTRODUCTION

A GREAT number of the subscribers to American magazines in the eighteenth century considered themselves patrons to these ventures in publishing. They were eager to advance the state of culture, to disseminate knowledge, and to support and preserve the literary and practical arts manifest in their young land. In a letter to Mathew Carey written in 1788, Washington expressed himself as being highly concerned in the success of magazines: "I consider such easy vehicles of knowledge," he wrote, "more happily calculated than any other, to preserve the liberty, stimulate the industry and meliorate the morals of an enlightened and free people." The files of magazines to which he personally subscribed, preserved at the Boston Athenæum, are a testimony of the sincerity of his conviction, which arose perhaps from his observation of the limited channels of communication. This conviction was in no way peculiar to him or the decade of the letter; the rosters of subscribers printed occasionally in some of the later magazines approximate lists of names of men well recognized as national or local leaders in politics, business, science, higher education, law, medicine, and religion. It is not unmeet that present-day readers of eighteenth-century magazines assume a point of view equally sympathetic.

The spirit of the majority of the editors was highly serious. They strove to make their magazines valuable "repositories" and "museums" of thought both current and past. Their ideal was to publish a "miscellany" of ample proportions, filled with subject matter as broad as the interests of a large group of cultivated men, and as carefully presented as in the encyclopedias which were the pride of the age. They hoped, also, that each number would "instruct and amuse," and thus perform the dual function of enlightenment and entertainment. They did not look upon the issues as ephemeral; often the intent was to publish periodically a collection of writings later to be appropriately bound and given an exalted place as fit "furniture" for every man's library. Before new magazines were launched, elaborate "proposals" were usually published, soliciting the kindly regard of all persons interested in the "preser-

vation" and "encouragement" of the noble estate of literature—
which embraced moral, political, and philosophical essays, fiction,
and poetry—and of the associated expository and narrative arts as
practised in the memoir, biography, history, narrative of adventure,
or account of discovery in science.

The men who were attracted to the idea of establishing or conducting magazines were not only of high purpose, but usually of
abilities somewhat distinguished, though their capacities were seldom
journalistic. Astute publishers, historians, ministers, lawyers, and
educators responded to the editorial urge: Benjamin Franklin,
Andrew Bradford, Jeremy Gridley, Thomas Prince, Jr., William
Livingston, William Smith, Samuel Nevill, Christopher Saur, Lewis
Nicola, Isaiah Thomas, Thomas Paine, Hugh Henry Brackenridge, Samuel Parker, Josiah Meigs, Noah Webster, Thomas Coke,
Francis Asbury, Joseph Nancrède, David Austin, and Mathew
Carey. Through their own writings and selections of extracts
from printed sources, or through the stimulus they incited in others
of established powers or of youthful ambitions, the service these
editors rendered to eighteenth-century literature and thought in
America was considerable. Only occasionally did subscription lists
attain one thousand to sixteen hundred names, and probably the
average list did not extend beyond five hundred; so doubtless the
total copies of magazines printed at any one time did not exceed
twenty-five hundred until the decade of the 1780's, when the lists
expanded rapidly and the number of magazines increased. But
they were a type of literary conveyance likely to be carefully preserved, and the total number of readers was comparatively large.
Furthermore, the important materal in any one magazine often was
reprinted in other magazines and newspapers, and thus came to be
widely distributed.

The leading printers of the eighteenth-century magazines, nearly
all of whom had been, or were at the time, publishers of newspapers, were moved to engage in the several projects in efforts to
extend their fortunes and serve American culture. In the former
endeavor they were almost uniformly unsuccessful. Advertising
was in its long infancy, and brief advertisements occasionally placed
on the covers, or in supplements, or in rare instances on the final
inside pages of the magazines, brought a negligible income. The
publishers, dependent on subscribers for support, soon tired of their

engagements, and most of the magazines were abandoned within a year or two; only two, *The Massachusetts Magazine* and *The New-York Magazine*, lived through a span of eight years. At most, a precarious living wage was the reward. But to these printers as agents serving American culture, their own age and ours owe a noteworthy debt.

The normal subscription price hovered around a shilling a number: the smaller journals sold for a trifle less and the larger miscellanies for slightly more, though the latter were frequently accompanied by such special inducements as supplements, gazetteers, or separately paged serial publications generally historical in content. The cost of postal delivery was slight; the usual practice was for the publisher to make special arrangements with the carriers or to present them with welcome gifts. No uniform system seems to have been in force until the tenth decade, when rates were established by law.

I

I have aimed chiefly to present the period in all its phases of thought and emotion as preserved in the miscellanies, to treat minutely of the histories of the magazines and their editors and publishers, and unstintedly to supply details and references which may be of service to scholars in their special investigations.

In the eighteenth century, as now, the vital political questions were largely economic in origin. Between 1741 and 1789 three wars were fought which culminated in major political adjustments —King George's War, the French and Indian War, and the Revolutionary War. Extension of territory, control of taxation, power of Colonial and later of State legislatures, treaties with Indian tribes, security of trade lanes, advancement of industry and commerce, and issuance of currency were among the problems of great moment, and the literature of economics and politics is a major element in the contents of the magazines. The student of fiscal matters alone will find hundreds of pages devoted to the subject. The magazines gave other hundreds of pages to interpretations of history and current events designed to convince readers at first of the advantages of the success of British arms over those of France and Spain, and later of the advantages of a sovereign federal government in America. Especially dramatic in theme and instructive in political wisdom are the magazines of the ninth decade, when came the recognition that independence had not brought equality or a happy solution of the ills of man in society. Considerations of state and federal constitutions, of division of legislative representation and authority, and of financial structures became vital, searching inquiries. The whole economic life seemed sick. Agriculture pointed accusing fingers at seaboard cities. Men in commerce and industry shook unavailing fists at English trade regulations. The bankers saw unsound currency and mounting debt everywhere. Fitful fires of internecine war cast lights on the horizon which some observers feared were direly prophetic. A young, incompleted political structure was called upon to quell and satisfy all these warring interests, and the magazines offer authentic, detailed pictures of these stirring times which are invaluable to historians.

Social history abounds in these records. In New York there was early agitation for a democratic structure in the administration of the college by means of trustees appointed by the legislature. Occasional rationalizations on curricula urged less of traditional discipline and more of "practical" content. In the Middle Colonies especially, the virtues of a collegiate education for the female mind were advanced, and the traditional theory of subservience of woman to man found opposition. A plan for a federal university was projected. Ideas on elementary education centered in discussions on home training and, among the Germans, on religious instruction. The evils of slavery were attacked by religious and humanitarian pleas coming from both America and England. Prohibition of the stronger alcoholic liquors found its champions. The administration of prisons and the punishments required by law for crimes were philosophically analyzed and discussed. Antiquarian lore was gathered diligently, and though adventure and exploration increased the interest in accounts of Indians, there did exist a genuine interest in the customs and history of the aborigines. Philadelphia was the center from which emanated more philosophical inquiries of social concern than from any other one place.

In religion, the magazines tell a story of the clash of conservative and radical forces in Protestant New England, of deism versus orthodoxy, of the rise and spread of "The Great Awakening" throughout the Colonies, of the potency of Anglican rule in New York and South Carolina amidst divers creeds, of the influence of Friends, German Mennonites, and Calvinists in and about Philadelphia, of the rise of Methodism, of a liberal Yale graduate's encyclopedic fervor in New Jersey, and of anti-Catholic sentiment merged with political hatred for France and Spain during the middle years—an aversion which was somewhat mitigated in the magazines during the Revolution because of French alliance, and which was absent from the two important magazines edited by Mathew Carey.

The century was alive with the spirit of scientific observation, and the magazines are ample testimony of the high regard held not only for men of science in the universities but for careful historians of natural phenomena everywhere. No publication worthy the title of miscellany failed to include numerous articles of interest to the medical profession. Hardly secondary was the mass of editorial content linking science and invention with better methods of manufacture and mining. Natural phenomena were everywhere collected or recorded. Correspondence among scientists was encouraged. At Philadelphia, the American Philosophical Society, as well as other societies for the promotion of manufacturing and of agriculture, offered the advantages of the collective findings of groups; and the publications of these societies were augmented in the magazines by selections from the publications of the Royal Society, the Dublin Society, and other foreign groups.

It is fair to the spirit of the magazines, however, to pay chief attention to the literary elements, and this book is chiefly concerned with these matters. The age was predominantly didactic; and the essay form, to which Addison and Steele had given both popularity and the touch of genius, throve lustily. Few could approach these great partners either in quality of idea or skill in treatment. In less capable hands, the light social essay for female readers too often frothed; the sentiment too often sickened, and in both idea and structure the essay would lose itself in vague ramifications. But the New World was not lacking in social, religious, political, moral, and fanciful thought. Coherent, incisive, and emotionalized were the styles of Gridley, Livingston, Dickinson, Jay, Hamilton, Ames, Ellsworth, Sherman, Coxe, Paine, the younger Lincoln, and William Smith of New York, to call but a partial roll. Greenleaf,

Witherspoon, Rush, Brackenridge, Stiles, and James Freeman, among others, controlled styles suited to the proper expression of their valued ideas. A native wit, a sound judgment, much practical experience, and the influence of Addison, the Bible, England, and France made Franklin the master essayist of his century. In the work of Dwight, Freneau, Hopkinson, Webster, Provost Smith, Crèvecoeur, Brown, and a score of others may be seen the results of conscious striving for literary artistry. Native essay-series were not uncommon. Wit, melancholy, satire, argument, and reason were borrowed from the works of, or the comments upon, such French and English authors of note as Voltaire, Rousseau, Montesquieu, Chateaubriand, Chastellux, Bacon, Locke, Hume, Swift, Chesterfield, Goldsmith, Johnson, Jenyns, and Burke.

Literary criticism was timid when dealing with contemporary authors; and Webster is to be noted as the first editor (1787-88) in America to engage considerably in careful, sincere criticism of native work. But the values of the classics were assayed, general trends in the current style were scrutinized, the anatomy of rhetoric was studied systematically, and several essays in etymology appeared. The neoclassicism of Boileau, the invective of Byles and Ladd against the Grub Street manner, the observations of Webster on language in general and the poetry of Dwight in particular, original and borrowed comment on the literary qualities of Vergil, Shakespeare, Milton, Richardson, Fielding, and Goldsmith, and selections from Hugh Blair's studies in rhetoric are found in the magazines, and are examples enough to indicate to the literary critic and historian that the content of the periodicals is worth his study.

The essay was a principal root of the fiction. In general a dramatic mode, such as the use of conversation, was not practised widely, though one complete drama and occasionally excerpts from plays were reprinted in the magazines. The illustrative incident so often imbedded in essays became the conventional story or "novel" by the simple process of raising and expanding it to a position of chief importance. The usual narrative point of view was that of the omnipotent author, though the first person singular was also frequently employed because of the popularity of the confidential letter and the memoir as narrative devices lending intimacy and verisimilitude to the stories. During the early decades of the period the amount of prose fiction in the magazines was meager, but Nicola in 1769 and Thomas in 1774 used stories in growing quantities. Sentiment and sensibility ruled in letters, memoirs, biographies, allegories, Oriental tales, and other forms of fiction. Richardson, Day, and Mackenzie were the tutors; the preservation of female chastity in a world of rakes, the tendency of wealth to breed avarice and arrogance, and the sad, ineffectual reactions of over-sensitized souls were principal themes. The bulk of the fiction was reprinted from British magazines, though some was written in America. Amidst the mediocre deluge, it is a pleasure to note during the eighth and ninth decades a thin stream of finished allegories by Hopkinson and others, and an occasional satire of quality, such as Belknap's *The Foresters.*

The history of English poetry in the eighteenth century is the history of Colonial poetry in the same general period, though the Colonies dragged behind by a score of years. In the earlier magazines are poems in the elder mode—translations from the Latin, heroic couplets, elegies, pastorals, songs, eclogues, epigrams, riddles, paraphrases, and general light verse. In the later magazines are found blank verse, Miltonic octosyllabics, political satire in several forms, and odes replete with romantic melancholy and a true regard for the out-doors. The influences of Horace, Milton, Dryden, Pope, Addison, Prior, Gay, Pomfret, Butler, Thomson, Macpherson, Gray, and Young are definite; selections from or parodies of their work appeared, and also excerpts from the pens of Cowley, Garth, Swift, Parnell, Duncombe, Goldsmith, Collins, Johnson, Falconer, Burns, Cowper, and many others. Shakespeare was parodied; Moschus, Vergil, Congreve and Racine were not unknown. Elaborate rhythms and rimes were attempted by Colonial poets; hymns, odes, epitaphs, and epithalamiums were not uncommon. No decade was without light verse, and it was especially popular in Boston in the middle decades of the century. The colleges bred light verse, translations from Latin poets, and lyrics and odes in the grand manner of Dryden and Pope. Patriotic lyrics, epics, and satires filled the years of the Revolution and after. An age which produced *M'Fingal, The Vision of Columbus, The Anarchiad,* and *The Conquest of Canäan* was an age convinced of the importance of poetry. To list the names of Sterling, Godfrey, Evans, Hopkinson, Davies, Freneau, Paine, Trumbull, Humphreys, Barlow,

Hopkins, Timothy and Theodore Dwight, Brackenridge, Richards, Wheatley, Coombe, and Ladd is to give but some of the many whose work appeared in the magazines either as original or selected fare for their readers.

Careful attention has been paid to the "embellishments" inserted by editors to attract subscribers. In main, copperplate engravings were used, though some work was done on wood. I have endeavored to list, so far as possible, all pictures, including music plates, cartoons, and illustrations of famous men and women, of homes of the great, of notable ceremonies, of major scenic attractions in America, and of inventions and discoveries in science, as well as scenes depicting interesting characters and events in the fiction. Some of the engravers, notably Paul Revere, Joseph Callender, John Norman, Robert Aitken, Amos Doolittle, and James Trenchard are worthy of special mention.

CHAPTER I

ENGLISH AND AMERICAN BACKGROUNDS

WITH unrestrained pride, the author of the preface to the eighth volume of *The Gentleman's Magazine*[1] (London, 1738) surveyed the history of the first eight years of the publication of magazines or miscellanies in England. "The Success of the *Gentleman's Magazine*," he wrote, "has given Rise to almost twenty Imitations of it, which are either all dead, or very little regarded by the World."[2] This statement, of course, and others which followed, were somewhat biased. Not all of the journals had come to a state of "primitive Nothing." If they were "little regarded by the World," at least *The Gentleman's Magazine* had regarded some of them as acceptable sources for much of its borrowed material. It seems not unlikely, moreover, as David Nichol Smith[3] has suggested, that the occasion for calling *The Grub-street Journal* an "Enemy of all Works of Merit" may have arisen from a previous complaint in the *Memoirs of the Society of Grub-street* (1737) that *The Gentleman's Magazine* was filching too profusely from its rivals. Then, too, the preface failed to view the condition of magazine publication from other possible angles; there was no mention, for example, of *The London Magazine*,[4] which for six years had been a truly successful rival. But if one views the scene in a larger perspective, he finds much in the preface which accurately conveys the journalistic atmosphere of the time. There had indeed appeared a flock of magazines imitating the first great miscellany,

[1] "To the Reader," page unnumbered. The editor of the magazine was Edward Cave, who adopted the pseudonym of "Sylvanus Urban," but the preface was written by Samuel Johnson, *The Works of Samuel Johnson, LL.D.* (1825), V, 345-47. The full title of the magazine is *The Gentleman's Magazine: or, Monthly Intelligencer.*

[2] A note lists the "imitations": "The *Weekly Magazine*, the *Gentleman's Magazine* and *Oracle*, the *Universal Magazine*, the *General Magazine*, the *Oxford Magazine*, the *Distillers Magazine*, the *Country Magazine*, the *Manchester Magazine*, the *Leeds Magazine*, the *Dublin Magazine*, and the *Lady's Magazine; with* several other of the like Kind, all dwindled to their primitive Nothing; to which we may add the *Bee*, and *Grub-street Journal*, that Enemy of all Works of Merit."

[3] *The Cambridge History of English Literature*, X, 183.

[4] *The London Magazine: or Gentleman's Monthly Intelligencer.*

The Gentleman's Magazine, shortly after its initial number (January 1731) had shown the way to a somewhat different method of appealing to the public. With more of belligerent zeal than originality of thought, these imitators had labored in a circumscribed literary area; consequently, the mortality had been great, and even the better members of the group, with few exceptions, had attained only to a precarious existence.

The true magazines or miscellanies of the 1730's were to a considerable extent enlargements of the essay-journals which had for the two previous decades carried on the traditions, though not the genius, of *The Tatler* and *The Spectator* (1709-12). During these decades the influence of Addison and Steele dominated the prose style, and the format as well as many of the essays of these two periodicals lived in the host of imitations which had followed them. The field was over-crowded, and in general the periodicals lacked the vitality worthy of existence.

Edward Cave made the real forward step, advancing beyond the highly competitive field of essay-journals bolstered with bits of news. The ethics which are expressed in the copyright laws of the present day were not conceived in the eighteenth century. Cave imagined a journal larger than its competitors, filled with extracts from them, and offering greater variety as well as bulk. There had been a kind of predecessor: Peter Motteux, thinking of *Le Mercure Galant*, had established an excellent literary journal, ill-managed financially, *The Gentleman's Journal; or Monthly Miscellany* (1692-94).[5] But for the second quarter of the eighteenth century *The Gentleman's Magazine* was a new departure; in it the subscribers could read an edited composite of the leading periodicals.[6] In addition to the essays, comprising about twenty pages of each monthly issue, there were several pages devoted to selected and sometimes original poetry, and a dozen pages consisting of "The Monthly Intelligencer," a department using newspaper reports as grist for its mill in presenting domestic and foreign news, vital statistics, prices current, and book lists.

[5] For a good presentation of the origins and developments of British literary periodicals, see Walter Graham, *English Literary Periodicals* (1930).

[6] During the first three months alone, Edward Cave, as "Sylvanus Urban," supplied his readers with essays from *The Craftsman, London Journal, Fog's Weekly Journal, The Grub-street Journal, The Universal Spectator, The Weekly Register, The Free Briton, The British Journal: or, The Traveller, Reed's Journal, The Daily Post, The Templer, Applebee's Journal,* and *The Hyp Doctor.*

By the close of 1740 certain minor changes had taken place. The leading feature of *The Gentleman's Magazine* had come to be an original contribution, made famous by Samuel Johnson, the "Proceedings and Debates in the Senate of Lilliput," a thinly disguised report of Parliamentary activities. Not only essays, but extracts from books and pamphlets were used, together with letters to the magazine and occasional engravings. *The London Magazine*, now the chief rival of *The Gentleman's*, was similarly edited, even to the publishing of a counterbalancing feature, the "Journal of the Proceedings and Debates of the Political Club." But the general scheme of conducting magazines had not been altered broadly. To the minds of editors and subscribers alike, a magazine was a repository of collected pieces of wit and learning selected for amusement or instruction: moral and political and economic essays, travelogues, visions and dreams, Oriental fables pointed with axioms of wisdom, light verse, wit directed against social foibles, instruction in the manners of etiquette, news, and, for the sentimental readers, tales of devotion which pointed the way of virtue, whether melancholy with false or blithe with true love. The successful editor was he who could present an attractive array of such "selected pieces," as the borrowed articles were called.

Exactly a decade elapsed between the establishment of *The Gentleman's Magazine* and the appearance of the first two magazines of British America. During this time the English periodicals circulated in the important centers of Colonial population, as newspaper advertisements testify. Later they maintained themselves as successful rivals of the Colonial magazines in the several provinces, and were, indeed, a main source from which the American editors selected materials.

Throughout this same decade (1731-41) the American newspapers continued, as in the past, to furnish their readers with the forms of literature current in the English periodicals, both original and borrowed.[7] The obstacles to easy communication in winter tended further to increase the literary content of the papers during this season, when news was secured with difficulty. The establishment of *The New-England Courant* (1721-27?) by James Frank-

[7] Elizabeth Christine Cook has written a delightful account of this phase of Colonial literary activity: *Literary Influences in Colonial Newspapers 1704-1750* (1912). See also Walter Graham, "Notes on Literary Periodicals in America before 1800," in *Western Reserve University Bulletin*, August 1927, pp. 5-27.

lin, who had recently returned to Boston from England, marked
the coming of an enlivened satirical force in Massachusetts.   With
his "Hell-Fire" club cronies, a library which was his boast, and a
challenging attitude against certain ecclesiastical powers, he mixed
some of the directness of Swift with some of the elegance of Addison, and created a little world of fictitious characters in the manner
of a *Spectator* grown satirical.   In this paper also appeared Benjamin Franklin's Dogood papers and many essays clipped from
English periodicals.

From a literary point of view, *The New-England Courant* easily
outshone its longer-established rivals, *The Boston News-Letter*
(1704-63) and *The Boston Gazette* (1719-41).[8]   But another
paper in the same city, *The New-England Weekly Journal* (1727-
41),[9] conducted by Samuel Kneeland, was a worthy contemporary
and successor.   Though the essayists who gathered about it more
closely imitated the mood and style in *The Spectator* than those
who wrote for *The New-England Courant*,[10] they were often fresh
in their choice of settings; and whereas the writers for *The New-
England Courant* were often limited to satire on local conditions,
the essayists in *The New-England Weekly Journal* were pleasingly
inclined to indulge their fancies in realms more purely imaginative.
It is probable that Judge Danforth and Thomas Prince, and certain
that Mather Byles, contributed prose or poetry to the paper,[11] as
did Matthew Adams,[12] formerly of the "Hell-Fire" group.   When
native art was lacking, clippings from English periodicals filled the
pages.   To the Boston group also belongs *The Weekly Rehearsal*
(1731-35).[13]   During the time of Jeremy Gridley's editorship—
somewhat over a year—the young Boston attorney gave to this
paper a distinctly literary cast.   His style was Addisonian, but he

[8] The paper was combined in the latter year with *The New-England Weekly Journal*
to form *The Boston Gazette and Weekly Journal*.

[9] See note 8.

[10] The Hon. Charles Gravely, Esq., and Mr. Honeysuckle are, for example, reminiscent
of Sir Roger de Coverley and Mr. Honeycomb.

[11] Isaiah Thomas, *The History of Printing in America* (1810 and 1874; the reference
is from the latter edition, II, 41-42.   See also Arthur W. H. Eaton, *The Famous
Mather Byles* (1914), p. 34, and Joseph T. Buckingham, *Specimens of Newspaper
Literature* (1852), I, 89-111, for definite attributions to Byles.   Miss Viola C. White,
of Brooklyn, N. Y., kindly corroborated this evidence in a letter dated Nov. 22, 1930.

[12] Delano A. Goddard, "The Press and Literature of the Provincial Period," in *The
Memorial History of Boston* (1881), edited by Justin Winsor, II, 396, note 2.

[13] The paper became in the latter year *The Boston Evening-Post*.

often drew from his knowledge of classical literature and his university studies, and though his work has some of the conceit of youth, it likewise has its fragrance.

In the Middle Colonies the usual traditions of the time were maintained. *The American Weekly Mercury* (1719-46),[14] owned and edited by Andrew Bradford in Philadelphia, copied selections from English books and periodicals,[15] contained many appropriations from American presses, and contributed in return its own original essays—among them the Busy-Body papers, of which six were written by Benjamin Franklin. On a far more limited scale, *The Universal Instructor in All Arts and Sciences: and Pennsylvania Gazette* (1728-29)[16] conducted by Samuel Keimer, followed the usual method of entertaining its readers with articles taken from other journals, and instructed them with solid material such as could be found in Chambers's *Universal Dictionary*. When Benjamin Franklin and Hugh Meredith took over Keimer's paper and rechristened it *The Pennsylvania Gazette* (1729-1845),[17] the journal gained in importance, competed successfully with *The American Weekly Mercury's* display of standard authors and contemporary periodicals, and was enlivened by Franklin's own schooled pen and editorial acumen. In a neighboring province *The New-York Gazette* (1725-73),[18] conducted by the experienced and conservative William Bradford, kept rather closely to a pattern of pure news, lightened by essays on morals and manners selected from English periodicals. But John Peter Zenger, at the helm of *The New-York Weekly Journal*, steered a more tempestuous course, creating on occasion fictitious characters as instruments to use in his satirical crusade against laws of libel, and filling many columns with the wit of dissent.

[14] Andrew Bradford died in November 1742, but the paper was continued by his widow. In 1746 the paper was discontinued.

[15] *The London Magazine, The Gentleman's Magazine, The Universal Spectator,* and others.

[16] The paper was sold in the latter year to Franklin and Meredith.

[17] During its long life it passed through several changes of name and was suspended on several occasions, but it did not lose its identity until merged in the latter year with *The Daily North American*.

[18] Charles Evans, *American Bibliography* (1903-   ), No. 2688, notes that Bradford continued the paper about sixteen years, and that *The New York Evening Post* (est. 1744) is said to be a continuation of Bradford's paper. Parker, who established *The New-York Weekly Post-Boy* in 1743, altered the name in 1747 to *The New-York Gazette, Revived in the Weekly Post-Boy*.

The South found the newspaper a channel especially apt for its needs, as it offered an outlet for literary energies otherwise somewhat checked by mechanical limitations. *The Maryland Gazette* (1727-30),[19] published at Annapolis by William Parks, who knew English methods first hand, has become justly famous for its original poetry and essays. Parks's English borrowings—which included ideas and material from *The Free-Thinker* of Ambrose Philips and *The Intelligencer* of Sheridan and Swift—reflect most of the types current in periodicals. Possibly the most remarkable series of native essays appearing in a Colonial newspaper of the time was the "Monitor" group in *The Virginia Gazette* (1736-50),[20] a paper established by Parks at Williamsburg upon his leaving Annapolis. These essays were full of verve and imagination, of odd types of ladies and gentlemen in their several humors, and of choice eighteenth-century phraseology. Their authors have never been ascertained, though it seems reasonable to suppose that a group connected with the College of William and Mary probably wrote them.[21] With Parks should be associated, in editorial ability, Thomas Whitmarsh, who made *The South-Carolina Gazette* (1732-33)[22] highly entertaining with the Meddler's Club series of moral essays. Both *The Virginia Gazette* and *The South-Carolina Gazette* followed the customary policy of using selections from English publications.

Thus passed the decades before 1740 in British America. It was a period conditioned by eighteenth-century English writers and periodicals, with manifestations of original work appearing in the efforts of individual editors and Colonial literary groups. The lack of inter-Colonial communication, the localized interests and sentiments of each of the Colonies, the literary tendencies of the newspapers, the universal leaning to an England of established literary fame—these were the handicaps to the establishment of a magazine in the Colonies. But the basic literary elements were present, finding expression wherever possibility offered and support encouraged.

[19] The paper was revived in 1732, with new number series; it ceased publication in 1734. With photostats, the file at the New York Public Library is complete.
[20] It was continued only a few months after the death of the founder in April 1750.
[21] Cook, *op. cit.*, p. 213.
[22] Discontinued at the death of the founder; re-established by Lewis Timothée later.

I

What constituted a proper degree of "liberty of the press" was a perturbed question in the eighteenth century, and a rather strict interpretation of existing laws curtailed the pens of a century noted for satire, and somewhat controlled the matter appearing not only in newspapers but also in magazines and pamphlets. Both Benjamin Franklin and Andrew Bradford, rival publishers of the first American magazines, had intimately experienced, while engaged in newspaper work, the power of the government over the press; and neither of them ever allowed his magazine to venture on unsafe ground.

In Massachusetts, James Franklin, whose articles in *The New-England Courant* in 1721-22 were occasionally vitriolic when referring to church or state, had criticized the government for tardiness in action against pirates operating off the coast of Rhode Island, and had commented harshly on the administration of the government, churches, and Harvard College. For these and other offenses he had been imprisoned for a short time, until he begged forgiveness for many items "reflecting on His Majesty's Government and on the Administration of it in this Province, the Ministry, Churches and Colleges."[23] But his spirit had remained unchastened, and on January 14, 1722 (O.S.) the Executive Council had forbidden his publishing any paper; whereupon James had surmounted this difficulty by using Benjamin's name.

In Pennsylvania, both William Bradford and his son Andrew had encountered several vexatious restrictions. In 1687 the Friends had passed resolutions requiring the elder Bradford to submit to them all matter relating to their society. Several years later, during a schism among the Quakers, Bradford had adhered to the Keith faction, and had been imprisoned for printing a pamphlet supporting George Keith. Disgusted, and in ill-favor in Philadelphia, Bradford had moved to New York. Andrew Bradford had printed, in *The American Weekly Mercury* of January 3, 1721 (O.S.), an item which caused him to be summoned before the Council for reprimand. In 1729 he had again been brought before the Council

---

[23] Livingston Rowe Schuyler, *The Liberty of the Press in the American Colonies before the Revolutionary War* (1905), p. 12, from MS. Records of the General Court.

for publishing a pre-election editorial urging voters to "firmness of mind and public spirit."[24]

In New York, as early as 1686, the governor had been instructed to allow no printing without special permit.   In 1701-02, in the case of Nicholas Bayard, an expelled member of the Council, the jury had taken into account the truth of the printed statements, and had rendered a verdict of not guilty.   Until that time, the judges had been inclined to apply the principle, not of truth or falsity of statement, but of "the greater the truth the greater the libel."   The ruling of the Bayard case had been confirmed in 1734, in the case of John Peter Zenger.

In his plan for publishing a magazine, John Webbe, hired by Andrew Bradford to edit America's first magazine, mentioned the Zenger case, and was careful to point out the liberal decision rendered.   However, he retreated in practice to safe ground, and protected his statements with many a limiting and conciliatory phrase. Franklin, in conducting his magazine, was even more heedful of the attitude of the period, but his judicial and practical mind, his political connections, and his business interests, rather than his fear of the law, probably determined his course.

[24] *Ibid.*, p. 29.

CHAPTER II

PHILADELPHIA: RIVALRY BETWEEN FRANKLIN AND BRADFORD

So FAR as may be ascertained, Benjamin Franklin was the first man in the British Colonies of America to conceive of the publication of a true magazine. This was in 1740. He was not able, however, until February 1741, to translate his purpose into the visible form of *The General Magazine, and Historical Chronicle, for All the British Plantations in America*;[1] and in the meantime his elder rival in Philadelphia, Andrew Bradford, succeeded in issuing *The American Magazine, or a Monthly View of the Political State of the British Colonies*,[2] probably three days before Franklin's magazine appeared. The history of the rivalry between Franklin on one side and Bradford and John Webbe on the other, with a full exposition of the points of view of the three principals, is both human and interesting.[3]

---

[1] See "Bibliography," p. 364. It is worthy of note that in 1723-24 Samuel Keimer published periodically in Philadelphia the first twenty numbers of Samuel Gordon's English periodical, *The Independent Whig*; he then bound these with the remaining numbers, which he issued in a volume. This publication has not been treated in this book as it was reprinted wholly from an English source. It is described by Charles R. Hildeburn in *A Century of Printing. The Issues of the Press in Pennsylvania 1685-1784* (1885-86), I, 68.

[2] *Ibid.*, p. 363.

[3] Biographers of Franklin, and others whose studies have led them to the subject at hand, have sometimes ignored, sometimes slightly mentioned, and sometimes treated briefly but acceptably of Franklin's magazine and the Franklin-Bradford controversy. Jeremiah Chaplin, *The Life of Benjamin Franklin* (1876); George Canning Hill, *Benjamin Franklin. A Biography* (1865); John T. Morse, Jr., *Benjamin Franklin* (1889), as well as the *Autobiography*, are silent. Jared Sparks, *The Life of Benjamin Franklin* (1844); James Parton, *Life and Times of Benjamin Franklin* (1867), and Paul Leicester Ford, *The Many-Sided Franklin* (1899) offer slight references. A good summary account may be found in John Bach McMaster's *Benjamin Franklin as a Man of Letters* (1887), pp. 129-35. Albert H. Smyth, in *The Writings of Benjamin Franklin, Collected and Edited with a Life and Introduction* (1905-06), X, 165-69, gives a summary account, but does not mention Webbe's final reply. However, the same author, in *The Philadelphia Magazines and their Contributors 1741-1850* (1892), does mention this reply in comments on pp. 24-26. John Clyde Oswald, *Benjamin Franklin, Printer* (1917), offers a brief description on pp. 72-81 (not all of which are devoted to the magazine). John L. Haney, "The Story of Franklin's Magazine," in *The General Magazine and Historical Chron-*

By 1740 Franklin, aged thirty-four, was justified in feeling a sense of satisfaction in his worldly achievements. He had begun in 1729 as part owner with Hugh Meredith of *The Pennsylvania Gazette*, "with at most only ninety subscribers,"[4] far eclipsed in every respect by Bradford's *The American Weekly Mercury*, which, established in 1719, circulated widely even beyond the borders of Pennsylvania. Meredith soon withdrew from the partnership. By 1731 Franklin had founded the Philadelphia Library and developed to a considerable extent his trade in London imprints; and in 1732 he had issued his first *Almanack*. He had secured a hold on the government printing in 1736, when he had become Clerk of the General Assembly. A year later Colonel Spotswood, the postmaster-general, removed Andrew Bradford from the postmastership of Philadelphia and appointed Franklin to the position. This was extreme ill fortune for the one and a distinct forward step for the other, as the position carried with it the privilege of franking newspapers through the mail. Bradford had previously refused Franklin the courtesy, and the latter had resorted to paying the carriers for personal service, a doubtful practice. When the tables were turned, Bradford found himself in Franklin's earlier predicament.[5] Though Bradford's *The American Weekly Mercury* was still larger than *The Pennsylvania Gazette* published by Franklin, and deserved a far more favorable description than appears in the latter's *Autobiography*,[6] the trend of affairs was distinctly in Frank-

---

icle (succeeding *The Alumni Register of the University of Pennsylvania*) for Oct. 1925, pp. 3-8, gives an excellent summary. Isaiah Thomas, *op. cit.*, II, 149, is in error in stating that Franklin's magazine preceded Bradford's by a month. Charles R. Hildeburn, *A Century of Printing. The Issues of the Press in Pennsylvania 1685-1784* (1885-86), I, 156, 159, gives an account of the dates of issue of the magazine. The account by Frank Luther Mott, *A History of American Magazines 1741-1850* (1930), pp. 73-77 is fairly complete.

[4] *Autobiography* (ed. Smyth, *The Writings of Benjamin Franklin*, I, 30).

[5] In the Autobiography (*ibid.*, p. 309) Franklin wrote: ". . . I did indeed receive and send papers by the post, yet the publick opinion was otherwise, for what I did send was by bribing the riders, who took them privately, Bradford being unkind enough to forbid it . . . and I thought so meanly of him for it, that, when I afterward came into his situation, I took care never to imitate it." This statement does not fully apply to Bradford, for Spotswood ordered Franklin not to receive Bradford's papers; whereupon Bradford was forced to resort to like bribery. According to Webbe, Franklin closed his eyes to this state of affairs until Bradford undertook to publish his magazine.

[6] *Ibid.* Franklin (p. 257) referred to Bradford as "poorly qualified" for his business and "very illiterate." Later (p. 303) Franklin remarked that his "first papers made

lin's favor. As the year 1737 drew to a close, he could count among his publication enterprises George Whitefield's *Sermons and Journals* in two volumes, *A New and Complete Guide to the English Tongue*, and a number of pamphlets. It is not surprising that three years later, revolving ideas of expansion in his mind, he should plan a magazine.

Conditions did appear hopeful. Centrally located, Franklin might indulge himself in the fancy of gaining a circulation extending both to the north and south. In 1737 a rider had been put on a run between Philadelphia and Newport, Virginia.[7] As early as 1726 Captain Nathaniel Uring had described Philadelphia as "near two miles in length, and in some places three-quarters of a mile broad, in which are reckon'd 4,000 houses . . . and . . . about 18,000 inhabitants."[8] It was only a matter of time until weekly service would be established between Philadelphia and New York, and fortnightly service between the former city and Annapolis.[9] The young publisher's boyhood in Boston, his experiences in London in 1725-26, and his practical success as publisher in Philadelphia should fit him well for the new enterprise. The population of the Colonies would seem to justify the experiment. The number of persons living in the Colonies in 1740 may be fairly clearly imagined by considering the approximate population of some of the provinces and sections of the country, based on data gathered during the middle of the century: in 1750 Pennsylvania, 150,000; in 1756 New York province, 96,790; in 1754 New Jersey, 80,000; in 1756 Connecticut, 130,000; Massachusetts, 145,000 in 1735 and 200,000 in 1755.[10] The Middle Colonies supported a total population in 1760

---

a quite different appearance from any before in the province; a better type, and better printed." These remarks may be construed in a way probably foreign to Franklin's intentions. Even at the time the magazines were being published, Bradford's paper was larger than Franklin's and better in appearance. On the other hand, Bradford lacked Franklin's natural ability to write.

[7] *The Pennsylvania Gazette*, Oct. 27, 1737.

[8] Oswald, *op. cit.*, pp. 3-4. Ellis Paxon Oberholtzer has written well of early social conditions in Philadelphia in *The Literary History of Philadelphia* (n. d., 1906) and *Philadelphia. A History of the City and its People* (1912).

[9] *The Pennsylvania Gazette*, in advertisement dated April 14, 1743.

[10] For statistics immediately preceding, see Franklin Bowditch Dexter, "Estimates of the Population in the American Colonies," in *Report of the Council of the American Antiquarian Society*, Worcester, Oct. 21, 1887: for Pa., p. 18; N. Y., p. 15; N. J., p. 16; Conn., p. 12; Mass., pp. 6-7.

of 405,000, while the number of whites north of Maryland was about 791,000, with about 419,000 to the south of this line.[11]

Commercially the Colonies were active. The need of capital for expanding enterprises was being supplied by the formation of partnerships. Perth Amboy and Burlington entertained a spirit of rivalry toward New York and Philadelphia; while Boston, Salem, Baltimore, and Charleston were still on a similar plane.[12] War with Spain had been declared in 1739,[13] but the only appreciable deleterious effect of this conflict upon the Colonies had been an increase in the tax rate. From Franklin's point of view, the turbulence of the world should only increase the interest in the news and articles his magazine was to carry.

Not wishing to add to his labors the work of editing the magazine which he now proposed to publish, Franklin conferred with John Webbe, "a conveyancer and a dull pedant"[14] who "had written heavy, prosy articles" for *The Pennsylvania Gazette*,[15] and who had been employed formerly by Bradford as attorney during difficulties with Colonel Spotswood.[16] Webbe was offered the editorship.[17] Franklin must have been thinking at the time of a magazine composed of selected extracts and simple news summary, for he told Webbe the editing should not require over three or four days a week; while Webbe's mind must have been imagining a magazine carefully edited and well supplied with articles and rewritten material by the editor, for he soon discovered that "every Moment of my Time would be necessarily engrossed in the Execution of the Undertaking."[18]

Memoranda for a later contract were set down by Franklin: "Magazine to consist of 3 Sheets 1000 to be printed at first.

[11] Edward Channing, *A History of the United States*, (1905-   ), II, 491-92.

[12] William Nelson, *The American Newspapers of the Eighteenth Century as Sources of History* (reprinted from *Annual Report of the American Historical Association for 1908*, I, 209-22), p. 213.

[13] For a lively account of the difficulties which beset enlistment, the reluctance of men to enlist and the equal reluctance of those possessed of indentured servants to yield the period of indentureship, see *The American Magazine*, Feb. 1741, pp. 58-59.

[14] McMaster, *op. cit.*, p. 129.

[15] *The Writings of Benjamin Franklin*, ed. Smyth, X, 165.

[16] *The Pennsylvania Gazette*, Dec. 11, 1740, in Franklin's reply to "The Detection" by Webbe.

[17] In the contention which followed, Webbe's tenuous defense for carrying the plan to Bradford without notice to Franklin appears to be his weakest argument, and the act the least justifiable.

[18] *The American Weekly Mercury*, Nov. 20, 1740, "The Detection."

Price 15s. a Year, or 15d. a piece single. 12s. a Doz. to those that sell again." Franklin was to bear the expenses of printing and paper, while "J. W. to dispose the Materials, make Abstracts, and write what shall be necessary for promoting the Thing, &c. The Money received to be divided thus—B. F. for and towards the Expense above mentioned to take first one half, the remainder to be equally shared between him and I. W. Bad Debts if any to be divided in the same Manner. To agree for a Term of 7 Years. The above Agreement to be for all under 2000; all above 2000 sold the Money to be equally divided; B. F. to be at all Expence."[19] Franklin justified his major share in the receipt of income on the grounds of expense and the possession of a "small letter" type which was necessary for the work and which no other printer in the colony possessed; he was, moreover, established in the peculiarly advantageous position of postmaster.[20]

Webbe took the memoranda and went his way, evidently satisfied for the moment.[21] Later he divulged the plan to Andrew Bradford, for whom he knew it possessed both a personal and a business interest. Bradford quickly offered Webbe a better proposition: the Franklin who had formerly worked in Bradford's own shop, who had later established a competitive business, and who had secured the postmastership, would not usher in this new scheme without meeting with some resistance.

As a consequence Franklin was chagrined and vexed when he read the first three pages of Bradford's *The American Weekly Mercury* of November 6, 1740, containing a long announcement of "The Plan of an Intended Magazine." It was the "Success and Approbation which the Magazines, published in *Great Britain*, have met with for many Years past," according to the announcement, which "*Encouraged* us to *Attempt* a Work of the like Nature in *America*. . . . It is propos'd to publish Monthly, *An Account of the publick Affairs transacted in His Majesty's Colonies, as well on the Continent of America as in the West India Islands*," which would include the proceedings of the various Assemblies, and their Constitutions and several interests and views. Also the "Situation, Climate, Soil, Productions, Trade and Manufactures of all the British Plantations" would be reported, as well as quotations

[19] *Ibid.*
[20] *Ibid.*
[21] *Ibid.*

of the prices of commodities and the exchange rate of money. Extracts of laws passed would appear, and likewise "Party-Disputes, carried on in the other publick Prints, which may tend to clear up any controverted Points, or discover the . . . Motives of Action. . . ." An impartial view of both sides of every question was promised, for "we shall *inviolably* observe an exact Neutrality, and *carefully* avoid mingling with the Arguments on either Side, any Reflections or Remarks of our own." Thus would be overcome the political biases of the various newspapers, which "cannot, without much Difficulty, be prevailed upon to publish any Thing against the Side of the Question they are of themselves." The editor promised to avoid the printing of libel: "Even where Faults are real, but private and meerly Personal; To drag them out of their Obscurity into open Day can only proceed from Malice or Envy." Yet "we would not be understood to refuse a Place to Satire," for satire which challenges "*proper* Objects, and attacks a vicious Tribe in general, but without singling from the Herd any Criminals in particular" would be acceptable, especially if treating of "Affectation, Foppery, Vanity, Impertinence or any reigning Folly." On the whole, the "Reader is desired to consider the Undertaking, as an Attempt to *Erect*, on *Neutral Principles*, A PUBLICK THEATRE in the *Center* of the *British* Empire in *America*, on which the most remarkable Transactions of each Government may be *impartially* represented. . . ." The size was to be equal to four sheets "of such as the *American Mercury* is printed on" (Franklin's plan had called for three), and the price was cut from Franklin's notation of fifteen shillings to twelve, Pennsylvania currency.

Franklin determined that Bradford and Webbe should not drive him from the field. In *The Pennsylvania Gazette* of November 13 appeared a curt half-column announcement on the fourth page: "In January next will be published, (to be continued Monthly) The General Magazine, and Historical Chronicle, For all the British Plantations in America: Containing (I) Extracts from the . . . Debates of the Parliament of Great Britain. (II) The Proclamations . . . of Governors; Addresses; Votes . . . of Assemblies. . . . (III) Accounts of, and Extracts from, all the new Books, Pamphlets, &c. published in the Plantations. (IV) Essays, controversial, humorous, philosophical, religious, moral or political. (V) Select Pieces of Poetry. (VI) A concise Chronicle of the most remarkable Transactions, as well in Europe as America. (VII) Births, Marriages, Deaths, and Promotions. . . . (VIII) Course of Exchange . . . Prices of Goods, &c." The advertisement announced further that the plan had been long projected and that "a Correspondence is settled with Intelligent Men in most of the Colonies, and small Types are procured." Franklin admitted that the magazine "would not, indeed, have been published quite so soon, were it not that a Person, to whom the Scheme was communicated *in Confidence*, has thought fit to advertise it in the last *Mercury*" without Franklin's participation and probably with a view toward thwarting him. As an inducement to purchasers, Franklin proposed to "desire no Subscriptions . . . which Method, we suppose, will be most agreeable to our Readers, as they will be at liberty to buy only what they like." He increased the size of his projected magazine to four large sheets, equal to Bradford's promise, and cut the price to nine pence, Pennsylvania money.

Franklin's advertisement brought forth a series of three articles in *The American Weekly Mercury*,[22] under the title of "The Detection," written by Webbe. In the first article Webbe admitted that Franklin had communicated his purpose to him, but stated that the ". . . Proposal neither obliged me to the writing of one [magazine] for him to print, nor restrained me from the printing of it at any other Press." There followed Franklin's memoranda for the contract, Webbe offering it as evidence that Franklin had tried to drive a hard bargain. The second article continued the diatribe; the writer admitted that Franklin's proposal somewhat interfered with his own plan, but assured his readers the proposal would none the less be carried out. In the third article Webbe charged that Franklin "has since my first letter, in Quality of Postmaster, taken upon him to deprive the *Mercury* of the Benefit of the Post, and will not permit it to travel with his *Gazette*." To this statement Franklin felt constrained to reply in *The Pennsylvania Gazette* of December 11, mentioning that his friends thought it necessary for him to take some notice of it. He explained that " 'tis now upwards of a Twelvemonth since I refus'd to forward Mr. Bradford's Papers free by the Post, in Obedience to a positive Order from the Hon. Col. Spotswood, then Post-Master General."

[22] Nov. 20, 27, and Dec. 4, 1740.

Spotswood's letter was printed in full; it revealed the fact that Bradford had been negligent in submitting reports when he was postmaster, and that Spotswood had ordered Franklin to refuse Bradford the post. Franklin closed his reply by mentioning that Webbe was "thoroughly acquainted with the Affair," as he was "employ'd as Attorney in the Action against *Bradford*."

Still the whole truth had not been presented to the public, for the following week *The American Weekly Mercury*[23] printed a two-page postscript. In it Webbe admitted that "it is true that after the Orders . . . Mr. Bradford never sent him any of his Papers to be forwarded in the Mail. But it is as true, that, as they were made up in unsealed Packets, he sent them to the Riders who used to distribute them on their several Routs. This Method . . . was NO SECRET; and consequently could not be *unknown* to Mr. *Franklin*; and therefore it must be presumed to have had his Approbation." Webbe also inferred from the remarks of a postman made to him since the last previous letter that it was evident Franklin had made known his disapprobation of continuing the policy.

The postscript to *The American Weekly Mercury* practically closed the issue; with approximate accuracy the case had been placed before the public and both sides had suffered somewhat by the remarks. Only one other personal rebuke appeared in print, and this was foolishly perpetrated probably by Franklin, in *The Pennsylvania Gazette* of February 26, 1741, after both magazines had appeared. In language which may have been intended as the dialectal speech of an inebriated Irishman (a conventional vehicle of satire), Franklin essayed to scoff at the phraseology of Bradford's first advertisement,[24] at the plan for using original rather than selected pieces in the magazine, and at the subscription price, which offered no reduction by the year.[25] The material for the

[23] Dec. 18, 1740.

[24] *The American Weekly Mercury*, Nov. 6, 1740.

[25] In part, "Teague's Advertisement," reads:
>"Arra Joy! My monthly Macasheen shall contain Sheets four,
>Or an Equivalent, which is something more;
>
> .   .   .   .
>
>Prishe shingle *One Shilling*: But shubscribe for a Year,
>You shall have it* sheaper, at de shame Prishe, Honey dear:
>'Tis true, my Book is dear; but Reashon is plain,
>The best Parts of it ish de Work of my own Brain:

satire seems poorly adapted for wit; the poetic execution was exceedingly crude; and Bradford, in a signed article, replied to the slur with dignity and justness.[26]

The race between the two publishers, each endeavoring to issue a magazine before the other, may be traced in the advertisements. *The American Weekly Mercury*, in the first announcement,[27] had advertised *The American Magazine* for March; Franklin had countered by offering *The General Magazine* in January.[28] On February 5, 1741, each paper advertised the magazine of its publisher as to appear the following week. In both cases limited printing facilities were insuperable barriers. On February 12 *The American Weekly Mercury* advertised the January number of *The American Magazine* as to be "Publish'd to-morrow"—Friday. On the same date the January issue of *The General Magazine* was advertised in *The Pennsylvania Gazette* to appear "on Monday next." In the newspaper issues of February 19, both magazines are advertised as published. Assuming that Bradford did not fail in his promise, *The American Magazine* may claim by a priority of three days the distinction of being the first magazine in America.[29]

But the vexations of publishing the magazines are clearly indi-

---

How can odher Men's Writings be Wort so much!
Arra! if you tink so, you're no vhery good Shudge.

    .   .   .   .

For de Buyer's Shake, and de Land's Reputaish,
No Shweepings, but dose of my own Shcull shall have plaish;

    .   .   .   .

"*The Word cheaper, I own, is not express'd in the Original, but it must have been intended to be understood. . . ."

The poem was signed "Shelah." That Franklin wrote it seems likely, for the references are to matters affecting Franklin most particularly: the four sheets (Franklin had originally planned for three), the price of subscription (Franklin had originally established a higher rate), the proper editing of a magazine (Franklin had planned to use only clipped and reprinted articles).

[26] *The American Weekly Mercury*, March 5, 1741.

[27] Nov. 6, 1740.

[28] *The Pennsylvania Gazette*, Nov. 13, 1740.

[29] M. Katherine Jackson, in *Outlines of the Literary History of Colonial Pennsylvania* (1906), termed *Der Hoch-Deutsch Pennsylvanische Geschicht-Schreiber*, established Aug. 20, 1739, by Christopher Saur, of Germantown, "a monthly magazine of four to eight pages" (p. 54). This publication, it seems to me, may be more properly classified as a newspaper, in spite of its infrequent appearance. Foreign and domestic news comprised nearly the whole interest. The aim of the publisher was to print in the German language the news of the time for the benefit of the German community. For several years it appeared less frequently than once a month; it then became a monthly, and finally a biweekly in 1748.

cated by the advertisements of the numbers which followed the initial issues. Bradford could not retrieve for the second number of *The American Magazine* any of the time he had lost for it, as the February issue was not advertised in *The American Weekly Mercury* as "Just Published" until March 19, and the third and final issue was not advertised at all. The advertisements in *The Pennsylvania Gazette* for the five numbers succeeding the first issue of *The General Magazine* indicate an increasingly difficult problem of printing, the numbers for March and June not being announced as published until *The Pennsylvania Gazette* issues of the thirtieth of the months following.[30]

I

John Webbe lacked the broadness of interests necessary for success in his editorial chair. Politics, theories of government, taxation, and immigration seemed to be the special stimulants to his mind. In an age when poetical epistles were currently popular, he found no room for light verse in *The American Magazine*; nor did he include any substitute appealing to feminine readers. He was conscious of public duty, and recognized his position as one of service to his time and the future historians; but he was so limited in his tastes that the magazine he conducted probably would not have lived had other conditions been even the most favorable.

Yet Webbe's weakness was also his strength. His "Remarks on the Maryland Government," which occupied eleven pages of the first number and sixteen of the second, is an able discussion of the republican system of political rule, and is superior to his article, "An Essay towards Explaining the Nature of Money in General, and of Paper Money in Particular," through which subject he has come to notice in historical and literary annals.[31] Maryland was functioning under a highly centralized system, with the popularly elected lower branch of the Assembly fighting for power against

---

[30] The February issue was advertised March 19 for "Tuesday next," and on March 26 as "Just Published"; the March issue was advertised April 30 as "Just Published"; the April issue was advertised May 28 as "Just Published"; the May issue was advertised June 25 to appear on "Saturday next"; the June issue was advertised on July 23 to appear "Monday next," and on July 30 as "Just Published."

[31] Moses Coit Tyler, *A History of American Literature during the Colonial Period 1607-1765* (1878) II, 240, mentions Webbe and notes the article under a later title; see note 58 below.

the upper. In contrasting the legislative formula as it operated bi-camerally in England and America, Webbe adroitly accepted the peerage in the mother country, as it perhaps had attained to a legitimate status; but he insisted that no upper house in the prov-inces had yet "equitably acquired a distinct Interest from their Fellow-Subjects,"[32] and he sincerely hoped that the House of Lords would never be imitated in America. In its entirety, the article presented the thoughts of a man democratic at heart, writing as forcibly as he thought the license of the press would permit. A characteristic but weak reply, "The Upper House of Maryland Vindicated," was made by "A. B." in March.

"An Essay towards Explaining the Nature of Money in General, and of Paper Money in Particular, with a Proposal for Obviating the Inconveniences Attending the Fall in Value of the Latter" was begun in the March issue,[33] and the death of the magazine left the essay unfinished. The first part of the intended article was re-printed by Bradford in 1743 under a different title,[34] though the second part never appeared. This essay has become one of the classic examples of Colonial reasoning in support of a practice help-ful to the debtor class.[35] The problem of currency was being livelily debated throughout the Colonies at the time Webbe's article appeared; not only Pennsylvania, but New York, and especially New Jersey and Massachusetts were suffering from unsound paper issues, and seeking to remedy the condition by issuing more paper, in opposition to executive orders from abroad.

Webbe's industry as an editor is to be noticed not only in his lengthly contributions, but in the pains he took to comment on excerpts selected from published works. In the first number, for example, an article written by Swift was copied so that the editor might reply to the writer's reflections on America as an unpleasant

[32] Jan. 1741, p. 29.

[33] Pp. 82-90.

[34] *A Discourse concerning Paper Money, in which its Principles Are Laid Open; and a Method, Plain and Easy, for Introducing and Continuing a Plenty, without Lessening the Present Value of it, Is Demonstrated.* See Tyler, *op. cit.*, note 55; also Charles Evans, *op. cit.*, No. 5308.

[35] Franklin himself had written *A Modest Enquiry into the Nature and Necessity of a Paper Currency* (1729), and was to write further on the subject in 1765, 1769, 1777, 1781 (see *The Writings of Benjamin Franklin*, ed. Smyth, I, 135-166). Though later Franklin retrenched his opinions somewhat from his stand in 1729, as "there are limits beyond which the quantity may be hurtful," he always defended the "utility of this currency" (see *Autobiography*, ed. Smyth, *op. cit.*, I, 306-07).

land for those contemplating emigration from Europe. Webbe
revealed himself here, naturally, to be an untrustworthy partisan,
for he suggested that one would "be *almost* tempted to swear" that
the Indians "are the same individual People, that Captain *Gulliver*
met with in his Travels, and allegorically describes under the Name
of Houynhnms."[36]   Nor would one dismiss so lightly as did the
editor, the difficulties of the borderland settlers, pushed into the
sparsely inhabited regions when they could not buy parcels of the
large land holdings owned by earlier settlers about more populous
centers.   In the majority of magazines which followed, many of
the editors were content to print selected articles without expend-
ing the labor, or sometimes incurring the danger, of commenting.
It must be noted, however, that Webbe's limited perspective rendered *The American Magazine* weak in this field of its composition.

As a repository of historical material, *The American Magazine*
is occasionally highly interesting.   Here one may trace the hesitation which characterized the mobilization in the Colonies to assist
England in the War of the Austrian Succession.   Only after repeated adjournments did many of the Assemblies, with grudging
illiberality, pass meager financial bills to support the war.   In the
February issue[37] is a clear picture of the attitude among the people
of Pennsylvania,[38] taken from *The Pennsylvania Gazette* of April
17, 1740: "On Monday his Honour our Governor, attended by
near 200 Gentlemen, came to the Court House, where a vast Con-
course of People were assembled, and published the King's Declaration of War against *Spain* together with the Proclamation. . . .
The People expressed their Joy in loud Huzzas; and the Cannon
from the Hill and the Ships from the Harbour, were discharged.
. . . Plenty of Liquor was given to the Populace; & in the Evening
they had a Bonfire on the Hill."   But though the Governor drew a
rich picture of the booty which would fall to the soldiers in the
Spanish West Indies, the men did not, even under the influence of
liquor and militant patriotism, eagerly respond to the call to enlist.
The Assembly, controlled by the Friends, would not pass an act
paying a lump sum for each enlistment; the Spaniards were well
known to be severe enemies; and when the Governor, pressed by his

[36] Jan. 1741, p. 7.
[37] Pp. 56-65.   The quotation immediately following is from p. 58.
[38] Although the Friends were responsible for Pennsylvania's attitude of extreme
pacifism, the other Colonies were fairly reticent also in matters of money and men.

comparatively wealthy constituents, published a proclamation to the effect that enlistment did not free indentured servants from their time contracts for service, but merely suspended them during the period of enlistment, nearly everyone lost what enthusiasm he may have had.

With the third and last issue of *The American Magazine* Webbe began printing correspondence, indicative that a broader appeal might have been attained in the magazine had it lived. One correspondent, for example, sought an answer to the question whether "private Persons have a Right to inquire into the Nature of Government;"[39] another wrote concerning the injustice of the present division of lands. Yet withal, it is doubtful whether Webbe possessed the catholicity of interest of a good editor. But the magazine he edited holds a firm place in the tight little area of interest it espoused, and vaunts a proportion of original material outranking many a subsequent, more ambitious, and successful miscellany.

II

Franklin's *The General Magazine* more closely followed the model of the English miscellany than did *The American Magazine*, and maintained a breadth of appeal far wider than its competitor. Formal essays, poetical epistles, letters, concise records of contemporary events, and a department of well-selected extracts from American books and pamphlets brought to the magazine a breadth of subject matter which Webbe, who used more original material by far, had not attained. The six numbers of Franklin's magazine truly became a selected anthology of native work. Nor was his perspective localized; New England and the South shared with the Middle Colonies the pages of the magazine.

Beyond the private concerns of its own life, the Colonial mind was engaged in contemplating three major states of affairs: the war with Spain, which might affect shipping to the east and stir up Indian hostility in the west; the problem of currency, which resolved itself into defeated attempts to supply everyone with paper money which would not depreciate; and the "Great Awakening," which was rising in the South, disturbing a complacent religious condition in New England, and giving the Middle Colonies a joyful, though

[39] P. 109.

tearful, mass emotional outlet. Webbe had been interested in the first two subjects; Franklin embraced all three.

With regard to the war, the reactions of the Colonies may be traced in the reports of the "Proceedings" of the legislatures. Unlike Webbe, Franklin aspired to no editorial comment or explanatory digest, but he did represent all sections of the country, printing the official messages. Of especial interest was the report of the speech of the Governor of New York, who, besides pleading for a stronger military establishment, urged that the Assembly loose the purse strings and pay officials a stipulated salary in advance— "only this, will remove, as to this Province, a Jealousy, which for some Years has obtained in *England*, that the Plantations are not without Thoughts of throwing off their Dependance [*sic*] on the Crown of *England*."[40]   In January appeared the Reverend Mather Byles's sermon on the "Christian Hero,"[41] delivered in Boston to those going to war. He asserted they would be "Calm of Mind" if they were assured (as Byles evidently was) that they were "venturing in the Name of the Lord of Hosts, and he is engaged for you!"[42]   For the February issue Franklin selected "The Crown of England's Title to America Prior to that of Spain,"[43] tracing the Welshman, Madoc ap Owen, to America in 1170; and in the same and succeeding numbers appeared Colonel Bland's "Manual Exercise,"[44] that the knowledge of military formations might be the better disseminated. To represent Colonial relations with the Indians, Franklin chose, among other selections, the important negotiations of Lieutenant-Governor Clarke of New York with the Six Nations, conducted at Albany in August 1740.[45]   This article was exceptionally interesting, for it treated of matters which would affect the Colonies directly should France enter the war, as indeed later she did. In this report may be traced the history of the gradual encroachment of the English on the hunting grounds of the Indians, the low ethics of barter, and the shrewd political maneuver of the tribes, who to their best advantage remained as neutral as possible, playing the English and French against each other. The

[40] April, p. 252.

[41] Pp. 34-45. "The Glories of the Lord of Hosts, and the Fortitude of the Religious Hero." The sermon had been printed in the form of a pamphlet.

[42] P. 45.

[43] Pp. 80-83.

[44] Pp. 127-31, 153-74.

[45] Feb., pp. 88-99.

importance of the negotiations extended to some of the Southern Colonies, as it was through the northern tribes that the English sought to deal with the Spanish Indians. Considering the military articles and historical reports as a whole, one may trace Franklin's own political opinions in favor of sound preparedness and concerted action against Indian barriers in the west and against limitations of trade imposed by foreign powers to the east. But never did he express an editorial sentiment.

Perhaps of greater importance in the public mind than the war was the "Great Awakening," which began about 1739 and swept across the Colonies during the middle years of the century, heralded by such divines as George Whitefield, Gilbert Tennent, and Thomas Prince.[46] In the Middle Colonies the movement met with especial favor; New England was divided, and localities in the South, under Episcopal organization, resisted. Franklin seems personally to have been mildly moved in favor of the revival, but he offered no comment in print, contenting himself by inserting representative articles for both sides. Just preceding the appearance of the magazine, the conflict had flared in sharp lights and shadows, probably somewhat occasioned by the printing of Whitefield's sermons, journals, and letters in two volumes in 1740. These books had been issued from Franklin's press. Was the spirit of the Creator manifesting itself with unusual energy in the world, turning men's hearts? Was the excitation of rampant revivalism expounded by Whitefield a true work of the Lord? Or was the emotional fervor entirely man-made and misleading, corrupting the eternal truths preserved in the various creeds and offending organized religion with undue license? There were many who answered these questions with a dogmatic fervency that brooked no reply.

In the January issue of *The General Magazine*[47] appeared articles against the tenets of Whitefield submitted by members of the Presbyterian Church, Whitefield's reply, and some notes by "Nathanael Love-Truth," who endeavored to point out Whitefield's error of emphasizing repentence rather than faith. One of the best contributions to appear in the magazine dealt with the same subject, being a satire against the "Great Awakening" en-

[46] A more complete discussion of the "Great Awakening" is undertaken in Chapter III, with special regard to the magazine, *The Christian History*.

[47] Pp. 45-57.

titled "A True and Genuine Account of a Wonderful Wandering Spirit,"[48] that had lately manifested itself in England, Germany, and America, possessing the mob so that "they swell and shake, like *Virgil's* enthusiastick Sybil," and "all that it bewitches generally bid farewell to Reason." In the April and June numbers the topic was aroused again when there appeared a reply to the essay on the wandering spirit[49] and a "Supplement to the History of the Wandering Spirit.[50] On the side of Whitefield in the February issue Franklin included a sermon by Dr. Benjamin Colman, of Boston,[51] who exclaimed that Whitefield had entered Massachusetts "even as an Angel of God," and that since the revival, people now came into churches "as Doves on the Wing in Flocks flying." In the same number was printed an excerpt from a pamphlet by the Reverend Isaac Chanler, of South Carolina, praising Whitefield's work.[52] To balance Colman's praise, Franklin selected four letters by the Reverend Alexander Garden, of South Carolina—the fourth an especially bitter attack on "the entire System of the Methodist Doctrine of Regeneration." These appeared in the issues of April, May, and June.[53] In the last number a reply to the Garden letters was begun, but the discontinuance of the magazine put an end to the squabble.

The liberal view which Franklin entertained with regard to relatively large issues of paper money[54] is to be observed in the articles he reprinted on this subject, though he made no personal comments in the magazines. Especially are to be noted the "New-England Scheme for Emitting Notes to Pass in Lieu of Money,"[55] and the "New-England Manufactory Scheme."[56] Both

[48] Feb., p. 120-22.

[49] Pp. 272-76.

[50] Pp. 406-09. Another interesting Whitefield item was William Brattle's objections to Whitefield's New England journal, Whitefield's reply, and Brattle's rejoinder, in the numbers for April, May, and June, pp. 265-68, 313-17, 401-06.

[51] Pp. 101-05. An extract by Colman on the character of Archbishop Tillotson appeared in the issue for Feb., p. 123; and articles by and to Colman on the doctrine of original sin in the issue for Jan., pp. 58-61. Articles and poetry favorable and unfavorable to Gilbert Tennent, who was more active even than Colman in the cause of proclaiming the "Great Awakening," appeared in Feb., pp. 123-24, 126, May, p. 351, and June, pp. 415-16.

[52] Pp. 105-12.

[53] Pp. 263-68, 300-12, 391-406.

[54] See note 59.

[55] Jan., pp. 10-16.

[56] March, pp. 175-84. See also "Proceedings in Parliament on the Affairs of the

plans were endeavors to arrange for paper issues against the instructions of the Crown.

Among the many other subjects Franklin selected in the hope
of entertaining or enlightening his readers were extracts from
Robert Beverley's *The History of Virginia*[57] and Patrick Tailfer's
and others' severe and effective arraignment, *A True and Historical Narrative of the Colony of Georgia*[58]—a book born of dis-
illusionment, frustration, hate, and the inability of the authors to
adapt themselves to circumstances. Typical of the love stories told
for a moral purpose was a feminine "confession" found among the
papers of Mrs. Martha Howard, of South Carolina,[59] wherein
"The Fate of the Writer is a strong Instance of the Violence of
human Passions, when they get loose from the Government of
Reason." The ostensible reason for printing the story was that
"Women may be more wise, and Men more honest."

The "Accounts of and Extracts from New Books, Pamphlets,
&c. Published in the Plantations" varied in bulk in accordance with
the need for filler. In the January number the ratio was about
thirty percent—exceedingly high. As time advanced, communications to the editor increased. Among them was a duplicate of
"A. B.'s" letter to Webbe supporting the aristocratic government
of Maryland,[60] the writer explaining that he was sending Franklin
a copy as Mr. Bradford's "Candour and Impartiality cannot be
depended upon"—a somewhat unjust comment which Franklin
printed. Another item was a letter by Joseph Morgan, pleading
for more good faith and less theological disputation.

The department of "Poetical Essays" was supplied largely from
clippings of American and English poems taken from Colonial
newspapers. War, religion, and the virtue of prominent men were
leading themes. Traces of light verse dotted the pages. The pre-

---

Paper Money in the American Colonies," April 1740, in magazine for Jan., pp. 6-8;
"Proclamation Issued in New York Relating to Coin," Jan., pp. 16-18; other proclamations and petitions, Jan., pp. 18-22, and 26-28; a letter to the magazine proposing a
method for issuing £100,000 loan secured by land or plate, Feb., pp. 117-20; the
report of the Board of Trade to the House of Commons respecting paper money in the
Colonies, April, pp. 258-60.

[57] Feb., pp. 83-88; March, pp. 147-53; April, pp. 217-28.

[58] The main narrative was cut short by the discontinuance of the magazine with the
June number. The preface, and some of the narrative appeared in the issues for
April, May, and June, pp. 260-63, 291-300, and 379-91.

[59] May, pp. 335-339; the quotation is from p. 335.

[60] March pp. 189-200.

dominant meter was the heroic couplet, which held undisputed first place in the minds of writers for years to come.   Chief timely reprints included Richard Glover's "Admiral Hosier's Ghost,"[61] an imaginary and patriotic reply[62] as by Admiral Vernon, commander of the British fleet in the region of the West Indies, and two poems in praise of Vernon.[63]   Mather Byles was represented by two reprints, "To the Rev. Dr. Watts, on his Divine Poems"[64] and "The Comparison, the Choice and the Enjoyment."[65]   John Wesley,[66] Gilbert Tennent,[67] and George Whitefield[68] were honored in poetic measures.   Of more local interest were "B.'s" "Verses to the Memory of Henry Brooke,"[69] and a Latin poem in praise of Governor Thomas which has been ascribed to William Lowry.[70]

Of the 426 pages comprising *The General Magazine*, less than ten percent can be definitely described as original with the publication.   The technique of editing was quite similar to that employed in the publishing of Colonial newspapers, though more care was

[61] Jan., pp. 63-65.

[62] Feb., pp. 137-38.

[63] March, pp. 207-09.

[64] March, pp. 209-10.

[65] March, p. 213.

[66] Jan., pp. 67-68.   The following lines exemplify the general type:
> "Mayst Thou, Great Man, withstand a misled Throng,
> And prove, with Aid divine, their Teachers wrong.
> May God a Blessing to thy Words impart,
> And deep engrave them on each Hearer's Heart.
> Our Saviour's Love to all the World declare,
> Nor all the Mighty Rage of Mortals fear:
> With Gospel-Truths their narrow Thoughts explode
> Who boldly stint the Mercies of their God.
> O Charity!   Oh whither art thou fled?
> Where wilt thou raise again thy drooping Head?
> When wilt thou abject Bigotry remove,
> And every Breast inspire with Social Love?"

[67] April, pp. 281-82; the poem was written by "Mrs. S. M."

[68] Jan., p. 70.

[69] Feb., pp. 136-37.   Henry Brooke was a younger son of Sir Henry Brooke of Cheshire.   For a time he was collector of customs in Pennsylvania; he was a famous politician and a man of "considerable sprightliness and social grace" (Tyler, *op. cit.*, II, p. 235).   He died at Philadelphia, Feb. 6, 1735-6.

[70] June, pp. 417-19.   Francis Howard Williams, in *The Pennsylvania Magazine of History and Biography* (1893), pp. 1-33, credits the poem, entitled "Carmen Gradularium" to Lowry with this reservation, "I believe the authorship is not undisputed" (p. 27).   In the comments the mistake is made of calling Franklin's magazine the *Universal Magazine*; evidently Williams confused the name of the newspaper Franklin and Meredith bought from Keimer, *The Universal Instructor*, with the magazine. Jackson, *op. cit.*, p. 51, falls into the same error.

taken to print material of enduring value. But there was no major motive or idea back of the magazine to give it life or render it much more serviceable than the weekly papers. Undoubtedly it was not a profitable venture, and so it died. What Franklin himself thought of the magazine can only be surmised. He did not mention it in his *Autobiography*.

CHAPTER III

BOSTON: ENGLISH HERITAGES, AND THE "GREAT AWAKENING"

THE second focus of activity for the publication of magazines in the American Colonies was Boston, provincial in many respects, but none the less the metropolis of education, finance, trade, and printing. The geographical disadvantage of partial isolation was in some measure overcome by internal self-sufficiency. The city was larger than New York; linguistic and racial cleavages did not exist to so great an extent in New England as in the Middle Colonies, and the territory was more populous and compact than the South.

In 1742, one year before the first three Boston magazines were published, the number of inhabitants in the city was approximately 18,000, and the valuation report listed 1,719 houses and 166 warehouses.[1] The city was at the apex of a period of fairly rapid expansion, and settling into staidness and slow growth. Though shipbuilding was slackening,[2] commerce continued active, and, exclusive of the coastwise trade, about a thousand vessels were entering or clearing port yearly.[3] The number of indigent persons was increasing, and wealth was accumulating in the possession of the aristocracy. Social distinctions were rigidly maintained, determining questions of precedence at Harvard and fixing the pattern of congregations in the churches. For the well-to-do, life flowed leisurely along, not lacking in pleasures. Afternoon teas, strolls along the mall, "turtle-frolics," and not unelaborate social entertainments at homes in lieu of "plays and music houses" dispelled the gloom which an English traveler imagined must enshroud the city until, on a visit, he found "they don't seem to be dispirited . . .

[1] Horace E. Scudder (quoting William Douglass's *Summary*), "Life in Boston in the Provincial Period," in *The Memorial History of Boston*, ed. Justin Winsor, II, 439. Of the total population there were 1,514 negroes and about 1,000 widows practically destitute.

[2] *Ibid.* (quoting Burke), II, 443. By 1760 the population had increased only to 20,000. In 1738 forty-one top sail vessels had been built; in 1749 the number had fallen to 15.

[3] *Ibid.*, II, 444.

for both ladies and gentlemen dress and appear as gay, in common, as courtiers in England on a coronation or birthday."[4]

The major interests stirring the Middle Colonies during the decade of the 1740's operated likewise in New England, though somewhat different conditions served to alter the emphases. Notwithstanding local commercial self-determinedness, New England's traditions and culture were actively allied to English ways. Had this condition not obtained, it seems doubtful whether *The American Magazine and Historical Chronicle; for All the British Plantations*[5] (1743-46), which often was hardly more than an American edition of numerous British magazines consolidated and abridged, would have received the support which gave it a comparatively long life and made it the outstanding miscellany of the decade. And had this magazine not been planned, it is barely possible that *The Boston Weekly Magazine* (1743)[6] would ever have appeared.

War against Spain and France also drew New England rather closely toward the mother country, for her eyes were turned not only toward the sea, but toward Canada, and she supported the hostilities with a greater sense of personal interest than did the other Colonies. But none the less, the strong gusto for enlisting in the ranks occasionally wavered, to be revived when pulses were temporarily quickened by local pageantries, internal conflicts between the legislature and executive, captures at sea, and victories in Canada.

Finally, the "Great Awakening" raged in New England against the embattled force of religious conservatism. In the Middle Colonies the emotionalized revivalism touched individual hearts; in New England it touched the spleens and heads of organized religious groups as well. Puritan ground became the field of battle. In the midst of the clash of beliefs, there appeared *The Christian History* (1743-45)[7] in support of the revivalists. It was bulwarked by the historically-minded Reverend Thomas Prince, internationalized by the Reverend James Robe's reports of the revival in Scotland, and fired and humanized by Gilbert Tennent, George Whitefield, Benjamin Colman, and a score of earnest ministers in the several Colonies who reported the progressive manifestations of

[4] *Ibid.*, II, 452-54.
[5] See "Bibliography," p. 364.
[6] *Ibid.*
[7] *Ibid.*

the spirit of the revival. In the end, conservatism emerged the victor, but the magazine remains as a testimony of the defeated party.

I

The Boston Weekly Magazine sprang into existence March 2, 1743, lived through three numbers within the month, and died. According to a contemporary account of the time, it was issued in an attempt to forestall the publication of *The American Magazine and Historical Chronicle*,[8] proposals for which had been announced the previous January, although the first number was not on sale until the following October. In seeking a basis for the rivalry, it is probably important to note the mixed publishing interests attending the preliminary arrangements to issue the two magazines. *The Boston Weekly Magazine* bore the imprint of Gamaliel Rogers and Daniel Fowle, who had established a partnership in 1742, and the name of Joshua Blanchard was added as a selling agent. The names appearing in the proposals for *The American Magazine and Historical Chronicle* were John Eliot, John Phillips, and Samuel Eliot.[9] Later, when *The American Magazine and Historical Chronicle* appeared, it was published by Samuel Eliot and Joshua Blanchard, and printed by Rogers and Fowle, who, according to Isaiah Thomas, were also interested in the publication, "and, after the first year . . . sole proprietors of it."[10] John Phillips and John Eliot, who had been listed among those interested when the original proposals were issued, did not appear later as vendors of the magazine, while the names of Blanchard and Rogers and Fowle were not associated with the journal until after their attempt to publish *The Boston Weekly Magazine.*

But the rivalry between the two magazines seems to have had a religious setting also, and it is to John Draper's *The Boston Weekly News-Letter* of March 17, 1743[11] that one must go to

[8] See letter under date of March 8, signed "J——— G———, &c.," in *The Boston Weekly News-Letter*, March 17, 1743. See also note 12.

[9] For proposals, see *The Boston Weekly News-Letter*, Jan. 20, 1743; the advertisement was repeated in the issue for Jan. 27, and other announcements appeared from time to time.

[10] *Op. cit.*, II, 67-68.

[11] The same paper, in the issue of March 10, contained a short announcement of the appearance of *The Boston Weekly Magazine*, and promised for the following week the letter by "J. G. &c."

discover some of the circumstances which preceded the publication of *The Boston Weekly Magazine*. In that issue of the paper, Draper printed a letter dated March 8, most probably written by Jeremy Gridley as it was signed "J—— G——, &c.", which stated that for some time enemies of the proposed *The American Magazine and Historical Chronicle* had "industriously propagated" the false statement that the magazine was to be printed in Philadelphia, and had hastily established *The Boston Weekly Magazine* to hinder, if possible, the sale of subscriptions for the other periodical.[12] Moreover, according to the letter, circumstances seemed

[12] A more complete résumé of the letter follows: "The Undertakers of the American Monthly Magazine, soon after their Proposals were publish'd were inform'd that an Objection was invented and industriously propagated that it was design'd to be printed in Philadelphia, with other Insinuations that manifestly tended to hinder Subscriptions to it. What Purposes were to be served by this Report, &c. we were not thoro'ly acquainted with, till Wednesday last, when there appeared a half Sheet intitled, The Boston Weekly-Magazine, in some measure copying our Title, and pursuing our Scheme: And now every Gentleman will readily see what design that Report was to serve without a Monitor. We are convinced from many concurring Circumstances that this Weekly Paper owes its hasty and immature Production, not only to a desire of hindering Subscriptions to the Monthly Magazine; but also from a Suspicion that the Compilers would not be so hearty and zealous in promoting and maintaining the Religious Controversies of the present Day, as it imagin'd the Exigencies of the Case required: And indeed with respect to us, they were not mistaken; for we had some Tho'ts of wholly omitting them for several Reasons, but chiefly because many think we have had eno' of them even to Satiety, if not to nauciousness already, and therefore don't intend (and if this *Weekly-Magazine* continues, shall be under no Temptation from the Importunity of angry contending Parties) to disoblige our Subscribers and mortify Paper with long trifling Disputes, wherein the Authors are frequently found asserting with great earnestness that which every Body knows; and laboring to prove what no Body denies; and as commonly offering Arguments, and dealing out such Censures and Reflections that . . . answer no end, unless to keep Feuds and Animosities alive; and convince their Readers that they are violently attach'd to a Party, their reasoning Powers debilitated, and overcome by Prejudice." The writer is aware that not all religious disputes are without purpose, "but we know that generally by how much any thing is more disputable, the less it is necessary or conducible to the Christian Life. . . . We shall not therefore appropriate much of our Magazine to those hot Disputes, or petty Questions, or turn to them ourselves, unless now and then for Diversion, and to exercise our reasoning Powers, which we trust may be done without stirring the Passions . . . being content that everyone should follow the Direction of his own Conscience in matters of Religion according to his present Light . . . being desirous our Endeavors might rather contribute to, than any ways impair that Love and Unity of Christians. . . . But as in our Proposals we have promis'd something of a controversial Nature, and by some the Work may be thought incompleat without inserting the Disputes of the present Day; we have determined to appropriate three or four Pages for that purpose, in which will be contained what is publish'd in the Month on both sides of the Question. If any should be so critical as to enquire how we propose to put such a Number of Things into so small a compass, they may know we have a Gentleman concerned in compiling the

to point to the probability that the supporters of *The Boston Weekly Magazine* wished to engage in the religious controversy which disturbed the scene almost to "nauciousness" already, and which those contemplating *The American Magazine and Historical Chronicle* had originally thought might well go unnoticed in their magazine.

The Boston Weekly Magazine's public statement as regards its own excuse for being appeared on the front page of its first issue: "It has often been wished by Gentlemen of Ingenuity and Learning," the announcement read, "that a Weekly Paper were published among us, something different in its Nature and Manner from those which already entertain us." Since newspapers are not easily bound, "many Pieces of Wit and Politeness, which perhaps we should have been willing to have preserv'd, are soon irrecoverably lost.

"To remedy these Inconveniences, and gratify the Curious and Intelligent, we propose a Weekly Pamphlet . . . in which, besides the most remarkable Passages of News, we shall endeavor to publish . . . Originals, and the best Collections, upon the most entertaining and useful Subjects; Essays of Wit and Humour, Poetry and polite Learning, so as to make the whole a Piece of valuable Furniture in the Library of a Gentleman." An invitation was extended to all who were "able and willing" to contribute articles for the "Embellishment of this Work"; and promises were made to print no "private Scandal" or anything "Inconsistent with Religion and Virtue," and to give fair attention to both sides in any matter of dispute. The subscription price was set at eight shillings a year, new tenor, with title page and index for the volume at the close of the year gratis.

The short life of the miniature magazine precluded any possibility of offering original material from a breadth of contributors. The bulk of the space in the three issues extant is devoted to such essays of a general nature of "Of Education," "Praise of

---

Work, whom we call our Condensor, from the Power he has with a little mechanical Instrument to extract the Air, . . . discharge the empreumatick Savour, collect the Sense of the Author, and place it in the least Room, and the most advantageous Light.
"(Signed) J——— G———, &c."

In connection with the subject of religion to which the letter makes reference, it is worth remembering that Gridley's leanings toward deism would make him not wholly acceptable to either of the two warring groups.

Cowardice," "Character of a Miser,"[13] "Of Impudence and False Modesty," "The Vanity of Humane Grandeur and the Œconomy of Life," "Man a Conceited Animal,"[14] and "On Honour."[15]   A slightly less general subject, yet one far distant, was "An Account of the Indians at Carolina," by a Frenchman, written in 1688.[16]   A page or two of each issue was devoted to poetry, the most notable reprint being Addison's "Ode on St. Cecilia's Day."[17] More characteristic of the quality of verse chosen was "To a Poetical Lady."

> "Yet still, to rule her House aright
>   Would better far become her,
> Than to surpass the noblest Flight
>   In *Milton* or in *Homer*."[18]

"Verses Made at Sea," in the second number, and "A Hymn to the Author of the Universe," in the third, are the chief poems of those issues.

The digest of news grew to occupy a page and a half, and though Boston was chiefly represented, some notes from other cities were included.   *The Boston Weekly Magazine* is one of the most trivial early periodicals, but it is a true magazine in the sense of the period.   It conformed to Edward Cave's conception of a magazine as a "storehouse" of material worthy (in the mind of the editor) of being ultimately bound in book form.

II

The launching of *The American Magazine and Historical Chronicle* was attended by a careful business supervision and editorial policy imitative of British journals.   Proposals for publishing the magazine were printed as early as January 20, 1743, in *The Boston Weekly News-Letter*,[19] but the first number (September)

[13] No. 1.
[14] No. 2.
[15] No. 3.
[16] *Ibid.*
[17] No. 1.
[18] *Ibid.*
[19] The advertisement was repeated Jan. 27; other advertisements appeared in the same paper from time to time in succeeding months.   It is interesting to note that the phraseology employed in the first advertisement is strikingly similar to lines in the advertisements used earlier by Franklin and Bradford; of perhaps greater interest

was not issued from the press until October. The proposals stated that the magazine would be published monthly on three sheets of large paper, and that no expense would be spared to secure the best materials and make the publication both interesting and instructive.

The editorial outline, as stated in the proposals of January 20, was broad, including: "(I) A summary Rehearsal of the Proceedings and Debates in the British Parliament. (II) A View of the Weekly and Monthly Dissertations, Essays, &c. selected from the publick Papers, and Pamphlets, published in London, and the Plantations, with Extracts from new Books. (III) Dissertations, Letters and Essays, moral, civil, political, humorous and polemical. (IV) Select Pieces, relating to the Arts and Sciences, viz., speculative and practical Mathematicks, astronomical, mechanical and experimental Philosophy, Physick, Surgery, Chymistry, Oratory, Musick, Painting, Architecture, Husbandry, Gardening, &c. (V) Governour's Speeches, with the Proceedings of the Assembly and an Abridgment of the Laws enacted in the respective Provinces and Colonies. (VI) Poetical Essays on variety of Subjects. (VII) The Monthly Chronologer. . . . (VIII) Price Current. (IX) Births and Deaths. (X) A Catalogue of new Books, &c." The whole was to be contained in a magazine which averaged forty-six pages each monthly issue, comparing favorably with the size of British journals of the same type.

Indicative of the sound business policy was the price set for subscriptions—forty-eight shillings a year, old tenor.[20] Furthermore, the magazine was not to be published unless a sufficient number of subscribers would encourage the undertaking. Some effort was made to secure a wide distribution: John Eliot, John Phillips, Samuel Eliot, in Boston; Benjamin Franklin, in Philadelphia; James Parker, in New York; Joseph Pomroy, in New Haven; and Captain Peter Franklin, in Newport, were named as agents to receive subscriptions which would be returned if the magazine failed to appear.

---

is the fact that the magazine fashioned its title by combining a part of the titles of both Franklin's and Bradford's magazines.

[20] *The Boston Weekly News-Letter*, Jan. 20, 1743. Ten shillings were to be paid on subscribing, fourteen at the end of the second quarter, and the remainder quarterly. When the magazine finally appeared, it was priced at three shillings per quarter, new tenor, and the name of Postmaster C. Campbell took the place of that of Captain Franklin as agent for Newport.

Occasional advertisements through the spring and summer of 1743 kept the proposals for *The American Magazine and Historical Chronicle* before the readers of Boston newspapers. On Thursday, October 20, the first number, for September, was advertised in *The Boston Weekly News-Letter* as "This Day . . . Published." The magazine was continued monthly through three years and four months, a record neither equalled nor exceeded (except by the specialized *Ein geistliches Magazien*) until *The Columbian Magazine*, begun at Philadelphia in 1786, achieved a longer existence. An examination of the files of the Boston papers shows that the magazine was issued throughout the whole span of forty months with surprising regularity.[21]

In his brief account of *The American Magazine and Historical Chronicle*, Isaiah Thomas[22] made a guarded statement relative to the identity of the editor: "Jeremy Gridley, Esq., who had edited the *Rehearsal*, it has been said, was also the editor of this magazine." Since then others, without presenting further evidence, have affirmed Gridley's connection, possibly by shearing Thomas's statement of its element of doubt. The signature attached to the letter in Draper's paper tends further, I believe, to confirm the connection of Gridley as editor, especially as not only the initials but the religious attitude and the somewhat belligerent and florid style of the letter are Gridley's.[23]

[21] The numbers represent the month and day advertisements appeared. The summary of the three incomplete files presents a clear picture of the publication dates. In some cases, because of lack of space in the newspapers, the advertisement appeared slightly irregularly, being omitted in one paper, but printed in another. The first number was advertised as late as Nov. 7 in the *The Boston Evening-Post*, but the second number, as noted, came out on time.

The Boston Evening-Post: 1743—10/24;11/21, 28; 12/19, 26; 1744—4/16; 8/13; 1745—2/18; 5/6; 6/10; 8/12; 10/14; 12/16; 1746—1/13; 2/10; 3/10; 5/12; 6/9; 7/7; 8/11; 9/15; 10/13; 11-10. *The Boston Weekly News-Letter*: 1743—10/20; 11/25; 12/8; 1744—1/12; 2/9; 3/8; 6/14; 7/12; 8/9; 9/13; 10/11; 11/15; 12/13; 1745—2/14; 3/14; 4/11; 6/6; 7/19; 8/8; 9/12; 11/7; 12/12; 1746—1/9; 2/6; 3/14; 4/10; 5/22; 6/26; 7/3; 8/7; 9/4; 10/9; 11/6, 28; 1747—1/1. *The Boston Weekly Post-Boy*: 1746—1/13; 2/10; 3/10; 5/7; 6/16; 7/7; 8/11; 9/15; 10/13; 11/3; 12/15.

[22] *Op. cit.*, II, 68.

[23] For general biographical references to Gridley (1702-67), see R. G. F. Candage, "Jeremy Gridley, a Paper Read before the Society, Oct. 22, 1902," *Publications of the Brookline Historical Society* (1903); Samuel L. Knapp, *Biographical Sketches of Eminent Lawyers, Statesmen, and Men of Letters* (1821), pp. 199-217; William T. Davis, *Bench and Bar of the Commonwealth of Massachusetts* (Vol. I, 1895); Francis S. Drake, *Dictionary of American Biography* (1872); Samuel Adams Drake, *The Old Boston Taverns and Tavern Clubs* (1886), p. 49; Samuel Gardner Drake, *The History and Antiquities of the City of Boston* (1854), II, 589, 618.

As Gridley's editorial hand is visible in the magazine also, even though the periodical was composed chiefly of material reprinted from British sources, the mind and attitudes of the man will serve somewhat not only to indicate the nature but to explain the history of the periodical. He was possessed of a true love for the classics. His graduation from Harvard (1725) had been followed by study in theology, but as his deistic beliefs triumphed over more orthodox concepts, he had drifted from the pulpit to the bar, to which he was admitted in 1731. During that year and the one following, he had found time, while establishing a legal practice, to polish his Addisonian style and gratify a natural haughtiness of spirit by editing *The Weekly Rehearsal*. Thereafter he had devoted himself to the law with a zest which characterized his life, and finally attained the office of attorney-general of Massachusetts. In 1743 he became interested in *The American Magazine and Historical Chronicle*. From a popular point of view, his place in history is connected with his defense, as attorney-general, of the unpopular Writs of Assistance against the arguments of James Otis, and with his support of British policies until his death. He impressed his acquaintances as a man of great erudition, excelling in the law and the classics, but possessed of an egotistic bearing which was his worst enemy, and dishonored by the deistic taint which spiritually associated him with Shaftsbury and Bolingbroke.[24]

Following the course of Gridley's mind, the magazine derived its source largely from its editor's fount of literary and legal authority—England. Even the articles concerning America were frequently copied from British magazines.[25] The American presses

[24] Shortly after the death of Gridley, the Rev. Ezra Stiles, President of Yale, wrote to his friend, the Rev. Charles Chauncy, "I had conceived him [Gridley] a Man of great Erudition, consummate Haughtiness, unbounded Ambition—and in Religion a Disciple of *Shaftsbury & Bolingbroke*: . . . an Antiamerican. . . ." To this letter Chauncy replied: "He was certainly a man of erudition; thô far from being an universal scholar. His learning was very much confined to the law, and the Classicks, in both w.ch he excelled. . . . Haughtiness of spirit accompanied him w.rever he went, and was all along in life a great dishonor as well as disadvantage to him. . . . His air, and whole manner of behavior were so haughty, forbidding and insolent, that but few cared to have to do w.th him. . . . The only way of access to him was by flattery. . . . As to his religion, I don't suppose he had any. . . ." (*Extracts from the Itineraries and Other Miscellanies of Ezra Stiles. . . . with a Selection from his Correspondence*, ed. Franklin Bowditch Dexter, 1916, pp. 443-44.)

[25] One should remember, of course, that books concerning America were often of London imprint, and to these the London magazines had earlier access.

were not lazy at this time. Pamphlets—the typical and practical mode for literary expression for this county—were numerous.[26] In them lay fundamental dramas of American life, religious, political, and economic. If Gridley could not summon a coterie of writers to his magazine, perhaps partly because his temperament was so "insolent, that few cared to have to do w.ᵗʰ him,"[27] he might have followed Franklin's lead in printing extracts from American sources. But this he failed in the main to do. He gazed eastward too steadily, and too eagerly awaited the literary cargoes from England. Thus the magazine did not adequately represent America in a period of ferment. Its long life was perhaps due to the lack of any other general magazine in America, and the power of England over the literary imagination of the Colonists.

A declaration of the policy of the magazine was expressed in the "Introduction" to the first number,[28] the writer prefacing his remarks with a statement of confidence in the success of the magazine, although the number of subscriptions was still insufficient to support the periodical. The program stirred him with enthusiasm. Those in authority contemplated "a Collection of the best and most approved Pieces, publish'd in *Great-Britain* and the Plantations, with summary Rehearsals and Quotations from the best Authors that treat of all Parts of polite and useful Learning; with such Originals as we have, or shall from Time to Time be furnish'd with from Gentlemen of Ingenuity and Erudition," and they hoped "that in a few Years these Collections will amount to a Treasury of various Knowledge and Learning, of the *serious* and *pleasant*, of the *instructing* and *diverting*, and help to furnish the Mind with Store of choice well-digested Apprehensions of Men and Things." In matters of religious and political controversy he recognized that "it is impossible in the Nature of the Things . . . and the Disposition of Mankind, who are passionately and almost universally fond of their own peculiar Sentiments, to touch upon them with so much Delicacy as that none will be displeased," but asserted that "we have no malevolent Design on the Character of Interest of any particular Persons, or Parties of

[26] An examination of Charles Evans, *American Bibliography* for this period will show a high percentage of religious works.

[27] See note 24.

[28] Sept. 1743, pp. i-iv.

Men whatever. . . ." The general status of the editors in these matters was to be largely that of "meer Reporters of Facts." The principle that "Every Man or Party of Men have a natural Right to be heard" would be respected, provided the comments contained "no blasphemous Tenets with respect to GOD, or tend to the Subversion of Government, or to vilify the just and regular Administrators of it."

It was, naturally, beyond the capacity of Gridley's temperament completely to carry out the policy just summarized. It is not to be supposed that one so conservative as to be considered by President Ezra Stiles of Yale as "Antiamerican"[29] in political affairs, and so deistic as to incline the Reverend Charles Chauncy of Boston to doubt whether he had any religion at all,[30] would maintain an editorial balance so delicate that the "natural Right to be heard" would operate fully.

In appearance *The American Magazine and Historical Chronicle* closely followed *The London Magazine*. For the first volume (and the first only) the publishers of the new magazine even adopted *The London Magazine's* plan of running capital letters from A to G vertically in the margin between the two columns of type on each page. When the first volume was issued the title page was embellished with an engraving by James Turner, silversmith, showing a part of Boston, the harbor, and the bridge across to Charlestown; this also was a close approximation of the picture of London on the cover of *The London Magazine*, in which the bridge was a focal center of interest.

From the English magazines, too, came much of the material in the magazine. During the first four months a fair amount of American copy was included; but in January 1744 the editor selected as a serial and leading article the "Journal of the Proceedings and Debates of a Political Club of Young Noblemen," appearing originally in *The London Magazine* to offset the Lilliput papers made famous by Samuel Johnson in *The Gentleman's Magazine*. This serial,[31] containing English political news, occupied usually from twelve to eighteen pages each month, and effectively diminished the amount of American material included. Among

[29] See note 24.
[30] *Ibid.*
[31] It ran from Jan. to July 1744; and from Jan. 1745 to May 1746 with fair regularity.

the other British periodicals and essay-books from which the magazine drew were: *The Present State of Great Britain; Common Sense, or the Englishman's Journal; The Universal Spectator; The Champion; The True Patriot; The Westminster Journal; The Daily Advertiser; The Dutch Spectator; The Grub-street Journal; The Free-Holder; The Drapier's Letters; The Occasional Writer; The Philosophical Transactions of the Royal Society; The Craftsman; The Gentleman's Magazine; The London Courant;* and *The Weekly Register.*

Great names in literature, and names so great that biographical sketches of the men were of universal interest, found their way into the magazine among the several hundred pages of selected pieces. Considerable space was given to Alexander Pope[32] and Jonathan Swift,[33] whose respective deaths in 1744 and 1745 stimulated the printing of short prose and poetical excerpts from their works as well as items regarding the authors. A favorite, though not the only source for biographies, was Bayle's *Historical and Critical Dictionary.* Most important and engaging are the accounts of the lives of John Milton,[34] John Calvin,[35] John Locke,[36] and Sir Isaac Newton,[37] which the editor undoubtedly believed would hold the attention of New England readers not only be-

[32] From his poetry were selected "The Universal Prayer" (Nov. 1744, p. 657) and "Messiah" (Dec. 1745, pp. 555-57); other items of interest were his last will (Nov. 1744, pp. 632-34), a letter to Joseph Addison (Sept. 1744, pp. 551-52), a letter to Richard Steele (Aug. 1744, pp. 505-06), part of a letter to Henry Cromwell dated Oct. 19, 1709 (Dec. 1745, pp. 544-45), a letter to Edward Blount (May 1745, pp. 210-11), an article on Pope's character (Nov. 1744, pp. 634-36), five poems occasioned by his death (Nov. 1744, pp. 653-58), and "Verses Prefix'd to the New Edition of the Essay on Man, . . . with Notes by W. Warburton" (Dec. 1746, pp. 570-71).

[33] Selections included Swift's poetical letter of advice to the Earl of Orrery (Nov. 1744, p. 658), the poem "The Furniture of a Woman's Mind" (June 1745, p. 266), "Lamentation for the Loss of his Hearing" (Oct. 1744, p. 608), an extract from *The Drapier's Letters* (Jan. 1746, pp. 19-22), "A Letter to a Young Lady on her Marriage" (Sept. 1746, pp. 399-404), and, in honor of Swift, the poem "On Dr. Swift's Death," by "C. B." (May 1746, p. 233), the poem "On the Death of Dean Swift," by "Philander," dated Spalding, Jan. 13, 1745 (May 1746, p. 231), and "The Scotsman's Yearning, for the Sight of the Rev. Dean Swift" (Sept. 1743, p. 37).

[34] June 1745, pp. 239-44.

[35] May 1744, pp. 366-69.

[36] Sept. 1744, pp. 540-44.

[37] Jan. 1745, pp. 9-18. Other accounts of lives included those of Robert Boyle (Oct. 1744, pp. 583-88), John Tillotson, Archbishop of Canterbury (Aug. 1744, pp. 490-95), Dr. Thomas Burnet (Feb. 1745, pp. 66-67), Peter Burman (Aug. 1745, pp. 336-41), and Bishop Jewell (Sept. 1745, pp. 395-96).

cause of the commanding personalities of the subjects, but because the "Great Awakening" had stirred a fresh interest in theological and philosophical speculations. Voltaire,[38] among the French writers, attracted the greatest attention for his wit and intellectual audacity. The usual references to Voltaire in magazines of the time reflected the popular conception of the man as brilliant but leagued with the devil; to read his works was to engage in an unholy excursion in religious unorthodoxy. But Gridley, with the gracious attitude of one deist to another, presented the man in intellectual moods not particularly antagonistic to the mass of readers who enjoyed thought mixed with satire. An extract from *The Persian Letters*[39] of Charles Montesquieu and a few lines from Jean Racine's *Esther*[40] are other excerpts from the French not unexpected in the magazine, though they might have been replaced by other selections. In the same class of pieces chosen by caprice from among many possibilities are lines from Mark Akenside's *The Pleasures of Imagination*[41] and Thomas Parnell's *A Hymn to Contentment*.[42]   On the other hand, Joseph Addison's essay in *The Free-Holder* No. 43, "A Popish King and Protestant Subjects Inconsistent,"[43] was clearly selected because of the invasion of the Young Pretender, Prince Charles Edward, into England in 1745-46, threatening the throne.

The American Magazine and Historical Chronicle did not confine the articles on governmental, military, and religious subjects to the "Chronicle" department. Indeed, this arbitrary division, occupying usually from five to eight pages monthly, contained little except short summaries of the acts of the provincial Assemblies and, for foreign intelligence, a digest of the news in the latest available number of *The Gentleman's Magazine*. Scattered throughout the body of the three volumes are many selected articles judged too important to be relegated to the "Chronicle."   Dis-

[38] Voltaire's speech when admitted to the French Academy (Nov. 1746, pp. 481-89), "Reflections with Regard to History" (Sept. 1745, pp. 391-92), and "The Vanity of Fame" (Feb. 1745, pp. 69-71) were printed; one controversial piece was selected, "Answer to M. Voltaire," from the "10th Tome of M. Rollin's Roman History" (Dec. 1745, pp. 540-41).

[39] Aug. 1745, pp. 341-44.

[40] *Ibid.*, p. 357.

[41] Nov. 1745, p. 507.

[42] Sept. 1745, p. 411.

[43] Jan. 1746, pp. 25-27.

putes between governors and their assemblies, financial appropriations, treaties with Indian tribes, matters relating to the conquest
of Canada and the capture of Louisburg under the leadership of
Massachusetts, the invasion of England by Prince Charles Edward
and the attending fear lest a Roman Catholic should again ascend
the throne, the provincial religious conflict—all these especially
engaged the attention of the editor, and he turned the blades of the
editorial shears to the cause of the English policies throughout.
Thus the speeches of William Shirley,[44] the governor of Massachusetts and vigorous prosecutor of the war, were carefully reported;
of major importance were his triumphal report delivered to the
legislature in July 1745, "A Particular Account of the Siege and
Surrender of Louisbourg," and his speech to the garrison at the
captured city, in which he urged the troops to remain beyond the
period of their enlistment until newly enlisted forces might be
brought to the scene of victory.[45] Other accounts, too, described
Cape Breton, traced the history of the conflict through to the capture of Louisburg and the attendant ceremonies, and, with an
insistence revealing the necessity for the propaganda, sought to
impress on the people at large the need of supporting the war
and retaining the captured territory.[46] Of these, the congratula-

[44] Note especially Shirley's speeches to the legislature in the magazine for March
and April 1744, pp. 282-87 and 316-26; his speech of April 3, 1745 in the magazine
for the same month, pp. 166-69, on the active measures taken to equip the expedition
and the progress of the war; his speeches on the further progress of the war (June
and July 1745, pp. 260-63 and 311-13), the latter being an account of the siege and
surrender of Louisburg; his speech to the garrison at Louisburg, Aug. 23, 1745 (Sept.
1745, pp. 403-05); his account of the victory to the Duke of Newcastle, dated Oct.
28, 1745 (Dec. 1746, pp. 553-58); his presentation of the king's thanks for the
Louisburg victory (Dec. 1745, pp. 549-52): his speeches urging further enlistment to
relieve those whose terms were expiring (April and May 1746, pp. 176-78 and 225-27,
and June, pp. 277-79 and 286); and other official speeches (Nov. and Dec. 1746, pp.
511-14 and 566-68).

[45] It became increasingly difficult to induce men to enlist, as the speeches by Shirley
indicate; Massachusetts came to feel that she had more than fulfilled her duty, and
that other Colonies should contribute more men.

[46] See accounts of Cape Breton (May and Oct. 1745, pp. 216-17 and 451-53);
accounts of the safe arrival at Louisburg and the siege and surrender thereof (May,
June, July 1745, pp. 223-26, 275-76, and 308-11); Peter Warren's speech to the
American troops at Louisburg, May 19, 1746 (June 1746, pp. 271-73); William Pepperell's "Congratulatory Address" to the victors (June 1746, p. 273) and his ideas of
"The Importance of Cape Breton" (July 1746, pp. 293-96); a statement of the
advantage of the French fishery on the Newfoundland banks (July 1746, pp. 293-96);
article on the importance of Cape Breton (Nov. 1746, pp. 490-92); the plea "To
Maintain a War with France, even without Allies, More Eligible than Restoring Cape-

tory speeches on the victory by General William Pepperell[47] and His Excellency Peter Warren, delivered May 19, 1746, are particularly interesting, as well as Pepperell's belief in "The Importance of Cape Breton" and Pierre Charlevoix's similar and earlier opinion, which he had expressed to his own country of France, and which Gridley reprinted to show the high regard of France for Canada.[48]

South of New England, where trade was not so distressed by the privateers lurking about the mouth of the St. Lawrence, there was less response to the war, and though Massachusetts had counted on considerable support from New York and Pennsylvania, the addresses of Governor George Clinton[49] and Governor George Thomas[50] indicate the difficulties the pro-war executives encountered with the far less belligerent legislatures. More active attention was paid to the Indian relations, however, as therein lay possibilities of danger. The most interesting article on this phase of the war was the report of "The Treaty Held with the Indians of the Six Nations at Philadelphia, July, 1742."[51] In this treaty the Indians pledged their friendship to Great Britain even though France should declare war against the British, but plainly showed their resentment of an economic system which bartered consumable goods for non-consumable Indian lands.

It is apparent that the editor of the magazine wished to maintain toward the local religious controversy a policy coolly objective, conservative yet conciliatory. In the initial number the first three articles concerned the provincial phases of the "Great Awaken-

---

Breton" (Nov. 1746, pp. 492-93); the journal of the siege of Louisburg (Dec. 1746, pp. 558-65); and three sketches by Pierre Charlevoix describing Cape Breton, Quebec, and Newfoundland, and insisting on the value of Canada to France (July 1746, pp. 289-93 and 313-18, and Sept. 1746, pp. 408-11.)

[47] Wealthy merchant of Kittery, Maine, and commander of the force against Louisburg.

[48] See note 46.

[49] See especially speeches reported in the following issues: Nov. 1743, pp. 129-31; Aug. 1744, pp. 516-17; June 1745, pp. 258-60; July 1745, pp. 306-08; June 1746, pp. 274-76.

[50] See especially speeches reported in the following issues: Aug. 1744, pp. 512-17; Sept. 1745, pp. 405-06.

[51] In magazine issues for October and November 1743, pp. 45-54 and 94-107. Other articles include an "Account of the First Confederacy of the Six Nations" as told by Conrad Weiser (Dec. 1744, pp. 665-69), and the declaration of war against the Indians by Lieutenant-Governor Spencer Phips, of Massachusetts (Aug. 1745, pp. 355-57).

ing." The first,[52] an editorial attempt to comprehend the whole situation, admitted that perfunctoriness and lethargy had characterized religious thought during the more recent past, when useless bickering over Calvinistic doctrines had been the chief attention. But the writer doubted the value of the "Great Awakening" and saw little virtue in the itinerant preaching of the winsome George Whitefield, the less intelligent Gilbert Tennent, and the wildly emotional James Davenport. He believed that a desire for personal glory was not lacking in the background of the emotionalism, and he stigmatized roundly the affectation of Davenport, who had "a Man always to attend him, . . . his *Armour-Bearer.*" The second and third articles[53] chronicled the conflict between the conservative ministers and the revivalists, the latter having held a convention of their own when they discovered they could not control the major assembly.[54]

A thin but important stream of essays ran through the pages of the magazine during the years 1744-46, counseling a rational attitude in the application of religious zeal in a world of many sects.[55] It was tributary to that loosely bounded but steadily flowing current of English and Continental thought which urged the adoption of a philosophical, historical, rationalistic point of view in the interpretation of religion. Undoubtedly this principle guided the editor in printing the lives of Milton, Calvin, Locke, Tillotson, and others,[56] thus supplying a broad historical background which might happily militate against specific and blind devotion. For the same reason were selected Locke's rationalistic study, "An Essay for the Understanding of St. Paul's Epistles,"[57] and Beran's "The Study of Scripture Recommended."[58] One who wrote in a way suggesting his not improbable connection with the church as a minister, "P. N." by signature, was continually urging moderation in original and clipped articles which he submitted. Of these,

[52] "A Dissertation on the State of Religion in North America," Sept. 1743, pp. 1-5.

[53] "The Testimony of . . . Pastors . . . of the Massachusetts-Bay . . . at their Annual Convention . . . Boston, May 25, 1743," and the "Testimony" of the dissatisfied revivalists at their meeting in Boston July 7, 1743 (Sept. 1743, pp. 6-13).

[54] For further comment, see section in this chapter devoted to *The Christian History.*

[55] It was displaced largely from Jan. to Aug. 1746 by a strong support of the existing establishment in England when the uprising of Prince Charles Edward brought sharply forward the possibility of a Catholic attaining the throne.

[56] See notes 34-37.

[57] Sept. 1744, pp. 529-40.

[58] Aug. 1744, pp. 485-90.

"Some Thoughts on Divisions"[59] pointing out the unnecessary sufferings incident to conflicts among churches, public societies, and
families, clearly applied to the condition in New England, while
"An Essay on Divine Judgments, Shewing the Wickedness and
Absurdity of Applying them to Men and Events"[60] cautioned the
superstitious in either camp not to consider acts of seeming misfortune as visitations of God's wrath on their rivals.[61]

The usual spirit of religious conciliation and toleration was
partially broken with the publication of the issue for January 1746,
as news had arrived of the success in Scotland of Prince Charles
Edward. Practically the whole issue was given over to articles reprinted from London and Edinburgh journals discussing the mixed
military, political, and religious phases of the uprising. Anti-
Catholic and anti-revolutionary articles were copiously printed
until late in the summer, although the April issue had carried the
news of the defeat of the invading forces. Pleas were made for
less separation and animosity among the Protestant churches;[62]
a great deal of fear was expressed over possible conditions under
"popish" rule; justifications of the Stuart reign and its right to
the rule of Scotland were printed, and reports of the military
activities and judicial decisions regarding rebels filled much space.[63]

[59] Dec. 1744, pp. 683-87.

[60] July 1744, pp. 458-61.

[61] Other essays under the aegis of "P. N." included "Of the Weakness of the
Human Mind" (March 1744, pp. 291-94), "An Essay on the Passion of Love" (April
1744, pp. 329-32), "An Essay on Eloquence" (Aug. 1744, pp. 495-98), and "Some
Thoughts on the Uneasiness of Life" (Nov. 1745, pp. 493-95), indicative of a broad,
mellow, but undistinguished reaction to life. "The Unreasonableness of Persecution"
(June 1745, pp. 255-57), by "Eusebius," and, in its way, "The Folly and Absurdity
of Atheism" (Sept. 1745, pp. 399-400) follow the same easy-chair trend. Occasionally,
however, the editor let the other side speak. "A Country Farmer," for instance
(Sept. 1745, pp. 397-98), took strong exception to the idea which "P. N." had slightly
treated (see note 60), that good or bad fortune came only through good or bad management. And in contradistinction to the first article published at the advent of the
magazine is "An Apology for Religious Zeal" (Nov. 1744, pp. 642-44), which supported
"a hearty and an affectionate Concern for the Service and Honour of God," as was being
manifested in the "Great Awakening," at a time when the "Fashionable World" had
refined us "at last into the most irrational Coldness and Indifference to Religion, that
was ever seen, since the Christian Religion was first planted." Isolated from the major
streams of thought, but consistent with the plan of broad education, was the article on the
Quakers which appeared in March 1745, pp. 118-21.

[62] See, for example, the Reverend Mr. Vines's treatise on the Lord's Supper, April
1746, pp. 150-53.

[63] See articles during 1746 against "Popery" (Jan., pp. 10-17, 19, 22-24); the
Archbishop of York's remarks on the sins of perjury and rebellion (Feb., pp. 74-77);

Not until August did the contents of the magazine resume their normal field of interest.

Scientific articles were copied almost exclusively from British magazines, and especially from the *Transactions* of the Royal Society and *The Gentleman's Magazine*. The eighteenth century was not unpossessed of an inquiring mind nor idle in exploring the physical world. Studies in geography, geology, and astronomy, descriptions of experiments in electricity, and accounts of the development of the microscope and advances in medical practice found their way into popular British journals and thence to *The American Magazine and Historical Chronicle*; and to this fund an occasional colonist would contribute.[64] From British sources, George Berkeley's presentation of the virtues of tar water[65] and John Arbuthnot's advice on foods occupied a goodly proportion of space.[66] American contributions included "Some Reflexions"[67] on

[64] an exceptionally long article on the settlement of the Crown in the Protestant line (Feb., pp. 52-65); the Bishop of Worcester's letter to his clergy on the rebellion (Feb., pp. 82-83); an extract on the rebellion from a sermon by William Warburton (March, pp. 117-20); his Majesty's speech to both Houses concerning the late rebellion and their answer (April, pp. 172-76); the right of the house of Stuart to the crown of Scotland defended (May, pp. 210-17); particulars of the Duke of Cumberland's victory near Culloden (July, pp. 330-32); the congratulatory address of the House of Peers to the King on his victory (July, pp. 323-24); speech of the Lord High Chancellor Philip Hardwicke at the sentence of the rebel lords (Oct., pp. 465-69); account of the Manchester rebels (Nov., pp. 503-06); accounts of the execution of Scotch rebels (Nov., pp. 506-09).

[64] Examples of the types during 1744 are Pere du Halde's description of China, an extract (Nov., pp. 615-32); a description of a burning volcano (Aug., pp. 503-05); an account of milk white Indians (July, pp. 465-66); a selection from Egede's account of Greenland (April, May, pp. 326-29, 359-65); a description of the Reverend Rector Clap's planetarium at Yale (Jan., pp. 202-03); a selection regarding comets from the Reverend Rowning's *Compendious System of Natural Philosophy* (Jan., pp. 207-09); a note on perpetual motion in matter (June, pp. 415-16); see also notes on microscopical discoveries (May 1744, pp. 369-72, Oct. 1746, pp. 439-40); a preservative against the plague (Dec. 1743, p. 160); a comical case of the "hyp" (Sept. 1743, pp. 29-31); a method to recover persons thought drowned (June 1746, pp. 265-67); a note on the bad effects of tea drinking (Aug. 1746, pp. 347-48); a physical account of the nature of distilled spirituous liquors (Sept. 1746, pp. 385-91); descriptions of experiments in electricity (Dec. 1745, pp. 530-37, Oct. 1746, pp. 461-64); an extract from Charles Bonnet's new observations on insects (June 1746, pp. 259-63).

[65] This account, with reflections by others, appeared in Oct. 1744, pp. 588-92, Nov., pp. 636-37, April 1745, pp. 145-52, and elsewhere. Berkeley's account first appeared in his *Siris*, 1744.

[66] A long extract from his essay on aliments was printed in Sept. and Oct. 1743, pp. 32-34, and 68-70. Although Arbuthnot's death occurred in 1735, his fame as Physician Extraordinary to Queen Anne lived after him.

[67] April 1745, pp. 145-52.

the adaption of tar water to diseases in America, "A Very Remarkable Case,"[68] by Dr. Nathan Hale, discussing peritonitis, and
Thomas Prince's gracious account of "The Late Mr. Edward Brom-
field, Jun's Microscope-Discoveries,"[69] the last being a memorial
article in honor of a young scientist of local repute whose death
terminated a promising career and whose labors in improving lenses
had already won him recognition in Boston.   But the articles
written by Colonial residents were few.   It would not be until
Provost William Smith of the College and Academy of Philadelphia should summon to *The American Magazine, or Monthly
Chronicle* (1757-58) the scientific intelligence of the college professors, and until Lewis Nicola should unite *The American Magazine, or General Repository* (1769) with the *Transactions of the
American Philosophical Society*, that America would take distinct
forward steps in the publication of scientific studies worthy of
respect.

In supplying literary substance, Gridley chose several essays
on criticism, a rather appalling number of moral essays, poems on
religious themes, translations and imitations from the ancient
classics and from the traditionally esteemed English authors, and
considerable *vers de société*, both original and selected.   The mode
of Addison was the beloved prose style, deft and aristocratic, not
in the "Bombastick" or "Grubstreet" manner;[70] Pope's *An Essay on
Criticism* was the bible for both critic and budding poet;[71] and extracts from the works of Vergil, Horace, Butler, Cowley, Prior,
Congreve, and Addison conjured the realms of literary art to the
mind.[72]   The moral essay or tale sometimes took the form of a

[68] July 1746, pp. 319-21.

[69] Dec. 1746, pp. 548-51.

[70] Particularly interesting was the selection of Mather Byles's criticism of prose composition introduced from the editorial office over the introductory signature of "L."
in the preface to the second volume (Jan. 1745, pp. 1-4), wherein two unhappy styles,
the "Bombastick" and the "Grubstreet," were criticized.   The latter was "easily
attained, provided a Man can but keep himself from thinking, and yet so contrive
Matters, as to let his Pen run along unmolested over a Sheet of White Paper, and drop
a convenient Quantity of Words, at proper Intervals upon it."   But the bombastic
writers were more particularly to be scorned, for "a Rattle of Words, and an Extravagance of Imagination, they look upon as a Perfection of Rhetorick. . . ."

[71] See "An Epistle to Myrtillo" (Sept. 1744, pp. 562-64), evidently an original poem
with the magazine, urging in heroic couplets the union of art and nature.

[72] See "An Epistle from Cambridge" (Feb. 1744, pp. 258-59), original with the
magazine, a poem containing the names given.

pensive story, as "The History of Florisa,"[73] emphasizing the sorrows of wealth; sometimes it embodied shape in a vision, as "Virtuous Love, and Lust"[74] and "A Consolatory Letter to a Friend upon the Death of his Mistress";[75] sometimes it became a satirical travelogue, tinged with national animosity;[76] often it was but a weakly conceived preachment, occasionally enlivened by a crusading spirit, as "A Caution against the Attempts of Libertine Wits."[77]

Religious themes in poetry were well diversified. Sometimes ministers were admonished, as in "A Charge to the Clergy,"[78] to employ more thought and less emotion in their sermons. Paraphrases from the Bible were popular, as exemplified in "David's Elegy upon Saul and Jonathan."[79] In "The Believer's Hope,"[80] "An Autumnal Hymn,"[81] and "A Hymn in a Spring Morning,"[82] as well as other poems of this type, the spirit of devotion rose. Occasionally, too, the themes were vividly emotional or terrible, as in "Our Saviour's Passion,"[83] describing minutely the scene on the cross, and a "Hymn"[84] by "S. T.," sent especially to the magazine, portraying the heavenly throne. In contemplating the large number of religious poems inserted in this periodical, one doubts whether

[73] Nov. 1743, pp. 114-16.

[74] Feb. 1744, pp. 245-48.

[75] Jan. 1745, pp. 23-28. The letter is signed "J. S.," and dated Stockbridge, Jan. 16, 1744-45; thus it is presumably original with the magazine.

[76] See the letter from "Sioeu Tcheou" at Paris, laughing at French immorality and costumes (Oct. 1743, pp. 62-65), and the letter from a Jew in Spain, condemning persecution (April 1744, pp. 338-39).

[77] Aug. 1744, p. 511.

[78] Oct. 1743, p. 80.

[79] March 1744, pp. 298-99. See also "Isaiah 35th Chapter Paraphrased" and the paraphrase on the 117th Psalm (Aug. 1745, pp. 358 and 361 respectively).

[80] Nov. 1745, pp. 504-05.

[81] Aug. 1745, p. 364.

[82] April 1745, pp. 172-73, by "J. D." Among reprints in the same mood, mention should be made of two excerpts from Edward Young's *Night Thoughts*, entitled "The Complaint" (March, April 1746, pp. 130-31, 178-79).

[83] Aug. 1746, p. 376.

[84] Nov. 1746, p. 518. In part, the lines read:

> "At God's right Hand there shines a Throne,
> And Jesus fills the Place:
> The Man the Deity infolds,
> Attempering all its Rays.
>
> . . . . . .
>
> Cherub or Seraph never saw
> So much of God before;
> And plunging in the milder Light,
> They burn and they adore."

Gridley, whose interests lay elsewhere, would have selected so many had the public not been so prolific in composing them or so active in clipping them from various sources and requesting him to print them.

Among all authors, Horace was the most popular for the young student and poet to imitate and translate. "Quintilian's Complaint"[85] offers variation, Ovid is briefly quoted,[86] Moschus is represented in "Cupid Ploughing,"[87] and a theme "On Homer"[88] praises a master of epic verse, but Horace appeared with the regularity of a fad pursued vigorously.[89] Representations of later periods, of course, may also be found—star-scattered efforts to attain true poetical expression. "An Epithalamium," wishing a happy life to Strephon and Charissa,[90] for instance, has not inconceivably qualities reminiscent of Spenser. Perhaps more interesting from a local point of view are two poems by "Myrtillo,"[91] original with the magazine, written in full knowledge of the preceding work of Addison and Philips.

Attention to the interests of women and the inclusion of a considerable body of society verse in the magazine emphasize a light and sentimental side to mid-eighteenth-century New England not usually recorded. Versified riddles and their solutions, epigrams, addresses to and from young ladies and gentlemen, and "advice" on conduct and love were somewhat fostered by the social life, legitimized by literary custom, and found suitable in theme and structure for juvenile literary attempts. These, together with the moral prose essay and occasional articles in praise of women, were the substance which a specialized magazine fashioned preëminently for ladies was soon to exploit in Boston.[92] In prose, "The Form of a Modern Love-Letter,"[93] the "Remarkable Instances of the Ex-

[85] Jan. 1745, pp. 37-38.

[86] March 1746, p. 136.

[87] Feb. 1746, p. 87.

[88] Ibid.

[89] See translations or imitations in the following numbers: Oct. 1743, pp. 74-76; March 1745, p. 124; April 1745, p. 172; Oct. 1745, p. 457; April 1746, p. 180; Aug. 1746, p. 373; and Dec. 1746, p. 572.

[90] May 1746, pp. 228-29.

[91] "Ode for St. Cecilia's Day" (June 1744, pp. 430-31) and "On Sappho's Hymn to Venus Attempted" (June 1744, pp. 431-32).

[92] The New-England Magazine (1758).

[93] Aug. 1744, p. 510.

tensive Capacity of the Fair Sex,"[94] "The Power of Beauty, and
the Influence the Fair Sex Might Have in Reforming the Manners of the World,"[95] and other similar articles certainly were
shrewdly included for the delight of feminine readers. In poetry,
a lighter vein was often struck. Men might enjoy an occasional
poem done in the spirit of the cavalier,[96] they might lightly instruct
in love,[97] they might pen short lyrics to sweethearts[98] and counsel
the young bride;[99] they might even allow their fancies to stray to
such odd themes as "On a Young Lady who Had Ill-Luck in the
Lottery"[100] and "Occasion'd by Seeing a Young Lady Drop a
Small Pin from Between her Fingers."[101] But women were as
interested in such work as the men, although their own themes were
not so frequently of love and courtship, and occasionally they struck
a militant attitude, as in "Verses . . . by a Young Lady on Woman
Born to be Controul'd,"[102] by one who highly resented the domination of the male in the marriage state. In fine, *The American
Magazine and Historical Chronicle* needed only to be somewhat
more restricted to the sphere of women's interests to become a lady's
magazine.

In the number for January 1746,[103] the editors published a proposal which presumably they hoped would place the magazine on
a less precarious foundation. Since maps[104] and historical accounts
of America were "generally so imperfect," they announced the publication "by Parcels" in the magazine of *A Summary, Historical
and Political, of the Beginnings, Progressive Improvements, and
Present State of the British Settlements in North America*, by
"W. D., M. D." This plan of printing William Douglass's work,
however, was slow in maturing. The year passed without a single

[94] Aug. 1745, pp. 344-47.

[95] Sept. 1745, pp. 400-03.

[96] "The General Lover," Sept. 1743, p. 34.

[97] "To a Lady who Ask'd, What Is Love?" Feb. 1744, p. 257.

[98] "To Amoret at Church," Feb. 1744, p. 257.

[99] "Advice to a Young Lady Just After her Marriage," by "A. Z.," evidently
original with the magazine, as it bore the same monthly date, Dec. 1744, pp. 698-701.
The poem urged the young lady "by submitting" to "bind him to your Will."

[100] June 1745, pp. 265-66. The poem is signed "R. F.," and is evidently original with
the magazine.

[101] Aug. 1744, p. 522.

[102] June 1744, p. 435.

[103] Pp. 1-2.

[104] Besides the illustration of Boston on the cover, the magazine contained in the issue
for June 1745 a drawing of the "Town and Harbour of Louisbourgh."

"parcel." In the meantime the publishers had decided to abandon the magazine as a monthly, and the last issue ever published (December 1746), failed to carry the usual line, "to be continued monthly."

Concerning plans for the future, *The Boston Weekly News-Letter* for February 12, 1747 printed an illuminating announcement: "Whereas many Gentlemen and others have appeared to subscribe for the *American Magazine* since the Advertisement for carrying on therein a *Summary* . . . and some of them being desirous it may be printed separate, . . ." it was therefore "judged adviseable [*sic*] for the more general Service to publish said *Summary* . . . by it self in Numbers, convenient afterwards to be bound: And the Subscribers for said *Magazine* are hereby notified, That the Undertakers (being also desired) are determined to publish the same but once in three Months, till said *Summary* or *History* is finished, and the Price is reduced to *Six Shillings* a Year *new Tenour*." The announcement requested any cancellations of subscriptions to be in the office of Rogers and Fowle by March 15, and set the publication of the first part of the *Summary* on "Saturday next" at the price of two shillings old tenor.

The magazine did not appear quarterly. The files of *The Boston Weekly News-Letter* show that the *Summary* was printed frequently though irregularly through 1747 and 1748, the twenty-eighth part being advertised on October 6 of the latter year. During this time Rogers and Fowle advertised many other works, and appeared to be doing a good business. It seems indubitable that public demand for the magazine had been found so slight that the presses were turned to other work. But the cessation of the magazine cost American readers only a few pages of original material each month.

III

Among the currents of interest which have been mentioned, none is more important in Colonial literary history during 1739-46 than the sweeping religious emotionalism which came to be termed the "Great Awakening" and brought into being *The Christian History*,[105] the first definitely religious magazine in the Colonies.

[105] See note 7.

Presses turned out pamphlet after pamphlet of sermons, counter sermons, reassertions, retractions, and appeals for peace among the combatants. Month after month the most important news in the Colonies pertained to religion. Even the war blazed only occasionally during short periods of victory or apprehension, and then dimmed before the multiple and steadier lights of hundreds of local religious controversies.

Chief among the figures in the movement was George Whitefield,[106] Oxford scholar and friend of John and Charles Wesley. After several years of itinerant preaching and revivalistic work, he paid visits to America in 1738, 1739-41, and 1744-48,[107] and his varying fortunes are a barometer indicating the state of the "Great Awakening" in the several provinces. On his second visit he brought with him a grant of land in trust for the establishment of an orphanage in Georgia, where immigrants had suffered from an inability to adapt themselves to an environment which had not proved to be the Eden advertised. He invaded New England, stronghold of conservatism, somewhat successfully, winning the friendship in Boston of Thomas Prince, Benjamin Colman, William Cooper, Thomas Foxcroft, and other divines of the liberal element. In the Middle Colonies he was phenomenally successful, appearing before 15,000 persons in Philadelphia, moving Franklin to eelemosynary deeds by his oratory, and firing Gilbert Tennent of New Jersey and James Davenport of Long Island to greater endeavors in itinerant revivalism. Although Whitefield was an ordained minister in the Church of England, his freedom from sectarianism turned the entrenched guns of the Anglican South against him, and a warrant for his arrest in South Carolina sent him to England in 1741. On his third visit to America he preached in New England during the winter of 1744-45, at one time officiating in Dr. Colman's Brattle Street Church. But by then the embattled forces of New England conservatism were ready to oppose him. Harvard, having paid

[106] There are two biographies: Joseph Belcher. *George Whitefield: A Biography*, American Tract Society, New York [1857], and Edward S. Ninde, *George Whitefield: Prophet-Preacher*, New York and Cincinnati [1924]. The latter is more complete, but probably too sympathetic. Neither biographer found it within his province to go fully over the contemporary publications. See also, S. D. McConnell, *History of the American Episcopal Church*, 10th ed. (1916), pp. 142-43.

[107] He made other visits to America: 1751-52; 1754-55; 1763-65; 1769-70. As a popular preacher Fielding (*Joseph Andrews*, bk. I, ch. 17) paid him the compliment of describing his works as one of the few good publishing risks in books of sermons.

him on his former visit the courtesy of an invitation to preach, closed her doors. Ministers in Massachusetts, assembled in meeting, went on record as opposed to inviting him to their churches; and in June 1745 the General Association of ministers in Connecticut followed the lead of their Massachusetts brethren.

It was during the strenuous years 1743-45 that *The Christian History*, organ of the adherents of the "Great Awakening," summarized the trends of religion in America and reported in detail the advancement of the awakening in the several provinces. In name, Thomas Prince, Jr. (1722-48), son of the famous historian and minister of the old South Church in Boston, was the publisher.[108] The young man, never robust, had been graduated from Harvard in 1740, and, entering his twenties, was permitted to associate himself editorially to assist in a religious enterprise dear to the heart of his father. There is no doubt that the elder Prince (1687-1758)[109] was chiefly responsible for the editing and the success of the magazine. From his sermons, pen, correspondence, and library came much of the material, and he and his friends were among those who led the early stages of the revolt against organized conservatism. His large collection of historical documents, his visit to England, his breadth of learning and experience and comparative freedom from sectarian prejudice, and withal his faith in recurring manifestations of heavenly grace made him a fitting guardian of the contents of the magazine. In New England in the winter of 1742-43 a crisis was approaching; and amidst the heat of an unhappy fray, Thomas Prince, Sr., undoubtedly felt that a calm survey of the religious history of New England and an appreciative and interpretative attitude toward the movement, expressed in print, would lessen the strife and assist generally the cause of religion in the Colonies. To his decision the Reverends Benjamin Colman

---

[108] See advertisement, *The Boston Weekly News-Letter*, March 3, 1743.

[109] He was born at Sandwich, Mass., and graduated from Harvard in 1707. After living for a time in England, he returned to Boston in 1717, and was the following year made a colleague of Dr. Joseph Sewall (himself a sympathetic worker in the cause of the "Great Awakening") of the Old South Church. Prince remained pastor of the church until his death. Good memoirs, but lacking in the discussion of *The Christian History* to any intimate degree, are Samuel G. Drake, *Some Memoirs of the Life and Writings of the Rev. Thomas Prince, Together with a Pedigree of his Family* (1851)', and Wm. H. Whitmore, *Catalogue of the American Portion of the Library of the Rev. Thomas Prince. With a Memoir, and List of his Publications* (1868).

and William Cooper, Jonathan Edwards of Northampton, and other friends and adherents of the cause, lent their hearty support.[110]

It was natural, too, that the printing of the magazine should fall to the firm of Kneeland and Green. Samuel Kneeland, a member of the Old South Church, of which Prince was pastor, was "pious, friendly, and benevolent,"[111] and his sympathies lay with the "new light" element. His partner, Timothy Green, "amiable," "much esteemed,"[112] joined him in the printing of pamphlets supporting the radical side.[113] Prince himself was an occasional contributor to their paper, *The Boston Gazette, or, Weekly Journal.*

The Christian History was first advertised in *The Boston Weekly News-Letter* of Thursday, March 3, 1743, to appear the following Saturday and weekly thereafter. The advertisement described the journal as a publication of eight pages octavo, priced at two shillings per quarter uninclosed, or six pence new tenor

[110] Benjamin Colman, pastor of the Brattle Street Church, submitted whatever material came to his hand. With William Cooper, his colleague, he was at the center of the radical group which held a special meeting in July 1743 to support the "Great Awakening," after the general body of Massachusetts ministers had frowned upon the idea the previous May. Cooper had written the "Preface" to the "new light" tract, *New Converts Exhorted to Cleeve to the Lord*, written by Isaac Chanler, of Georgia, and printed by Kneeland and Green in 1740. Jonathan Edwards's most important contribution to the magazine was his report of the Northampton revival in Numbers 46-48. The depth of emotional antagonism accompanying the religious disturbances may be imagined by noting the contents of a letter from the Reverend Charles Chauncy (conservative adherent and author of *Seasonable Thoughts on the State of Religion in New England*, 1743) to Ezra Stiles, dated Boston, May 6, 1768. Professing himself "considerably intimate" with Colman, Cooper, Sewall, and Joshua Gee of the Old North Church, he continued: "Dr. Colman was of too complaisant a make, too unsteady and variable. We found the disadvantage of this in the Whitefieldein times. After the coming of Whitfield [*sic*] M.ʳ Cooper and I had little to say to one another unless in a way of wrangling; and the same loss of friendship took place w.ᵗʰ respect to M.ʳ Gee and my self." (F. B. Dexter, *Extracts from the Itineraries and Other Miscellanies of Ezra Stiles . . . 1755-1794*, 1916, pp. 445-46.)

[111] Thomas, *op. cit.*, I, 108.

[112] *Ibid.*, I, 187.

[113] In 1730 the firm printed Thomas Foxcroft's *Observations, Historical and Practical, on the Rise and Primitive State of New-England*; the author later identified himself with the radical party when it came into being at the close of the decade. In 1739 the firm published John Callender's *An Historical Discourse on the Civil and Religious Affairs of the Colony of Rhode-Island*. In 1743 they published *The Testimony and Advice of an Assembly of Pastors of Churches in New-England, at a Meeting in Boston July 7, 1743. Occasion'd by the Late Happy Revival of Religion in Many Parts of the Land. To which Are Added, Attestations Contain'd in Letters from a Number of their Brethren who Were Providentially Hinder'd from Giving their Presence. By Order of the Assembly.*

extra if sealed and directed. Subscriptions were taken by the publisher and "at his Father's." Payment in advance was urged, as "it would be a great Encouragement to go on with the Work and enable us to it." The same advertisement outlined the general scheme of contents: "I. Authentick Accounts; from Ministers and other serious and creditable Persons, of the Revival of Religion in the several Parts of New-England. II. Extracts of the most remarkable Pieces in the weekly Histories of Religion, and other Accounts, printed both at London and Glasgow. III. Extracts of written Letters, from all parts of Great Britain and the American Plantations, of a religious Nature. . . . IV. In Intervals of fresh Occurances [*sic*] . . . it is proposed to give the Reader the most remarkable Passages, out of the Books of the most famous old Writers even from the Reformation, both of the Churches of England and Scotland, as also the first Settlers of New-England; that we may see how far their Doctrines and Spirit are revived at this Day." On March 10, *The Boston Weekly News-Letter* announced that the first number of the magazine had appeared on Saturday as advertised; the second number was advertised March 17, but thereafter, possibly because the numbers appeared as frequently as did the newspapers, no advertisements were carried.

The appearance of *The Christian History* three days after the initial number of *The Boston Weekly Magazine* stirred premonitions of a conflict between them over religious issues. Gridley, thinking of his own project, had darkly hinted that the latter magazine might fan the flames of an unhappy controversy.[114] Rogers and Fowle, who published *The Boston Weekly Magazine*, were printers of pamphlets supporting the conservative group,[115] and they were therefore aligned with those who were antagonistic to the supporters of Kneeland and Green, publishers of *The Christian History*. Had *The Boston Weekly Magazine* lived beyond a month, some quarrel might have ensued. The prospect seemed imminent, and a contemporary account offers an interesting point of view of a bystander. Thomas Fleet, publisher of *The Boston*

---

[114] See note 12.

[115] In 1743 they printed *The Testimony of the Convention of Ministers, May 25, 1743. Against Several Errors and Disorders in the Land.* This pamphlet attacked the "new lights" and supported the very position which the convention of July 7 denied. (See note 113.) Nathanael Ells was moderator of the convention held in May.

Evening-Post, a man of "Understanding and Industry in . . . his own Profession," of "general and extensive Knowledge of the World," and of a "friendly and benevolent Disposition,"[116] was not inclined toward enthusiasm. So, perceiving a certain incongruity between the professions of many of the enthusiasts and their daily practices,[117] he could not control his desire to express his thoughts with some irony and gruff-humored sarcasm.

"Last Wednesday," he wrote for his paper of March 7, "was published . . . a Paper called the *Boston weekly Magazine*, containing some pieces from the *Magazines* formerly printed in *London*, . . . an Ode by Mr. *Addison*, . . . and two Advertisements: And on Saturday *another* Paper made its Appearance among us, entitled, *The Christian History*. . . . Both Papers are design'd to come out weekly. The *first* offers Room for Disputes on both Sides, (which is fair enough) so that our religious Controversies are more likely to increase than subside. The *last* seems a *Party Paper*, and design'd only for the Use of *special Friends*, it being with great Difficulty that we could obtain one, they refusing (for some Time) to sell 'em either at the *Printer's* or the *Publishing Office*, but on Conditions too hard to be complied with by many, who were yet desirous to see the *Specimen*.

"The *sudden* Appearance of these two Papers, without the usual previous Proposals for Encouragement, must needs be very mortifying to the Rev. Gentleman, who more than a Year ago published Proposals for printing a weekly Casuistical Paper, but has not yet found sufficient Encouragement to begin it. And as we are now favoured with a Paper *every* Day except *Friday* . . . it behoves that Gentleman to bestir himself, lest some other Person,

[116] The quotation is taken from the obituary notice in *The Boston Gazette* at the time of his death in July 1758.

[117] Only in the acts and writings of the more temperate men, of whom Prince was a representative, did the revival assume a dignified bearing. Occasionally, though rarely, the services of the revivalists even became maudlin. For instance, the Reverend Timothy Cutler (whose opinions were those of a conservative Anglican) wrote from Boston under date of September 24, 1743: "Whitefield has plagued us with a witness. . . . It would be an endless attempt to describe that scene of confusion and disturbance occasioned by him,—the division of families, neighbors and towns. . . . Our presses are forever teeming with books, and our women with bastards, though regeneration and conversion is the whole cry. . . .

"After him came one *Tennent*, a monster! impudent and noisy, and told them they were *damn'd*, damn'd, damn'd; this charmed them, and in the most dreadful winter I ever saw, people wallowed in the snow night and day for the benefit of his beastly brayings. . . ." (McConnell, *op. cit.*, pp. 142-43.)

out of *pure Love to his Country*, should put out a Paper on *that* Day, and thereby be utterly excluded."

In the first issue of *The Christian History*, the editor, besides restating the general editorial outline as it had been presented in the first advertisement,[118] further elaborated the reason for the existence of the periodical: "Tis at the earnest Desire of many Persons of Piety and Judgment, *Lovers* of the peculiar Doctrines Power and Practice of the Christian Religion, as they were promoted by the *purer Part* of the *old Church* of *England* from the Days of the Reformation, and by the renowned *Settlers* of New-England; *who* therefore heartily rejoyce to see and hear of their Revival both in *Great Britain* & *America* . . . that the PRESENT WORK is undertaken: Which therefore will be wholly confined to Matters of Religion. . . .

"*Ministers* and *other* Persons of Credit and of religious Dispositions in the several Parts of the *American Plantations* where there has been a Revival of Religion, are desired to send *their* Informations . . . to the *Publisher* of this Paper; studiously avoiding Personal Reflections and angry Controversy . . . but subscribing *their Names*: Since to a *nameless Relation* of *Matters of Fact*, no wise Man can give any Credit. . . ."[119]

In the seventeenth number of the magazine,[120] the editor defined the periodical as a "*Treasury* of Pious History, collected from authentick Books, Pamphlets, Papers, and Letters both in *Print* and *Manuscript*." Prince was endeavoring to publish a chronological history of religion in America, as well as maintain a present-day interest in the periodical by the inclusion of material which would define and report the "Great Awakening."

The first seven numbers were given over to "A Faithful Narrative of the Extraordinary Work of the Spirit of God, at Kilsyth," Scotland, by the Reverend James Robe, later editor of *The Christian Monthly History* at Edinburgh,[121] who described what he

---

[118] New correspondents had been secured; thus letters from New York, New Jersey, Pennsylvania, South Carolina, and Georgia were promised.

[119] P. 2.

[120] P. 129.

[121] Pp. 3-56. *The Christian Monthly History* was first published in Nov. 1743. For it Robe copied from *The Christian History* some of the more important articles, including "The Testimony and Advice of an Assembly of Pastors" (Jan. 1744, pp. 7-60), an account of the death of William Cooper (Jan. 1744, pp. 61-64), Edwards's account of the revival at Northampton (June, July 1745, pp. 86-114), and accounts of many other

considered to be an outwelling of the new religious spirit in the parish. At the same time, he cautioned his readers against maudlin expressions of frenzy.[122] To this latter word of warning Prince added a few words of approval, admonishing the new movement against forsaking method, instruction, and doctrine to engage only in vehement outcries.[123] The eighth number, a kind of preface to the history of religion in New England which was to continue through the fifteenth number,[124] comprised an extract from a sermon by the Reverend Prince on the religious principles of the early New England settlers. "In Points of *Doctrine*," he said, "they entirely held with the *Church* of ENGLAND. . . . But they apprehended it to be the sole prerogative of GOD Himself . . . to appoint the Orders of his own House, and the acceptable Ways of his own Worship."[125] The ninth number began printing extracts from the sermons of early ministers to illustrate the period of spirit and power,[126] when unanimity of religious belief and ecclesiastical power had been most nearly attained; and the account of this phase of New England history was followed by selected extracts from sermons pointing out the *"great and lamented* DECAY" of religion, with *"Instances of the transient* REVIVAL."[127] Having thus etched an historical panorama as a background, the next consideration was to show, contrary to the expressed opinions of opponents, that there had been "The Remarkable Revival in This Country Before Mr. Whitefield's Arrival Hither in Sept. 1740";[128] and among the exhibits of evidence tend-

---

local revivals in America. Another Scottish magazine which carefully reported the awakening in America was *The Glasgow-Weekly-History, Relating to the Late Progress of the Gospel at Home and Abroad; Being a Collection of Letters, Partly Reprinted from the London-Weekly-History and Partly First Printed Here at Glasgow. For the Year 1742*. For an excellent account of this magazine, see a descriptive article by Mr. J. H. Tuttle in the *Proceedings of the Massachusetts Historical Society, 1919-20*, LIII, 192-216.

[122] In his closing paper, the Reverend Robe dwelt on *"some Disorders* I could not forsee"; public confession, he wrote, might result disastrously.

[123] P. 13.

[124] Pp. 57-112.

[125] P. 59.

[126] Pp. 65-72. The Reverends John Higginson, William Stoughton, and James Fitch were among those quoted.

[127] Nos. 12-14 (May 21, 28, June 4, 1743), pp. 93-112. Quotations from sermons by Prince, Stoughton, Samuel Danforth, Increase Mather, Samuel Torrey, Samuel Williard, and Cotton Mather were among items selected.

[128] Nos. 15-17 (June 11-25, 1743), pp. 113-36.

ing to conform the general fact, Jonathan Edwards's "A Faithful Narrative" of the revival in Northampton and other towns has become the most famous.[129]

More vital yet was the report which followed, "An Account of the Late Assembly of Pastors" in favor of the revival, held in Boston July 7, 1743.[130]   As the majority of the organized assembly of ministers of Massachusetts had testified the preceding May against the validity of the "awakening,"[131] a separate meeting, composed of pastors of the militant minority in sympathy with the emotional trend, was called in July.   The leading organizers of this group were Cooper, Colman, and Prince, and, with Prince as "Scribe," the magazine reported the affairs of the assembly fairly completely.[132]

The journal was now prepared to offer more complete accounts of contemporary revivals and regenerations as manifested in many parts of the land,[133] and especially in Massachusetts, New Jersey,

[129] Edwards's communication had been sent as a letter to Dr. Colman in 1736.   It appeared on pp. 114-28, 367-81.

[130] No. 20 (July 16, 1743), pp. 155 ff.   This group of ministers, "being *persuaded there has of late been a happy Revival of Religion*" (p. 156), held it fitting that testimony should be given and the revival acknowledged and supported.   That some of the revivals had been attended by undue emotion was frankly admitted by the assembly; for "who can wonder, if . . . Satan should intermingle himself, to hinder and blemish a Work so directly contrary to the Interest of his own Kingdom?" (P. 162).

[131] See note 115.

[132] Nos. 20-26. (July 16-Aug. 27, 1743), pp. 155-201.

[133] Chief accounts of revivals, places, and reporters, are as follows: Wrentham, Mass., Revs. Messenger and Haven (Nos. 30-32, pp. 236-52); Newark and Elizabeth-Town, N. J., Rev. Jonathan Dickinson (Nos. 32-33, pp. 252-58); Halifax, Plimouth Co., Rev. John Cotton (Nos. 33-34, pp. 259-70); Bridgewater, Mass.; Rev. John Porter (Nos. 50-51, pp. 396-408); Somers, Mass., Rev. Samuel Allis (Nos. 51-52, pp. 408-12); Harvard, Mass., Rev. John Seccomb (Nos. 54-55, pp. 13-21); among Indians at Westerley and Charlestown, R. I., by Joseph Park (Nos. 55-56, pp. 21-28); progress of Christianity in East Indies (Nos. 56-57, pp. 28-37); Glocester, Mass., Rev. John White (No. 58, pp. 41-46); Middleborough, Mass., Rev. Peter Thatcher (Nos. 63-64, pp. 87-99; see also No. 52, pp. 412-16); Lyme and New London, Conn., Rev. George Griswold, (Nos. 66-67, pp. 105-18); Lyme, Conn., Jonathan Parsons) Nos. 67-73, pp. 118-62); Sutton, Mass., David Hall (Nos. 73-74, pp. 162-72); New Londonderry, Pa., Rev. Samuel Blair (Nos. 83-85, pp. 242-62); Germany, Augustus Hermannus (Nos. 85-88, pp. 262-84); New Jersey and Pennsylvania, Rev. Gilbert Tennent (Nos. 88-90, pp. 285-98); New Jersey, Rev. William Tennent (Nos. 90-91, pp. 298-310); Plymouth, Mass., Rev. Nathanael Leonard (No. 92, pp. 313-17); Taunton, Mass., Josiah Crocker (Nos. 93-97, pp. 321-58); Boston, Rev. Thomas Prince (Nos. 99-104, pp. 374-415).   Items other than reports of revivals include three articles by John Wilson defending the belief of special operations of the Holy Spirit on men, supernatural illumination, and regular zeal from the charge of enthusiasm (Nos. 53-54, pp. 1-13; Nos. 61-62, pp. 65-77; Nos. 80-82, pp. 220-34); a letter from Rev. Howell Harris to the Society at the London Taber-

and Pennsylvania. Occasionally an article or series of articles appeared describing revivals in Scotland,[134] in England, or in Germany, implying the universality of the spirit of the "awakening" throughout the Protestant world. But the interest in the reports waned as similar details piled monotonously upon one another through the second year of life of the magazine, and the decease of the publication in February 1745 meant little else than the end of a monotonous chronicle.

There was, however, one brief flair toward the close of the career of the magazine which quickened the heartbeats of those on either side of the controversy. Whitefield disembarked on one of his visits to America at York, Maine, October 19, 1744. And although *The Christian History* had printed evidence showing that the "awakening" had not been started by him, it nevertheless welcomed his coming most heartily. This welcome, printed in the issue for December 15, 1744, when the major powers of New England had turned bitterly against him, was not lacking in elements of bravery, and deserves to be preserved as a picture of the man as his friends saw him, and as a restatement of the religious attitude of the revivalists:

"The Rev. Mr. *Whitefield* was so far reviv'd [he had been stricken ill while preaching at Portsmouth] as to be able to take Coach with his *Consort*, and set out from *Portsmouth* to *Boston*; whether he came in a very feeble State . . . since which he has been able to preach in several of our largest Houses of public Worship, particularly the Rev. Dr. *Colman's*, D. *Sewall's*, Mr. *Webb's*, and Mr. *Gee's* [all supporters of the revival spirit], to crowded Assemblies of People, and to great and growing Acceptance. At Dr. *Colman's* Desire, and the Consent of the Church,[135] on the *Lord's day* after his Arrival, he administered to them the

---

nacle (Nos. 59-60, pp. 52-57); a memorial of the life of Rev. Peter Thatcher by Rev. Thomas Prince (Nos. 62-63, pp. 77-87); a selection from the confessions and retractions of Rev. James Davenport (Nos. 82-83, pp. 236-41); and some accounts of Rev. George Whitefield (Nos. 97-99, pp. 358-74).

[134] Besides Rev. Robe's accounts in Nos. 1-7, 38-45, pp. 300-36, 341-52, 355-60, see other accounts as follows: Nos. 36-38, pp. 286-99; No. 45, pp. 353-57. For Germany and England, see note 133.

[135] In Thomas Fleet's *The Boston Evening-Post* for Dec. 24, 1744, appears an article asserting that the congregation was surprised into accepting Whitefield, and did not consent.

Holy Communion . . . [Later] he preach'd for the Rev. Mr. *Emerson*, of *Malden*.

". . . He comes with the same extraordinary Spirit of Meekness, Sweetness, and universal Benevolence as before. In Opposition to the Spirit of *Separation* and *Biggotry*, is still for holding Communion with all Protestant Churches. In Opposition to Enthusiasm, he preaches a close Adherence to the Scriptures, the Necessity of trying all Impressions by them. . . . In Opposition Antinomianism,[136] he preaches up all Kinds of relative and religious Duties, tho' to be perform'd in the Strength of Christ, and in short, the Doctrines of the Church of *England*, & the first Fathers of this Country. As before, he *first* applies himself to the *Understandings* of his *Hearers*, & then to the Affections: And the more he preaches, the more he convinces People of their Mistakes about him, and increases their Satisfaction."

Thomas Prince's private copy of *The Christian History*, now in the New York Public Library, contains a number of his own penned annotations. Some of these merely correct errata,[137] one offers a glimpse into a tender incident of home life which effected the inclusion of a hymn in the magazine,[138] one identified the author of an article on the life of William Cooper,[139] while others, as they deal with important phases of the history of the revival, throw a clearer light upon the events than do printed documents. It is interesting to note that it was Cooper who drew up the invitation extended to the dissenting pastors to meet in Boston in July.[140]   Prince himself wrote the "Vote" which the assembly passed affirmatively, thus acknowledging the revival but discountenancing the errors in doctrine and disorders in practice which

[136] Antinomianism opposed the doctrine that the moral law is obligatory, on the ground that faith alone is necessary to salvation.

[137] Prince began by marking errata carefully, and these were corrected in the following issue of each number through No. 19; thereafter no errata were printed, and Prince gradually ceased to be so meticulous.

[138] No. 52 (Feb. 25, 1743-4), p. 416, carried this annotation by the side of a hymn by Dr. Watts: "This Hymn was inserted Here upon ye Suggestion of my Dear Daughter Deborah Prince, junr; Saying it at ye same time by Heart with a modest, pious & pleasant Voice and Countenance."

[139] No. 43 (Dec. 24, 1743), p. 341. "R[ev.] Mr Gray."

[140] No. 20 (July 16, 1743), p. 156: "This Invitation was drawn up by ye Rev. Mr Wm Cooper at his House, I & others being with Him at the same time, & yrin concurring & assisting."

accompanied excessively emotional meetings.[141]   The final "Result"
or summary of the "Testimony and Advice of an Assembly of
Pastors," comprising the ultimate platform and point of view of
the assembly of July 7, 1743, was drawn up by Cooper, and modified by Prince and a committee.[142]   It would seem, therefore, that
Cooper and Prince were the guiding powers of the revival in New
England.

In his personal copy of the magazine, Prince annotated his account of the revival in Boston with considerable care.   Beside a
long paragraph defending Whitefield and describing his first visit
to Boston, he noted by hand: "He was kindly received by y⁰
Associate Pastors of y⁰ Town in General; & upon Invitation
Preached in most of y⁰ churches."[143]   A further note listed nine
pastors who asked him to preach.[144]   Finally, Prince proved the
power of Whitefield and Tennent as emotional speakers, and offered a detailed picture of emotional reactions during the revival in
Boston, by listing in the margin of a leaf religious manifestations
among converts through an indicative period of one month."[145]

[141] *Ibid.*, p. 156.   The account contains the following printed note: "We Pastors of
Churches in the Provinces of the *Massachusetts-Bay* & *New-Hampshire* in NEW-
ENGLAND, met at *Boston* this 7th Day of *July* 1743, being perswaded there has of
late been a happy Revival of Religion, thro' a remarkable divine Influence in many
Parts of this Land, and apprehending it our *Duty* to give an open conjunct TESTI-
MONY, to the GLORY of GOD, to an *Event so surprising and gracious*, as well as
against those *Errors* in Doctrine, and *Disorders* in Practice which thro' humane *Frail-
ties* and *Corruptions* and the permitted Agency of *Satan* have attended it, and in any
Measure blemish its Glory and hindered its Advancement; came to the following
RESOLUTION, *that a* COMMITTEE *be chosen to consider the* Premises *and make
a* Report *to* Morrow Morning at nine *of the Clock.*"   The annotation reads, "This vote
was drawn up by me."
[142] *Ibid.*, p. 157: "This Substance of this Result was drawn up by y⁰ Rev Mʳ Wᵐ
Cooper before y⁰ meeting of y⁰ sd assembly & communicated to me, & had some Correc-
tions from me, & then some more from sd Committee, & then diverse [*sic*] allevations
[*sic*] from sd assembly."
[143] No. 100 (Jan. 26, 1744-5), p. 380.
[144] *Ibid.*, pp. 380-81: "The 9 Eldʳ associate Pastors of y⁰ Town affectionately embraced Him; viz Dʳ Colman & Sewall, Mʳ Webb, Cooper, Foxcroft, Checkley, Welsted,
Gee & Prince; & invited Hᵐ into yʳ Pulpits; tho He pray'd & Preached in y⁰ cannoni-
cal Habit.   Both Ministers & People wʳ so intent on y⁰ more important Points of
Religion yᵗ yʸ wʳ got wholly above those trivial Matters, & cared not whether He had a
Gown on or no: nor did I ever hear any move him to lay it aside."
[145] Nos. 101 and 102 (Feb. 2-9, 1744-5), pp. 391-94.   Marginal pen note reads: "While
Mʳ Whitefd wˢ Here & aftʳ some began to put up to y⁰ Pulpits *Notetes* [*sic*], tho wᵗʰ- o
a Name, fʳ earnst Prayers; expressᵍ yʳ Convicˢ: wᶜ hᵈ bⁿ so rare among us, yᵗ

Thomas Fleet's *The Boston Evening-Post*[146] was the only paper in the city which opened wide its columns to articles strongly attacking the revival. It was Fleet who mentioned his difficulty in procuring the first issue of *The Christian History*.[147] Cheap banter, mixed with some legitimate criticism, was frequently printed

yr seemed to be a new Sort of Bills we surprized many; espy wn in Mr. *Tenant's* Preachg yy increas'd so much yt on Tuesday Evening Lecr at Dr *Colman's*, Jan. 27, I read to ye No. of 29 such Persons: On Fryday aft·noon, Feb. 27, at ye *S. ch* to 34: & on a Tuesd Eveng at Dr Colman's yr wr betwn 60 & 70—And tho some opposers suggested as if ys *notes* wr forged; yet ye writg was very various, & several Ministers knew by ye numbers resortd to ym in concern of Soul yt yr wr a gt many more in ye like Conditions than ye *Notes* mentioned, & ye *Notes* described ye Real Cases of ye awakened Ppl wo repaired to us for Pity & Help.

"I hv abv 100 of yee *Notes* still by me, & yy beg expresv of ye State of yr Souls at that Season; I may gv ye Readr a Specimen of yos in ye Month of *February* only ——

"A *little Boy* abt 8 or 9 Years old, desires Prayers to G fr his Soul. A Boy undr slighty Convics & ye Sense of an hard Heart, &c.

"A *Young Lad* undr Fears least ye Holy Spirit shd withdraw fm Hm, ——. A Youth wo has bn for some time undr Convics ——.

"A *Young Man* labourd undr Spiritual Blindness & Hardness of Heart.—— A *Young Man* undr slighty Convics Hardness of Ht & concern for his Soul. —— A *Youg Man* undr strong Concern fr his Soul Sensib of ye Hardn of his Ht. A *Youg Man* undr strong Convics & gt Temptas ——. A *Y M* havg quenched ye Motions of ye H Sp, & beg distressed least He shd depart ā Hm ——. A *Y M* havg bn undr Convics for sm Months ——. A *Y M* wo has bn sm tm undr Convics, & undr apprehensn of a vile Ht, & fearg ye withdrawg of ye H Sp ——.

"A *Young Woman* undr Convics, Hardn of Ht & Blindn of Mind,—A *Young W* in gt concn for her Soul, & Sensib of ye Hardn of her Ht.—— 3 Sists & 2 near Relas undr slighty Convics & Sensib of ye Hardn of yr Hts.

"*Two Young People* in gt Concern for yr Souls & Hardn of Ht.—*3 Young Perns* beg for a long Time undr Convics ——.

"An *Indn Wom* wo has bn undr Convics, & afrd of yr warg off & Sensib of a hard Ht. A *Negro Wom* in Concn fr her Soul.—A *Negro Man* undr Convics & Sensib of ye Hardness of his Ht ——.

"One yt is *Head of a Famy* undr gt Concn for his Soul.—One *in Years* undr a deep Sense of an hard Ht·—. An *Aged Persn* in Concern for her Soul—. *Three Persons* havg gn on in a Course of Relign fr some Years, now fearg yyr still in ye Gall of Bittern & Bond of Iniqy ——. One *in full comun* in a Distress of Mind for Fear of being uncoverd ——. One havg bn *in full Comun 14 Years*, & fearg He has all along bn buildg on a Righteousn of his own ——. A Persn far advanc'd in Years desires ur earn prayrs, yt He may not be left behind wn oths r going to X, but may be thorôly humbd & brot to Repnc for Grievg ye H Sp & all his othr Sins.

"These notes indeed described but a small Part of yr Cases, or presented only a general View yr of. But wn yy resorted to my Study, yy gave abundantly mr particr accounts of yr vars Cases, wth ye vars operas of ye Sp of Concicn in ym & yr vars Effects; as described in Scriptr, & by ye most pious, judics & experimental writers I hv conversed wth, & shall by and by delineate."

[146] See note 116 and text appertaining thereto.

[147] *The Boston Evening-Post*, March 7, 1743.

in the paper, the barbs striking the revivalists in general, their leaders, and the magazine.

In January 1743, before *The Christian History* was begun, *The Boston Evening-Post* was running articles by the Reverend Jonathan Ashley, a conservative of Deerfield, Massachusetts, who had recently engaged in a pamphlet war with Cooper. In March the newspaper was ready to attack *The Christian History*. In the issue for the 14th, for example, a writer, hinting unfairly at the disorganized nature of the revival with regard to creed and authority, remarked: "There is one singular Advantage that will attend this *Work*, (*viz.*) its being read instead of the *Bible*, or any Religious Book." The same article attacked the elder Prince with unwarranted irony, inferring that he wished to hide behind his son's editorship: "It is said his honoured Father is concerned in the Paper, and that it will hinder his Ministerial Office . . . but . . . I perswade my self that it is not true . . . for it is impossible that a Gentleman who in his *Ordination Sermon* has said: *That the Work of the Ministry is of such great Importance, Difficulty and Variety, that they had need apply themselves Entirely to it, and allow no other to divert and hinder them:* I say, it is impossible that after a Man had said this, he should engage in other Business in conjunction with that." The elder Prince certainly did not hide his attitude with regard to the revival or his friendship with Whitefield, nor did he keep his name out of the magazine. Actually, it would seem that he honored his son, just attaining manhood, with a title as a reward for assisting in the details of publication. The attack just mentioned was unsigned, but in the paper for July 4 there appeared an equally vicious article, signed by Fleet, which addressed the young editor in such bantering terms as "Master Tommy," "little Master," and "Child," and insisted that the youth was writing beyond his depth, knowing nothing actually about affairs in Scotland.

A somewhat fairer criticism appeared in the paper for August 22, 1743, in a letter addressed to Fleet: "I have now before me the *Testimony and Advice* of a Number of Pastors respecting the late happy revival of Religion, and must confess I am *stumbled at the Threshold*; for I find in the *Title-Page* 'tis represented as coming forth with *Authority—By order of the Assembly*." Even in this case, however, facts were twisted, for if the full title of the publication had been quoted,[148] the date would have met the eyes of the readers. The subsequent assembly was not trying to fly the colors of the first.

Through 1744 *The Boston Evening-Post* continued printing assaults. On January 30, for example, appeared a reply to Jonathan Edwards's account of the "Work at Northampton"—a reply which conceived the whole matter in an entirely different and unfavorable light.[149]   Whitefield and excessive emotional disturbances were assailed frequently, sometimes with a degree of truth, sometimes unfairly, and nearly always with emotional rancor.[150] Unfair, certainly, was the mood of the writer who thus attacked Whitefield for soliciting funds for the famous Orphan House in Georgia: "A matchless Event [the establishment of the orphanage] for answering every Purpose of the Man's Heart! Furnishing a specious Pretence not only for the Exercise of his Talent for Begging and collecting for Charity; but also for managing or dispensing the same when collected, in the darkest Corner of all the *British* Dominions. . . ."[151]   The writer patently had no evidence to support his implications other than perhaps his having observed in Whitefield a mixed sincere and egotistic delight in giving largess. Another attack, coming late in the year and directed against Colman and *The Christian History*, deserves special mention.[152]   It would seem that in this case the writer had some justice on his side, for I have found no concrete evidence that Colman gave the anti-Whitefield faction in his church, however small it may have been, opportunity to express its opinion with regard to Whitefield's taking part in the church services.   The aggrieved writer thus explained the situation, quoting a sentence from *The Christian History*: " 'At Dr. *Colman's* Desire, and with the Consent of the

[148] *The Testimony and Advice of an Assembly of Pastors of Churches in New-England, at a Meeting in Boston July 7, 1743. Occasion'd by the Late Happy Revival of Religion in Many Parts of the Land—To which Are Added, Attestations Contain'd in Letters from a Number of their Brethren who Were Providentially Hinder'd from Giving their Presence.* By Order of the Assembly. This pamphlet was a reply to that of the earlier convention: *The Testimony of the Convention of Ministers, May 25, 1743. Against Several Errors and Disorders in the Land.*

[149] "Some Serious Thoughts on the Late Times."

[150] For articles against Whitefield and emotionalism, see *The Boston Evening-Post* Dec. 10, 17, 24, 1744, and Jan. 21 and Feb. 11, 18, 1745. Pro-Whitefield articles appeared in the same paper for Dec. 24, 1744 and Jan. 21, 1745.

[151] *The Boston Evening-Post*, Nov. 19, 1744.

[152] *Ibid.*, Dec. 24, 1744.

Church . . . he [Whitefield] administered to them the holy Communion.' This Passage contains an absolute Falsehood. . . . The Church were surpriz'd into the Thing. . . . The only Thing that look'd like *Consent* was, that they did not all, or the greatest Part of them, immediately leave the House. But the Surprise they were under, and the Fears of making a Disturbance prevented them from doing this. . . ."

By 1745 events had so shaped themselves that the magazine could not well be continued beyond its second year. The months to come were to be full of heated discussion, with the conservative forces ever increasing in power. To have represented editorially the forces of the "Great Awakening" longer would have required an iconoclastic temper which Thomas Prince, concerned with rather broad aspects of life, could not easily summon. Defeat, at least in New England and the South, was inevitable. *The Christian History* had presented a chronicle of the religious life in New England and had reported the evidences of the spirit of revival faithfully, according to the sincere opinions of its editors. It had not attacked the opposing forces. Let the contest wax hot in congregations, assemblies, pamphlets, and newspapers. It was time for the non-challenging magazine to withdraw, leaving the field to more blustering knights.

CHAPTER IV

NEW YORK: RELIGION AND EDUCATION

FROM the discontinuance of *The American Magazine and Historical Chronicle* (Boston) at the close of 1746, to the appearance of *The American Magazine, or Monthly Chronicle* (Philadelphia) in October 1757, American magazine activity was limited to New York city, a new area of enterprise. During this decade, only one true magazine was published, *The Instructor*[1] (1755) a diminutive four-page weekly. But in 1752, in the midst of this fallow period, an essay-journal was begun, the original plan of which, before local controversy emphasized certain topics of discussion, was broad in scope though provincial in appeal. With the appearance of this journal, *The Independent Reflector*[2] (1752-1753), a weekly, four-page folio, leading in its wake *The Occasional Reverberator*[3] (1753) and *John Englishman*[4] (1755), American essay writing for periodicals attained a new height in cogent exposition and argument. It is interesting to note, however, that this blossoming in New York was short-lived, continuing only through the years 1752-55, and the city was not again represented in magazine production for thirty-two years, when Samuel Louden commenced publishing *The American Magazine*.

Certain conditions had retarded the publication of periodicals in New York. The large proportion of Dutch inhabitants, the close regulation of affairs of the colony by the Crown, the close literary association of the English tradesmen with England, and the manorial nature of the hinterland were handicaps. The Reverend Andrew Burnaby,[5] who visited the colony in 1760, reported the population to be about 100,000, whereas he had given an estimate of 400,000

---

[1] See "Bibliography," p. 365.

[2] *Ibid.*, p. 364.

[3] *Ibid.*, p. 365.

[4] *Ibid.*

[5] For statistics and comment, see *Burnaby's Travels through North America*, reprinted from the third edition of 1798, with introduction and notes by Rufus Rockwell Wilson (1904), pp. 110-18.

to 500,000 for Pennsylvania. Of the 100,000, a "considerable part" were negroes, and more than half of the total were Dutch. The city itself, somewhat over a mile in length and half a mile in breadth, he described as being "tolerably well built" and containing 16,000 to 17,000 inhabitants. Besides agriculture for the colony as a whole, trade rather than manufacture was the important economic pursuit. The trade lane from Oswego, Albany, and New York to England was the vital center of the colony's life.

I

The publishing of the New York periodicals of 1752-55 is associated principally with the names of James Parker and Hugh Gaine; while William Livingston, assisted by William Smith, Jr., John Morin Scott, and others, became the center of a militant editorial force. James Parker[6] had come from Woodbridge, New Jersey, to New York to serve his apprenticeship in *The New-York Gazette* office under William Bradford the elder. In January 1742-3 the young man had established his own *The New-York Weekly Post-Boy*, and on Bradford's retirement and the discontinuance of *The New-York Gazette*, both printing and newspaper patronage fell to Parker, and the paper became known as *The New-York Gazette, Revived in the Weekly Post-Boy*. He began publishing *The Independent Reflector* in November 1752, and the following January took into partnership William Weyman, likewise a past apprentice of Bradford's, and the firm continued until 1759. In the meantime Parker expanded his holdings to include presses at Woodbridge, New Jersey, and New Haven, Connecticut. The New York office was influential, the newspaper was held in good esteem, and books and government printing issued from the press. For their own advantage, it was necessary for Parker and Weyman to support the existing régime. This fact explains, to a large degree, the discontinuance of *The Independent Reflector* at the close of its first year; for this publication, originally formulated on principles which Parker must have thought would be innocuous to himself and the governing powers, soon became

[6] For references to Parker, see Thomas, *op. cit.*, I, 298-301 II, 125, and Frederic Hudson, *Journalism in the United States from 1690 to 1872* (1873); p. 111; see also comments in C. M. and B. E. Martin, *The New York Press and its Makers in the Eighteenth Century* (1898).

a disturbing polemic against certain phases of the existing order, exercising itself especially against the power which the Episcopal Church wished to hold over the establishment of King's College.

During the same year *The Independent Reflector* was founded, Hugh Gaine, a young Irish immigrant who had been an apprentice of Parker's, and had thereafter set up a printing office, established a paper, *The New-York Mercury,* in opposition to *The New-York Gazette, Revived in the Weekly Post-Boy*.[7] This paper drew to its columns opinions antipodal to those being formulated by *The Independent Reflector,* and as the contest grew heated with the rising ire of the disputants, the conflict descended from the plane of reason to that of ridicule. That Gaine's paper should occupy this position in the discussion of public affairs was solely the result of competitive dissent; temperamentally, Gaine should have been on the side supported with growing reluctance by Parker and Weyman. Normal adjustment was attained a year later, when an actual shift in support occurred.

William Livingston, a descendent of an early and wealthy New York family and a man of energy and talent, had risen to a position of legal prominence in the city by the time he had begun to edit *The Independent Reflector* in 1752. He had been graduated from Yale in 1741, had published both prose and poetry, and had been admitted to the bar in 1748. With William Smith, Jr., who also assisted him on the magazine, he published, during his first year in an editorial capacity, the first digest of the laws of the colony.[8]

[7] *The Journals of Hugh Gaine, Printer,* edited with biography and bibliography by Paul Leicester Ford (1902), presents a lively and documented account of interesting phases of New York publishing life of the times; for a description of circumstances bearing upon this book, see especially I, 10-17, 211-21.

[8] William Livingston (1723-90) was a descendant of John Livingston, a Scotch Presbyterian minister who fled to Holland on the restoration of Charles II. John's son Robert, born in Scotland and reared in Holland, came to America about 1673, where fortunate connections and royal grants made him one of the wealthiest men in New York—his holdings along the Hudson amounting to 150,000 acres. Philip Livingston, the second Lord of Livingston Manor, was the father of William. In 1745, William Livingston married Miss Susanna French, whose father had been a large proprietor of land in New Jersey. In 1772 the family moved to Elizabethtown, N. J.; in 1774 and 1775 he was a delegate to the Continental Congress; and in 1776 he became governor of New Jersey. For biography, see Theodore Sedgwick, Jr., *A Memoir of the Life of William Livingston . . . with Extracts from his Correspondence* (1833); *cf.* Lucius Q. C. Elmer, "The Constitution and Government of the Province and State of New Jersey," in *Collections of the New Jersey Historical Society,* VII (1872), 56-76. Livingston, Smith, and Scott

As a writer of trenchant prose in *The Indepent Reflector*, William Livingston made a distinct contribution to American essays. If his style is slightly oratorical in form, this element is held well in check, and serves rather to lend order, brevity, and strength, than verbosity. No essays had appeared previously in American magazines so fitting to the time, place, and idea. In the factor of civic improvement, his remarks still ring with a modern tone. His discussions on law and the process of courts are equally modern. In his religious comments he stood forth valiantly against an established church; while in the field of education he proposed and fought gallantly, though quixotically, for a state college governed ultimately by the legislative body. In the midst of severe and scurrilous remarks printed against him in the press, he directed the magazine-journal remarkably high above the plane of petty disputation. The plan of the periodical forbade reply, and, except in one or two instances, the editor succeeded in restraining himself from engaging in incivilities. At no time did he name an adversary. *The Independent Reflector* is to be commended for its balanced judgment in the main and for its directness and clearness. It maintained a fairness in point of view seldom elsewhere encountered in its time.

For style, and to some extent for content, however, it is not to be supposed that Livingston's literary background cannot be traced. Like others of his time, he had absorbed the universally prevailing influence of Addison and Steele, mentioning the former with high respect,[9] and occasionally writing in the manner of *The Spectator*. Moreover, both in style of composition and in agreement in religious thought, Livingston was indebted to Thomas Gordon, the writer of *The Independent Whig*, the four volumes of which, under London or New York imprints, were well known in the Colonies. From these volumes he sometimes paraphrased, as comparison readily shows,[10] and in his essay No. 41, he

---

were known as "The Triumvirate"—Yale graduates, associates at the bar, and young lawyers of energy and promise.

[9] *The Independent Reflector*, "Preface," p. 25.

[10] *The Independent Whig: or, a Defence of Primitive Christianity*, fifth edition, London (1732). In the "Introduction," I, 1-2, the following statement is made: "Whoever goes about to reform the World, undertakes an Office obnoxious to Malice, and beset with Difficulties. It speaks a Confidence of his own Capacity, which prompts him to set up for the School-master of Mankind; and it infers a Charge of Corruption or Ignorance in his Pupils, out of which he assumes to whip them." *The Independent Reflector*, No.

glowingly praised Gordon, who, he said, had "gone farther towards shaming Tyranny and Priestcraft . . . with downright Banter, than would have been effected by austere Dogmas, or formal deductions."[11]   Among the classical figures whom he enjoyed mentioning or quoting were Socrates, Plato, Cicero, Horace, Milton, and Pope, while Roman history and law often served his pen.

William Smith, Jr., has never been given sufficient credit for his work on the *Independent Reflector, The Occasional Reverberator*, and "The Watch-Tower" column of Gaine's *The New-York Mercury*. It is doubtful if all his essays can be definitely reclaimed.[12] But at least there is evidence in the Smith manuscripts at the New York Public Library that some of the material formerly attributed in a general way to Livingston belongs more properly to his coworker in the fields of law and essay composition. A preliminary stage in the launching of *The Independent Reflector* is revealed in Smith's "New York in its Natural Advantages Shortly Considered," the major part of which appeared in the periodical in Nos. 8 and 52. At the top of the first page of the manuscript of this article, Smith wrote the title, "The New York Guardian," and below this the date line, "Number [blank] Thursday, November [blank] 1752."[13] It is evident that the later title, *The Independent Reflector*, was not chosen until close to the time of

---

1, p. 1, stated the idea in these words: "Whoever sets up for a Reformer of Public Abuses, must expect to encounter innumerable Difficulties. It seems to carry with it an Air of Superiority to which Mankind submit with the greatest Reluctance. The Office of giving Advice, is naturally Obnoxious to Ill-Will, as it implies either some Fault, or a less Degree of Understanding, in the Person who is to take it; for which Reason it is seldom taken." While other paraphrased passages may be found (*e.g., The Independent Whig*, No. 2, I, 8, and *The Independent Reflector*, No. 34, p. 136), Livingston more usually adapted the general ideas of *The Independent Whig*, finding them after his own heart; *e.g., The Independent Whig* No. 4, *The Independent Reflector* No. 31; *The Independent Whig*, Nos. 35, 39, and *The Independent Reflector*, No. 41. *The Independent Whig* was sufficiently well known in New York to attract the sale of Francis Squire's reply, which was advertised in *The New-York Mercury* for June 25, 1753.

[11] *The Independent Reflector*, p. 163.

[12] Maturin L. Delafield, in a biographical sketch, *William Smith* (reprinted from *The Magazine of American History*, April and June 1881), has written a brief account of the life of William Smith, Jr., see pp. 418-39. The son was graduated from Yale in 1745; he was appointed a judge of the Supreme Court of the Province of New York in 1763; he was made a member of the Council as early as 1769, and following the Revolutionary War became Chief Justice of Canada.

[13] Smith Papers, box numbered 198-206.

publication, and that Smith was interested in the periodical before its name had finally been determined.

There was no particular reason why Parker should be afraid to undertake the publication of the new journal. At its inception there was no indication that stirring animosities would develop. Both Livingston and Smith had been educated according to conventional standards, and were rising young attorneys. Livingston had written acceptably for Parker's *The New-York Weekly Post-Boy* as early as August 19, 1745, and had published in 1747 *Philosophic Solitude*,[14] a long poem deriving its inspiration partially from Pomfret and Horace. He was apparently interested in literary matters. Finally, if Parker had not accepted the proposal, it was probable that another publisher would have been secured.

No clear allocation of authorship which may not be challenged has ever been made for the essays in *The Independent Reflector*.[15]

[14] Sedgwick, *op. cit.*, p. 61.

[15] Initials and pseudonyms attached to all essays of consequence are as follows: No. 1, "Z."; No. 2, "B."; No. 3, "M. K.," "X. & Z."; No. 4, "Z."; No. 5, "T. D.," "B."; No. 6, "Z. & B."; No. 7, "X."; No. 8, "A.," "Z."; No. 9, "Z.," "Ralph "Syntax"; No. 10, "L.," "Eboracus,"· "Z. & A.," "Publicolus"; No. 11, "Z."; No. 12, "A."; No. 13, "Z.," "Timothy Freeheart"; No. 14, "Agricola," "O."; No. 15, "Philalethes"; No. 16, "Publicus"; No. 17, "Z."; No. 18, "A."; No. 19, "B."; No. 20, "B."; No. 21, "A."; No. 22, "Z."; No. 23, "N."; No. 24, "X.," "A."; No. 25, "B." (a continuation of No. 24); No. 26, "X."; No. 27, "A. & Z."; No. 28, "G. R.," "A."; No. 29, "Shadrech Plebianus," "Academicus"; No. 30, "Z.," Phileleutherus"; No. 31, "Z."; No. 32, "Z."; No. 33, "B."; No. 34, "Z."; No. 35, "A. & Z."; No. 36, "Z."; No. 37, "B." (a continuation of No. 36); No. 38, "Z."; No. 39, "B." (a continuation of No. 38); No. 40, "A."; No. 41, "Z."; No. 42, "Z."; No. 43, "Z."; No. 44, "A."; No. 45, "Z.," "Shadrech Plebianus"; No. 46, "Z."; No. 47, "B."; No. 48, "T. T.," "J. F."; No. 49, "Z."; No. 50, "A."; No. 51, "Z."; No. 52, "A. & X."

The contents of numbers may be thus briefly described: No. 1 promises a policy "vindicating the *civil and religious RIGHTS*"; No. 2 opposes annual sale of office of collector of excises; No. 3 urges a more efficient police system; No. 4 argues for limited as opposed to absolute monarchy; No. 5 pleads for strict construction of immigration law, so that mendicants will be prohibited entry; No. 6 is "A Vindication of the Moravians"; No. 7 proposes more efficient fire protection; No. 8 presents advantages of New York over Philadelphia; No. 9 compliments New York as being free from vice of sale of public offices; No. 10 exposes unfair petition pleading for endorsement of land titles; No. 11 is a vindication of the author against attacks of the clergy; No. 12 discusses the practice of medicine, and the *"dismal Havock"* of quacks; No. 13 urges men not to subscribe wholly to any party; No.. 14 is a reply to No. 10, showing fairness of petition; No. 15 supports "The Independent Reflector" against his adversaries; No. 16 applies itself against "Transportation of Felons"; Nos. 17-22, "Remarks on our Intended College," declare the advisability of the establishment of a non-sectarian college governed by the legislature; No. 23 treats "Of Patriotism"; No. 24 urges state regulation of beef and pork, and an act to inspect butter; No. 25 resumes discussion of No. 24; No. 26 sets forth the principle that bad money drives out good money; No. 27

It is certain, however, that Sedgwick[16] was too sanguine in believing that Livingston wrote under the initials "Z.," "B.," "X. & Z.," "Z. & B.," "X.," and "A." Manuscript or other evidence clearly shows that the four letters involved in the signatures were employed to indicate the work of Livingston, Smith, and John Morin Scott. To the essay, "New York in its Natural Advantages Shortly Considered," which has been shown by manuscript evidence to belong to Smith, are attached the initials "A." and "A. & X." respectively.[17] It is quite probable that "A.," at least, represents Smith's contributions, and that he was the sole author of nine essays, and joint author of four others.[18]

There is no doubt that Livingston, as chief editor, wrote over the initial "Z." The essay entitled, "The Vanity of Birth and Titles," which appeared in Number 43, lies still preserved in manuscript, in Livingston's handwriting, and signed "Z.," in the Smith Papers. On the last sheet, Smith, his legal and literary associate, has signed an initial "A." following the notation, "perused 26 May, 1753." No. 1, which was the "Introduction," as well as No. 11, "The Author's Vindication of himself," and other characteristic essays, are signed "Z." This assignment alone grants to Livingston the authorship of twenty-one essays, and the joint

is "A Prayer" suitable for a non-sectarian college; No. 28 applies itself "On Delays in Chancery"; No. 29 criticizes expensive funerals; No. 30 laments the "Levity" in which "The Multiplicity of Oaths" are administered; No. 31 is of "Primitive Christianity Short and Intelligible, Modern Christianity Voluminous and Incomprehensible"; No. 32 pleads for free elections; No. 33 defends the English compound of monarchy, aristocracy, and democracy; No. 34 treats of veneration and contempt of the clergy; No. 35 arraigns the "pettifogger" attorney; Nos. 36-37 deal with the absurdity of civil magistrates interfering in matters of religion; Nos. 38-39 undertake to discuss the theories "Of Passive-Obedience and Non-Resistance" to laws; No. 40, "Of the Use, Abuse, and Liberty of the Press," closes with an attack on the *New-York Mercury*; No. 41 is "A Defence of Ridicule" to stir men to upright action; No. 42 sets forth importance of the office of justice-of-the-peace; No. 43 is on "The Vanity of Birth and Titles"; No. 44 refutes arguments in support of an ecclesiastical establishment in New York; No. 45, "A Catalogue of Sundry Grievances," discusses in main the problems at issue in Nos. 17-22; No. 46 offers a broad creed for religion; No. 47 treats "Of Credulity" in religion; No. 48 generalizes on the "Waste of Life"; No. 49 propounds the immortality of the soul; No. 50, of "The Advantages of Education," urges the necessity of instituting grammar schools; No. 51 recurs to the discussion in Nos. 17-22; No. 52 concludes No. 8.

[16] *Op. cit.*, p. 83.

[17] I am indebted to Mr. W. R. Leech, of the manuscript department of the New York Public Library, for his assistance in considering the handwritings of Livingston, Smith, and Scott among the Smith Papers.

[18] Author of an essay in Nos. 8, 12, 18, 21, 24, 28, 40, 44, 50; joint author of an essay in Nos. 10, 27, 35, 52.

authorship of five others.[19] It is likewise evident that Livingston assumed general responsibility for the contents of the journal. In the "Preface" to the bound volume, written after the essays had appeared, he wrote in a manner indicating he considered himself "The Independent Reflector."

In the second number of *The Occasional Reverberator*, "The Independent Reflector" (Livingston) contributed two letters defending himself, in one of which he wrote that, although he had signed the first essay in *The Independent Reflector* "Z." and in the second number had used the initial "B.," he wished to correct the impression of multiple authorship, as he had "never conceived himself to consist of a *Duality* of Persons."[20] This statement seems to imply at least the assumption of authorization of all articles, and also of the use of "B." as well as "Z." for a personal signature. The assignment of "B." to Livingston would yield to him the authorship of ten more essays, as well as the sole authorship of one signed "Z. & B."[21] It will be noted that essays signed "Z." and "B." complement subject matter on more than one occasion; and that when this is not the case (as in the extended essay, "Remarks on our Intended College," which extended through six numbers and was signed variously "Z.," "A.," "B.," "B.," "A.," and "Z."), the association is with Livingston's closest editorial companion, Smith.

The importance of John Morin Scott in the editing of *The Independent Reflector* may be safely rated as next to that of Livingston and Smith, though evidence other than general tradition seems to have been lacking heretofore. That Scott assisted Smith in the controversy is certain. A signed article in *The New-York Mercury* for September 3, 1753, in behalf of "The Independent Reflector," links their names. That they should expose their identities thus publicly regarding the controversy, while all others were hiding and continued to hide behind pseudonyms, speaks strongly for their interest and association. Moreover, manuscript evidence points to the association of the three in the conduct of *The Inde-*

[19] Author of an essay in Nos. 1, 4, 8, 9, 11, 13, 17, 22, 30, 31, 32, 34, 36, 38, 41, 42, 43, 45, 46, 49, 51; joint author of an essay in Nos. 3, 6, 10, 27, 35.

[20] Published Sept. 14, 1753.

[21] Author of an essay in Nos. 2, 5, 6, 19, 20, 25, 33, 37, 39, 47. Note that Nos. 37 and 39, signed "B.," are conclusions of Nos. 36 and 38 respectively, signed "Z."; however, No. 25, signed "B.," is a continuation of No. 24, signed "X., A."; and No. 6 is signed "Z. & B."

pendent Reflector. At the bottom of Smith's manuscript copy
of "New York in its Natural Advantages Shortly Considered,"
there appears the lines "perused & approved by Z.," and "Octo^r.
15, examined & emended—X.," indicating the association of three
men. The handwriting of "X." appears almost certainly to be
that of Scott. Furthermore, in the manuscript of the editor's
"Preface" to the Craftsman, a sermon from *The Independent Whig*,
likewise among the Smith Papers, the handwriting of three men
is evident, the "Preface" being written by Livingston and Smith,
and the marginal notes by Scott. On the two manuscripts the handwritings of Scott and "X." appear to be identical. The assumption
of "X." as the mark used by Scott makes him the author of three
essays, and the associate author of two others.[22]

Who the other writers of the group may have been is a matter
of conjecture. Sedgwick[23] included the name of William Peartree
Smith, a friend of Livingston, as a possible contributor, and
Thomas[24] added the "reputed" names of another friend, the Rev-
erend Aaron Burr, later President of Princeton, and General
William Alexander,[25] Livingston's brother-in-law. The "Watch
Tower" column in Gaine's *The New-York Mercury*, to which
The Independent Reflector group turned when their journal was
discontinued, was written, according to Livingston, principally
by "men of business,"[26] but their identities remain concealed.

To the policies of "vindicating the *civil and religious RIGHTS*
of my Fellow-Creatures" and "displaying the amiable Charms of
Liberty"—without the "blemish" of "personal Reflection"—the editor so completely set his mind and ardor that the "World of Science" went begging, though promised when other things should
fail.[27] But though civil matters filled many an essay, nearly half
of the numbers of *The Independent Reflector* were concerned with
religion and education,[28] and these were the subjects which drew

---

[22] Author of an essay in Nos. 7, 24, 26; joint author of an essay in Nos. 3 and 52.
[23] *Op. cit.*, p. 83.
[24] *Op. cit.*, II, 125; *cf.* Mott, *History of American Magazines*, pp. 47-48.
[25] *The Life of William Alexander*, by his grandson, William Alexander Duer (Vol. II
of the *Collections of the New Jersey Historical Society*, 1847), contains no reference to
this point.
[26] P. L. Ford, *The Journals of Hugh Gaine, Printer*, 1902, I, 18, quoting a Livingston
letter to Noah Welles.
[27] *The Independent Reflector*, No. 1.
[28] See note 15.

hot fire from opponents. Livingston was a member of the Presbyterian Church, whose congregation numbered many of Dutch
descent; Smith, his able assistant, was a thorough critic of the
Episcopal establishment, and his manuscripts abound in religious
discussion.[29]

Andrew Burnaby's summary (1760) of the religious establishments in the city is interesting from the point of view of an English Episcopalian minister. "There are," he wrote, "two churches
[Episcopalian] in New York . . . both of them large buildings.
. . . Besides these, there are several other places of religious worship; namely, two Low Dutch Calvinist churches, one High Dutch
ditto, one French ditto, one German Lutheran church, one Presbyterian meeting-house, one Quaker ditto, one Anabaptists [sic]
ditto, one Moravian ditto, and a Jews [sic] synagogue."[30] The
complexity of religious elements is evident.

The Episcopal Church had been established in New York in 1664,
but hereafter for a time it had lain nearly dormant. In 1692
Governor Fletcher had induced the Assembly to pass an act making
provision for ministry in each county, the ministers to be appointed
by the governor.[31] Fletcher had used his authority to appoint
Episcopalians only, who were supported by a state grant of forty
to sixty pounds a year. The Church was still in the minority by
the middle of the eighteenth century, but it was strong in influence and seeking to make its creed the creed of the "intended College." To assist in this design, Trinity Church had offered a
grant of land, providing the college should comply with certain
religious restrictions.

[29] See particularly, among the Smith Papers, "Thoughts Relating to Bishops in
America," and the paper on religious "Oppressions in 1719-20," containing a reference
to *The New-York Mercury* of Feb. 17, 1755.

[30] Burnaby, *op. cit.*, pp. 112-13.

[31] S. D. McConnell, *History of the American Episcopal Church*, tenth ed. (1916),
pp. 64-65. From this work, as well as from William Stevens Perry, *The History of the
American Episcopal Church 1587-1883* (1885) and Arthur Lyon Cross, *The Anglican
Episcopate and the American Colonies* (*Harvard Historical Studies*, Vol. IX, 1902)
the remarks are based. Perry, *op cit.*, I, 296 (note), 414, 417, 438, 457, is inclined to
present Livingston's anti-Episcopalian attitude in an unfavorable light; Sedgwick, *op.
cit.*, presents the point of view of a sympathetic biographer. The remarks of Cross,
op. cit., seem to me the most judicial. He who reads the papers and journals of
the period must feel convinced that Livingston was fully as fair, rational, and sincere in
his arguments as his opponents. On the other hand, the fact that the Dutch groups, so
far as written evidence is concerned in the papers of the period, remained quietly indif-
ferent to the contest, suggests that Livingston was somewhat quixotic.

Through the six numbers of *The Independent Reflector* devoted to "Remarks on our Intended College," Livingston and Smith waged combat against restrictive religious ordinances, entirely private financial support, and a limited curriculum. The college should offer courses "to qualify Men for the different Employments of Life,"[32] rather than a concentrated program of Greek, Latin, and rhetoric. The evils of sect rule which surrounded Harvard and Yale should not operate in New York, especially as the city was composed of many sects. Moreover, the college should not be established by charter, but by an act of the Assembly, which should choose the trustees, who in turn should appoint a president. Such an establishment, Livingston believed, would bring to the college both public and private support.

So many were the replies to "The Independent Reflector's" program that the subject immediately became dominantly important in succeeding numbers of the journal.[33] Of special interest is the "Prayer" by Smith and Livingston, printed in No. 27, which was printed with liberal marginal references to the Bible in an endeavor to refute what "hath often been asserted by those for a partial College [Episcopalian], that no Prayer could possibly be formed, but what would be rejected by all other Denominations." Of a less controversial nature was the educational policy supported by the fiftieth number, wherein were presented "The Advantages of Education, with the Necessity of Instituting Grammar Schools for the Instruction of Youth, Preparatory to their Admission to our Intended College."

Though an aura of sweetness and light did not wholly pervade the religious discussion, there was considerable fire and strength in the democratic liberalism diffused through the essays of Livingston and Smith relating to religion and government.[34] The major salvo, "Primitive Christianity Short and Intelligible, Modern Christianity Voluminous and Incomprehensible" (No. 31), attacked the Thirty-

---

[32] No. 17.

[33] For engagements of the pen by others than Livingston, Smith, and Scott, see especially "Phileleutherus" in No. 30, and the letter to "Z." in No. 51.

[34] Important essays discussing religion but not embracing the religious-educational conflict, appeared in Nos. 6, 11, 15, 31, 34, 36, 37, 41, 44, 46, 47, 49, 51. In No. 15, "Philalethes" compliments "The Independent Reflector" for supporting the Moravians; in No. 41, "Z." (Livingston) compliments "The Independent Whig" for shaming tyranny and undue power of priests; in No. 51, a letter criticizing a lazy minister is printed; see note 15 for contents of the other numbers.

Nine Articles, the idea of a state church, and the tendency of a highly organized sect to assert bloc power. There is no doubt that Livingston had real and active adversaries in the Episcopal group, some members of which were openly insisting that by law the Church of England was established in the province of New York with prerogatives similar to those enjoyed in England.[35] Smith, probably, undertook a reply to this attitude of the Church members in his essay, "The Arguments in Support of an Ecclesiastical Establishment in This Province, Impartially Considered, and Refuted" (No. 44). Other essays served Livingston in advancing further tenets. Although he held the clergy in "profoundest Reverence," he did not hold a brief for any of their possible demands for "unreasonable Respect, persecuting Fury, and holy Grimace,"[36] and "being priest-ridden was worse than having no Religion at all."[37] He fought against interference with individual religious beliefs by civil government, citing the "memorable Test-Act" as a case at point.[38] He defended the privilege of skepticism,[39] issued his personal "Creed"[40]—a broad and tolerant one—and stated his belief in the immortality of the soul.[41]

The Episcopalian interests found an organ for retaliation in Gaine's *The New-York Mercury*, and as the weeks advanced, the articles against *The Independent Reflector* waxed decidedly warm. Letters appeared in support of an Episcopalian college.[42] Other challenges to "The Independent Reflector's" views were issued with fair regularity, some of them well written and well pointed in thought. On June 18, 1753, came the reply to the non-sectarian "Prayer,"[43] the writer pointing out that it possessed "the Spirit, the Order, and the very Words . . . that are generally in Use by that Sect among us, which goes under the Denomination of Independents, in New-England, Congregationalists, and by none other Sect."[44]

[35] See particularly *The New-York Mercury*, July 30, 1753, p. 1.

[36] No. 11.

[37] No. 34.

[38] Nos. 36-37.

[39] No. 47.

[40] No. 46.

[41] No. 49.

[42] See especially *The New-York Mercury*, June 4, 1753.

[43] For the "Prayer," see *The Independent Reflector*, No. 27.

[44] Livingston's residence at Yale perhaps accounts for his familiarity with the point of view of the Congregationalists. It is likely he fully believed the prayer to be as broad as he represented it to be.

A week later "Mosche Vecalessh Ethan," who wrote as a Quaker, took issue against "The Independent Reflector"—an unkind cut, as at least the writer professed himself to belong to a sect usually associated in its interests with the Protestant churches which were not Episcopalian. On July 9 was printed a direct accusation that "The Independent Reflector" was still pilfering from *The Independent Whig* and *Henry on Prayer*, the article containing also a challenge to the statement that the positive precepts of Christianity were but two,[45] and an exhortation to the Episcopalians and the Dutch to "hold steadfast" against "The Independent Reflector" and his principles.[46] Among the Episcopalian writers, this essay group, using the signature "X.Z.&." (to which the later "Z.&." is evidently related), was able to deal the most effective blows. The full signature appeared under a subsequent essay, in which Butler was used to characterize "The Independent Reflector" as Hudibras:

> " 'He rose, dred Foe to Priests and Fetters,
> Deep-skill'd in Church and civil Matters;
> For he had read all Cato's Letters.' "[47]

Livingston's belief in the absurdity of civil magistrates interfering in matters of religion[48] was attacked in a series of four essays, signed "Z.&," in *The New-York Mercury* during September.[49] The writer developed the thesis that the state should take cognizance of religion in so far as it endeavored to assist the state for the good of mankind, and closed by charging "The Independent Reflector" with promulgating "Notions, that tend to overthrow that Constitution which himself has given the Preference to."[50]   In the meantime Gaine had replied to *The Independent Reflector*, No. 40, on the liberty of the press, admitting that every printer set up for personal advancement, but denying that he had ever received the value of ten shillings for everything he had printed for or against

---

[45] The "positive precepts" are given in *The Independent Reflector*, No. 31.   The challenger offered the New York edition of Squire's *Answer to the Independent Whig* in reply.

[46] Episcopalians were addressing the Dutch Church as a "sister church" because the latter was also a state institution.

[47] *The New-York Mercury*, July 23, 1753.

[48] *The Independent Reflector*, Nos. 36-37.

[49] Sept. 3, 10, 17, 24, 1753.   The author was given the front page, not an unusual position for challenging essays of all types.

[50] Sept. 24.

the essay-journal.[51] Other issues of *The New-York Mercury* attacked not only "The Independent Reflector," but "Philo-Reflector" (William Smith),[52] his staunch defender. A particular point in the dispute involved the question whether the Dutch Church, as a state institution in Holland, was a "sister-church" of the Episcopalian sect, or more nearly akin in doctrine to the other Protestant churches, as Livingston and Smith asserted, pointing to the refuge of English Protestant bodies in The Netherlands during the seventeenth century. *The New-York Mercury* printed the last word: the final issue of *The Independent Reflector* appeared November 22, while an anonymous "J. F.," in the paper for December 3, accused "The Independent Reflector" of forging his name to an epistle, writing what had never entered "J. F.'s" heart.

Through the files of Parker's *The New-York Gazette* one may trace the printer's change of attitude from early enthusiasm to a growing aversion for *The Independent Reflector*, issuing from his press. With the exuberance born of initial enterprise, he had devoted, on December 4, 1752, the whole of the first page of his newspaper to the "Design" of the essay-journal, which had already made its appearance on November 30, the price to be ten shillings per annum, "so calculated . . . as barely to pay the Printer, without any Commission for his [the editor's] own Time and Labour."[53] The following week Parker printed in *The New-York Gazette* an essay urging the organization of schools in the country districts and the teaching of practical subjects in the intended college— evidently the first draft of Smith's essay which appeared nearly a

[51] *The New-York Mercury*, Sept. 3. The reply contained the letter to Gaine mentioned in Section II, signed by Smith and Scott, requesting Gaine to publish two letters by "The Independent Reflector"—a request not granted.

[52] That William Smith was "Philo-Reflector" there is no doubt, though the essays over that name (as also in the case of "The Independent Reflector") were sometimes group-written and edited. Among the Smith Papers is the "Editor's Preface" to *The Craftsmen, a Sermon from the Independent Whig*, by "Philo-Reflector," in the handwriting of Smith and Livingston, with marginal notes probably by Scott. "Heirocles," in *The New-York Mercury* for Oct. 8, and "Z. &.," in the same paper for Oct. 22, reply to "Philo-Reflector's" pamphlet, *The Craftsmen, a Sermon from the Independent Whig*, the former charging the writer with an attempt to tear down the structure of religion, and the latter insisting that the Dutch Church was very similar to the Episcopalian Church, especially as "In Point of Doctrine, the Dutch agree with the 39 Articles of the Church of England."

[53] The "Design" in *The New-York Gazette* was a reprint of *The Independent Reflector*, No. 1.

year later in *The Independent Reflector*.[54]   Then came his most
audacious move in support of Livingston.   On February 19, 1753,
he opened *The New-York Gazette's* front page to "Philo-Reflector"
(Smith), who defended "The Independent Reflector" in a reply to
a "Reverend Clergyman, who last Week appeared in Print, and
honoured the Public with a little Sermon entirely his own," in which
he had argued "that blasphemous Position, that *whoever despises
a Minister, despises Jesus Christ.*"

The effect of "Philo-Reflector's" reply was immediate.   Several
irate Episcopalian subscribers cancelled their subscriptions; and
Parker, as government printer and leading publisher, saw danger
ahead if he did not remain neutral.   On February 26 *The New-
York Gazette* printed a letter from one who wrote as a Quaker,
appealing for an end to religious discord and insisting that "Philo-
Reflector" (as well as "Bull-Dog," "Layman," "Dreamer," and
other correspondents of the press) was to Parker an enemy in sheep's
clothing.   On April 16 *The New-York Gazette* carried another
letter to Parker, signed "A.P.," which inclosed a message to "The
Independent Reflector," whom the writer addressed in an Irish
brogue, conventional dialect of ridicule, assuring him that the religion of the college was "a shmall Mattersh of great Importantsh."
Parker's name continued to appear on the journal as the printer,
but beginning with No. 39, for August 23, he withdrew a succeeding line which had heretofore announced, ". . . by whom letters
to the author are carefully delivered."

Number 52 of *The Independent Reflector*, the final issue, bore
the date November 22, 1753.   Livingston later wrote a long
"Preface," which was added to the volume as a valedictory explanation of the difficulties encountered by the editor in his relationships
with his publisher and critics.[55]   According to his remarks in the
preface, Livingston had lost his publisher without warning.   Parker,
he wrote, had promised to continue the essay-journal until June
1754; but after the publication of the fifty-second number, the
printer had instructed the distributor boy to collect all past dues,

[54] No. 50 (Nov. 8, 1753).

[55] The preface printed in the bound volume is dated Jan. 19, 1753; an advertisement
printed in the volume at the New York Public Library is dated Feb. 29, 1754.   The
volume was priced at two shillings, and sold by Robert McAlpine, bookbinder, in
Hanover-Square.   It was not advertised in *The New-York Mercury* or *The New-York
Gazette*

assuring the customers they were to expect no more numbers. The reason Parker gave Livingston for discontinuing publication was that he had been threatened with loss of public business if he should persist. The loss of a publisher cost Livingston much pain, for there was a great deal which he must now leave unsaid, in proof of which he attached to the preface fifty-seven titles he had intended to make the subjects of essays.[56] The rest of the preface was concerned principally with that "venerable tribe" of clergymen whose attitude had established, among the "immutable and eternal truths," the fact "That tho' the order is of divine institution, and therefore to be greatly revered; many of it's [sic] members are the most abandoned of the species, and therefore to be greatly abhorred."[57] The paper on "Primitive Christianity Short and Intelligible" had been widely attacked and falsified by the writer's enemies as a "latent attempt to discredit religion itself."[58] Finally, Livingston revealed in the preface a reason why *The New-York Gazette* had been closed to his friends. In an early stage of the contest, Parker had, indeed, opened his columns in *The New-York Gazette* to "Philo-Reflector," but had thereafter refused his support when the article had cost him twelve subscribers. Thus it was that "Philo-Reflector" had been driven to the publication of a pamphlet, *The Craftsmen, a Sermon from the Independent Whig*, to support his friend.[59]

II

As the editorial policy of *The Independent Reflector* prohibited replies to the attacks of adversaries, the friends of Livingston felt the need of some journal to support their battered comrade. Parker's *The New-York Gazette* and Gaine's *The New-York Mercury* were both closed to them, and so a new four-page journal, *The Occasional Reverberator*,[60] was established, the first number

[56] Among the proposed articles were several dealing with the importance of a free college, a history of the religious establishments in New York City and neighboring counties, and essays on persecution, on civic beauty, on the right of British subjects on plantations to privileges enjoyed by those in Great Britain, on the defenseless nature of New York City and the frontiers, and on importation of negroes (which Livingston opposed).

[57] P. 3.

[58] P. 4.

[59] P. 8; see also note 52.

[60] See note 3.

appearing September 7, 1753, and the fourth and last[61] on October 5, when *The Independent Reflector* had still seven more numbers to run. Parker, though unwilling to open the columns of his newspaper to "The Reverberator," was still printing *The Independent Reflector* and balancing himself between the contending parties. So he agreed to print the new essay-journal, and announced its publication in *The New-York Gazette* of September 17: " 'The Enemies of Liberty . . . having by the most iniquitous Arts, engrossed the *New-York Mercury*, and utterly excluded their Antagonists from a fair Hearing in that Paper; and the Printers of the *Gazette* declining the Insertion of any Thing that savours of political or religious Controversy,' another Paper, entitled, *The Occasional Reverberator*, has been set up to be published every Friday, as often as Occasion shall require: the First Number was printed the 7th Instant, and the Second on Friday last. Any Person inclining to take them . . . may have them at the Rate of 2/6 per Quarter . . . or at 3d. a Piece single."

The first number of *The Occasional Reverberator* (written by Smith, who signed himself "The Reverberator"), besides containing an appeal for the "frequent Assistance" of "so pure and disinterested a Writer" as "The Independent Reflector," printed a reply,[62] signed "F. & G." and written in part probably by Smith,[63] to a letter which had been published in *The New-York Mercury* September 3, in defense of Gaine, who had been crudely attacked in *The Independent Reflector*, No. 40.[64] This reply, although containing severer strictures than decency might warrant, was not wholly wrong in surmising that Gaine, who had during his life turned from the Episcopalian Church to the Presbyterian and back to

[61] *The Independent Reflector*, "Preface," p. 14, gives Livingston's testimony that the "paper was not continued beyond four numbers."

[62] "A Letter to Mr. Gaine, on his Notable Address to the Publick, in *The New-York Mercury*, No. 56."

[63] Among the Smith Papers are No. 1 of "The Reverberator," written by Smith, and also Smith's article on religious "Oppressions in 1719-1720," containing a reference to *The New-York Mercury*, No. 132, published Feb. 17, 1755. The article is signed "F.," showing that Smith did use that letter on occasion.

[64] In No. 40 (Aug. 30, 1753) of *The Independent Reflector* there appeared a reference clearly intended to describe Gaine as one who "deserted his Religion, made himself the Tool of a Party he despised . . . slandered half the People of his Country . . . promised afterwards to desist . . . continued the Publication of his Lies, Forgeries and Misrepresentations . . . obstinately refused to print the Answers or Vindications of the Persons he had abused; and yet even this Wretch, had the Impudence to talk of the *Liberty of the Press*."

the Episcopalian, "would readily forsake the Service of the latter provided . . . [he] could be assured of a constant Employment from the former."

Livingston himself, as "The Independent Reflector," contributed the two letters comprising the second number of *The Occasional Reverberator*, answering "Z. &.'s" strictures in *The New-York Mercury*[65] against Livingston's attack on the power of civil authority to regulate religious affairs.[66] It is not unlikely that Livingston would have been a fairly regular contributor to the journal had it continued any length of time, for he elsewhere mentioned the periodical as one which, having been "set on foot to give my friends an opportunity of being heard," was likewise one in which "I was determined to try my hand."[67] The third number contained two letters also, the first, probably by Smith as it bore the signature "F.,"[68] urging the Reformed Dutch congregations to conduct their services in the English tongue so that they might interest their children, and the second, a hoax dated from New-Windsor, arraigning "The Independent Reflector's" ideas with ridiculous argument.[69] The final number of the journal contained as the principal article a reply to an essay in *The New-York Mercury* of July 30, 1753, which had sought to prove that the Church of England was by law established with similar prerogatives in the province of New York.

From the evidence at hand it is certain that Smith and Livingston were the chief instigators of *The Occasional Reverberator*, and that Smith was "The Reverberator," for whatever is blazed in the trail leads to his manuscripts. Evidence also points to the implication that the editors may well have been disappointed at the short duration of the journal, for plans included the possibility of its continuance for a year or longer.[70] But one can only conjecture that external circumstances put an end to the publication.

[65] See note 49.

[66] In these letters he assured "Z. &.," whom he believed to be a clergyman, that the then "Bishop of Winchester, Mr. Locke, Sir Algernon Sidney, Mr. Hooker, and many more" were opposed to civil interference.

[67] *The Independent Reflector*, "Preface," p. 9.

[68] See note 63.

[69] This article is preserved in manuscript among the Smith Papers; it is dated Aug. 15, 1753, and signed with the initials "H. W."

[70] The prefatory announcement in *The Occasional Reverberator*, No. 1, announced a price of ten shillings per annum for fifty-two papers.

III

Exactly one year after the death of *The Independent Reflector*, the whole controversy sprang again into journalistic life. Gaine's *The New-York Mercury* opened its columns to the anti-Anglicans, and to it the group around *The Independent Reflector* turned, giving Parker an opportunity soon to print the views of the Episcopalians. *The New-York Mercury* initiated the conflict with a group of essays under the title of "The Watch-Tower," which began November 25, 1754, and continued through fifty-two numbers to November 17, 1755, coming to an end while the negotiations for the college were still pending. "The Watch-Tower" from the very beginning was an energetic section of the paper, usurping the front page, and on occasion relegating the news of the week to a supplement.[71] The chief burden of its weekly messages was its uncompromising fight against the organization of King's College as an Episcopalian school.

Against "The Watch-Tower" soon appeared *John Englishman*,[72] usually issued as a two-page broadside, its ten numbers being printed between April 9 and July 5, 1755. The sheet, whose imprint bore the firm name of Parker and Weyman, had been advertised in Parker's *The New-York Gazette* of April 7, as to be published "on Wednesday next," and priced at "two coppers."

John Englishman had begun as an essay by "John Englishman" in *The New-York Mercury* in reply to "The Watch-Tower" in the same paper.[73] But evidently the exigencies of the occasion seemed to call for independent publication, though regular issues were not anticipated, as an announcement at the close of the first number stated, "The Public may expect a Paper of this Length, as often as shall be thought needful." Correspondence was solicited. The writers for the publication have never been ascertained; "The Watch-Tower" for April 14 was pleased to designate an editorial group consisting of "a Conclave of Eight Reverend Clergymen," but the second number of *John Englishman* replied that in

[71] "The Watch-Tower," No. 4, *The New-York Mercury*, Dec. 16, 1754.
[72] See note 4.
[73] *The New-York Mercury*, Jan. 27, 1755, printed a letter by "John Englishman," who contended that the Church of England and the Dutch Church were "sister" churches. For a reply by "F.," see "The Watch-Tower" in the same paper, Feb. 10, 1755.

this conjecture "The Watch-Tower" labored, "as in most other Things, under a grand Mistake."

From its point of view, *John Englishman* was consistent. Its basic tenet was never more clearly expressed in the paper than in the ninth number: "All the *Watch-Tower's* Clamour of Ill-Treatment and Persecution, arises from his mistaken Apprehension, that the religious Constitution of this Province, is an absolute and intire Equality among all the different Professions and Denominations." Acting on the assumption that the establishment existed in New York as in England, the paper requested articles "in Defence of the College and the English Constitution,"[74] assuming an Episcopalian college[75] and state church the proper commitments of the province. As "Old England" remarked, the dissenters had little reason to speak of loyalty to the constitution, as they had murdered a king, "voted the House of Lords useless, and turned two-thirds of the Commons out of Doors."[76] In an effort to win support, *John Englishman* was eager to prove the Dutch Church a true "sister" to the Church of England,[77] as by a common religious ancestry "Nations . . . whose established Religion may be truly called Christianity, are properly called Sister Churches, notwithstanding much Dissimilitude in their forms of Government."[78]

Something of literary value still may be found in the fifth and sixth numbers, by "Agricola," leavening a journal filled otherwise with specious reasoning. In the form of a narrative essay, the writer offered a scene wherein "a mixed Company of almost every Sect and Denomination of religious Professions among us"[79] gathered to discuss the vexed college question. Out of the conversation

[74] "Advertisement" at close of No. 1.

[75] No. 4 ironically offered "Forty Unanswerable Reasons, against the Bill Relating to the College."

[76] No. 3.

[77] Nos. 1, 2, 7. A reply in "The Watch-Tower" to No. 1 appeared in *The New-York Mercury* for May 5, 1755, wherein "Dordracensis" pointed out that the sisterhood was not perceptibly closer than that of any other dissenting group, for "By the Test Act, are not the Members of the Dutch Church as effectually excluded from Offices civil and military, without taking the Sacrament in the established Church, as any other Sect whatsoever?" During March and April other letters on the same subject appeared in the same paper, variously signed: "Joseph Plain-Truth," "W.," "R. A.," "Philo-Demos," "F.," and "J. V. D."

[78] No. 1. Next in importance to the claim of sisterhood was the effort to justify Governor Fletcher's administration, which *The Independent Reflector* had termed tyrannical.

[79] No. V, first page.

which ensues arise the personalities of the Quaker who felt that "The Independent Reflector" had written with too much acrimony and of the rough and cursing Captain who agreed with "The Independent Reflector's" religious ideas, but who could not see "what Occasion there was for granting this £500 a Year, for Seven years" to build the college.[80]   These characters are worthy of remembrance in Colonial essay literature of the period.

As a challenger of an old order supporting the ideals of the influential Episcopalian group, Livingston suffered the usual fate of being personally berated by some of his opponents, who sought to unite their invective with moral indignation—a sincere union, perhaps, but not persuasively rational.   Though Livingston sometimes replied in kind, the sum of his written expression is on a definitely higher level.   The phases of Livingston's life now under review seem to show the man's strength to have lain in his argument and in a theory which a later decade adopted; while his weakness is revealed in his failure to estimate the mood of the time.   His voice lacked the magic to arouse the masses to follow a flag which may have been theirs, but which they did not care to advance.   On the whole, the journalistic energy surpassed for a time the energy of achievement, for only one wing of the college had been erected by 1760, though in 1753 the Assembly had appointed trustees and voted a yearly grant of £500, and the royal charter had been given in 1754.   Livingston himself was made a trustee, probably partly to silence opposition, but under the Episcopalian rule he could not conscientiously take the oaths of office, and so "never frequented their meetings."[81]

IV

About six weeks before *John Englishman* made its appearance, Parker and Weyman commenced a small literary experiment of their own which was in no way connected with local politics or religion. The publication was called *The Instructor*,[82] and it was conducted on an editorial policy partaking of the traditional characteristics of both the essay weekly and the magazine formula as developed by Cave.   The blending was not fortunate.   It had not the origi-

[80] *Ibid.*
[81] Sedgwick, *op. cit.*, p. 95, quoting a Livingston letter.
[82] See note. 1.

nality of the former, as it adopted the reprint policy of the latter; and it had not the variety and breadth of appeal of the latter, as it adopted the restricted four-page weekly policy of the former. It was frankly an experiment, the first five numbers bearing the announcement that the periodical was "To be continued Weekly, (if suitable Encouragement)" were forthcoming. The parenthetical phrase was dropped from the remaining numbers, but no evidence has been found that the publication was continued beyond the tenth; nor was it, so far as I can discover, advertised for sale at any other shop than that of the publishers.

The design of the little journal, as Parker's *The New-York Gazette* announced,[83] admitted of two general types of cultural matter—the light essay and the historical summary: "Select Pieces on the Social Duties, and such Historical or Speculative Remarks as may be thought useful, to be collected from the best English Writers." The plan thus proposed by Parker and Weyman was the reprinting of such material as could ultimately be bound into an acceptable book, for in the same article the publishers announced that if at the close of the year subscribers would return a complete file "neat, clean, and entire," the publishers would give them a rebate of a copper a number. It is also worthy of note that, in the midst of considerable local religious and educational agitation, the following stipulation was likewise made in *The New-York Gazette's* advertisement; "N. B. No Controversy of any Kind will have Admittance." The public evidently did not respond to so placid an editorial policy.

However, with as much force as its plan and diminutive size could summon, *The Instructor* fought the territorial claims of France and Spain in the New World with the ponderous literary weapons of the Johnsonian Age, the rational essay and the encyclopediac article filled with historical fact and interpretation. Although the Seven Years' War in Europe was not to commence until a year later, the preliminary skirmishes of the French and Indian War had already been fought, and the French had emerged the victors. The Colonists coveted the Saint Lawrence, the western valley frontiers, and the southern lands held by France and Spain, and they looked with increasing concern on the strength of France

[83] March 10, 1755. The item referred to the first issue as of "Last Thursday." Two weeks later the newspaper briefly referred to *The Instructor* as "Now publishing in the City." I have found no other reference.

at the north and west.   Braddock, prepared for the western invasion, arrived on the Potomac in the very month *The Instructor*
began its short career, and hopes were running high.   Historians,
with more prejudice than reason, were engaged on what appeared
a great thesis: the proving of the English title to America over
the titles of the French and Spaniards.[84]

Five numbers[85] of *The Instructor* were largely concerned with
the international conflict in America, and the burden of the thought
was often presented with devices of rhetoric.   Why stood the English Colonies idly by, while France, secure in the north, was rapidly
establishing new settlements to the west of the Middle Colonies
and down the Mississippi?   If France should possess both Canada
and Louisiana, with free communication between, the doom of
England would be sealed.   Consider the prospect: "Thus Great
Britain being deprived of its Subjects, Dominions and Trade in
and to America, our Merchants will be ruined, our Customs and
Funds will sink, our Manufactures will want Vent, our Lands
will fall in Value, and, instead of decreasing, our Debts will
increase, without the least Prospect of the Nation's emerging."[86]

The lighter aspects of *The Instructor* were typical of the period
in several aspects.   Misanthropic observations of human miseries
in the manner of Swift and Johnson,[87] moral essays,[88] discursive

[84] The Colonists were actively engaged in trying to justify their desire to expand, and
seeking to awaken British sentiment across the ocean.   Much propaganda was included
in historical discussions, and considerable stress was placed on the alarming "present
state" of the Colonies.   William Douglass's historical *Summary*, heretofore mentioned,
which had been cut short by his death, was issued by Fowle of Boston, 1747 *passim*; in
1755 Fowle issued a reprint from the London edition of E. Huske's *Present State of*
North America.   In the same year James Franklin published Stephen Hopkins's *Plan*
for Uniting the Colonists, and Benjamin Franklin and David Hall published Lewis
Evans's *Geographical, Historical, Political, Philosophical . . . Essays*.   Samuel Nevill's
The History of the Continent of America was issued serially in *The New American*
Magazine (Jan. 1758-March 1760), a history abruptly terminated by the discontinuance
of the magazine.

[85] Nos. 1, 2, 3, 5, 6.   The first two issues were occupied by "Historical Remarks on
the Present State of Affairs on the Continent of North-America," viewing French
activity along the Mississippi River and Gulf of Mexico with alarm.   The third number
presented "A Geographical Description of Those Parts of This Continent, as Are Now
in Dispute, with the Rights of the Several Claimants."   The fifth and sixth numbers
were devoted to the encroachments of France in the east, being a reprint of a "letter
published in the Year 1712, just before the Treaty of Utrecht."

[86] No. 3.

[87] "A Sketch of Human Life," in No. 7.

[88] "Of Youthful Intemperance," and "The Rule of Life," both in No. 4.

observations,[89] lightsome social banter in the style of Addison and Steele,[90] fables,[91] and an occasional poem[92] were selected for the edification of the gentle readers. Most noteworthy and surprising of all, perhaps, was a short quotation from Milton's *Paradise Lost*[93] in support of a brief essay on wedded love. But though mainly typical, the offerings were too few and too slight to be taken seriously by the public as worthy of purchase or preservation, and today there is only one known file of the periodical.

[89] "Of the Sciences," in Nos. 8-9.

[90] "Tears an Infallible Method to Conquer the Fair Sex," in No. 9; and "New Sect of Evites," in No. 10.

[91] "The Orang-Outang," in No. 4; and "The Party-Colour'd Shield," in No. 7.

[92] "An Ode," selected as suitable to the distressing times, in No. 4; "The Pious Sailor," No. 7.

[93] No. 9.

CHAPTER V

FROM a political point of view, the year following the beginning of the Seven Years' War (1756-63)[1] was disastrous for the British Colonies. As early as 1755 campaigns against the French and Indians in western Pennsylvania and New York had failed; and a year later the important English trading post of Oswego fell. During 1757 an expedition against Louisburg was driven back by the French, and Fort William Henry, at the southern end of Lake George, was captured by Montcalm. Outer evidences pointed somewhat to another weak termination of traditional hostilities not unlike that which followed King George's War. But there was a difference in the English and Colonial outlook which was manifest even in this period. First, England was now more concerned and sent stronger expeditions to the New World. Secondly, a new spirit was stirring among the Colonies. Not only Massachusetts, but other of the Colonies also, were more conscious of a desire for industrial and commercial expansion, and they looked more covetously on the French possessions to the west and north.

This growing tenacity of purpose against the French was both abetted and reflected by the two most important magazines of the time. They were edited by men who had grown to manhood in Great Britain, one a doctor of divinity and the other a journalist. These men, who rose to stations of considerable influence in America, one as a college president and the other as a jurist, brought from across the ocean a strong English hatred of the French and a strength of emotional animosity toward England's Continental enemies beyond that which stirred the mind of the average Colonial-born citizen.

The American Magazine, or Monthly Chronicle for the British Colonies (1757-58)[2] was an able exponent of the renewed military

---

[1] Hostilities between the French and English had begun in America in 1754, and the conflict is usually called the French and Indian War. In Europe, France, Russia, Austria, and Poland finally united against Great Britain and Prussia.

[2] See "Bibliography," p. 365.

endeavors against France. It was edited by William Smith, provost
of the College and Academy of Philadelphia, which became the
University of Pennsylvania after Smith's resignation in 1779 because of his Tory sympathies. The editor, a Scot doctor of divinity,
so strenuously fought the Friends' program of peace in Pennsylvania that less than a year after the magazine was launched he
found himself twice in prison. But Smith was more than a belligerent propagandist; he was a lover of *belles-lettres* and an
eighteenth-century romanticist at heart. His magazine bore the
influence of college professors and students, received many contributions from colonies to the south, and achieved the distinction of
being the most vital and original literary magazine published in
America before the War of the Revolution. Less distinguished
from a literary point of view, but even more completely concerned
with the war, was *The New American Magazine* (1758-60),[3] published at Woodbridge, New Jersey, by James Parker, and edited
by Samuel Nevill, who had been engaged in journalism in London
during his young manhood. In the first year of his editorship in
America, Nevill became a judge of the Supreme Court of New
Jersey. *A History of the Continent of America*,[4] which he compiled from various sources, is the most significant collection of selected articles in the magazine and abounds in specious pleading
for the rights of Great Britain. A fitting companion serial, quite
as full of propaganda, is Thomas Gage's "The Traveller," a narrative of adventure and travel mixed with hatred of Spanish rule in
the Americas. The only other magazine published between the
years 1755 and 1764 was *The New-England Magazine* (1758),[5]
edited in Boston by Benjamin Mecom, a youthful dilettante who
spent so much time choosing between the "Turkey's Wing . . .
and Leg" of polite essay literature that he took no cognizance of
the war.

I

The personality of William Smith[6] was the chief force determining the nature of *The American Magazine, or Monthly Chronicle*

[3] *Ibid.*
[4] See note 3; also Chapter IV, note 86.
[5] See "Bibliography," p. 366.
[6] His great-grandson, Horace Wemyss Smith, has written the *Life and Correspondence of the Rev. William Smith, D.D.* (1879-80), which has served me as a basis for

for the British Colonies. He was born of well-to-do parents in Aberdeenshire, Scotland, in 1727, and following his graduation as Doctor of Divinity from the University of Aberdeen in 1747, he busied himself for a time in London and elsewhere in the interest of Scotch parochial schools. Finding his efforts thwarted, he embarked for New York in 1751 as the tutor of the two small children of a Colonel Martin. The following year he wrote a newspaper article on education, and in 1753 he published *A General Idea of the College of Mirania*, which he intended as a sketch for the proposed college to be established in New York. He did not fail, however, to mail copies of the pamphlet to Franklin, the president of the Board of Trustees of the Academy and Charitable School of Philadelphia, and to the Reverend Richard Peters, who was likewise interested in the school. In 1754, having returned from a trip to England, where he had been ordained a priest in the Church of England and had sought financial aid for the foundation to be laid at Philadelphia, he assumed the office of provost of the institution which became, the following year, the College and Academy of Philadelphia.

Smith's energetic activities in support of the French and Indian War, his defense of the proprietary rights against the wishes of the Friends, and his indignation at "Whitefield's Mob," "Hellfire Tennent,"[7] and the attitude of the Quakers[8] won him many enemies. One could not happily live in Philadelphia and be of a mood to write such lines as these: "The Province is powerful in Men, in Money, and in all Sorts of Provisions. From twelve to twenty Thousand Men might be raised in an Emergency. . . . And yet we have not a single Man in Arms, but our Lives & our all left at the Mercy of a Savage Crew, who are continually Scalping around us & among us."[9] Of the Quaker doctrine of peace he wrote: ". . . if these Scruples unfit such Men for that which is the chief End of all Government (Protection of the Governed), they ought in Conscience to resign to those who are better qualified."[10]

---

statements of biographical facts. The plan of this biography did not include a careful study of the magazine.

[7] Horace Wemyss Smith, *op. cit.*, I, 103.

[8] *Ibid.*, I, 109.

[9] *Ibid.*, I, 118.

[10] *Ibid.* These sentiments Smith expressed in a letter to the Archbishop of Canterbury in Oct., 1755. Smith's reactions to affairs in Pennsylvania were violent, as his letters show. His point of view is probably more English than strictly

During the years 1756-58 Smith continued to fight for the support of the war and of the proprietors in sermon, pamphlet, letter, and magazine.[11] He was accused, in the summer of 1756, of teaching doctrines inimical to the welfare of the colony and supporting the proprietors against the Assembly, but the senior class of the college came to his aid, and the trustees agreed to stand by him. However, Franklin and Hall, publishers of *The Pennsylvania Gazette*, refused to print anything concerning the charges and vindication.[12] Franklin, although a supporter of the war, was friendly toward the Quaker-controlled Assembly in its contest with the proprietors; thus a breach of friendship developed between him and Smith.

As the rupture between the two men widened, Smith was naturally drawn toward William Bradford the third, grandson of the founder of the family in America, who, after a period of residence in England, had returned in 1742 to establish *The Pennsylvania Journal* in Philadelphia.[13] The paper was successful, and a bookstore, which he added to his printing plant, became a chief mart of its type in America. Bradford, like Smith, carried on stern political

Colonial. On Sept. 23, 1756 the Reverend Thomas Barton, of Carlisle, Pa., wrote an answer to a communication from Smith. In part, the letter reads: "I am not surprised that all is Confusion with you, for the British Interest seems to totter! Braddock defeated!—Minorca taken!—Oswego destroyed,—I had liked to have said sold!—Our Fellow Subjects daily murder'd, & carried into Savage Captivity;—and a great Part of Pennsylvania already depopulated & laid waste!" (*Ibid.* I, 132-33.)

[11] Of special note is Smith's sermon, "The Christian Soldier's Duty," delivered before the forces of General Stanwix immediately preceding their departure for the frontier towns after Braddock's defeat. Note also, "An Earnest Address to the Colonies, Particularly those of the Southern District; on the Opening of the Campaign, 1758: Written and Published, at the Desire of Brigadier-General Forbes, When Levying Forces for the Expedition against Fort Du Quesne." Both appear in *The Works of William Smith* (1803), the former in II, 157-175, and the latter in II, 17-25.

[12] Horace Wemyss Smith, *op. cit.*, pp. 126-29.

[13] William Bradford, the third, was a nephew of Andrew Bradford, who adopted him as his son and heir. It is recounted that Andrew Bradford's second wife, Cornelia, made her husband dissolve partnership with William Bradford, and alter his will to the young man's detriment. William went to England in 1741, but on the death of his uncle in 1742 he returned to Philadelphia and commenced the publication of *The Pennsylvania Journal and Weekly Advertiser* in December of the same year. The newspaper flourished and became widely influential. He was chosen a lieutenant in the militia in 1748, and in 1756 he was made a captain. Though aged, he took part in the Battle of Trenton as a major of militia. See Thomas, *op. cit.*, I, 242; also Smyth, *The Philadelphia Magazines and their Contributors 1741-1850* (1892).

warfare against the Quakers; *The Pennsylvania Journal* supported the military activities, and from the bookstore emanated pamphlets criticizing pacifist Pennsylvania and portraying the "shocking inhumanities" of the Indians.[14] Thus Bradford's imprint on *The American Magazine, or Monthly Chronicle* is easily explained.

Who the others were of the "Society of Gentlemen" associated for editing the magazine can probably best be surmised by considering some of the known contributors. It may be that four men were chiefly responsible, as the "Postscript" at the close of the issue for October 1758—the last—was signed "A. I. O. M." The Reverend Ebenezer Kinnersley, professor of English and oratory at the college, contributed to "The Philosophical Miscellany" department, and may have conducted it. The Reverend Francis Alison, minister of the First Presbyterian Church and vice-provost of the college under Smith, probably was not directly concerned with the editing, but he did solicit editorial matter and subscriptions when requested.[15] It is not impossible that Judge William Moore, of Chester County, whose daughter, Rebecca, became Smith's wife in June 1758, may have lent his assistance. Some of the students may have helped. But the whole situation is a matter of conjecture. The chief editorial stimulus was given by Smith, however, and

[14] See Bradford's bookstore advertisement in *The Pennsylvania Journal*, Jan. 6, 1757.

[15] In a letter to Ezra Stiles written from Philadelphia Sept. 17, 1757, Alison commented on the magazine as follows: "A Society of Gentlemen in this City have undertaken to publish a monthly magazine (a plan of which I send you enclosed) & they promise themselves the Countenance and encouragement of all Gentlemen of letters on the Continent.

"Some of them applied to me to mention such of my acquaintances as I thought qualified & inclined to promote this useful undertaking, and as I could not in Justice to y^r. Character omite y^r. name, they requested me to write to you to procure them Subscriptions & to favor them with any papers you think worthy of the publick attention.

" 'Tis to be hoped that this undertaking may encourage some men of abilities to publish their sentiments or Observations, who thro modesty might otherwise deprive y^e. world of that benefit—that it may encourage our young students to become litterary [*sic*] adventurers, when it can be done with so much safety— that it may promote a friendly intercourse among men of Learning in our different Colonies, & possibly produce some papers worthy y^e. approbation of Great Britain famed for arts and sciences." (Dexter, *op. cit.*, pp. 421-22.)

The letter just quoted appears to be strong evidence that the "Society," by whomever constituted, was more than a group consisting of "Dr. Smith and several of his pupils in the College," as Oberholtzer assumed in *The Literary History of Philadelphia* (1906), p. 63.

he labored under difficulties. In January 1758, three months after the first issue of the periodical, he was arrested and sentenced to jail for "aiding and promoting the publishing of a libel," the charge being made by the Assembly as the result of Smith's assistance to Judge Moore during the latter's contest with the legislative body over its authority to try him.[16] While he was in prison he conversed with many friends and instructed many students. In April, when the Assembly adjourned, he was liberated, but on the convening of the body again in September he was confined once more until the end of the session, when he was released and seized the opportunity to sail for England in December, where he remained for some time. The magazine, having in November completed a year's publication with the October issue, came to an end with the printing of a thirteenth number, called the "Supplement."

Although Bradford, in his *The Pennsylvania Journal* of October 27, 1757, announced the first issue of *The American Magazine*,

[16] In August 1757, Moore, who opposed the Friends, was called to appear before the Assembly to answer to charges of injustice. He refused to obey, contending the demand was beyond the power of the Assembly. The House prepared an address to the governor, praying for Moore's removal, and Moore prepared an address in reply. Both addresses were published in *The Pennsylvania Gazette*, the official paper, and Moore's address likewise appeared in *The Pennsylvania Journal*. In January 1758 the Assembly ordered both Moore and Smith confined, the latter for a libel entitled "The Address of William Moore." Smith denied the charge, saying that his only connection with the affair was to tell a gentleman that he thought it was not improper to translate Moore's address into German for publication. Moreover, Smith challenged the right of the Assembly to try a case of libel. This move was circumvented by the Assembly when it charged him with "breach of privilege." After months of wrangling, Moore was acquitted by the governor in August 1758, and Smith went to England in December of the same year. Later the governor communicated to the Assembly "his Majesty's High Displeasure at the unwarrantable behaviour of the said Assembly" over the whole issue. (See Horace Wemyss Smith, *op. cit.*, I, 167-96.)

But behind the recorded facts of the contest, it is not impossible to surmise that Smith's personality was unhappily suited for contests, and that his English rather than Colonial point of view and the manner he employed in advocating his principles stirred personal rancor. The friendship of his students, the ministerial zeal of his sermons, and the pensive eighteenth-century romanticism in his religious and nature essays reveal one side of his temperament. The reactions of Ezra Stiles offer other testimony, probably warped by the passions of the War of the Revolution. In 1772 Stiles termed Smith a "jovial Priest." But in 1776 he accused him of "A ministerial Stratagem to excite Confusion"; and in 1779 he wrote, "Provost Smith is a contemptible drunken Character! of tolerable academic general Knowledge. But immoral, irreligious & profane, *avaricious* and covetous, a consummate Hypocrite in *Religion* & *Politics*. I know him personally, tho I am not a Witness to his Immoralities." (For the three quotations above, see *The Literary Diary of Ezra Stiles* (1901), ed. Franklin Bowditch Dexter, I, 323, 660; II, 338.)

or Monthly Chronicle to appear on the first of November,[17] the newspaper of November 3 advertised the publication date as of the next day, indicating a slight delay. There were fifty-two pages to each number. The price was a shilling a copy, Pennsylvania currency. Advertisements through the year show that the magazine was published with fair regularity, though toward the end there were increasing delays.[18]

Both the justification for the new enterprise and the editorial policies were contained in the "Preface." An international note was struck at the first. "It has long been a matter of just complaint," wrote the author, "among some of the best friends of our national commerce and safety, that the important concerns of these *Colonies* were but little studied and less understood in the mother-country."[19] Thus "it was proposed by some booksellers and others in *London,* soon after the commencement of the present war, to some persons in this city who were thought to have abilities and leisure for the work, to undertake a Monthly Magazine for the colonies." Some difficulty in procuring a sufficiently intercolonial representation had been apprehended because of expense and time involved in securing correspondents, but this obstacle had been overcome, and "proper persons" were "now engaged in the design not only in all the different governments on this continent, but likewise in most of the *West-India* Islands." The subscribers were assured that the local society of managers, as well as the correspondents, were persons whose "talents and views in life are very different, and that neither religious nor party distinctions . . . had any share in pointing them out. . . ." Some of the society were gay; others were grave. Some were interested in commerce, agriculture, and the mechanic arts; others were wrapped in the abstruser phases of philosophy and science. Always a proper "veneration of our holy, undefiled Christianity" would be upheld. Together with the departments usual for magazines of the time, the editors promised

[17] Among the papers of William Bradford at the Historical Society of Pennsylvania ("List of Subscribers to the American Magazine—1757") is a broadside containing the preface and advertising the day of publication as "Wednesday the 2d of November."

[18] The monthly numbers were advertised as follows in the issues of *The Pennsylvania Journal*: 1757—11/10, 17; 12/8, 15, 22; 1758—2/9, 16; 3/2, 9; 4/13; 5/11; 6/15, 22; 7/13, 20; 8/17; 9/14; 10/19, 26. The "Supplement" for Oct. was advertised Nov. 30. Advertisement for Dec. 1757 not found.

[19] For "Preface," see No. 1, pp. 3-8.

an emphasis on the present war and European affairs. The preface closed with an invitation to contribute articles, sending them post-free to William Bradford.

Among the William Bradford manuscripts[20] is a subscription list for the magazine for 1757; and although New England is not listed, over 850 names appear. The circulation was concentrated principally in Pennsylvania and New Jersey,[21] but a goodly number of copies were sent to Delaware,[22] Virginia, and North Carolina.[23] One file inspected[24] had a cover for the December issue of the magazine on which the names of those delegated to take subscriptions were printed. Some copies circulated in New England—especially in Connecticut and Massachusetts,[25]—the West Indies,[26] and England, Scotland, and Ireland. But numbers alone do not tell the story of the influence of the magazine, for a great many of the subscribers were educators, physicians, ministers, and merchants of high standing, whose contacts were numerous and whose opinions were highly respected.

[20] MSS. are in the Historical Society of Pennsylvania, in two volumes, arranged by John William Wallace.

[21] The Philadelphia list accounts for 247 copies at least, the list for Lancaster and Chester Counties about 38 copies, that for Carlisle about 37 copies, that for York County, about 17 copies. The New Jersey list credits to Elizabethtown about 16 copies, Trenton about 15 copies, Princeton 11 copies, and Bordentown and Brunswick about 9 each. Bradford kept the subscription book in a way serviceable to himself for refreshing his memory, but it cannot be definitely interpreted by readers today.

[22] The Delaware list included for Wilmington about 44 subscribers and for Newcastle about 13 subscribers. A letter from Matthew Wilson of Lewes, contributor to several magazines during his lifetime, dated Feb. 10, 1758 ("A Collection of Papers Relating to Col. William Bradford," manuscript Volume II, p. 98) suggests the interest some well-wishers took in the magazine: "Please to take *Mr. Tho*[s]. *Till Esq*[r]. in Sussex as another Subscriber for y[r] *American Magazine*. 'Tis all I have since had an Opportunity to get for you.—He is a Gentleman of a plentiful Fortune; and indeed all the Subscriptions I have taken in, are from Persons able at any Time to pay you, when you shall give Notice. . . . I hope to prevail with more yet, to subscribe, but am not certain."

[23] In his own handwriting, George Washington (*ibid.*, II, 96) sent in subscriptions for himself, Lord Fairfax, John Funk, and John Hope. Twelve copies were sent to Suffolk, Va.; at least 70 copies seem to have been regularly sent to North Carolina.

[24] A file in the Library Company of Philadelphia.

[25] In Connecticut Rev. Wells, Stamford; Mr. Johnson, Stratford; Chauncey Whittelsey, New Haven; John Beveridge, Hartford, and Postmaster Chew of New London took subscriptions for the magazine; in Massachusetts the same function was performed by Prof. Winthrop of New-Cambridge, and in Boston by Dr. Hooper, Rev. Cooper, Rev. Caner, and the publishing firm of Edes and Gill.

[26] Agents were secured at Jamaica, Antigua, Barbadoes, and St. Christopher.

A picture of an Indian, pressed on the one side by an Englishman offering a Bible and some cloth and on the other by a Frenchman proffering gunpowder and a tomahawk, was the fitting ornamental device on the title-page for *The American Magazine, or Monthly Chronicle.*[27] The general international conflict of the Seven Years' War interested Smith and his editorial board, and European history both past and present was the subject of a number of articles.[28] So, too, American history, including a wide range of contemporary events, was given much space.[29] But more particularly Smith was aflame with the desire to organize Pennsylvania and other colonies into units for fighting the French and Indians. The Indians, though cruel, attracted the Colonists not a little as ethnological specimens; it was felt, too, that they could be rather easily dealt with if the French did not interfere.[30] But the French were powerful and natural enemies; a war must be fought, and the Quakers were a strong, internal impediment.

One of the moot problems was the organization and duties of militias. "T. K.," in "On the Uses and Abuses of Militias,"[31] urged that these bodies be reserved for times of civil dissension and peril, but that the frontiers should be guarded by soldiers hired for the purpose, the costs to be paid from a general tax levied in proportion to wealth. "Agricola," who, for general information,

[27] The details of the illustration on the cover are hardly distinguishable in many of the files; but the picture is very clear on the broadside mentioned in note 17.

[28] As announced in the "Preface," the first issue of the magazine contained a department of "European Affairs" as the first article. This department consisted of historical material at first, "A Short Sketch of the Principal States of Europe" (pp. 7-8, 51-56, 99-107, Oct., Nov., Dec. 1757) to serve as background; thereafter, reports of the present war were featured, much attention being paid to Prussia and Frederick the Great. The department was merged with the "Monthly Chronicle" in January.

[29] The "Monthly Chronicle," reporting the events of the war in America, ran somewhat under ten pages an issue. "The History of the War in North America" became a separate department in Feb. 1758, running three to ten pages an issue; the subject matter ranged from reviews of past history and war to Indians, militias, and slaves. (For slavery, see "Short Dissertation on the Ancient and Present State of Slavery," May 1758, pp. 397-402.)

[30] Articles included: "Account of the North American Indians" (a reprint), Oct. 1757, pp. 9-23; "Disquisition concerning the Original and Transportation of the Indians," by "H. J. R. SS.," of Maryland, Jan., Feb. 1758, pp. 195-98, 246-50; "Directions for Obtaining a Better Knowledge of Indians," by a South Carolina governor, June 1758, pp. 447-53; and "Observations concerning the Nature of Indian War," by "Agricola," July 1758, pp. 468-70.

[31] The editor refers to the article as by an unknown hand (Nov. 1757, pp. 71-75).

had abridged a plan for bettering militia organization in England,[32] appended a "Proposal for a Militia in Pennsylvania,"[33] urging that it be supported by moderate fines imposed on certain classes exempted from bearing arms: Catholics, Moravians, Quakers, and Mennonites.[34]

Directly outspoken against the predominant power of the Quakers in the Assembly were the "Case of William Moore"[35] and the anonymous series of essays by "The Watchman" which began in Bradford's *The Pennsylvania Journal* February 23, 1758 and were occasionally selected for reprinting in the magazine.[36] Moore's case was necessarily somewhat personal in its implications, but "The Watchman" voiced in no mistakable terms the sentiments held by the party of which Bradford and Smith were members. In his opinion the Friends should either assume the burden of defense of Pennsylvania or resign from the Assembly.[37] Empires had fallen in the past because of misrule, and might again.[38] Those who misapplied the power invested in them were traitors.[39] Now was the time to awake from lethargy, to fight "our ambitious and bloody French neighbours," and save the Protestant civilization.[40]

Dissatisfaction with the Quaker doctrine of non-resistance was not the only religious phase of the conflict. Smith was emotionally in agreement with the principles of the Church of England, and was alarmed lest the lack of coherence among the various Protestant churches in America should render encroachments by French Catholics easy of attainment. Therefore he pled for whatever bases of harmony might be attained among the dissident churches, and the magazine reflected this attitude. One series of articles, beginning with "Some Account of the Covenants,"[41] after seeking to explain the beliefs of the covenanters and seceders, closed with

[32] *Ibid.*, pp. 57-63.

[33] *Ibid.*, pp. 63-68.

[34] The first for political reasons, the second by Act of Parliament, the last two by reason of their religious tenets.

[35] Feb. 1758, pp. 210-27. Though marked to be continued, the "Case" was dropped. See note 16 for biographical comment.

[36] "The Watchman" Nos. 3, 5, 6, 7, 8; April 1758, pp. 307-15 and 349-54; June, pp. 433-36; July, pp. 492-97; Aug., pp. 546-50.

[37] See note 10. A note appended to No. 3, signed "W.," and dated Chester County, expresses sentiments quite in agreement with Smith's.

[38] No. 7.

[39] No. 6.

[40] No. 5.

[41] April, July, Aug., Oct. 1758, pp. 315-19, 480-83, 537-41, 617-21.

a plea for Protestant accord rather than schism. And in an editorial note appended to the "Plan of Union" of the synods of New York and Philadelphia,[42] confidence was expressed that subscribers would be heartened to see "Protestants and Britons united among themselves, especially at a crisis time when our best and warmest efforts are necessary for the defence and support of our common Christianity."[43]

Besides the historical and political essays, two other departments of prose flourished, the "Philosophical Miscellany" and the "Monthly Essays." The former embraced the sciences, and the magazine was fortunate in its connection with collegiate circles. Among others, William Smith, the Reverend Ebenezer Kinnersley, of the Department of English, and John Winthrop, professor of mathematics and natural philosophy at Harvard, contributed. Letters by Thomas Godfrey and James Logan relative to Godfrey's invention of the quadrant added a local touch of importance. There were speculations on the laws governing the wonders of the heavens, seas, land, and mankind. English magazines supplied some of the material, notably the list of premiums offered by the Society at London for the encouragement of the arts, manufactures, and commerce of the Colonies, by which means the Society endeavored to stimulate the production of goods that would supplement rather than compete with British trade.[44]

But by far the more important department was the "Monthly

[42] By Gilbert Tennent, May 1758, pp. 387-90. For further comment see "Remarks on the Union of the Synods," by "J. E.," Aug. 1758, pp. 534-37.

[43] P. 387.

[44] Following are listed the more important articles. "On the Invention of the Quadrant . . . Commonly Called Hadley's," being an account of Thomas Godfrey's invention, and a letter concerning it from James Logan; also a letter by Godfrey to the Royal Society, and one by Logan to the same society relating to Godfrey's improvement of Davis's quadrant (July, Aug. 1758, pp. 475-80, 527-34). "Concerning the Latus Rectum of the Ellipsis," by William Smith, and another article on the same by "A. E." (Dec. 1757 and March 1758, pp. 108-11, 272-74). "New Experiments in Electricity," by "D. C.," and another article on the same by "E. K."—Ebenezer Kinnersley—(Jan. and Oct. 1758, pp. 164-66; 627-30). Two essays on agriculture by "Agricola" (Feb. and May 1758, pp. 234-36, 382-87). "On the Eclipses of Jupiter's Satellites" (Nov. 1757, and Jan., March, April 1758, pp. 68-69, 161-64, 269-72, 321). "The Philosophy of Earthquakes," by a member of the Royal Academy of Berlin, and "On the Causes of Earthquakes," by John Winthrop (Oct. and Dec. 1757, pp. 23-24, 111-16). Articles on the increase of mankind and peopling of the Colonies (July 1758, pp. 470-75); on yaws (May 1758, pp. 374-82); on the aurora borealis (Oct. 1757, pp. 25-28); on sea animals (Oct. 1757, pp. 28-33).

Essays," offering an incentive and outlet for four major serial essayists of the mid-eighteenth century. In their respective rôles as "The Antigallican," an opponent of the French, "The Planter," an ubiquitous commentator and philosopher on human society and politics, "The Prattler," a character who began his literary life in the "Will Honeycomb" tradition, and "The Hermit," the nature-loving Smith himself, this quartette made distinct contributions to American essay literature of the period.

"The Antigallican"[45] was the most politically prejudiced of the group, proud to flaunt himself as "an irreconcilable foe to *French power, French* customs, *French* policy," ready to devote himself "to reluminate the dying virtue of our country, and bear my testimony against every sentiment, notion, measure or thing, either in *Religion, Manners* or *Government*, whereby the unrighteous designs of our enemies may be promoted against us."[46] But "The Antigallican" was too musingly philosophical to fulfill dramatically his militant purpose. In the first five numbers he accomplished little more than to review the history of a Rome fallen through luxury and discord, to remark sadly on the debilitating effects of gaming, operas, and plays, and to plead that America awake from her sin and dissension and follow the example of Holland in virtuous thrift. At a time when "our country calls aloud for our united efforts to save her from distruction [*sic*],"[47] if our internal animosities are too great for permanent renouncement, "let us at least suspend them."[48] He closed the series with a final virulent attack on the French, cautioning his countrymen to remember that they "are alike celebrated for their skill in making treaties, and infamous for their perfidy in breaking them"; it was therefore imperative, when peace should come, to watch the commitments at the treaty table, so that the Colonies might "secure by our wisdom, what we have acquired by our valour."[49]

[45] There are seven essays, appearing respectively in the issues of Nov., Dec. 1757, Jan., Feb., April June, July, 1758, pp. 78-82, 116-19, 166-69, 231-34, 321-24, 428-31, 484-86. John William Wallace, in *An Old Philadelphian. Colonel William Bradford* (1884), p. 66, felt confident enough to "suppose" "The Antigallican" may have been William Smith. Although the general sentiments expressed are those entertained by Smith, I strongly doubt the validity of the attribution. The articles were not marked by Smith in his private copy.

[46] No. 1.
[47] No. 4.
[48] No. 5.
[49] No. 7.

More typical of the broad-minded eighteenth-century man of culture and practical affairs was "The Planter,"[50] whose interests comprehended matters of government, Indian relations, social vices, agriculture, human prejudices, finance of the "Poor Richard" school, and the beauties of love and nature. He wrote as one practised in the style of long, round sentence structure; and although afflicted with a tendency to indulge in philosophical generalizations, he restrained himself in the use of the prevalent mood of pensive melancholy, and did not unduly display his knowledge of history and literature, though he seems to have been a man of much reading.[51] His essays are enlivened by his alert public interest. His apt illustrations, drawn from simple imaginary or real occurrences which he presented as passing before his observation, give to his work a narrative style similar to Addison's.

Like "The Antigallican," "The Planter" employed historical reference to illustrate the evils of civil discord, which sometimes "grows so warm that both parties are too intent upon weakening one another to take proper notice of a common enemy";[52] but from thoughts of the French he turned to the problem of the Indians,[53] who, he asserted, had been shamefully treated, whereas they should be civilized, Christianized, and induced to settle on the western borderlands, where they might either live in peace or act as buffers against encroachments from the far west. The evils of a liberal voting franchise interested him also, for he had heard much heated argument and hot political disputation lacking both information and reason. But he was a democrat at heart and believed that education would solve the difficulties.[54] Then, too, the vice of inordinate drinking, which he had observed on his business trips throughout the colony, was a grief to his heart. It was not his wish to disrupt a profitable intercolonial trade, nor to pose as a reformer and live on the vices of others, but he did desire, in the cause of temperance, to call attention to the excesses he witnessed

[50] "The Planter" was the most regular of the serial essayists, appearing in twelve numbers; Oct.-Dec. 1757, Jan.-April, June-Oct. 1758, pp. 33-37, 82-84, 119-22, 173-77, 227-30, 274-77, 324-28, 425-28, 486-92, 541-46, 597-600, 621-23.

[51] Among other references, note those to Otway (Oct. 1757) and Don Quixote (Dec. 1757).

[52] Oct. 1757, p. 36.

[53] Oct. 1757, March, 1758 (Nos. 1, 6).

[54] Dec. 1757, April, 1758 (Nos. 3, 7).

everywhere about him.[55] Local difficulties he treated with the tact of generalized comment: in the case of Judge Moore, for instance, he left to those living nearer to Pennsylvania than he the decision as to whether the Assembly had exceeded its powers. But he cautioned his readers to remember that illiberal and ignorant groups may at any time attain positions of power, and the personal affairs of the more intelligent private citizens must not be unwarrantably circumscribed.[56] Unlike his other essays, the one for June discovered him in a sentimentally romantic mood similar to that of "The Hermit," for it recounts a "dialogue, between two young Females of my neighbourhood, in an evening's walk, after entertaining company,"[57] the conversation turning to the beauties of sunsets and stars and the glory of love.[58]

Left to himself, "Timothy Timbertoe," who wrote most of "The Prattler"[59] and described himself as being twenty-three years of age and a native of the region of Philadelphia, would have followed the footsteps of "Will Honeycomb." But the dramatic element of a lively adventure was introduced into the series, giving plot and event and adding the interest of suspense seldom found in American essays of the period. Hiding behind the assumed reticence of an egotistic simpleton, the author permits himself to be introduced to the readers by a friend, "Richard Dimple."[60] A conventional diatribe on the scantiness of female dress[61] wins the approbation of a Quaker but is so thoroughly attacked by "Miss Barbara Shallow"[62] that "Timothy" is thrown into almost inescapable dejection. The following month he is silent, and in the March issue of

[55] Jan. 1758 (No. 4).

[56] Feb. 1758 (No. 5).

[57] June 1758 (No. 8), p. 425.

[58] After the issue for June, "The Planter" yielded his columns to correspondents. No. 9, for July, contained two articles, one by "Agricola," who explained the principle of rotation of farm crops, and the other by the gentleman who had written on the origin of Indians (see note 30) and the lawfulness of slavery (see note 29), who discussed the virtues of black walnut lumber. In the August issue "Agricola" wrote about wood culture and fertilization of land; the September number was given over to a correction of a statement by "Agricola"; and he was back in the October issue, writing of "this province of Pennsylvania" and urging the use of oxen.

[59] There are five numbers of "The Prattler," which appeared in the issues of Nov., Dec. 1757, Jan., June, July, 1758, pp. 76-78, 125-28, 169-73, 431-33, 497-99. Other references to "The Prattler" series appeared in March and April 1758, pp. 255-56, 328-29.

[60] Nov. 1757.

[61] Dec. 1757.

[62] Jan. 1757.

the magazine, "A. Blockhead," his cousin, announces that "Timbertoe" has been found lying in a state of coma, evidently the result of "Miss Shallow's" withering remarks. In the April issue "Hymenaeus Phiz" gives notice that he has resuscitated the stricken man; and a month later the visions of "Timbertoe" while in a lignified state are promised for June. The final two numbers describe the visions, the victim having dreamed that in an enchanted castle he had been brought to trial before a body of irate women—a scene reminiscent of the predicament of Euripides in Aristophanic comedy.[63] The whole structure of "The Prattler" series would indicate that the numbers were written by a small group, possibly four persons;[64] and the contents and moods suggest that they may have been local college students.

Smith's literary and romantic instinct saved him at first from presenting unadorned sermons in his own series of eight essays entitled "The Hermit."[65] The "Preface" to the magazine had promised a religious article for each issue, Smith having anticipated the use of several of his sermons which he considered appropriate for general publication, as well as a number of new essays. He called to his aid, also, a spirit which he had already been able to catch in literary form in *A General Idea of the College of Mirania*,[66] for as the Hermitage at Long Island had served to feed a romantic mood in his writing of educational theories, so he now employed a Schuylkill hermitage as the locale from which emanated his religious musings. The effect he strove to secure was one of

[63] June, July, 1758.

[64] No. 1 is signed "S. and O."; No. 2, "S., O., and I."; No. 3, "O. and H."; Nos. 4 and 5 are unsigned.

[65] There are eight numbers to "The Hermit, or Theodore," appearing respectively in the issues of Oct., Dec. 1757, Jan., March, April, July, Sept., Oct. 1758, pp. 37-43, 123-25, 181-84, 290-94, 330-31, 505-07, 600-02, 623-27. The original is reprinted in Horace Wemyss Smith's edition of *The Works of William Smith* (I, 93-152), and a copy of the magazine in the Library of Congress (Oct. 1757, p. 43) contains an ascription in pencil to "Wm. Smith, provost."

[66] Jacob Duché (Smith manuscript among the Hawks Papers at the New York Historical Society), in a letter to William Smith dated July 31, 1755, bore testimony to the influence of the Long Island Hermitage: "I think Hermitage the most agreeable Place that ever I was in in my Life. . . . The Mansion-House from the Road appears very grand and venerable, like the Temple of some Sylvan Deity in the midst of a bowery Wood. The whole is . . . perhaps rendered more so [beautiful] to me, by considering, that these hallowed Walks . . . inspired you with many a noble Sentiment, & many an elevated Idea, while you were painting in harmonious Prose the incomparable Pleasures of Mirania,—while you sung in elevated Verse the Blessings of Science & a polite Education."

pensive melancholy rising occasionally to apostrophic utterance in the contemplation of God and the solemn grandeur of Nature.

"The Hermit" devised for himself a romantic past. His father, dying, had asked him to prepare for the ministry. The young man had soon seized an opportunity to travel abroad for two years, but penitently returned to his aging mother. Then he had met Amelia, but their plighted love had been occasion for the wagging of calumnious tongues, and, torn between her love and the current slanders, the fair girl had died. His mother also dying, he became a hermit. Learning that the editor of the magazine intended to keep sacred one paper monthly for the propagation of "our holy and undefiled Christianity," "The Hermit" determined to write one sermon monthly which should be general enough for the public at large, and written in a "manner that can never create prejudices against my person or performances, as I am to be forever concealed."[67] The assistance of ministers of every denomination was solicited.

In the midst of his first sermonic soliloquy touching upon the heavenly teachings of "amiable *nature* . . . and divine *solitude*,"[68] the proprietors of the magazine visited "The Hermit," and he turned to a discussion of editorial matters.[69] Especially did he instruct them in the treatment of the subjects of religion and politics, fit topics for able pens, but requiring tactful treatment, allowing passing events to suggest something to editorial purpose. None the less, these subjects must not be handled in a vacillating manner, for occasions always arose when one must lift up his "voice like a trumpet," and, convinced of the rightness of "British religion and British Government let no motive on earth ever induce" one "tamely to suffer them to be infringed."[70] The remaining numbers by "The Hermit" were written entirely in the form of sermons. "On the Perfection and Efficiency of the Christian Religion"[71] was a clear interjection, and only slightly joined with the series was "A Solemn Meditation on the Late Fast,"[72] a prayer in praise of the Reformation, Protestantism, and liberty. The final two sermons empha-

[67] Oct. 1757 (No. 1), pp. 42-43.
[68] Dec. 1757 (No. 2), p. 124.
[69] Jan. 1758 (No. 3).
[70] *Ibid.*, p. 183.
[71] March, April 1758 (Nos. 4, 5).
[72] July 1758 (No. 6). This number, as well as the eighth, was signed "M.," the final of the four initials attached to the announcement by the proprietors of the suspension of the magazine.

sized the wonders of God's providence and his glory as expressed in the world about. Years later, while preparing to publish the series among his works, Smith slightly revised the first four numbers, the alterations in main adding to felicity of expression and enhancing the descriptive passages.[73]

American poetry of the mid-eighteenth century owes a considerable debt to Provost Smith, as he secured for the pages of his magazine much native material ranking high in the current production. Besides a number of unknown contributors, Francis Hopkinson, Thomas Godfrey, John Beveridge, and probably Colonel Joseph Shippen (or a "Mr. Hicks"), James Sterling, and Samuel

[73] Smith's personally annotated copy of the magazine at the Boston Public Library contains a manuscript insert describing the contents of "The Hermit," a part of which reads as follows:

"The HERMIT, (first published about 45 Years ago,) was among some of the Author's earliest Writings; and having been well received, by the more *serious part of his Readers*, at that time, He resolv'd to give it a Place among such Works of his, as he might afterwards be induced to think, in any Degree, worthy of being collected from their original *fugitive* State, & of being preserved and bequeath'd to Posterity (or at least to his *surviving friends*) in a more permanent way, by means of the *Press*.

"The Subjects treated of, by the *Hermit*, in his 4th and 5th Numbers & his *Soliloquies* in the 2nd and 6th having so close a relation to some of the foregoing Sermons [of the contemplated edition], and especially to those from Thess. Ch. IV (on *Death*, a *Resurrection* from the *Dead* a *future Judgment*, & an *eternal World* to come) determine the Author's Choice of this Volume, as the proper Place, to give the *Hermit's* Speculations a Chance for longer Life. . . ."

Nos. 1, 3, and 4 were only slightly revised. No. 2 carried the longest insertion, a descriptive passage of Smith's hermit home on the Schuylkill as viewed for the first time by the proprietors when they came to visit him:

"We flattered we could without much Difficulty discover the Place, from our Knowledge of the Country, in the environs of the Metropolis; & more especially from the Description given, & the Landscape delineated by the Hermit himself, in his first Number.

"Anxious to be assured that no accident, among the Changes and Chances, incident to our Mortality, had deprived us of so valuable a Correspondent; we struck off from the great Road down a Lane, which terminates on the Banks of one of those Rivers, that wash the Borders of our City. Then bending our course upwards, by the various Windings & Turnings of this romantic River; panting & ascending many a cragged height, & descending again through many a rough & briery thicket, till at Length a little before *Night-fall*, we found ourselves in the middle of a small Vale; hemmed in by a gently-rising Hill on one Side, & by the River, pouring its rapid Torrent, over rough Rocks on the other side, and fretting and roaring its Complaints at the Resistance it met with in its Way, to mix its Tribute with its Parent-Ocean!

"By the Foot of the aforesaid Hill, a small Brook ran babbling thro' the Vale, over a pebbly [*sic*] Bottom, till it lost itself in the River. Directing our view through a little Openening [*sic*], cleared of the Shrubs & Underwood, up the [sloping?] Side of the Hill, we on its brow observ'd a Tuft of Trees, embracing in their Bosom, a little Log-built Cottage, its Ivy-cover'd Walls almost buried from human Sight."

Davies supplied the department of "Poetical Essays" with a number of original poems.

Hopkinson's contributions[74] were among the poet's earliest work. In "L'Allegro" and "Il Penseroso" he paid to Milton a youthful tribute of imitation, inscribing the first to Benjamin Chew, under whom he studied law, and the second to Provost Smith, under whose tutelage he had completed his bachelor's degree but a few months previously. It was almost certainly these poems, too, which won the praise of Lieutenant-Colonel Henry Bouquet in a friendly

[74] "Ode on Music," Oct. 1757, pp. 44-45. It was described as "written at Philadelphia by a young Gentleman of 17, on his beginning to learn the Harpsicord." Thus, as George Everett Hastings has noted in his admirable volume, *The Life and Works of Francis Hopkinson* (1926) p. 100, the poem was written three years before publication. A copy of the magazine at the Library of Congress contains a penciled note ascribing the poem to Hopkinson (p. 84).

"L'Allegro" and "Il Penseroso," Nov. 1757, pp. 84-88. The former was inscribed to "B. Ch——w, Esq." (Benjamin Chew), "By the Author of the Ode on Music, published in our last"; while the latter was "By the Same, Humbly inscribed to the Rev. Mr. S——th" (Provost William Smith), and referred to "The Hermit," No. I. A notation in a copy of the magazine at the Library of Congress ascribes the poem to Hopkinson (p. 84).

"Ode on the Morning" (Jan. 1758, pp. 187-88), "By the Author of L'Allegro and Il Penseroso." A notation in a copy of the magazine at the Library of Congress ascribes the poem to Hopkinson (p. 187).

"On the Taking of Cape-Breton" (Aug. 1758, pp. 552-54), signed by "F. H."—the first time these initials were used.

All the above poems appear in Hopkinson's *The Miscellaneous Essays and Occasional Writings of Francis Hopkinson, Esq.*, published in three volumes in 1792 by T. Dobson. Certain other pieces in the magazine not appearing in the above collected edition have been ascribed to Hopkinson. He almost surely wrote "Verses Inscribed to Mr. Wollaston" (Sept. 1758, pp. 607-08), for the poem is signed by the initials "F. H." Hastings (*op. cit.*, 102) remarks that the attribution to Hopkinson of the poem "Upon Seeing the Portrait of Miss xx——xx by Mr. West" (Feb. 1758, p. 238), "though entirely circumstantial, seems very plausible" because of the poet's friendship with the painter. But Moses Coit Tyler (*A History of American Literature During the Colonial Period*, 2 Vols. in 1, 1893, p. 240) and Albert H. Smyth (*The Philadelphia Magazines and their Contributors 1741-1850*, p. 33), both referring to Rufus Griswold's *Poets and Poetry of America*, attribute the poem to Joseph Shippen. Theodore Hornberger (*The Pennsylvania Magazine of History and Biography*, LIII, 1929, 343-51) upon the authority of an annotation in the copy of the magazine at the British Museum, has advanced the conjecture that a Mr. Hicks, possibly William Hicks, of Philadelphia, was the author. The annotator credits the poem to "Mr. Hicks"; and as he made other notations which have since been proved true to fact, or provisionally accepted, it would seem that the case for Mr. Hicks is possibly as strong as that of any other. The portrait was of Anne Hollingsworth Wharton, and the name attached to the verses was "Lovelace." Finally, if Hopkinson was the author of the prose article "The Properties of a Gardener" (June, 1758, signed by the initials "A. B.," which he later employed, the piece is noteworthy as an early attempt of the author in the field of the humorous essay. Hastings (*op. cit.*, p. 476) notes that the tone has "something to suggest" Hopkinson.

letter to Smith.[75] But Hopkinson's work was not entirely in the
mode of the lyric Milton. He caught the spirit of Addison's
"Blenheim" in the poem "On the Taking of Cape-Breton";[76] and
he attempted light verse in "Verses Inscribed to Mr. Wollaston,"
in which, as in also "Upon Seeing the Portrait of Miss xx——xx by
Mr. West" (the authorship of which is widely disputed),[77] the
famous painter is lauded affectionately. To compare his poems in
the magazine with the collected edition of 1792 is to note many
revisions in the later form which improve them according to the
ideas of poetic craftsmanship of the time, both in precision of expression and conciseness of treatment. The "Ode on the Morning" became "A Morning Hymn," greatly altered in wording and
trimmed by omissions. "L'Allegro" underwent a similar though
less drastic revision; "Il Penseroso" and the "Ode on Music" were
marked by substitutions of words; and "On the Taking of Cape-
Breton" became "On the Late Successful Expedition against Louisbourg," though otherwise it was only slightly altered.

An unusual ability for poetic expression in the classic traditions
of the ode and pastoral as exemplified by Dryden, Pope, and Gray,
and for weaving in a romantic melancholy in the mood of a Young

[75] Among the Hawks Papers at the New York Historical Society is a letter from
Bouquet to Smith, dated Charlestown, Feb. 22, 1758, which, besides containing other
comment as regards the magazine, makes kind reference to "my ingenious young neigh-
bor"—Hopkinson, I am convinced. In part, the letter reads:

"I had long ago wished to see this Scheme executed, and as an individual of the
gratified Society, I return you my hearty thanks for the great Share I suppose you have
had in promoting so usefull & entertaining a Work.

"If it can be Supported with the same Spirit, I could answer that it will be Superior
to any of the kind in Europe.

"I have seen with particular Satisfaction the two Pieces of my ingenious young neigh-
bor, he has a peculiar talent for that chief Part of true Poetry, the *Imitation*. I wish
for my own taste, (tho' it would perhaps not be very general) that he would confine himself to that imitation of real objects, and not indulge to (*sic*) far that Seducing imagination, grounded merely upon empty *fictions* too often met with in modern Poets.

"The Hermit has won my heart, his affecting narrative of his loss, tho' I hope
imaginary, is so well adapted to my present thoughts, that I read with infinite delight my
own sentiments—expressed by so masterly a hand.

"I shall as far as in my Power forward the Subscriptions, amongst which, I have
taken care to insert several of my acquaintances here."

Bouquet had come to America in 1756, and was given command of the troops in
Philadelphia. In May 1757 he was ordered to South Carolina with a detachment of the
Royal Americans.

[76] The poem closes with the not unconventional reference to God's part in battles:
"*He* guides the conqu'ring sword, *he* governs in the fight."

[77] See note, 74, final paragraph.

or a Blair, brought to the young Thomas Godfrey[78] the sincere favor of Smith, who took unusual pains to commend the contributions[79] which so clearly appealed to his own literary taste. Through these poems poetic justice was attained in fact, for they won for the later author of *The Prince of Parthia* an introduction into the pleasant literary circle in Philadelphia from which his lack of educational advantages might otherwise have held him distant. "The Invitation" came to Smith unsolicited, and the editor's fancy was so captivated by its pastoral dialogue treating of the beauties of the countryside in spring that he prefaced the poem with comment.[80] "This little poem," he wrote, "was sent to us by an unknown hand, and seems dated as an original. If it be so we think it does honour to our city; but of this we are not certain. All we can say is that we do not recollect to have seen it before." Then came "A Pindaric Ode on Friendship," replete with classical allusions and drawing upon the legend of the death of Achilles to support the theme that friendship is purer than wild desire. Warmer still in poetic fancy, and stronger in both conception and performance, was the succeeding piece, "A Pindaric Ode on Wine," and Smith wrote for it a long introduction crediting the poet with the powers of genius.[81] One other poem, "A Night Piece," was published in

[78] Besides references to Godfrey in Smyth's *The Philadelphia Magazines and their Contributors 1741-1850*, see Oberholtzer, *The Literary History of Philadelphia* (pp. 67-69) and "Pennsylvania Poets of the Provincial Period," in *The Pennsylvania Magazine of History and Biography*, Vol. XVII, 1893 (pp. 11-14).

[79] "The Invitation," signed "Junius," and dated at Philadelphia, Jan. 20, 1758 (Jan. 1758, pp. 185-86); "A Pindaric Ode on Friendship," announced as by "the Author of the Invitation" (Aug. 1758, pp. 554-56); "A Pindaric Ode on Wine," noted in the table of contents as "by Mr. Godfrey, author of the Invitation" (Sept. 1758, p. 604); "A Night Piece; by Mr. Godfrey" (Oct. 1758, pp. 644-45). The first two are ascribed to Godfrey by annotations in the file of the magazine at the Library of Congress.

Professor R. L. Rusk has called my attention to a slight error of fact in Archibald Henderson's "Introduction" to his *The Prince of Parthia* (1917), p. 33: "During his sojourn of three years in North Carolina, Godfrey often contributed verse to the *American Magazine* of Philadelphia, edited by his friend and patron, William Smith." The magazine suspended publication in 1758, and Godfrey did not leave for Wilmington until the spring of 1759.

[80] Jan. 1758, p. 185.

[81] In part, Smith wrote (p. 602): "There is something very unaccountable in the propagation of Genius. . . . This is the case with respect to the sole surviving son of the late Mr. *Thomas Godfrey*. . . . *Nature* seems not to have designed the father for a greater *Mathematician*, than she has the son for a *Poet*." It is quite remarkable, Smith thought, that this young man, about twenty years of age, "without any other advantage than that of natural genius, a common education in his mother-tongue, and an attentive

the supplement. The allegorical treatment of the beauties of night, with allusions to Philomel, Cynthia, Zephyr, and others, shows the retention of the pastoral machinery, while the introduction of a religious plea against atheism shows the influence of such poems as Young's *Night Thoughts*—and perhaps also of Smith's slight rebuke that the matter and machinery of the "Pindaric Ode on Wine" might with reason be disapproved by rigid critics.

John Beveridge, who had taught school in Edinburgh, and who was, while at Hartford, Connecticut, an early subscriber to the magazine,[82] began contributing Latin poems to the periodical before his appointment under Smith as the professor of languages in June 1758.[83] The Provost was elated to receive these poems, not only because he enjoyed Latin exercises in verse, but also by reason of the fact that their author had contributed to English magazines. He prefaced Beveridge's second contribution, to which was attached a translation by Dr. Jonathan Mayhew, of Boston, with a commendatory note;[84] he likewise paid tribute to "Psalm CIV" as an improvement in concise statement over the famous rendition by

perusal of the works of *Dryden*, *Pope*, and one or two more *English* poets, has exhibited such proofs of *poetical* capacity as really surprize us.

"Our readers may recollect, in our *January* magazine, a most beautiful and delicate little performance called 'the *Invitation*,' and likewise in our last magazine '*An Ode on Friendship*.' Both these were the production of young Mr. *Godfrey*, as is the following '*Ode on Wine*,' which is written with much *poetic warmth*, tho' a rigid critic may perhaps find reason to object to the *Matter* and *Machinery* of it." Smith closed by predicting that another poem, the "Court of Fancy," yet unpublished, would be highly appreciated, as it exhibited the "spirit of true creative Poetry."

[82] See note 25.

[83] Beveridge contributed five poems: "Ad Mr. Gardner," by "I. B.," dated Falmouth, 1753 (Jan. 1758, pp. 186-87); "Ad Rev. Jacob: Innesium, V. D. in Parochia de Merton at Ripam Tuedae in Britannia Septentrionali," dated Jan. 1753, and signed "I. B.," accompanied with a translation by Dr. Jonathan Mayhew (June 1758, pp. 437-38); "Ad Illustrissium . . . Guielmum Shirley . . . ," by Johamn. [*sic*] Beveridge (Sept. 1758, pp. 609-10); "Eulogium," in praise of the Canadian campaign (Sept. 1758, p. 609); "Psalm CIV," by Joh. Beveridge (Oct. 1758, p. 641). A notation in a file of the magazine at the Library of Congress ascribes "Ad Mr. Gardner" to "I. Beveridge" (p. 186).

[84] In part, Smith wrote: "We flatter ourselves that the author of the following performance, Mr. John Beveridge, will not be thought unworthy to be mentioned after the above names [Buchanan, Erasmus, and Addison]. The notice that has already been taken of his several productions in the English magazines, Boston news-papers, etc., with the translation of many of them, by eminent hands, is a sufficient proof of their merit. The reverend translator of the following piece, is a gentleman whose name and genius are well known in the world." (P. 437.)

Blacklock, the blind poet, a former pupil under Beveridge.[85] Beveridge's poems, moreover, stimulated the writing of two other Latin contributions sent in from Kent, Maryland,[86] the first, "from an eminent hand," praising Smith, and the second, evidently by the same author, an imitation of Horace, inscribed to the wife of "his late Excellency, Samuel Ogle, Esq."

The attribution to Joseph Shippen[87] of several poems in the magazine rests upon surmise and the fact that the file of the magazine at the Library of Congress contains a penciled ascription.[88] There is rather convincing evidence, however, both internal and external, that the Reverend James Sterling of Maryland, the author of *The Rival Generals* (1722) and *The Parricide.* (1736), contributed poetry to the magazine.[89]   A. H. Smyth discovered,

---

[85] Smith remarked in his comment that Blacklock's paraphrase had appeared in the *Lives of the Poets* (Vol. IV) with a statement that Blacklock's paraphrase was the most successful of some forty attempted. Beveridge's paraphrase contains only about a hundred lines (pp. 640-41).

[86] Oct. 1758, pp. 642-43.

[87] Joseph Shippen was born at Philadelphia in 1732, was graduated from Princeton in 1753, and thereafter entered military service, serving during 1756-58 at Fort Augusta, Clapham, and Fort Duquesne. Following the War of the Revolution he became a judge of the Common Pleas Court of Lancaster County. He was a writer of some verse, notably "The Glooms of Ligonier," and probably "Lines Written at the Assembly, Philadelphia." See Thomas Willing Balch, *The English Ancestors of the Shippen Family* (1909), pp. 16-17, reprinted from the *Pennsylvania Magazine of History and Biography* for Oct. 1904; also "The Shippen Family and the State," in the same journal for 1926, p. 23, and "Military Letters of Capt. Joseph Shippen," in the same journal for 1912, p. 367.

[88] The doubtfulness of Col. Joseph Shippen's authorship of the poem, "On Seeing the Portrait of Miss xx——xx by Mr. West," has been discussed in the final paragraph of note 74. The poem is credited to Shippen in a penciled annotation in the file at the Library of Congress. Smyth, *The Philadelphia Magazines and their Contributors 1741-1850* (p. 33), has attributed "On the Glorious Victory . . . Near Newmark in Silesia," dated March 11, 1758 and signed "Annandius" (March 1758, p. 280) to Shippen, and a penciled note in the file at the Library of Congress adds its weight of confirmation. On the other hand, Theodore Hornberger (*op. cit.*, note 74) records that the annotator of the copy in the British Museum credits the poem to "Mr. Hicks of Philadelphia." Three other poems by "Annandius" credited to Shippen by notations in the file at the Library of Congress are: an "Answer" to an enigma, "Winter," and "Ode on the Late Victory Obtained by the King of Prussia," dated Philadelphia, Feb. 10, 1758, all in the issue for Feb. 1758, pp. 238-40. "Winter," "By the same," is written in the discursive, pictorial manner common to eighteenth-century nature poems; the two poems using military themes attempt a fiery strength which is lost by imitation and convention in idea and form.

[89] The poems which have been attributed to Sterling are "On the Invention of Letters and the Art of Printing," dated Kent County, Md., Dec. 15, 1757 (March 1758, pp. 281-87); "A Pastoral," lamenting the death of Mr. Pope and inviting the Muses to America, inscribed to George Thomas, then Governor of Pennsylvania (May 1758, pp. 390-97);

while reading a copy of the magazine in the British Museum, that someone had noted by hand that Sterling was the author of "On the Invention of Letters and the Art of Printing,"[90] a long poem done in heroic couplets and addressed to Samuel Richardson, "the Author and Printer of Sir Charles Grandison, and other works, for the Promotion of Religion, Virtue, and polite Manners, in a Corrupted Age." The poem was accompanied by three pages of notes explaining references in the context. Editorial comment explained that "The author of the following poem is a gentleman of acknowledged taste and learning, in a neighboring government. . . . His intimacy with Mr. Pope, he says, obliged him to tell that great Poet, above twenty years ago, that it was peculiarly ungrateful in him, not to celebrate such a subject as the Invention of Letters, or to suffer it to be disgraced by a meaner hand."[91] Sterling's acquaintance with Pope before the former's coming to America, as well as the nature of Smith's editorial comment and the notation in the British Museum copy of the magazine, tends to convince one that Sterling was the author. Smyth has also credited Sterling with the authorship of two other poems in the periodical:[92] one, an "Epitaph on the Late Lord Howe," because history bears out an introductory statement to the poem that "the grandfather of the late Lord Howe, when in a high employment in the reign of Queen Anne, was a generous patron to the father of the author of these lines," and the other, "A Pastoral," lamenting Pope's death and inviting the muses to America, because it was inscribed to George Thomas, governor of Pennsylvania, and because it refers to Pope and is accompanied by editorial comment applicable to Sterling.[93] It was, moreover, like the poem "On the Invention of Letters and the Art of Printing," attended with many annotations—a most unusual procedure.

There are three other major poems in the magazine which I am

---

and an "Epitaph on the Late Lord Howe," dated Kent, Md., 1758 (Sept. 1758, p. 605). To these I have added three poems, for reasons explained in the context: "The Patriot" (April 1758, pp. 332-34), "The 22 Ode of the First Book of Horace Imitated" (Oct. 1758, p. 643), and "The Royal Comet," dated Kent, Md., July 14, 1758 (Aug. 1758, p. 550). The last two are ascribed to Sterling in penciled notations in the file at the Library of Congress.

[90] Smyth, *The Philadelphia Magazines and their Contributors 1741-1850*, note 88, pp. 35-41.

[91] P. 281.

[92] See note 90.

[93] P. 390.

inclined to place along with those just mentioned.[94] They are well annotated—a factor unique to the group—and they are written in the same rather pronounced, individual style, roughly buoyant, strong, and ready though crude in expression. One of these poems, "The Royal Comet," done in heroic couplets in honor of Frederick the Great, was "hastily composed," the author informed his readers, "at the request . . . of a select company of publick-spirited friends, who gave me a short notice of their intention to dine with me, and drink the Protestant champion's health. . . ." This poem is ascribed to Sterling in the copy at the Library of Congress. The second, entitled "The Patriot," was, like Sterling's verses, full of familiar English references. The third, "The 22 Ode of the First Book of Horace Imitated," is credited to Sterling in the copy at the Library of Congress.

Over the pseudonym of "Virginianus Hanoverensis," the Reverend Samuel Davies,[95] dissenting minister of Hanover County, Virginia, submitted a group of poems,[96] largely paraphrases and hymns, with an accompanying letter[97] expressing his interest in the magazine and promising to investigate his library for other possible contributions, especially "criticisms on the sacred classics (my favourite study)." His paraphrases were pleasingly successful as exercises; but this cannot be said of a poem of his own conception, "A Father's Reflections on the Birth of a Son," more typical of Wigglesworthian times.

A few other poems deserve mention by name as examples of native work of contemporary merit. "Roxana to Alexander at the Siege of Tyre,"[98] written by "a young lady in a neighboring government,"

[94] See note 89.

[95] Smyth, *The Philadelphia Magazines and their Contributors 1741-1850* (p. 45). Davies (1723-1761) had gone to England with Gilbert Tennent in 1753 to secure funds for the College of New Jersey. Tyler, *A History of American Literature During the Colonial Period 1607-1765* (II, 241), described him as probably the most "brilliant" of Southern ministers of his time. He succeeded Jonathan Edwards as president of the College of New Jersey.

[96] "A Father's Reflections on the Birth of a Son," dated Aug. 20, 1752; "A Paraphrase of Jer. XXXI, 18, 19, 20"; "Psalm CXXXIX, A Translation"; "The Invitations of the Gospel," dated April 9, 1753; an extract from "a hymn sung at the initiation into the Eleusinian mysteries"; "A Hymn Adapted to the Present State of Public Affairs"; "A Criticism on I Thess. v, 19"; and a poem of poetical definitions of the principal tropes in rhetoric, by another hand, but sent in by Davies. All the poems appeared in the issue of July 1758, with foreword, pp. 499-505.

[97] P. 499.

[98] Oct. 1758, pp. 645-48.

and containing "too much real feeling and beautiful perplexity of thought in it for a *feigned* story"—so an editorial note informs the reader—is noteworthy as an infrequent example of the use of blank verse. "A Pindaric Ode. On the Compleat Victory Gain'd by his Prussian Majesty over the French and Imperial Army,"[99] ranks among the several serious efforts in verse using a military theme. A pretty lyric, "On the Nativity of Christ,"[100] beginning "Awake, my heart! Awake, my lyre!" was probably composed under the influence of Milton. Examples of poetry in a lighter vein are "Ode, on a Late Marriage,"[101] and "To a Young Lady at a Boarding School."[102]

The American Magazine, or Monthly Chronicle was the only magazine before the Revolution to meet with any substantial measure of success; it was the only pre-Revolutionary magazine terminated for other reasons than inadequate support. A "Postscript"[103] explained the cause for discontinuing the publication: "The *Proprietors* take this opportunity once more to express their grateful sense of the unmerited reception this magazine has met with from all quarters; which has been such, that if reputation or profit had been their motive, the work would have been long continued. But the design was at first set on foot by a number of gentlemen, merely with a view to promote a taste for *Letters* and useful *Knowledge* in this *American* world, and as several of the principal hands who first engaged in it, are now obliged to give their constant attention to other matters, the carrying on the work falls too heavy on the remainder, so that it has been determined to discontinue it, at least for some time." The farewell note was dated Philadelphia, November 14, 1758, and was signed by the four initials "A. I. O. M." It may be of some significance to note that Smith had occasionally used the initial "M." as his signature in "The Hermit" series,[104]

[99] Feb. 1758, pp. 240-42.

[100] Dec. 1757, pp. 131-32.

[101] Oct. 1757, p. 45.

[102] Nov. 1757, p. 88. Occasionally English material was reprinted. In drama, the magazine devoted much space to the dispute raging in Edinburgh as to whether John Home's tragedy, *Douglas*, should be allowed on the stage, and likewise printed selections from the play (Jan., Feb. 1758, pp. 151-61, 203-09); extracts from Home's later play, *Agis*, were also printed (June 1758, pp. 411-17). Note may also be made of poet laureate William Whitehead's "Elegy on the Mausoleum of Augustus" (Oct. 1758, pp. 43-44).

[103] Oct. 1758, p. 656.

[104] See note 72.

and that "I." and "O." had appeared in signatures to "The Prattler."[105]

II

The interest of Judge Samuel Nevill,[106] of Perth Amboy, New Jersey, in a happy destiny for British power in America and the advancement of Colonial well-being was the motivating spirit which brought *The New American Magazine*[107] into existence. James Parker,[108] the publisher, was primarily concerned with the venture only as a method of furnishing work for his Woodbridge printing establishment. Nevill had been in America nearly twenty-two years when the magazine was begun, in January 1758. The death in 1735 of his sister, widow of a landed proprietor of New Jersey, had left him as the sole inheritor of large holdings and brought him to the colony the following year from England, where he had been an editor of *The Morning Post* in London. In New Jersey he became a member of the Assembly, of which he soon rose to the speakership. In the Assembly he was a strenuous supporter of the rights of the proprietors of East Jersey, and of the legislative body in its contests with Governor Lewis Morris. He was made a judge of the Supreme Court and assumed the duties of editor of *The New American Magazine* in the same year.

Nevill was a compiler,[109] politician, statesman, and judge, and the magazine he edited reflects both his capacities and limitations. As a chronicle of the times the periodical is valuable. Joel Barlow was not ill-advised by a friend who, on hearsay, recommended it to the poet as a possible source for material for his *Columbiad*.[110]

[105] See note 64.

[106] For biographical data, see Richard Stockton Field, "The Provincial Courts of New Jersey, with Sketches of the Bench and Bar," *Collections of the New Jersey Historical Society*, III (1849), 155-58, who is in error in stating that the magazine was the second of its kind in America; see also *ibid.*, IV (1852), "The Papers of Lewis Morris"; *ibid.*, IX (1916), "New Jersey Biographical and Genealogical Notes," by William Nelson; Thomas, *op. cit.*, II, 129; and Barber and Howe, *Historical Collections of the State of New Jersey*, pp. 44-46.

[107] See note 3.

[108] See Chapter IV.

[109] He had published the first volume of *The Acts of . . . New Jersey* in 1752, to which he added a second volume in 1761.

[110] Abraham Baldwin, in a letter to Barlow written in March 1780, stated that a friend, Mr. Kemble, had told him that "the best account he has ever seen of this continent is in the *New American Magazine* for the years 1758-59. It also contains the

But as a literary journal it attracted few contributors; and though the editor asked for original work, he was forced to draw most of the material used from the storehouse of current and past English periodicals. The magazine consequently was never very popular, and lack of support put an end to publication after a trial of two years and three months.

Parker first published the "Proposals" for undertaking the new magazine in *The New-York Gazette: or, the Weekly Post-Boy* for August 29, 1757.[111] As the advertisement was dated from Perth Amboy, it presumably was drawn up by Nevill. As outlined, the magazine, edited by "Sylvanus Americanus," was to be a monthly of six half-sheets octavo, priced at a shilling "Proclamation" a number. It was proposed to divide the periodical into two sections. The first three half sheets were to be a "complete History of the *Northern Continent of America*, from the Time of its first Discovery to the present: Compiled with that Impartiality and Regard to Truth which becomes a faithful Historian, and carefully extracted from Authors of the best Credit both ancient and modern."[112] As it was to be separately paged, it might be handsomely bound and handed down to posterity as a "*Family Chronicle* and *Historical Legacy*." The second half of the magazine was to contain "*Amusements and Essays, serious, entertaining, philosophical, mechanical, historical, political and poetical*, with the most *material News* and *authentic Occurrences*, Foreign and Domestic, which shall happen during the Month." Furthermore, "whatsoever *New Pieces* any Gentlemen may be so kind to furnish us with, shall always have the Preference in our *Magazine*, out of a peculiar Emulation to satisfy the Publick that even this *New World* is not destitute of *Learning* and *Learned Men*." To assist in promulgating the new magazine, the first number of which was to be published for January 1758, subscription agents were listed for the principal towns in New Jersey, and for New York, New Haven, Rhode Island, Boston, and Philadelphia.

---

travels of Mr. Thomas Gage through the greater part of South America. . . ." (Charles Burr Todd, *Life and Letters of Joel Barlow*, 1886, p. 27.)

[111] Reprinted in issues of Sept. 5, 12, 26. Oct. 10, Dec. 19.

[112] More specifically, the *History* was to contain accounts of the first settlements by the English and French, of the disputes, wars, battles, treaties, boundaries, and of the present war between the English and the French and Indians, "with the Murders and Cruelties committed by the Savages upon the British Subjects,"

The magazine appeared according to specifications,[113] but though it lived for two years and three months, it was never widely popular.[114] Nevill's conscientious editorial labor may be witnessed in each issue, but he lacked, as had Gridley, the genius to raise a magazine above the plane of a failing mediocrity.

At the close of the first year, the editor announced that all was not well.[115] As he reviewed his work, he found "great reason to think he hath failed" in answering the expectations of the readers and "his own engagements." Complaints had been made that "too many grave Essays" had been printed, crowding out polite wit and humor. To this fault Nevill pleaded guilty, and promised that "though *Morality* be his principal favourite, yet any sprightly humorous pieces, which may engage the attention of his *Readers*, and not inconsistent with decency and modesty, shall always meet with an acceptable place in his Miscellany." In the future he hoped "to improve the method of his scheme by observation and experience"; and as he had extended his correspondence, he begged leave "to assure his *Readers*, that his Magazine shall be a *Conservatory* for those pieces of literature, wit, and useful knowledge, . . . which by being published in loose papers, would otherwise perish. . . .'

In January 1760 a most imposing array of topics to suit divers tastes was announced for the coming year,[116] and for the first time in American magazine history the subject of agriculture was accorded the dignity of a serial treatise.[117] But the public did not respond. Income from subscriptions failed to defray the expense of printing,[118] and the periodical was discontinued with the March

[113] No. I, for Jan. 1758, was first advertised in *The New-York Gazette: or, the Weekly Post-Boy* for Feb. 20, 1758. Parker did not advertise the issues regularly, probably because the magazine was sold by subscription only, according to the announcement.

[114] The subscription agencies were never thickly distributed excepting over New Jersey, and Vol. II designates in a special way only three: those at Woodbridge, New York and Philadelphia.

[115] *The New American Magazine*, Dec. 1758, "The Author to the Publick," on the final printed but unnumbered sheet.

[116] See second unnumbered page following p. 40. Among the subjects were to be "entertaining Histories; the Lives of famous Men; the innumerable *Wonders* of the Universe; an accurate Account of the *various* Curiosities . . . in the known World . . . *approved* Improvements, in Husbandry, Gardening, and other Arts and Sciences . . . , pieces of Poetry . . . , the freshest and most material Occurrences that shall happen during the Course of the Month. . . ."

[117] "A Course of Experiments and Improvements in Agriculture, Made by a Person who Lately Occupied Many Hundred Acres of Land of All Sorts" began in the issue for Jan. 1760. The treatise had been published originally in England.

[118] March 1760, inside of title page.

issue. When the proprietors had first conceived a magazine which would entertain the public with a "Miscellaneous Collection of Essays, Moral, Political, Geographical, and Historical . . . they conceived great Hopes so necessary a Work would have met with a suitable Reception." It was, therefore, with "Concern" that they admitted their hopes had exceeded their success—a concern which did not arise from a desire to make money, "but from the Reluctance which seems to prevail in these Parts towards acquiring that Education and Knowledge, which is absolutely expedient to form the truly serviceable Man."[119] Nevill had evidently come to realize that a journal of selected reprints could satisfy only a comparatively few persons. He could not summon for his work the vital originality which had caused Smith's magazine to flourish.

Still, as a storehouse of eighteenth century thought *The New American Magazine* did perform a service for a number of readers, and the selections are often worth an analysis or a record. The first number established a general outline of departments for the subsequent months, embracing seven divisions: "The History of North-America," "The Traveller," by Thomas Gage, "The Monthly Miscellany," "Poetical Essays," "The Chronological Diary," "The Historical Chronicle," and "Naval Engagements." In general, the contents embodied articles and news concerning the war, with contingent historical and geographical material, general essays, and poetry.

"The History of the Continent of America,"[120] which Nevill himself compiled from works supplying "the greatest Probability of Truth," appeared in every issue of the magazine, and was concluded in the last number. It was paged continuously for separate binding. During the first year, sixteen pages were usually inserted in each number, and thereafter eight pages. Beginning with a life of Columbus, the articles progressed from accounts of John and

[119] *Ibid.*, from the same announcement.
[120] See note 3. On the inside of the title page of the Jan. 1758 issue Nevill ran "A List of the Authors upon whose Credit the History of the Northern Continent of *America* is principally founded. . . . The Rev. Mr. Richard Hackluit. The Rev. Mr. Samuel Purchas. Mather's Magnalia Anglicana. De Mont's Voyage to New-France, in 1604. Collections of Voyages and Travels, Vol. 2. History of the Discovery of the British Colonies in America. Neal's History of New-England. Stith's History of Virginia. Beverley's History of Virginia. Colden's History of the Five Nations. Douglas's [*sic*] Summary of the first planting and present State of the British Settlements of North-America. Campbell's Naval History. Salmon's Modern History of America. And some others."

Sebastian Cabot, Sir Humphrey Gilbert, Sir Walter Raleigh, Jacques Cartier, Henry Hudson, John Smith, and Nathaniel Bacon through to the second half of the eighteenth century, with numerous selections on Indians, Canada, and Florida, as well as the British Colonies. As favorable a point of view as possible for the English always emerged from the selected discussions; British claims always seemed more rational and substantial than those of the French, and British civilization the more progressive and fair to the natives. As Nevill avoided "Prolixity and Contradiction," one could not expect an unbiased, judicial attitude toward the French, especially during the years of the French and Indian War. But he labored earnestly in his work of compiling the historical accounts, and it is not unlikely that this serious attitude toward American history sustained his endeavor in editorial work, and possibly prolonged a general interest in the magazine.[121]

"The Traveller,"[122] by Thomas Gage, also separately paged for binding, began with the first issue and continued through May 1759. Though the peregrinations of the hero led the readers through Mexico, Central and South America, and instructed them in the customs, history, and social states of the Indians and Spaniards—to the shame of the latter—the feature was not so popular as the editor had anticipated, for in the issue for July 1759[123] Nevill announced that some readers had complained that the long narratives of "The Traveller" had been "dull and burthensome." He promised he would "carefully avoid giving any distaste that way" in the future, and would spare no effort to select pieces of highest repute and credit which would be agreeable and interesting, promising to proceed with the magazine if the returns would "barely defray the expences."

Of the departments paged within the magazine proper, only two were essentially literary,[124] "The Monthly Miscellany" of articles, essays, and tales, and the "Poetical Essays." Both were largely

[121] Douglass's *Summary*, it will be remembered, was to have been printed in *The American Magazine and Historical Chronicle*, but the magazine was abandoned and the historical treatise issued separately, indicating their relative popularity.

[122] See note 3; also Evans, *op. cit.*, No. 8136.

[123] P. 519.

[124] The three others performed functions in the digest of news. "The Historical Chronicle," never skipping an issue, occupied from four to twenty-four pages—usually eight or twelve—and was the principal news digest. For "Naval Engagements," see note 3. "The Chronological Diary" was soon changed in name to "Meteorological Observations," and recorded the usual data.

compiled by clipping from current and standard books and periodicals the material which Nevill felt should go into a magazine designed to inform, instruct, and entertain. The department of poetry was held fairly steadily at about four pages an issue, but the space allowed to the miscellaneous essays varied from twelve to twenty-nine pages.[125]

Among the prose essays, for which Nevill expressed his preference, three serials sprang up, but none approached any distinction. Only one of the essayists, "Publicola," of Philadelphia, who wrote "The Occasional Writer,"[126] was in any manner original; and he, after sedately writing of marriage, good roads, and respectability, resorted in the fifth number to the clippings in his commonplace book, from which he never emerged during the remaining of his score of essays.[127] Nevill himself started the other two. In deference to agriculture, he began "The Country Farmer"[128] in the first issue with a clipped article, and asked his readers for original contributions. As none was submitted, the serial was abandoned after the third number until January 1760, when the first of the three final essays, none of which was original with the magazine, appeared. The third serial, "The Impartial Politician,"[129] was begun in January 1759. It never aspired to originality, being made up of reprints of "such political pieces as relate to the constitution of Great Britain; extracted from the present most able Ministerial and Anti-ministerial writers in those parts."[130]

Other miscellaneous prose, principally selected from various sources but occasionally original, shows a tendency to fall into four

[125] The upper reaches in space allotment were begun in Jan. 1759, shortly after "The Historical Chronicle" was reduced; a further expansion was made when "The Traveller" came to an end.

[126] Nos. 1 to 6 and 8 to 21 inclusive; No. 7, unless misnumbered as 8, never appeared. Jan., March, May, June, and Aug. through Dec. 1758, pp. 10-11, 52-54, 113-14, 137-38, 197-98, 229-30, 251-52, 274-77, 297-98; Feb. through July, and Oct. through Dec. 1759, pp. 357-58, 390-92, 430-32, 466-67, 501, 534-36, 657-59, 681-83, 745-47; Feb. and March 1760, pp. 50-52, 101-03.

[127] Fifteen, as No. 7 did not appear.

[128] Nos. 1 to 6 inclusive. Jan.-March 1758, pp. 9-10, 27-28, 54-56; Jan.-March 1760, pp. 14-18, 55-60, 93-97. Nos. 2 and 3, concerning cattle, were from R. Bradley's treatise on husbandry; the last three numbers were from a treatise describing a course of experiments and improvements in agriculture.

[129] Jan. through July, and Sept. through Dec. 1759, pp. 319-21, 364-66, 383-85, 415-18, 458-60, 485-88, 529-31, 614-15, 655-56, 678-81, 742-44; Jan. through March 1760, pp. 18-20, 54-55, 89-91.

[130] Editorial note, Jan. 1759, p. 319.

classes: matter regarding the war and the related topics of geography and the Indians, *belles-lettres,* expositions in science, and sentimental tales. Other subjects, such as the economic condition of New Jersey,[131] the possible evil of slavery,[132] the conspiracy against the life of the King of Portugal,[133] and Freemasonry[134] could not obscure the accounts of Indian skirmishes and treaties,[135] sieges in the west and north,[136] and the conflict in Canada.[137] The magazine would have been well supplied with militaristic narrative and propaganda even if it had not carried "The Traveller" and "The History of the Continent of America" as separate features.

Polite prose literature was drawn almost wholly from English sources, among which *The Monitor, The Idler, The Spectator, The Connoisseur,* and *The World* offered a varied assortment of sophisticated wit, anecdote, and speculation both rationalistic and sentimental.[138] When well-known names were involved, as those

[131] Evidently original with the magazine is "Philo-Patria's" article urging the young men of New Jersey to wake up to their opportunities; Philadelphia is taking Burlington's trade, and New York, Perth Amboy's; the application of industry is essential for the fair name and economic health of the colony. See March 1758, pp. 50-52.

[132] "On the Use and Abuse of Negro Slaves," emphasizing a doubt as to the propriety of keeping slaves, especially those who had embraced Christianity (Jan. 1760, pp. 25-27).

[133] Nov. and Dec. 1759, pp. 665-72, 727-31; Jan. 1760, pp. 1-9.

[134] In poetical form, Freemasonry became a subject of light verse; "Esop Coon," writing of ladies who wished to become members of the fraternity (Jan. 1760, pp. 29-30), was answered by "Clorinda Cora" the following month (p. 69).

[135] Most important of the accounts of the Indians are the treaties made at Easton (Oct. and Nov. 1758, pp. 269, 287-92), at Albany (April 1759, p. 445), and with the Cherokees in South Carolina (Jan. 1760, pp. 35-38), though further hostilities in the southern state were reported later (March 1760, pp. 118-19). Other articles include Cherokee peace with the Chickasaws (Feb. 1758, p. 45), the journal of Major Robert Rogers regarding his proceedings against the Indians (Nov. 1759, pp. 701-02), the war with the Indians in South Carolina (Nov. 1759, pp. 695-700), and the discourses between "Ponderous" and "Pertinax" and "Ponderous" and "Mistrust" regarding Indians and their ways (Feb. and April 1759, pp. 362-64, 432-34).

[136] For DuQuesne, see magazine for Dec. 1758, pp. 315-17; for Ticonderoga, see issues of July, Aug., and Sept. 1759, pp. 545-46, 595-97, 626-28; for Niagara, see issues of Aug. and Sept. 1759, pp. 593-95, 628-31.

[137] See accounts of the progress of the war in Canada (Oct. 1758, pp. 266-69), affairs at Louisbourg (July-Oct. 1758, pp. 178-84, 210-15, 240, 265-66; April 1759, pp. 441-42), the country of Canada (Aug. 1759, pp. 573-84), reasons for insisting upon the cession of Cape Breton (Sept. 1759, pp. 606-07), capitulation of Quebec, Sept. 18, 1759 (Nov. 1759, pp. 700-01; Feb. 1760, pp. 44-47). For indications of national prejudices, see two articles regarding the "French Nation" and the "French and English" (Dec. 1759, p. 742; March 1760, pp. 97-99).

[138] For *The Monitor,* see issues of April 1758, pp. 73-75, Nov. 1759, pp. 685-87, and Aug. 1759, pp. 586-87; for *The Idler* No. 39, Dec. 1759, pp. 739-41; for *The Spectator,*

of Pope, Gay, and Edward Young, there was an inclination to select personal anecdote;[139] however, satire based on racial differences and interest in history and adventure were not uncommonly found, as the excerpts relative to Voltaire, Walpole, Captain John Smith, Van Sloetten, and Selkirk indicate.[140]

In science, medical subjects comprised the major theme. Especially interesting were Coxe's treatise on inoculation for smallpox,[141] and "Philanthropos's" discussion of the epidemical diseases in Dorchester County, Maryland, the latter undertaken by a practising physician in that section of the state.[142] The interests were occasionally somewhat economic, embracing articles on the salt mines of Poland[143] and the precious metal mines of Potosi, Bolivia.[144]

The popular sentimental stories selected for the magazine were usually in the form of the confidential letter made beloved by Richardson. Longest of these was the sad history of Lucinda, whose love of Clerimont was finally thwarted by death after the

---

Nos. 132 and 166, Jan. and Feb. 1758, pp. 1-3, 25-27; for *The Connoisseur*, No. 68, April 1758, pp. 75-76; for *The World*, May 1758, pp. 114-16.

[139] For Pope, see extract of a letter to Addison (Feb. 1758, pp. 28-29); for Gay, see his letter relating the incident of two lovers killed by lightning (*ibid.*, pp. 31-32); for Young, referred to as the author of *Conjectures on Original Composition*, see his discussion of Addison (Dec. 1759, pp. 747-48).

[140] Five selections were taken from the writings of Voltaire: his description of the character of the King of Prussia (March 1758, p. 60), his select thoughts presented to a minister of state in France (June 1758, pp. 138-39), his observations on this world (Nov. 1758, pp. 279-80, misnumbered 277-78) and on a custom in Holland (May 1759, pp. 462-63), and an "Anecdote from Le Siecle de Louis XIV" (Aug. 1759, pp. 563-64). From Horace Walpole's works was extracted a portion of one of the letters of Xo Ho to Lien Chi (Jan. 1758, p. 11); the life of Captain John Smith before his arrival in America is reprinted (June 1750, pp. 479-81); and perennial interest in the isolation of an individual or group on uninhabited islands was supplied by accounts from Alexander Selkirk's experiences (Feb. 1759, pp. 359-62) and Cornelius Van Sloetten's remarks on a group of English marooned in 1569 (Jan. 1759, pp. 335-40).

[141] Nov. 1759, pp. 674-78.

[142] Aug. 1759, pp. 564-69. Other subjects included discussion of natural marks in children (Aug. 1758, pp. 189-90), lepers in Guadaloupe (March 1759, pp. 385-89), cures for gout, rheumatism (Sept. 1759, p. 618) and bloody-flux (Jan. 1760, p. 24), as well as electrical virtue in cure of palsy (March 1759, pp. 400-01), and an essay on the progress of the science of medicine (Feb. 1760, pp. 47-50).

[143] Oct. 1759, pp. 639-41.

[144] Feb. and March 1758, pp. 32 and 56, the first credited to Don Ulloa. Two other articles should be mentioned, an "Essay on Some Remarkable Phaenomena in the Late Earthquake" (June-Aug. 1758, pp. 134-36, 160-64, 191-96), and "D. C.'s" justification of his electrical experiments, which Ebenezer Kinnersley had attacked in *The American Magazine, or Monthly Chonicle*—see note 44—(April 1759, pp. 422-25).

young lovers had overridden the prejudices of the groom's father.[145] Different in form, but more essentially interesting in that it partook of reality, was the account of the escape of Miss Juliet West from the wiles of a voluptuary, which closed with an application of the *Comus* moral to the narrative.[146]

From a young poet's point of view, *The New American Magazine* had "but small traffic with the nymphs of *Helicon*."[147] Yet the selections chosen by the editor are particularly interesting from the aspect of literary history. The mid-eighteenth century was a changing age for English poetical expression; and though "the dawn of a new era was not coming up quite so like thunder" as some Romanticists might wish, and though the qualities in the work of the newer major poets of the middle years were "none too common in that of their contemporaries,"[148] still, a change is to be noticed, and the newer tone was reflected in Colonial America as quickly as it appeared in England. Less than a score of years had passed since *The American Magazine and Historical Chronicle* had filled its pages with verse in the elder mode—with translations from the Latin, with paraphrases, songs, eclogues, elegies, and light verse more conceited than delicate and more bantering than friendly.[149] In Smith's *The American Magazine, or Monthly Chronicle*, preceding and contemporary with *The New American Magazine*, the modification of the poetical mode is visible.[150] The older phase was present in a major degree—in Beveridge's translations, Sterling's poems in the manner of Pope, Davies's paraphrases, and imitations of Dryden—but changing stresses in forms and moods are apparent also in the Miltonic octosyllabics of Hopkinson, the blank verse of "Roxana to Alexander at the Siege of Troy," the romantic, somewhat personalized melancholy of Godfrey, and in the apparent regard for the out-of-doors shining occasionally in old pastoral designs.

The New American Magazine carried on the change normally. The widening stream of original blank verse in the magazine is

[145] For the story, sequel, speculation as to the author, and declaration of his name as Turlough, see issues of March, July and Sept. 1758, pp. 58-59, 167-68, 223, and May, Aug., and Sept. 1758, pp. 116, 200, 223-24.

[146] Aug.-Oct. 1758, pp. 198-200, 225-28, 249-50.

[147] Nathaniel Evans, in a letter introductory to a submitted poem, printed in the magazine for March 1760, p. 105.

[148] Raymond D. Havens, "Changing Taste in the Eighteenth Century," *Publications of the Modern Language Association of America*, Vol. XLIV (June 1929), p. 528.

[149] Chapter III, section II.

[150] Chapter V, section I.

one of the indications of America's contemporaneousness with the motherland. Something of the religious, tragic mood of a Young, turning to the contemplation of the wayward life, lies in "The Convert's Soliloquy";[151] and, however weakly sentimental the idea poetized, blank verse served a nimble rimester, "Fil. Nass. Ale—s," of East Jersey, in tracing her pensive thoughts, at early morn, as she contemplated a world from whence all innocence had fled.[152] More important still is the work of "Martius Scriblerus," of Hunterdon, New Jersey, who was among the more frequent contributors. In "The Moonlight Night,"[153] a poem crying for the awakening of conscience, his control of unrimed pentameter lines is well illustrated in the introductory lines:

> "Hail! Empress of the star-bespangled sky!
> At thy benign approach Night throws aside
> Her raven-colour'd vest, and from her cave
> Starts forth to visibility. . . . "

"Scriblerus" deserves mention, too, for his rimed poems. They are florid and possess more of youthful frenzy than the harmony of high poesy; yet they are stirring in their ardor, and they are native to America in their portrayal of the famous Indian council at Easton and in their expression of the loyal sentiments of young British Americans toward the war.[154]

Pastorals, too, are frequently met with in the magazine. They

[151] Signed "R.," from Berks County, Pa., Sept. 3, 1758; see magazine for Oct. 1758, p. 258.

[152] "The Solemn Pensive" (March 1759, pp. 406-07). The author was ambitious in her work, though barren of high emotional qualities. Three other poems in the magazine are signed by the same pseudonym. One, "A Night Piece" (Jan. 1759, p. 332), like Parnell's earlier poem by the same title, closes with a religious strain. Another, "True Politness" (May 1759, pp. 467-68), riming *aabccb* in octosyllabics and trimeters, and a third, "Louisburg Taken: An Ode" (Sept. 1759, pp. 621-22), in variant stanzaic rime as *ababccddee* and *ababcccdddd*, indicate metrical ingenuity and reveal occasional felicities in expression.

[153] Nov. 1759, pp. 692-93.

[154] His first poem, "A Poem . . . Inscribed to his Excellency Francis Bernard," governor of New Jersey (Oct. 1759, pp. 665-67), in heroic couplets, relates the speeches of two Indians at the council at Easton, one counseling war in self-defense, the other pointing out that a Bernard or a Denny would treat them fairly, whereas the French were not to be trusted. The same number printed the poet's "A Loyal Prayer: or, an Ode" (pp. 667-68), written to be set to the tune of "God Save the King." In the November issue (pp. 690-92) "An Ode," by the same author, related the success of the war on the European continent; while in the December issue (pp. 752-53) appeared an extract from Racine's *Esther*, for which "Scriblerus" wrote an imitation in English.

are usually crowded with traditional characters and with a mixture of both the light and the serious in conventional thought. But occasionally octosyllabics take the place of heroic couplets, indigenous scenes are substituted for literary landscapes, and moods toward nature occur which are not entirely conventional.[155]

More especially significant from the standpoint of later popularity are three poems: "A Panegyric Ode, on the Late General Wolfe, on the Taking of Quebec,"[156] the earliest known printed poem by Nathaniel Evans, of Philadelphia; "The Glooms of Ligonier [157] by "an Officer of the Pennsylvania Regiment, station'd at Ligonier (formerly Loyalhanning) in the winter of 1759"— Joseph Shippen, of Philadelphia—; and "The Bard,"[158] by Thomas Gray. Evans, aged seventeen, accompanied his poem with a letter, signed "N. E.," youthful in the intensity of its bravado and self-negation: "I cast it at your feet, either to stamp with oblivion, or preserve with your collection." As his poetry is more classically correct though less intense than that of his fellow townsman, Godfrey, and as a collection of his verse was gathered in a posthumous volume, it is important to note the text of the poem in the volume shows that Evans's technique involved laborious filing of lines and compression of ideas.[159] Shippen's contribution, a popular lyric

[155] From Brunswick, N. J., came an original poem, "A Pastoral Ballad" (Jan. 1758, p. 16), in praise of Daphne; the same author (see verse 23) later contributed "A Pastoral" (May 1758, pp. 117-18) in heroic couplets, carefully annotated as to "imitations," and "A Pastoral Ballad" (June 1758, p. 143), in octosyllabics. Local in name is "Schuylkill Side" (June 1758, pp. 143-44), in octosyllabics and trimeters describing the place where Philadelphia's nymphs and swains will build. In the older tradition is "The Spring" (June 1758, p. 144), by "C.," depicting in heroic couplets Florio and Clarissa in a vernal setting more literary than local; but "On the Approaching Spring" (April 1759, pp. 434-35) sent in by "Philo-Musaeus," was done in octosyllabics alternately rimed. He was in spirit, if not in practice, an early proponent of American materials and genius for poetry. The poem, he wrote, was "the product of *North-America*," and he did "heartily wish I could see polite literature flourish in this part of the world, as well as in Europe, since I am well assured a proper genius is not wanted here to propagate the same. . . ." (P. 434.)

[156] March 1760, pp. 105-06.

[157] *Ibid.*, p. 106. See notes 87 and 88. The poem is reprinted, among other places, in *The Pennsylvania Magazine of History and Biography*, Vol. XXIV (1900), p. 120.

[158] March 1759, pp. 404-06; the poem was given the title of an "Ode," as the real title was not known.

[159] The original poem is of a hundred lines. It was reduced to eighty-six, and only the fifth stanza remains but little altered. The first three stanzas underwent nearly total modification, while the fourth, sixth, and seventh were carefully worked over. See *Poems on Several Occasions, with Some Other Compositions*, by Nathaniel Evans, A. M., (Philadelphia, 1772), for which Goldsmith, among others, was a subscriber.

of love and war, exploited the old theme of men's valor on the field being sustained by maidenly hearts at home. Gray's famous poem was sent to the magazine by a frequent correspondent, "Z.," who, having received it in the form of manuscript, did not know whether it had ever been published, and evidently considered its merits unique.[160]

It is not to be inferred that the characteristics of the earlier part of the century, and of the century as a whole, are not evident throughout the pages. Besides numerous original and selected poems of no distinction but typical of the period, poems and excerpts were reprinted from the works of such men as Alexander Pope, John Gay, Matthew Prior, Samuel Garth, Joseph Green, Thomas Parnell, Edward Young, and the recently appointed poet-laureate, William Whitehead.[161] Quite surprisingly, however, Shakespeare is accorded for the first time in American magazines the honor of two parodies,[162] the latter in imitation of Hamlet's celebrated soliloquy, debating whether to print and risk the fortunes of living with Pope or "to sleep perchance with Quarles"—a problem which, in the clash of the traditions of Pope and Milton in this middle period, might indeed be distressing to imitators. Two narrative extravaganzas, raucously humorous, should also be mentioned: "The Pig: a Tale"[163]—followed by a sequel written by a "Gentleman of Virginia"[164]—and "The Cobler: a Tale."[165] Typical, too, were the many original and clipped poems falling under two convenient classifications by subject matter, religious and military.

[160] The poem was published in Aug. 1757, in London.

[161] Extracts from Pope's works were "On the Frailty of the World" (Jan. 1758, p. 15), "The Wife of Bath" (Feb. 1758, pp. 37-38), his epitaph on two lovers killed by lightning and "The Story of Sir Balaam" (March 1758, pp. 61 and 63), and "Messiah" (Dec. 1759, pp. 749-51). From Gay's works was taken "The Jackall, Leopard, and Other Beasts" (March 1758, pp. 61-62); but the fable was a popular form, and a number of them, not credited to anyone, were printed (see especially those in issues of April and Sept. 1758, pp. 79, 235-36; and April and Nov. 1759, pp. 437, 689-90). From Prior's works were taken "The Vanity of Attempting Supernatural Knowledge" and "On Excessive Drinking" (Jan. 1758, pp. 13-14). Garth was included with "Honour" (Jan. 1758, p. 13), Green with "Poet's Lamentation for the Loss of his Favourite Cat" (Sept. 1758, p. 234), Parnell with "I pass with melancholy state" (April 1759, p. 437), Young with "The Happy Man"—a great favorite—(March 1758, pp. 62-63), and Whitehead with "Ode for his Majesty's Birth-Day" (July 1759, pp. 546-47) and "Ode for the New-Year, 1759" (Aug. 1759, pp. 587-88).

[162] Jan. 1759, p. 334; May 1759, pp. 470-71.

[163] June 1759, pp. 508-09.

[164] July 1759, pp. 548-50.

[165] Sept. 1759, pp. 619-21.

The writers of the former class frequently employed a background of nature, while the brighter side of the war in progress engrossed the belligerent pens.[166]

In summary, it is apparent that *The New American Magazine*, though edited without brilliance, was distinctive for its articles on history and the war, for the reprints selected by one familiar with editorial life in London, and for poetry definitely valuable to the student of a changing age.

III

In 1757 Benjamin Mecom, aged twenty-five, having returned from the island of Antigua, where his uncle, Benjamin Franklin, had assisted him financially in the establishment of a paper, set up a printing office in his native city of Boston.[167] A year later, being equipped to do pamphlet and small book work, he yielded to an inner urge to publish a periodical, *The New-England Magazine of Knowledge and Pleasure* (1758-59).[168] This magazine became in fact also a lady's magazine and gift book long before gift books, as such, were common.[169] Isaiah Thomas, while an apprentice eight years of age in the office of Zechariah Fowle, watched Mecom with a boy's own interest in odd characters, and, knowing him through a number of years following, assayed him with ma-

---

[166] Among the religious poems, see especially "Psalm CXXXIX" (Aug. 1759, p. 588); "Part of a Funeral Elegy . . . Now Justly Ascribed to his Excellency, Jonathan Belcher . . . Deceas'd, Late Governor of New-Jersey. By a Particular Friend" (Jan. 1758, pp. 15-16); "The Prospect" (Feb. 1758, pp. 38-39), stressing the need of holy living, as death may come at any time; "Life a Bubble" (March 1758, p. 64), telling in octosyllabics the constant round of pain on earth and joy in heaven; "A Hymn to the Creator. By a Youth under Seventeen" (July 1758, pp. 169-70). Among the poems relating to the war, see especially "An Elegy . . . to the Memory of Brigadier-General Prideaux" (March 1760, p. 108); "On the Death of General Wolfe," by "Massachutensis" (Oct. 1759, p. 668); "On the Late Defeat at Teonderoga" (Aug. 1758, p. 201); a "Hymn" on the reduction of Louisburg, Fort DuQuesne, and Fort Frontenac, by "Z." (Dec. 1758, p. 309); and two poems in honor of General Amherst (Jan. 1759, pp. 333-34).

[167] Isaiah Thomas (*op. cit.*, I, 32, 142-43, 189, 260, II, 69-70, 85-86, 192) knew Mecom well enough to offer valuable personal opinion regarding him, as well as to trace his business experiences. See also *The New-England Historical & Genealogical Register*, Vol. XXVII (1873).

[168] See note 5.

[169] Frederick W. Faxon, *Literary Annuals and Gift Books* (1912), lists the *Forget-me-not* (1823) as the first English gift-book annual, and the *Atlantic Souvenir* (1826) as the first annual American gift-book. Hundreds of annuals appeared in the immediate decades following, and it is interesting to note that over-stocks of magazines were sometimes sold in the guise of gift-books.

ture judgment. He was, Thomas testified, a gentleman, honest and sensible, and an accurate printer, though lacking in ability to manage a business profitably; yet there was "something singular in his work, as well as in himself. He was in Boston several months before the arrival of his press and types from Antigua. . . . During this interval he frequently came to the house where I was an apprentice. He was handsomely dressed, wore a powdered bob wig, ruffles and gloves; gentleman-like appendages which the printers of that day did not assume, and thus apparelled, would often assist for an hour, at the press."[170]

The cover design of the new magazine, a hand bearing a bouquet and accompanied by the motto "Prodesse E Delectare. E Pluribus Unum," was copied directly from *The Gentleman's Magazine*; and Mecom's pseudonym, "Urbanus Filter," seems to be a modification of Edward Cave's "Sylvanus Urban." But in many respects the publication was treated as a gift book. Each number contained sixty small pages—a greater number than comprised magazines generally. It was published irregularly; each number was separately paged; and it was offered for sale, not by subscription, but by the copy at eight pence or by lots at a reduced rate. Moreover, it was advertised as a publication which might "recommend itself as a suitable Present for Youth,"[171] and the mass of material—on such topics as good taste and habits, virtue, envy, perseverance, extravagance, parsimony, contentment, love, friendship, enmity, glory—though treated with a lack of any distinction, was suited precisely to the gift-book idea.

Mecom's thoughts were so completely alive to his new venture that the first number was taken up largely with his ideas relating directly to the magazine or to the printing trade. He composed, as prefatory pieces, a rimed description of the contents,[172] a poeti-

[170] Thomas, *op. cit.*, I, 142-43.
[171] *The Boston Weekly News-Letter*, Aug. 31, 1758.
[172] No. 1, p. 1. He sketched the contents thus:
"Old-fashioned Writings and select Essays,
Queer Notions, useful Hints, Extracts from Plays,
Relations wonderful, and Psalm, and Song,
Good-Sense, Wit, Humour, Morals, all *ding-dong*;
Poems, and Speeches, Politics and News,
What *Some* will like, and other *Some* refuse;
Births, Deaths, and Dreams, and Apparitions too;
With some *Thing* suited to each different *Goû*,
To humour Him, and Her, and *me*, and You."

cal epistle to the readers,[173] and a "Poetical Dedication to a Good Old Gentleman,"[174] as well as a prose address "To the Honourable Republic of Letters, in New-England."[175] Then followed the "Design,"[176] through which may be traced in Mecom's mind a firm imprint of the critical ideas of the neo-classical school. No-

---

[173] No. 1, p. 3. He expressed the miseries of an editor in these words:

"*Kind Reader*,—Pray, what would you have me do
If, out of Twenty, I should please but Two?
One likes the Turkey's Wing, and one the Leg,
The Vulgar *boil* (the Learned *roast*) an Egg."

[174] No. 1, pp. 4-5. In part the "Dedication," possibly describing Benjamin Franklin, who had assisted Mecom and was later to do so again, reads:

"*You are the Man* who Counsel can bestow,
Still pleas'd to teach, and yet not proud to know;

Bless'd with a *Taste* exact, yet unconfin'd;
A Knowledge both of Books and Human Kind;

The *old*, you still retain your manly Flame;
Your Energy of Mind is still the same.
Virtuous and wise you are, not sternly wrong,
And still remember that *you once was YOUNG*.

You e'en the Dissolute admire and court,
(Attracted by your *Freedom* of Deport).

Much have you read and heard, much more have seen,
And seldom ask *What does the Author mean?*

To you the Wit of *Greece* and *Rome* is known,
And every Author's Merit—but your own.

The filial Thought, fond Wish, and Kindred Tear,
Make *You* the Parent, and the Friend sincere:"

"I am," Mecom wrote at the close of the dedication, "with the *utmost Gratitude* for all your Favours,—the *profoundest Regard* for your Person,—and the *greatest Esteem* and *Veneration* for your Understanding . . . Urbanus Filter."

[175] No. 1, p. 6. A plea for "Learning" and "Piety."

[176] "The chief Design of this Magazine," wrote Mecom, "is to increase, collect and amplify old and new and entertaining and useful Remarks; to conform, improve and illustrate established Doctrines; to communicate uncommon Truths and *Intelligence*, consisting of such Parts as may gratify the Curiosity and improve the Minds of Persons of all Conditions, and of each Sex.—To promote which good Design, we may reasonably hope for the Assistance of Genius, in order to illuminate several *Numbers* . . . to form a *Pocket Volume* or *Volumes* containing . . . Instruction and Entertainment for all Persons, in all Places, and at all Times." The article continues with an expression of hope that ladies may derive much satisfaction from the magazine, although the material is "almost universally applied to one Sex"—the male. (No. 1, pp. 7-12.) Note should be made that Mecom gave up the idea of publishing a department of historical chronicles, and that, as the first number did not sell well, the editorship of "Urbanus Filter" was dropped, and the line, "By various Authors," substituted.

where in American magazines of this period is neo-classicism so fully expressed as a credo as in this article in *The New-England Magazine*, though in performance other editors, especially Gridley, had based their editorial decisions on its rules. Most definitely Mecom called attention to "what Mr. Boileau has so well enlarged upon in the Preface to his Works: That Wit and Fine Writing doth not consist so much in advancing Things that are *new* as in giving Things that *are known* an applicable or agreeable Turn. . . . A *new* Author's *Expression* and *Application* is what we are chiefly to admire. . . ."

Regardless of the general weakness of the periodical,[177] its three numbers are truly distinctive for other reasons than Mecom's critical essay. It was, so far as I can discover, the first American magazine to contain major examples of three types of eighteenth-century literature heretofore disregarded: dramatic prose, the moral epistle written for young children, and the moralistic story of humanitarian cast. While Mecom was in Antigua he was at one time connected with a play house,[178] and his interest led him later to establish in his magazine a department of "Dramatic Entertainment," in which was printed "The Toy-Shop,"[179] exhibiting in dialogue a fop on a purchasing tour. The second type mentioned is represented by "A Letter from Father Abraham to his Beloved Son,"[180] in which the admonitions of the father were intended to serve as a sermon for youthful readers, already familiar with the characters involved. "The History of Tom Varien,"[181] representing the third type, is the story of a pampered boy on the island of St. Christopher, whose early youth was spent absenting himself from school, beating negro slaves, and indulging in willful deviltry of all sorts. Young manhood found him discharged from an English university and lodged in a debtor's prison. On his return to St. Christopher, he spent the family fortune and hastened the

[177] The expanding intervals between the dates of publication (see note 5), indicate that the method of selling by hawkers and over counters, as advertised, proved unsuccessful. Advertisements appeared as follows: *The Boston Weekly News-Letter*, No. 1 of the magazine, Aug. 31, 1758; No. 2, Oct. 26, Nov. 2, 1758; *The Boston Evening-Post*, No. 1 of the magazine, Sept. 4, 11, 25, 1758; *The Boston-Gazette, and the Country Journal*, No. 1 of the magazine, Sept. 4, 18, 1758; No. 2, Oct. 30, Nov. 6, 13, 1758; No. 3, March 12, 1759.

[178] Thomas, *op. cit.*, II, 192.

[179] No. 1, pp. 43-44.

[180] No. 1, pp. 20-28.

[181] No. 3, pp. 3-13.

death of his parents by causing them infinite grief. The shades of Defoe and Richardson, and the dawning shadow of Day, hover in this story, and as the century advanced this sort of tale increased widely in popularity.

Certain other selections are worthy of mention. From the twenty-seventh number of the *Independent Reflector* Mecom took Livingston's famous prayer, retitling it "Thirty-nine Articles of a New and Uncommon Creed,"[182] and the fortieth number served him for "The Use, Abuse, and Liberty of the Press."[183] Excerpts were also printed from the works of Benjamin Franklin, David Hume, Jonathan Swift, and John Leland.[184] The anthem, "Morning and Evening Devotion," in heroic couplets, by a "Gentleman educated at Yale College,"[185] and "The Power of Innocence,"[186] renewing the theme of *Comus*, are essentially characteristic of the poetical selections.

With the discontinuance of *The New-England Magazine* so far as we know in March 1759, and of *The New American Magazine* in the same month of the succeeding year, American magazine publishing entered a period that is fallow in comparison to the one just described. *The American Magazine, or Monthly Chronicle* had issued valiant calls for support of arms in the earlier phases of the war, and *The New American Magazine* had celebrated Amherst and Prideaux along Lake Ontario and Lake George, and Wolfe at Quebec. But the entrance of Spain into the war, the capture of Havana and the Philippines, and the Treaty of Paris of 1763, with the cession of the Canadian lands and Florida to the British, came at a period when there was no magazine in British America to publish the accounts and revel in the spirit of victory.

[182] No. 2, pp. 19-22.

[183] No. 1, pp. 33-41.

[184] "Advice to a Young Tradesman," by Franklin (No. 3, pp. 27-28); extract from Hume's *History of England* (No. 2, pp. 3-12); on vice, by Swift (No. 2, p. 50); extract from "View of Deistical Writers" and on the "Behaviour" the Abbé de Paris, by Leland (No. 2, pp. 48-50, 38-47).

[185] No. 1, pp. 50-51.

[186] No. 3, p. 54.

CHAPTER VI

RELIGION, SCIENCE, JOURNALISM, AND POLITICS

BETWEEN 1760, when *The New American Magazine* came to a close, and 1774, when Isaiah Thomas, Boston newspaper publisher, began *The Royal American Magazine*, American magazine publishing was rather weakly represented by two periodicals which were essentially repositories of religious material, two modifications of true newspapers, one genuine magazine somewhat given over to science, and one political essay journal. No magazine appeared which would extend *belles-lettres* as such, or reflect the moods of the time in a comprehensive editorial plan. Of the religious type were *Ein geistliches Magazien* (1764-72),[1] edited and published by Christoph Saur, of Germantown, Pennsylvania, and *The Royal Spiritual Magazine* (1771),[2] issued at Philadelphia by John M'-Gibbons. The two newspapers which somewhat resembled magazines were *The North-Carolina Magazine* (1764-?)[3] published at New Bern by James Davis, printer and newspaper man, and *The Penny Post* (1769),[4] edited and published by Benjamin Mecom, formerly the editor and publisher in Boston of *The New-England Magazine*. The one true miscellany was *The American Magazine, or General Repository* (1769),[5] edited by Lewis Nicola, of Philadelphia, whose membership in the American Philosophical Society gave him the opportunity to publish his magazine partially under the aegis of the society. Of the political essay type was *The Censor* (1771-72),[6] printed by Ezekiel Russell in Boston for Tory

[1] See "Bibliography," p. 366.

[2] *Ibid.*, p. 367.

[3] *Ibid.*, p. 366.

[4] *Ibid.*, p. 367.

[5] *Ibid.*

[6] *Ibid.* Mention should perhaps also be made here of *The Bee*, by "William Honeycomb" (*pseud.*), the three issues of which were published Feb. 12 and 19, and March 7, 1765, at Philadelphia, by Anthony Armbruster. The plan contemplated a weekly periodical of eight pages. The Historical Society of Pennsylvania and New York Public Library have complete files (Hildeburn, *op. cit.*, II, 37, and Evans, *op. cit.*, No. 10006). *The Bee* was not a miscellany, but rather an essay journal, containing one essay a number. The essays were directed against the proprietary government of

sympathizers attempting to justify the principles of English rule which were being severely criticized by trenchant newspaper essayists.

I

In 1764, when *Ein geistliches Magazien* was founded, social conditions among the German communities of Pennsylvania were isolative and self-sufficient. Farms, trades, and small manufactures engaged the labors of the majority of the hundred thousand immigrants and their descendants.[7] The settlements already bore marks of staidness, for immigration had begun in earnest as early as the ninth decade of the previous century, Germantown having been founded in 1683. Since religious persecution and desolation following military activities had been the chief factors for moving to America, the groups comprised those who wished to live quietly, worshiping simply and devoutly, but without much formula, in the manner of Mennonites, Friends, Dunkers, and Moravians, believing largely in the separation of church and state and a social order disinclined to war at any cost.

Leaving Westphalia, the elder Christoph Saur had arrived in Germantown in 1724, accompanied by his wife and a son of his own name, who was then three years of age.[8] After engaging in various occupations, he secured control in this city of a press and types which had been sent to the New World for the propagation

Pennsylvania. They closely resemble in style and attitude several other essays, which have been attributed to Isaac Hunt, notably *A Humble Attempt at Scurrility: in Imitation of Those Great Men of the Art, the Rev. Dr. S[mi]th; the Rev. Dr. Al[iso]n; the Rev. Mr. Ew[i]n[g]; the Irreverend D. J. D[o]ve, and the Heroic J[oh]n D[ickinso]n, Esq.*, and *The Substance of an Exercise, Had This Morning in Scurrility-Hall*, which was extended by "continuations" to eight numbers. Both were published in 1765 (Evans, *op cit.*, Nos. 10014-22).

[7] Albert Bernhardt Faust, *The German Element in the United States* (1909), I, 128-29, 284-85, records the German population of Pennsylvania in 1775 as 110,000, or one-third of the total inhabitants; Maryland and Delaware, 20,000; New York, 25,000; Virginia, 25,000; South Carolina, 15,000. For a detailed description of the settlement of the Germans in Pennsylvania, see *ibid.*, I, 112-48.

[8] For general reviews of the lives of the Saurs, both father and son, see Faust, *ibid.*, II, 366-67; Thomas, *op. cit.*, I, 270-82, and II, 153; and particularly Oswald Seidensticker, *Bilder aus der Deutsch-pennsylvanischen Geschichte* (1885), pp. 105-66. None has carefully studied the magazine, however, and errors are to be found: *cf.* Seidensticker's references to *Ein geistliches Magazien* (pp. 153-54), confused in titles, issues, and dates.

of the gospel, the operator to receive the usual emoluments for general printing providing he would also print and distribute free of charge certain religious books. Steady and devout, the elder Saur began in 1738 faithfully to perform this requirement, along with his other printing. Calendars, pamphlets, a newspaper, and books emanated from his press, the most famous being the Bible in German, in ·1743, which was the first time the book had been printed in America in any European language.

When the elder Saur died in 1758, his son, who had engaged in bookbinding and merchandising, acquired his father's business; he engaged not only in printing, but also in paper making and type casting, and was remarkably successful.[9] Like his father, he was sincerely concerned with religious interests, on occasion filling a pulpit, and publishing religious works. Probably the most outstanding of his publications was a new edition of the Bible in 1763, which he followed by two subsequent editions. More typical, however, were lesser religious works, such as the popular *Geistliches Blumen-Gärtlein inniger Seelen* (1747, 1769, 1773).[10]

There is little difference in the nature of the content between the type of book just mentioned and *Ein geistliches Magazien,* which was a periodically issued[11] repository of religious observations, essays, sermons, poetry, simple catechisms, and narratives designed for reading about the fireside. Having recently completed his first edition of the Bible, it was natural that the younger Saur should turn his mind to the problem of his next free production, and that the publication of a magazine should seem a feasible project, being a convenient vehicle for the printing of a varied collection of material without unduly taxing the facilities of his press. He did not assume for his readers an interest in religion from historical and creedal points of view, nor did he presume their interest in the church as an organization, as Prince had done in editing *The Christian History.*[12] Rather did he endeavor to supply his German readers with selections from the works of such men as William Law, Hans Engelbrecht, Johannes

[9] Thomas, *op. cit.*, I, 277, 279-82, notes that when difficulties during the War of the Revolution led to the confiscation of Saur's properties, he lost about $90,000; he removed to Mathatchen in 1780, where he kept house, assisted by his daughters. He died in 1784.
[10] The Historical Society of Pennsylvania has these three editions.
[11] See note 1.
[12] See comments on *The Christian History,* Chapter III, section III.

Ernst Stolten, Jacob Janneway, Andrew Rivet, Christopher Dock, and the German-American Theophilus. Thus he offered religious thoughts, simply expressed, for parents and children gathered in family circles—matter which could be preserved for conning, and stored in the memory to feed Christian faith and justify and emotionalize belief in the purposefulness of the work-a-day life.

It had been widely observed by Saur, he announced in the "Vorrede" to the magazine, that general readers were too careless of godly things and often too poor to buy many books. He cherished the thought, however, that if he placed in the hands of people, free of charge, concise pieces of a religious and moral turn of thought, the readers might reflect thereon. Thus he planned to issue gratis a magazine of eight pages, pledging himself neither to time or number, but printing the issues as circumstances permitted, and choosing his selections broadly, beyond the narrow limits of any single sect.[13]

Saur's long introductions to the various selections in the magazine testify to the editorial humility with which he approached the conduct of his religious publication and the labor he was willing to bestow upon it. Occasionally, too, when the spirit seemed truly to move him, he wrote essay-sermons of his own thoughts, and urged others to do likewise.[14] But as the issues progressed, he seems to have become somewhat disturbed by what he believed to be an insufficient interest in the magazine on the part of the public, and lamented the paucity of contributions to a work in which no less a man than Johannes Einfältig had originally inspired him.[15] However, the distinguishing marks of a diligent editor are noticeable throughout the whole life of the periodical, and even the lesser selections and contributions, both originals and reprints, fulfill not unmeetly the purpose Saur had outlined for his publication.[16]

[13] Vol. I, No. 1, first four unnumbered pages.

[14] See especially Vol. I, Nos. 5, 15, 21, 30.

[15] In Vol. I, No. 30, p. 240, Saur wrote: "Es ist doch nicht zu glauben, dass keine solche Schatzmeister Göttlicher Geheimnisse mehr übrig, seyn solten, welche aus denen ihnen vertrauten Schätzen nicht auch dann und wann etwas Altes oder Neues aus Erfahrung auftragen könten, dass zum allgemeinen Besten gereichen könte [sic]."

[16] The following descriptive references are typical of the contents of the first volume: No. 6 contains an exhortation by Johannes Einfältig to a fundamental conversion (pp. 49-56); No. 7 embraces an essay, "Die Nutzbarkeit der Armuth," by "A. W. H." (pp. 57-60); No. 15 includes "Ernstliche Ermahnung an Junge und Alte," by Benjamin Padin (pp. 127-28); No. 17 consists in part of "Erbauliche Nacht-Andacht oder ernst-

First among the more important selections to appear was a German translation from the Reverend William Law's *A Serious Call to a Devout and Holy Life*,[17] originally published in English in 1729. In making this choice the editor exhibited well his own ability, for Law's work was one of the more influential books of the century. Samuel Johnson, picking it up at Oxford, found it "the first occasion of my thinking in earnest," and, among others, both John Wesley and George Whitefield were profoundly moved by it. Following close upon this consideration of the evidences of holiness in useful works, Saur printed "Das Leben Hans Engelbrechts," more dramatic and pictorial in its appeal, as it engaged the reader with the sorrows, death, and resurrection of Christ, with admonitions to repentance, and with the vision of the new heaven and earth and of celestial joys.[18]

Although in succeeding numbers English divines were occasionally given space in German translation,[19] the usual selections were from the work of devout Germans. Of especial length among the latter were the excerpts from Gottlieb Weigen's *Das Geheimniss der geistlichen Geburt Christi in uns*,[20] and a series of sermons by Gerhardtte Stegen[21] which, taken together, supplied the material for nine numbers. More valuable by far from a literary point of view were the selections from the work of Theophilus, Mennonite member of the Ephrata colony, whose poetry, although largely translations, is especially noteworthy and remains a major

liche Beherzigung der Ewigkeit, von einem Christlichen Krancken-Wärter," in fifty-seven numbered stanzas of rhythmical prose (pp. 137-42); Nos. 18-20 contain a reprint, "Von der Möglichkeit die Gebote Gottes zu halten" (pp. 145-68); No. 35 presents a dialogue by the "blessed German preacher," Theodore Brackel, in which a father and his son advance a story concerning "Die Möglichkeit einer frühzeitigen Bekehrung" (pp. 279-86); Nos. 43-44 consist of "Ernstliche Ermahnung zur Keuschheit," sent in by a reader who had perused the magazine with joy, and hoped that this submitted piece would prove useful (pp. 343-58); No. 45 contains "Einladung zu der wahren Gottseligkeit," by "N. B." (pp. 359-63).

[17] *Ernstlichen Ruff zu einem andächtigen und heiligen Leben.* For references to Law and the selections, see Vol. I, Nos. 1-4, through p. 40.

[18] Vol. I, Nos. 8-13, pp. 65-112.

[19] For the Reverend Andrew Rivet's "Die Macht der Religion in Krankheit und im Tode" two numbers were given, 31 and 32 of Vol. I, pp. 248-62.

[20] Vol. I, Nos. 46-50, pp. 367-406.

[21] With the exception of Dock's poems in No. 15, and the selections from Theophilus in No. 10, these sermons, in Nos. 5 to 8 inclusive, are the only noteworthy selections in the second volume.

example of *belles-lettres* among the German writings of the time in Pennsylvania.[22]

Considerable attention was paid by the editor to articles pertaining to the religious education of children. Reprints from the work of Johannes Ernst Stolten,[23] beginning with "Eine höchstnöthige Anweisung zu einer vernünfftigen und Christlichen Erziehung und Unterrichtung der Jugend," undertook to consider the religious and moral instruction of the growing generation through the agencies of the home, school, and church; while Jacob Janneway's *Kinder-Buch* furnished good "Exempeln" for the instruction of youthful readers.[24] The writings of Samuel Lucius were also drawn upon to present the scene of the terrible departure of a herdsman from this life after twenty-three years of ignoble living,[25] which was a "Warnung an die Jugend vor Verführung zum Bösen."[26]

Closely associated in part with the articles printed with reference to children were the contributions and selections which bore the name of the Mennonite, Christopher Dock, who arrived in America about a decade before the Saurs, and became a noted schoolmaster.[27] He was a close friend of Saur the father and so influential a teacher of Saur the son that he deserves the recognition of the final paragraph in the discussion of the magazine his pupil later edited. Dock's first article was a letter to his former pupils, urging them not to be attached to the selfish joys of the world.[28] Saur appended a kindly note to the contribution, writing

[22] See the poems under the titles of "Reim-Gedichte vom rechten Gebrauch des innern und aeussern Gottesdienstes" and "Von der Freyheit zu gedencken" (Vol. I, No. 34, pp. 271-78), and "Warnung vor Selbst-Mord, und wichtigkeit der Lebens-Frist" (Vol. I, No. 36, pp. 287-94); in the second volume appeared "Ernstliche Betrachtungen vom unterschied zwischen Zeit und Ewigkeit" (No. 10, pp. 73-80).

[23] Stolten's work was printed in Vol. I, Nos. 22-25.

[24] Credited selections from Janneway's book occur as parts of Vol. I, Nos. 25 (pp. 207-08), 27, and 28 (pp. 217-32). Typical of the subject matter is the record of a reply a young girl is reported to have made to her mother's weeping statement that the husband and father was dead: "Nein . . . ihr habt keine Ursach so viel zu weinen, denn Gott ist und bleibet ein guter Gott für euch" (No. 27, p. 217).

[25] Vol. I, Nos. 38 and 39, pp. 303-10, 315-18.

[26] Vol. I, No. 42, pp. 335-42.

[27] See *The Life and Works of Christopher Dock . . . with a Translation of his Works into English Language,* by Martin G. Brumbaugh. . . . Introduction by Hon. Samuel W. Pennypacker (1908), pp. 12-14. For general comment, see also Faust, *op. cit.,* II, 204-05.

[28] Vol. I, No. 33, pp. 263-70, "Copia einer Schrifft welche der Schulmeister Christoph Dock, an seine noch lebende Schüler zur Lehr und Vermahnung aus Liebe geschrieben hat."

that "der liebe Author einen solchen guten Wandel geführt, und thut es noch in seinem hohen Alter, dass es nicht unerbaulich, und ihm nicht nachtheilig seyn wird, dass man seinen Namen wisse. Gott gebe, dass alle die es lesen, sich einen würklichen Nutzen daraus mögen."[29] This was followed by two hundred worthy rules for children, embracing the whole category of their possible daily actions at home, school, church, and at play, together with a number of rules for Christian living.[30] Later, when the second volume of the magazine was printed, two songs were included which Dock had written for his pupils and all others who might care to read them.[31]

II

While Saur was engaged on the second volume of his non-creedal magazine in Germantown, *The Royal Spiritual Magazine*,[32] edited, as the title page indicates, by "Several Divines," sprang up in Philadelphia and propounded Calvinistic doctrine in the sole offering of the two extant numbers, a dialogue between Truth and Friendly, conducted in the manner universally popular in the medieval period. Joseph Crukshank, the printer of the publication, was a Quaker "honest in his dealings, punctual in his payments, and amiable in his manners."[33] John M'Gibbons, the publisher, was a bookseller of Philadelphia who engaged also in publishing. As the issues are not numbered, it is not likely that he planned to publish a magazine in the modern sense of the word, but considered

---

[29] P. 270.

[30] "Hundert nötige Sitten-Regeln für Kinder" (Vol. I, No. 40, pp. 319-26) and "Hundert christliche Lebens-Regeln für Kinder" (Vol. I, No. 41, pp. 327-34).

[31] "Zwey erbauliche Lieder, welche der Gottselige Christoph Dock, (Schulmeister an der Schipbach) seinen lieben Schülern, und allen andern die sie lesen, zur Betrachtung hinterlassen hat." (Vol. II, No. 15, pp. 153-57.) The first is of twenty-two, the second of twenty-four stanzas. The first poem seems to have been written very late in life, for Dock describes the scene of a man on his death-bed who cannot refrain from instructing children and survivors in the manners of proper moral conduct; thus it may, perhaps, serve somewhat in correlating the date of issue of the magazine, for Dock died in the autumn of 1771.

[32] See note 2.

[33] See Thomas, *op. cit.*, I, 261-62. William McCulloch, who new Crukshank, wrote Isaiah Thomas, quoting the above phrase the latter had written, and assuring him the statement had been well bestowed (*Proceedings of the American Antiquarian Society,* April 1921, p. 94).

the work rather as simply "a compendious treasure of the most interesting knowledge to mankind"[34]—a repository to be published in convenient installments. Whether more than two numbers were issued has not been ascertained, as only a part of the second is known to exist. I can find no advertisements of the venture in the newspapers. Evidence points to an early relinquishment of the project, however, for in January 1772 M'Gibbons was advertising proposals to issue *The Works of Flavius Josephus* in four octavo volumes,[35] a more lucrative method, probably, of issuing "treasure" to the public, for the proposals were greeted with sufficient favor to cause the set to be published.

The dialogue which comprises the contents of the magazine discovers Friendly, learned but unhappy, being instructed in the Calvinistic interpretation of Christianity by Truth, who explains the tenets so convincingly, and so ably supports them by Biblical citations, that Friendly attains finally to a state of rapture and adoration. One's state in nature, says Truth, is "without hope"[36] and "lost,"[37] redeemable only through Christ.[38] In reply to Friendly's query why the Word is preached to everyone, when grace and glory extend only to the elect,[39] Truth answers that if a mountain held both precious stones and pebbles, one would surely search the whole mountain; furthermore, even the elect are by nature the children of wrath, "but distinguishing love makes them the jewels in God's esteem."[40] Throughout the dialogue occasional poetry is inserted, including several songs, one being a hymn by Watts.[41] Broadly considered, and disregarding the material which the "Several Divines" may have originally planned to print had the project lived, it would seem that the content of the magazine could have been more advantageously published in a single book, in which form it might have enjoyed a wider sale, especially in the northern Middle Colonies, Delaware, and Connecticut.

[34] See the "Preface," pp. I-VI. "We shall endeavour," he wrote further, "to open those everlasting springs of life, love, and peace, contained in the word of GOD. . . ."
[35] *The Pennsylvania Gazette*, Jan. 23, 1772.
[36] P. 22.
[37] P. 23.
[38] P. 27.
[39] P. 67.
[40] *Ibid.*
[41] P. 51.

III

Both *The North-Carolina Magazine*[42] and *The Penny Post*[43] were so slightly modified from the newspaper type of publication that they deserve but scant space in this study. James Davis, the editor and publisher of *The North-Carolina Magazine*, had set up the first press in the colony at New Bern in 1749.[44] In May 1755 he established, in the same town, the colony's first newspaper, *The North-Carolina Gazette*, which ran until some time near or after the close of the decade.[45] In the first week of June 1764 he commenced publishing *The North-Carolina Magazine*, which he conducted as a weekly quarto of from six to eight pages until December 28 of the same year, when he reduced it to four pages.[46] It is evident that he contemplated nothing more than a small news journal, for the first two pages, given over to essays selected from various sources[47] and to texts of important legislative acts, are similar to the front pages of many weekly newspapers of the time, while the remainder of the "magazine" contained news and advertisements. How long the journal was continued is unknown; the thirty-third number of the second volume (January 18, 1765) is the last known to be preserved, though a later date of termination has been inferred.[48] As it was succeeded on May 27, 1768, by *The North-Carolina Gazette*, a reversion to the title of the earlier newspaper, it may properly be classed with the papers which preceded and succeeded it.

The Penny Post, published by Benjamin Mecom at Philadelphia for a few weeks in 1769, was a diminutive magazine of four pages issued three times a week.[49] All but the first and a part of the

[42] See note 3.

[43] See note 4.

[44] For reference to Davis and his publications, see S. B. Weeks, *The Press of North Carolina* (1891), pp. 9-23.

[45] Clarence S. Brigham, "Bibliography of American Newspapers, 1690-1820," in *Proceedings of the American Antiquarian Society*, new series, Vol. 28, Part 2, p. 306.

[46] *Ibid.*, p. 308.

[47] These treated largely of historical, social, political, and religious subjects; Nos. 5 and 6 of the first volume, for example, carried the Bishop of Salisbury's "Discourse of the Use and Intent of Prophecy" (pp. 37-38, 43-45).

[48] For brief references, see Francois-Xavier Martin, *The History of North Carolina* (1829), II, 186, and *North Carolina University Magazine* (III, 40).

[49] Thomas, *op. cit.*, II, 150, never having seen the publication, described it somewhat inaccurately.

second pages were devoted to foreign and domestic news. Short pieces, epigrams, poems, and brief essays on general subjects[50] gave it the tinge of Mecom's earlier failure, *The New-England Magazine*.[51] But the frequency of issue and the emphasis on news place it among the newspapers. To mention some of the contents is to pay it sufficient respect. Probably the most interesting factor to be observed in the editing is Mecom's adherence to the British political point of view. A letter to Old England by "New England"[52] railed against the "calumniators on either side of the water, who would (for the little dirty purposes of faction) set brother against brother, turn friends into enemies, and ruin an empire, by dividing it." Still more important is an original three-column poem, signed "R." and dated from Philadelphia, January 25, 1769, purporting to be an address to Parliament by George III, who, as a man delighting in peace, is distraught at the uprising in Boston, which, of course, must be quelled.[53] Among other selections, "The Properties of a Gardener" is noteworthy for its possible relation to Hopkinson,[54] and another reprint, "On the Death of General Wolfe,"[55] adds one more item of poetry to the long list of references to the valiant commander which were published in the periodicals of the time.

IV

As Lewis Nicola,[56] merchant and bookseller of Philadelphia, was both a member and a curator of the American Philosophical Society in 1769,[57] he was able to win the support of some of its members

[50] Subjects in prose included discussions on contentment (No. 5, p. 19), temperance and intemperance (No. 6, p. 22), of the proper balance of custom and opinion in the influencing conduct (No. 7, p. 26), and, by Mecom himself, an "Essay on Habits" (No. 2, p. 5); in poetry were included an imitation of Horace (No. 4, p. 14), some Latin lines pinned to a lady's bed-curtain on her wedding night (No. 7, p. 26), and an epitaph on the late Lord Howe (No. 8, p. 30).

[51] See Chapter V, section III.

[52] No. 3, p. 10.

[53] No. 9, p. 31.

[54] No. 5, p. 19. See Chapter IV, note 74 for previous appearance of the selection. A letter to Theophilus on the subject of love (No. 5, p. 17) is signed "A.B."—initials which, although by no means limited to Hopkinson, were a favorite of his.

[55] No. 4, p. 13.

[56] See note 5.

[57] *Early Proceedings of the American Philosophical Society . . . 1744-1838* (1884), p. 24.

to supplement the periodical he edited in the same year, *The American Magazine, or General Repository*,[58] with a separately paged department, "The Transactions of the American Philosophical Society." The publication thus gained the distinction of being the first and foremost magazine in America during the third quarter of the eighteenth century adequately to represent American scientific thought. Since the *Early Proceedings* does not contain reference to the magazine, but does mention the separate publication of the *Transactions*,[59] it seems probable that no official action was taken by the society to make the magazine an official organ, but that a general acquiescence was given to Nicola to bind sections of the *Transactions* with the monthly issues of the periodical, by which method the magazine might attain a higher status, the society receive favorable publicity, and copies of the *Transactions*, separately bound, be thereafter more cheaply manufactured. Proposals for establishing the new magazine, which appeared in the local papers January 12, 1769,[60] refer only to Nicola as the man responsible for the enterprise. An imposing array of distributors was announced, firms and individuals having been secured from Halifax to Savannah;[61] in these arrangements it is probable that the printers of the magazine, William and Thomas Bradford, father and son, proprietors of *The Pennsylvania Journal; and the Weekly Advertiser*, lent their assistance. The general plan, as announced in the advertised proposals, contemplated the publication of thirteen numbers a year (including a supplement) at a shilling a number Pennsylvania currency, each issue to contain three sheets of paper, printed in octavo. The first magazine was dated the month the proposals appeared, and though only nine numbers were printed, it would seem that Nicola entertained high hopes for the success of his periodical during the first few numbers; at least in May he advertised his intention of quitting the branch of his business involving his general store, at which he had vended "Wines, Rum, Tea, Dye Stuffs, Salt, Spirits, Molasses, Sugars, Lamp Oyl,

[58] See note 5.

[59] *Op. cit.*, p. 84. The reference is of 1773.

[60] *The Pennsylvania Journal; and the Weekly Advertiser*; also *The Pennsylvania Gazette*.

[61] Other cities listed included: Trenton, Burlington, Princeton, Elizabethtown, New York, New Haven, New-Providence, Newport, Portsmouth, Boston, Baltimore, Charles-Town, Annapolis, Williamsburg, George-Town, Lancaster, Carlisle, York, Wilmington, Edenton, and Newbern.

Rice, and sundry other Wet Goods," as well as a "variety of dry goods."[62]

Nicola's personal tastes entered so largely into the editorial structure of the magazine that the publication attained a characteristic quality which may partially be explained in the light of his known life history, although biographical accounts of the man are meager.[63] He was born in France, educated in Ireland, and accepted an appointment in the British army. Subsequently, coming to America with his wife and four children, he opened a store in Philadelphia in 1767, in the same year publishing proposals for conducting a new circulating library supported by subscriptions and dues. His interest in the "Society held at Philadelphia, for the promotion of useful knowledge," which merged with the American Philosophical Society in 1769, was nearly immediate, for he became a member in 1768. He later contributed articles to the Society,[64] served in a military capacity in support of the Revolutionary War, wrote the famous "Nicola Letter" urging Washington to become king, went on a diplomatic mission to England under the direction of Washington, and occasionally took active charge in the civic affairs of Philadelphia, most notably on the occasion of the political disturbances in July 1795. He maintained an active interest in scientific discoveries, and was a capable leader in military affairs. He possessed a good knowledge of current popular literature, was helpful in civic matters, and associated with important men of his time.

In accord with the policy of most other editors, Nicola proposed to issue a magazine built "To instruct, and innocently amuse," promising to print nothing "derogatory to the principles of the christian religion," nor anything savoring of private disputes.[65] Later, in the two-page preface to the first number, he announced the principle that magazines, though "they do not entirely reject the article of news" were chiefly literary publications. Consequently the departments of "British and Foreign Intelli-

[62] *The Pennsylvania Journal*, May 18, 1769.

[63] References have occasionally appeared in *The Pennsylvania Magazine of History and Biography* which have served me for some of the biographical details; see IV (1880), pp. 181, 255, 400; XV (1891), p. 300; XXIV (1900), p. 11; XXVII (1903), p. 395; XLII (1918), pp. 213-16; XLVII (1923), p. 265.

[64] See *Early Proceedings of the American Philosophical Society . . . 1744-1838*, pp. 103, 123, and the *Transactions of the American Philosophical Society* (1771), I, 244-46.

[65] *The Pennsylvania Journal*, Jan. 12, 1769.

gence" and "American Occurrences" were edited with uncommon succinctness. As the editor had been in America but a short time, and as he hoped to secure a wide inter-Colonial circulation for his magazine, he decided to steer an even course, and the preface proclaimed his "determination to keep clear" of party connections, presenting both sides of whatever arguments might arise among the Colonies.

None the less, the magazine adequately represented Colonial opinion as expressed in authoritative documentary statements, and in the "American Occurrences" one may trace the rising animosity which later led to the rupture with the mother country, and which was being fed fat by British military occupation and the insistence of Parliament that the Colonial legislatures were under its authority and in no way co-equal with it under the Crown.[66] Outside the department, too, articles mirroring political affairs appeared, especially important being those relating to the petitions to England by the legislatures of Pennsylvania and New York against certain taxes[67] and the petition of the town of Boston to the King apologizing for its late disorders.[68] Nicola was careful, however, that the excursions in the field of politics should be limited to the formal expression of the various bodies themselves. The unauthorized rantings of individual protagonists and antagonists he let strictly alone; neither did he care to don the gown of a judge in the court of public opinion, but remained a clerk, merely preserving the records.

Though the magazine was a miscellany of generous proportions, religious subjects, which not infrequently had occupied considerable space in former magazines, were given only slight recognition, a fact for which the period was somewhat responsible. The emotions which had stirred the "Great Awakening" and invoked *The*

[66] The news from Boston reporting petitions denouncing the behavior of the British troops and the maintenance of the military and naval forces assembled there (Jan., March, April, June) was augmented by printing also the message in support of the city's stand by the lower house of Georgia (April) and followed by various official messages from several sources in New England demanding constitutional freedom (July). Very distressing to the several Colonial legislatures was the act of Parliament suspending the New York legislature The printing of the resolutions of that assembly that it possessed certain rights from the Crown alone, and that the suspension was a "high infringement" of these rights (Feb.) was followed by similar statements from other assemblies, notably Virginia (April) and Rhode Island (June).

[67] Feb. 1769, pp. 46-51, and April 1769, pp. 127-30.

[68] Sept. 1769, pp. 321-24.

Christian History were now being turned toward considerations of theories of government, though "On a General Providence" was a subject which stirred some interest, however, and the writer's conviction that God did not supersede His general providences on occasion by particular acts, brought some dissenting opinions into print.[69] But other articles, such as the attempt to plumb the mind of Moses in "On the Egyptian Magicians"[70] and the warning in "A Caution on Jesuitical Conversions"[71] that many Indians adopted Christianity out of fear for the French governmental power, must have been very little regarded.

In the more popular field of fiction, Nicola indulged not only a public desirous of the excessively romantic, sentimental, pathetic, and tragic in theme,[72] but likewise his own interest in French and other Continental personages, who were frequently of the decadent or perturbed aristocracy. Thus a phase of yellow journalism crept into the magazine, and the maladjustments of love, the exhibitions of the baser passions, and the inhumanities of blind justice were presented in the guise of history and biography in a lurid manner. There was a practical moral in the "History of M. de St. Ignan,"[73] who, having married for wealth and being later enamoured of another woman, was won back to the domestic hearth of his wife by her judicial treatment of the affair; there was a saving grace of atmosphere attached to the love elements in "The History of Abelard and Heloisa"[74] and "The History of Mademoiselle des Vignoles";[75] but less may be said of some of the other selections, such as "The Tragical History of the Marchioness de Grange,"[76] whose husband attempted to poison her, and the "Tryal of the Czarewitz,"[77] containing an account of a father killing his sons.

[69] For essay and replies, see June, Aug., and Sept. 1769, pp. 174-77, 237-42, 303-06.

[70] July and Aug. 1769, pp. 209-13, 244-48.

[71] March 1769, pp. 83-87.

[72] William and Thomas Bradford advertised in *The Pennsylvania Journal* of Jan. 12, 1769, among other books, the following: *The Fool of Quality, The Distressed Wife, History of Lucy Watson, Woman of Honour, The Happy Extravagant,* and twelve plays, including *Zenobia, The Good-Natured Man, The Royal Merchant,* and *The Indiscreet Lover.*

[73] May 1769, pp. 137-39.

[74] July 1769, pp. 203-06.

[75] June 1769, pp. 172-74.

[76] March, April 1769, pp. 76-80, 101-04.

[77] April-June 1769, pp. 113-17, 133-37, 169-71.

But it was in science that the magazine ranked supreme among its contemporaries of the period. Emphasis was given to natural history, physics, agronomy, geography, astronomy, and medicine. In the magazine proper most of the articles were reprints, as Nicola drew frequently from the publications of the Royal Society,[78] the Dublin Society,[79] and various books.[80] His interest in science, and his connections with the Continent and Ireland, as well as England, deepened his sensitivity to many sources. In these borrowings he took care usually to announce in forewords the particular services to America the selections were intended to give; he considered especially vital the continued articles on flax and silk worms,[81] for the textile industry particularly intrigued the minds of many persons at the time. Original articles also appeared, the respect in which the magazine was held inducing unsolicited contributions. Among them were "D. C.'s" essay on the importance of natural history,[82] a discussion dated from Philadelphia "On the Increse [sic] of Continents"[83] considering the phenomena of the eastern coast of North America and the delta of the Mississippi, a communication "On the Putrid Sore Throat"[84] written by a "gentleman of the Faculty" in Philadelphia, and a commendatory article in company with Dr. Jacobus Winslow's "Dissertation on the Symptoms of Death, and the Abuse of Hasty Burials or Embalmings."[85] The most renowned among the group, however, was Dr. Hugh Williamson's essay, "A Dissertation of Comets,"[86] which tended to prove that comets were not burning bodies, but received their light from the sun.[87]

[78] See especially "Observations on Animals . . . Called Amphibious," by D. Parsons, Jan., Feb. 1769, pp. 11-13, 31-34.

[79] See especially "Directions for Raising Banks against Tides and Floods," Jan., Feb. 1769, pp. 1-6, 38-41 (misnumbered 46), and the longest continued article of all, discussing the culture and dressing of flax, March-Sept. 1769, pp. 87-90, 117-19, 153-55, 186-88, 216-19, 258-61, 313-15.

[80] See especially an article on an "Extraordinary" manner of catching birds (with full page engraving), from Pentoppidan's *Natural History of Norway* (March 1769, pp. 80-83), and a long continued discussion of the care of silk worms, taken from the work of Pullein and other sources, May-July 1769, pp. 147-52, 183-85, 214-16.

[81] See notes 79 and 80.

[82] Jan. 1769, pp. 6-9.

[83] Feb. 1769, pp. 34-38.

[84] May 1769, pp. 164-68.

[85] Feb. 1769, pp. 65-67.

[86] Sept. 1769, pp. 307-12.

[87] Dr. Williamson, a native of Philadelphia and a graduate of its college, had gone to Edinburgh and Utrecht to complete his studies, had returned home, and in Jan. 1769

In addition to the scientific articles in the magazine proper, the "Transactions of the American Philosophical Society," embracing twenty studies added in the desire to render the knowledge they contained "more generally known,"[88] gave great emphasis to natural history. The chief contributors were Moses and Isaac Bartram, David Rittenhouse, Henry Hollingsworth, John Ewing, Peter Miller, Lionel Chalmers, and Landon Carter, among whom, Chalmers, a physician of Charleston, South Carolina, was the most indefatigable, five papers coming from his pen.[89]

In poetry the Horatian attitude on contentment was a dominant theme. The homage of poetic idealization was frequently paid to the simple life.[90] Of the poems in this mood, "The Choice,"[91] opening with two lines quoted from John Pomfret's poem by the same title, is a noteworthy example: a well-stocked farm, six slaves, a gracious wife, and the opportunity to revere God and country were the elements of the author's requirements for a state of happiness. In some ways the author of this poem was provincially patriotic, for he chose American rather than English cheese for his palate; but he turned to England for literature, declaring he would pay "most attention" to "Swift, Shakespeare, Pope, Young, Addison, and Gay." Another important class of poetry in the magazine was composed of ambitious eclogues in heroic

---

had been appointed as one of a commission of the American Philosophical Society to observe the transits of Venus and Mercury.

[88] So I noticed in an announcement on the cover of an issue for June 1769.

[89] No. 1, by Moses Bartram, discussed silk worms, No. 2, by David Rittenhouse, described an orrery; No. 3, by William Henry, described a self-moving register; No. 4, by Richard Wells, described a machine for pumping vessels at sea; No. 5, by an Englishman in communication with John Morgan, discussed the eruption of Mt. Vesuvius in 1767; No. 6, by Henry Hollingsworth, presented experiments in destroying wild garlic; No. 7 discussed means of destroying flies injurious to wheat; No. 8, by John Ewing, discussed the projection of the transit of Venus over the sun; No. 9, by Peter Miller, discussed the right time to sow peas; Nos. 10, 16, 18, 19, 20, by Lionel Chalmers, discussed medical virtues of American vegetation, effect of weather on disease, nervous colic, peri-pneumony, and catarrhal consumption; No. 11, by Landon Carter, discussed the nature of the fly destroying wheat; No. 12, by Dr. Otto, described an oil made from the sunflower; No. 13, continued the discussion of sunflower oil; No. 14 by John de Normandie, described mineral water at Bristol, Pa.; No. 15, by Isaac Bartram, discussed distillation of persimmons for making a substitute for rum; No. 17, by John Ewing, described a magic square.

[90] See "The Man's Wish" (March 1769, pp. 92-93), "The Bachelor's Reasons for Taking a Wife" (March 1769, pp. 91-92), and "The Ingredients of Contentment" (April 1769, p. 123).

[91] Feb. 1769, pp. 54-55. This is not the rather popular poem of the same title originally appearing in 1757 from the pen of Benjamin Church.

couplets, which furnished as good poetry as any the magazine contained.[92] Another type of poetry especially favored of the editor, and heretofore more dominant in Gridley's magazine than any other, was light verse, fanciful, sentimental, sophisticated, and sometimes humorous; in this group "Verses Sent to a Young Lady" by "E.," has occasionally been credited to Nathaniel Evans.[93]

V

While, in and around Philadelphia, Saur was spreading the gospel of love and peace and M'Gibbons was publishing Calvinistic doctrine, and shortly after Mecom's dapper bantam paper and Nicola's miscellany had been discontinued, men in Boston were taking up the pen in preparation for the sword. As active Whig imaginations rapidly heightened the colors of the pictures of their grievances and ideals, the Tories grew so concerned at the state of mind of their opponents that they organized an essay periodical, *The Censor*,[94] to support Governor Thomas Hutchinson and his council and to justify established eighteenth-century political doctrines, especially those pertaining to the prerogatives of the parent over Colonial governments.

The Tory party was not spiritedly served by the Boston newspapers. *The Massachusetts Gazette; and the Boston Weekly News-Letter*, whose roots lay in the old *News-Letter*, followed a dignified, conservative policy under the guidance of Richard Draper, and supported the government but could not be jubilantly partisan. *The Boston Evening-Post*, published by Thomas and John Fleet, sought to maintain a strict neutrality, and found little support.

The other two papers actively supported the Whig party and

[92] See especially "A Pastoral Elegy on the Death of a Young Lady" (April 1769, pp. 120-22), and "Jealousy, an Eclogue" (June 1769, pp. 188-90); "Hope, an Eclogue," the only poem in the magazine for May 1769 (pp. 156-57), is probably the best representative of the group.

[93] April 1769, pp. 122-123. The copies of the magazine at the Historical Society of Pennsylvania and the New York Public Library bear annotations designating "E." as Evans; on the other hand, Evans died in 1767, and I do not find the poem in Evans's *Poems on Several Occasions* (1772), collected by his friend, Provost William Smith. Other examples of light verse are "Lines" from a gentleman to a lady who had ridiculed him (March 1769, p. 93), "Advice to a Young Lady" (July 1769, pp. 223-25), a young lady's lament of man's domination over her sex, with a reply by a gentleman (August 1769, pp. 271-72), "On Belinda" (Aug. 1769, p. 272). More purposeful was Wilkes's satiric elegy on William Pitt (Jan. 1769, pp. 15-20).

[94] See note 6.

throve on the articles of the essayists, both occasional and serial, who were busily engaged with principles, emotions, and grievances. One of these papers, *The Boston-Gazette, and the Country Journal*, published by two able Whigs, Benjamin Edes and John Gill, was supported by a sane group of their party "who were experienced statesmen, and had a particular object in view; to make people understand the nature of government, the rights of the colonies, the oppressions of Great-Britain. . . ."[95] But in no way did it refuse to place chips on its shoulders, for in it "Valerius Poplicola" could assert that "nobody can have a power to make laws over a free people, but by their own consent,"[96] "Sincerus" could dub Governor Hutchinson's proclamation of thanksgiving to God "for the continuation of our civil and religious privileges" as an "impious mockery,"[97] and "An American" could urge patriots of Great Britain and Ireland to come to America to escape tyranny, for no American would tolerate it.[98]

Still more valiant in the cause of the Whigs was *The Massachusetts Spy*, organized in 1770 by Zechariah Fowle and his erstwhile apprentice, Isaiah Thomas.[99] Within the year Thomas had assumed full ownership of the paper, and the year following it became the most violently radical and increasingly popular among the Boston journals. The proprietor, although only in his twenty-second year, had previously identified himself with anti-British interests, as he had run afoul of civil authorities in Halifax for criticizing the Stamp Act in a paper of that city.[100] During 1771 *The Massachusetts Spy* repeatedly attracted the opinions of several of the fiercest essayists of pre-Revolutionary years. In it were printed a number of essays by "Monitor," who viewed the Hutchinson administration with indignant alarm. "Massachusettensis" showed himself to be no less dissatisfied. Greater than either was "The Centinel," who brought to the controversy a keen pen, a legal sense, and a tone which in the heat of the con-

[95] For full discussion, see *Collections of the Massachusetts Historical Society*, first series, VI, 73-75; the quotation is from p. 73.

[96] Oct. 28, 1771.

[97] Nov. 4, 1771.

[98] Nov. 25, 1771.

[99] The title of the paper embraced the description, "A Weekly, Political, and Commercial Paper; Open to all Parties, but Influenced by None."

[100] For a brief sketch of the life of Isaiah Thomas see *Biographical Encyclopedia of Massachusetts of the Nineteenth Century* (1879), pp. 176-80.

test seemed singularly charged with a cool, convincing logic.[101] He, above the rest, would soon be able to meet *The Censor* on its own ground of rationalistic, restrained argument. Not even "The Centinel," however, possessed the magic pen of "Mucius Scævola," best suited for the time. Joseph Greenleaf, of Abington, justice of the peace for Plymouth County, was accused by Governor Hutchinson of writing over this pseudonym, and never denied the charge. Having warmed himself to his task in October,[102] "Scævola" became so virulent in *The Massachusetts Spy* for November 14 that Hutchinson was obliged to order first Thomas, who refused, and then Greenleaf to appear before the Council.[103] Greenleaf was dismissed from office;[104] the Governor could hardly do otherwise than institute proceedings against one who called him an "Usurper."[105]

The first issue of *The Censor* appeared on Saturday, November 23, 1771,[106] and, not waiting to introduce itself in the customary manner of new periodicals, hurled a spear at "Scævola's" article in *The Massachusetts Spy* of November 14. This was a signal for increased activity on the part of the Whigs, although *The Censor* was not mentioned. One commentator in *The Boston-Gazette* of November 25, referred to "Scævola" as "a writer

---

[101] Years later, when the perspective of time could come to the aid of history, the essays were described as "direct attacks on all authority and law." (See reference in note 95.)

[102] Issues of Oct. 24 and 31 respectively.

[103] The summons was printed in *The Massachusetts Spy* for Nov. 22, 1771.

[104] Notice of dismissal appeared in *The Massachusetts Spy* Dec. 12 and 19, 1771.

[105] In part, the essay read: "We have need of the wisdom of serpents, who are concerned with such rulers; to be considered by them as fools, is irritating; for fools they must think us, if they can imagine that we can complain of loss of liberty in one breath, and with the next solemnly thank God for the preservation of it. . . ." The allusion is to the governor's proclamation for thanksgiving.

"A ruler, independent on the people, is a monster in government; and such a one is Mr. Hutchinson. . . . A Massachusetts Governor, the King by compact, with his people may *nominate* and *appoint*, but not pay: For his support, he must stipulate with the people, and until he does, he is no legal Governor; without this, if he undertakes to rule, he is a Usurper."

[106] *The Massachusetts Gazette: and the Boston Weekly News-Letter* took cognizance of it in its first succeeding issue, announcing it as a folio weekly selling at two cents a number, and remarking, "The Reception this Paper has already met with, gives the Publisher Encouragement to hope for a large Subscription." In this hope the publisher, Ezekiel Russell, was disappointed (Thomas, *op. cit.*, II, 71). No advertisements were printed in *The Censor* proper, but the larger-paged postscripts carried advertisements, and might easily have developed into a newspaper had the new publisher received sufficient public encouragement.

whom I very much admire," and the following week the same paper copied a "Scævola" essay. On November 28 "Monitor" began a series of essays in *The Massachusetts Spy*, and by December 12 had so far nursed his wrath as to condemn the acts of the Hutchinson government as "TREASON," while in the same newspaper the steadily contributing "Massachusettensis" was ready, in the issue of December 5, to charge the governor with "TYRANNY."[107]

Against an overwhelming array of public opinion *The Censor* engaged in journalistic battle for nearly six months. At first it attempted to counter-thrust with rationalistic argument and with appeals to support conservative, eighteenth-century conceptions of government. But as time wore on the explanations of the Tory point of view grew less studied. The editorial drive, at first well organized and pointed, was dissipated in useless, short arguments; and the tone changed from one of paternal, aggrieved dismay toward the wayward beliefs of the Whigs to a truculent self-defense mixed with self-pity. One senses in its petulance a feeling that it deemed itself to be unjustly the victim of an opposing force which would not recognize ordinarily accepted doctrines. It thus adopted in dismay the mien of the vanquished.

How far Ezekiel Russel, the publisher, was concerned in the editing of *The Censor*, it is difficult to surmise. Now in his middle twenties, he had established a small printing office in Boston only two years previously. His political associations were apparently being determined largely by business interests, for he had already engaged in an ill-fated attempt to publish a Whig paper at Portsmouth, New Hampshire, and his printing of *The Censor* in behalf of Tory interests came at a time when he was in need of financial assistance.[108] In the printer's introductory remarks to the periodical, published in the second number,[109] he expressed "his most unfeigned thanks to his generous BENEFACTORS," whose assistance made him "now possessed of every re-

---

[107] On the Tory side, "Chronus," in a series of essays in *The Massachusetts Gazette*, was defending the policies of the government with something more of dignity but much less power.

[108] According to Thomas, Russell was born in 1744. In 1765, with Thomas Furber, he published a Whig paper in opposition to the somewhat conservative newspaper issued by Daniel Fowle. He returned to Boston subsequently, opening a print shop there in 1769. (Thomas, *op. cit.*, I, 154-55, 178, 206; II, 71, 75, 94-96.)

[109] I, Nov. 30, 1771, pp. 5-6.

quisite in the Printing Business" after the Whigs had "precluded him the use of the press which had been heretofore open to him." He justified his position as a Tory by proclaiming himself a "hearty friend to his country" and a lover of constitutional liberty who considered those who were heaping "detraction" and "virulent" abuse upon the magistrates as "destructive pests to the pupblick peace." In contradistinction to the Whig papers, the designs of the new journal were "To weight every sentiment . . . with temper and decency: to compare discordant opinions, and give birth to truths which the temper of the times may have hitherto confined to the honest but timid bosom of the patriot: to blunt the arrows of envy, malice, and revenge, and detect the designs of the conspirator against his country's peace." Russell was, therefore, the public target and shield from behind whom the Tories might fire their volleys; he assumed the details of publishing, and apparently considered himself in the light of an editor bound by close ties to his benefactors. It is probable that he wrote most if not all of the editorial announcements[110] and at least some of the several unsigned articles, and that he chose some if not all of the occasionally selected reprints.

Certain principal essays in *The Censor* are worthy of description. Following the reply to "Scævola's" article in *The Massachusetts Spy* of November 14 and to Cotton Mather's defense of "Scævola,"[111] a group of six essays over the pseudonym of "Freeman" appeared, which is by far the most important contribution made by *The Censor* in support of Tory principles.[112] Tradition has connected the "Freeman" essays to the pen of Andrew Oliver, lieutenant-governor of Massachusetts, though definite assignment seems never to have been carefully supported.[113] In any case, the

[110] In the first volume he expressed his thanks for the articles by Freeman (No. 10, Jan. 25, 1772, p. 37), set forth the difficulties of the Crown (No. 13, Feb. 15, 1772, pp. 49-50), and offered the use of the magazine to William Molineux to reply to charges made against him (No. 17, March 14, 1772, p. 67); in the second volume appeared a statement by the publisher that Joseph Greenleaf never contributed to the periodical (No. 6, April 25, 1772, p. 91).

[111] "Scævola's" article, with the reply, was printed in Nos. 1-3, pp. 1-4, 6-8, 9-12, the reply being signed by the letter "A."

[112] Nos. 5-9, Dec. 14, 1771-Jan. 18, 1772, pp. 13-36.

[113] Thomas, *op. cit.*, II, 71, records that Oliver was the "reputed" author of the series. Delano A. Goddard, "The Press and Literature of the Provincial Period," in *The Memorial History of Boston*, ed. Justin Winsor, II, 409, mentions Oliver and Benjamin Church as general contributors. An article in the *Collections of the Massachusetts Historical Society*, first series, VI, 73-75, definitely assigns (though

author was intimately acquainted with the laws passed by the legislative assemblies, with leading English legal commentators, and with conservative theories of government. He maintained poise amidst argument, and a style cool and rational; and he urged that redress of grievances be accomplished through "moderation . . . and perseverance in some steady plan of opposition."[114] He was, moreover, somewhat familiar with the operation of the governments of some of the other colonies, and used his knowledge of current practices to refute the Whig argument that the Colonial legislatures possessed certain powers independent of Parliament.[115] The later numbers of the series were concerned particularly with the question of the powers and privileges of governors and with a portrayal of the unpleasant aspects of occupying the executive chair,[116] a subject again discussed by "Censor" and "Marcus Aurelius" in the thirteenth number.

The other essayists were less prolific. One, who termed himself "A Son of Liberty," settled down through two numbers[117] to discuss the history of the charters of Massachusetts and the events transpiring in the period of the Commonwealth, but he was pushed aside to make room for "The Ladies Protest,"[118] in which the "Ladies of New-England, over the *tea-table* assembled," voiced their solemn declaration against an article in *The Boston-Gazette*[119] by "Eleutherina," who, they asserted, had exhibited "unparalleled *effrontery* . . . in presuming to *represent* the whole sex" in an article which treated "His Majesty's *Servants* . . . most illiberally and scandalously." Still more in the vein of ironic humor was an open letter of the "Honourable Patrick McAdam O'Flagharty," one of the many illiterate but egotistic Irishmen of satiric fiction used to heap ridicule on the side of misguided democracy; in keeping with his rôle as ubiquitous representative of the Whigs, he

without offering proof) the "Freeman" series to Oliver, but refuses to associate Church with Tory articles until the beginning of the war. The copy of *The Censor* in the library of the Massachusetts Historical Society contains in pen writing of an early hand the ascription of the "Freeman" essays to Lieutenant-Governor Oliver (p. 13).

[114] I, No. 4, Dec. 14, 1771, p. 16.
[115] I, No. 5, Dec. 21, 1771.
[116] I, Nos. 6-9, Dec. 28, 1771-Jan. 4, 11, 18, 1772.
[117] I, Nos. 10-11, Jan. 25, Feb. 1, 1772, pp. 38-44.
[118] I, No. 12, Feb. 8, 1772, pp. 45-48.
[119] Jan. 27, 1772.

addressed the "sweet Electors" of Boston, promising, if awarded a political post, to make government difficult for both king and governor.[120]   More worthy of sober thought was an article by "D. W." defending the court processes of Massachusetts.[121]   But in general the later numbers of *The Censor* lacked both wit and reason, and the abusive epithets of "Tullius" hurled at the Whigs— the "discontented Vultures"—for reducing Boston "almost to penury" by their "tragic" acts, tokened the coming demise of the journal.[122]   On May 2, 1772, the final number appeared, and the Tories fell back to *The Massachusetts Gazette*, from which vantage point Andrew Oliver, William Brattle, Daniel Leonard, Jonathan Sewall and others opened fire on John Adams and a score of other Whig challengers of Tory doctrines.   No other magazine was to appear for nearly two years, when the nearness of the Revolution precluded any political views other than anti-British.

[120] I, No. 15, Feb. 29, 1772, pp. 57-59.

[121] II, Nos. 2, 3, March 28, April 3, 1772, pp. 75-82.

[122] II, No. 5, April 18, 1772, pp. 87-90. Equally abusive was the "Recipe" to make a patriot, sent in by "T. N.," who wrote that a mixture of "impudence, virulence . . . groundless abuse . . . atheism, deism . . . libertinism . . . groundless alarms . . ." would bring forth "a Y[oung], an A[dams], an O[tis], and a M[olineux]." (See I, No. 12, Feb. 8, 1772, p. 48; the insertions within brackets are those written by hand in the copy at the American Antiquarian Society.)

CHAPTER VII

THE BELLIGERENT YEARS

FROM 1772 to 1783 only three magazines were published in British America; two of them were discontinued at the brink of the War of the Revolution, while the third, begun in the midst of hostilities, was abandoned at the close of a year. *The Royal American Magazine* (1774-75),[1] published at Boston first by Isaiah Thomas and later by Joseph Greenleaf, reflected a broad editorial policy; it was an inclusive miscellany of ample proportions, running Thomas Hutchinson's *The History of the Colony of Massachusetts-Bay* and copious extracts from British magazines, as well as some original American contributions. But conditions gathering around the approach of the war, especially the closing of the port of Boston, and an evident lack of general interest in the magazine, in part revealed by the paucity of original articles, left the journal without justifiable financial or literary reason to exist. *The Pennsylvania Magazine* (1775-76),[2] published at Philadelphia by Robert Aitken and edited by Thomas Paine, was much more distinctive; not since the time of William Smith's *The. American Magazine, or Monthly Chronicle* had America supported a magazine of equal native worth. Not only Paine, but, among others, John Witherspoon, Francis Hopkinson, David Ramsay, Matthew Wilson, Benjamin Rush, and Samuel Chew served in their several capacities to enliven the pages with seasoned wit, opinion, humor, and instruction. But Paine resigned probably in dudgeon, and turned his pen to other things, and the prospect of continuing the magazine after the Declaration of Independence came into force did not appeal to its Scot publisher. *The United States Magazine* (1779)[3] was published at Philadelphia by Francis Bailey, and edited by Hugh Henry Brackenridge, both of whom had but recently arrived in the city. This magazine printed a

[1] See "Bibliography," p. 367.
[2] *Ibid.*, p. 368.
[3] *Ibid.*

remarkable mock-epic, "The Cornwalliad," and followed with diligence the progress of the war and the problems facing the new nation. It managed also to carry an aura of peaceful literary distinction which the winds of war could not dispel. It appropriated articles from the pens of some who had contributed to *The Pennsylvania Magazine*, including Ramsay, Witherspoon, and Wilson. But it also drew other names into its list, and the importance of such men as Philip Freneau, Charles Lee, William Livingston, and the editor brought a lasting eminence to the magazine. Nevertheless, the times were inauspicious for the publishing of a costly literary magazine, and war conditions, notably the falling value of currency, brought an end to the journal.

I

The success of *The Massachusetts Spy*, an anti-British newspaper established in Boston in 1770 by Isaiah Thomas and Zechariah Fowle, probably induced Thomas, now in his early twenties, to consider enlarging his printing activities by publishing *The Royal American Magazine*. He was a young man of a practical turn of mind, well schooled by adversity in his trade. The desertion of his father had thrown him early in life into a Boston printing office as an apprentice, and subsequent wanderings from Halifax, Nova Scotia, to Charleston, South Carolina, had broadened his experiences. His return to Boston had been greeted by immediate good fortune in the printing business; he had assumed full ownership of *The Massachusetts Spy* within a few months after the paper was begun, and by 1773 it was the equal of any journal published in the city.[4] In it, on June 24, 1773, he printed his proposals for the publishing of *The Royal American Magazine*, consuming nearly two columns of space on the front page in an explanation of the project. Newspapers, he averred, were not well "fit to convey to posterity the labours of the learned." So he proposed a monthly periodical of about fifty pages, large octavo,

---

[4] See Chapter VI, section V, for statement of Boston press conditions of the period; see same chapter, note 100, for reference to Thomas's life. For brief references to *The Royal American Magazine*, see Thomas, *op. cit.*, II, 72-73, and Charles Deane, "Hutchinson's Historical Publications," in *Proceedings of the Massachusetts Historical Society* for 1855-58, pp. 141-44.

embellished with engravings, to be sold at seven shillings nine pence sterling per annum. He had secured the promise of several worthy gentlemen to contribute to the magazine. He had, moreover, subscribed to "all" of the magazines and reviews of Great Britain and periodicals of America, and from them would select the most interesting material for his own periodical. He was ready, finally, to issue serially in his magazine, in a manner suitable for separate binding, Thomas Hutchinson's *The History of the Colony of Massachusetts-Bay*, which alone was "worth the cost of the magazines." Thus equipped, and being convinced that literature was "the grand fountain head from whence springs all that is requisite to accomplish rational beings," he felt capable of issuing a magazine worthy of American support.

The response was sufficient to encourage Thomas to proceed with the enterprise. In *The Massachusetts Spy* of September 9, he announced that the magazine was "likely in a short time to make its appearance," and, having requested his agents and friends in the several provinces to turn in their subscription lists,[5] he stated in the paper of November 26 that the new periodical would "undoubtedly appear on the first of January next," and asked that all newspapers in the Colonies copy the advertisement. But unforeseen difficulties delayed the program. Thomas had sent to England for new types for the magazine; the ship was wrecked on the shore of Cape Cod, and though the cargo was salvaged and the types recovered, delivery was delayed "until the Day intended for Publication," and the issue of the first number was advertised for "the first Day of February next."[6] But mechanical obstacles must have intervened, for *The Massachusetts Spy* of February 3, 1774, contained no advertisement relative to the magazine, and the issue of February 10 announced the first number as "This Day Published" at ten shillings eight pence a year.[7]

The publishing of *The Royal American Magazine* grew burdensome beyond endurance for Thomas. The May issue was tardy in its appearance, not being advertised until June 23 in *The Massachusetts Spy*, and the June number was not announced in the

---

[5] *The Massachusetts Spy*, Nov. 4, 11, and 18, 1773.

[6] *Ibid.*, Jan. 6, 1774; the advertisement appeared in other Boston newspapers also.

[7] The price originally established was ten shillings four pence lawful money, or seven shillings nine pence sterling (*The Massachusetts Spy*, June 24, 1773).

newspaper until the issue of August 4, when it was promised for the following Saturday.[8] Thomas was then ready to cease publication, and printed an announcement of suspension on the reverse side of the title page of the magazine. The "shutting up of our Port, and throwing all Ranks of Men into Confusion" had "so embarrassed those good Gentlemen . . . who kindly promised to assist the Editor with their various Lucrubrations [*sic*]" that lately he had been "favoured with but few original Pieces." As the editor could not, therefore, publish a magazine of a quality befitting his established standards, he proposed a temporary suspension of the periodical for a few months until "the Affairs of this Country" should be "a little better settled."

Had the elderly Joseph Greenleaf been as astute in business matters as his friend Isaiah Thomas, *The Royal American Magazine* would have died at the time of its suspension. But the pride of editing a periodical and a patronal interest in Colonial literary and political activities seized him. He had been an early contributor to *The Massachusetts Spy*, and, accused of being the virulent writer of anti-Hutchinson articles under the pseudonym of "Mucius Scævola," his commission as justice of the peace of Plymouth County had been withdrawn in 1771.[9] At the time of the suspension of the magazine he was the owner of a printing office in Boston which was managed by his son, who had learned the printing trade under Thomas.[10] Urged by friends of the periodical and by his own interest, he assumed ownership of the magazine in August, Thomas yielding all unpaid subscriptions "for value received."[11]

Greenleaf zealously pushed forward his new enterprise. He called upon the star-scattered "sons of Harvard" to help him; he hoped to receive accounts of improvements in "mechanical arts, husbandry, in natural and experimental philosophy, and the mathematics"; he asked for "materials from which to continue the History of this country"; and in order to make the world "Better as well as wiser," he promised "to intersperse subjects of a Moral

[8] Issues for Feb., March, and April were respectively advertised in *The Massachusetts Spy* for March 10, April 7 (for the following Monday), and May 5 (for the following Tuesday).

[9] Notice of dismissal appeared in *The Boston News-Letter* of Dec. 12, 1771.

[10] For a personal account, see Thomas, *op. cit.*, I, 174-75; II, 72-73, 119, 255-58.

[11] *The Massachusetts Spy*, Aug. 25, 1774.

and Religious nature."[12]   He was "near two months" behind the publication schedule, and set diligently to work retrieving the time lost, being "obliged" to publish an issue "oftener than once in three weeks."[13] The process of his labors may be followed through advertisements in *The Massachusetts Spy*. He was not able to advertise the July number until the newspaper issue of September 15, but the November number was promised on December 8 as ready the following day, and the issue for December was advertised on January 5, 1775. To the year's volume he shortly after added a supplement, a common practice, but not promised by Thomas in his proposals.[14]

On December 31, 1774, Greenleaf was still looking forward to another year's life for the magazine. In an announcement of that date, appearing with the supplement,[15] he proposed new plans. If three hundred of his subscribers would pay a little more, he would increase the number of pages of Hutchinson's *History* bound with the magazine each month; on the other hand, he would omit the *History* to subscribers not desiring it, charging them less. An "almost new" type had been procured, and all indications pointed to the publication of another complete volume. Even the issue of March 1775—the last—carried no notice of suspension. But the financial burden was too great. Subscription money for the current year would not be due until August; payments of past dues came in with evident slowness, for it was necessary to "plead" for them;[16] a possible, though distant competitor, *The Pennsylvania Magazine*, had bid for support in New England.[17] With prospects so drear and funds so low as to weaken his fine energy, it was well

[12] Announcement of plans was made by Greenleaf on reverse side of title page of magazine for July 1774, from which quotations are taken.

[13] See announcement on reverse side of title page for Dec. 1774. Issues for Aug., Sept., Oct., and Nov. 1774 were respectively advertised in *The Massachusetts Gazette: and the Boston Weekly News-Letter*, Oct. 6, 27, Nov. 17, and Dec. 16.

[14] Advertised in *The Massachusetts Gazette: and the Boston Weekly News-Letter*, Jan. 26, 1775.

[15] See page following title page for the volume.

[16] See reverse side of title page for March 1775.

[17] Thomas advertised *The Pennsylvania Magazine* in *The Massachusetts Spy* of Jan. 19 and 26, and Feb. 2 and 9, 1775. Greenleaf did not advertise *The Royal American Magazine* in *The Massachusetts Spy* after Jan. 12, though he continued to announce the monthly issues in *The Massachusetts Gazette: and the Boston Weekly News-Letter*, the latter advertising the numbers for Jan., Feb., and March on Feb. 23, March 17, and April 13 respectively.

that Greenleaf heeded the disheartening signs and stopped publication with the third number of the second volume.

Thomas endeavored to combine in *The Royal American Magazine* both original articles and the popular features of the current British periodicals. In the first phase of his effort he was in the main unsuccessful, for notwithstanding his continued appeals, he was unable to gather for the forty pages of each number over ten pages of original work, and the nature of the submitted material was mostly too imitative, too general, or too pompous to be in any sense distinctive.[18] But in the second phase of his editorial plan he was successful, for he exhibited considerable catholicity of taste.

For one thing, he was the first editor in America to offer the public a really important series of twenty-two engravings,[19] executed, at least in the main, by Paul Revere, who received about £3 for each engraving,[20] and by Joseph Callender, both citizens of Boston.[21] Though crudely executed, these engravings have become famous for their historical interest, and include busts, portraits, illustrations to accompany articles on natural history and new inventions, cartoons satirizing the English and French, and scenes to vivify popular, romantic, and confessional love stories.

Equally important as material somewhat extraneous to the con-

[18] Greenleaf followed Thomas's policies as best he could, though his interests were less broad. He realized that he was in a position of importance as an aid to future historians, but under his editorship the magazine did not contain much material of historical value. The newspapers are more important.

[19] See note 1. In order, the illustrations included: 1) a view of Boston (Revere), 2) a thunder storm (Reverse), 3) Sir Wilbraham Wentworth (Revere), 4) a night scene (Callender), 5) bust of John Hancock (Revere), 6) illustration of "The Fortune-Hunter" (Callender), 7) bust of Samuel Adams (Revere), 8) "The Hill-Tops," illustrating a song (Callender), 9) an Indian gazette (unsigned), 10) cartoon, "The Able Doctor, or America Swallowing the Bitter Draught" (Revere), 11) "The Hooded Serpent" (unsigned), 12) Spanish treatment at Carthagena (Revere), 13) a method of refining saltpetre (unsigned), 14) a water-spout (unsigned), 15) "The Mitred Minuet (The Dancing Bishops)" (Revere), 16) a Russian Rabbit (Revere), 17) Mademoiselle Clairon (Revere), 18) "The Bees" (unsigned), 19) Col. Bouquet conferring with Indian chiefs (Revere), 20) "A Certain Cabinet Junto" (Revere), 21) illustration for "History of Lauretta" (Revere), 22) "America in Distress" (Revere). Nos. 1 and 19 are unsigned, but were executed by Revere (see Clarence S. Brigham's discussion in *Proceedings of the American Antiquarian Society*, new series, XXIX, 1919, pp. 210-11).

[20] See Brigham as above, p. 210.

[21] The chief occupation of Callender (1751-1821) seems to have been that of engraver of bookplates, bill-heads, and dies for the Massachusetts mint. The activities of Revere (1735-1818) were more varied. See David McNeely Stauffer, *American Engravers upon Steel and Copper* (1907), I, 40, 220-21.

tent of the magazine proper was the Hutchinson *History*, which Thomas believed would be desired by the public since only two editions of the first and one of the second volume had been printed.[22] In this he guessed correctly, as a subsequent offer indicated that a number of subscribers wished the "Supplement" to be entirely comprised of it, and Greenleaf planned to furnish it in added quantities if desired.[23]

There were other features in process and selection. It is important to note, for instance, that Thomas carefully designated the articles contributed "To" or "For" the magazine, and that in arranging the sequence of material he gave precedence to original work. He was, too, the first in America to insert in a magazine an engraving of the words and music of a song,[24] a type of specialty which English editors were including occasionally, and which other American editors introduced into their magazines later. Moreover, he was the first Colonial editor to offer many confessional and love stories heavily laden with sex, sorrow, and sentimentality. These he borrowed from English magazines, which were sensitive to the public taste. The stories were narrated almost entirely in the third person, the writers refusing to give the principals a voice. In an age of light essay prose, this method might well be expected. For story-telling, the illustrative incident of the essay was raised to a position of chief importance, while the commentary was relegated to the service of supplying occasional observations impeding the flow of incident and furnishing a statement of the self-evident moral at the close. The dramatic method of carrying the story forward by conversation and holding steadily to an objective point of view, was seldom used. There were, it should be noted, several classes of short stories. The most prevalent was the biographical story based on an incident from a life-pattern or fashioned from imaginary experiences sentimentally conceived.[25]

[22] Thomas and John Fleet, of Boston, printed the first volume (to 1691) in 1764, and under a London imprint the volume was reprinted in 1765. The Boston publishers issued the second volume (to 1750) in 1767, and printed a new edition of two volumes in 1795. See also note 1.

[23] See note 15.

[24] "The Hill-Tops," April 1774, opposite p. 152.

[25] Outstanding illustrations of this type of story include the following: "The Thunder Storm" (Jan. 1774, pp. 26-30), in which a bolt of lightning prevents rape; "Justice and Generosity" (Feb., March 1774, pp. 53-56, 91-93), in which all ends well following an episode wherein the heroine, uttering a "violent shriek," falls "lifeless on the floor"; "The Fortune Hunter" (Feb.-Aug. 1774, pp. 57-61, 101-05,

A second type was the Oriental tale. This kind of story was becoming increasingly popular; and as it was built to a set pattern widely recognized, the structure of these stories was commendable even when told by ill-gifted writers. A rather careful attention to diction and description and the use of some degree of restraint in the portrayal of emotions were likewise noticeable.[26] A third class was the memoir. Incidents selected from the experiences of those whose lives were full of wild romance or tragedy were not infrequently printed for their sensational story value, and the type lost in good taste whatever advantage it gained in the attainment of a closer approach to an artistic illusion of reality.[27]

The general literary content of the magazine, both original and selected, exhibited little creative power. At first a philosophical interest in *belles-lettres* and language was evinced, and articles considered the birth of writing, periodical publications, the history of literature, and the desirability of founding an American Society of Language somewhat on the order of the French body.[28] But active production was another matter.

Political discontent furnished the chief stimulus to thought and action. But it was not generally in the mind of the time to consider politics proper substance to translate into a magazine as

141-45, 169-73, 209-12, 261-66, 305-07), in which the hero, discovering the troubles incident along the pathway of lust for wealth, finds happiness when he marries a girl for love alone; "The Unhappy Lovers," signed by "Irenius" and sent in by "I. X." (Aug. 1774, pp. 297-302), in which the tragedy following a girl's foolish hiding of true love is given a setting which includes a massacre and life in a cave (both popular in American stories); "The Stage-Coach: A Moral Tale" (Oct. 1774, pp. 378-80), in which haphazard acquaintanceship leads to sorrow; and the "History of Lauretta" (Nov. 1774-Feb. 1775, pp. 426-28, 459-64, 12-14, 49-54), in which seduction and elopement lead to a penitent life on a farm, followed by a reunion and happiness. Mention perhaps may be here made of an extract from Henry Brooke's *The Fool of Quality* (May 1774, pp. 179-82), and to an advice-to-the-lovelorn service extended by the magazine under the title "The Directory of Love" (Feb., April, May 1774, pp. 68, 148-49, 189-90).

[26] See "Hamet: or the Insufficiency of Luxury to the Attainment of Happiness" (May 1774, pp. 173-75); "Anecdote of an Eastern Emperor" (Nov. 1774, pp. 420-21); "A Turkish Tale" (Aug. 1774, p.—misnumbered—328).

[27] See extracts from the memoirs of Mademoiselle Clairon (Nov. 1774, pp. 422-24), and the Marchioness de Lambert's advice to her daughter (June 1774, pp. 219-21).

[28] See extract on the history of literature from Dr. Adam Ferguson's *An Essay on the History of Civil Society* (Jan. 1774, pp. 15-20); an essay on periodical publications (Feb. 1774, pp. 68-69); an attempt to prove use of letters known before the Flood (Feb. 1774, pp. 50-51); and "To the Literati of America" regarding possible founding of a society (Jan. 1774, pp. 6-7).

prose literature, which was conceived as a field of art somewhat too restrained in manner and sublimated in its interpretations of life to use such grist. ₁ Proclamations and speeches were more normal to the period, and these the magazine reported, along with a monthly digest of news, mainly as a matter of course for permanent record.[29] Controversial essays, the most important literary product of the time, seemed to their authors more fitting in newspaper columns. Such attempts as were made to write of politics with patrician grace of manner and thought usually were weakly conceived and tritely expressed observations on historical or philosophical verities.[30]

However, the thunder of the approaching storm did ride on the winds of one traditional literary form which was a distinct contribution of the magazine: the descriptive dream or vision essay. Occasionally the allegorical implications were strikingly bold. In "A Dream"[31] the writer reports his visit to the "Person, Palace and Courtiers of King Tyranny" (the court of George III), where Avarice remarks to the visitor that he hopes to see America succumb to the hell-dwelling type of government envisaged by the dream. In another dream essay[32] the author beholds a beautiful garden (America), to be entered only by a long and difficult route. In this garden he comes upon a stately "fabrick" (the English Constitution), one side of which is new in structure, the other side old. And near by is a serpent (England), already battered into three parts, the head of which stays the hands of a group of per-

[29] See the "Address" of the Council of Massachusetts Bay to Gov. Hutchinson concerning Indian affairs in Martha's Vineyard, boundaries of the province, and rights of the Council (Feb. 1774, pp. 73-75); the remonstrance of the House and petition for removal of Peter Oliver (chief justice of the Superior Court of Assize), with Hutchinson's replies (Feb. 1774, pp. 77-79); John Hancock's "Oration" of March 5, 1774, delivered at Boston to commemorate the "bloody Tragedy" of March 5, 1770 (March 1774, pp. 83-87); the Boston Port Bill (May 1774, pp. 163-67); Rev. Jonathan Shipley's speech on the bill for altering the Charter of Massachusetts Bay (Aug., Sept. 1774, pp. 321-27—misnumbered—and 328-32). The "Historical Chronicle," embracing about five pages monthly, ran throughout the life of the magazine, and included news both foreign and domestic, meteorological observations, and marriages and deaths.

[30] See especially "Character of an American Patriot" (Feb. 1774, pp. 44-45), "An Essay on the British Government" (Dec. 1774, pp. 456-59), a "Summary" view of the sufferings and deliverances of early Americans (Jan. 1775, pp. 20-29), and an essay on the origin and nature of government (Feb. 1775, p. 64).

[31] Dec. 1774, pp. 443-45.

[32] Ibid., pp. 471-72; the interpretation appeared in the issue of Jan. 1775, pp. 3-4. Another example of the type is "A Vision" concerning the tea tax, by "Fiat Justitia," together with the "Vision Realized," by an "American" (Nov. 1774, pp. 414-15).

sons about to throw stones at it by announcing that it is already dead. These dream stories are rather elaborately and carefully worked out. They and their fellows of the decade constitute an interesting though slight phase in literary expression merging fancy with political upheaval.

On problems and topics other than governmental, *The Royal American Magazine* took a normal interest. Comments regarding the slave trade were opposed to the practice.[33] Though contrary statements inspired debate, a broad education for girls was valiantly upheld on occasion,[34] and light social banter occupied some space in discussions on desirable female traits.[35] Thomas Goldthwaith, Robert Eastburn, and others were drawn upon for Indian material, which was sometimes colored with adventure and danger and sometimes sentimentalized with romantic associations.[36] Though usually short, the articles on religious themes were considerable in number, offering philosophical observations, textual interpretations, and anti-Catholic harangues, the last being emphasized by the indignation of the Colonies against Great Britain's successful political move in granting a liberal extension of privileges to the Catholics of Quebec.[37] Very little was chosen on the basis of reputation of the author; seldom does one find such names as Goldsmith, Francis Bacon, and Voltaire, and even then the subject matter may have been a deciding influence over the choice.[38]

Science played an important rôle. The most frequent contribu-

[33] See "Queries" concerning negro slavery, by "Philanthropos" (May 1774, pp. 175-76), and "The Dying Negro," a poem written by Thomas Paine (Feb. 1774, pp. 71-72).

[34] See "On Female Education," by "Clio" (Jan. 1774, pp. 9-10), "Leander's" considerations of education and the fair sex (April 1774, pp. 131-32), and "Sylvia's" reply to the latter (May 1774, pp. 178-79).

[35] See especially Jack in a "Dilemma" and "To Jack Dilemma" (Nov., Dec. 1774, pp. 406-07, 445).

[36] For Goldthwaith's talk with a Mattugwessauwack Indian, see issue of Feb. 1775, pp. 55-59; for Eastburn's captivity, see issue of Dec. 1774, pp. 449-54; for another adventure among Indians, see issue of Feb. 1775, pp. 59-61, and for an Indian's sentiments on venality and bribery, see issue of June 1774, pp. 215-18.

[37] For articles on the Bible as a book of knowledge and on philosophical reasons for observing the Sabbath, see respectively issues of Jan. and Feb. 1774, pp. 11 and 45; for an example of textual interpretation, see issue of July 1774, pp. 241-42; for an example of anti-Catholic sentiment, see issue of Oct. 1774, pp. 365-66.

[38] Selections from Goldsmith on friendship, Bacon on judicature, and Voltaire on the life of Charles XII appeared respectively in issues of June and Oct. 1774 and March 1775, pp. 206-07, 384-86, 104.

tor was Dr. Thomas Young, of Newport, whose experience in the treatment of fevers, rickets, and contagious diseases led to a number of "Observations."[39] Other original articles appeared in the interest of medicine, but usually the selections were borrowed, and thus the work of well-known men is often to be found, including Joseph Priestley, Samuel Tissot, and Mark Akenside.[40] The greatest name for husbandry in the magazine was that of Bernard Romans, who wrote on the culture of madder and indigo.[41] As Massachusetts spent annually $234,151 on indigo alone, according to Romans's estimate, the economic weight of the article may be appreciated. The need for powder emphasized the interest in saltpetre, its properties and the methods of making it;[42] and the market for salt suggested the worth of an article describing a distillation process.[43] The editor resorted to the works of Franklin for an article on waterspouts, and mixed adventure with natural science by using Everard's "Adventure . . . at the Quicksilver Mine of Idra," and a selection from Captain Samuel Wallis's account of his trip around the world.[44]

Although an excerpt from Parnell's *A Hymn to Contentment* was published in the magazine, neither Thomas nor Greenleaf was generally inclined to select the work of major poets of the century,[45] and although Phillis Wheatley, who was known by a book of poetry issued in 1773, contributed two light poems printed "By particular request," the editors were unable to secure distinctive original contributions to supply the department of poetry.[46] The heroic couplet and simple forms for light verse predominated.

[39] Young's contributions were printed in issues of Feb., March, April, Sept., Oct. 1774 and March 1775, pp. 47-48, 98-100, 129-31, 339-40, 366-68, 89-91.

[40] Priestley, on tea (March 1774, pp. 96-98); Tissot, on recovering drowned persons (March 1774, p. 100); Akenside, on use of ipecacoanha in asthmas (Oct. 1774, pp. 381-84).

[41] See respectively issues of April and Jan. 1774, pp. 138-40, 12-13. Romans also sent in a poem, which gave a description of America (Jan. 1774, pp. 32-33). The longest article on the culture of madder was by "A Husbandman" (Sept.-Dec. 1774, Jan. 1775, pp. 332-33, 372-73, 409-12, 464-65, 11-12).

[42] See issues for Aug. 1774 and Jan. 1775, pp. 285-88, 18-19.

[43] March 1774, pp. 95-96.

[44] For Franklin, see Sept. 1774, pp. 341-49; for Everard, July and Aug. 1774, pp. 243-44, 302; for Wallis, Jan., Feb., and April 1774, pp. 21-26, 62-67, 134-38.

[45] For Parnell, see Aug. 1774, pp. 313-14.

[46] Phillis Wheatley's poems consist of two short pieces addressed to "a Gentleman of the Navy" (Dec. 1774 and Jan. 1775, pp. 473-75, 34-35).

Chastity,[47] religion, [48] the seasons,[49] happiness,[50] the night,[51] and the sea,[52] were the usual themes. Of local contributors, "Hilario" and "Juvenis" were the most prolific, but they lacked both aptitude and ideas.[53] American patriots, wading in the blood of thousands slain, were extolled in "A Prophecy of the Future Glory of America," which bore a New Haven postmark,[54] while "Thoughts on Tyranny," by "W."[55] and a "Song for America," by "Philomusus"[56] added to the fanfare. Some "Verses" found among the manuscripts of the late Benjamin Pratt, former chief justice of New York, written in the conventional couplet and expressing conventional philosophy, were distinguished in authorship only.[57]

II

Robert Aitken planned the publication of *The Pennsylvania Magazine; or American Monthly Museum*[58] when he was forty years of age and when he had been for four years a resident of Philadelphia.[59] The first "Proposals" appeared in *The Pennsylvania Packet* of November 21, 1774, and in *The Pennsylvania Gazette* and *The Pennsylvania Journal* of November 23, 1774.

[47] See, as an example, a "Hymn to Chastity," by "G. S.," March 1775, pp. 111-12.

[48] See, as an example, a poem on the Ascention (April 1774, pp. 153-54).

[49] See, as an example, "Winter, a Pastoral Ballad" (Dec. 1774, p. 475).

[50] See, as an example, "On Happiness" (Nov. 1774, p. 433).

[51] See, as an example, a poem on "Night" (April 1774, p. 154).

[52] See, as an example, "A Sea-Piece" (Oct. 1774, p. 393).

[53] "Hilario" wrote a poem to the author of "A Thought on the Connubial State"; also "On Happiness," "The Wish," "Autumn," "To Philander, Discontented," and "To Miss, on her Haughty Carriage." (Feb., April, Sept. 1774, pp. 70, 151, 353-54). "Juvenis," who needed not the pseudonym to assert his youth, addressed poems to three young ladies: to one on the birth of a son, to another on her recovery from the smallpox, and to a child on New Year's Day (March 1775, pp. 108-09, 109-111, and Jan. 1775, pp. 31-32); another poem, "On Winter," appeared in issue for Jan. 1775, p. 33.

[54] Jan. 1774, p. 31.

[55] Feb. 1775, p. 67.

[56] Nov. 1774, p. 429. To this group should be added one written "nearly fifty years" previously, when no thought of war engaged the mind, Dr. George Berkeley's "To the Honour of America" (March 1775, pp. 114-15).

[57] March 1774, p. 106.

[58] See note 2.

[59] Aitken was born at Dalkeith, Scotland, in 1734, and died at Philadelphia in 1802. He came to Philadelphia as a printer in 1769, but returned shortly to Scotland and came again to the city in 1771. See Stauffer, *op. cit.*, I, 4, and Thomas, *op. cit.*, II, 151-52, 239.

The plan therein outlined proposed the printing of "original American productions" extending "to the whole circle of science, including politics and religion as objects of philosophical disquisition, but excluding controversy in both."[60]   Select essays from British and Scotch magazines were also promised, as well as lists of new books "with remarks and extracts," a request being made for critical commentaries.   However, American publications, although listed, would not be criticized; thus the editor would "avoid the suspicion of party or prejudice."[61]   To this offering were added a department of poetry and departments of news, vital statistics, meteorological diary, prices current, and the course of exchange.   It was proposed to print six half-sheets large octavo monthly, embellished with a copperplate, at thirteen shillings a year Pennsylvania currency, which would include the price of the customary supplement. The date of publication of the first issue was set for the first Wednesday in February 1775.   Robert Aitken's name was the only one signed at the close of the announcement.[62]

The year seemed an auspicious one for the printing business at Philadelphia, and plans were expansive.   While the magazine was in the offing, two new weekly newspapers were being proposed,[63] and Aitken, in *The Pennsylvania Gazette* of March 1, 1775, not only announced the first number of his magazine, but reported a large and increasing list of subscribers and editorial contributions.   He was ambitious, therefore, "not only to *equal,* but to *excel* every former attempt of this kind."   Under such enchanting prospects he was willing to admit an editorial assistant, Thomas Paine, who had arrived in the city in November 1774, bearing let-

[60] The announcement elaborated on the point of controversy: political controversy would be printed as news, and religious controversy, "particularly between the different denominations," would be wholly excluded.

[61] Under such restrictions an opening was offered for the publication of current literary criticism in American magazines.

[62] Occasional advertisements indicate that the magazine was published on time; *The Pennsylvania Gazette* advertised the Feb. number in the issue of March 1, and the March number in the issue of April 5, and the June number in the issue of July 5; *The Pennsylvania Packet* issues of Jan. 30, Feb. 27, and April 3, 1775, advertised respectively the Jan., Feb., and March numbers of the magazine to appear on the following Wednesday, March 1, and April 5.

[63] See *The Pennsylvania Journal* of Jan. 25, 1775, proposing *The Pennsylvania Mercury, and Universal Advertizer* (Enoch Story and Daniel Humphreys) and *The Pennsylvania Leidger, or, the Maryland, Pennsylvania, and New-Jersey Weekly Advertiser* (James Humphreys, Jr.).

ters of recommendation by Franklin, and, casting about for an occupation, began his editorial duties with the second number.[64]

Paine's active mind brought merit to the magazine. His personality and opinions yielded him many active enemies as well as friends, however, and the testimonies of his time are partisan and sometimes violent, though a fairly clear pattern can be distinguished. Among his early biographers, Chalmers and Cobbett were unfriendly and unfair to him, and mention his connection with Aitken only as a "shopman" at twenty pounds a year.[65] Cheetham had the fairness of mind to write to Dr. Benjamin Rush, who knew Paine fairly well, concerning the man's life in Philadelphia; and Rush's remarks are authoritative evidence that Paine had been considering the opening of a private school, that he was made editor of the magazine after the publication of his essay on slavery, and that he was to receive fifty pounds a year for his editorial work.[66] Paine's own comments are illuminating. In a letter dated March 4, 1775, addressed to Benjamin Franklin, Paine remarked that Aitken, "having little or no turn" for editing a magazine, had "applied" to him for assistance, since which time the number of subscriptions had increased from "not above six hundred" to "upwards of fifteen hundred." He also stated that no terms of remuneration had as yet been agreed upon, but that he "was not concerned" in the first number, and the present issue was only the second.[67] Added information is contained in a letter from Paine to the Honorable Henry Laurens, in which the writer mentioned that Dr. John Witherspoon, president of the College of New Jersey, "had likewise a concern" in the magazine, and that the venture "turned out very profitable," and continued: "At the end of six months I thought it necessary to come to some contract. I agreed

[64] Paine was thirty-eight years of age at the time. Both Rush and Paine are definite in their statements that Paine was not an editor of the first number; however, he was a contributor. See Moncure D. Conway, *The Life of Thomas Paine* (1892), I, 40-41. For the date of Paine's arrival in America, see article by Albert Matthews on Paine in *Proceedings of the Massachusetts Historical Society*, XLIII, 245 *n.*

[65] *The Life of Thomas Pain* [sic] . . . *by Francis Oldys* [George Chalmers], *A. M. of the University of Pennsylvania*. Sixth edition (1793). *The Life of Thomas Paine . . . with Remarks and Reflections, by Peter Porcupine* [William Cobbett]. Philadelphia, printed; London, reprinted (1797). The latter book quotes Oldys, p. 28.

[66] James Cheetham, *The Life of Thomas Paine* (1809), pp. 34-40. Also Conway, *op. cit.*, I, 41. The anti-slavery tract was published March 8, 1775.

[67] Conway, *op. cit.*, I, 40-41.

to leave the matters to arbitration. The bookseller [Aitken] mentioned two on his part—Mr. Douché, your late chaplain, and Mr. Hopkinson. I agreed to them and declined mentioning any on my own part. But the bookseller getting information of what Mr. Douché's private opinion was, withdrew from the arbitration, or rather refused to go into it, as our agreement to abide by it was only verbal. I was requested by several literary gentlemen in this city to undertake such a work on my own account, and I could have rendered it very profitable."[68]

It seems not unlikely that Paine may have terminated his connection with the magazine about September 1775, and that assumptions that he remained with the publication until its demise can hardly be justified.[69] Not only does the letter just quoted suggest an impasse, but no article appearing in the magazine later than the issue for August 1775 has been definitely assigned to Paine,[70] and *Common Sense*, the outline of which had been formed and first part of which had been nearly finished by October 1775,[71] was published by Robert Bell[72] rather than Aitken. Furthermore, Dr. Benjamin Rush, whose statements are fully as accurate as those of any other commentator,[73] noted that Paine's editorial connection was conducted "with great ability and success for several months,"[74] which is hardly the phraseology he would have used had Paine stayed with the magazine throughout its life. Incidentally, too, it is not amiss to note that the association of Aitken and Paine was, according to current report, fraught with some difficulty, for Thomas mentions that Aitken (who did not "at all

[68] Conway, ed., *The Writings of Thomas Paine* (1894), IV, 429-32.

[69] Ellery Sedgwick, *Thomas Paine* (1899), p. 13, wrote that Paine conducted the magazine a year and a half, perhaps basing his statement upon Conway's *The Life*, I, 41, 82, which so infers.

[70] Paine's article signed "Humanus" and containing the word "Independency" appeared in *The Pennsylvania Journal* of Oct. 18, 1775, and not in *The Pennsylvania Magazine* of that date, as a misprint reads in Frederick James Gould, *Thomas Paine* (1925), p. 34.

[71] F. Sheldon, "Tom Paine's First Appearance in America," *The Atlantic Monthly*, Nov. 1859, pp. 565-575.

[72] Jan. 10, 1776.

[73] Both were members of the American Philosophical Society, and knew each other fairly well. Rush wrote of Paine in terms of friendship, and suggested to him the title of *Common Sense*. See *A Memorial Containing Travels through Life or Sundry Incidents in the Life of Dr. Benjamin Rush . . . Written by himself* (1905), pp. 84-85, and Harry G. Good, *Benjamin Rush and his Services to American Education*, Witness Press, Berne, Indiana, n. d., pp. 40-44.

[74] *A Memorial, op. cit.* note 73, p. 84.

times evince the most amiable manners")[75] "often found it difficult to prevail on Paine to comply with his engagement" to contribute for the magazine, once taking him supervisionally in hand while Paine wrote for an issue, which he did "with great rapidity" after "he had swallowed the third glass."[76]

Time and place conspired with the contributors to set *The Pennsylvania Magazine* high in importance among its eighteenth-century kin. A general destiny swept it along. But the magazine was not conceived of the restless spirit of the approaching war. Aitken's memories of Great Britain were still fresh in his mind, and he commonly remarked he was "na a fechting mon."[77] He desired to emphasize literature, manufacturing, science, and the arts and trades of peace while he chronicled the passing show of political events. He was pleased to print a letter from one writer, probably Paine, making a gesture for recognition,[78] who saw no reason why America could not produce articles both useful and entertaining. The British magazines, the writer averred, had been "repositories of ingenuity" at their commencement, but were "now the retailers of tale and nonsense. From elegance they sunk to simplicity, from simplicity to folly, and from folly to voluptuousness."[79] The times were already beginning to try men's souls. If the new magazine would cling to the earlier principles, it could perform a mission of value for the occupations and spirit of man which its over-seas competitors had relinquished. And Aitken himself, as he was about to launch the first issue, looked with some concern on the turbulence of the year, and hoped that an amicable solution would soon be found. All who would normally write for the magazine, he said, "now turn their attention to the rude preparations for war—Every heart and hand seem to be engaged in the interesting struggle for *American Liberty*." It was "the sincere wish—the earnest prayer of the Publisher" that "all public contentions may find a speedy and equitable reconciliation, and that this once happy country may again enjoy the unviolated blessings of the *British Constitution*."[80]

[75] William McCulloch (correcting and elaborating Thomas's remarks), *Proceedings of the American Antiquarian Society*, April 1921, p. 96.

[76] Thomas, *op. cit.*, II, 151-52.

[77] McCulloch, *op. cit.* in note 75, p. 96.

[78] "To the Publisher of the Pennsylvania Magazine," Jan. 1775, pp. 9-12; credited to Paine by Conway, *The Writings*, and reprinted therein, I, 14-19.

[79] *The Pennsylvania Magazine*, Jan. 1775, pp. 9-12.

[80] *Ibid.*, Jan. 1775, in "The Publisher's Preface."

Aitken's prayer was unanswered. But he kept the magazine marching steadily in pace with the times. It caught the thunders of the approaching war as they pealed more and more loudly. Hopkinson, Paine, Witherspoon and others gave it tongue to speak in defense of Colonial points of view, and though the tones were positive, reason prevailed. Amidst the chatter of the "Select Passages" and the "Monthly Intelligence," Hancock, Dickinson, Gage, Burgoyne, Lee, Church, and others gave authentic expressions on the passing scene.[81] In the final issue was printed the "Declaration of Independence."[82] A feature for a subsequent issue was announced, and no notice of suspension was printed, but the state of actual war brought a termination to the periodical.

The chief contributors to the magazine were the three who were principally interested in it—Aitken, Paine, and Witherspoon—and Francis Hopkinson and Matthew Wilson. Beyond making publisher's statements, Aitken seems to have limited himself to the cutting of engravings. In the earlier numbers, engravings by John Poupard and Caleb Lownes (both residents of Philadelphia, the

[81] Among the "Select Passages," note particularly the reprint of the "Appendix" to John J. Zubly's *The Law of Liberty*, an account of the manner the Swiss recovered their liberty (Oct. 1775, pp. 471-76); the extract from Thomas Simes's *The Military Guide for Young Officers* (March 1776, pp. 137-41); and an extract from *A New System of Military Discipline*, by a "General Officer" (May 1776, pp. 229-32). In the "Monthly Intelligence," note Connecticut's letter to General Gage regarding his military activities in Boston, his defense and request for advice (May 1775, pp. 233-35); John Dickinson's "A Declaration by the Representatives of the United Colonies . . . Setting Forth the Causes and Necessity of their Taking Up Arms," signed by John Hancock (July 1775, pp. 334-36); the "Rules and Articles" passed by Congress for "the better government of the Troops" (Sept. 1775, pp. 433-39); the letters to the inhabitants of Great Britain and Ireland, presenting the Colonial grievances, by the "Delegates in Congress" (Aug. 1775, pp. 379-86); General Charles Lee's letter of July 7, 1775, to his former commander in Portugal, General Burgoyne, urging him to recognize the rights of America, and Burgoyne's reply, stating that if relief from taxes be the issue, the quarrel was at an end, but if freedom from Parliament be the issue, a contest must follow, and Lee's reply (Aug. 1775, pp. 375-79); accounts of Washington's command at Cambridge, and the capitulation of St. Johns and Montreal (Nov. 1775, pp. 530, 532-36); Dr. Benjamin Church's "traiterous" letter to an officer at Boston, stating that the people of Connecticut were up in arms, with 280 pieces of cannon at Kingsbridge, that the people of New Jersey were "not a whit behind the Connecticut in zeal," that he saw 2,200 men in review at Philadelphia, with 1000 riflemen and 40 horsemen, and that Washington and Lee in Massachusetts had 18,000 men (Jan. 1776, pp. 49-50); the speech of Governor Johnston in the House of Commons, urging conciliation (May 1776, pp. 235-44); the description of the reorganized government of South Carolina (June 1776, pp. 289-94); the new constitutions of New Jersey, Virginia, and Connecticut (July 1776, pp. 330-38).

[82] July 1776, pp. 328-30.

former an engraver and jeweler, the latter a die-sinker and seal-cutter),[83] and by J. Smither and Christopher Tully were used. But from late in the summer of 1775 to the close of the magazine, Aitken engraved plates regularly for the magazine, though he was ill-skilled in the art.[84]

It is more than hazardous to proclaim, as some in their zeal have done, that Paine was "first" in the expression of a number of social and political opinions which have since become fact, law, or custom. The origin or expression of these ideas is not so easily traced. He was, none the less, a leader among the bolder spirits of the time. Following Cheetham and Sherwin,[85] and searching independently of them, Conway has with good judgment ascribed to Paine the prose and verse in the magazine appearing over the pseudonyms of "Atlanticus," "Esop," and "Vox Populi," and he has also, from internal evidence, attributed to him a number of unsigned pieces which it were more logical to accept, at least provisionally, than to decline, though final proof be sometimes lacking. Some of these items have since been proved by Mr. Frank Smith

[83] A brief description of engravings and those who made them follows. The decorative design, first edition of the first number, was executed by John Poupard, that for the second edition by J. Smither, and the title-page for the first volume was designed by Pierre E. du Simitière, cut by Aitken. Monthly illustrations included: a rotating glass plate machine for generating and storing electricity, by J. Smither, and a picture of Oliver Goldsmith to accompany "Retaliation," by Poupard (Jan. 1775); a new threshing instrument consisting of revolving flails (Feb. 1775), by Smither; engraving by Smither to accompany Paine's song, "Death of General Wolfe" (March 1775); a new machine for spinning cotton and wool, by Christopher Tully, and a view of a frame house (April 1775); a new machine for deepening docks (May 1775); "A New Plan of Boston Harbour from an Actual Survey," by Caleb Lownes (June 1775); a plan of the town of Boston and the American camp (July 1775), by Aitken; an "Exact" plan of Gage's lines on Boston Neck, by Aitken (Aug. 1775); the battle at Charlestown, June 17, 1775, by Aitken (Sept. 1775); the "Present Seat of the War" on the borders of Canada, by Aitken (Oct. 1775); a plan of the town and fortifications of Montreal, by Aitken (Nov. 1775); a new device for delivering persons from houses on fire, by Aitken, and a plan of Quebec, by Aitken (Dec. 1775); a furnace for distillation of sulphur, and an apparatus for distilling fresh water from salt water (Jan. 1776); a cut showing manual alphabet for the deaf and dumb (Feb. 1776); a plan of a salt works, by Aitken, and a perspective view of salt works at Salisbury, New England (March 1776); a map of the maritime region of Virginia, by Aitken (April 1776); a map of North Carolina, South Carolina, and Georgia, by Aitken (June 1776). For critical remarks on some of the plates above enumerated, see indexed volumes by Stauffer, op. cit.

[84] See Stauffer, op. cit. I, 4, 228.

[85] For Paine's contributions as listed by W. T. Sherwin, see his *Memoirs of the Life of Thomas Paine* (1819), pp. 22-25.

to be definitely from Paine's hand, and he has pointed out internal evidence to support the other ascriptions to Paine, as well as to hazard the placing of an occasional new title in the group.[86]

[86] The following contributions are credited to Paine by Conway in his *Life* of the author (I, 43-45) or are reprinted in Conway's edition of Paine's *Writings* (I, 14-64; IV, 477-85). "To the Publisher of the Pennsylvania Magazine" (Jan. 1775, pp. 9-12) is unsigned, but in *Writings*, I, 14-19; the introductory letter "To the Public" in the January issue, unsigned but dated Jan 24, 1775, at Philadelphia, containing the simile of a "snow-drop"—a simile later utilized by Paine in an unsigned poem, "The Critic and Snow Drop"—is credited by Conway in *Writings*, IV, 481, and by Smyth, *Philadelphia Magazines*, p. 49; the "Description of a New Electrical Machine" (Jan. 1775, pp. 31-32) is signed "Atlanticus"; "Useful and Entertaining Hints" (Feb. 1775, pp. 53-57) is signed "Atlanticus" and reprinted in *Writings*, I, 20-25; "New Anecdotes of Alexander the Great" (Feb. 1775, pp. 61-62) is signed "Esop" and reprinted in *Writings*, I, 26-28; "Reflections on the Life and Death of Lord Clive" (March 1775, pp. 107-11) is reprinted in *Writings*, I, 29-35; "Cupid and Hymen" (April 1775, pp. 158-61) is signed "Esop" and reprinted in *Writings*, I, 36-39; "Reflections on Titles" (May 1775, pp. 209-10) is signed "Vox Populi" and reprinted in *Writings*, I, 46-47; "Cursory Reflections on the Single Combat" (May 1775, pp. 226-29) is reprinted in *Writings*, I, 40-45; "The Dream Interpreted" (June, 1775, pp. 259-61) was sent in from Bucks county (from whence "R. S.," who praised the magazine, threatened to write—see April 1775, pp. 164-65), is reprinted in *Writings*, I, 48-50, but the attribution, it seems to me, may be doubtful; "Thoughts on Defensive War," by "A Lover of Peace" (July 1775, pp. 313-14) is reprinted in *Writings*, I, 55-58, as "probably" by Paine, and it is well to observe the caution; "An Occasional Letter on the Female Sex" (Aug. 1775, pp. 362-64) is reprinted in *Writings*, I, 59-64, but Mr. Frank Smith (see below) has proved this attribution unjustified; "The Old Bachelor," No. 2, containing a poem (April 1775, pp. 168-72) is listed among the poetical works in the *Writings*, IV, 484, and No. 4 of the series, containing reflections on unhappy marriages (June 1775, pp. 263-65) is listed with reservation in *Writings*, I, 51-54. Of the poetry only three pieces are signed "Atlanticus": "The Monk and the Jew" (March 1775, p. 137), in *Writings*, IV, 482-83; "Liberty Tree" (July 1775, pp. 328-29), reprinted in *Writings*, IV, 484-85, and "Farmer Short's Dog: Porter" (July 1775, pp. 331-32), reprinted in *Writings*, IV, 478-81. The other poems, unsigned but admitted by Conway, are "The Critic and Snow Drop" (Feb. 1775, p. 85), in *Writings*, IV, 481; and "Death of General Wolfe" (March 1775, p. 134), in *Writings*, IV, p. 477.

Mr. Frank Smith, "New Light on Thomas Paine's First Year in America" (*American Literature*, Jan. 1930, pp. 347-71) has greatly clarified the problem of Paine's contributions, proving a number of Conway's surmises. He has pointed out that in the two-volume edition of Paine's works published by James Carey in 1797, Aitken designated the following pieces in *The Pennsylvania Magazine* as having been written by Paine: "Description of a New Electrical Machine," "A New Method of Building Frame Houses in England" (April 1775), the introduction to *The Pennsylvania Magazine*, "To the Publisher on the Utility of Magazines," "Useful and Entertaining Hints on the Internal Riches of the Colonies," "New Anecdotes of Alexander the Great," "The Critic and the Snowdrop," "An Account of the Burning of Bachelor's Hall ("The Old Bachelor" No. 2), "Liberty Tree," "The Farmer's Dog Porter." From the London edition of 1819 of Paine's works Smith adds "A Mathematical Question Proposed," in the magazine for June, 1775, and "Cupid and Hymen." From Rush's letter of July 17, 1809, to Cheetham, Smith adds "The Death of General Wolfe" and "Reflections on the Life and Death of

Paine's service to the magazine, aside from his general editorial point of view and his interest in science, lies in his iconoclasm, florid prose style, fancy, romanticism, militant democracy, and a solid, plebeian humor which, though often coarse, was fundamentally sound. For "Useful and Entertaining Hints," in which he indulged the fancy that earth hides her luxuries underground, being prodigal only of those gifts she can annually recreate, he engaged a sentimental style as choice of its type and period as it is mannered. Satiric fantasy conceived "New Anecdotes of Alexander the Great," who, in the realm beyond the Styx, assumed in the eyes of the writer the aspects of a horse, dung, and a bug; and in style the essay is a good example of the type of the earlier William Smith and the later Washington Irving: "In one of those calm and gloomy days, which have a strange effect in disposing the mind to pensiveness, I quitted the busy town and withdrew into the country. As I passed towards the Schuylkill, my ideas enlarged with the prospect, and sprung from place to place with an agility for which nature hath not a simile."[87] Still more mannered is the style of "Reflections on the Life and Death of Lord Clive," which employs dramatic scenes not unlike the method of Carlyle, though more oratorical and less trenchant, lacking that " certain magnitude" found in great works.

The lesser pieces which Conway and Smith have ascribed to Paine establish in the magazine the thought of the man in several aspects: "Cupid and Hymen" portrays the virtues of romantic love as against marriages of convenience, especially in cases of great disparity in the ages of the contracting parties; "Reflections on Titles" asserts the democratic principle of individual worth; "Thoughts on Defensive War" entertains favorably the idea of a

Lord Clive"; and "The Monk and the Jew" is admitted because the pseudonym "Atlanticus" is attached to it. Smith has accepted provisionally other titles admitted by Conway, together with new titles, as follows: "Duelling" or "Cursory Reflections on the Single Combat," "Reflections on Titles," "The Dream Interpreted," "Reflections on Unhappy Marriages," "Thoughts on Defensive War," "A Whimsical Anecdote of the Late Duke of Newcastle" (Oct. 1775), "The Dying Negro" (Jan. 1776), the last two being unsigned. In a subsequent article (*American Literature*, Nov. 1930, pp. 277-80), Smith proved that "An Occasional Letter on the Female Sex" was not written by Paine, but was taken from the preface to Antoine Léonard Thomas's *Essay on the Character, Manners, and Genius of Women in Different Ages*, as translated by Russell; so that "Except as editor of the magazine, he [Paine] had no hand in the matter at all."

[87] Feb. 1775, p. 61.

state of world disarmament, but insists on preparedness until such a time when universal agreement can be attained; and "Cursory Reflections on the Single Combat" mocks the lip-service of Christians engaging in duels.

Just how many numbers of "The Old Bachelor" series[88] were written by Paine, and how many were contributed by Hopkinson and others, cannot be definitely told. Conway has credited Paine with the second and fourth at least.[89] The series rose to no distinction, however; the rough, irascible bachelor of fifty odd years never became vitalized in the imaginations of his creators. But it is interesting to note that the earlier numbers are less refined than the later ones modified by the hand of Hopkinson, and that among these the third is perhaps the most interesting. In this essay the author used servants for his characters and was able to draw upon a literary background established by the novelists of his century.

Dr. John Witherspoon was one of the "promoters" of the magazine along with his "compatriot and protégé," Aitken,[90] and with Paine, toward whom he at first entertained a "sympathy."[91] Witherspoon became the outstanding contributor on social, moral, educational, and political subjects, and on occasion wrote articles on science.[92] Some of these essays, the "Letters on Educa-

[88] This series appeared during 1775-76: No. 1 (March 1775, pp. 111-13), No. 2 (April, p. 168), No. 3 (May, pp. 213-15), No. 4 (June, pp. 263-65), "Consolation for the Old Bachelor" (June, pp. 254-57) by "A. B." (Francis Hopkinson's first, probably), No. 5 (July, pp. 311-12), No. 6 (Oct., pp. 455-57), No. 7 (Nov., pp. 511-13), No. 8 (Dec., pp. 551-54), "To the Bachelor" (Jan. 1776, pp. 28-32) by "Aspasia," No. 9 (April, pp. 177-80), "To the Old Bachelor" (June, pp. 267-68).

[89] See note 86.

[90] For quoted words, see Varnum Lansing Collins, *President Witherspoon. A Biography* (1925), I, 199. Witherspoon (1723-94) was born in Scotland, and received his licensure from the University of Edinburgh in 1743. In 1768, when already a well-known writer and divine, he came to America to become president of the College of New Jersey, which office he held until his death. In 1776 he was a member of the Constitutional Convention of New Jersey, and for six years was a member of the Continental Congress.

[91] For quotation, see Collins, *op. cit.*, I, 199. Later, in 1777, when John Adams nominated Paine for secretary to the Committee on Foreign Relations, Witherspoon objected, saying that he knew Paine well, that originally he had been pro-English, and that, although he was now anti-British, he was very intemperate and "could not write 'until he had quickened his thoughts with large draughts of rum and water. . . .'" (*Ibid.*, II, 25-26). In reference to the early pro-English attitude of Paine, William Jay reported (*The Life of John Jay*, 1833, I, 97) that Paine, while editing the magazine, had "struck out several passages in papers composed by Dr. Witherspoon, as being too free."

[92] "The Druid" series of three numbers appeared in the issues for May, June, and July, 1776, pp. 205-09, 253-57, 301-05. These were reprinted in *The Pennsyl-*

tion,"[93] offering sound counsel to parents on sane living and rational conduct toward children, had been written some time before while in Scotland, but were "wholly original."[94] The decision to print this series may possibly have been hastened by the fact that Hopkinson,

---

vania Journal of Feb. 14, March 14, and March 21, 1781, and four new papers added (Collins *op. cit.*, I, 200). The seven were included later in *The Works of the Rev. John Witherspoon* (1802), IV, 425-75. The basic idea of "The Druid" No. 3, and the thirteenth lecture, "Of the Law of Nature and Nations" (*Works*, 1802, III, 439-45) is the same, as Collins has pointed out in his edition of Witherspoon's *Lectures on Moral Philosophy* (1912), pp. 99-109. The "Letters on Education" appeared in the issues of April-June, Set. 1775, pp. 149-53, 197-202, 245-49, 399-405, and Jan. 1776, pp. 9-15. The first was signed "X. Y.," but the second, which admits authorship of the first, and all the succeeding numbers were signed "Epaminondas," Witherspoon's most frequently used pseudonym in the magazine. They were reprinted in the *Works* (1802), III, 125-59, and several other publishers reprinted them also, even *The American Museum* including them among its pirated treasury; see Collins's bibliography appended to *President Witherspoon*. The "Reflections on Marriage" appeared in the issues of Sept. and Dec. 1775, p. 408-13 and 543-48, and March 1776, pp. 109-14, and were signed "Epaminondas." Replies by Witherspoon to letters received from interested readers of the articles were printed in the issues of Dec. 1775, pp. 557-59 and July 1776, pp. 319-23. The "Reflections," but not the replies, were reprinted in the *Works* (1802), IV, 161-83, and likewise by several other publishers; see Collins's bibliography noted above. The "Dialogue on Civil Liberty" (April 1776, pp. 157-67), was not signed; the ideas, however, appear in partial form in the twelfth lecture, "Of Civil Society," in Collins's edition of Witherspoon's *Lectures*, pp. 87-99, and Collins notes (p. 99n) that the "Dialogue," which was delivered by students at Nassau Hall in January 1776, was revised, if not actually prepared, by Witherspoon. Three other essays, lighter in nature than the foregoing, can be identified by the pseudonym of "Epaminondas": "A Comparison of the Passions of Pride and Vanity" (Jan. 1775, pp. 12-15), "A Letter from Epaminondas" on "firmness and obstinacy" (March 1775, pp. 115-19), and "On Public Speaking" (June 1775, pp. 262-63); the first is unsigned, but the second and third carry the pseudonym, and the second owns the authorship of the first in a reference. They are not in the edition of his *Works* (1802). One scientific article, at least, in the magazine, signed "J. W.," was written by Witherspoon, "A Few Thoughts on Space, Dimension, and the Divisibility of Matter in Infinitum" (May 1776, pp. 225-29), written in support of and addition to ideas advanced by Matthew Wilson in "A Proposal for Reducing Natural Philosophy to a System," which had appeared in the magazine the previous March, pp. 123-28; Witherspoon's article attacked a part of Newton's law of gravitation, and an unknown correspondent, who signed himself as "R." replied in support of Newton (June 1776, pp. 282-83). One poem, "On the Death of a Young Lady," dated from Philadelphia (Aug. 1775, p. 373), is signed by the initials "J. W.," but I know of no other evidence which possibly relates it to Witherspoon.

[93] For this and other titles of articles by Witherspoon, see note 92.

[94] April 1775, p. 149. The first letter, dated Oct. 2, 1765, is very general in its remarks. The second and third assert the necessity of employing servants who will not teach children disloyalty to parents, of gaining discipline without blows or exhibitions of passion, and of controlling the conduct of adults. The fourth and fifth declare the virtue of friendship and religion.

in March 1775, had opened the general topic with "A New Plan of Education."[95] But usually Witherspoon's articles were written specifically for the magazine. It is worth conjecturing, in this connection, that his "Reflections on Marriage" might never have been written had "The Old Bachelor" series not displeased him. The bachelor, in belittling marriage, had been rather more vulgar than witty, and although Witherspoon referred sadly to *The Spectator* as an erring case in point, he lectured broadly against all articles discouraging marriage, however facetiously they might be conceived. Then, surveying the subject of marriage and literature from another angle, he attacked the sentimental love stories current at the time for stressing physical beauty and painting impassioned or romantic scenes more affected than real.[96] In "The Druid" series Witherspoon concerned himself with the political conflict between Great Britain and the Colonies. As he was only eight years removed from the mother country, he often indulged a tendency to reflect in a personal way upon the crisis. The magazine had been remarkably temperate, but by May 1776, when "The Druid" first wrote, war was clearly seen to be inevitable. The writer first reviewed his condition in the world: a man in late middle life, born in Great Britain, long resident at one of its major seats of learning, and long engaged in public business, now found himself settled of his own choice in America, where he was likely to remain until his death. He loved both England and America. He was grieved at the displays of ignorance, prejudice, and malice between the two countries, and hoped they were only temporary aberrations. Yet he was ready to acknowledge that "When liberty, property, and life are at stake, we must not think of being scholars but soldiers."[97] In the second number, replying to appeals for him to assert his loyalty to America, he sanctioned the uprising and outlined a fair manner of carrying on the war; while in the third he turned his thoughts to a contemplation of

---

[95] March 1775, pp. 101-04.

[96] Witherspoon undertook also in the articles to point out conditions which might lead to unhappy marriages, including hastiness in choosing a spouse, lack of good health, and variability in rank, education, or taste. He believed the chief cause of failures to enjoy a happy state of matrimony was due to a lack of care in choosing mates, men erring in this manner more frequently; and he felt constrained to emphasize, too, his opinion that a delicate physique was no asset, thus inferring that many sought to attain a sylph-like figure.

[97] May 1776, p. 208.

civil wars. It is interesting to note that when the series was re-printed in *The Pennsylvania Journal* in 1781,[98] he found it un-necessary to alter the three numbers in any way.[99] Not only "The Druid," but the series on education and the series on marriage were later reprinted, the latter two more than once;[100] no other such mass of material written by one man for original printing in an American magazine had yet enjoyed this distinction. Witherspoon contributed other essays to the magazine also,[101] but they were not, so far as I know, reprinted; and of these only the "Dialogue on Civil Society" deserves more than a passing regard.

To Francis Hopkinson, who wrote half facetiously to Aitken that he wished to be "an Author of some sort,"[102] *The Pennsyl-vania Magazine* offered again an opportunity to employ his gentle humor as a poet and essayist, and no American writer of the time responded more to the stimulus of the presence of literary peri-odicals. Not only poetry—new, old, and revised—but the prose essay was assiduously cultivated, as Hastings has shown.[103] He

[98] See note 92.

[99] However, a new strain of thought ran through the four added numbers, the fifth, sixth, and seventh dealing with grammar and philology.

[100] See note 92.

[101] *Ibid.*

[102] See magazine issue of Jan. 1775, p. 15.

[103] To Hastings's carefully selected list of titles of the writings of Hopkinson ap-pearing in the magazine (*op. cit.*, 184-91, 476-77), hereinafter described, may I add the almost certain essay on "The True Value of Crosses and Afflictions" (Oct. 1775, pp. 467-70), signed "C. Philomenes," the very possible "Vulgar Errors Recti-fied" (Nov. 1775, pp. 503-06), signed "C.," the "Description of a New Machine for Enabling Persons to Escape from the Windows of Houses on Fire" (Dec. 1775, pp. 554-57), signed "C. A. B.," and perhaps "Arabella's Complaint of the Con-gress" (Sept. 1775, pp. 407-08), signed "C." All these bear signatory devices known to have been used by Hopkinson in the magazine.

The following prose pieces have been definitely proved by Hastings (*op. cit.*, pp. 184-91) to have been written by Hopkinson; they appear either in *The Miscellaneous Essays and Occasional Writings of Francis Hopkinson, Esq.*, (1792), or in the Huntington Collection of Hopkinson manuscripts. Titles below carrying asterisks may also be found in the three volumes of manuscript material of Hopkinson's works I have examined in the library of the American Philosophical Society, at Philadel-phia. "Extraordinary Dream" together with an accompanying letter,* signed "A. B." (Jan. 1775, pp. 15-19)—the "Dream" was criticized in the magazine by "N. T. R." (Nov. 1775, pp. 513-17) and defended by "C. A. B.," most probably Hopkinson himself (Dec. 1775, pp. 560-61)—; "A New Plan of Education," by "A. B." (March 1775, pp. 101-04); "On the Late Continental Fast" (July 1775, pp. 309-10); "Con-solation for the Old Bachelor,"* by "A. B." (June 1775, pp. 254-57); "Affectation Instanced in a Variety of Characters," by "C. Philomenes" (Aug. 1775, pp. 343-46); "Humorous Incidents Occasioned by the Ambiguity of the English Language,"* by "A. B." (Oct. 1775, pp. 460-63); "The Old Bachelor No. VI,"* by "C." (Oct.

was to become fully as successful in prose as in verse, tutoring himself with *The Spectator, The Tatler, The Guardian* and their ilk. His first essay in the magazine, an "Extraordinary Dream,"[104] presented an elaborate picture of a garden wherein departments had been marked off for Religion, Law, Painting and Poetry and Music, Logic, Physics, and Natural Philosophy and Astronomy; and the author commented on the various states of repair and development of each of the departments. Especially interesting is his comment on poetry, as it contains a reference to Shakespeare; in general, Hopkinson thought that the glories of ancient poetry could not be matched by the moderns, though one, Shakespeare, had "cultivated here a few flowers and evergreens." Once again Hopkinson employed the vision type of essay in the magazine, creeping into the mind of a miser to expose its base reflections in "A Revery."

In prose, Hopkinson is best known for his allegories, to which kind of work his vision essays belong. But he did not limit himself either in subject matter or form, though often his essays, including those I have added to Hastings's list of possibilities, are slight in import.[105] In other essays, however, he proved himself able to handle character with considerable sureness of touch, and he practised this art in *The Pennsylvania Magazine*. In "Consolation for the Old Bachelor" two characters emerge on a story-trail stretching from Philadelphia to New York: a wife whose domineering quali-

---

1775, pp. 455-57); "The Bachelor No. VIII,"* by "C." (Dec. 1775, pp. 551-54); "Considerations on the Use and Abuse of Mottos [*sic*],"* by "A. B." ("Supplement" for 1775, pp. 587-89); "A Revery,"* by "C. A. B." (April 1776, pp. 186-88).

The following poems have been positively identified by Hastings (*op. cit.*, pp. 184-91). "The Nest," by "A. B." (June 1775, p. 279); "The Wasp," by "C. A. B." (Aug. 1775, pp. 372-73); "To Celia on her Wedding Day," by "C. A. B" (Oct. 1775, p. 480); "A Riddle," by "C. A. B." (Oct. 1775, p. 481); "A Riddle," (Nov. 1775, p. 527); "A Morning Ode," by "C. A. B." (Nov. 1775, p. 526); "An Answer to a Riddle in the Last Magazine, by a Lady," (Nov. 1775, p. 527); "An Evening Hymn," by "C. A. B." (Dec. 1775, p. 576); "An Answer to the Riddle in the November Magazine," by "Eudocia" (Jan. 1776, p. 41).

The following prose and poetry have been cited by Hastings, (*op. cit.*, pp. 475-77), as having something to suggest Hopkinson's authorship: "On Hearing the Rev. Mr. D.——é [Duché] on Good-Friday and Easter-Day," poem (June 1775, p. 280); "L'Allegro," (untitled) poem (Sept. 1775, pp. 429-30); "To Mr. Aken" (*sic*); being "Susannah Trapes's" letter urging a cleaner Front Street (Nov. 1775, pp. 510-11); "To Eudocia, An Ode," by "A. B." (Dec. 1775, pp. 575-76); "Scheme for Taxing the Colonies in 1754," by "A. B." (March 1776, pp. 133-34); "An Account of a Remarkable Fish," by "C. A. B." (May 1776, pp. 212-13).

104 For this and other titles by Hopkinson, see note 103.

105 For the additions, see note 103.

ties are matched only by her gracelessness, and a wife-dominated husband whose sensitive but sunken features have been, in type, perennial in the books of the humorists and the galleries of caricaturists. He elevated the mood of "The Old Bachelor" in the sixth number of the series, and brought him, albeit by a threadbare device, to a state of love in the eighth number. The better to preach the virtues of civic cleanliness, he probably gave literary form to "Susannah Trapes." And in "Affectation Instanced in a Variety of Characters" he tried his ability to hold a fair number of characters in the confines of a single essay. Had he possessed more of invention and lived in America in an age less cribbed by the essay form and the essay types of characters, it is not unlikely he would have become a reasonably good novelist; he was at least on the verge of weaving literary substance by crossing threads of lives and events within a definite structure.

Matthew Wilson, like Hopkinson, was stimulated by the presence of magazines to write articles which otherwise never would have been done.[106] The energy of his pen made his home town, Lewes, Delaware, well known among readers of monthly periodicals; and as he was a minister, physician, teacher, and scholar of a kind, his contributions reveal a versatility of interest which *The Pennsylvania Magazine* reflected.[107] Inspired by patriotism and supported by medical knowledge, he attacked tea-drinking as both unpatriotic and injurious to health, and his knowledge of herbs enabled him to offer substitutes, including sassafras, red rose bush leaves, mistletoe and wild valerian, white oak leaves, golden rod

---

[106] He was born in Pennsylvania in 1731, and for a time was a student under Francis Alison at New Haven. As has been noted, he contributed to *The American Magazine, or Monthly Chronicle* of 1757-58, and his contributions to *The Pennsylvania Magazine* were succeeded by other articles appearing in later magazines. He died at Lewes, Del., in 1790. There is a sketch of his life by the Rev. Edward D. Neill, a copy of which is preserved among biographical pamphlets at the New York Public Library, but no attempt has ever been made to gather carefully his complete writings.

[107] "Substitutes for Tea," by "Philanthropist" (Feb. 1775, pp. 72-76); "The History of a Malignant Fever . . . in Sussex County, Delaware," by Matthew Wilson (April 1775, pp. 165-68); a report on a "Remarkable Instance of . . . Longevity," in which the writer discussed the harmful effects of tea, by "M. W." (July 1775, pp. 314-15); "A Fact Proposed to the Investigation of Philosophers," suggesting the possibility of the human body acting as a medium for sustaining young snakes, which might feed on the liver (Nov. 1775, p. 519); "A Proposal for Reducing Natural Philosophy to a System, with Remarks on the Cartesian and Newtonian Theories," by "M. W." (March and April 1776, pp. 123-28, 173-76).

and betony, and pepper and mint and yarrow[108]—but none of these, according to a story current at the time, would satisfy a visiting sister of Philadelphia, who carried her own supply of tea to his table and announced herself both patriot and drinker of the taxed beverage.[109] In science Wilson was often unfortunate in his opinions. Superstition was mingled with clear observation in his medical inquiries,[110] and in "A Proposal for Reducing Natural Philosophy to a System, with Remarks on the Cartesian and Newtonian Theories" not even the approbation of Witherspoon saved him from a rebuttal as convincing as the original proposal.[111]

Besides the work of the chief writers considered in the preceding section, *The Pennsylvania Magazine* printed a varied assortment of prose, often borrowed from English sources, which is of some literary, biographical, adventurous, commercial and scientific, and historical and political interest. Eighteenth-century "sensibility" appeared in several shades—sometimes in outright sentimentality, as in the letter by "Eliza" to her betrayer,[112] "The History of Amelia Gray,"[113] and "Mirtil and Thirsis";[114] sometimes amidst rather fanciful trappings of allegory, as in "The Dream of Irus";[115] and once, in "The Oracle,"[116] molded amidst the substance of a Greek near-tragedy. As Paine had remarked, the sentimental tale was being exploited in English magazines, and, chiefly through selections from the inexhaustible over-sea supply, America was growing used to the fare. But in main, *The Pennsylvania Magazine* inclined toward eighteenth-century "sense." The shears which clipped the philosophy of David Hume,[117] the historical observations of Lord Kames,[118] the homely expressions of Franklin's "Poor Richard Improved,"[119] critical and descriptive pieces by

---

[108] See especially "Substitutes for Tea," note 107.
[109] An Article in *The Delaware Register, and Farmers' Magazine* for Oct. 1838 relates this anecdote.
[110] See "A Fact Proposed," note 107.
[111] See note 107.
[112] March 1775, pp. 113-15.
[113] Jan. 1775, pp. 22-24.
[114] From the German; Aug. 1775, pp. 359-60.
[115] Feb. 1776, pp. 57-63.
[116] May 1776, pp. 216-24.
[117] June 1776, pp. 274-77.
[118] Jan. 1775, pp. 77-80.
[119] Sept. 1775, pp. 419-22.

Samuel Johnson,[120] and, an inscription to the memory of Tobias Smollett[121] were guided by a mind which did not reckon time by heart-throbs. Something besides sentimentality controlled the selection of biographical extracts and anecdotes surrounding such men as the Earl of Chesterfield,[122] John Churchill,[123] Archbishop Laud,[124] George Psalmanazar,[125] Voltaire,[126] and Robert Walpole.[127] And it was a somewhat adventurous editorial spirit which chose for reprinting the accounts of the shipwreck of Emanuel Crespel,[128] the experiences of Nathaniel Wraxal in northern Europe,[129] and Patrick Brydone's journey through Sicily and Malta.[130] In short, Aitken published a magazine which reflected well the many interests of his century.

Congressional action against the importation of British goods and a consciousness of the need of being self-sufficient in case of war gave an emphasis to the already strong sentiment for increasing the manufacturing power of the Colonies; and associated with this interest was the attention being given to science. As a publisher whose presses turned out publications on divers subjects, Aitken was situated amidst circumstances which kept his economic interests broad. Economic problems were discussed in the magazine in a number of articles, some of which were emphasized by engravings.[131] The formation of the United Company of Philadelphia for promoting American manufacturing was duly reported,[132] and Dr. Benjamin Rush's speech of March 16, 1775, before the subscribers of the Company, urging the production of woolen, cotton, and linen fabrics,[133] was given good space. The production of saltpetre and salt, to which were attached the names of Rush and

[120] A fairly long discourse on the epitaphs of Pope (April 1775, pp. 174-80), two extracts from Johnson's journey to the western islands of Scotland (May and June 1775, pp. 221-22, 274-75), and an extract on agriculture (Feb. 1775, pp. 69-70).

[121] By John Armstrong, Jan. 1775, p. 30.

[122] March 1775, pp. 120-21.

[123] June, July 1775, pp. 249-54, 300-03.

[124] June 1775, p. 258.

[125] May, June 1776, pp. 209-12, 257-59.

[126] Jan. 1775, pp. 19-20.

[127] Nov. 1775, p. 511.

[128] Feb., March, April, June, July 1776, pp. 69-73, 134-37, 180-84, 263-67, 312-18.

[129] Feb. 1776, pp. 81-89.

[130] Jan., Feb. 1775, pp. 35-37, 80-84.

[131] See note 83.

[132] March 1775, pp. 140-41.

[133] Oct. 1775, pp. 482-85.

Dr. William Brownrigg, was explained in detail, as it had been in previous and would be in future magazines.[134]   Flora and fauna were represented by excerpts from the hackwork of Oliver Goldsmith[135] and Bernard Romans's account of the natural history of East and West Florida.[136]

In common with the general practice of magazines, *The Pennsylvania Magazine* published each month a condensed account of the news of the world.[137]   Articles long since published were occasionally reprinted, when the sentiments suited the current spirit; it was fitting, for instance, to reprint "The Lawfulness of Defence Evinced," by one who had been nominally a Quaker, the late Judge Samuel Chew.[138]   But the usual pieces were born of the passing time, such as youthful academic expostulations,[139] matters surrounding George Washington,[140] Burgoyne,[141] Gage,[142] Colonial legislatures,[143] or the reports of battles fought.[144]   Considered in summary, the selected and casual articles, news digests, engravings by Aitken, and the work of the leading writers for the magazine make it of considerable importance as an agent to perpetuate the

[134] For Rush's article on saltpetre, see issue of June 1775, pp. 266-68; for another article on saltpetre, see issue of Aug. 1775, pp. 360-61. For Brownrigg's article on salt, see issue of March 1776, pp. 128-33; for another article on salt, see issue *ibid.*, p. 146.

[135] Sept. 1775, pp. 423-26.

[136] Jan. 1776, pp. 33-36.

[137] For engravings illustrating centers of military interest in Massachusetts and Canada, see note 83; for articles of military interest already mentioned, see note 81.

[138] Aug. 1775, pp. 346-53.

[139] William Moore Smith, "On the Fall of Empires," a commencement oration, May 1775, pp. 236-38.

[140] New England's address of welcome, with Washington's reply (April 1776, pp. 194-95); the Washington-Patterson interview concerning prisoners (July 1776, pp. 343-44); Washington-Gage correspondence concerning prisoners (Oct. 1775, pp. 486-88).

[141] Gen. John Burgoyne to Lord Stanley, regarding Massachusetts (Nov. 1775, pp. 528-29).

[142] Gen. Thomas Gage to Gov. Trumbull, of Connecticut, urging his influence in an attempt to persuade Massachusetts against hostilities (May 1775, pp. 234-35).

[143] See, for example, the Governor of Virginia's presentation of North's conciliatory plan to the Assembly, and the Assembly's rejection of it (June 1775, pp. 282-84).

[144] Lexington (April 1775, pp. 189-92), Bunker Hill (June 1775, pp. 284-85, misnumbered 287), Louisburg and Ticonderoga (July 1775, pp. 310-11, 315-17); interest in Canadian campaigns lay back of a descriptive and historical article on Montreal and Quebec (Nov., Dec., and "Supplement" for 1775, pp. 517-18, 563-66, 604-08).

mood and temper of those who were loyal to the American interest but of a conservative type of mind.[145]

Very little poetry of high importance by English writers was printed, for *The Pennsylvania Magazine* did not often reach backward for material, and the current English periodicals and the pens of a fair number of native contributors supplied an adequate amount of copy. Yet both in manner and matter the magazine was equal to the years of its century. It held poetic criticism in sufficient esteem to publish not only Johnson's remarks on Pope's epitaphs,[146] but also some considerations of John Hughes on harmony in English verse[147] and "Remarks on Epithets," by "E. S.," the latter a definite contributor to the magazine who, using examples from lines by Pope, Thomson, Goldsmith, and Milton, reasoned in accord with the school of precise diction of his century and declared that "a race of synonymous epithets gives no beauty either to prose or poetry."[148] Probably the recent death of Goldsmith was the occasion for including "Retaliation"[149] (together with his portrait) and an extract from "The Tears of Genius,"[150] in memory of Goldsmith, Gray, Young, Shenstone, and others. But other among the greater English names were attached to very short pieces. Smollett's "Ode to Independence"[151] was appropriate enough for July 1776, but Swift was more honored by imitation[152] than by his own "Description of Dr. Dellany's Villa."[153] The name of Pope was accorded a place only by virtue of a Philadelphian's parody of "Ode to Solitude";[154] perennial interest in "The

[145] Despite the wide selection of clipped material, it is interesting to note that Aitken failed to include excerpts from a number of publications which were of importance in his time as well as today; *e.g.*, the second edition of the works of John Woolman, Mrs. Mercy Warren's *The Group, a Farce*, and John Trumbull's *M'Fingal*, all of which were published at Philadelphia in 1775, and may presumably have been known to him. Aitken was inclined to choose from among his own imprints.

[146] See note 120.

[147] March 1775, pp. 125-27.

[148] April 1775, pp. 155-57; the quotation is from p. 156. "Epithets" was used to designate modifying words, particularly those used adjectivally.

[149] Jan. 1775, pp. 42-45. Goldsmith died in 1774.

[150] *Ibid.*, pp. 37-38.

[151] July 1776, pp. 325-27.

[152] "The Sale," in imitation (July 1775, p. 332).

[153] May 1775, p. 231.

[154] Aug. 1775, p. 373.

Happy Life" alone bought a place for Sir Henry Wotton;[155] and Anna Laetitia Aikin was the sole one among the group who ranked with Goldsmith in amount of space yielded—and this honor had been less had her publications not been recent.[156]

Among the Colonial writers of some importance, representative poems of four appear: Hopkinson, Paine, Phillis Wheatley, and Mrs. Elizabeth Graeme Fergusson; others may be hidden in anonymity. Mrs. Fergusson supplied an "Ode to Spring," and Miss Wheatley's pen is exhibited only in one uncontributed piece, her "Letter and Verses . . . to his Excellency Gen. Washington," which through association has become, with the possible exception of Paine's "Death of General Wolfe," the most noted of the several eulogies to men of some renown printed in the magazine.[157] Paine's song in honor of Wolfe,[158] set to music, stands along with his "Liberty Tree"[159] as the best lyrical expression of this man of prose. Some of the poems he inserted in the magazine, among them "The Monk and the Jew" and "Farmer Short's Dog: Porter," he had written under a stimulus to entertain his cronies of the *Headstrong Book* group of the White Hart inn at Lewes, England.[160] The two mentioned are narratives which turn on sturdy but crude points of humor, and belong to a type which, often indulging a love for fable, maintained a place in the period,

[155] March 1776, p. 146.

[156] June and July 1775, pp. 273-74, 327-28. Her *Poems* appeared in 1773, and *Miscellaneous Pieces in Prose*, written jointly with her brother, was issued in the same year.

[157] For Mrs. Fergusson's poem, see issue for April 1776, p. 191; for identification of the pseudonym, "Laura," I am indebted to Mr. C. T. Hallenbeck, of Columbia University. Miss Wheatley's poem appeared in the issue for April 1776, p. 193. Others of interest include anonymous poems to Thomas Penn (Oct. 1775, p. 479), Jacob Cheesman (March 1776, pp. 143-45), and Benjamin Franklin, for his electrical discoveries (May 1776, pp. 233-34).

[158] For this and all subsequent titles by Paine, see note 86.

[159] The first stanza reads:

> "In a chariot of light from the regions of day,
>   The Goddess of Liberty came;
> Ten thousand celestials directed the way,
>   And hither conducted the dame.
> A fair budding branch from the gardens above,
>   Where millions with millions agree,
> She brought in her hand, as a pledge of her love,
>   And the plant she named, *Liberty Tree*."

(July 1775, pp. 328-29).

[160] See Conway, *Life*, I, 25.

and are to be met with elsewhere in the magazine.[161]   Though they deserve short comment in themselves, they carried the spirit of the race which had built ballads and stag hornbooks with glorious recklessness, and they usurped a few pages which might otherwise have been devoted to Delia, Sylvia, and their sisters.   Hopkinson, like Paine, reached back into the past for a number of his most pleasing poems when the opportunity came to publish them in the magazine:[162] especially among the group should be noted "To Celia on her Wedding Day," "The Nest," "To Eudocia," and an imitation of "L'Allegro"—four fancifully light but sincere poems with sentiments neatly turned—and the more solemn endeavors of "A Morning Hymn,"[163] and "An Evening Hymn."   As a whole, his poetical contributions, though outstanding among the offerings of the magazine, reflect the Hopkinson of the period of William Smith's *The American Magazine* of 1757-58, and do not reveal, as does his prose, a growing command of his art.

The magazine was fortunate, in a comparative sense, in being able to act as a polarizing agent for the poetic urge of a number of anonymous contributors whose efforts in verse are laudatory examples among the mass of vicarious material submitted by the general public.   Among these poems there is a variety in structural forms which is pleasing to contemplate.   The attitudes and subject matter are sharply limited and undistinguished, as they are in most popular productions, but the manners of expression are commendable and supported by a certain imitative dexterity in craft and a fair degree of popular wit or moral earnestness.

Philadelphians were the most sensitive to the opportunity for publishing.   "Amanda" wrote only in one mood of religious peace and contentment, but her art was comparatively schooled and delicate.[164]   A "Clergyman" of the city wrote on the same theme with

[161] For strictly sedate fables, see "The Two Peacocks," by "T. W.," of Philadelphia (June 1775, p. 279), "Jove and the Farmer," by "I. W." (Feb. 1775, p. 86), and "The Sheep and the Bramble-Bush," by John Cunningham—a reprint (Jan. 1776, pp. 42-43).

[162] For complete list with page references, see note 103, third paragraph.

[163] Hastings (*op. cit.*, p. 189) refers briefly to this poem as being "republished" from Smith's *The American Magazine*. It is worth noting that the later form varied greatly from the first, being reduced from twelve to nine stanzas, with lines altered, transposed, and omitted, and new ideas introduced.

[164] "Poem on Christmas Day" (Jan. 1775, pp. 41-42), and an untitled poem (Feb. 1775, p. 86), from which the following stanza is quoted to indicate her mood:
"Oh lead me to some humble cell,
Where innocence with peace does dwell

equal power in "A Hymn to Resignation."[165] "Delia," a true conventional moralist in verse, to whom love in gentle bosoms seemed to burn "Like lamps plac'd near sepulchral urns," sang not unmeetly of charity and tender passion.[166] "J. W.," in "On the Death of a Young Lady," summoned the aid of an internal dramatic monologue in pastoral machinery to offer sentimental lament indited with a fervency that lacked only creative capacity.[167] More ambitious yet was "The Teacher's Birth-Day," containing three recitatives and three airs, which chanted introspectively of religious ardor and a sincere moral attitude of helpfulness.[168] "T. W." contributed with some regularity, but he was more ambitious than gifted, and when he was not engaged in narrative, his poems were too full of sentimentality, or of bombast in shaky imitation of Lear's desolate agony, to be exhibited favorably among their peers.[169] From outside the city came a thinner stream, some of which is commendable. One would not lose, for instance, "A Hymn to Monimia" on her leaving the author, in which four-foot lines are well handled by a Marylander in the complicated riming structure of *ababccdeed*;[170] while from New York came excellent light verses "To S——y W——n."[171]

Certain themes and materials among the poems catch the attention of the historical chronologer. Through "Hermes," the magazine was able to continue the custom of offering classics in translation. The odes of Anacreon were his problem, which he

---

And rose-lipp'd sweet content;
There smiles shall cheer the frugal meal
And I shall greater pleasure feel
Than those on wealth intent."

[165] Jan. 1775, p. 45.

[166] "Ode to Charity" (Feb. 1775, p. 87); "To a Young Lady" (April 1775, p. 183), from which the quotation is taken.

[167] Aug. 1775, p. 373. The initials are those of John Witherspoon, a frequent prose contributor, but I know of no other evidence to support this suggestion.

[168] April 1775, pp. 181-82. The author was a Philadelphian who was born on a January 27.

[169] "The Two Peacocks," a farce (June 1775, p. 279); "Hopeless Love," an elegy imitative of Lear's speech (Nov. 1775, pp. 525-26); "Elegy on the Death of Phibba," a cook (Jan. 1776, p. 42).

[170] May 1775, p. 230.

[171] Jan. 1776, p. 43. The following lines are typical:
"From her rural retreat the goddess of wit,
Like a bee from the lawn hath return'd:
Her friends that surround her, soon will forget:
How they in her absence have mourn'd;".

introduced with a preface indicative of his own limitations, as he hoped he had "given them such a *paraphrase* as . . . would preserve his principal *beauties*, without retaining his *blameable* levities."[172]   Sentiment against cruelty may be traced in an extract from "The Dying Negro,"[173] and again in "Cruelty to Animals Exposed,"[174] the latter poem being dated from Philadelphia. Finally, the shadows of war and the actual repercussions of battle brought an assortment of poetry both good and bad.   On occasion, as in "The Irishman's Epistle to the Officers and Troops of Boston," celebrating the British retreat from Concord, a rough, rollicking humor was admitted into the magazine which never would have appeared associated with any other theme.[175]   Concord, too, was treated in a serious manner by "Sylvia," of Philadelphia, who saw crimson slaughter followed by famine, with pleasure, hope, and love decaying, and mercy bowing her head.[176]   Other poems bore this burden of mood.   Phoebe, a character in "A New Song" of love and war, was less thoughtful than "Sylvia," for she would love only "Who saves himself and me" by going to war, and thus gave an added motive for Colinet's departure to the field.[177]   Typical, also, were poems seeking to rationalize the passing scene, as "A Song on the Times,"[178] and others, too, in which the patriotic emotions were old enough to be tinged with earlier nexus, as the "Ode to the British Empire."[179]

III

The United States Magazine, issuing from Philadelphia, illuminates but the single year 1779, from January through December;

[172] For the preface and Odes Nos. 37, 3, 20, 23, 39, 19, see issues of April, May, and July 1776, pp. 189-91, 232-33, 327.   For another example of a translation, see "Juvenis's" Fifteenth Ode of Horace (June 1776, p. 288).

[173] Jan. 1776, pp. 36-38.

[174] May 1775, pp. 231-32.

[175] *Ibid.*, p. 232.   The following quotation is indicative of the spirit of the time:

> "How brave you went out with your muskets all bright,
> And thought to befrighten the folks with the sight;
> But when you got there how they powder'd your pums,
> And all the way home how they pepper'd your bums,
> And is it not, honies, a comical farce,
> To be proud in the face, and be shot in the a——se."

[176] "An Elegy to the Memory of the American Volunteers" (June 1775, pp. 278-79).

[177] Feb. 1776, pp. 89-90.

[178] April 1776, pp. 192-93.

[179] June 1776, pp. 285-87.

indeed, after August its fine fervor of the earlier months begins to wane, for the engaging editorial visions of Hugh Henry Brackenridge needed the substance of financial support which did not materialize. And yet the editor gave to his journal a strong, individualized tone which, augmented by the interest attached to the militant year of its publication, makes the magazine more vital than earlier ones which were edited with the assistance of several persons and enjoyed a longer life.

Brackenridge's occupancy of the new editorial chair was a fitting culmination to the decade of his twenties, for the journal reflects many of the interests and friendships of his college and early post-college years. In early life he had enjoyed few of the advantages of those whose families were in more fortunate circumstances,[180] but he managed to attend the College of New Jersey, where he came to know its president, John Witherspoon, and, among other students, Philip Morin Freneau, William Bradford, Jr., and James Madison, all of whom save Madison later contributed to the magazine. His patriotic emotions were centered in the Colonies, and, possessed of a love of poetry, he wrote as his Commencement exercise, in conjunction with his friend Freneau, "A Poem, on the Rising Glory of America," which was delivered in September 1771 and published by Aitken the following year. He became a tutor and student of divinity at his *alma mater*, and the urge to write being still strong within him, he expressed his literary proclivities in an ambitious theological poem published in 1774. His training was molded on the classics, including Greek tragedy and plays in the grand manner of Dryden; and the battle of Bunker Hill and the death of General Montgomery fired him to write two poetic dramas cast in the shape and mood of heroic tragedy, which were published in 1776 and 1777. Religion and war then mingled in the current of his life, and there came from his pen six political discourses based on Scripture, which he delivered before Revolutionary soldiers and later published at the press of Francis Bailey, at Lancaster, in 1778. His publications now numbered five, the

---

[180] The family had emigrated from Scotland to York County, Pa., when Hugh was five years of age. A biographical sketch has been written by his son, H. M. Brackenridge, which is attached to some editions of *Modern Chivalry*. A misleading statement in this account has confused E. A. and G. L. Duyckinck and others as to the date of the magazine. See *Modern Chivalry* (Getz and Buck, 1851), II, 153, (pp. 151-89 containing the biography).

last being issued by the man who would soon undertake the publishing of *The United States Magazine*.[181] In the spring of 1778 Brackenridge advertised that he had "opened an Academy at Frederick-Town, Maryland," and that school exercises would begin "the first Day of June next,"[182] but the academy soon gave way to the more congenial work of editing. The printers who had abandoned Philadelphia during the British occupation had now returned, and in January 1779, when the magazine was first being printed, the city was supporting three newspapers. During 1778 Francis Bailey, who had learned the printing trade in Ephrata Colony, decided to move his printing office from Lancaster to Philadelphia. The transfer was accomplished in the fall of the year, and the succeeding year he commenced *Freeman's Journal*.[183] It must have been approximately at the time the shift was accomplished that he and Brackenridge determined to publish the magazine, and arranged that the new enterprise should be under the control of the latter, leaving Bailey free to attend to the newspaper and other printing.

The first number of *The United States Magazine* was advertised for sale in Hall and Sellers's *The Pennsylvania Gazette and Weekly Advertiser* of February 10, 1779, but received less publicity than any major magazine preceding it.[184] The announcement stated that the journal was "This day" published, indicated several of the more important articles, asked for the "favours of the Ingenious," and established a first-month price scale of three dollars the single copy, two and one-half dollars the copy in lots of twelve, and two dollars a copy for those who advanced twenty-four dollars; the price for the future, it was announced, would rise or fall with the prices of other articles and commodities in general.

---

[181] *A Poem, on the Rising Glory of America* (Robert Aitken, 1772); *A Poem on Divine Revelation* (Robert Aitken, 1774); *The Battle of Bunkers-Hill* (Robert Bell, 1776); *The Death of General Montgomery* (Robert Bell, 1777); *Six Political Discourses Founded on the Scripture* (Francis Bailey, 1778).

[182] *The Pennsylvania Gazette* (published at Yorktown, May 2, 1778). H. M. Brackenridge wrote that his father left Frederick-Town in 1777 to publish a magazine in Philadelphia; this is a somewhat misleading statement. See note 180.

[183] William McCulloch, *Proceedings of the American Antiquarian Society* (April 1921, p. 103), in a letter to Thomas.

[184] *The Pennsylvania Gazette* alone of the three Philadelphia papers advertised the magazine. The advertisement was repeated in the issue of Feb. 17. The issue of the magazine for February was advertised in the same paper of March 3, and the March issue in the issues of April 7 and 14; thereafter announcements ceased.

Three introductory articles by Brackenridge in the first number, and a valedictory in the last, serve as indices of his editorial craft and policies. Incidentally, too, they reveal the wavering hand of maladroit youth now writing with modesty, now delighting to exhibit academic learning, now defiantly egotistic as he conquers his fears or explains his failures. In his "Preface,"[185] which he introduced with a quotation from Cicero, he complimented the public on the good taste it undoubtedly would show in supporting the magazine, defended the price as most reasonable, and assured England that independent Americans would not become "Ouran—Outans" lacking culture, for indeed there were some "*d-mn'd* good writers" among them. "It was the language of our enemies," he wrote, "at the commencement of the debate between America and what is called the mother-country, that in righteous judgment for our wickedness, it would be well to leave us to that independency which we seemed to affect, and to suffer us to sink down to so many Ouran-Outans of the wood, lost to the light of science which, from the other side of the Atlantic, had just begun to break upon us. They have been made to see, and even to confess the vanity of this kind of *auguration*. The British officers who are, some of them, men of understanding, on perusal of our pamphlets in the course of the debate, and the essays and dissertations in the news-papers, have been forced to acknowledge, not without chagrin, that the rebels, as they are pleased to call us, had some *d-mn'd* good writers on their side of the question, and that we had fought them no less successfully with the pen than with the sword. We hope to convince them yet more fully, that we are able to cultivate the *belles-lettres*, even disconnected with Great-Britain; and that liberty is of so noble and energetic a quality, as even from the bosom of a war to call forth the powers of human genius, in every course of literary fame and improvement."

In the "Introduction"[186] Brackenridge became the first of American magazine editors to advertise his journal as a short cut to culture and learning of a profitable nature.[187] "The honest hus-

---

[185] Jan. 1779, pp. 3-4.

[186] Jan. 1776, pp. 9-11.

[187] The usual advantages were also presented, the statement reading in part: "It will contain writings of the sage historian; it will convey the thoughts, remarks, proposals, theories and reasonings of the politician; it will collect the genuine letters of the hero; it will communicate the observations of the curious traveller; it will

bandman who reads this publication," he asserted, "will rapidly improve in every kind of knowledge. He will be shortly capable to arbitrate the differences that may arise amongst his neighbours. He will be qualified to be a Magistrate. He will appear a proper person to be appointed Sheriff in his county. He will be equal to the task of legislation. He will be capable of any office to which the gale of popularity amongst his countrymen may raise him." And in the fourth article, a "Letter to the Poets, Philosophers, Orators, Statesmen and Heroes of Antiquity,"[188] the editor indicated his definite editorial aspirations, for he solicited contributions from certain essayists who were appearing in print under various pseudonyms, some of which had been selected from among illustrious ancients. "Junius," "Lycurgus," "Hampden," "Solon," "Sidney," "Harrington," "Russel" were called upon, and especially the "Theban General Epaminondas" (John Witherspoon) and "Hortensius" (William Livingston, the former "Independent Reflector," now serving his third year as the governor of New Jersey).[189]

In this effort to attract the work of notable persons Brackenridge was happily successful, and he himself poured a patriotic, religious, tutorial fervor into the pages of the magazine. If his labors to produce men equal to the tasks of sheriffs and legislators were in vain, the fault rather lay in the essential ignorance of those to whose cupidity his promises might appeal than in a lack of good sustenance in the journal. And while at the task of instructing his readers and furnishing England with yet more undeniable proofs of the literary prowess of Americans, the editor was educating himself. For with the war came a new sense of the value of satire and a new interest in constitutional law and processes of government, both of which were mirrored in the magazine; and thus the Brackenridge of the courts was evolving from the Brackenridge of the chair and pulpit, and the future satirist in prose from the poet

---

unfold the new discoveries of philosophers . . . ; it will comprise the most remarkable events in Europe and America. . . . Amusements will desport in every form of letters, tales, dreams, scraps and anecdotes. . . ."

[188] Jan. 1779, pp. 11-14. It was reprinted, somewhat reduced, in *Gazette Publications*, pp. 221-23.

[189] "Hortensius," he wrote, was "a writer of the first magnitude," and had "drawn his pen with a fine vein of wit and humour in the controversy with the tyrant. His pieces published in Collin's [sic] Gazette of New-Jersey are admirable. That particularly, in which he proposes the exchange of General Burgoyne, is equal to the best performances of Lucian."

of religious and heroic verse. But the public did not adequately support the magazine, and the saddened editor was forced in the December issue to take a disgruntled farewell, blaming a depreciating currency and assuaging his wound by assuring the public that two classes of people would rejoice in the failure—the friends of Britain and those who "inhabit the region of stupidity."[190]

Attached to Brackenridge's personal and somewhat hand-marked file of *The United States Magazine* at the Library of Congress is a letter by his son, H. M. Brackenridge, identifying the copy and markings as those of his father, who, he wrote with some exaggeration in the approximation, "was the author of nearly all the Original articles." It is probably impossible to reclaim every piece which came from the editor's hand, but a number can be recognized by internal evidence, by previous allied publication, or by their having been later republished in *Gazette Publications* (1806), in which the author gathered a number of his scattered compositions. There is no doubt, for instance, that Brackenridge was the author of "The Cave of Vanhest,"[191] for even if the reference to it in *Gazette Publications* were ambiguous,[192] the narrator describes himself as a tutor, and in the last number admits Miss Muse as his first love, Miss Theology his second, and his third and present, Miss Law. The central theme of this discursive story lies in an account of the battle of Monmouth and the rebuke Washington gave to General Charles Lee (whom Brackenridge disliked) for ordering a retreat; and into this account the author wove the setting of a rustic mountain retreat inhabited by a charming family to which Mrs. Sarah Bache, daughter of Benjamin Franklin, has given a habitation and name.[193] Neither is it difficult to find the

---

[190] Dec. 1779, pp. 483-84.

[191] Jan.-July 1779, pp. 14-15, 61-63, 106-10, 149-50, 213-16, 253-55, 311-13.

[192] P. 177.

[193] On Oct. 2, 1779, Mrs. Sarah Bache wrote to her father, Benjamin Franklin, then at Paris, that she was sending him some newspapers and *The United States Magazine*. "Tell Temple that the Cave of Vanhest is a very romantic description of Mr. and Mrs. Blair's House and family. The young Ladies that the Traveller describes and is in love with, are children, one Seven Months younger than our Benjamin—and the [one word illegible] just turned up five. Miss Blair was in town last week, enquired very kindly after you both, and begged when I wrote to remember her affectionately both to you and Temple. As I have mentioned her being in the Country, you may think it some other Miss Blair—'tis necessary to tell you 'tis my old friend Suky Shippen who has never returned to town since they were driven out by the enemy, but has rented a farm on the Raritan." This

hand and mind of Brackenridge in the religious articles justifying the war. His *Six Political Discourses*, which Bailey had issued in 1778,[194] as well as new ones of the same type, he thought well enough of to consider reprinting in the magazine,[195] and he so far accomplished his scheme as to print the seventh, ninth, and tenth.[196] He likewise delivered on July 5, 1779, "An Eulogium of the Brave Men who have Fallen in the Contest with Great-Britain," in a church at Philadelphia, and published it in the magazine, and again later in revised form.[197] In view of his clerical training and the nature of his patriotic emotions, it is not surprising that these sermons, and others which Brackenridge chose to include of other men's writing,[198] should be quite orthodox in tone. There is a change which should be noted, however, in the nature of the allusions made to the morality and the religious faith of the French. Heretofore the French had been vilified as knaves, moral lepers of cunning intrigue, and envoys of dreaded Catholicism. Those views were now softened. With France joining with the seceding Colonies, toasts were drunk to "His Most Catholic Majesty" and to

---

quotation is taken from a copy of the letter in one of the files of *The United States Magazine* at the New York Public Library.

[194] See note 181.

[195] The religious justification of the war is to be frequently met with, not only in the magazine and in newspapers, but in pamphlets and reports of speeches of the time.

[196] Jan. and Feb. 1779, pp. 25-29, 58-61; May 1779, pp. 197-99; Sept. 1779, pp. 371-73. The seventh also appeared, slightly cut down, in *Gazette Publications*.

[197] Aug. 1779, pp. 343-52. It was printed separately by Bailey in a pamphlet in 1779; it was translated into German as *Eine Lobrede auf diejenigen tapfern Männer, welche in dem Streit mit Gross-Brittannien gefallen* and published by Steiner and Cist in 1779; and it was included in Brackenridge's *Gazette Publications*, pp. 162-68, greatly reduced.

[198] See "The Address of the Chaplain of his Excellency the Minister of France" before Congress on July 4, 1779 (July 1779, pp. 313-14); see also Matthew Wilson's "A Breviate of Scriptural Prophecies, Relating to the Revolutions of Nations, and More Particularly of This at Present in America" (July 1779, pp. 299-308), in which he proved to his own satisfaction that Scripture has prophesied all the major events of nations and, as did Brackenridge in his *Discourses*, saw the hand of God specifically fulfilling events. As one in sympathy with the religious atmosphere of the College of New Jersey, Brackenridge was against an established or state church, and he had no sympathy for the excessive elements of "enthusiasm" which accompanied some of the revivals; he was thus of a mind to include Matthew Wilson's "A Genuine Letter on the Danger and Evils of All Religious Establishments" (April 1779, pp. 155-59) and "Some Remarks on the Infectious Spread of the Present Religious Enthusiasm in America," by "Philo-Aletheias," dated also from Lewes (Oct. 1779, pp. 411-21).

the perpetual union of France and the United States,[199] and *The United States Magazine* reflects this change.

A most distressing problem of the year was the decreasing value of currency, which fell the lower the more desperately it was printed in order to keep armies in the field. To start a debate on the subject, Brackenridge wrote an initial article in the first number of the magazine, "The Representation and Remonstrance of Hard Money,"[200] an allegory in which "Hard Money" supported his cause against "that paper-wasted, rag-born, kite-faced fellow, *Continental Currency*."[201] An editorial note requested an answer (for Brackenridge certainly did not in his heart sympathize with the hard-money point of view), and the following month a reply, written in the same style but with more zest, appeared.[202] One inestimable achievement did "Constitutional Currency" claim for himself—he alone had made war possible: "Did I not bring an army into the field, and cloathe them? . . . Where in the meantime was Hard Money? was [*sic*] he not chiefly in the cities of Boston, Philadelphia, and Baltimore, sending out his sloops to the West-Indies, or *speculating with the Tories*?"[203] This second article must have been written for lack of any other reply, since before the March forms were closed William Livingston, as "Hortensius," had contributed what Brackenridge designated as the "true" answer of "Continental Currency."[204] It lacked the play of wit and argument of the second, but so pleased the editor that it was included in the *Gazette Publications*, along with his own January article.[205] Other discussions on the monetary affairs also appeared. Through two numbers "The Adventures of a Continental Dollar," written by himself, traced his autobiographical his-

---

[199] A list of thirteen toasts drunk on one occasion is given in *The Pennsylvania Gazette* of Feb. 10, 1779, p. 3, from which these two have been selected.

[200] Jan. 1779, pp. 28-31. It was "Addressed to the People of America" and the contents indicate that the author was at least somewhat acquainted with Shakespeare's works.

[201] P. 28.

[202] "Reply of Continental Currency, to the Representation and Remonstrance of Hard Money" (Feb. 1779, pp. 72-81).

[203] P. 73.

[204] March 1779, pp. 110-21.

[205] Theodore Sedgwick, *A Memoir of the Life of William Livingston* (1833), pp. 327-28, notes that "not long subsequent to this period" Livingston, who had been contributing to *The Pennsylvania Packet* and especially to Isaac Collins's *The New-Jersey Gazette*, ceased writing popular articles because certain legislators of New Jersey thought the practice unbecoming to a chief executive.

tory from the time he had been born in America "(God be thanked)" to his present lustihood, though the Tories had made his early life difficult.[206] John Jay's "Address to the Inhabitants of America"[207] and "A Circular Letter,"[208] asserting the need of a new loan and the necessity of supporting the sorely tried fiscal system, may have been printed in the routine of reporting, but certainly the magazine was in agreement with Jay; and Matthew Wilson's optimistic belief that real wealth was based on produce, which in quantity had remained fairly steady, was a contribution calculated to inspire confidence amidst chaotic price levels.[209]

A more unlovely side of Brackenridge emerged in the letters surrounding General Charles Lee's famous *jeu d'esprit*, the "Genuine Letter of an Officer of High Rank in the American Service, to Miss F——s [Franks], a Young Lady of This City," which Lee had written in high spirits to this lovely young Jewess, and which, coming by some devious route to the hands of Brackenridge, found its way into the magazine.[210] Had the letter not been private, the printing of it had been fortunate, for it was neatly turned; and if the writer was not equal to Franklin in deftness of touch, he at least possessed a dashing impetuosity which enlivens the missive. But it may be presumed that the circumstances attending the publication made Brackenridge all the more eager to insert it, when he should have been hesitant. Miss Franks had attended a gorgeous ball given by the British officers—who came as knights of Mischianza—to General Howe before the evacuation of Philadelphia, and at this ball tilts and tournaments had been played in favor of the ladies.[211] Lee wove both these circumstances into his letter to Miss Franks, who, he heard, had laughed at the quality of clothes the American general wore. "If you had accused me," he wrote, "of a design to procrastinate the war, or of holding a treasonable correspondence with the enemy, I could have borne it. . . . If you had accused me of getting drunk . . . or even if you had given the plainest hints that I had stolen the soldiers [*sic*] shirts, this I could have put up with, as the great duke of

[206] June, Sept. 1779, pp. 264-68, 385-87.
[207] June 1779, pp. 247-53.
[208] Oct. and Nov. 1779, pp. 408-10, 436-38, 448-50, 477-78.
[209] "On the Present Money-Dilemma" (Sept. 1779, pp. 389-93).
[210] Jan. 1779, pp. 41-42.
[211] See also Smyth, *The Philadelphia Magazines*, pp. 58-59.

Marlborough would have been an example. . . . But the calumny you have, in the fertility of your malicious wit, chosen to invent, is of so new, so unprecedented, and so hellish a kind, as would make Job himself swear like a Virginia colonel. Is it possible that the celebrated Miss F——s . . . should assert it in the presence of these respectable personages, that, I wore green breeches patched with leather?" Lee assured her he wore pure Sherryvallies, that his dress was more fashionable than that of the knights of Mischianza, and he challenged her to a duel: "I insist on the privilege of the injured party, which is to name his hour and weapons, and as I intend it to be a very serious affair, I will not admit of any seconds. . . ." Several newspapers immediately copied this letter; Lee grew rightfully indignant, and prepared a reply. In the April issue of the magazine appeared two letters which Lee had written, and which had appeared in *The Pennsylvania Gazette, and Weekly Advertiser.*[212] The first spoke of the "impertinence and stupidity" of the editor of the magazine, asserted the highest regard for Miss Franks, lamented the fact that the original letter had been "misinterpreted by the malicious, and misunderstood by the blockheads," noted a garbled passage, and cast aspersions on "The Cave of Vanhest" and Brackenridge's "damnable verses." The second letter was a copy of Lee's letter to Miss Franks, begging her pardon, with a postscript assuring her of his refusal to believe that a certain published letter was, as purported, an answer by her. To these letters Brackenridge appended an elaborate reply,[213] later reprinted in revised form, in which he asserted he never believed *The United States Magazine* would please Lee: "The list of the members of Congress which it contains in the first page of it, must be to you what a list of the angels in paradise would have been to Lucifer after he had been precipitated headlong. Moreover, that portion of whiggism pretty largely interspersed in it, must have operated on your olfactory nerve like the smell of a burnt fish to Tobit's devil. . . ." Having warmed to the attack, Brackenridge descended in the latter part of the reply far below all bounds of decency.

[212] See *The United States Magazine*, pp. 163-65, for the reprinted letter.
[213] April 1779, pp. 165-72. This reply, greatly shortened, much of the latter part especially being cut out, was reprinted in *Gazette Publications*, pp. 179-87.

But it was not the editor's usual practice to give permanent form to scurrilities directed against individuals of whatever stamp who supported the Revolution. Political and military matters of a larger scope were his main concern, with a secondary but an assured interest in purely literary work. He was inattentive to agriculture and the sciences, both of which other magazines had striven to represent. It seemed to Brackenridge more to the point to print such articles as President John Witherspoon's satire against James Rivington, the New York printer whose location rendered his opinions of the war more Tory than Whig,[214] or Matthew Wilson's account of the excellence of peach leaves as a substitute for tea,[215] or Dr. David Ramsay's "Oration" delivered July 4, 1778, at Charleston, South Carolina, together with accompanying laudatory "Remarks" regarding it.[216] With regard to the last, it may be noted that Ramsay's place in *The United States Magazine* may be somewhat explained by reason of his birth in Pennsylvania, his attendance at the College of New Jersey, and his subsequent study of medicine at Philadelphia before moving to Charleston. But it must also be recognized that his oration stands as one of the best of its kind of the time, and that it was widely popular.

Then too, general disquisitions on history were begun, but some of these attempts were abortive. A "History of the Present War," copied from a "British Publication," was started, and included remarks on Lexington, Bunker Hill, Washington, Lee, and the invasion of Canada; but the serial was discontinued after three numbers.[217] Similarly was begun an American account of the "Establishment of These United States," but this never reached beyond attaining to a philosophic conclusion that the aborigines had little right to the soil.[218] A department of "Domestic Affairs" was included in each number, but the usually accompanying "Foreign Affairs" did not always find space. Of more permanent worth was an account of the taking of Fort Mifflin,[219] and espe-

[214] "The Humble Representation and Petition of James Rivington" (Jan. 1779, pp. 34-40).

[215] "Green Tea in America" (May 1779, pp. 216-17, misnumbered). For other of Wilson's contributions, see notes 198 and 209, with text attending.

[216] Jan.-March 1779, pp. 20-25, 53-58, 101-06. Ramsay subsequently wrote one of the most popular histories of the war.

[217] April-June 1779, pp. 151-55, 199-202, 245-47.

[218] *Ibid.*, pp. 159-62, 202-04, 260.

[219] May and July 1779, pp. 204-08, 314.

cially instructive was the publishing of the "Constitutions of the Several States."[220]

Of other prose, little need be said. "Thoughts upon the Enfranchisement of the Negroes,"[221] quoting Montesquieu against slavery, is indicative of the attitude of the magazine on this problem, though the inclusion was not based on any spirited editorial policy, and was probably perfunctory. The "vision" type of essay occasionally appeared, as in the "Vision of the Paradise of Female Patriotism,"[222] by a lady of Philadelphia, who saw in mental parade not only the patriotic women of antiquity but such women as Mrs. John Adams and Mrs. Samuel Adams. Most consistent of the correspondents dealing with lighter social phases of life was "Sylvius," whose letters came from Baltimore. Whether he advised his sister of the dangers incurred in social life in a city,[223] or urged that fiction attend more to the virtues than the duplicities of women,[224] or turned his hand to poetry in the presentation of the *Comus* plot,[225] or defended the head-dress of ladies,[226] he wrote adroitly though not with distinction, and, according to the editor,[227] his contributions pleased many female readers.

The poetry of Freneau and "The Cornwalliad" have given *The United States Magazine* a distinction in the department of verse which no preceding magazine can enjoy. Of "The Cornwalliad, an Heroi-comic Poem," which terminated unfinished after running through seven numbers,[228] little seems to have been recorded, and

[220] During the year the magazine published reports of the constitutions as follows: May, Pennsylvania, pp. 217-29; June, New Jersey, pp. 255-60; July, Delaware, pp. 291-99; August, New York, pp. 332-42; September, South Carolina, pp. 373-84; October, North Carolina, pp. 421-29; November, Virginia and Maryland, pp. 451-55, 455-72; December, Connecticut, pp. 488-90.

[221] Dec. 1779, pp. 487-88.

[222] March 1779, pp. 122-24.

[223] April 1779, pp. 172-80.

[224] June 1779, pp. 260-640.

[225] *Ibid.*, pp. 276-78.

[226] July 1779, pp. 290, 308-11.

[227] June 1779, p. 244. For other pieces by or about 'Sylvius," see May, p. 234; July, pp 319-20; Sept., pp. 387-89, 368-70, 406.

[228] Jan.-July, Sept., Oct. 1779, pp. 15-18, 63-65, 133-34, 181-82, 232-33, 278-79, 317-18, 394-400, 431-33. Accompanying the poem was a satirical "Apology" and some remarks (pp. 15-18, 63-65) in which the author was caused to reveal himself as one who had borne a gun against Dunmore while he lay on Guyns Island, and helped to suppress several insurrections of Tories on the eastern shore of the Chesapeake, and had written articles against "the tyrant" and the men he had chosen to represent him, but who had changed his mind entirely since the

its author has remained anonymous. The narrative is confined to the circumstances surrounding Cornwallis's march into New Jersey, his inability to take Philadelphia, and his successive defeats as he proceeded "From Trenton hills to Brunswic, retrograde." It is an engaging satire of sufficient length and worth to rank high among its fellows of the period, and is the equal of some of the work of Freneau, or Brackenridge, or Trumbull.

The contributions which Philip Freneau made to the magazine have been gathered in Professor Pattee's three-volume edition.[229] Freneau's fellowship and collaboration with Brackenridge during their college days made the periodical a natural recipient of the pieces. It is worth noting again that in the first number was begun Freneau's prose "Account of Some of the West-India Islands," by a "young American Philosopher and Bel Esprit, just returned from several small Voyages amongst those islands," the first letter, addressed to "R. H." and dated May 10, 1778, being concerned with Bermuda, and the second, addressed to "A. P.," with Santa Cruz.[230] In these sketches Freneau clearly identified himself with the romantic attitude: in his essay on Bermuda, for example, he spoke of the ill-blood which congestion of population fostered, and contrasted the thickly inhabited portion of the island with the southern side where, amidst green valleys, there was no gold to "allure the greedy eyes of the English tyrant," and the inhabitants lived in peace unbroken by bloodshed.

The second prose essay was followed immediately by the original "Poem on the Beauties of Santa Cruz,"[231] and his subsequent contributions were in verse. "King George the Third's Soliloquy,"[232] "The Dying Elm,"[233] and "Columbus to Ferdinand"[234] followed shortly, an editorial note announcing them as by the author of the prose articles on the West Indies.[235] It is well known that Freneau

Declaration of Independence had been passed, and now, in hope of reconciliation, had written some cantos "in honour of the great Cornwallis."

[229] Fred Lewis Pattee, ed., *The Poems of Philip Freneau* (1907). For comment, see especially I, xvii-xxx.

[230] For description of Bermuda, see Jan. 1779, pp. 31-34; for Santa Cruz, Feb. 1779, pp. 81-84.

[231] Feb. 1779, pp. 84-88.

[232] May 1779, pp. 230-31.

[233] June 1779, pp. 281-82.

[234] *Ibid.*, pp. 282-83.

[235] *Ibid.*, p. 244.

often revised his poems for subsequent editions. Major alterations have been noted by Pattee, who sometimes disregarded lesser modifications; among the latter it may be well to point out that the original "Columbus to Ferdinand" is lacking the eleventh stanza of later editions, and that other lines were altered.[236] "The House of Night: or, Six Hours Lodging with Death" followed, the August number devoting all of its department of poetry to the original seventy-three stanzas.[237] It is important to record that an editorial comment, probably by Brackenridge, indicates that the distinctive nature of this poem was immediately perceived, for the note expressed confidence that "readers of taste will no doubt be pleased with it, as perfectly original both in the design and manner of it."[238] "Psalm CXXXVII, Imitated"[239]—later called "The Jewish Lamentation at Euphrates,"—"The Sea-Voyage,"[240] and "A Dialogue between his Britannic Majesty and Mr. Fox"[241] complete the known contributions of Freneau to the magazine. There remains, however, one interesting suggestion relative to the man in "Remarks on the Magazine for August, in a Conversation of Ladies,"[242] in which a group of Whig women are reported to have expressed their wish that the author of "The House of Night" would "go on and employ his poetic and descriptive vein, in like manner, on the *prison-ship* at New York"—a suggestion later fulfilled in title though actual incarceration left nothing for imaginary development and considerably altered his mood.

The remaining poetry in the magazine is representative of the period but not distinguished. Brackenridge solicited William Bradford, Jr., a college friend then just opening a legal practice at Yorktown, for something from his pen; the latter responded with "A Pastoral Song"[243] in imitation of Shenstone, concerning which

---

[236] See stanzas eight and nine.
[237] Pp. 355-63.
[238] P. 330.
[239] Sept. 1779, pp. 402-03.
[240] Oct. 1779, pp. 435-36.
[241] Dec. 1779, pp. 495-501.
[242] P. 406.
[243] June 1779, pp. 273-74. It was reprinted with credit in *Gazette Publications*, pp. 341-43. Bradford had joined the army in 1776, but resigned because of ill health in 1779. He later became attorney-general of the United States. That he held Brackenridge in good esteem for his literary ability may be inferred from a letter by James Madison, Jr., to Bradford in the manuscript collection of Wallace Papers (I, 42) at the Historical Society of Pennsylvania: "I entirely acquiesce in

he wrote a letter to his sister, Rachel: "With this you will receive a letter for Mr. Breckenridge [*sic*] which I request you will be so good as to send to him as soon as you have an opportunity. It contains a small piece of poetry which he requested me to send him—& if he publishes it, you may perhaps think me in the way you are pleased to wish me [in love] . . . but I assure you it was written long ago (a verse or two excepted) and that the subject of it, is now a *married* lady.—Oh Benedict . . . but I forbear— Surely the *brave* deserve the *fair*."[244]   Governor William Livingston, of New Jersey, who had contributed an article to the magazine on the currency problem, also sent in a poem, "A Morning Hymn,"[245] under the pseudonym of "Hortensius," which in its religious and romantic melancholy is reminiscent of his *Philosophic Solitude*, published in 1747.   Brackenridge himself wrote in dainty octosyllabics his "Genethlicon of the United States Magazine,"[246] a companion in purpose to the design cut for the magazine by Pierre E. du Simitière: an arch supported by pillars and studded with stars representing the states, beneath which is the figure of Fame.   Besides these, a large number of odd verses were printed, among which "The Loyalists,"[247] "The Unhappy Consequences of a Precipitate Duel,"[248] and "An Ode on Masonry"[249] may be named to illustrate some of the more special subjects among many bits of verse bearing lighter burdens of social wit and various love situations.

your opinion of our friend Brackenridge's Talents and think his poem an indubitable proof of what you say on that Head.   It certainly has many real beauties in it and several strokes of a strong original Genius but at the same time as you observe some very obvious defects which I am afraid too are more discernable to common Readers than its excellencies."   The letter was written Jan 20, 1775.

[244] Wallace Papers (see note 243), I, 77.

[245] June 1779, pp. 274-76.   It was reprinted as a memorial to Livingston in *Gazette Publications*, pp. 343-44.

[246] Jan. 1779, p. 43.   See also *Gazette Publications*, p. 177.

[247] July 1779, pp. 315-16.

[248] Sept. 1779, pp. 400-02.   Dueling was being occasionally criticized in public prints as an evil practice.

[249] April 1779, pp. 182-84.   Masonic articles are not uncommonly found in the public prints; *The United States Magazine* printed a prose account in the issue for Aug. 1779, pp. 353-54.

CHAPTER VIII

RENEWED ACTIVITY IN BOSTON: 1783-1786

BOSTON did not support a magazine comparable in value to *The American Magazine, or Monthly Chronicle*, of Philadelphia, until 1783, twenty-six years later. Then a combination of circumstances led to the formation of a well-informed editorial board, which was able to induce leading men of various occupations to supply *The Boston Magazine.* (1783-86)[1] during 1784 with an unusually rich amount of native work, especially in prose. When in 1785 the support of the group was withdrawn, the magazine deteriorated, becoming less original and relying more on the sentimental essay and anecdotal story characteristic of the popular English magazines which Paine had condemned in his introductory remarks to *The Pennsylvania Magazine*. The existence of *The Boston Magazine* stirred Job Weedon and William Barrett, of Boston, to publish *The Gentleman and Lady's Town and Country Magazine* during most of 1784,[2] hoping to profit thereby in their print shop. In its prose, the magazine was imitative of the cheaper sentimentalism of the period, although it offered a fair range of topics, often excised from other publications, which gave it the right to the title of a miscellany; in its poetry it was somewhat more fortunate, being supported by a group of contributors. But it was never distinctive or successful, and when Weedon withdrew near the close of the year, Barrett alone issued the final number for December, and turned to publishing a newspaper. One other Boston magazine was published during this period, *The American Monitor: or, the Republican Magazine*, for October, 1785,[3] over the imprint of Ezekiel Russell. Although it aspired to become a miscellany of permanent value, it was more like a newspaper in every respect but form. It contained three pages of advertisements in the single number that was ever published, and the special interest

---

[1] See "Bibliography," p. 369.
[2] *Ibid.*
[3] *Ibid.*

of the publisher in matters commercial is to be noticed. Russell's inability even temporarily to win the support of a small public saved him from the fate of all his more astute predecessors—a grander failure.

I

John Norman and Joseph White, printers in Boston, issued over the date of September 20, 1783, proposals for the publishing of *The Boston Magazine* in an advertisement appearing in one of their publications, *Weatherwise's Town and Country Almanack* for 1784.[4] The announcement stated that they had been urged to the attempt by a number of men who were "desirous to see a work of this kind published," and, asking for the assistance of gentlemen of leisure and learning, they promised "a Miscellaneous exhibition of the most valuable productions that can be procured," to appear each month in forty pages, embellished by two copperplates and a song set to music, at a price of one shilling four pence a number. By profession Norman had been bred an engraver; he came from London to Philadelphia to ply his trade as early as 1774, and was residing in Boston by 1781.[5] His special task was to make the engravings for the new magazine.

The first number proved the need of an efficient editorial board. An abstract of Linnæus's *System of Natural History* was begun,[6] and also a series of essays harboring the usual characters of Thomas Fool, Squire Nonsense, Jack Blunderbus, and James Numskull;[7] an essay "On the Seduction of Young Women,"[8] and a poem on the "Character of Anacreon"[9] came from Cambridge. The sponsors of the magazine were primarily concerned in printing, and they were glad to yield the entire editorial policy to a group of important local men, who met November 25, 1783, and organized an editorial board consisting of the Reverend Simeon Howard, the Reverend Samuel Parker, Benjamin Guild, the Reverend John Eliot, Dr. Nathaniel Walker Appleton, John Bradford, the Rev-

[4] See advertisement on cover.
[5] Stauffer, *op. cit.*, I, 190-93.
[6] Pp. 5-8.
[7] Pp. 15-17.
[8] Pp. 18-20.
[9] P. 33.

erend John Clarke, Dr. Aaron Dexter, Thomas Dawes, Jr., Dr. James Freeman, Benjamin Lincoln, Jr., and George Richard Minot.[10] Thus the clergy, Harvard graduates, and professional and business men of various ages were represented in this group willing to occupy some of their time with current interests and literature; and in a special room lighted and warmed by candles and a fire, and surrounded by the good cheer of each other's presence and accompanying wine, spirits, and tobacco, they planned the processes of their newly assumed duties.[11] If any single tendency of thought predominated, it was toward history, for, as Dr. Samuel Green has noted,[12] half of this original group later became members of the Massachusetts Historical Society. At the first meeting Mr. Norman "appeared and engaged for himself & Mr. White that the Boston Magazine should in the future be entirely subject to the directions of this Society both as it might respect the time & manner of printing & the selecting & arranging of the materials to be published,"[13] and, having decided to disregard the October issue, a new numbering was begun with the issue for November.

During fourteen months—November 1783 through December 1784—the group functioned, meeting first twice a month and later weekly,[14] and appointing committees of five or three to take charge of each issue,[15] though the whole group passed upon the final selections. For the first half-year Simeon Howard was president and George Minot secretary;[16] during the second half-year Samuel Parker and James Freeman held these respective offices,[17] and for the final two months Parker was president and Nathaniel

[10] From the minutes of the meeting preserved in a manuscript column of the "Society for Compiling a Magazine," at the Massachusetts Historical Society.

[11] A receipted bill, dated Jan. 30, 1784 in the volume of manuscripts, refers to the following items: three gallons of wine, one-half gallon of spirits, one-half dozen pipes, smoking tobacco, candles, and the charge for the meeting room.

[12] *Proceedings of the Massachusetts Historical Society*, second series, XVIII, pp. 326-30.

[13] Minutes of Nov. 25, 1783.

[14] Minutes of Jan. 29, 1784, record that meetings would be held every week thereafter, rather than semimonthly, as had been the custom. This arrangement, rigidly obeyed, was probably irksome to some of the members after awhile, and was perhaps one cause for dissolving after the issue for December 1784.

[15] Minutes of Jan. 29, 1784, record that the number comprising the committee for each monthly issue should be reduced from five to three, and that appointments to the committee each month should rotate alphabetically.

[16] Minutes for Nov. 27, 1783.

[17] Minutes for April 30, 1784.

Appleton secretary.[18] Occasionally new members were admitted, so that the group finally included Dr. Thomas Welsh,[19] Dr. Oliver Smith, Christopher Gore, Major-General Lincoln,[20] Dr. John Warren,[21] and the Reverend Oliver Everett.[22] By the close of the first year, interest had waned and circumstances had somewhat changed; and the members voted to continue to assist the printer only until fourteen numbers had been printed.[23] Attendance at the editorial meetings declined, and on December 17, 1784, a motion was carried to "withdraw our Patronage from the *Boston Magazine* after the publication of the present Month."[24]

In the meantime certain changes in the printing firm and the publishing policy had taken place. Very soon after the establishment of the magazine Edmund Freeman was admitted into partnership with Norman and White, his name first appearing among the publishers on the issue for February 1784. In July Norman and White sold out their interests to Freeman and Thomas Greenleaf.[25] The new publishers announced a decrease in the yearly subscription rate from sixteen to fourteen shillings, an increase from forty to forty-eight pages per month,[26] and the continuation of the policy of running two engravings an issue executed by Norman. The editorial board had sometime since voted against inclusion of the music plates. These latter adjustments were undoubtedly due to the appearance of the competing periodical, *The Gentleman and Lady's Town and Country Magazine*. The first number, for May, had been put on sale in June, and the third, containing forty-eight pages, had offered a yearly rate of twelve shillings.[27] Comparing the merits of the two magazines, one readily acknowl-

[18] Minutes for Nov. 12, 1784.
[19] Minutes for Dec. 2, 1783. The meeting of Nov. 27, 1783, had set a minimum and maximum number of members at 7 and 21.
[20] Minutes of Dec. 16, 1783.
[21] Minutes of Dec. 30, 1783.
[22] Minutes of Feb. 6, 1784.
[23] Minutes of Nov. 12, 1784.
[24] In a letter to Jeremy Belknap, dated Dec. 30, 1784, John Eliot, a member of the group, wrote: "The Magazine will continue, but the present editors will drop it. It is now in the hands of a good printer. Give me your opinion of the Gazetteer." (*Collections of the Massachusetts Historical Society*, sixth series, IV, 279.)
[25] See announcement in *The Boston Gazette*, Aug. 2, 1784, the advertisement dated July 15.
[26] *Ibid.*, Aug. 2, 1784.
[27] See advertisement of *The Gentleman and Lady's Town and Country Magazine* in *The Boston Gazette* of Aug. 9, 1784.

edges that *The Boston Magazine* was greatly superior. It contained, as the publishers noted at the close of 1784, one-third original to two-thirds borrowed material. It was also more securely entrenched. But none the less, the support it received was provincial with respect both to contributors and subscribers;[28] so the proprietors looked with concern on the newer magazine, and might have met their competitors on an even subscription price level had they not announced in the July number proposals for including with *The Boston Magazine* a *Geographical Gazetteer of the Towns in the Commonwealth of Massachusetts*, which they were able to begin issuing with the October number, and which proved to be of considerable popular interest.

Greenleaf and Freeman, as equal partners, found their profits so slight that a few weeks after the partnership was formed in June 1784, Greenleaf offered to buy Freeman's interest or sell his own, but was refused.[29] In this unsatisfactory state the partnership continued throughout the editorship of the board, and into the year 1785, when the publishers were forced to rely more upon the support of women, for in the February issue they requested "the *Favours* of those *Ladies* whose brilliant Geniuses and literary Productions are so great an ornament to the Republic of Letters . . . in order to communicate a sprightliness and vivacity to the Publication."[30] But during the year the intellectual quality of the pieces deteriorated, and they were often imitations of the school of sentimentality. The magazine was also suffering by January 1785 because of the omission of engravings, which Norman had continued to supply through the issue for September 1784, although he had earlier withdrawn from direct connection with the periodical.[31] By February 1785 the loss had become so acute that

[28] *The Boston Gazette* of Aug. 2, 1784, carried an advertisement for the magazine listing two Boston sales places, and representatives in the following cities only: Salem, Newburyport, Worcester, Providence, Hartford, Springfield, Portsmouth. The magazine was also sold "by all Post Riders."

[29] So Greenleaf stated in a signed notice in *The Independent Chronicle*, Oct. 20, 1785.

[30] *The Boston Magazine*, cover of month indicated.

[31] The following titles describe plates engraved by Norman: "Unexpected Surprise" and "Long-Tailed Scarlet Lory" (Oct. 1783); "A Glass House" and "The Interview" (Nov. 1783); "Emblematical Frontispiece" commemorating battles of Lexington, Bunker Hill, Saratoga, Brandywine, Guilford, Camden, and "Tombeau de Madame Langhan's" (Dec. 1783); "Dr. Franklin" and "Maternal Affection" (Jan. 1784); "Hon. John Adams" and "Air Balloon, with Sails" (Feb. 1784); "Time" and "Rev. Dr. Cooper" (March 1784); "Genius of Liberty" presenting medal to George Washington, and

the publishers of the magazine announced in *The Boston Gazette* of the 7th: "Many of the Customers having found great fault with the Cuts, as being badly executed, has induced the Publishers to omit them, untill an Engraver can be procured to do them in an elegant manner. In the mean time, to do justice to the Subscribers, the price will be reduced to Twelve Shillings per annum."[32] Norman was not an excellent engraver, but it is probable that lack of elegance was not the chief cause of the discontinuance of his work. His statement of the case may be found on the cover of *The Gentleman and Lady's Town and Country Magazine* for December 1784, wherein he stated in part that the printers "were always ready to accept of his services *gratis*, but when after repeated refusals to pay his account, he was obliged to seek his redress through the law, they then found it an œconomical measure to omit the plates. Whether the difficulty of finding an *accurate engraver* to work *without pay*, is, or is not the true reason of the present nakedness of this work he leaves the world to judge. . . ."

In September 1785 Greenleaf again tried to secure Freeman's consent to a dissolution of the partnership, but being refused, in anger he made over his shares to Joseph Greenleaf, his father, and went on a journey to Providence.[33] Freeman resented Greenleaf's action so keenly that he could not refrain from intimating in a published announcement that Greenleaf had somewhat unfairly treated him in the desertion, and publishing in *The Boston Gazette* of October 3, 1785, a statement to the effect that Greenleaf had gone into the country for his health and that Freeman alone would continue the magazine and the *Gazetteer*. In January 1786 Free-

"Major-General Warren" (April 1784); "The Faithful Shepherd" and "The Justice of Frederic" (May 1784); "Chevalier D'Éon" and "Coluber Cerastes" (June 1784); "Voltaire" and "Monkey" (July 1784); "Peace Crowned by Victory," "Ascent of the Air Balloon," "Henry Laurens, Esq." and "Descent of Air Balloon" (Sept. 1784). Four other engravings, "The Plan of the Town of Boston" (Oct. 1784), "Commencement of the Liberties of Switzerland" and "Animal Flower" (Nov. 1784), and "The Monument of Joseph Gascoigne Nightingale, Esq." (Dec. 1784) were not signed by Norman. In addition, four musical sheets were furished: "A New Song," set to music by A. Hawkins (Oct. 1783); "Rosline—Castle" (Nov. 1783); "Advice to the Fair" (Dec. 1783); and "The Married Man" (Jan. 1784).

[32] The same slurring announcement is on the cover of *The Boston Magazine* for Feb. 1785.

[33] *The Independent Chronicle*, Oct. 20, 1785, printed an explanatory advertisement, written by Greenleaf from New York on Oct. 8, defending himself against Freeman's point of view.

man was still determined to succeed with the magazine. He bought new types and asserted he was "using the *utmost* exertions" to make the periodical "still more respectable and useful," flattering himself that his efforts would meet with "*ample* encouragement from lovers of SCIENCE, and the patriotic friends of AMERICAN LITERATURE."[34] But a notice on the cover for June revealed that subscribers failed to pay amounts due. The issues for September and October were combined in one number of regular size, the editor explaining he had suffered "a fit of sickness." The same difficulties caused him to telescope the issues of November and December,[35] and the close of the year brought a termination to the life of the magazine.[36]

If James Freeman, a member of the editorial board, had not annotated his private file of *The Boston Magazine* during 1783-84,[37] it is probable that many of the pieces which may now be identified as to authorship would still be anonymous. Among the contributors designated by Freeman are several whose names are well known at the present day, as well as others equally famous in their time. It is pleasing to note that Boston's earlier Holmes, the aged Mather Byles, who had suffered the abuse of his townsmen for his Tory convictions during the war, was still admired for the wit of his masterly light essays, and that his work was included in the magazine.[38] In "Criticism on Nonsense"[39] he discussed two types of writers, the "Bombastick and the Grubstreet"; the former, he asserted, missed the truly sublime by their "noise and clamour; a rattle of words, and an extravagance of imagination," while the style of the latter was "easily attained, provided a Man can but keep himself from thinking, and yet so contrive matters, as to let his pen run along unmolested over a sheet of

[34] Cover of issue for Jan. 1786.

[35] Cover of issue for Sept.-Oct. 1786.

[36] It had been, at least in the earlier period, published with fair regularity near the beginning of each month, as advertisements in *The Boston Gazette*, *The Salem Gazette*, and *The Massachusetts Centinel* show. Regular advertisements disappear with the issue for Sept. 1785, when Freeman assumed sole control.

[37] In the library of the Massachusetts Historical Society.

[38] Byles (1707-1788) is best known for his *Poems on Several Occasions* and for his contributions in *A Collection of Poems. By Several Hands* (1744). Professor R. L. Rusk has suggested that *Poems on Several Occasions* was probably first published in 1744, and not in 1736, as given by Arthur W. H. Eaton, *The Famous Mather Byles* (1914).

[39] Nov. and Dec. 1783, pp. 8, 49-51.

white paper. . . ." In main, he cautioned young writers against falling into bombast, and indulged himself in the essay by doing some lines of mock bombast to please his humor. His other essays are not so full of wit, though he managed, in his whimsical and oblique way, to write pleasingly of the unreasonable period of courtship, when men "impose upon themselves" and women make themselves ridiculous trying to be what their lovers say they are;[40] and in his "Essay on Flattery"[41] he cautioned everyone against that subtlety of expression which deceives even the most adept at the art when practised upon themselves. Selections were also printed from a letter by Mather Byles, Jr. to his three daughters—pieces of poetry which have little save associative value.[42]

Among others whom Freeman noted as being represented were Jeremy Belknap, Vicesimus Knox, Soame Jenyns, Hugh Blair, J. Hector St. John Crèvecoeur, Joseph Green, and Timothy Dwight. Some of the pieces of this group were original with the magazine, others were reprints. Belknap, a young Harvard divine then preaching at Dover, New Hampshire, was especially petitioned by John Eliot[43] to send in an article on the advantages and disadvantages the discovery of America had yielded to civilization.[44] Among the disadvantages Belknap pointed out the extension of slavery, the unfair appropriation of Indian lands, and Spanish attitude of domination over colonies; the advantages included an extension of political and religious liberty to the English who had left the mother country, increased trade, and a wider knowledge of geography. The two essays from the works of the English divine, Vicesimus Knox, were reprinted undoubtedly because of his current fame,[45] and Soame Jenyns's work was reprinted for the same

[40] Feb. 1784, pp. 140-42; it was signed "A."

[41] March 1784, pp. 183-85; it was signed "Honestus."

[42] Byles the son fled to Nova Scotia with Howe's fleet in March 1776. The manuscript is in the library of the Massachusetts Historical Society. The title in the magazine (May 1784, pp. 296-97) is ". . . Lines . . . Wrote . . . for . . . Samplars of Three Young Ladies . . . by their Papa, a Gentleman Residing at Nova Scotia."

[43] Letter from Eliot to Belknap, *Collections, Massachusetts Historical Society*, sixth series, IV, 271-72. Belknap (1744-1798) was at the time especially interested in historical studies. In 1784 he published *A History of New-Hampshire*. He moved to Boston in 1787, and was later identified with a magazine enterprise.

[44] May 1784, pp. 280-85. Belknap also started but did not finish "An Essay on Bottled Cyder," by "Tristram Spintext" (May 1784, pp. 287-89), the title of which was not to be taken literally.

[45] Knox (1752-1821) was famous for his *Liberal Education* (1780). The magazine printed an "Essay on the English Universities" (March 1784, pp. 180-83), "On the

reason.[46]   The latter's efforts to prove the divine nature of the Bible by "internal marks of Divinity," since upon these "the credibility of the prophecies and miracles in a great measure depends,"[47] was hotly resented by many of the orthodox, and Professor Aaron Dexter, of Harvard, who signed himself "A Rational Christian," could not keep his pen idle when he saw Jenyns's deistic ideas in the magazine.[48]   The fame of Timothy Dwight and the popularity of "Columbia"[49] explain its inclusion, and "The Poet's Lamentation for the Loss of his Cat"[50] was sufficiently well known to preserve the memory of Joseph Green.   Current interest in the work of Crèvecoeur was reflected in the magazine,[51] and the renown of the Edinburgh rhetorician, Dr. Hugh Blair, was indicated by selections from his essays on literary style, taste, and criticism, with some special remarks on the work of Shaftsbury, Bolingbroke, Temple, Addison, Tillotson, and others.[52]

Freeman's annotations are particularly serviceable in defining the contributions of the men of local importance who gathered in support of the magazine.   Colonel Thomas Dawes wrote a number of articles on the making of brick and mortar.[53]   His son, an

Folly and Wickedness of War" (April 1784, pp. 242-43), and a later piece, not noted by Freeman, on good character (July 1786, pp. 304-06).

[46] Jenyns (1704-1787) was well known for *A View of the Internal Evidence of the Christian Religion* (1776)—for a Philadelphia reprint, see Evans, *op. cit.*, No. 16812—and for *Disquisitions on Various Subjects* (1782). The magazine reprinted "Disquisition on Rational Christianity" (Nov. 1783, pp. 5-8) and "Disquisition on the Nature of Time" (Jan. 1784, pp. 89-90, Feb. 1784, pp. 143-47).

[47] *A View*, second London edition, p. 5.

[48] "To the Printers of the Boston Magazine" (Jan. 1784, pp. 102-04). Dexter was professor of chemistry and materia medica.

[49] Dec. 1783, p. 71. His *The Conquest of Canäan* was yet unpublished.

[50] Green (1706-1780), a Boston business man and poetic wit, had enjoyed considerable recognition for this poem. It had appeared in *The London Magazine* in 1733. *The Boston Magazine* printed it in the issue for Aug. 1784, pp. 438-39.

[51] *Letters from an American Farmer* (London, 1782) from which the magazine selected excerpts on snakes (March 1784, pp. 171-73) and whale fishing (April 1784, pp. 243-45).

[52] Blair's *Lectures on Rhetoric and Belles Lettres* was so well known as to call forth an edition in Philadelphia in 1784 (Evans, *op. cit.*, No. 18369); for selections in the magazine, see Nov., Dec. 1783, Jan., Feb. 1784, pp. 27-29, 53-55, 90-92, 136-37, 148-49.

[53] Dawes, a mechanic, was made a colonel in 1773 and served until 1778. He later was elected to the legislature. The *Boston Directory* of 1789 associated him with the Massachusetts Bank. For articles in the magazine, see issues for April, May, June, July, Aug., Nov., 1784, pp. 219-20, 292-94, 339-40, 382-83, 432-33, 555-56.

attorney,[54] contributed two poems, one a mock elegy recalling "The Death of Grey-Toby," a horse associated with Dawes's Harvard days, and the other a sprightly flowing piece, "The Temple of Love."[55] Major-general Benjamin Lincoln, who after an active military and political life had retired to his farm, wrote about the shiftings of land and sea and the value of frost as a soil-conditioner.[56] His son, bearing the same name, was a truly important contributor, as he sounded a strong federal note in a series of essays entitled "The Free Republican."[57] Lincoln the son was no thorough democrat. He recognized the tyranny of the majority as well as of the minority, and warned his readers that though autocracies had fallen through tyranny, the same fate had overtaken democracies through lack of intelligence. He was firm in his belief that a system of checks and balances, built somewhat on the system of the British bicameral parliament, would best serve the nation. The series as a whole may be described as a pro-federal tract by a young man of fair ability and attainments. Riper and more personal judgments characterize the contributions of Judge Samuel Sewall and Judge James Sullivan, the former bringing his experience to bear on a "Proposal for a More Speedy and Less Expensive Method of Deciding Causes Judicially through the Commonwealth, of Massachusetts,"[58] and the latter upholding freedom of worship in "An Essay upon the Right to a Free Exercise of Conscience in Religious Matters."[59] Phenomena of the physical sciences were recorded and considered. Edward Wigglesworth, the professor

[54] Dawes the son (1757-1825) was graduated from Harvard in 1777; the *Boston Directory* of 1789 records him as an attorney.

[55] Both poems appeared in issue for March 1784, pp. 199-201.

[56] Lincoln is famous for clearing Boston Harbor of British ships in 1776, for his engagements during the Revolutionary War, and for his years as Secretary of War (1781-84); thereafter he retired to his farm. For contributions, see issues of Dec. 1783 and March 1784, pp. 62-64, 186-88.

[57] For the seven numbers, see issues for Feb., March, May, July, Aug., Nov., Dec. 1784, pp. 138-40, 192-95, 271-74, 375-78, 420-23, 546-49, 589-90.

[58] Sewall, as Chief Justice of Massachusetts, believed that the common pleas courts were ineffective, and that the Supreme Court should be increased to nine members, and that these nine should constitute three circuit courts of three judges each. See issue for April 1784, pp. 226-28.

[59] Sullivan was made a member of the Supreme Court of the state when he was thirty-one years of age; he became the attorney-general of the state in 1790. For the article, see issues for Dec. 1783, Feb., March, April 1784, pp. 59-61, 140-51, 175-76, 230-33. Sullivan also wrote (Jan. 1784, pp. 107-09) an essay on natural history, discussing geographical changes in the earth; he held a literal belief in the account in Genesis.

of mathematics and natural philosophy at Harvard, conducted the department of meteorological observations. A rather spirited discussion arose concerning the reasons for differences in stature, form, and color among the races.[60] Dr. Aaron Dexter, who had replied to the "rational" methods of Jenyns's study of the Scriptures,[61] wrote also on the expanding power of water under heat,[62] and took issue with Benjamin Lincoln, not being convinced, as was the latter, that the introduction of air in the ground acted as a fertilizer.[63] Dr. Thomas Welsh, physician and orator,[64] wrote not only of the "destructive consequences" of private academies— since they led to a degeneration of the public school system—[65] but "On Animal Heat,"[66] concerning himself with the phenomena of bodily temperatures. Literary criticism occasionally crept in. The Reverend John Clarke, Jr., pastor of the First Church of Boston,[67] in "Remarks on Sir C. Grandison,"[68] added his testimony in behalf of the book, as it taught him "the emptiness of those pleasures to which young persons are generally devoted," and showed him that "a man might be virtuous, without being austere. . . ." And a Mrs. Warren, in "A Letter from an American Lady to her Son in Europe,"[69] while admitting that Lord Chesterfield had the "correct stile, the elegant diction, the harmony of language," disdained him for being of the school of Voltaire and "exerting the powers of brilliant talents . . . to arouse corrupt passions in the bosom of his son," and recommended that Addison's works be read instead. Variety of subject matter was more characteristic of the writings of the ministers than any other one group. True, religious topics had their place; the Reverend

[60] Dr. Mather (Oct. 1784, pp. 523-25), answering an inquiry in the magazine for Aug., p. 436, referred to Genesis for an explanation of the differences among races. Justice Greenleaf (Dec. 1784, Jan. 1785, pp. 596-601, 14-18) was evidently not convinced by Mather's article, and under the pseudonym of "Mosches" he wrote in support of the theory that climate and other natural causes were responsible for variations.

[61] See note 48.

[62] Jan. 1784, pp. 105-06.

[63] April 1784, pp. 239-42.

[64] Boston Directory for 1789; Evans, op. cit., No. 18302.

[65] "On Education" (March 1784, pp. 176-78).

[66] Jan. 1784, pp. 84-86.

[67] Clarke (1755-1798) is represented by at least two pamphlets; see Evans, op. cit., Nos. 17492 and 18399.

[68] March 1784, pp. 185-86.

[69] June 1784, pp. 326-28.

William Hazlitt, fearing "popish invention" in the use of only one doxology, submitted fifty-five benedictions and twenty-eight doxologies from the New Testament,[70] and to this the Reverend Samuel Parker, an Episcopalian, made reply.[71] But the essays of John Eliot, Samuel West, and James Freeman embrace a variety of interests ranging from a Trumbullian castigation of an educational system pampering "Dunces" to a dispute between an Indian and a Negro.[72]

The poetry which Freeman credited to the several authors was not distinguished by any special qualities. George Richards wrote

[70] "Scriptural Benedictions and Doxologies" (Oct. 1784, pp. 517-22.) The Rev. Hazlitt was "now residing in this Town" (*The Boston Magazine*, Sept. 1784, p. 457).

[71] "Elakistoteros's Answer to the New Testament Christian" (Nov. 1784, pp. 567-68). Parker (1744-1804) was a Harvard graduate of 1764. He became a deacon in 1774, and during the Revolution made himself conspicuous by adhering to the American cause. One other article, a humorous essay on "engines" to assist writers, appeared in the issue for Feb. 1784, pp. 142-43.

[72] Eliot (1754-1813) was the most prolific of the three. He had already published pamphlets (Evans, *op. cit.*, Nos. 17526 and 17960), and he wrote for the magazine "Triumph over Old Age" (March 1784, pp. 195-96, "Memoirs of Major-General Warren" (April 1784, pp. 221-22), an "Essay on Vanity" (April 1784, pp. 223-24), and an essay "On Education" (April 1784, pp. 238-39) in which his attitude toward dunces was not unlike John Trumbull's. West (1730-1807) contributed "A Dispute between an Indian and a Negro, Respecting the Natural Right of Pre-eminence" (Nov. 1784, pp. 565-66), and Freeman (1759-1835) wrote "Cupid Turned Fisherman" (Nov. 1783, pp. 18-21) in praise of the virtuous young man as opposed to the dashing coxcomb.

Freeman's credit extends to other prose writers. One of the most faithful to the magazine was George R. Minot, who was graduated from Harvard in 1778, held several judicial posts from 1782 on, and became an historian of prominence. His essay under the pseudonym of "Facetus" (Dec. 1783, pp. 61-62) pledged his support of the enterprise; an essay signed by the same pseudonym (May 1784, pp. 285-86) urged the editors to disregard religious and philosophical pieces and include the light, sentimental, and romantic; he was also responsible for the "Proceedings of the General Court" of Massachusetts for July 1784, and probably for its record as reported in other issues. The Rev. Oliver Everett, ordained at the New South Church in 1782, contributed "On Love of Fame" (April 1784, pp. 217-19), in which, as a young minister, he lamented the sad lack of intelligence in the ministry, which required only adherence "to a particular system of opinions"—under which he was evidently rebelling. Dr. John Warren (1753-1815), professor of anatomy and surgery at Harvard (see *The Boston Magazine* for July 1786, p. 320), who had already published pamphlets (Evans, *op. cit.*, Nos. 17526 and 18292), wrote a long treatise "On Man" (March, April, May 1784, pp. 178-80, 228-30, 289-92), bearing the refrain that human beings, living in a vale of tears, must take consolation in the belief that "man never is but always to be blest"; he also wrote an essay more in keeping with his profession, a discussion of the "Fatal Effects of Drinking Cold Water" (July 1784, pp. 368-71). Benjamin Austin, Jr., who is listed in the *Boston Directory* of 1789, contributed a "Description of Amsterdam" (March 1784, pp. 188-89).

verse for several occasions, but he was a pedantic rhymster, unin-
spired.[73] Harrison Gray Otis, who was admitted to the bar in
1786, contributed "Elegiac Lines, Occasioned by the Much Lamented Death of Miss N——A."[74] Youthful S. C. Johonnot, a
Harvard student, solved a poetical enigma.[75] Other selections were
similar in types and manners.[76] Whatever genius the members
of the group possessed lay rather in prose.

Although during 1785 and 1786 *The Boston Magazine* lost
much of its originality, it occasionally received outstanding contributions of original prose and poetry. Especially to be noted are
the two long series of essays written by rival literary groups at
Harvard under the respective titles of "The Nursery"[77] and "The
Competitor."[78] The Attick Bud Society conceived the idea of
"The Nursery," and soon under this head two essays were contributed every month, each essay separate but the second often a
partial reply to the idea advanced in the first. The value of ambition, the service of knowledge, the fatal effects of luxury, the
virtue of generosity, the blessings of an agricultural life, the harmful effects of a civilization based on an "absolute equality amongst
men,"[79] the evils of slavery, and the pleasing outlook for the
future of America were discussed by "Lenander," "Horatio,"

[73] The *Boston Directory* of 1789 lists a George Richards, who was a schoolmaster.
He contributed an "Elegiack . . . to the Memory of . . . Michael Knies" (Nov. 1783,
pp. 31-32), an "Imitation of Horace" (Dec. 1783, pp. 69-70), a "Thanksgiving Hymn"
(Dec. 1783, pp. 70-71), and an "Ode for the New Year" (Jan. 1784, pp. 111-12).

[74] The *Boston Directory* of 1789 lists him as a practising attorney. The poem appeared in the issue for Feb. 1784, pp. 157-58; the same issue reported (p. 166) the
death of Miss Nancy Amory, aged fourteen.

[75] Harvard conferred the degree of Master of Arts on him in 1786 (*The Boston
Magazine*, July 1786, p. 320). The solution appeared in issue for Feb. 1784, p. 159.

[76] Note "An Elegy," by Samuel Barrett (Dec. 1784, pp. 621-22); an "Ode to
Liberty" and an "Ode to Fortitude," by G. Apthorp (April 1784, pp. 249-51); a
translation from Horace by J. Mascarenc (April 1784, p. 251); "A Ballad," by Dr.
Haven (May 1784, p. 206); "To a Young Lady who Appeared in a Plain Dress at a
Ball" and a paraphrase of the third chapter of Habakkuk, by Dr. Caner (Nov. 1784,
pp. 571-74), and a "Monody" by Dr. Cutting (Jan. 1784, pp. 114-15).

[77] Nos. I-XXIII, Jan.-Dec. 1785, pp. 19-20, 55-57, 99-100, 133-35, 180-81, 224-26,
251-52 and 256-57, 290-92, 328 and 345-46, 385-86, 418-20, 458-59 and 461-62). For
notes and references to the Attick Bud Society and "The Nursery," see issues of Feb.
and March 1785, pp. 38-39, 84-88.

[78] Nos. I-XIII, April, June-Aug., Oct., Nov. 1785, Jan. 1786, pp. 139-41, 212-14
and 217-18, 257-58 and 261-62, 286-87 and 301-02, 372-73, 421 and 427-28, 25-26
and 33-34.

[79] Pp. 180-81.

"Eugenio," "Eumenes," "Florio," "Palemon," "Altamont," "Philo," "Uranio," "Ardelio," "Lysander," "Fidelio," and perhaps others. The group writing "The Competitor"—"Euphranes," "Alberto," "Anaximander," "Vicento," "Castalia," "Armine"— was probably the smaller of the two, but it was the more enterprising. While "The Nursery" men wrote of vague generalities in the main, "The Competitor" group singled out more definite issues. One among them advocated the extension of female education;[80] another pointed out that deists "in general . . . have more exalted ideas of the Deity than the most sincere christians";[81] another blamed a reputed dearth of ministers upon the meager salaries received;[82] another emphasized the great worth of scientific knowledge;[83] another discoursed on the close association of the mind and the senses;[84] another, basing his argument on the thesis that nature (realism) rather than imitation should be sought in literature, set Homer above Vergil, found blemishes in Milton, whose use of long periods and energetic style were the language of the poet "but not of an enraged seraph,"[85] and, though he dreaded to censure Shakespeare, found that "in almost every instance he has fallen short of nature; nor with his extensive genius been able to copy the anger of a fool. . . ."[86]

There were other outstanding original contributions. An unimpassioned but pro-Colonial survey of the British attitude, by an "American Clergyman," written in 1774 but never published hitherto, is to be found in "The Contest between Great-Britain and the Colonies Reviewed."[87] Increasing activities among circles in Boston interested in music sprang up during the winter of 1784-85, as accounts in newspapers testify, and these are reflected in *The Boston Magazine* by three humorous essays, based on musical discussions of the times, peopled in allegory by the Messrs. Semibreve, Quaver, Minim, Crotchet, Adagio, Largo, Allegro, Accent, Swell, Emphasis, and others.[88] And "Constantia," inspired

---

[80] No. III, pp. 212-14.
[81] No. V, pp. 257-58.
[82] No. IX, p. 372.
[83] No. X, p. 373.
[84] No. XI, p. 421.
[85] No. IV, pp. 217-18, quotation from 218.
[86] P. 218.
[87] Feb.-June 1786, pp. 76-81 (misnumbered 68-73), 111-17, 153-59, 204-10, 241-45.
[88] Feb., March, May 1785, pp. 44-45, 85-86, 178-80.

by "The Vision of Mirza," dreamed a dream of her own, and saw a world of men whose diverse fates seemed unattended by a justice based upon fitting rewards and punishments, until an angel approached and showed her a broader economy in which right prevailed.[89]

Short excursions up the side of Mount Parnassus were taken by many contributors, and the magazine was able to print a large amount of original light verse, together with a few more ambitious pieces. From a manuscript volume of poems by Phillis Wheatley was selected "To Mr. and Mrs. —— on the Death of their Infant Son," an editorial note explaining that it was "inserted as a Specimen of her Work: should this gain the Approbation of the Publick, and sufficient encouragement be given, a Volume will shortly be published, by the Printers hereof. . . ."[90] An ambitious ode by James Allen, "The Retrospect," in four-line stanzas of pentameter lines rhyming alternately, recounted in detail the rise and progress of the war.[91] Quite as patriotic is "The Agreeable Prospect, or, a View of Charlestown, from the Adjacent Hills of Boston; Interspersed with Moral Reflections,"[92] expressing at the close the hope that the burned city might rise again like the Phœnix, more beautiful. On the same subject was the "Ode, Written by Thomas Dawes, jun., Esq; and sung by Mr. Rea and several other gentlemen . . . after the 4th toast, was given at the entertainment on the opening of the bridge,"[93] the writer using the simile of the Phœnix for the city then "sunk in Night."

[89] June, July 1785, pp. 203-06, 254-56. The pseudonym is that employed by Mrs. Judith Sargent Murray only a few months before, in *The Gentleman and Lady's Town and Country Magazine.* See note 129.

[90] For announcement and poem, see issue for Sept. 1784, pp. 462, 488. Her death was occasion for a poem by "Horatio" (Dec. 1784, pp. 619-20).

[91] Dec., Jan., March 1785-86, pp. 471-72, 35-37, 132-35. Allen (1739-1808) was the son of a wealthy merchant of Boston.

[92] Aug. 1785, pp. 309-12.

[93] June 1786, p. 261. Other poems of merit—mainly elegies—included an "Elegy on the Death of Mrs. O——" (May, June 1786, pp. 226-30, 263-66), an elegy by "Zaca" sacred to the memory of Elisha Brown (Oct. 1785, pp. 389-90), an "Elegiack Ode, Sacred to the Memory of Major General Nathaniel Greene," by George Richards (Sept.-Oct. 1786, pp. 393-96), a "Dialogue . . . Occasioned by the Death of the Late Mrs. C." (Aug. 1784, p. 440), "On the Last Day," done in heroic couplets (Jan. 1785, pp. 30-31). "By a Young Lady, on the Death of her Father"—imitative, as were many in the magazine, of the Graveyard School, especially Gray—(Jan. 1785, pp. 33-35), and "The Death of General Montgomery," by "W. Z.," who had written the poem on the occasion of the death but had never had it printed (June, July 1785, pp. 230-32, 269-70.

The magazine published many interesting pieces clipped from printed sources. The "Reflections" of the Philadelphia physician, Dr. Benjamin Rush, on the life and death of Edward Drinker, was popular.[94] The recent death of Samuel Johnson was cause for the appearance of a continued series by "L." on "Memoirs of the Life and Writings of Dr. Samuel Johnson."[95] Franklin's "Information" to those who would remove to America, his "Remarks" concerning Indians, his very recent "A True Description of the Interest and Policy of the Continent of America," and a reprint from his almanac of 1758, "On Œconomy and Frugality" were normal selections.[96] Voltaire and Goldsmith also appeared as a matter of course.[97] Of exceedingly practical value was "An Address from the Philadelphia Society for Promoting Agriculture; with a Summary of its Laws: and Premiums Offered," to which the name of Timothy Pickering was attached as secretary.[98] Other selections are interesting because they were unusual. It is rarely one's experience, for instance, to meet with an as elaborately outlined aesthetic discussion as "An Essay on Beauty," which undertook to consider color, form, expression, and grace.[99] Unexpected, too, was the report of the Shakespeare jubilee of 1769.[100] And quite as surprising was "Philological Remarks," by "E.," a Harvard professor, a painstaking treatise on tenses which had originally appeared about seventeen years previously.[101]

As original prose decreased, borrowings increased, and a major portion of these consisted of tales of sensibility, reflecting the type of narrative which had caught the popular imagination. Among these, one pattern was devoted to an exhibition of the unhappiness

[94] Jan. 1784, pp. 86-88.

[95] May-July 1785, pp. 172-76, 209-12, 249-51.

[96] The four pieces appeared respectively in issues of Oct. 1784, pp. 505-09, Nov. 1784, pp. 556-57, Sept.-Oct. 1786, pp. 383-86, Jan. 1786, pp. 11-16.

[97] For Voltaire, see "A Prayer" (June 1784, pp. 338-39), and an engraving of his portrait and comment on his life (July, Sept. 1784, pp. 461-62, 511-13). For Goldsmith, see selections from his *Natural History* (Dec. 1785, Jan. 1786, pp. 443-47, 1-5).

[98] March 1786, pp. 121-26.

[99] July-Sept. 1784, pp. 363-66, 429-32, 463-66.

[100] March 1785, pp. 90-93.

[101] April-June 1785, pp. 125-28, 169-71, 214-17. Rather unusual, too, was a long essay "Of Women," by Dr. Alexander (Dec. 1784, Jan.-March, May, and July 1785, pp. 605-08, 24-26, 39-40, 106, 181-83, 246-47), which was a sociological study of the various types of the marital relations which had obtained in the several modes of life from savage times to the present.

which attends wealth, whether it be that one marries for money,[102] or, becoming possessed of wealth, moves among the degenerate idlers fashioned by the city's abnormal life.[103] Another pattern treated of "The Lost Daughter Recovered."[104] Still another painted scenes in the lives of the French nobility.[105] The Oriental tale, with its attendant moral, persisted.[106] For two other patterns, prose invaded traditional sanctuaries of verse, laying a heavy hand on the pastoral poem and the historical drama. The writers of the prose pastoral, remembering that God made the country, offered happy fates to the pure-hearted characters, but they forgot that poetry may achieve artistic reality in moods which, done in prose, become weakly sentimental.[107] Equally inclined to pathos was such an "historical novel" as "The Prince of Brittany."[108] In this long story, which revolves around the love of Giles, third son of John VI, Duke of Brittany, and Alicia, niece of the Marshal of Brittany, the dislike of the Marshal for Giles leads to a tragic conclusion which might have been better supported in verse.

Among the selections of poems which had hitherto been printed, at least four are outstanding. Chief of these is David Humphreys's *A Poem, on the Happiness of America*, seized upon and given a most unusual amount of space, indicating its popularity and the value the editor attached to it.[109] Second in importance is William Livingston's *Philosophic Solitude*, a poem of many years' standing which was printed on request.[110] The fame of Laetitia Aikin was bright, and she was represented by "The Invitation";[111] and, interesting to note as being somewhat unexpected, *The Feminead; or, Female Genius*, by the English divine, John Duncombe, which had originally appeared in 1754, was printed for the pleasure of women readers.[112]

[102] "Elvira and Jacintha" (Aug. 1784, pp. 425-29). This story was submitted to the magazine, and may have been original.

[103] "The Cruel Deception" (Aug., Sept. 1785, pp. 283-86, 329-30).

[104] Feb.-April 1785, pp. 49-52, 96-99, 134-39.

[105] "The New Pygmalion" (Jan.-March 1785, pp. 3-5, 41-44, 89-90).

[106] See especially issue for Feb. 1785, pp. 57-58.

[107] "Virtue Rewarded: A Pastoral Tale" (Aug. 1785, pp. 287-88), and "Elvira; or the Happy Shepherd" (Jan. 1785, pp. 27-28).

[108] Jan.-April 1786, pp. 27-33, 57-66, 105-11, 164-74.

[109] July, Aug., Sept.-Oct. 1786, pp. 306-11, 348-52, 396-401. The poem had appeared in several editions at home and in England.

[110] March-June 1785, pp. 107-09, 147-48, 189-90, 227-28.

[111] May, June 1784, pp. 298, 341-43.

[112] Oct.-Dec. 1785, pp. 387-89, 429-31, 468-70.

II

Commercial rivalry among publishers was probably at the base of the establishment of *The Gentleman and Lady's Town and Country Magazine*,[113] which ran from May through December 1784. Most of the contents came from printed sources, and there was only one major editorial policy in mind: definitely to appeal to feminine readers. For the first time in American magazine history this policy governed the title of a periodical. As *The Boston Magazine* during the plural editorship in 1784 was masculine in its major appeal—although some women wrote for it and undoubtedly found in it many articles and poems congenial to them—Job Weedon and William Barrett were astute in soliciting the special regard of women. In their announcement to the public in the first issue, over date of June 1,[114] the editors wrote: "The Ladies in particular, are requested to patronize this Work, by adding the elegant polish of the Feminine Pencil, where purity of sentiment, and impassioned Fancy, are happily blended together." This request was not intended, however, to discourage male readers, for "the Learned and Ingenious" were urged to contribute, and the publishers promised to note all pieces of merit and assured everyone that they would not blast "by indelicate Censure, or solemn Criticism" the contributions which could not be used.[115]

The program as outlined must have received some encouragement from the public, as the issue for July[116] announced an increase in size to forty-eight pages octavo at an annual price of twelve shillings "Lawful Money." Editorially, the publishers expressed the hope soon to "adorn" the periodical "entirely with original Composition," but, failing this, they promised European selections "from the most approved Authors."[117] In the issue for August they called attention to the new "Elegant Type," asked that scientific subjects be the topic of some of the contributors, and, assuring business men of an "extensive circulation," offered space on the

[113] See note 2.
[114] Pp. 3-4.
[115] All quotations are from p. 4.
[116] Pp. 83-84. See also *The Boston Gazette* of Aug. 9.
[117] P. 83.

cover for general advertisements.[118]   In the October issue they referred to the engraved plate accompanying the number, and asked their readers to pay their subscription dues, six months having now passed.[119] The following month brought forth an indication of an early demise for the journal, for the November issue was not honored, as had been the others, by advertisements in the public papers.[120] The issue for December bore the name of Barrett only as the publisher, and he printed no more numbers. It would seem that he had determined to try publishing a newspaper as being possibly more lucrative, for in February 1785 he began a weekly, *The American Journal, and Suffolk Intelligencer*.[121]   It was a small paper, however, and was poorly edited, containing many reprints. The last issue located is for July 12, 1785—containing, by some circumstance, one of the major articles that had appeared in the magazine, "A Walk through the City."[122]

As a periodical containing many selections from a number of printed sources, *The Gentleman and Lady's Town and Country Magazine* was more typical than original. An analysis of its contents is an analysis of the contents of the average magazine of the period. Specifically, Weedon and Barrett show by their choices the current popularity of Eastern tales, moral tales, moral essays, and certain books, especially those of adventure and discovery. The Eastern tale can be divided into several types. Long a growing favorite in magazines, it attained to full bloom in the 'eighties. Such stories as "The Discontented Man,"[123] like *Rasselas*, chronicled a story of the search for happiness, and closed in the realization that within oneself alone lodges a world sufficient for all desires.

---

[118] See cover for announcement. Advertising in magazines carrying the typical blue cover was still confined to the cover, but the case at hand is interesting as an early attempt to broaden the nature of the advertisements. Heretofore, publishers' announcements had constituted nearly the sole copy.

[119] See cover for announcement.

[120] The magazine had been published regularly, as advertisements indicate, and the numbers announced in *The Boston Gazette* and *The Salem Gazette*. The first issue, for May 1784, was advertised in *The Salem Gazette* of June 15, and subsequent issues were advertised in *The Boston Gazette*, as follows: June, July 5; July, Aug. 2; Aug., Sept. 6; Sept., Oct. 4; Oct., Nov. 15.

[121] No. 5 is dated March 22, 1785; Barrett probably, therefore, issued the first number in February. See Brigham, *op. cit., Proceedings of the American Antiquarian Society*, April 1915, p. 196.

[122] See note 131.

[123] Oct., Nov. 1784, pp 253-56, 281-84.

Others, like "The Story of Hamet and Sophonisba"[124] and "Unbounded Tyranny Punished,"[125] dwelt on the avarice and lust of Eastern potentates and described the suicide of heroines to escape lascivious rulers. Others were more philosophical and, like "Zaman,"[126] the personification of Truth, who learns that bigots and women can not endure it, pointed to foibles and attitudes.

Often the moral tale revolved around a story of illicit sexual relations, and English magazines were the chief source for such pieces. But Weedon and Barrett were careful to exclude the more lurid of these stories. "The Exemplary Daughter" and "The False Step" are representative titles.[127] The editors were sometimes able to print a story evidently original, an example being "The History of Auretta; or the Fatal Effects of Impatience,"[128] which supported the romantic theory for enduring love—the heart of youth rather than the head of age—and illustrated the point by a tragedy as old as that of Pyramus and Thisbe.

Among the essays, three original contributions stand out prominently. Appealing to women, the editors were pleased to publish "Constantia's"—Judith Sargent Murray's—"Desultory Thoughts upon the Utility of Encouraging a Degree of Self-Complacency, Especially in Female Bosoms,"[129] in which the positive virtues of ambition were noted and a plea was made to re-order a society which caused too many women to suffer the "depression of soul" accompanying an inferiority complex. "A Simple Layman," in "Serious Thoughts on a Serious Subject,"[130] glorified the Psalms

[124] June 1784, pp. 70-72.

[125] May 1784, pp. 9-12.

[126] June, July 1784, pp. 47-48, 96-98.

[127] For the first see issues of Aug., Sept. 1784, pp. 135-36, 183-84; for the latter, which may be original, see issue of Aug. 1784, pp. 159-62. Note also such titles as "The Merited Disappointment" and "The Fair Recluse" (Aug. 1784, pp. 138-42 and 144-46).

[128] May, June 1784, pp. 17-20, 54-57. The story was, at least, submitted "for" the magazine.

[129] Oct. 1784, pp. 251-53. For identification, see Vena B. Field, "Constantia, A Study of the Life and Works of Judith Sargent Murray, in *University of Maine Studies*, Feb. 1931, pp. 18, 24, 106. Mrs. Murray later employed the pen name "Constantia" in contributing to *The Massachusetts Magazine*, beginning in 1790. In the meantime Sarah Wentworth Morton had used the same pseudonym for three poems printed in *The Massachusetts Magazine* during 1789. See Chapter XI, note 85. Another article in the magazine, especially noteworthy as it places women on an equal plane with men, is "On the Virtues of Women," sent in by "W. J." (Dec. 1784, pp. 337-39), which asserts that genius knows no sex.

[130] July 1784, pp. 85-87.

and called attention to the necessity of living in "an habitual sense of his Maker's Omnipresence." And in the mode of John Gay was a prose essay, "A Walk through the City."[131] The editors enjoyed this description of street scenes which embraced dousings and cane fights in a municipality reputed to be "the best regulated City in America," and they asked for more "favours."[132] Excerpts from books of current interest included selections from Crèvecoeur's *Letters from an American Farmer*[133] and Northey's *Voyage* in the South Sea.[134]

Poetry came more readily to the editorial desk than prose, and *The Gentleman and Lady's Town and Country Magazine* offered in its department of verse an array the equal of other periodicals which had been more fortunate in securing original prose. A great many of the writers contented themselves with riddles, Latin imitations, short epitaphs, brief sentiments on love, and light verse; but some were moved to more ambitious endeavors. In the magazine, for example, lie the poems of "the late" Heman Harris, of Wrentham. "The Thunderstorm,"[135] in heroic couplets describing the approach, deluge, and retreat of a storm of rain, is one of the earlier American poems treating a moving force of nature with elaborate panoramic detail, and is suggestive of the slowness with which mid-eighteenth century English nature poetry was imitated in some details in the Colonies. In another poem, "Philander and Sabrina,"[136] Harris used a pastoral setting to describe, in blank verse, a love idyll in the manner of a dramatic bucolic. "On Friendship"[137] and "An Epitaph on an Only Son"[138] followed, and,

---

[131] Sept. 1784, pp. 209-12.

[132] P. 212. Other essays embraced such subjects as advice to a young lady approaching matrimony, by "B. W." (May 1784, p. 27), "Prudes Preferable to Coquettes," by "J. S." (July 1784, pp. 115-16), Sir Charles Grandison and Clarissa Harlowe as characters (July 1784, pp. 90-92), correspondence of Sterne (Aug. 1784, pp. 137-38), and a letter by Addison to a lady (Sept. 1784, pp. 197-98).

[133] June 1784, pp. 58-61.

[134] May-Sept. 1784, pp. 13-16, 63-66, 104-06, 147-49, 189-91. From the works of the Abbé Guillaume Raynal were selected essays "On Agriculture" (July, Aug. 1784, pp. 101-03, 157-59) and "On Manufactures" (Sept., Oct. 1784, pp. 192-93, 240-42). From the works of Nicholas A. Boulanger was taken an "Epitome" of his inquiry into the origin of despotism in Oriental governments (May-Sept. 1784, pp. 5-8, 43-46, 92-95, 142-44, 184-85).

[135] July 1784, pp. 117-18.

[136] Aug., Oct. 1784, pp. 168-69, 261-63.

[137] Sept. 1784, pp. 214-15.

[138] Oct. 1784, p. 268.

in order to preserve all of Harris's poems together,[139] the publishers reprinted on request "The Choice,"[140] traditional in both title and content, but containing a flattering reference to Phillis Wheatley. Harris traced the paths of others, blazing no trails, but he followed carefully, conscientiously, and deftly.[141]

Certain anonymous writers submitted meritorious work. Very unusual, being a ballad, was "The Snow Love Walk,"[142] a narrative of love. "The Beauties of the Mall,"[143] offering a rather charming picture of Boston street life, came as a poetic rebuke to the prose essay of the previous month, "A Walk through the City."[144] "Birth-Day Thoughts,"[145] by "Lorenzo," of State Street, Boston, far from conveying festive associations, was an early American imitation of the Graveyard School, turning thoughts to the "clay-cold tomb." Going back several decades, the author of a "Sacred Anthem for the Anniversary of Peace"[146] revived the manner of the musical numbers of Dryden and Pope, in caroling his joy at the state of peace following war. Interesting chiefly as another example of imitation of Hamlet's most quoted soliloquy is "The Bachelor's Deliberation."[147]

Eulogistic poems were popular, and the attention of the publishers to women gave to them as well as to men places in the subject matter. "An Address . . . Inscribed to Madam Hayley"[148] on her arrival in Boston, though ostentatious, has a rousing, even a

[139] See p. 311.

[140] Nov. 1784, pp. 311-13. Reprinted from *The Independent Chronicle* of May 20, 1784.

[141] The Rev. Cummings's epistle to Harris, done in heroic couplets, was also printed (Dec. 1784, pp. 350-52); in the same issue appeared another poem by the minister, "On the Choice of a Wife" (pp. 353-54).

[142] Nov. 1784, pp. 309-10.

[143] Oct. 1784, pp. 265-66. It was signed "K. K.," and dated Oct. 20. In part, it read:

> "Mild as the Zephyr, on a violet bed,
> Bright as the dew drop, on the Jonquil's head,
> Bostonia's Daughters sweetly move along,
> Pride of the muse, and glory of her song.
> Then ev'ry look, good sense and wit displays
> And souls replete with virtue's warmest rays. . . ."

[144] See note 131.

[145] Nov. 1784, pp. 313-14.

[146] July 1784, pp. 120-21.

[147] Nov. 1784, pp. 310-11.

[148] May 1784, pp. 34-35. Notice of her arrival appears in a news item of the same issue, p. 40.

ringing tone the while it celebrates the sister of Wilkes, who "stood forth the Champion of insulted laws." "E. E.," of Boston, in "Stanzas Inscribed to a Celebrated Female Historian,"[149] saw in Berkeley's death the downfall of British genius until Mrs. Macaulay Graham rose to the plane of the elect and, probably because of her republican sympathies in her *History of England*, "Reigns Nature's equal on the throne of time." Among the men celebrated in poems were John Bradford,[150] John Hurd,[151] and General Joseph Warren.[152] Interest in the first poem centers in a quotation from Burns, certainly one of the earliest in America; the second is a well-turned elegy in the pastoral tradition; the third adds another title to the list of commemorative verses to the fallen leader at Bunker Hill.

Imitations in the manner of Horace or translations from his works appeared frequently. This magazine, like *The American Magazine and Historical Chronicle* edited by Gridley,[153] attracted versifiers who indulged rather playfully in exercises of wit and dexterous phrasing. Most important of this class of poems in *The Gentleman and Lady's Town and Country Magazine* was an imitation, "Virginia's Invitation,"[154] dated from Boston and dedicated to Washington, which opened with the following lines:

> "Hero and Statesman, friend to virtue's cause,
> Guardian of Freedom, when opprest by pow'r,
> Virginia's sons unite in just applause,
> Ask thy return, and wait the blissful hour."

Other poems based on Horace came from Boston, Waltham, and Newport, one of which, by "G. R.," was probably by George Richards, who had contributed over the same initials to *The. Boston Magazine*.[155]

[149] July 1784, p. 120. A prospectus of her *History* (six volumes) was being advertised in American newspapers in 1784; see, for example, *The Boston Gazette, and the Country Journal*, Nov. 8, 1784.

[150] June 1784, p. 74.

[151] Sept. 1784, pp. 215-16. Hurd had served in the Revolutionary army.

[152] July 1784, pp. 121-22.

[153] For the vogue of Horace in this magazine see Chapter II, note 89, and text to which note is appended.

[154] June 1784, pp. 73-74. The poem is dated June 10, from Boston, and is an imitation of Horace, Ode 5, Book 4.

[155] Ode 16, Book 2, by "G. R.," and an ode from Book 9, by "R. G.," of Boston (May 1784, pp. 29-30, 32); Ode 1, Book 2, by "E. S.," of Newport (July 1784, pp.

In summary, it may be said of the contributors of poetry that, though they lacked the powers which make for great individual work, they were somewhat schooled and of good intellect; and though they borrowed tools, patterns, and materials from English writers, they wrote with commendable skill.

III

The ill-starred Boston printer, Ezekiel Russell,[156] whose Whig newspaper enterprise at Portsmouth, New Hampshire, had failed, and whose Tory connections with *The Censor*[157] had proved unfortunate, could not stand by while *The Boston Magazine* held the field. Nine months after the failure of *The Gentleman and Lady's Town and Country Magazine*, and just as Greenleaf withdrew from *The Boston Magazine*, leaving Freeman as the sole and unhappy editor and publisher, Russell published *The American Monitor: or, the Republican Magazine*, which he discontinued after the first issue for October 1785.[158] The new magazine contained sixteen pages octavo. It was not advertised in the newspapers, but the first number was in itself a prospectus, and following the title Russell announced the plan of printing "the greatest Variety of the most useful, entertaining and agreeable Matter, both in Prose and Poetry," to be published, on suitable encouragement, at least once a month, and more often if occasion permitted, at nine pence a single number.

The American Monitor was the first magazine in the United States with a definitely commercial appeal. Russell promised to "make it our constant study . . . to promote COMMERCE," to give the latest mercantile intelligence from Europe, and to report the commercial proceedings "of every Trading Town throughout the United States in general, but of Boston and other Sea-Port Towns in this Commonwealth in particular." He promised also "to serve the interest of the honest and industrious HUSBAND-MAN" and the merchants, and he was planning to include Jeremy Belknap's *A History of New-Hampshire* and many "kind favours"

118-19); Ode 3, Book 2, by "B. A.," of Waltham (Aug. 1784, pp. 167-68); Ode 24, Book 1 (Sept. 1784, p. 216); Ode 14, Book 2 (Nov. 1784, p. 310).

[156] See Chapter VI, note 108.

[157] See Chapter VI, section V.

[158] See note 3.

of the "Sensible and Polite" and the "Witty and Grave," but the failure of the magazine put an end to all hopes.[159]   How much of this plan was Russell's own, and what ideas were supplied by others, it is impossible to determine.   But on the first page plural editorship was admitted, for an announcement was signed by "The Editors and Publisher."

The commercial emphasis was normal for the times.   When the magazine was started, the excellent Boston newspaper, *The Independent Chronicle: and the Universal Advertiser*, was running a number of anonymous articles and essays on business, written by men who exhibited sound judgment in their writings.   But the scene quickly shifted.   Hardly had the first number of the magazine appeared when internal political difficulties and unrest among the less fortunate classes (which led later to Shays's Rebellion) assumed grave proportions.   Interest turned dramatically to the militia.   A newspaper might shift with the times, reporting the news.[160]   But a magazine could not veer so easily.   The general aim of the articles printed in the first issue was an attempt at exuberant satire of court decisions, of whipping posts, and of crabbed maliciousness stalking in the garb of piety.   In "Observations on the Liberty of the Press,"[161] the sixpence tax on advertisements was attacked as unfair to business.   In "The Downfall of American Religious Tyranny: or, the Total Repeal of the Warden-Act in the Town of Rocksburgh, Not Thirty Miles from the City of Bostonia; Commonly Called the Parish of Piety, in the City of Reformation and County of Somefolks"[162] was the beginning of what probably would have been a religious satire.   In a prologue called "The Silver Age,"[163] courts were criticized and magistrates accused of basing their judicial decisions on factors of self-enrichment.   News of the turns in events, politics, commerce, and business could be more quickly and frequently supplied by the news-

[159] For quotations and the statement of plans for the magazine, see the issue for October 1785, pp. 1-2.   Belknap's *History* was published separately; see note 43.   Russell broke away from the general practice by devoting three pages of the sixteen to advertising.   The rate (see pp. 1-2), single column, not exceeding six lines, was a shilling four pence a single insertion, and nine pence per issue thereafter.   Special rates were offered to term subscribers.

[160] A comparison of the file of *The Independent Chronicle* during Sept. and Oct. 1785 with the issues for Nov. 1785 clearly reveals a major change in events.

[161] Oct. 1785, pp. 3-7.

[162] *Ibid.*, pp. 9-10.

[163] *Ibid.*, p. 10.

papers. So Russell abandoned the project. Magazines of a kind sprang up in Worcester and New Haven, and true magazines came into being at New Brunswick, New York, and Philadelphia; but with the demise of *The Gentleman and Lady's Town and Country Magazine* in 1785 and of *The Boston Magazine* in 1786, the city was without a miscellany until 1789, when Isaiah Thomas, whose experiences as publisher of *The Massachusetts Spy*, *The Royal American Magazine*, and *The Worcester Magazine* had given him a broad background, founded *The Massachusetts Magazine*.

CHAPTER IX

NEW ENGLAND HYBRIDS

DURING 1786 five magazines were established in the United
States: two in Connecticut, and one in each of the states of Massachusetts, Pennsylvania, and New Jersey. But it is convenient to
discuss in this chapter only the New England group, for the three
founded in Connecticut and Massachusetts were in a sense variations of other types of publications, while the remaining two[1] were
true monthly miscellanies, readily associated by time and district
with two other magazines begun in 1787 at New York and
Philadelphia.[2]

The New-Haven Gazette, and the Connecticut Magazine (1786-
89),[3] published by Josiah Meigs and Eleutheros Dana, and *The
Worcester Magazine* (1786-88),[4] published by Isaiah Thomas,
were the successors of newspapers which their respective publishers
had conducted. Meigs and Dana, in changing their newspaper to
a weekly quarto magazine of eight pages, seem to have slightly
altered their attitude in making their selections. Thomas, however, frankly admitted that he had changed only the format of the
paper he had been publishing, and that he had done this in order
to dodge the stamp tax on newspapers, which he held to be as
abominable as the British tax of Colonial days. *The American
Musical Magazine.* (1786-87)[5] published at New Haven by Amos
Doolittle and Daniel Read, contained only selections of music,
with accompanying lyrics. Both men were somewhat familiar
with the details of music-book publishing, and their plan was nothing more than a method of marketing a book of music by issuing
it in parts, and receiving payment in the form of subscriptions. In
its restricted field it indicates the popular interest in New Eng-

---

[1] *The New-Jersey Magazine, and Monthly Advertiser* and *The Columbian Magazine,
or Monthly Miscellany.*
[2] *The American Magazine* (edited by Noah Webster) and *The American Museum.*
[3] See "Bibliography," p. 369.
[4] *Ibid.*, p. 370.
[5] *Ibid.*

land in vocal music, especially hymns. As a magazine of music it was the first representative of its class in America; but if considered as a book of music, it becomes one of several publications during the 'eighties which fed an awakening regard for music that gathered momentum during the succeeding decade.

Both *The New-Haven Gazette, and the Connecticut Magazine* and *The Worcester Magazine* exhibit the tense political atmosphere of 1786-88. Neither *The Pennsylvania Magazine* of 1775-76 nor *The United States Magazine* of 1779 conveys a more disturbed sense of fearful apprehension. A foreign adversary had been a tangible assailant, easy to hate and definite to combat; but the causes of domestic confusion following the war, shattering the dreams of those who had built visions of happiness, prosperity, and progress, were internal enemies not so easily attacked. Imposed on all the other burdens pressing on the relatively new state governments and the largely impotent, still unfinished structure of the national government, lay the financial crisis. The soldiery had been dismissed unpaid. New foreign loans had been required to pay interest on old foreign loans. Descending values had ruined the hopes of those who had thought to escape difficulties by issues of currency. Payments of interest on the domestic debt had long been suspended. The farming population looked apprehensively, at times belligerently, at efforts to redeem outstanding currency, much of which had been drawn to the cities; and commercial centers, lacking domestic manufactories, were practically forced to trade with England under impositions of duties which yielded a heavy balance in her favor. When in the early autumn of 1786 Shays's Rebellion broke out in Massachusetts, possibilities of a more general internecine war disturbed some minds. States clung tenaciously to their new-gained powers, and minor but determined groups were obstructing movements toward a closer federation of the states.

In Connecticut, where conflicting forces seemed rather evenly matched until the genius of her statesman, Oliver Ellsworth, found a working compromise to safeguard the interests of the smaller states, *The New-Haven Gazette, and the Connecticut Magazine* became a tireless advocate for the adoption of a strong federal constitution and the stabilization of the financial structures. It summoned to its pages logic, satire, and pure passion to support its convictions. In it appear essays by such men as Oliver Ellsworth, Roger Sherman, and Noah Webster. It indulged more strenuously than did its contemporaries in ironic satire, chief examples being the prose of "Lycurgus" and the prose and verse of David Humphreys and his collaborators in *American Antiquities*, a part of which, *The Anarchiad*, may be aptly called the *M'Fingal* of the post-war reign of distress.

The Worcester Magazine could not print satire with the abandon of its fellow in Connecticut. Worcester lay at a center of Shays's Rebellion. Thomas and the major contributors to his magazine clearly realized the necessity of maintaining a conciliatory and sympathetic attitude toward all, while they pressed the claims of the agencies of stabilization; besides, the publisher was himself smarting under the Massachusetts tax on newspapers, and he appreciated the state of mind of those who might find fault with certain governmental practices. "Tom Taciturn," "The Worcester Speculator," "Tom Tinker," "Nestor," "A Citizen," and others supported the principles of federal cohesion and a sound financial structure, each in his own manner and measure of wit and reason. But the imperative need for domestic tranquillity governed the tone of their utterances, and the magazine best served the public weal by serving least the literature of forensic and satire.

I

Proposals for issuing *The American Musical Magazine* in monthly numbers of four pages, printed from copperplates at a price of two-thirds of a dollar a year, were addressed to all "Lovers of Musick," and appeared in *The Connecticut Journal* of March 29, 1786.[6] A "variety of the newest, and most approved Pieces . . . both from British Authors, and American Composers" was promised. Perhaps most important of all was the assurance that "no Piece will be Published without being previously examined and approved by the *Musical Society* of *Yale College*." It seems that no advertisements heralded the first or the early succeeding numbers, but *The Connecticut Journal* of September 13, 1786, con-

---

[6] The advertisement was dated February. One-half the subscription price was due with the first number, the remainder at the close of the year. Those subscribing for lots of six were offered a seventh gratis. The agencies for sale of the periodical seem to have been limited largely to the state.

tained an announcement that four numbers were "already published"; so if they were issued in accordance with the custom of the time—each month's number during the early part of the succeeding month—the first appeared in May. In *The New-Haven Gazette* of September 6, 1787, Doolittle and Read informed "their customers" of the completion of the first volume, but made no statement of a desire to continue publication. Evidently success had not greeted the publishers, and it seems possible that the numbers had not been issued regularly with the march of the calendar months.

As a singing master, organist, and editor of *The American Singing Book* (1785), Daniel Read,[7] tradesman of New Haven, was a well-known figure in musical circles before he undertook, in his twenty-ninth year, the publication of *The American Musical Magazine*, associating himself with Amos Doolittle, an engraver, in the enterprise. Doolittle, then thirty-two years of age, had come to New Haven as a young man to ply his trade as a silversmith, and, self-taught, had engraved a number of copperplates and been associated with Simeon Jocelyn in the publishing of a music book.[8] He lent his support to Read's enterprise by engraving the plates for the magazine and becoming associated with him as a publisher.

[7] Read was born at Rehoboth, Mass., in 1757. He moved to New Haven during the Revolutionary War, and engaged in business as a comb maker and later as proprietor of a general store. Before he was twenty years of age he had taught psalmody. In New Haven he became a leader of a choir, an organist, and a teacher of music, as well as a composer of some note. Following the publication of the magazine he issued other musical publications, the most famous being the three sections of *The Columbian Harmonist*, first editions of which appeared respectively in 1793, 1794, and 1795.

Read's manuscripts at the New Haven Colony Historical Society embrace his Song Book (1777), Letter Book (1793-1807, 1829-32), and Journal (well kept through 1796-98, then sketchily done through to 1812). The most interesting account of his life is by J. M. Hoppin (who in his boyhood often saw Read at the North Church), in a chapter of *History of the City of New Haven* (1887), edited by Edward Elias Atwater, pp. 211-12. For a bibliography of Read's publications, see Champlin and Apthorp, *Cyclopedia of Music and Musicians*, III, 186-87. See also Frank J. Metcalf's *American Writers and Compilers of Sacred Music* (1925), pp. 94-99.

[8] Doolittle was born at Cheshire, Conn., in 1754, in which place he learned the trade of silversmith. He saw duty at Cambridge, Mass., at the outbreak of the Revolutionary War, and published a series of copperplate engravings of scenes of early battles. Other engravings followed. In 1782, in association with Simeon Jocelyn, who was the editor, he published *The Chorister's Companion*. He sold likewise Chauncy Langdon's *The Beauties of Psalmody* (1786) and did plates for Read's *The Columbian Harmonist*,[c] first published in 1793. Later work included engravings for geographies, an encyclopedia, and books on mechanics and chemistry. For a short biography, see William A. Beardsley's *An Old New Haven Engraver and his Work: Amos Doolittle* (read in 1910 and privately printed to the number of 31 copies, of which No. 13 is at Yale).

Undoubtedly the success of *The American Singing Book*, which by 1787 had passed into a third and enlarged edition, as well as the general activity in music-book publishing,[9] in which New Haven was a most important center, led Read to conceive the idea of the magazine. Certainly there is no essential difference in type of content between *The American Singing Book* and the magazine, nor between the latter and Read's later successful compilation, *The Columbian Harmonist*,[10] for which Doolittle engraved the plates.

The churches and colleges were the chief organizations in which musical expression was fostered for the mass of people; so nearly the whole interest resided in devotional music, principally vocal. Read's manuscript Song Book,[11] much of which had been prepared by 1776, shows the nearly complete sway of Isaac Watts, and is an example of selective tendency which the compiler shared with his age. *The American Singing Book*, well supplied with selections from Watts, was a collection of psalms, hymns, and spiritual songs compiled—so Read wrote in the preface—to assist congregations in their singing, a "Duty encumbent upon all Denominations." No song used in the singing book was reprinted in the magazine; but only five of the thirty-four pieces in the magazine may be classified as non-devotional: a minuet, a plaint of love's general sadness, and three songs treating of pastoral themes.

Most of the songs in the magazine are short, occupying not over a page. The longest, "An Anthem Taken out of the 57th Psalm" (Williams), extends over seven pages;[12] only three other source-credited songs cover four pages each, "The Seasons Moralized" (Dwight), "An Anthem Taken out of the 26th Psalm"

[9] Some idea of the vitality of the movement may be gained by noting not only the New Haven imprints already cited (*The Chorister's Companion, The American Singing Book, The Beauties of Psalmody,* and *The Columbian Harmonist*), but also certain of the important books published in the several states during years approximating those of the magazine: *Select Harmony* (Oliver Brownson, 1783), *A Collection of Anthems and Hymn Tunes* (Daniel Bayley, 1784), *The Psalm Singer's Assistant* (ibid., 1785), *The New Harmony of Zion* (ibid., 1788), *Select Harmony* (Andrew Law, 1779, 1784), *The Suffolk Harmony* (William Billings, 1786), *Laus Deo! The Worcester Collection of Sacred Harmony* (printed by Isaiah Thomas, 1786), *Select Psalms and Hymns* (Andrew Adgate's Pupils, 1787), and *A Compilation of the Litanies and Vespers* (printed by John Aitken, 1787).

[10] For the last, see note 7. Both *The American Singing Book* and *The Columbian Harmonist* are rectangular, 4½ x 7¼ inches; the larger magazine is nearly square, 8½ x 10½ inches.

[11] See note 7, 2nd paragraph.

[12] Pp. 35-41.

(Adams), and "An Ode for Christmas" (Atwell).[13] From his own compositions, Read selected seven songs, all short and devotional in theme, three of which he later republished in *The Columbian Harmonist*.[14] Next to himself, Read honored William Billings, including four songs by this famous Boston tanner who by 1786 had published four books of music and won for himself a most important place among early American composers of church music.[15] The other selections in the magazine are sufficiently broad in variety of subject and number of composers represented to make the periodical an ecumenical collection.[16] Whether or not the advertisement in *The New-Haven Gazette* of September 6, 1787 indicates that the twelfth number appeared approximately four months late, at least the project was more successful than the subsequent musical magazine planned by Read's fellow Connecticut publisher of music books, the Reverend Andrew Law, the first number of which appeared in 1792, the second in 1793, and the sixth in 1801.

II

The New-Haven Gazette, and the Connecticut Magazine[17] is more closely associated with Josiah Meigs than with his partner, Eleutheros Dana, as the latter withdrew from the firm at the beginning of August 1787. Moreover, Meigs's connections in New

[13] These appear respectively on pp. 3-6, 19-22, 27-30.

[14] The seven are: "Devotion" (p. 8), "Russia" (pp. 9-10), "Greenwich" (pp. 13-14), "Windsor" (p. 31), "Unity" (p. 46), "Condescension" (p. 48), "Stonington" (pp. 48-49). The three reprinted are "Russia," "Greenwich," and "Windsor."

[15] Selections by Billings are: "Phoebus" (p. 23), "Golgotha" (p. 25), "Manchester" (pp. 32-33), "Worcester" (p. 33). For comment on Billings see Metcalf, *op. cit.*, pp. 51-61.

[16] "New-Milford" (Bunnel, pp. 7-8), "Contemplation" (Read, W., p. 47), "Hopewell" (Seaver, pp. 9-10, the only love song in the magazine), "Danbury" (Canfield, p. 10), "Southwell" (Carpenter, pp. 12-13), "New-Stratford" (Gillet, p. 24), "Crusifixion" *sic* (Harris, p. 26), "Medfield" (Adams, G. W., p. 46), "Autumn" (Fisher, p. 43), "Fischer's Minuet" (p. 18), "Berwick" (Thomas, p. 11), "Andover" (*ibid.*, pp. 24-25), "Walpole" (*ibid.*, p. 34), "Pastoral Nymph" (Arne, p. 15), "Sweet Echo" (*ibid.*, pp. 17-18), "The Morning" (Hook, pp. 16-17), "Anthem" 126th Psalm (Adams, pp. 44-45), "Vernon" (*ibid.*, p. 49), "Jerusalem" (anonymous, pp. 41-42). It should be noted that in the cases of Thomas, Arne, Hook, Adams, and Billings, Read's attributions as given in this note refer to the collections by the several composers and editors in which the songs appear, not necessarily to the composers. The other songs are identified as composed by the several men.

[17] See note 3.

Haven were more favorable for editing an important periodical.[18] He was a native of Connecticut, in which state he was born in 1757, and graduated from Yale at the age of twenty-one. Three years later he received an appointment as tutor in the college, and he remained there until 1784, when he formed a partnership with Daniel Bowen and Dana for the publication of a weekly newspaper, *The New-Haven Gazette*. In the meantime (1783) he was admitted to the bar, and at the beginning of the first year of his editorship he became Clerk of the city, a position he held until 1789. His associations at Yale, a stronghold of federalism, were an undoubted assistance to him in many ways. Among his classmates were Noah Webster and Joel Barlow—men whose writings later appeared in Meigs's magazine—as well as the jurist and statesman, Uriah Tracy, Zephaniah Swift, later Chief Justice of the state, and Oliver Wolcott, who succeeded Hamilton as Secretary of the Treasury. Timothy Dwight, a contributor to the magazine and later President of Yale, Meigs came to know when the former was a tutor at the college; and the Reverend Ezra Stiles, who was most friendly to him, became President of Yale the year preceding Meigs's graduation.[19]

The linage of the eight-page issues of *The New-Haven Gazette* was greater than that of its New Haven competitor, *The Connecticut Journal*, with its four larger-sized pages; but the latter had been strongly entrenched since its establishment in 1767, and maintained its patronage. Another but less competitive paper, because of its distance from New Haven, was *The Connecticut Courant*, at Hartford, a vital force in the field since 1764. During two years *The New-Haven Gazette* won and maintained a solid

[18] For chief details of chronology I have used the *Life of Josiah Meigs* (1887), written by his great-grandson, William M. Meigs, as well as certain associative background as recorded in Richard J. Purcell's *Connecticut in Transition: 1775-1818* (1918). Neither source engaged to any extent on the study of the magazine. Of the later life of Meigs—his contentions and rather stormy experiences in the Bermudas and as a professor at Yale and as the president of the University of Georgia—this study has no concern except possibly to point out that the pattern emphasizes a combativeness perhaps ill adapted to the working out of major administrative policies. This crusading spirit was more happily engaged when fighting antifederalism in the first bloom of his powers as editor, and makes the magazine the most important medium among its fellows for satire.

[19] Stiles wrote commendingly of Meigs, was interested in his aeronautical experiments, and made him a pallbearer at the funeral of his daughter in 1785. See the *Diary* edited by Dexter, *op. cit.*, III, 157, 158, 160, 321.

place among the newspapers. But internal dissension arose among its three owners; and when with the issue for February 16, 1786, the words *"and the Connecticut Magazine"* were added to the title and some reorganization of style was made, Bowen terminated his association and addressed himself to the establishment of *The New-Haven Chronicle*, the first issue appearing April 18, 1786.

According to the "Proposals" issued, two principles induced Meigs and Dana to make the change. First, subscribers were complaining that advertisements usurped too much space, and the new scheme, with the subscription price set at nine shillings a year, provided for advertisements in supplementary pages only. Secondly, the smaller eight-page quarto size, indexed for binding, would offer a form in which men of "genius and ability will be more willing to place their writings."[20] The plan was not wholly successful, for at the close of the first year, in accordance with an announcement,[21] the price was reduced to eight shillings, and the advertisements were carried without supplementary pages. At the time, between four and five hundred papers were being delivered to the post.[22] Several months later more definite statements of circulation were made; in June 1787 nearly nine hundred papers were being printed weekly, and in September the figure was raised closer to a thousand.[23]

When the transition from the newspaper to the newspaper-magazine was made, the first four or more pages were reserved for essays, poetry, and general magazine material of other kinds; and the news, which did not occupy over a fourth of the total space, was issued under the usual magazine heading, "Historical Chronicle." Much original material was printed, and the magazine became the source of many clippings for *The Connecticut Courant* at Hartford and *The American Museum* at Philadelphia; even the local competitor, *The Connecticut Journal*, clipped articles from it on occasions when Meigs was waging his liveliest journalistic war with the state legislature and governor over the question of national federation. Gradually the original plan was abridged. The abandonment of supplementary advertising pages was the first indication

---

[20] Dated Feb. 15, 1786. The first volume contained only 399 numbered pages plus five pages of index, and the supplements of advertisements.

[21] See magazine issue for Jan. 11, 1787, p. 364.

[22] *Ibid.*, Jan. 18, 1787, p. 366.

[23] *Ibid.*, June 14 and Aug. 7, 1787, pp. 135 (misnumbered 137), 199.

of weakening; Dana's withdrawal from the partnership with the twenty-fourth number of the second volume further curtailed the enterprise, and as the second volume drew to a close Meigs announced, while pleading for subscribers to pay their accounts, "If this paper is continued, the size of it will probably be reduced."[24] Though the periodical was continued undiminished in size during a third year, even the early numbers contained less of original substance, and as the weeks progressed the clippings lost their vitality, and instead of being timely native discussions on important subjects, they became merely filler lifted almost at random from any source, often foreign.

The New-Haven Gazette, and the Connecticut Magazine looked on a seaboard nation newly formed and complicated by a snarl of interrelating disturbances: public debts, a lack of manufactures, agricultural distress, an impotent national government. Factions were quick to anger when shifting circumstances seemed to operate unfairly against them. Men like Josiah Meigs, David Humphreys, Joel Barlow, John Trumbull, Thomas Paine, Roger Sherman, Oliver Ellsworth, Noah Webster, Benjamin Rush, Tench Coxe, James Wilson, William Williams, the anonymous "Cato" and "Spectator," and others had spoken or were to speak with an emphasis applicable to the times, and the magazine gave them a new or an extended public. It is worth while at this point to note that the editors recognized their strategic position, and while conducting a journal filled with the satire which was the traditional mode in both England and America, they still remembered that good will was a necessary antidote for the public's distraught mind. In a note explaining why extracts from David Humphreys's *A Poem on the Happiness of America* were reprinted, the editors announced that "Amid the tumultuous proceedings and existing troubles . . . the Editors of News-Papers are called upon to select such . . . good-humoured entertainment, as may tend to put their Readers in better temper with respect to themselves, their neighbours, the community at large, and their fellow creatures in general."[25]

[24] *Ibid.*, Dec. 27, 1787, p. 358 (misnumbered 340).
[25] For announcement and one excerpt, see magazine issue of Dec. 7, 1786, pp. 337-38; for other excerpts, see issues of July 13, 1786 and Jan. 18, 1787, pp. 172, 372. The poem was published in London and Hartford in 1786, in Portsmouth in 1790, and in *The American Museum* in March 1787, pp. 240-62. (Frank Landon

The most important literary item in the magazine is *American Antiquities*, which embraced principally *The Anarchiad, a Poem on the Restoration of Chaos and Substantial Night*, conceived by David Humphreys, John Trumbull, Joel Barlow, and Lemuel Hopkins, and conducted through twelve numbers and an epilogue.[26] Of this work, the most trenchant literary outgrowth of the fight against antifederalism and the most outstanding mock epic of the early post-war period, David Humphreys wrote to his friend, George Washington: "I would have sent you several of the late papers from the same press, which contained performances written by Mr. Trumbull, Mr. Barlow, & myself, in a style & manner, I believe somewhat superior to common newspaper publications: but the demand has been so uncommonly great for those papers that there is not a single one to be obtained. In some instances the force of ridicule has been found of more efficacy than the force of argument, against the Anti-federalists & Advocates for Mobs & Conventions. It was pleasant enough to observe how some leading

---

Humphreys, *The Life and Times of David Humphreys*, 1917, II, 461.) The ninth edition appeared in *The Miscellaneous Works of David Humphreys* (1804), pp. 23-43.

Humphreys's fame was so great that other of his poems were printed in the magazine: "Elegy on the Burning of Fairfield" (June 29, 1786, p. 159), "Mount Vernon" (Nov. 16, 1786, p. 314), "The Genius of America" (Jan. 25, 1787, p. 373), and the uncredited "It Rains" (Sept. 20, 1787, pp. 243-44). Note also the letter of the Marquis de Chastelleux to Humphreys on Chastelleux's prose translation of Humphreys's poem addressed to the American armies, together with a review (Nov. 9, 1786, pp. 305-06).

[26] See issues of Oct. 26, 1787, pp. 287-88; Nov. 2, pp. 294-95; Dec. 28, 1786, pp. 353-54; Jan. 11, pp. 357-58; Jan. 25, p. 380; Feb. 22, p. 3; March 15, p. 26; March 22, pp. 30-31; April 5, p. 49; May 24, pp. 105-06; Aug. 16, p. 201-02; Sept. 13, 1787, pp. 233-34; Feb. 21, 1788 (issues for the year were not paged). Frank Landon Humphreys (*op. cit.*, I, 382) wrote that "it may be safely assumed that the majority of the papers" were by Humphreys, a statement perhaps too rash for evidence at hand; that Humphreys was a major contributor and perhaps the most prolific of the group may possibly be stated. The biographer was in doubt whether Dr. Lemuel Hopkins contributed to the series, but wrote that to say Hopkins did not contribute "cannot positively be said" (*ibid.*, I, 384-85). The series has been edited with notes and appendices by Luther G. Riggs, *The Anarchiad: A New England Poem* (1861). Vernon Louis Parrington (*The Connecticut Wits*, 1926, "Introduction," p. xxxi) has considered Hopkins as "chiefly responsible" for the substance of the poem, following the opinion of Samuel Kettel (*Specimens of American Poetry*, 1829, I, 272-83). Kettel's attribution was rather speculative, however. "Dr. Hopkins suggested the plan of the work, and has always borne the credit of having written the most striking passages," Kettel wrote. "Its authorship being more closely connected with his name than any other, the extracts from the poem are given under the present [Hopkins's] head." (*Ibid.*, I, 274.)

Men, of erroneous politics, were stung to the soul by the shafts of satire."[27]

In manner, like other mock epics of the period, the scheme was somewhat Miltonic, though the immediate inspiration seems to have sprung from *The Rolliad* (1785), which Humphreys had seen on a visit to England.[28] The first number proclaimed the discovery in the West of an ancient manuscript in twenty-four books, some of the prophetic parts of which, since they dealt with the current transpiring year, would be published. In the second number reference was made to Shays's Rebellion, and Anarch expressed his confidence of continued anarchy in Massachusetts. The third and fourth numbers treated respectively of the currency problem and of selfish, hypocritical, job-seeking politicians. The succeeding number undertook a discussion of patriotic songs and Humphreys's "The Genius of America" was considered as an example. Wronghead, in the next installment, delivered a sad soliloquy on his fear lest a federal constitution should yet be devised, but is consoled by Anarch. In the seventh and eighth numbers mock satire was pointed against the Cincinnati, and sincere satire was thrust at the Connecticut jurist and state senator, William Williams, who was the butt of an unusual amount of ridicule on the part of the magazine, yet so far triumphed as to win again his seat in the senate at the succeeding election.[29] In

[27] Frank Landon Humphreys, *op. cit.,* I, 380.

[28] *Ibid.,* pp. 381-82; also Luther G. Riggs, *op. cit.,* "Preface," p. v.

[29] As a judge and state senator, William Williams was a leader of the antifederalists and an opponent of the organization of army officers known as the Cincinnati. In main his followers were of the opinion that a highly organized federal scheme would curtail democracy and be negligent of the rights of the smaller states, and that the Cincinnati would operate to establish a kind of aristocracy and an invisible force subversive to democracy and dangerous to the civil government. They remembered the project of Gates and his associates to coerce legislators by turning the army against the representatives of the public. As regards both federalism and the Cincinnati they harbored a real fear.

Humphreys was both a federalist and a member of the Cincinnati. Meigs had gathered around his magazine a strong group of federalists, and in the attempt to defeat Williams at the approaching election they wrote many satirical articles against him. (See Luther G. Riggs, *op. cit.,* Appendix C, pp. 104-20.) The controversy started when a manuscript of a speech by Williams, while being transmitted to Joseph Hopkins for comment, was intercepted. *The Connecticut Courant* printed the letter in a form designated as true, and likewise a satire on it in verse. *The New-Haven Gazette, and the Connecticut Magazine* also printed the satire (Oct. 12, 1786, p. 276), and followed this with a reputed genuine copy of Hopkins's reply and a satire thereon (Oct. 19, 1786, pp. 281-82). Next came Williams's accusation that Gen. S. H. Parsons unfairly secured the letter from the carrier, Col. David Smith, and Parsons's reply

the ninth and tenth numbers the writers returned to the thread of the narrative in the epic; Night, mother of Anarch, animates anew the discouraged spirit of her son in his fight for a chaotic world; and Hesper, archenemy of Anarch, delivers a strong plea for federal government. The eleventh number, concerned with "The Land of Annihilation," is one of the most powerful of the satires in the whole magazine, picturing vividly a country destitute of leadership and credit, and close to chaos, and containing pointed references to William Williams. The twelfth number prophesied the writings of the Abbé Raynal, who would not name, among men of genius in arts or sciences, one from America, and of Robertson, who should observe that American soil produced only reptiles and serpents. But the fashioners of *American Antiquities* were loath to close the series in this situation. Filled more with political consciousness than with a sense of art, they had hitherto more than once shattered the illusion of reality in the structure; and an epilogue, the "Edict of Penance," was attached, in which Anarch was caused to order three coffins, one each for the antifederalists, the paper-moneyites, and the insurgents.[30]

The work of Humphreys, Trumbull, and Barlow in the magazine is not limited to *American Antiquities* and possibly some of the other satirical thrusts at William Williams.[31] Besides minor poems,[32] Humphreys is represented by his speech to the state legislature on the encouragement of agriculture and manufactures,[33]

(Nov. 2, 1786, pp. 293-95). David Smith wrote then in defense of himself, and Williams corrected the errors in the original letter as published (Nov. 9, 1786, pp. 306-07). Mock defenses of Williams followed by "Benevolence Junior," "Trustless Fox" (Nov. 23, 1786, pp. 317-18), and by "Benevolence, Sr." (Dec. 14, pp. 343-44). The issue for Jan. 11, 1787 (pp. 358-59) reprinted *The Connecticut Courant's* New Year's "The News-Boys: an Eclogue," filled with barbs against Williams and mentioning Dwight, Trumbull, Humphreys, and Barlow.

[30] The series is occasionally reflected in other contributions to the magazine. One who signed himself as an admirer of *American Antiquities* undertook in "The Soliloquy of Spectator" (imitative of Hamlet's popular soliloquy) a blank-verse reply to "Spectator," who had defended the actions of the Connecticut Assembly against the criticisms of "Cato." The soliloquy, which appeared in the issue of Feb. 1, 1787, pp. 386-87, was represented as a part of a manuscript of tragedies discovered by a man in Kentucky. A female contributor, whilst Anarch slept, seized a pen and attempted to mount Parnassus, but was told that woman's place was in the home ("The Female Patriot," Feb. 15, 1787, pp. 397-98).

[31] For a survey of the items regarding Williams, see note 29.

[32] See note 25.

[33] Oct. 26, 1786, p. 290. The extreme need for development of manufactures because of unfavorable foreign trade barriers made the problem a major concern; Humphreys's connections with trade lent weight to his opinions.

in which he was personally interested, and by his defense of his former chief, George Washington, in the famous Captain Asgill case.[34] As secretary to General Washington during the war, Humphreys was familiar with the details, and he submitted the official correspondence to indicate the necessity under which Washington had acted. From the works of Trumbull and of Barlow, Meigs chose two extracts from *M'Fingal* and a critical reference to the poem,[35] and three extracts from *The Vision of Columbus*, together with two critical comments on the epic.[36]

Well-wrought satire was by no means the only weapon used by the magazine against disorder. Appeals to reason, though often filled with passion and sometimes lacking cogency, were valuable aids in the battle. At Hartford young Noah Webster, in two summaries entitled "Political Paragraphs," surveyed the record of the state legislature in the manner of a gruff and ancient patriarch.[37] As he glanced over the shoulder of the immediate past, in June 1786, he could pen no more salutary remark than that "We feel happy that while our public measures are unfederal and our national faith sinking into infamy, some regard is paid to commutative justice. Our legislature has not been knavish enough to adopt that pernicious principle . . . of placing private debts on a footing different from what the parties intended at the con-

[34] Nov. 16, 1786, pp. 309-12. The case arose when an American prisoner, Captain Joshua Huddy, while under the care of the British Captain Lippencut, was killed as the result of British indignation when the life of one of their soldiers, Philip White, was taken because, having laid down his arms, he immediately picked up a musket and shot one of his approaching American captors. Washington's demand that Lippencut be surrendered was refused, and he ordered a reprisal by causing lots to be drawn by British prisoners of equal rank. The fatal lot fell to the young and admirable Captain Charles Asgill, whose death was postponed until waves of sympathy in England and America brought his release. The letters submitted by Humphreys were reprinted in *The Columbian Magazine* (Jan.-Feb. 1787, pp. 205-09, 253-55). A complete survey appears in David Humphreys's *The Conduct of General Washington, Respecting the Confinement of Capt. Asgill, Placed in its True Point of Light* (1859). See also Frank Landon Humphreys's *Life, op. cit.*, I, 252-53. Washington wrote Humphreys a personal letter of thanks for the manner in which he explained the necessity of a reprisal.

[35] (Citations from Vol. III (1788) hereinafter made will not be given with folio numbers, as this volume was unpaged.) Aug. 24, 1786, p. 220; Sept. 21, 1786, p. 249; Jan. 17, 1788.

[36] April 19, Aug. 30, 1787, pp. 65, 219; Jan. 10, Sept. 4, 1788.

[37] In the Hoadley copy of the magazine at the Connecticut Historical Society, Noah Webster affixed his initials "N. W." to the first article (June 22, 1786, p. 151); to the second article (Nov. 30, 1786, pp. 330-31) he wrote both "N. W." and "N. Webster."

tract."[38] In November of the same year he commented sadly on the injustice done the army, "cheated" of pay when disbanded and still awaiting the partial sum promised. He was also concerned that "*jealousy*, thou child of hell and father of all mischief," operated uppermost in the councils of both federalists and antifederalists, and he was ready to proclaim himself an advocate of a limited monarchy: "I was once as strong a republican as any man in America. *Now*, a republican is among the last kinds of government I should choose. I would infinitely prefer a limited monarchy, for I would sooner be subject to the caprice of one man, than to the ignorance and passions of a multitude."[39]

Much more important, rational, and authoritative were the articles of other Connecticut men. Roger Sherman, Connecticut legislator and member of the committee which had drafted the Declaration of Independence, wrote a series of letters "To the People of Connecticut," under the pseudonym of "A Countryman," which were so carefully prepared that they rank among the best of their kind, and their influence in securing an early adoption of the Constitution by the state was considerable.[40] Meigs also published Sherman's strictures on the judicial establishment of the state[41] and his "Observations on the Alterations Proposed as Amendments to the New Federal Constitution," the latter, commended by John Adams, appearing over the pseudonym of "A Citizen of New-Haven."[42] No less important a figure was Oliver Ellsworth, whose compromise plea for equal representation of states in the proposed national senate had greatly facilitated the drafting of the Constitution when the convention had nearly broken up in dissension. In the magazine Meigs reprinted two of a series of thirteen letters by Ellsworth in support of a strong national govern-

[38] P. 151.

[39] Pp. 330-31.

[40] Nov. 15, 22, 29, Dec. 6, 20, 1787, pp. 305-06, 313-14, 321, 329-30, 345. Annotations in the P. L. Ford file of the magazine, owned originally by Simeon Baldwin, resident of New Haven at the time, attribute the first three to Sherman. See Sabin, *A Dictionary of Books Relating to America*, No. 80405 note.

[41] Nov. 6, 27, 1788. Signed "A Countryman," and attributed to Sherman in the Baldwin copy.

[42] Dec. 18, 1788. Signed "A Citizen of New-Haven," and attributed to Sherman in the Baldwin copy. John Adams wrote to Sherman that he had read the letters "with pleasure" (*The Works of John Adams*, ed. Charles Francis Adams, 1851, VI, 427-36, 437-42). The letters are also mentioned in *The Writings of James Madison*, Gaillard Hunt (1900-1910), V, 346 note.

ment.[43] Perhaps more popular, as it possessed the characteristics of personal combat, was the controversy between "Cato," a strong federalist, and "Spectator," a defender of the recalcitrant state legislature. The questions at issue—the legislature's apparent anti-federalism and its adjournment without voting to the federal government the sum of money requisitioned for the latter's support—[44] were discussed so heatedly that in the issue for March 15, 1787, "Cato's" remarks usurped the leading position usually held by *American Antiquities.*

Meigs himself was quite possibly the author of the series of ten articles, "Observations on the Present Situation and Future Prospects of This and the United States," by "Lycurgus."[45] This series was original with the magazine and held first position during the first nine issues of the periodical in its new format. It was not inspired as to method, nor did it display unusual fertility of invention; but it made good reading for the time and was a peer among the better class of offerings published for politically-minded readers. The ironical rationalizations of the modified Lycurgus pled for a glorious age of penury. He was in favor of the loose confederacy, for only in poverty lay democracy, and impotency assured the desirable seizure of western lands by foreign powers and a loss of riches.[46] He felt that young America should be congratulated in attaining a place half way between pure democracy and representative government, as federal legislators and executives were elected but given no power.[47] He was pleased to yield the eighth number to Anarchus "in manly opposition to the sentiment of Washington and the late Governor Trumbull."[48] Probably the most interesting of the series is the ninth, in which the author seized upon a current article of news—the discovery of white negroes—and turned it to the service of satire. The first white negroes, said he, were the serfs of ancient times. But they had

---

[43] Dec. 20, 1787, pp. 345-47, March 13, 1788.

[44] Nov. 30, 1786, Jan. 18, Feb. 8, March 28, 15, April 5, 1787, pp. 331-32, 365-66, 389-91, 391-92, 17-20, 25-26, 51-52.

[45] Feb. 16, 23, March 2, 9, 16, 23, 30, April 6, 13, 20, 1786, pp. 5-6, 9-10, 17-18, 25-26, 33-34, 41-42, 49-50, 57-58, 65-67, 79-80. Wm. M. Meigs (*op. cit.* p. 21) is inclined to believe that the first article of biography by "Lycurgus" fits in general Meigs's own life, and that Meigs may have written under that pseudonym.

[46] Feb. 23, 1786, No. II of the series.

[47] March 23, 1786, No. VI of the series.

[48] April 6, 1786, p. 57.

risen in rebellion, and the method of continuing in the world the happy social state of servitude lay now in burdening the populace with debt and keeping them in debt by issuing paper money and refusing to fund existing obligations.[49]

The editors of the magazine reached also beyond the boundaries of the state and reprinted articles whenever the contents and authors lent weight to the principles of federalism and sound money, or offered ideas of assistance in the development of manufacturing and agriculture. Paine's "Dissertations on Government, the Affairs of the Bank, and Paper Money" was used, an editorial introduction, designed to make peace with the religiously orthodox, proposing that his "patriotism, and . . . elevated reputation as a writer, will render acceptable to our readers any productions of his which may have a general application."[50] Some "Thoughts of Paper Money," by Benjamin Rush ("Nestor"), were clipped from *The Pennsylvania Gazette*.[51] The arguments of James Wilson, who had helped to frame the Constitution, were used in its defense, and a panegyrical peroration of his was likewise reprinted to encourage those engaged in agriculture and commerce.[52] The impassioned but restrained logic of Tench Coxe, of Philadelphia, in his "On the Federal Government," was reprinted from *The American Museum* during five numbers;[53] and to approach the problem from another point of view, "An Essay on the Means of Promoting Federal Sentiments in the United States, by a Foreign Spectator, Native of Sweden" was selected.[54] Meigs also published during 1787 a long series, "Political Establishments of the United States of America, in Candid Review," originally issued in a pamphlet from the press of Robert Bell in 1784, so that the readers of the magazine might easily acquire a solid background of constitutional knowledge to serve them in considering problems of government and political policy.[55]

But the new nation, as seen through the eyes of *The New-Haven*

[49] April 13, 1786, pp. 65-67. No. III (March 2, 1786, pp. 17-18) dealt also with the problem of paper money.

[50] June 1, 22, July 6, 13, 1786, pp. 121-22, 146-47, 163, 171-72.

[51] July 27, Aug. 3, 1786, pp. 188, 189-90.

[52] Oct. 25, 1787, pp. 283-85; Aug. 7, 1788.

[53] Oct. 18-Nov. 15, 1787, pp. 276-77, 282-83, 289-90, 297, 306-08.

[54] Sept. 6, Oct. 18, 1787, pp. 225-26, 274-76.

[55] May 10-June 7, 21, July 5, 12, 1787, pp. 89-90, 97-98, 106-07, 113-14, 121-22, 137-38, 153-54, 161-63.

Gazette, and the Connecticut Magazine, was not all political, financial, and commercial chaos. Meigs was the first American magazine editor to point with humorous mockery at the Connecticut "Blue Laws." "The Friend" offered harborage for the literary essay, criticism, and poetry. Accounts of frontier life and exploration were utilized. Negro slavery was severely criticized, almost raised to a point of issue. Topics on religion were not shunned. American letters and criticism, education, and other topics were given liberal representation.

"The Editor," in presenting "to his readers some extracts from the ancient Records of New-Haven" which would "most strongly mark the singular character and genius of the first settlers," offered "New Haven Antiquities, or Blue Laws" to his readers during four numbers;[56] and in doing this he was the first to usher this sort of iconoclastic policy into American journalism of the magazine type. During the first two numbers he chronicled such records as the punishments of whipping for stealing, and of fines for kissing, and of public shame for illicit relations between the sexes; then, becoming more interested in other than the grotesque elements of history, he printed in the final two numbers the original constitution of the colony, dated June 4, 1639.

Because of original comments on Shakespeare, Milton, Goldsmith, and style and taste, and because of the poetry of Timothy Dwight, "The Friend," conducted through fifteen numbers possibly by Meigs himself under the pseudonym of "James Littlejohn," is the most important literary department in the magazine.[57] The conductor described himself as a native of the state, born in an inland town in 1748; he had attended college, pursued but aban-

[56] Feb. 28, March 6, 13, 20, 1788. The quotation is taken from the first number.

[57] Nos. I-XV, March 23-April 6, April 20-May 4, 25, June 8-22, July 6, Sept. 21, Oct. 12, 19, 1786, and Oct. 4, 1787, pp. 42-43, 50-51, 58-60, 73-74, 81-82, 89-90, 113-14, 129-30, 137-38, 145-46, 161-63, 245-46, 269-70, 277-78, 257-58. Elihu H. Smith, the Connecticut physician and compiler, reprinted from the series Timothy Dwight's "The Trial of Faith" in *American Poems* (1793) and assumed (p. 33) Dwight to be the conductor of the whole series. William Meigs, *op. cit.,* p. 21, was inclined to believe that Meigs was the "James Littlejohn" because of the biographical description in the second number. The biographical details will not wholly suit either man. Of the two, it might seem that Meigs is the more likely candidate, else Dwight resorted to most intricate deception in writing to "Littlejohn" an introductory letter signed "Z." Dwight was living at Greenfield. Though the critical references to the poets might be those of the minister, Meigs was equally fond of Milton, as indicated by his reprinting copious excerpts from the works of Milton during 1788, when he was sole editor.

doned the study of medicine, and, assisted by an inheritance, was able to engage his time as a "spectator of human life."[58] The contribution on epic and pastoral poetry is among the first important critical references to Milton's art in poetry to appear in an American periodical.[59] The writer is convinced that had Milton and Shakespeare changed their birth dates with Homer, Aristotle would have considered their works for the source of pleasure derived from them, and founded his maxims upon the evidence revealed in their work. Thus the dispute would be later whether the *Iliad* and *Æneid* were entitled to be termed epic poems. Reasoning in the same manner, the author found fault with the school of criticism in pastoral poetry which classified the quality of work according to a single standard, for had Theocritus not been taken as an inviolable model, certainly Goldsmith's *Deserted Village* now "would hold the first rank in Pastoral Poetry."[60] It was not the purpose of the author to bring discredit to the genius of Aristotle, but to insist that nature, not Aristotle, should be the basis of critical thought on works produced since his day. The essays on taste were reared on the definition of the term to mean the perception of propriety and beauty in objects, especially those of the imagination, and the author traced the development of the qualities of taste through the enlightening path of experience richly cultivated.[61] Of specific authors, Addison was characterized as possessing "pencil-like beauty" and Johnson as deficient in art.[62] Among other prose contributed to the series, the story by J. Alby, recounting the tale of an old man who married a young wife, is especially distinctive in its qualities of swift action well developed by the use of direct discourse ably handled.[63] Most important of the whole series in the field of literature was Timothy Dwight's "The Trial of Faith," a paraphrase in heroic couplets of the book of Daniel, running in three parts through the twelfth, thirteenth, and fourteenth numbers.[64] "The inclosed poem," Dwight wrote,

[58] No. II, p. 51.
[59] No. IV, p. 74.
[60] *Ibid.*, p. 74.
[61] Nos. X and XI (misnumbered XI and XII).
[62] P. 162.
[63] No. VIII (misnumbered IX).
[64] The first three chapters of the Book of Daniel correspond to the three parts of the poem. *The Conquest of Canäan,* based on the Book of Joshua, had been published in 1785.

"is handed you for publication. I have long thought that the Bible furnished many subjects for poetry, far more deserving the ambition and efforts of genius, · than those to which it is commonly dedicated."[65] In the susceptible mind of Dwight played the stylistic qualities of Pope and the men of his age, as well as the manner and imagery of Milton and the elder writers of the epic as indicated in Vergil.[66] Though he did not attain the higher reaches of originality, Dwight more inclusively brought European tradition to America than did his contemporaries, and "The Trial of Faith" possesses so many associative qualities with respect to literary tradition and to Dwight's own *The Conquest of Canäan* and *The Triumph of Infidelity* that it lends considerable stature to the magazine.[67]

Attention to the West and to slavery was due somewhat to the state's western land holdings and the prospect of immigration, and to the state law enacted in October 1788 to prevent slavery. The adventures of Daniel Boone among Indians ran through four numbers,[68] and John Filson's history of Kentucky was used to describe roads and settlements.[69] Indian treaties were a subject of interest,[70] but the materials of legendry of the noble Indian were wanting, the space being given to the official orders for the regulation of Indian affairs and for troops to combat the tribes who resented peaceful penetration.[71] Poetry was on occasion employed to combat slavery,[72] but in main the matter was one for prose. British[73] as well as native[74] sources were used, and the issue came practically to a close with the printing of the state anti-slave law and the petitions of the Africans to the Sons of Liberty.[75]

[65] P. 244.

[66] *The Conquest of Canäan* owes a considerable debt to Vergil, Milton, and Pope; *Greenfield Hill*, published in 1794 but contemplated long previously, indicates Dwight's familiarity with such other writers as Spenser, Thomson, Denham, Beattie, and Goldsmith.

[67] Dwight was also represented by two extracts from *The Conquest of Canäan* (Jan. 10, Feb. 21, 1788). A critical essay in praise of his poetry and Barlow's also appeared (Sept. 4, 1788), reprinted from *The Connecticut Courant*.

[68] April 17, 24, May 8, 22, 1788.

[69] April 17, 1788.

[70] March 30, April 13, May 25, 1786, pp. 55, 70-71, 118.

[71] Aug. 24, Dec. 28, 1786, Jan. 11, 18, 1787, pp. 215-16, 355-56, 359-60, 367-68.

[72] Feb. 21, Sept. 25, Nov. 27, 1788, the last being a reprint of a poem by William Cowper.

[73] May 29, June 5, 1788 (misdated May 29).

[74] Aug. 24, 1786, p. 216.

[75] Both were in the issue of Oct. 30, 1788.

In its religious attitude the magazine was broadly tolerant. A friendly letter regarding the Moravians at Bethlehem, Pennsylvania, by a girl in her teens, was printed to quiet scandal-loving tongues.[76] "A Dissertation on Miracles" sought to prove their validity but emphasized the foolishness of looking daily for signs in the sky or of following self-appointed prophets.[77] A reprint of the law establishing religious freedom in Virginia was printed with an attached commentary on the progress of the modern world against malicious cruelty and persecution.[78] Two excerpts from the works of Soame Jenyns were used, although his name was anathema to the orthodox because of his insistence on scholastic and historical scrutiny of the text of the Bible.[79] The creed of Chesterfield found a place,[80] and the list of references to Voltaire, though most of the items are on other than religious topics, is not short.[81]

For miscellaneous American selections the editors chose by name as well as by topic, reaching out widely as they thumbed magazines, newspapers, and books. From the works of Franklin were reprinted the "Speech of Miss Polly Baker," "Advice to a Young Tradesman," a maritime observation, the essay on how to make money plenty in every man's pocket, another on state sovereignty (linked with Chastelleux's account of Franklin), and a note on the origin of tobacco.[82] Extracts from the works of the versatile, crusading Benjamin Rush, of Philadelphia, included "The Life of Edward Drinker," his letter to Dr. Price on government and religion, his plea for a federal university, his thoughts on paper money, and his argument for abolishing spirituous liquors.[83] Francis Hopkinson's witty exemplification of modern learning by a specimen of a collegiate examination, his "The New Roof," his celebrated report of the grand Federal procession at Philadelphia, July 4, 1788, and his "Thoughts on the Diseases of the Mind" were all given

[76] Sept. 11, 1788.

[77] Nov. 30, Dec. 7, 14, 21, 1786, pp. 325-27, 333-36, 341-42, 345-46.

[78] Feb. 16, 1786, p. 6.

[79] Essays on virtue (May 18, 1786, pp. 109-10) and a preëxistent state (May 15, 1788).

[80] Nov. 30, 1786, pp. 327-28.

[81] Feb. 16, Sept. 7, 1786, pp. 8, 230-31; March 6, 13, Aug. 14, 1788.

[82] Items appear respectively in issues of April 27, July 27, Aug. 31, Sept. 7, 1786, March 22, 1787, pp. 86-87, 182-83, 224-25, 231, 31-33, and July 10, 1788.

[83] Items appear respectively in issues of April 27, May 18, June 22, July 27-Aug. 3, 1786, pp. 83-84, 109, 149, 188, and 189-90, and July 31 and Aug. 7, 1788.

places.[84] Two letters of John Witherspoon ("Epaminondas") on marriage were chosen.[85] Of perhaps equal interest are the reprints from the works of Dr. David Ramsay of Charleston, South Carolina, William Livingston, Benjamin Lincoln, Thomas Jefferson, Thomas Dawes, Jr., Jedidiah Morse, and William Hillhouse, and an anonymous article in praise of leading American painters and writers.[86]

Among the numerous selections in the magazine still unmentioned are many by writers of note from across the Atlantic. These pieces were readily available to the editors, and in the press of conducting a miscellany, ease of clipping may have somewhat determined the items. But in any case, the selections represent acts of choice, and they reflect the spirit of the current age at the Yale literary center which nursed the Connecticut Wits and was in turn nursed by them. Surely Meigs must have felt the pride which came from the knowledge of shears well handled (in an age when the use of them was an advertised virtue), when from the pages of the magazine he could assemble a roll call which, though one exclude Milton[87] because of his century and Adam Smith[88] because of his subject matter, includes such eighteenth-century writers as Charles Montesquieu, Matthew Prior, William Collins, James Thomson, Samuel Johnson, William Falconer, Samuel Richardson, Jonathan

[84] Items appear respectively in issues of April 5, 1787, pp. 53-54, and Jan. 17-24, July 17, Sept. 25, 1788.

[85] Aug. 28, Sept. 18, 1788.

[86] Items include Ramsay's remarks on Col. Isaac Hayne (March 9, 1786, p. 29) and an extract from his oration to celebrate adoption of the Constitution by South Carolina (July 24, 1788), Livingston ("Hortensius") on "Deism" (June 22, 1786, pp. 147-49), Lincoln on springs in Pennsylvania and Virginia (June 1, 1786, p. 124), extracts from Jefferson's *Notes on Virginia* (April 26, May 3, 1787, pp. 73-75, 81-83), Dawes's "Ode" sung at completion of the Charlestown Bridge (June 29, 1786, p. 159), the Morse-Daggett debate on sumptuary laws (Oct. 5, 12, 1786, pp. 261-63, 270-74), Morse's plan for a geographical grammar (Sept. 6, 1787, pp. 226-27), and Hillhouse's oration in commemoration of Major-General Nathaniel Greene (Sept. 28, 1786, pp. 253-56). The anonymous piece, "An Essay on American Genius" (Feb. 1, 1787, pp. 381-82) announced "The time is come to explode the European creed, that we are infantine in our acquisitions and savage in our manners, . . ." and refers with pride to Ramsay's history, to the triumphs of Barlow, Humphreys, Dwight, and Trumbull in verse, and of West, Copley, Trumbull, Taylor, Steward, and Brown in painting.

[87] "L'Allegro" (March 13, 1788), "Il Penseroso" (March 20, 1788), "Song" (May 22, 1788), extract from *Paradise Lost* (May 15, 1788); a critical piece on the first two poems appeared in the issue of March 27, 1788.

[88] Selections from the *Enquiry into the Nature and Causes of the Wealth of Nations* appear in the issues of July 13-27, Nov. 2, 9, 1786, pp. 169, 177-78, 181-82, 293, 302-03, and Feb. 7, 21, 1788.

Swift, Thomas Warton, Thomas Gray, William Hayley, Oliver Goldsmith, William Cowper, Hugh Blair, and Robert Burns.[89]

III

Isaiah Thomas dated the initial number of his weekly journal, *The Worcester Magazine*, for the first week in April 1786.[90] He had already been a publisher in Worcester for eleven years. In May 1775, having been driven from Boston for attacks against the British policies published in *The Massachusetts Spy, or, Thomas's Boston Journal*, he had established in Worcester *The Massachusetts Spy: or, American Oracle of Liberty*, slightly changing the title in 1781.[91] In 1786, after the state legislature passed an act taxing newspaper advertisements, in lieu of a tax on paper, Thomas indignantly suspended *The Massachusetts Spy* and turned it into the format of an octavo magazine of twelve to sixteen pages as a "substitute."[92] He charged the same price as for newspapers, nine shillings a year unstitched, and printed ad-

[89] Items appear as follows: extract from Montesquieu's *Persian Letters* (May 18, 1786, p. 107); Prior, "On his Death Bed Poor Simon Lies" (April 10, 1788); Collins, "Fidele" and "The Passions" (April 6, 1786, p. 61, Aug. 17, 1786, pp. 208-09); extract from Thomson's *The Seasons* (June 26, 1788); Johnson "A Prayer" and "Anacreon's Dove" (April 6, June 1, 1786, pp. 61, 125); extract from Falconer's *The Shipwreck* (June 8, 1786, p. 132); Richardson's description of a brothel (July 13, 1786, pp. 169-70); Swift's "Causes of a Country's Growing Rich," "The British Wizard," "The Musical Contest," "Imitation of Horace," (June 1, 1786, Aug. 9, 1787, pp. 122, 193-95, April 10, Oct. 2, 1788); Warton's "Ode for the New Year" (Sept. 4, 1788); Gray's "The Fatal Sisters," "The Triumphs of Owen" (May 22, July 10, 1788); extract from Hayley's "Essay on Epic Poetry" (April 27, 1786, p. 82); extracts from Goldsmith's *The Citizen of the World*, etc. (Aug. 10, 1786, pp. 197-98, April 3, 1788); Cowper's "The Rose," and an excerpt against slavery (Oct. 26, 1786, p. 285, May 1, 1788); Burns's "Winter" (Jan. 1, 1789); extract from Blair's *Lectures on Rhetoric* (May 18, 1786, pp. 107-08). Perhaps one should also mention Marquis Beccaria's *Essay on Crimes and Punishments*, which, begun in the newspaper, was concluded in the magazine (Feb. 23, March 2, 9, 16, 23, 30, April 6, 13, 20, 27, May 4, 11, 25, June 15, 29, Aug. 3, 1786, pp. 10-11, 18-19, 27-28, 34-35, 44-45, 51-53, 60-61, 67, 74-75, 82-83, 90-91, 98-99, 114-15, 138-39, 154-55, 191-92).

[90] For bibliography of the magazine, see note 4; for biographical references to Thomas, see especially Chapter VI, note 100; see also Chapter VII, section I, and note 4.

[91] Thomas, *op. cit.*, II, 77-79; I, 180-81. He came to Worcester in 1775, where he had shortly before established a printing press. He left the city in 1776 to go to Salem, but soon returned. The new title was *Thomas's Massachusetts Spy: or, the Worcester Gazette*.

[92] *Ibid.*, II, 77-79; for quotation, see p. 79.

vertisements on the first two and last two pages on "reasonable" terms because "at present advertisements accompanying Magazines are not subjected to a duty."[93]

The first number of the new magazine announced itself as "the *Offspring* of the *American Magazine*, which appeared in Boston, in 1774, and a distant Relation, although unknown to you, of your old publick servant the *Massachusetts Spy*," which had suffered "an attack upon its vitals," and would not appear again until the state should repeal the unfair tax.[94] In the second number Thomas's sentiment welled: sixteen years had elapsed since he had first published the *Spy*; always he had "zealously and religiously endeavoured to support the Cause he from *Choice* engaged in," and the stopping of the paper was "like the parting of dearest friends to meet no more."[95] Real sentiment lay beneath this statement, for Thomas had made *The Massachusetts Spy* the greatest Boston paper in support of the issues of the Colonists in the months preceding the war, and he had struggled through the Revolutionary years with colors flying. The tax issue was a real one to him, the more so as it reminded him of the British stamp taxes; and there is more than a lack of chivalry in the satire *The American Herald* of Boston published in humorous mockery against his stand, suggesting that the dangerous wound *The Massachusetts Spy* had suffered now showed signs of *"Mortification."*[96]

Through two years Thomas bided his time, waiting to revive his beloved paper in name and shape. He was not passive during this period, as his manuscript records show. In 1786 he was appointed deputy postmaster of Worcester for a three-year term. In the same year he entered into contract to extend his printing plant,

[93] *The Massachusetts Gazette*, advertisement, April 24, 1786.

[94] P. 14.

[95] P. 24. The announcement is rephrased in a printed handbill which was distributed and copied in *The Massachusetts Centinel* (April 12, 1786), *The Massachusetts Gazette* (April 24, 1786), *The American Recorder, and the Charlestown Advertiser* (April 14, 1786).

[96] In part, *The American Herald* (April 3, 1786) commented: "The Massachusetts Spy (which it is acknowledged has been of very essential service to the cause of the United States, and to this Commonwealth in particular, before, at, and since the late Revolution) is now languishing with a *dangerous Wound*, given it by the *Legislature of Massachusetts,* on the second day of July last. . . . The wound grows worse daily —*Mortification* has taken place, and in all probability will soon prove fatal to the existence of that *Old Publick Servant!*"

purchased considerable type from England, and traded actively in English imprints.[97] The day of release finally came. On April 2, 1788, he wrote jubilantly ·that he had the happiness to renew *The Massachusetts Spy, or Worcester Gazette*, now "restored to its Constitutional Liberty—(thanks to our present Legislature). . . . Heaven grant that the FREEDOM of the PRESS, on which depends the FREEDOM of the PEOPLE may, in the United States, be ever guarded with a watchful eye. . . ."[98] There was, of course, no real change in the contents—the "History of the Late War," "Worcester Speculator," "Pegasus of Apollo," and "Chreston's Miscellany," all features of the magazine, continued uninterruptedly to inform the readers of the restored paper, which still sold at nine shillings a year.

Times were in greater disorder in Massachusetts than in Connecticut. The inland rural inhabitants looked with distrust on the capitalists and merchants of the cities, who were in main, like Fisher Ames, Federalists, advocates of sound money, and staunch believers in the basic virtue of property rights. The farmers pressed their representatives for lower taxes and for the issue of currency, both inconsistent with the federal policy of stability. They saw in the erection of a strong national government a lessening of state power; this troubled them, as indeed it did even such men as John Hancock and Samuel Adams. In the autumn of 1786 "embattled farmers" again took up arms, and under the leadership of Daniel Shays they broke up the courts at Northampton and Worcester, besieged Springfield, and did not disband until Governor Bowdoin sent General Lincoln with 4400 men against them in the winter of 1786-87. *The Worcester Magazine*, conducted precisely as a weekly newspaper, naturally became a storehouse for the expression of the views of the public on these issues, and its columns are principally concerned with courts, paper money, federalism, antifederalism, rebellion, civil order, and the federal Constitution.

Though tradition held the major serial essayists of the magazine to discursive treatments of multifarious topics, they occasionally commented on the perplexities of the situation of the state and nation, offering their several counsels. "Tom Taciturn," most probably

[97] Isaiah Thomas manuscripts at the American Antiquarian Society, I (1754-1792).
[98] This notice was printed the following day in the first issue of the restored newspaper.

Edward Bangs, a leading citizen of Worcester,[99] contributed eighteen essays during the first year. Chiefly, he was Addisonian in style, and given to sane but insignificant discussions on knowledge, religious disputes, prejudices, liberty, labor, language riches, virtue, marriage, and labor. But sometimes he rose to more original treatments of the current scene. In one dramatic sketch in which "Tom," his wife, Dr. Pull, Esquire Selfish, and Deacon Honesty discuss the unhappy judicial establishment of the state, Honesty is of the opinion that lawyers and courts could well be abolished, leaving the administration of justice to the local ministers.[100] In a later conversation held at a tavern, Candid, a friend of "Taciturn," admits that the wheels of justice turn slowly and at considerable cost, but notes that a reasonable amount of time is necessary to discover truth and that any system of court procedure is unavoidably expensive.[101] Still later, in the midst of public hysteria, "Taciturn" remained fearlessly democratic, asserting that there could be no danger of anarchy; and he urged administrative officers to permit mass meetings, for any single tyranny would be worse.[102] This essay brought a stern reply by one who signed himself as "S.," and "Taciturn," after dreaming that the garden of America was endangered by the poison tree of Discord, quietly withdrew.[103]

"The Worcester Speculator," who was indirectly if not directly connected with Pliny Merrick, of Brookfield,[104] was as prolific as

[99] The Brinley copy at the Yale Library has the name of Edward Bangs appended by hand to the "Tom Taciturn" articles. For definite reading of the chirography I am indebted to Clarence S. Brigham of the American Antiquarian Society, who has written me that Bangs was "a leading Worcester citizen, one of the incorporators of this Society and much interested in history." The essays appear with fair regularity from April to September 1786, Vol. I, pp. 35, 46 (misnumbered 42)-47, 58, 67, 82, 92, 102, 118-19, 150, 161, 179, 201, 227, 238, 248-49, 272-73, 286-87, 297-98.

[100] No. X, June 1786, pp. 118-19. Bangs wrote dramatic dialogue well. In a style similar to Sterne's and with good narrative effect, he portrayed the characters of a squire, a young gallant, and Miss Affectation discussing charity and considering whether a beggar should be fed (No. XV, July 1786, p. 179).

[101] July 1786, p. 201.

[102] No. XXIV, Sept. 1786, pp. 286-87.

[103] No. XXV, Sept. 1786, pp. 297-98.

[104] Under date of Dec. 23, 1788, Merrick wrote from Brookfield to Thomas that he was sending some material which "springs from the same source as the 'Worcester Speculator.' I have the honour, by permission, to submit it to you for a place in the proposed Massachusetts Magazine." He further announced that Thomas might "expect a succession of Numbers—your kind correction of any inadvertencies in this or the Speculator will be esteemed a favour—I have further to request that you will

"Tom Taciturn," whom he followed in point of time; but he was considerably less democratic. In the latter half of his series of essays he grew ubiquitous, treating uninspiredly of happiness, seduction, marriage, medical quacks, whims of women, ambition, and contentment; but after preliminary introductions, the earlier numbers of the series strike a strongly federalistic note. In the third essay, for example, he asserted the need of the balancing effects of a represented landed class, and hoped a Lycurgus would arise to lead with single strength the development of commerce, agriculture, and manufactures.[105] The succeeding number set forth the theory of social contract for the establishment of government, but insisted that, once the people had accepted a form, "be the majority ever so great," they "have no right to act counter thereto."[106] The next four essays addressed themselves to the purpose of urging the adoption of the federal Constitution, which was not ratified by the state until February 6, 1788, when the measure was passed by the relatively small margin of nineteen.[107] The ninth number rebuked all printers chafing at the tax on advertisements, and to this Thomas attached a note in reply;[108] thereafter the essays became less vital.

"Tom Tinker," the third important serial essayist whose work was original with the magazine,[109] did not possess the legal mind of "The Worcester Speculator" or of Fisher Ames, nor did he govern his thoughts by theoretical principles in the manner of "Nestor" or Bangs. It was his purpose to show the foolishness of the current hysteria in a somewhat humorous manner, and to recommend an end of introspective examination of the "intestine struggles" of state, and a beginning of an era of work. He saw no advantage in tinkering with the Constitution, or, as did the

conceal the origin of each of the productions." (Isaiah Thomas manuscripts, I (1754-1792), at the library of the American Antiquarian Society.) The sixteen numbers of "The Worcester Speculator" appeared in the magazine as follows: Sept.-Dec. 1787, Jan.-March 1788, pp. 311-13, 323-25, 337-38, 6-7, 31-32, 56-57, 85-87, 91, 115-17, 169-70, 184-86, 195-96, 247, 290-91, 305, 335-36.

[105] Pp. 337-38.

[106] P. 6.

[107] Pp. 31-32, 56-57, 85-87, 91. For a long report on the ratification of the Constitution of Massachusetts, see Nos. XX and XXVI, Feb., March 1788, pp. 254-58, 331-35.

[108] Pp. 115-17.

[109] March, April 1787, pp. 629, 645, 23-24, 31-32.

politicians, gathering at every public house, "where characters are arraigned, laws canvassed, and liquor consumed."[110] He disapproved of the mood of the time, which disrupted churches and schools and suspiciously interpreted innocent sentences.[111] He plainly saw that in state feuds those who were in the right often hurt their cause by obstreperously asserting their rightness,[112] and he advised the rebellious in spirit to think less of their difficulties and more of their work.[113]

Besides the commentaries of the serial essayists, many other important articles treat of the turmoil. Some were original with the magazine; some were selected from printed sources. Some were definitely attributed; others not. The confusion of issues made clear thinking difficult. The fiscal and tax problems were bound with discussions of the judicial system, for the courts were agencies of law enforcement; and the conventions and mass meetings ran counter to the courts, for they sought to reconsider laws and the methods of enforcement. Thomas desired order and stability.[114] He gave space to those who opposed his opinions, for he was not blind to the injustices arising from the application of new laws; but a universal order was, he thought, a prime necessity. From *The Independent Chronicle* four essays "On Publick and Private Credit" were copied to assert the need of sound money and funded debts;[115] extracts from the works of Paine, Franklin, and Witherspoon, as well as "An American's" "Conventions! And Paper Money," the last written originally for *The Massachusetts Centinel*, were selected for the same purpose.[116]

In September 1786 mass meetings and conventions had become so frequent in Massachusetts that during the third week reports of the gatherings crowded out a major serial, a "History of the Late War in America," which was being copied from *The An-*

[110] P. 629.

[111] P. 645.

[112] Pp. 23-24.

[113] Pp. 31-32.

[114] None the less, he was fair. "A Conventioner" wrote to him expressing his pleasure to note that Thomas was not so subservient to the great and powerful as to refuse articles favoring conventions. See issue of Oct. 1786, pp. 349-50.

[115] May, June 1787, pp. 80-82, 91-93, 103-05, 134-36.

[116] For Paine, see issues of April, Dec. 1786, pp. 32-33, 449-50; for Franklin, Oct. 1787, p. 45; for Witherspoon, Aug. 1786, pp. 236-37; for "An American," Aug. 1786, pp. 251-52.

nual Register of London.[117] Many citizens were against the conventions because they feared the violence of mob spirit. One writer, who addressed himself "To the Inhabitants of Massachusetts," and wrote "From the humble Cell of Consideration in the Town of Benevolence, County of Honesty, State of Good Government," though he treasured the democratic ideal in government, was convinced that the "lawless invaders" must be put down.[118] Among the many supporters of federalism, none was more logical or wrote with greater precision than Fisher Ames, the "Camillus" of *The Independent Chronicle*, whose essays Thomas occasionally reprinted. "It is an Herculian labour," wrote Ames, "to detail our political absurdities"; and he felt certain the conventions and insurgents would "continue to destroy the pillars of their security, until they are buried in the ruins."[119] But the spirit of the public was not a little in favor of conventions, and the members of these groups held their patriotism to be pure. Forty-one towns were represented in the convention at Worcester, and the report of the chairman, Willis Hall, indicated popular dissatisfaction toward the general sessions and common pleas courts and a conviction that taxes were not equalized nor lawyers' fees reasonable.[120] Those who were bold enough to infer that the actions of the conventions were treasonable were quickly given replies.[121] The Chief Justice of Middlesex might charge his grand jury to stand for law and order and interpret convention methods as tyrannical,[122] but many an honest man, like "Ploughjogger,"[123] could not be convinced that land taxes were not too high or that conventions were not disloyal to the best interests of government. So it was

[117] April 1786 through Jan. 1788, with hiatuses, pp. 1-4, 15-18, 27-32, 39-42, 51-54, 63-66, 75-77, 87-90, 99-101, 111-16, 123-25, 135-37, 147-50, 159-61, 171-73, 183-85, 195-98, 207-09, 219-22, 231-33, 243-45, 255-57, 267-70, 279-81, 291-92, 303-06, 315-18, 355-57, 367-69, 379-81, 391-93, 403-04, 454-56, 467-69, 479-81, 503-04, 515-16, 527-29, 541-44, 555-58, 569-71, 583-85, 597-600, 611-13, 625-26, 639-41, 1-3, 15-17, 27-28, 39-42, 53-54, 77-79, 89-91, 101-03, 115-17, 129-31, 141-42, 155-56, 169-70, 183-85, 197-99, 211-13, 267-69, 281-83, 295-97, 309-11, 321-23, 335-37, 3-5, 17-19, 29-31, 41-43, 53-55, 65-67, 77-79, 89-91, 101-03, 113-15, 127-29, 193-95.

[118] Sept. 1786, pp. 291-92.

[119] March, April 1787, pp. 613-15, 645-47, 3-4; for quotations, see pp. 647 and 615.

[120] Oct. 1786, pp. 334-35.

[121] "Monitor," for example, replied to "Citizen," who had declared conventions treasonable (Nov. 1786, pp. 369-71).

[122] Nov. 1786, pp. 406-10.

[123] *Ibid.*, pp. 385-87.

of little avail for "Nestor," a man of calm temper, to generalize on the virtues of a republican form of government for nations of large areas, and to point out that democratic systems of rule were necessarily more expensive than autocratic establishments, thus hoping to quiet the more actively dissatisfied man.[124] The difficulties continued, in spite of the efforts of such men as James Sullivan in the interests of peace.[125] The uprising led by Shays added many official and non-official reports growing out of the "vigour, decision and energy" used by Governor Bowdoin to "terminate this unnatural, this unprovoked insurrection."[126] The progress of the struggle, the gradual success of the state over the insurrectionists, the fear of a gale of revolt by many who had been pleased to fan the lighter breezes, and the public demand for leniency on the part of the civil authorities towards those who had taken up arms are all copiously written on the pages of *The Worcester Magazine*.[127]

As dissension within the state quieted, the problem of national cohesion arose. During the latter part of 1787 and on into 1788 Thomas carried on a policy of reprinting a number of the most important addresses and letters by delegates to the national convention and others expressing views both for and against the proposed Constitution. Dissenters, such as Elbridge Gerry,[128] George Mason,[129] Richard Henry Lee,[130] Edmund Randolph,[131] and "A

[124] For "Nestor's" series, see issues of Dec. 1786-Jan. 1787, pp. 431-32, 462-64, 469-71, 484-86, 505-06, 517-20.

[125] For Sullivan's article, see issue of Jan. 1787, pp. 481-82.

[126] Quotations are from Governor Bowdoin's speech to the legislature, delivered Feb. 3, 1787; see magazine issue of Feb. 1787, p. 540.

[127] Among the items are: proceedings of the Worcester and Springfield conventions (Aug., Oct. 1786, pp. 246-47, 340); insurrection in Vermont (Dec. 1786, p. 460); Shays's petition to the town of Holden (Jan. 1787, pp. 507-11); insurgent papers by Shays and others (Feb. 1787, pp. 534-35); Act declaring rebellion (Feb. 1787, p. 559); insurrection at Lancaster (*ibid.*, pp. 532-34); skirmish in Berkshire County (March 1787, pp. 619-20); insurrection at Stockbridge (*ibid.*, pp. 648-49); General Lincoln's reports on his success in combating the insurgents (Feb. 1787, pp. 563-66); petitions of Daniel Shays and Eli Parsons praying to be restored to rights and liberties (March 1788, p. 330); sentences of death for treason of John Wheeler, Henry McCullock, John Parmiter, Daniel Luddington, Alpheus Colten, and James White (June 1787, pp. 117-19); article by "Theophrastus" urging that men in the insurrection be not deprived of jury rights for a year (Oct. 1787, pp. 20-23).

[128] Nov. 1787, pp. 79-80.

[129] Dec. 1787, pp. 130-32.

[130] Jan. 1788, pp. 181-84.

[131] *Ibid.*, p. 205-10.

Philadelphian"[132] were well represented, while those in favor of the instrument took consolation in the words of James Wilson,[133] Roger Sherman,[134] Oliver Ellsworth,[135] Benjamin Franklin,[136] and others. Moreover, the proceedings of the Massachusetts Convention were reported in detail, crowding out much else for several issues.[137]

Miscellaneous prose was frequently selected in a haphazard fashion, though famous names were often caught. The subjects were diverse; however, concentrations in science and agriculture are to be noted, and religious topics were not wholly neglected. In "Chreston's Miscellany" Thomas was supplied during twenty issues with "a small variety of *Sentimental Observations, detached Sentences, and instructive Apothegms*" which the compiler gathered from books.[138] Items from the works of Samuel Johnson,[139] Jonathan Swift,[140] St. Jean de Crèvecoeur,[141] Francis Hopkinson,[142] Benjamin Franklin,[143] and Ezra Stiles[144] lent variety. Indian affairs,[145] Masonry,[146] commercial treaties,[147] and the Russian Empire[148] were among the topics needing no well-known hand to insure for them a place in the magazine. The movement for prison reform, started by Benjamin Rush and others at Philadelphia with the organization of a society for alleviating the miseries of prisoners, met with favorable response in Massachusetts. "Phil-

[132] Dec. 1787, pp. 160-62. He presented twenty-three objections.

[133] Nov. 1787, pp. 80-84; Dec. 1787, p. 47.

[134] Nov. 1787, p. 85.

[135] *Ibid.*, p. 85 (in conjunction with Sherman); Dec. 1787, pp. 132-34, 155-60; March 1788, pp. 306-07.

[136] Dec. 1787, p. 112.

[137] Jan.-March 1788, pp. 199-201, 211-15, 219-30, 233-42, 248-59, 265-68, 275-85, 293-97, 307-14, 317-25, 331-35.

[138] Dec. 1786-March 1788, with hiatuses, pp. 461, 481, 506-07, 520, 531-32, 558, 571-72, 627, 644-45, 31, 79, 117, 131, 147, 156-57, 171, 286, 67, 336-37; quotation from letter accompanying first number.

[139] "Meditations on a Pudding" (June 1786, p. 104).

[140] Analysis of causes for a country's growing rich (June 1786, p. 155).

[141] Graces of a country life (Oct. 1787, pp. 57-58).

[142] "Nitidia's" reply to humorous essay (June 1787, pp. 145-46).

[143] "Advice to a Young Tradesman, from an Old One" (Aug. 1786, pp. 247-48).

[144] Extract from an election sermon (Oct. 1786, p. 360).

[145] May, June, Aug. 1786, pp. 95-96, 133, 263-64.

[146] Oct. 1786, pp. 360-61.

[147] See especially treaty between the United States and King of Prussia (June 1786, pp. 140-44).

[148] Continued from *The Massachusetts Spy* (April, May 1786, pp. 18-20, 42-44, 54-55, 67-69, 77-79).

anthropos," in an article original with the magazine, urged that the movement be imitated,[149] and he was heartily supported by "Philologus."[150]

In science, borrowed articles on diseases were the most numerous. Discourses on cancers or malignant tumors were frequently used, including Dr. Benjamin Rush's "Account of Dr. Hugh Martin's Cancer Powder," in which he stated that arsenic was an active ingredient of the formula, and offered the advice that the knife was more efficacious than caustics.[151] Malignant sore throat, according to one writer, had been raging epidemically for three years, and a long article was inserted on the treatment of the disease.[152] Many short pieces on various ills were published, showing an appeal to the public interest similar to that made by syndicated newspaper articles of the present day, and news accounts of the proceedings of such organizations as the Massachusetts Medical Society and the American Academy of Arts and Sciences were used.[153] Other scientific subjects than medical were diverse, extending from Benjamin Lincoln's "Account of Several Remarkable Springs in Pennsylvania and Virginia,"[154] written to President Willard of the American Academy of Arts and Sciences, to an extract from Franklin's letter to Miss Stevenson on barometers.[155]

Though the notes on agriculture, which included comments on field crops, fruit, vegetables, live stock, and dairy produce, were many in number, they were usually short insertions published at random to interest the general agrarian reader. It is worthy of noting, however, that the selections not infrequently had been written under the ægis of the agricultural committee of the American Academy of Arts and Sciences.[156]

[149] June 1787, pp. 163-64.

[150] July 1787, pp. 187-88.

[151] For Rush's article, see issue of Jan. 1787, pp. 524-25; for other articles on cancer, see especially issues of May and Sept. 1787, pp. 93, 302-03. Hugh Martin was a surgeon in a Pennsylvania regiment during the Revolutionary War.

[152] July, Aug. 1787, pp. 185-87, 199-201, 213-15, 245.

[153] For the former, see issue of June 1786, p. 131; for the latter, see, for instance, issues of June 1786 and March 1788, pp. 132, 339-40.

[154] May 1786, pp. 81-82.

[155] July 1786, pp. 173-74, reprinted from *The Columbian Herald*, Charleston, S. C.

[156] See especially John Spooner's article on cultivation of carrots (April 1786, p. 48), article by Samuel Barton, Jr., and Joseph Blaney on raising hemp (April 1786, pp. 55-56), Joseph Greenleaf's experiment in corn raising (May 1786, pp. 80-81), and another article on hemp culture April 1787, pp. 34-35), which are among the pieces sponsored by the Academy. See also such pieces, selected at random, as Decius Wads-

Thomas would not fight religious battles in his publications with the spirit he evidenced in political affairs. Orthodoxy marked his selections, without undue challenging of the opposition. One of his most interesting choices was an extract from Dr. Richard Watson's *Theological Tracts*. Watson, as a man of attainments in science before he became a bishop of most orthodox views, was a valuable aid to those who were opposed to the deists and free-thinkers, for he presumed, as a man of science, to strike at the views of Bacon, Newton, Grotius, Locke, Addison, Hartley, Jenyns, Voltaire, Bolingbroke, Helvetius, and others.[157] Less impressive but equally descriptive of the time and of Thomas's selective tend-encies was a rather superstitious article by Matthew Wilson, of Lewes, Delaware, entitled "Notices from the Invisible World,"[158] reprinted from *Freeman's Journal*. "In this age of infidelity," Wilson felt that "any Notices given us from the World of Spirits, when sufficiently proved to be genuine," were not to be overlooked; and he offered what he deemed to be two instances from occur-rences in his native county of Sussex.

"Pegasus of Apollo," the title for the department of poetry which Thomas brought over from *The Massachusetts Spy*, harbored dis-tinguished poetry, but most of the selections were taken from printed sources, and political matters frequently usurped the muses' wonted space. In the category of well-known reprints may be mentioned an extract from Thomas Coombe's "The Peasant of Auburn; or, the Emigrant,"[159] a popular lament for the homeland in imitation of Gray and Goldsmith; an extract from Dyer en-titled "Trade";[160] "The Creation," from Timothy Dwight's *The Conquest of Canäan*;[161] three pieces from the pen of David Hum-phreys—"An Elegy on the Burning of Fairfield," a selection from "Mount Vernon. An Ode," and a lyric from *The Genius of*

worth's method of destroying the Hessian fly (July 1787, pp. 215-16), and articles on mules (April 1787, pp. 17-18), sheep (May 1787, pp. 93-94), and cheese making (Aug. 1787, pp. 274-75).

[157] Aug. 1786, pp. 209-10.

[158] Aug. 1787, pp. 287-88.

[159] May 1786, p. 73. Coombe was a minister of Philadelphia. His poem was pub-lished in that city in 1786 by Enoch Story (who spelled the name "Combe"), and by Shepard Kollock at New York in the same year. *The Worcester Magazine* spelled the name "Coomes."

[160] May 1786, p. 85.

[161] June 1786, p. 145.

America—;[162] a selection from Samuel Butler's *Hudibras*,[163] and two pieces from the work of Jonathan Swift,[164] as well as a bit of John Trumbull's *M'Fingle*.[165]

Political motives, born of the current controversies, governed the choice of many of the selections in verse. Of the poems already mentioned, those by Swift attacked the bestiality of many politicians, the excerpt by Trumbull bore a lament that the national legislative body was lacking in proper powers, and the third selection by Humphreys was an impassioned utterance against political discord. Short lyrics of the Revolutionary War period and patriotic verse of all kinds were reprinted; so the magazine became a minor storehouse of popular songs.[166] Here is preserved, too, "A Fair Bargain," wherein, Satan asking Columbia for a state, is offered Vermont, whom he refuses on the ground of present possession, and is thereupon conceded Rhode Island.[167] Two poems carry on the humanistic attitude toward negroes which later was to increase in favor.[168] Another piece, an "Ode for the Festival of Saint John the Baptist," dated Philadelphia, June 24, 1786, was an elaborate structure of recitative, song, and air in praise of Masonry.[169]

But there was no generative force in the poetical department, and, languishing on reprints, it passed practically into a state of desuetude during the third volume. Of original contributors, perhaps only one is worthy of mention—Daniel George, of Portland, Maine, whose "An Ode on Spring"[170] appeared in an early

---

[162] The three appeared respectively in July and Nov. 1786 and March 1787, pp. 180, 376, and 607.

[163] Jan. 1787, p. 501.

[164] Aug. 1786, pp. 252, 264. They are political satires.

[165] Sept. 1786, p. 276.

[166] One should note particularly the ode by Thomas Dawes, Jr., on the occasion of the opening of the Charles River bridge (June 1786, p. 139); "Columbia," a cantata in honor of America and George Washington, written at New York, June 3, 1786 (Aug. 1786, p. 228); the popular "Address to the Ladies," urging them to be patriotic and wear homespun (Sept. 1786, p. 312); "Come, come, my bold boxers, 'tis Liberty calls" (March 1787, p. 607), and Selby's poem for Independence Day, recited at Boston on July 4, 1787 (July 1787, p. 194).

[167] May 1787, p. 95; written in 1782.

[168] One is an imaginary farewell to his wife by an African slave condemned to die (June 1786, p. 156); the other is a poem by a Jamaican mulatto sixteen years of age (Aug. 1786, p. 264).

[169] Aug. 1786, p. 216.

[170] June 1786, p. 121; dated from Falmouth, May 15, 1786.

issue, and who was sufficiently interested in his own poetry to write Thomas in 1789 a letter of thanks for having commented favorably on another poem of his riming.[171]

[171] This letter, among the Isaiah Thomas manuscripts, I (1754-1792) at the library of the American Antiquarian Society, is dated Aug. 15, 1789, and refers to an ode.

Mention should be made, before closing, that this library also possesses a limited collection of manuscripts, filed as "Worcester Magazine 1786-1790," containing a number of contributions. Among them are articles by "Nestor," "A Yeoman," "Monitor," "Paper Money," "Juvenis," "A Conventioner," "A Member of the Convention," "Modertur," "Philadelphus," "A Farmer," "Common Sense," "Protestor," "Retribuo," "Cato," "A Ploughjogger," "Philologus," "Philanthropos," "Observator," "A Soldier," "An Independent Elector," "Philo," "Thoughtful," and "Z. Z." There are also letters from M. Wimby, B. Whipple, and the town clerk, Abel Brown.

CHAPTER X

WEBSTER, CAREY, TRENCHARD, AND OTHERS

THE men of the ninth decade discovered that the Revolutionary War was not an end of labor, but the beginning, and that, as in the past, the "happiness of America" still lay in the future. The combined forces of the "Age of Reason" and "Enlightenment," and the spirit of revolt which opened the "Romantic Age," had not produced a finished world; affairs were greatly disordered, keeping young men humbly industrious and old men from their naps.

It was a new age, with pertinent matters to discuss, if not to settle; and no magazine at this time could be patterned on the elderly scheme of Mecom's *The New-England Magazine* or Gridley's *The Boston Magazine*, as Frederick Quequelle and James Prange soon discovered at New Brunswick, New Jersey, when they tried to conduct *The New-Jersey Magazine, and Monthly Advertiser* (1786-87)[1] on those old principles. They reprinted selections from the works of John Filson, William Ellis, and George Whitefield, but such matter would not now sustain a magazine otherwise offering only the withered flowers of a decadent poesy and weak, general essays on morals and manners. More closely approaching the ideal of the period was *The Columbian Magazine* (1786-90),[2] published at Philadelphia under shifting managements which included Mathew Carey, William Spotswood, and James Trenchard, and edited at different times by Carey, Trenchard, Francis Hopkinson, Alexander Dallas, and perhaps others. Much of the content of the magazine was original, and some was paid for, so there was an air of distinction to the periodical. Original and selected pieces from the pens of such men as Jeremy Belknap, Benjamin Rush, Charles Brockden Brown, Israel Putnam, James Wilson, David Ramsay, David Rittenhouse, Trumbull, Barlow, Hopkinson, and Dallas suited the temper of the readers. The public wished to read articles on federalism, currency, manufac-

[1] See "Bibliography," p. 371.
[2] *Ibid.*, p. 370.

tures, agriculture, inventions, and science; and *The Columbian Magazine* furnished them. Because of the number of contributors and contributions, the editorial care lavished on it, the duration of publication, and the expenditures of the publishers, this magazine may be considered the most important of its type in the seventeen eighties.

But there were two challenging competitors. One, *The American Magazine* (1787-88),[3] published at New York by Samuel Loudon and industriously edited by Noah Webster, who had attained to his thirtieth year, was most deserving of success, though its fortunes were never bright. Webster gave to an American periodical the first distinguished department of literary criticism, for which he himself wrote. He was the first to insist on respect for a copyright law; he treated literary productions as private property and insisted that others do the same. He had the spirit of a gladiator, and he had visions of editing a federal magazine which would be supported by sub-editors in the several sections of the United States; but he could not summon a group interested in writing, or get various individuals to contribute to his magazine. He himself wrote much and well, and he turned his pen to many subjects, but he could not make his magazine universal in its appeal, though he gave it distinction. The other, and more important, competitor was *The American Museum, and Monthly Advertiser* (1787-92),[4] which, under the care of Mathew Carey as both publisher and editor, throve longer than any other magazine of its time, and was the most successful of all the magazines of the decade. It was not the purpose of this periodical to print original material, and there is little among its contents which had not been published elsewhere. Carey planned to supply more pages of printed matter monthly than any other publisher had dared, and he succeeded in issuing numbers of a hundred pages. He planned to select his material from the choicest pens, and to preserve in his magazine the most distinguished productions of the years immediately preceding, during and following the war. He accomplished his aim remarkably well, considering practical limitations. He made of his magazine a true museum.

[3] *Ibid.*, p. 372.
[4] *Ibid.*, p. 371.

I

The New-Jersey Magazine, as its name partially suggested in the sub-title,[5] was a substitute for a newspaper. Though dedicated to literary expression and suffused with the perfumes of rosemary and mignonette, Frederick Quequelle and James Prange would most probably have published a newspaper in New Brunswick rather than the state's first magazine if they had been able to do so. The history of newspaper publishing in the state had been rather disheartening, the towns being large enough to tempt but not to sustain any of the trials, and the successful papers in 1786 could be numbered on the fingers of one hand. At Trenton *The New-Jersey Gazette*, which had been established at Burlington by Isaac Collins in 1777, was discontinued in November 1786. *The Princeton Packet*, established in the summer of 1786, was faring little better, and came to a close in 1787. At Elizabethtown *The New-Jersey Journal*, begun at New Brunswick by Shepard Kollock in 1783 as *The Political Intelligencer*, was in a fair state of health following its remove. Shelly Arnett, who had been associated with Kollock, launched *The New Brunswick Gazette, and Weekly Monitor* in October 1786, and it was against this competition that Quequelle and Prange inaugurated their magazine. But they found it unprofitable and stopped its issue with the third number. Quequelle moved to Trenton, open since the failure of *The New-Jersey Gazette*, where he and George M. Wilson began *The Trenton Mercury and Weekly Advertiser* in May 1787, and Prange moved to Philadelphia to publish *The Evening Chronicle*.[6]

The magazine need never have existed as an outlet for local literary productions, for *The New Brunswick Gazette* had been

[5] See note 1.

[6] For a bibliography of newspapers in New Jersey, see Brigham, *op. cit.*, in *Proceedings of the American Antiquarian Society*, Vol. XXVI (Oct. 1916), pp. 413-60. See also William Nelson, "Some New Jersey Printers and Printing in the Eighteenth Century," in *Proceedings of the American Antiquarian Society*, new series, Vol. XXI, Part I (1911), pp. 15-56. The cities of New Jersey were small and had not long been incorporated as such by royal charter. Perth Amboy had been incorporated in 1718, but New Brunswick had waited until 1730, Burlington until 1732, Elizabeth until 1740, and Trenton until 1746 (see Austin Scott's "Foreword" to "The Charter of the City of New Brunswick," in *New Brunswick, N. J. Historical Club Publications*, No. 3, p. 4. For Prange's association with *The Evening Chronicle* of Philadelphia, see Brigham, *op. cit.*, April 1922, p. 111.

organized to include such work; Arnett had announced in the first
number that "A part of the paper will always be devoted to the
use of such gentlemen as will please to favour him with their
lucubrations, either in prose or verse,"[7] and the same issue had
included in its offerings a column of poetry and a general essay
gracing the first page. But Quequelle and Prange were bold
enough to endeavor against odds, and they proclaimed in the first
number of their magazine: "We propose to carry on this *Work;*
with a view to inform, improve & please our *Readers;* and as we
have made it our business to transplant from several Parts into
this our garden, such flowers as for their beauty or sweetness may
delight, and such herbs & fruits only as for their useful and salutary virtues may benefit mankind; so we have established it as a
maxim . . . that no noxious poison, no useless *bramble* to perplex,
shall ever knowingly be admitted." Asking to be "favoured by the
Learned & Ingenious with any scheme for the public good, any
essay or poem for the amusement, any discourse or dissertation for
the improvement of Mankind," they closed their salutatory with a
proposal to publish advertisements also, which would be inserted
"gratis for Subscribers only."[8]

The printers of the magazine were in no way good editors, not
being inclined to use their own pens or able to secure the contributions of others. So the flowers and herbs in the garden of
the magazine were plucked almost entirely from other plots during
the three wintry months the magazine sustained life. Some space
was yielded to excerpts from two widely popular books of travel
and adventure, William Ellis's *An Authentic Narrative of a Voyage to the Pacific Ocean,*[9] and John Filson's *The Discovery, Settlement, and Present State of Kentucke.*[10] The selections from
the former were accounts of the dishonorable practices which led
to the murder of Captain James Cook and of the conditions of life

[7] Oct. 5, 1786, p. 1.

[8] For quotations, see "Introduction," in the issue for Dec. 1786, p. 2.

[9] See issue of magazine for Dec. 1786, pp. 11-14. Ellis's book was translated into
the French and German and published at Paris and Göettingen as early as 1749 and
1783 respectively; an edition printed at Philadelphia appeared in 1783 (Evans, *op.
cit.,* No. 17921).

[10] See issue of the magazine for Feb. 1787, pp. 102-10. Filson's book was published
first at Wilmington in 1784, and by the following year had been translated into
French at Paris (see Sabin, *op. cit.,* No. 24338). For an extended account, see Reuben
T. Durrett, *The Life and Writings of John Filson,* especially pp. 15, 16, 29, 38.

among the Indian tribes on the western shores of Hudson's Bay, and the excerpts from the second book were relations of explorations in Kentucky by James M'Bride, John Finley, and Daniel Boone, with expostulations on the geographical virtues of this land, an Eden awaiting those who felt the lure of new removes.

The editors revealed an avid taste for sentimental essays and melancholy love stories, many of which were confessional in type, and nearly all were taken from printed sources. Typical of this group is "The Man of Fashion, and the Country-Gentleman," by Thomas Mulso, a "confession" story of Callistus and Sophronius, the former seducing a gentleman's wife and subsequently deserting her, letting the unfortunate lady endure alone the obloquy of the world. Of this story the editors naïvely noted that it was "one of the most valuable publications that have of late supported the credit of the Press. The subject, the moral, the discourse, are most interesting; the language is genteel and elegant. . . ."[11] Equally typical is "An Interesting Adventure between a Young Gentleman and a Young Lady," being her letter exhorting him to avoid spirituous liquors and the company of lewd women, with his reply.[12]

All other kinds of offerings, including poetry, were of minor importance, though the subjects were diversified. Of medical interest were two articles on smallpox—one supporting inoculation and the other endorsing "adhesion"[13]—and "an Essay upon the nursing and management of Children," a study of nutrition which rather mildly discouraged including wine, sugar, or spices in the diet.[14] Within the range of social morality, the evils of alcoholic

[11] Jan. 1787, pp. 29-35; quotation from p. 29.

[12] Feb. 1787, pp. 97-102. Other anecdotal essays and stories include the following: "Story of Orestes & Almeda," in which the envious Almira is taught the qualities of virtue by the presence of Almeda (Dec. 1786, pp. 52-53); "Story of Eudocius and Clarinda" (Jan. 1787, pp. 4-6); "Infidelity of a Wife," being a tale of a queen's unholy love of a court dwarf (Jan. 1787, pp. 19-22); "An Oriental Tale," being a version of the story of the three greedy companions who find gold, and, plotting against one another, are all killed (Feb. 1787, pp. 114-17); "A Warning to the Fair Sex" (Dec. 1786, pp. 35-36); "Cautions concerning Marriage"—together with the story of Eugenio and Theana, who led gay and licentious lives, in contrast to Euphorbus and Sophronia, a virtuous pair (Dec. 1786, pp. 40-43); and "Of the Pernicious Custom of Telling Lies in Conversation" (one of the few original pieces in the magazine), which seems to have relation to a local quarrel (Feb. 1787, pp. 131-32).

[13] See issues for Dec. 1786, pp. 38-40 and Feb. 1787, pp. 127-31.

[14] Feb. 1787, pp. 122-26.

beverages were presented in "The Drunkards [sic] Looking-Glass."[15] Religion was duly recognized by a selection from an account of the life of George Whitefield, thus editorially introduced: "He was universally esteemed the principal teacher of the Methodists, & was the first of them, that endeavoured by the most extraordinary efforts of preaching in different places . . . to rouse the lower class of the people from the last degree of inattention and ignorance to a sense of religion, among whom he hath left an impression, which cannot soon be effaced."[16] In literary criticism, an essay on Fielding's *Amelia* revealed no appreciation of the story, or of the manner, or of the novel as a type, but offered the opinion that many of the reflections were useful and parts of the story amusing, though anachronisms—such as the reference to the siege of Gibraltar—sometimes marred the story, for "A novel, like an epic poem, should at least have the appearance of truth. . . ."[17] The poetry was inconsequential; the prevailing selections were light and capricious in thought, or didactic, or religious.[18]

II

A long and intricate drama lies behind the establishment and publication of *The Columbian Magazine; or, Monthly Miscellany* (1786-90),[19] which achieved distinction above *The American Magazine* by reason of the variety of its editorial content. Announcement of a proposal to publish the new magazine appeared in *The Pennsylvania Gazette* (Hall and Sellers) of August 9, 1786, the statement being signed by Thomas Seddon, Mathew Carey, William Spotswood, Charles Cist, and James Trenchard, all of Philadelphia. The announcement commented on the advantages of commencing a magazine at that time, "when the genuine spirit of liberty has extended its benign influence over these independent and highly favored republics," and promised a monthly issue of forty-eight pages beginning October 1, "elegantly printed," and

---

[15] *Ibid.*, pp. 86-87.

[16] "Memoirs of the Life of the Rev. Mr. George Whitefield," taken from his journals (Dec. 1786, pp. 44-52); quotation from p. 49.

[17] Synopsis and remarks on *Amelia* occupy pp. 15-34 of the issue for Dec. 1786; the critical references are taken from p. 34.

[18] See, for examples, "Sophia" (Jan. 1787, p. 71); "On Happiness" (Jan., Feb., 1787, pp. 69-70, 142-43); and "Hymn" (Feb. 1787, pp. 143-44).

[19] See note 2.

"adorned with two engravings on copper-plate, executed by an American artist," with as much original material as possible (eminent men having already promised to contribute), at twenty shillings a year to subscribers.[20] The proprietors were soon more than able to fulfill their pledge, for the monthly installments grew to over fifty pages, and a yearly supplement was added. The current expense has been said to have been £100 monthly.[21]

The publishers of the magazine had been severally associated with various phases of the publishing business. Thomas Seddon conducted a well-stocked book and stationery store in Philadelphia, his wares including engravings, jewelry, and optical instruments.[22] William Spotswood was a printer of means. Charles Cist was likewise a printer in good standing.[23] James Trenchard, who, with Carey, was probably more vitally concerned in the magazine than the others, had been located in Philadelphia about ten years, where he had engaged himself as an engraver and seal cutter. His major concern in the new project lay in the fact that the magazine would offer him work as an engraver.[24] Mathew Carey, who became the most prominent of the group as a publisher of magazines, had recently ceased publishing *The Pennsylvania Herald*, and was particularly interested in the magazine since he was to print it; it would, moreover, present him an opportunity for public expression, to which he was accustomed.[25] Carey's life had been color-

[20] Outside Philadelphia, subscription agents were listed for New York, Baltimore, Charleston, Savannah. In general the magazine was not so widely advertised in the newspapers as was *The American Museum*. Unlike the latter, it was not advertised in *The Pennsylvania Gazette* during 1787-88. Neither magazine was advertised in *The Pennsylvania Journal*, a semi-weekly. Both magazines were advertised in the New York papers, where Webster's magazine offered competition, but *The American Museum* invariably received a much larger space.

[21] Smyth, *The Philadelphia Magazines and their Contributors*, p. 62.

[22] A four-page advertisement in *The Columbian Magazine* for Oct. 1786 is attached to some copies.

[23] He was a friend of Benjamin Rush, who contributed to the magazine; several of Rush's pamphlets were issued from the Cist press. Ebenezer Hazard characterized Cist to Jeremy Belknap as "a man of sense, and a scholar; he is a printer who has lived a number of years in America, married in Philadelphia, and is among the foremost in his profession" ("The Belknap Papers," *Collections of the Massachusetts Historical Society*, fifth series, II, 451). See also Faust, *op. cit.*, I, 146.

[24] He went to England in 1793, after the definite failure of *The Columbian Magazine* and *The American Museum*. See Stauffer, *op. cit.*, I, 276.

[25] The best account of Carey is by Earl L. Bradsher, *Mathew Carey: Editor, Author and Publisher* (1912). Dr. Bradsher's plan did not embrace an exhaustive study of the magazine.

ful, and an undertaking of his earlier career serves to explain some of his operations while engaged with *The Columbian Magazine* and *The American Museum*. He was born in Dublin in 1760, and when fifteen years of age was apprenticed to a bookseller. In 1779 he published a pamphlet in defense of his fellow Irish Catholics which caused such a disturbance that his friends shipped him to France, where Franklin employed him for a time as a printer at Passy. Carey returned later to Dublin, where in 1783 he began to publish *The Volunteer's Journal*, in which he boldly defended Irish manufactures and commerce, and asserted for the Irish political rights beyond those England was prepared to admit. This political iconoclasm led him into further difficulties. He was imprisoned at Newgate for a month, and on his release he determined to sail for America, where he made his residence until his death in 1839. During his early struggles for a livelihood in Philadelphia, Carey was assisted by Lafayette, who loaned him $400, with which he started *The Pennsylvania Herald* in 1785, a paper whose early demise was perhaps in some measure due to the editor's belligerent antifederalism during the first years of his residence in America. Later, he supported the federalist cause.

There is no doubt that Carey was the first principal editor of *The Columbian Magazine*, although perhaps no definite title was assigned to him. Not only does the announcement of the plan of the magazine in *The Pennsylvania Gazette* of August 9, 1786, contain the phrase, "these independent and highly favored republics," characteristic of Carey's early antifederal conception of the Union, but in the same newspaper of August 16th the advertisement was repeated with an appended sentence: "The Editor of the Columbian Magazine shall esteem it a very particular favor, if any Gentleman will furnish him with anecdotes, or documents, for writing the Life of that much regretted hero GENERAL GREENE." Carey was the author of the account of Greene's life printed in the magazine later, and he called himself the editor of the periodical in the advertisement. He did not long remain satisfied with the arrangement, however; he determined to publish a magazine of his own, *The American Museum*, based on the plan of Almon's *Remembrancer for Fugitive Pieces*,[26] and the first issue

---

[26] Postmaster-General Ebenezer Hazard, of New York, who was fairly well acquainted with Carey, mentions Almon's periodical as the prototype of Carey's in a letter to

of the new magazine appeared for January 1787. By this time he was contemplating also the publication of an *American Annual Register* and searching for men who would contribute to it.[27] Some time before he quit *The Columbian*, it was known he would not remain with the magazine after March 1787.[28]

Upon Carey's recommendation, as early as January 1787 the proprietors were considering the advisability of securing a new editor, and Postmaster-General Ebenezer Hazard, of New York, a close friend of the youthful Reverend Jeremy Belknap, of Boston, offered to try to secure this literary post for his friend, if he should desire it. He informed Belknap that the proprietors were planning to pay for original articles at a rate which Carey estimated would amount to two guineas for four or five columns. He wrote further that he had heard the position of editor might pay about £100 a year, and it was possible that with this post might go also the keepership of the library at Carpenter Hall at £60 a year.[29] To this doubtful offer Belknap replied that a Congregational church at Boston had offered him £125, and so he must refuse the editorship; but he would greatly enjoy contributing to the magazine.[30] In January 1787 the proprietors made Belknap a definite offer of £100 for editing, revising, and writing for the magazine,[31] but Belknap again refused, though "What I have said above is not intended as if I would *decline* having a *share* in the Magazine. . . ."[32]

By March 1787 an editor had been employed. Belknap mentioned in a letter to Hazard that he was glad the office had been filled, but he did not give the name of the man who had taken the

Jeremy Belknap, of Boston, "The Belknap Papers," Part I, *Collections of the Massachusetts Historical Society*, fifth series (1877), II, 449-53.

[27] Hazard wrote to Belknap on Feb. 3, 1787 (*ibid.*, II, 459), that Carey would pay Belknap about 20 guineas a year to edit the historical section of the *Register*; to this offer Belknap replied favorably in a letter dated Feb. 16, 1787 (Belknap Papers, Vol. V of the manuscripts at the Massachusetts Historical Society, p. 77).

[28] Hazard to Belknap, Jan. 20, 1787 (*op. cit.* note 26, II, 449-53).

[29] Hazard to Belknap, Jan. 20, 1787 (*ibid.*, II, 449-53).

[30] Belknap to Hazard, Feb. 2, 1787 (*ibid.*, II, 453-57).

[31] Hazard to Belknap, Feb. 3, 1787, quoting letter from Carey dated Jan. 23, 1787 (*ibid.*, II, 459).

[32] Belknap to Hazard, Feb. 16, 1787 (*ibid.*, II, 461). Later (March 10 and April 29, 1787) Belknap again expressed his desire to contribute to the "Magazine, Museum, or Annual Register," emphasizing his strong inclination to write (*ibid.*, II, 465, 473).

position.[33] The new man was Francis Hopkinson, for Hopkinson himself affirmed his "Management of the Work" as early as March 1787, in a letter to Thomas Jefferson dated April 14: "The Proprietors of the Magazine have engaged me to undertake the Management of the Work—to which they are by no means competent themselves. The Month of March is my first Exhibition. In the Magazine this Month I shall take the Liberty of giving an Extract from your valuable Notes on Virginia. . . . I hope this will not displease you. I hope further that you will give me some Assistance now and then. I have a very curious Drawing & Account of the Remains of an ancient fortified town on the Muskingum. . . ."[34]

It seems likely that Hopkinson was not editor of the magazine beyond the period of a very few months. It is interesting to note that though his contributions to the magazine commence with the issue for March 1787 and continue through May, they then abruptly cease for over a year, beginning again in July 1788 and appearing intermittently thereafter through September 1792.[35] It

[33] Belknap to Hazard, March 10, 1787 (*ibid.*, II, 465).

[34] Hastings (quoting Jefferson Papers, Library of Congress, XXIX, 4950-52), *op. cit.*, p. 433.

[35] For the years 1786-88 Hastings (*ibid.* pp. 434-35) lists the following poetry and prose by Hopkinson appearing in the magazine, and to these items I have affixed the page numbers: "To Myrtilla; the Nest" and "The Birds, the Beasts, and the Bat" (March 1787, p. 346); "Nitidia's Answer" ("Nitidia's Defense of Women and White-Washing") and "The Temple of Minerva" (April 1787, pp. 375-77, 391-92); "Description of a Candle Case," "An Improved Method of Quilling [Tonguing] a Harpsichord," "An Evening at Sea," and "Verses Wrote Near the Conclusion of a Very Tedious Voyage" (May 1787, pp. 420-21, 421-23, 446); "Ode" from "An Account of the Grand Federal Procession" (July 1788, p. 409). In addition to this list of known poetry and prose, Hastings (*ibid.*, pp. 479-80) suggests the possibility of Hopkinson's authorship of two other poems printed in the magazine during this period, the first signed "A. B." and the other "H.," both initialings being devices commonly used by him: "To a Lady" (Dec. 1786, p. 199); and "Epigram" (March 1787, p. 346). Hastings has omitted mentioning "A Fair Bargain" (April 1787, p. 392). For the years 1789-92 Hastings (*ibid.*, p. 435) has listed the following pieces in the magazine by Hopkinson, to which I have affixed the page numbers: "Song" (Aug. 1789), "A Description of a Floating [Chamber] Lamp Invented by Hopkinson" (March 1790, pp. 136-37), "To Miss Lawrence" (March 1792, p. 198), "On Public Speaking," "Description of a Church," "Disappointed Love," and "To Delia, Wrote on a Leaf of her Pocket-Book" (Aug. 1792, pp. 79-80, 119-20), and "To the Rev. Dr. White" on the conduct of a church organ (Sept. 1792, pp. 53-55). To this group mentioned by Hastings, I may add a song "Come, Fair Rosina" (Nov. 1789), printed as an insert, with music, which is included in *The First American Composer. 6 Songs by Francis Hopkinson*, edited and augmented by Harold V. Milligan (Arthur P. Schmidt Co., n. d., copyright, 1918).

would appear doubtful to infer, with Hastings,[36] that Hopkinson was still editor of the magazine in January 1788. It is more probable that his connection ceased in 1787 at about the same time as did his contributions. Belknap, who was smarting under the information that the editor was receiving £50 more than had been offered to him, asked Hazard, in a letter dated May 4, 1787, if he knew who the editor was, and reported that Spotswood was displeased with the man, having said that the magazine still lacked "a *capable* editor" and refusing to commit himself as to the continuance of the periodical beyond the current year.[37] In reply, Hazard wrote to Belknap on May 12th, saying: "I am told their editor is John O'Connor," an Irish counselor at law for whose abilities he had small respect.[38] Hazard may have been misinformed, but whether or not O'Connor followed Hopkinson, or assisted him as editor, or did not edit the magazine at any time, it is at least certain that one or both were soon supplanted, for two letters between Belknap and Hazard (August 2 and September 14, 1787) refer to Alexander James Dallas, the second letter definitely attributing the editorship to him;[39] and Dallas still held the position in March 1788, for Belknap, who contributed to the magazine, mentions his name as editor during that month.[40] Dallas was born in Jamaica in 1759, and was later educated in England. He came to Philadelphia in 1783, and was shortly afterward associated with Carey, reporting convention proceedings for *The Pennsylvania Herald* and later for *The Columbian Magazine*.[41] As he was, like Carey, during his early years in America, an antifederalist, the magazine suffered the alienation of sympathy of a great many persons of opposite political faith. On this matter Benjamin Rush wrote to Noah Webster February 13, 1788: "From the impudent conduct of Mr. Dallas in misrepresenting the proceedings and speeches in the Pennsylvania Convention, as well as from his deficiency of matter, the *Columbian Magazine*, of which he is editor, is in the decline"; and the statement must have con-

[36] Hastings, *op. cit.*, pp. 433-34.
[37] "The Belknap Papers," *op. cit.*, II, 474.
[38] *Ibid.*, II, 477.
[39] *Ibid.*, II, 485, 489.
[40] Belknap to Hazard, March 19, 1788 (*ibid.*, III, 27).
[41] Dallas also wrote pamphlets on public affairs, and became widely known. He later was appointed to the secretaryships of the Treasury and War for the United States, and his second son, George M., became Vice-President.

tained some element of truth even though penned by one ardent Federalist to another equally ardent.[42]

In January 1789 James Trenchard became the sole proprietor of the magazine.[43] Spotswood, who was never sanguine regarding the enterprise, withdrew for a time, and Trenchard resolved to carry on alone. At the time, Noah Webster, who for several months had known that his magazine in New York would be modified or discontinued, was planning an extensive federal magazine. He hoped to unite his New York publication with Isaiah Thomas's project for the establishment of *The Massachusetts Magazine* in Boston and also with one of the publications in Philadelphia. So Trenchard probably believed that a continuance of *The Columbian Magazine* might serve him to good purpose if some merger were effected, and in the meantime he could maintain an outlet for his engravings and hopefully nurse a weak enterprise. Webster's project failed. Thomas was wealthy enough to publish *The Massachusetts Magazine* alone. Trenchard added the name of Stewart to the imprint of his magazine for the issues of May and June, and with the issue for December, Spotswood again became the printer for "the Proprietors." The appearance of *The Massachusetts Magazine* restricted the sales of *The Columbian Magazine* in Boston, where it had enjoyed some patronage through the efforts of Belknap, but this misfortune was compensated by the discontinuance of Webster's magazine in December 1788, leaving the New York field open until the establishment of *The New York Magazine; or Literary Repository* in 1790, whose four hundred sixty-nine subscribers as listed at the close of the first volume, though scattered somewhat throughout the states, probably represented the capacity of this territory to support a magazine.

The distinction accorded to *The Columbian Magazine* came through the adoption by the proprietors of an elaborate, expensive policy at a time when financial support by the public was growing less inadequate.[44] The recommendations of Carey brought to the

[42] For quotation, see Smyth, *The Philadelphia Magazines and their Contributors*, p. 66.

[43] Not only does the imprint indicate this fact, but Belknap mentions the change in a letter to Hazard dated Jan. 3, 1789 ("The Belknap Papers," *op. cit.*, III, 89).

[44] Increasing population and a growing sense of national cohesion were probably factors helping to support magazine enterprises. On the other hand, the mood of the time was still not such as to support magazines freely, a sense of patronage on the

magazine an editor on salary and at least one contributor who was paid for his work. Trenchard kept the magazine well supplied with copperplate engravings, and the size of the periodical offered space for an appeal to many interests. A healthy stress was placed on the policy of publishing a large amount of original material, and contributors supported the magazine well.

Besides the pieces by Hopkinson (which were mainly reprints),[45] the reports by Dallas,[46] and Carey's pieces in the early numbers,[47] the magazine drew to its pages important papers by Jeremy Belknap and Benjamin Rush. Belknap achieved his desire to receive payment for his work, and under this contract he wrote *The Foresters: An Historical Romance* during 1787-88. It was conceived, as his references to Hazard indicate, in the manner of John Arbuthnot's *The History of John Bull*, and it appeared anonymously because the author wished to deal with "sad truths" harshly. None the less, he was anxious to learn of its public reception, and he was pleased when Hazard commented favorably regarding it and when the proprietors asked for an extension of the numbers after the series had been tentatively drawn to a conclusion.[48] Using elaborate

---

part of the public being marked. The technique of popular authorship, popular editing, and advertising was for a future age.

[45] See note 35.

[46] See note 41 and text appertaining.

[47] Carey's early account of the life of Major-General Nathaniel Greene (Sept., Oct. 1786, pp. 1-3, 53-60), for the preparation of which he advertised for materials, is noteworthy though not extensive. Smyth (*The Philadelphia Magazines and their Contributors*, pp. 62-63) credits Carey also with "The Shipwreck," "An Extravagant Reason for Hard Times" (Sept. 1786, pp. 6-8, 31-32), and a "Chronicle of the Year 1850," being "A Philosophical Dream" of the development of the country in 1850, with a suggestion for uniting the Ohio and Delaware Rivers (Sept. 1786, pp. 5-6).

[48] *The Foresters* was printed in the issues for June-Dec. 1787, and Feb. and April 1788, pp. 453-56, 514-17, 565-69, 618-22, 706-10, 737-41, 790-93, 58-60, 183-86. Belknap wrote to Hazard May 4, 1787 ("The Belknap Papers," *op. cit.*, II, 474), that Spotswood had offered him a guinea for each installment of three pages of "*John Bull*," as he termed the papers, a price which Hazard, who had also communicated with Spotswood, affirmed in a letter to Belknap dated May 12, 1787 (*ibid.*, II, 577). In a letter dated May 18, 1787 (*ibid.*, II, 482), Belknap mentioned to Hazard that he had sent the first installment of the "Bulliad" by sea, with instructions not to print it if it were not worth the premium. Hazard wrote to Belknap Nov. 17, 1787 (*ibid.*, II, 496), that *The Foresters* was arousing some interest, as a friend had pressed him to reveal the author, and had asked him whether Francis Hopkinson or Dr. Clarkson had written the papers. On Dec. 8, 1787, Belknap wrote to Hazard (*ibid.*, II, 497) that it remained with the editors whether *The Foresters* would be continued or not; and on Jan. 2, 1788, he informed Hazard (*ibid.*, II, 500) that Spotswood had written for another guinea's worth. The confirmation had come too late, however, to serve the

but obvious allegorical machinery, and representing the Foresters as the people of the United States, Ontontio as Canada, Robert Lumbers as New Hampshire, John Codline as Massachusetts, Peter Bull-Frog as New York, Walter Pipegood as Virginia, his grandson as George Washington, Charles Indigo as South Carolina, and Ethan Greenwood as Vermont, Belknap was able to review the history of the Colonies—their internal and external bickerings, intolerances, grievances, and greediness—in a humorously satirical manner not bitter enough to arouse anger.

Belknap contributed other pieces also. Under the standing title of "The American Plutarch, or a Biographical Account of the Heroic and Virtuous Men . . . of the United States," he conducted a biographical series consisting of the lives of John Winthrop, Sir Ferdinando Gorges, and Captain John Smith.[49] These sketches suggested to his mind the publication of a book containing rather elaborate accounts of the lives of eminent Americans, a plan which he later executed.[50] He replied at length to Noah Webster's conjectures regarding the travels of Ferdinand de Soto,[51] and to this article Webster responded in *The Columbian Magazine*

magazine for January 1788, an omission Hazard noticed with regret (*ibid.*, II and III, 2, 15). Belknap remained anonymous throughout the series for the reason that he had confided to Hazard in a letter dated May 4, 1787 (Belknap Papers, manuscript at the Massachusetts Historical Society, V, 83): "I must not be known as the author, for I shall take great Liberty & tell some sad truths, in pretty coarse Language. I shall pass it thro' your hands." Later Belknap wished to publish *The Foresters* in book form, and he wrote to Hazard and Spotswood regarding possible rights Spotswood might have in the production by virtue of its original appearance in the magazine. Spotswood agreed to advance expenses for printing the book, the profits to be divided, and these terms Hazard considered quite fair, although Belknap was rather inclined to the belief that the nine guineas he had received for the series hardly entitled Spotswood to any book rights (Belknap to Hazard, June 6, 1789; Hazard to Belknap, June 12, 1789; and Belknap to Hazard, June 20, 1789, "The Belknap Papers," *op. cit.*, III, 136-38, 141-43). *The Foresters, an American Tale: Being a Sequel to the History of John Bull, the Clothier,* appeared anonymously under a Boston imprint in 1792 (Evans, *op. cit.*, No. 24086).

[49] Jan.-Aug., Oct.-Dec., and supplement for 1788, pp. 3-5, 55-57, 121-23, 178-80, 237-39, 297-301, 357-62, 418-21, 549-54, 637-41, 699-703, 721-27. In a letter to Hazard dated Jan. 3, 1789 ("The Belknap Papers," *op. cit.*, III, 89), Belknap inquired of his correspondent whether he had full right to publish the "Lives" again.

[50] The first volume of his *American Biography* appeared in 1794 (Evans, *op. cit.*, No. 26637).

[51] For Webster's articles in *The American Magazine* see especially notes 147-50. Belknap's article appeared in *The Columbian Magazine* for Sept. 1788, pp. 477-89, under the title, "Observations on the Travels and Transactions of Ferdinand de Soto, in Florida."

with his "Further Remarks on the Travels of Ferdinand de Sote (sic)"[52] which Belknap considered to be a retraction.[53] There appeared likewise one article by Belknap earlier published in *The Boston Magazine*, his "Enquiry" whether the discovery of America had been useful or hurtful to mankind.[54] He was also responsible for the appearance in the magazine of John Quincy Adams's "Oration" delivered at the Harvard Commencement on July 18, 1787,[55] for he prevailed upon the hesitating young man to yield him the manuscript for publication.

The contributions of Benjamin Rush[56] are far more interesting than Belknap's because of Rush's energetic and crusading spirit, which neither his middle forties nor the attacks of his political enemies could tame. Late in life he wrote that Scotland had given him his republicanism while he was studying medicine in that country, and that this "same republican ferment produced similar commotions and I hope a similar precipitation of the feculencies of error, upon the subjects of education, penal laws and capital pun-

[52] Nov. 1788, pp. 645-46. At least one other piece by Webster appeared in the magazine, "Anecdotes of Pocahunta" (July 1787, pp. 548-51), which had been published hitherto.

[53] On Dec. 20, 1788 Belknap wrote Hazard ("The Belknap Papers," *op. cit.*, III, 85) that he did not intend to carry on the controversy regarding De Soto, since Webster had conceded that none of the fortifications still remaining was De Soto's.

[54] For reference to *The Boston Magazine*, see Chapter VIII, section I, note 44. The article appeared in *The Columbian Magazine* for June 1788, pp. 303-08.

[55] Sept. 1787, pp. 625-28. In *Life of Jeremy Belknap*, by his granddaughter, Jane Belknap Marcou, pp. 156-58, the account of Belknap's repeated requests for the manuscript is told in detail.

[56] Rush was born on a farm near Philadelphia in 1745. He studied medicine at the University of Edinburgh, receiving his degree in 1768. In the same year he met Franklin, Johnson, Goldsmith, and others in London, and he visited Paris in 1769, before returning to Philadelphia, where he practised medicine and held professorships in the medical school of the University of Pennsylvania during a long, active life. He was widely recognized not only in his profession but for his interest in government, politics, and social reform. He opposed the Constitution of Pennsylvania in 1776, and the same year served as a member of the Continental Congress, signing the Declaration of Independence. In 1777 he was appointed surgeon-general of the Middle Military District. A strong Federalist, he was a member of the Convention of 1787 which met to frame the Constitution. He advocated free schools and higher education for women. He opposed slavery, capital punishment, and the use of distilled liquors and tobacco. Typically energetic and dramatic was his fight against the yellow fever epidemic in Philadelphia in 1793, during the course of which he often visited over a hundred stricken patients daily and devised a treatment strongly condemned by a number of members of his profession. Materials for the study of Rush are chiefly at the Ridgway Branch of the Library Company of Philadelphia. See also *A Memorial Containing Travels Through Life or Sundry Incidents in the Life of Dr. Benjamin Rush . . . Written by himself* (1905).

ishments,—upon each of which I published a number of essays in the 'American Museum,' the 'Columbian Magazine,' and other periodical works. A selection of them has since been published in an octavo volume by Samuel Bradford of Philadelphia."[57] By the time *The Columbian Magazine* was begun, Rush had been for over a decade withdrawn from the political ferment of the days when he had signed the Declaration of Independence and helped in drafting the Constitution, and was devoting his pen largely to social reform.

Rush's articles in the magazine are usually unsigned, but from several sources a number of them can be positively identified. He contributed at least two pieces against slavery. One of these, "The Paradise of Negro-Slaves," after picturing the grossest cruelties, contains an elaborate compliment of the work of Anthony Benezet, who had circulated a petition for the abolition of slavery.[58] The other, a report which Rush wrote as secretary of the Society for the Gradual Abolition of Slavery, deals with "Certificates of Mental Improvement in Negroes."[59] His aversion to alcoholic liquors is manifest in "A Moral and Physical Thermometer," in which he condemned all liquors stronger than beer as contributing to degeneracy, vice and disease.[60] In "The Benefits of Charity,"[61] one of his most highly wrought allegorical satires, he endeavored to persuade the General Assembly to establish free schools: the city, he said, had been saved from the visits of the Destroying Angel by the fact that the Angel of Mercy had been able to point to the City's hospital, dispensary, and the societies for the abolition of slavery and for the alleviation of the miseries of public prisons; but unless the Angel of Mercy could cite the establishment of free schools in the city by May 1788, the havoc of retribution would descend. He paid his highest respects to the frugality, industry, kindness, and religious zeal of the German immigrants in the state

[57] *A Memorial*, p. 64.

[58] Jan. 1787, pp. 235-38; reprinted in *Essays, Literary, Moral & Philosophical*, by Benjamin Rush (1798).

[59] "Supplement" for 1788, pp. 742-44.

[60] Jan. 1789, p. 31. Belknap mentions this article in a letter to Hazard dated Feb. 18, 1789 ("The Belknap Papers," *op. cit.*, III, 106), stating that Rush had inclosed a proof-sheet of it in a recent communication to him.

[61] Aug. 1787, pp. 578-81. This also appears as No. 10 in a collection of pamphlets and clipsheets once in the library of James Rush, now at the Ridgway Branch, lettered "Works of Dr. Benjamin Rush" (see note 56).

in "An Account of the Manners of the German Inhabitants of Pennsylvania," one of his longer articles.[62] The field of his profession offered occasional subjects for his pen, as in his "An Inquiry into the Methods of Preventing the Painful and Fatal Effects of Cold upon the Human Body,"[63] in which he digressed to attack the slave trade.[64] Other of his essays and reports were more in the nature of occasional writings on subjects of less continuous interest to him. His "Account of a Curious Sermon," on the rash requests of women, he had written down on returning from a church he had visited while on a trip through the South.[65] He wrote also "Causes Which Produced the Ruin of States,"[66] "An Enquiry into the Consistency of Oaths with Reason and Christianity,"[67] and a choice bit of descriptive writing entitled "Description of the Entertainment, Given by the Minister, on the Account of the Birth of the Dauphin of France," at Philadelphia on July 15th, for which celebration eleven hundred tickets had been distributed and many of the ladies "were obliged to have their heads dressed between four and six o'clock in the morning, so great was the demand."[68]

Without exception, the articles by Rush are the most lively expressions on social problems in the magazine. There are others of

[62] Jan. 1789, pp. 22-30. Belknap mentions this article (see note 60).

[63] May 1787. pp. 427-31. It is signed "A Customer."

[64] The magazine also republished an extract from his "Observations on the Duties of a Physician, and the Methods of Improving Medicine," delivered at the University of Pennsylvania Feb. 7, 1789 (March 1789, pp. 163-69).

[65] Feb. 1787, pp. 271-72. It is signed "A Customer" and is listed as No. 27 in the bound volume of pamphlets lettered "Works of Benjamin Rush" (see note 61).

[66] Dec. 1787, pp. 816-18. It is signed "B. R."

[67] Feb. 1789, pp. 104-08. Belknap, in a letter to Rush dated June 26, 1789 (Vol. 30, p. 10, of manuscript correspondence of Benjamin Rush at the Ridgway Branch) announced that this essay, which Rush had sent him, had appeared in Fenno's *Gazette* and *The Columbian Magazine*.

[68] Feb. 1787, pp. 260-63. This is listed as No. 4 of the bound volumes and pamphlets lettered "Works of Benjamin Rush" (see note 65). Other articles by Rush appearing in *The Columbian Magazine* in years subsequent to the bounds of this study include an essay on female education addressed to the visitors of the Young Ladies' Academy at Philadelphia (April, May 1790), a Commencement address delivered at the medical school of the College of Philadelphia Dec. 15, 1790 (Dec. 1790), and an account of the sugar maple tree of the United States (March 1792). Harry G. Good, in *Benjamin Rush and his Services to American Education* (n. d. Witness Press, Berne, Ind.), has traced Rush's ideas on education in large part directly to Fénelon's *De l'Education des Filles* (1688), and has listed a number of Rush's magazine articles in his study.

merit—"A. Z.'s" "Considerations on Religion,"[69] various articles on slavery,[70] Matthew Wilson's "On a Liberal Education,"[71] and the anonymous "An Essay on Genius"[72] and "A Dialogue between a Meeting-House and a School-House,"[73]—all probably original with the magazine. And there were the usual serial essayists, "The Trifler,"[74] "The Retailer,"[75] and "The Rhapsodist" (Charles Brockden Brown),[76] among whom the last was able to infuse a romantic sincerity and humility into his work not unlike that found in William Smith's "Hermit" papers. But the essays of all these others cannot approach those by Rush, in whom were united a nature outspoken, a precise pen, and a mind worthy of record.

Selected pieces not original with the magazine introduced the names of eminent Americans and Europeans discovered in many of the periodicals. Franklin's essay on the handsome and deformed leg, his letter to the Governor of Massachusetts concerning Shays's Rebellion, and some of his maritime observations were used.[77] Items by Washington included his speech on accepting the command of the army, and his letters regarding the Asgill case.[78] Not only

[69] April-Dec. and "Supplement" 1787, pp. 351-56, 401-07, 459-61, 519-21, 571-73, 623-24, 683-85, 750-53, 795-97, 839-52.

[70] Among the pieces bearing on the subject were Theophilus Rowe's "The Slave," a poem (Feb. 1787, pp. 293-94), an account of the introduction of slavery into England (Aug. 1788, 465-66, the Marquis de Chastellux's description of slavery in America, from his *Travels* (June 1787, pp. 479-80), "A Summary View of the Slave Trade" ("Supplement" for 1787, pp. 870-72), an answer to an argument in favor of slavery (May 1788, pp. 266-68), and "An Account of a Free Settlement of Negroes, Now Forming at Sierra Leona," by Granville Sharpe (April 1789, pp. 234-40).

[71] Feb. 1787, pp. 263-67.

[72] March-June 1789, pp. 176-79, 249-52, 293-96, 344-52.

[73] Jan. 1789, pp. 36-38.

[74] Dec. 1786, June, July, Sept., Nov., 1787, Jan., March, May, June, Aug. 1788, pp. 164-65, 461-63, 526-29, 628-30, 758-60, 33-37, 137-41, 273-75, 336-40, 449-50.

[75] Feb.-June, Dec. 1788, Feb.-April, July, Sept.-Nov. 1789, pp. 83-85, 150-53, 202-06, 263-66, 318-23, 695-98, 111-14, 181-85, 252-55, 401-04, 522-24, 586-89, 646-50.

[76] Aug.-Nov. 1789, pp. 464-67, 537-41, 597-601, 661-65. "A Rhapsodist," wrote Brown, "is one who delivers the sentiments suggested by the moment in artless and unpremeditated language. . . . But he is equally remote from the giddy raptures of enthusiasm, and the sober didactic strain of dull philosophy." He loved, he said, "to converse with beings of his own creation," and would withdraw from the commerce of the world if he were not by his nature compelled to seek the comfort of his friends at certain seasons.

[77] See especially issues for Oct. 1786, and April and May 1787, pp. 61-62, 396, 434-36.

[78] See respectively issues for Sept. 1786, p. 39; Jan. and Feb. 1787, pp. 205-09, 253-55.

was *Notes on Virginia* drawn upon at the request of Hopkinson,[79] but other references indicate Jefferson's importance.[80] Selections were printed from the writings of Generals Israel Putnam and Joseph Warren;[81] James Wilson's temporarily famous "Oration" of July 4, 1788, occupied seven pages;[82] and short extracts were taken from the histories by Thomas Hutchinson and David Ramsay.[83] Among European writers, Johnson, Whitefield, Penn, Hume, Burke, Voltaire, Montesquieu, and Rousseau were included, either in special references or by selections from their works.[84]

It was logical for *The Columbian Magazine*, as a periodical serving a new nation, to pay special attention to geography, agriculture, manufactures, science, and invention; and it was with reference to these subjects that the copperplate engravings were chiefly concerned.[85] There was little of literary criticism either original

[79] April, May, Aug. 1787, Feb., March 1788, pp. 366-69, 407-16, 573-75, 75-77, 86-89, 141-44.

[80] See issues for July, Oct., Nov. 1787, pp. 555-56, 705-06, 767.

[81] For Putnam, see David Humphreys's "Singular Adventure by General Putnam" (Oct. 1788, pp. 591-92) and "Extracts" from the life of Putnam (Nov. 1788, pp. 628-37). For Warren, see his "Oration" (July 1787, pp. 529-37).

[82] July 1788, pp. 304-400.

[83] See respectively issues for Sept. 1788 and Sept. 1786, pp. 497-501, 22-25.

[84] For Johnson, see issues for Dec. 1786 and May 1788, pp. 170-71, 283; for Whitefield, April and June 1788, pp. 224-25, 313-14; for Penn—his thoughts on government and an account of his life—July 1787, pp. 543-45 and April, June-Sept. 1789, pp. 223-28, 337-41, 397-401, 479-84, 517-22; for Hume's essay on civil liberty, Jan. 1788, pp. 9-13; for a digest of "A Concise History of the Late War in America" published in *The Annual Register* and ascribed to Burke, March-Dec. 1789, pp. 146-52, 209-16, 269-76, 329-36, 389-96, 449-56, 509-16, 569-76, 633-39; for Voltaire, March 1787 and Aug. and "Supplement" for 1788, pp. 338, 445-47, 749-50; for Montesquieu and Rousseau, "Supplement" for 1788, pp. 749-50.

[85] Probably because of Trenchard's association, *The Columbian Magazine* is the most profusely illustrated of early American periodicals, two to four engravings and etchings appearing each month. Following is a descriptive list, with the sculptor's name, when given on the illustration, in parentheses. Sept. 1786: frontispiece entitled, "While Commerce Spreads her Canvas O'er the Main"; portrait of Nathaniel Greene; arms of the United States (Trenchard). Oct.: reverse of great seal of the United States (Trenchard); plan of a farmyard; medal presented Col. Morgan (Trenchard). Nov.: bones found near Ohio River (Trenchard); representation of eclipse of moon, Jan. 3, 1787. Dec.: plan of a granary; plan of Fitch's steamboat; lane of the annual passage of herrings. Jan. 1787: plan of proposed bridge over the Schuylkill River; portrait of Washington. Feb.: view of Ohiopyle Falls; illustration of ruby-crowned wren. March: Chalybeate Spring near Saratoga (Trenchard); drawing of new solar dial. April: view of country between Wilmington and Delaware. May: plan of new candle case; plan of ancient works on Muskingum River. June: plan of new machine for raising water by wind; illustration of armorial bearings of Pa. and N. J. July: view of state house in Philadelphia

or selected,[86] and though many sentimental love stories, memoirs, and tales exploiting moral virtues were copied from old-world sources, they were used largely as "filler."[87] But accounts of the

in 1778 (Trenchard). Aug.: view of Gray's Ferry on the Schuylkill (Trenchard). Sept.: view of Natural Bridge in Va.; draught of newly invented plotting instrument; draught of remarkable tooth found on banks of the Susquehannah River; draught of helmet crab. Oct.: illustration for story "Amelia: or the Faithless Briton" (Trenchard); illustration of armorial bearings of Mass. and N. Y. Nov.: view of Christ Church, Philadelphia. Dec.: view of Boston; draught of newly invented drill plough. Jan. 1788: frontispiece entitled "Behold! a Fabric Now to Freedom Rear'd" (Trenchard); map of Pa. Feb.: view of new market, Philadelphia (Thackara); view of lighthouse on Cape Henlopen. March: engraving of profiles of Washington and Franklin; engraving of fossils found in Pa. April: view of meeting house on Hollis Street in Boston (Bullfinch and Vallance); engraving of implements used to assay ores. May: pass over South Mountain between Yorktown and Carlisle (Bedwell); illustration of Rumsey's new boiler for generating steam; engraving of ores and fossils in the United States. June: Newbold's plantation on Indian River (Trenchard); draught of lead smelting furnace. July: engraving of transit of Mercury over the sun; draught of Wall's trigonometer. Aug.: view of Juniatta River; engraving of American fossils. Sept.: view of Pulpit Rock between Huntingdon and Bald Eagle Valley in Pa.; plan of new method of reaping. Oct.: view of a pit at Sinking Spring Valley, Pa.; plan of Winlaw mill. Nov.: Baron Trenck chained in dungeon at Magdeburg; plan of Campus Martius at Marietta, Ohio. Dec.: view of ancient colleges at Cambridge, Mass.; view of Fort Robertdeau in Sinking Spring Valley, Pa. Jan. 1789: frontispiece entitled "America! with Peace and Freedom Blest"; a mud iguana; a horizontal spinning wheel; illustration of a moral and physical thermometer, by Benjamin Rush. Feb.: ground plan of the state house at Annapolis; Schuylkill River; design representing circle of the social and benevolent affections. March: specimens of snow; view of Canaan, Conn. April: six specimens of fossils found in America; a prospect of Paysaïck Falls, N. J. May: Gray's Ferry on the Schuylkill, with decorations in honor of Washington (Trenchard); triumphal arch erected at Trenton in honor of Washington. June: Cook's patent drill plough; rural scene looking from the green woods toward Canaan, in Conn. July: map of seat of war in Mass.; plan of a varied landscape. Aug.: plan of a federal edifice at New York; words and music of a new song by Francis Hopkinson. Sept.: chemical furnaces; Indian works on the Huron River or Bald Eagle Creek. Oct.: new carriage springs invented by Mr. Jacobs; view from road near New Windsor. Nov.: view on the Schuylkill; illustration of the four temperaments; words and music of a song in "Rosina," by Francis Hopkinson. Dec.: houses in Albany; male and female remiz.

[86] For examples, see "Strictures on Pronunciation," by "P.Q." (March 1787, pp. 313-14); "On the Literature, Wit and Taste of the European Nations" (July, Aug. 1788, pp. 384-88, 423-30), and "Strictures on the Style of Doctor Blair" (Jan. 1789, pp. 43-49).

[87] For examples, see "The Contemplant. An Eastern Tale" (Nov. 1786, pp. 130-33; "Perrin and Lucetta, or Rural Probity" Nov. 1786, pp. 133-37); "Charlotte, or the Prudent Choice" (Dec. 1786, pp. 191-96); "Bathmendi: A Persian Tale" (Jan.-Feb. 1787, pp. 241-43, 289-92); "History of Kitty Wells" (March, April 1787, pp. 339-42, 381-89); "Constantia, or, Unexampled Magnanimity" (June 1787, pp. 481-88); "Chariessa: or, a Pattern for the Sex" (Jan. 1788, pp. 40-45); "Ela; or Delusions of the Heart" (Sept.-Dec., 1788, pp. 525-35, 592-602, 648-57, 706-11).

progress of Pennsylvania,[88] David Rittenhouse's description of the Ohiopyle Falls,[89] Richard Champion's consideration of the best situations for settlements in America,[90] William Morrel's summary of the natural advantages of New England,[91] a narrative of New Smyrna in Florida,[92] William Byrd's "Description of the Dismal Swamp,"[93] and accounts of the Dunkards and Swedes in America[94] held more pertinent command of the readers' attentions. Agricultural notes were many in number, and scattered throughout the pages; any subject seemed acceptable, from short notes on the culture of grain and the rehabilitation of soil to the care of orchards and bees.[95] In the reports on manufactures, the Pennsylvania Society for the Promotion of Manufactures played an important part.[96] Science and invention were accorded much space. John Pennington's "Chemical and Economical Essays" on earths and salts is perhaps the most outstanding single series,[97] but David Hartley's comments on iron,[98] S. Latham Mitchill's observations on peat and evaporation of water,[99] David Rittenhouse's letter on the generation of clouds,[100] Jonathan Elmer's dissertations on chemical bodies and air,[101] John Gilpin's notes on the migration of herrings,[102] a summary account of the donations and communications of the American Philosophical Society,[103] a description of John Fitch's steamboat,[104] and long articles on ores and fossils in

[88] Nov. 1786, pp. 117-22.

[89] Feb. 1787, p. 284.

[90] Oct., Nov. 1787, pp. 685-87, 753-54.

[91] July-Sept., 1788, pp. 407-08, 470, 535-38.

[92] Aug., Dec. 1788, pp. 440-43, 683-88.

[93] April 1789, pp. 230-34.

[94] Jan. 1788, pp. 28-33.

[95] Note particularly George Morgan's "Essay on Bees" read at Princeton (Jan. 1787, pp. 216-19), and J. Beale Bordley's "Experiments" with wheat (Nov. 1786, Jan. 1787, pp. 128-30, 222-26).

[96] See, for examples, issues of the supplements for 1787 and 1788, pp. 865-68, 736-40.

[97] Sept.-Dec. 1789, pp. 525-31, 577-82, 643-46, 694-96. See Smyth, *The Philadelphia Magazines and their Contributors*, p. 64.

[98] "Supplement" for 1787, pp. 868-69.

[99] Aug. 1787, pp. 581-87.

[100] March 1787, pp. 301-03.

[101] Sept., Dec. 1788, pp. 493-97, 677-82.

[102] Dec. 1786, pp. 157-59.

[103] For 1789 alone, items appear in issues for June, July, Aug., Oct.-Dec., and "Supplement," pp. 360-61, 412-13, 484-85, 602-03, 673-74, 703-06, 763-66.

[104] Dec. 1786, p. 174.

America,[105] and on lead,[106] indicate the variety of appeal and the attention paid to investigations which might offer practical benefits.

From an historical point of view, probably the most interesting among the offerings of *The Columbian Magazine* in poetry are a dozen versifications and imitations of *The Ossian*, which suggests the sudden and wide interest taken in this unusual form of narration.[107] Selections from the poems of David Humphreys,[108] Joel Barlow,[109] Francis Hopkinson,[110] and John Trumbull[111] are to be expected, though Trumbull's "The Wedding, an Epithalamium," written in four-foot couplets, was an unfortunate choice, as it was done in a manner to provoke the loud laugh that speaks the vulgar if not vacant mind. Poems by Elizabeth Graeme Fergusson,[112] an epistle to Samuel Seabury[113] a translation from the Latin of Thomas Gray,[114] a poem in honor of William Collins,[115] an Italian sonnet by Dominico Bertini in praise of Washington,[116] and translations

---

[105] March-May,1788, pp. 153-56, 208-11, 282-83.

[106] June, July, Sept., 1788, pp. 333-34, 389-90, 509-10.

[107] Jan., Feb., July, Aug., Nov. 1787, May, June, July, Nov., Dec. 1788, April 1789, pp. 248, 292, 558, 608-09, 781, 289, 347-50, 408-09, 660-61, 712-13, 261. The first was by Dr. Joseph Brown Ladd.

[108] "Elegy on the Burning of Fairfield" (Oct. 1786, pp. 93-94), "Mount Vernon" (Jan. 1787, pp. 246-47), and an extract from "A Poem on the Happiness of America" (March 1788, p. 165). The last had been accorded a long review in the issue for Oct. 1786, pp. 67-71, in which year editions were printed in London and Hartford.

[109] Two extracts from *The Vision of Columbus* (May 1787, Jan. 1788, pp. 443-44, 47).

[110] See note 35.

[111] June 1789, pp. 373-78.

[112] Mr. C. T. Hallenbeck, in a letter dated Oct. 25, 1930, has kindly listed the four poems positively identified: "On the Death of Leopold, Prince of Brunswick" (Dec. 1786, p. 198), "Lines by a Friend, on Reading Mrs. M. Moore's Printed and Unprinted Extracts for the Use of Schools" (June 1788, p. 350), "On a Beautiful Damask Rose; Emblematical of Love and Wedlock (May 1789, p. 312), and "A Song" (Dec. 1789, p. 746). Mr. Hallenbeck also stated that he was "fairly certain" Mrs. Fergusson is the author of four others: "Nathan's Parable. Paraphrased from the 12th Chapter of the 2nd Samuel" (Sept. 1787, p. 667), "III. Chapter of Job Paraphrased" (Feb. 1789, p. 127-28), "On the Mind's Being Engrossed by One Subject" (July 1789, pp. 437-38), and "A Paraphrase on the 16th Chapter of of [*sic*] St. Luke's Gospel" (Sept. 1792, pp. 189-91). Mrs. Fergusson's favorite pen name was "Laura."

[113] Sept. 1786, pp. 44-45.

[114] Oct. 1787, p. 833.

[115] Oct. 1786, p. 92.

[116] June 1787, p. 506. A translation appeared in the issue for Feb. 1789, p. 128.

from Cervantes[117] and Quevedo[118] are more distinctive in their personal than in their literary associations. Lyrics accompanied by music were occasionally inserted.[119] The tradition of printing imitations of Horace, though waning, still persisted.[120] But in broad survey there is little to notice in "The Columbian Parnassiad," the section devoted to poetry. Rondeaux, elegies, lyric and narrative verse, purely ephemeral and rising from slight personal relationships and experiences, comprise most of the selections. The versifiers had little to say of value to anyone excepting themselves. It was by virtue of the prose rather than the poetry that the magazine attained a foremost place among the American magazines of distinction in the eighteenth century.

III

On October 26, 1787, Noah Webster, aged twenty-nine, arrived in New York from Philadelphia to confer with two printers, Samuel Campbell and Samuel Loudon. Five days later he contracted with the former to print his *Spelling Book*, and on December 4, having taken tea with Loudon the previous day, he made "the bargain for printing the American Magazine," and got the paper on shore.[121] During the past several years he had established a wide acquaintanceship, and was already well known as a strong Federalist and as an educator. He had been graduated from Yale in 1778, where President Ezra Stiles had observed his powers in "serious disputing" and marked him along with Josiah Meigs and Joel Barlow, as among the better students. Thereafter he had studied law, opened a private school in Connecticut, and published his popular *Spelling Book* (1783). He was a Federalist both by environment and by nature, and the difficulty he had encountered in attempting to collect royalties from the sale of his book in the several states emphasized in his mind the advantages of a strong central government.

[117] July 1787, p. 559.

[118] Nov. 1787, p. 780.

[119] Besides the two songs by Hopkinson (see note 35), "The Bud of the Rose" appeared in the issue for Nov. 1789. In prose, an appreciation of "two Americans of extraordinary Genius in poetry and music" (Robert Bolling, of Chellow, Va., and William Billings, of Boston) appeared in the issue for April 1788, pp. 211-13.

[120] See, for examples, the imitations in the issues for Nov. 1787 and March 1788, pp. 782, 167.

[121] Manuscript Diary at the New York Public Library, July 2, 1786-Sept. 19, 1820.

His *Sketches of American Policy* had appeared in 1785. During 1787 he had taught mathematics and English at the Episcopal Academy in Philadelphia, and in the same year he had published *An Examination into the Leading Principles of the Federal Constitution Proposed by the Late Convention Held at Philadelphia* as well as the third edition of his grammar and the seventh edition of his speller.[122] He now removed to New York in the hope of bettering his fortunes and launching a magazine which should hold first place throughout the states.

Webster's manuscript Diary[123] for the latter part of 1787 and the succeeding year affords the reader a rather intimate glimpse into his editorial work and social life in New York, from a somewhat introspective point of view. Having agreed to terms with Loudon, who had come to New York before the Revolutionary War,[124] Webster set himself diligently to writing. Recreation seems to have been largely confined to teas at the Loudon and other homes, an occasional ball or evening party, and the theatre. On January 2, 1788, he was busy sending the first number of the new magazine eastward. His interests were not confined wholly to the periodical, for in March he wrote of being engaged on the second part of his *Institute*, and in June he read his second lecture before the Philosophical Society. In August he made a visit to Boston, staying at the home of Rebecca Greenleaf, whom he married the following year. Since the beginning of the magazine, Webster had been planning to secure a more national reputation for the publication, and on this trip to Boston he surveyed the

[122] For biographical details, see *Notes on the Life of Noah Webster* (1912) compiled by Emily Ellsworth Fowler Ford and edited by Emily Ellsworth Ford Skeel. For an excellent bibliography of Webster's works, see Gorden Lester Ford, *Websteriana* (1882).

[123] See note 121.

[124] Loudon was born in Ireland. In New York he was a member of the Scotch Presbyterian Church. He was an ardent Whig, and left the city when it fell under British control during the Revolutionary War. Later he returned, and engaged in publishing a newspaper. He kept a bookstore, and printed books and pamphlets occasionally. William McCulloch, in a letter to Isaiah Thomas (*Proceedings of the American Antiquarian Society*, April 1921, pp. 135-36) stated that Louden was poor in worldly goods, and retired from business because of financial failure. He died in 1813, well advanced in years. Thomas (*op. cit.*, I, 311-12, 410, and II, 124, 235, 276) has recorded a fair outline of Loudon's life, though the facts presented occasionally conflict (*cf. ibid.*, I, 312 and II, 124). See also Hudson, *op. cit.*, p. 115.

northern prospects, but he met with little if any encouragement. On October 16, back at New York, he awoke to find "30 years of my life gone," and as he reviewed the past he discovered that though he had "read much—written much—& tried to do much good," he had made little money; so he was now determined to "leave writing & do more lucrative business." He was disconsolate, too, by reason of his state of bachelorhood, and his resolution to earn more money led him to prosecute vigorously his plan of an elaborate, federal magazine. On November 7 and 8 he confided the fact that he was busy "endeavoring to form a Society for publishing The American Magazine & Universal Register," and he believed he was on the verge of success; and a month later (December 5 and 6) he signed a contract with Francis Childs and Ebenezer Hazard for the publication of the magazine, but the plan failed. By December 15 he must have completed his editorial work on the final issue of *The American Magazine*, as he prepared to leave New York for Boston, where, on January 4, 1789, he waited on Isaiah Thomas, seeking to secure his approval to a union of *The American Magazine* just discontinued and *The Massachusetts Magazine*, the first issue of which was in preparation. This merger was not consummated, and in February Webster was studying law intently. That autumn he was married to Rebecca Greenleaf, and on November 4 they arrived at Hartford, where the young attorney had resolved to practise law.

From more external sources than the Diary, public announcements during the same period explain other plans and endeavors. The initial appearance of *The American Magazine* was not widely heralded in the public press, and the correspondence which has been preserved bearing upon the periodical indicates that Webster was never satisfied with its reception, hoping to merge with Boston and Philadelphia groups. Meanwhile he bided his time, doing whatever seemed necessary to maintain a cheerful front. The first issue, for December 1787, was advertised in a small space in *The Daily Advertiser* (Francis Childs) of December 29, 1787, to appear "On Tuesday next," at a subscription price of twenty shillings a year or ten shillings for six months. A similar announcement was printed in *The New-York Journal, and Weekly Register* (Thomas Greenleaf) of January 3, 1788. For several months brief announcements of new numbers were printed in the papers, but even these were discontinued after the issue for May.[125] *The American Museum*, on the other hand, was regularly advertised in the New York papers, and *The Columbian Magazine* followed suit on a less extensive scale. On the evidence of the newspapers, it would appear that the competitors in Philadelphia were successfully combating Webster in his own territory, and that he grew hopeless of single-handed success as early as July 1788.

In the "Introduction" to the first number, Webster outlined his general policy. He was "determined to collect as many original Essays as possible; and particularly such as relate to this country, and contain useful and curious discoveries in the history, or geography of America, or ingenious remarks upon the science of Government, and the peculiar institutions and customs of the people, in the different States." He wished to appeal to "every class of readers—the Divine, the Philosopher, the Historian, the Statesman, the Moralist, the Poet, the Merchant and the Laborer," and his "fair readers" were "assured that no inconsiderable pains will be taken to furnish *them* with entertainment." Wit, satire, and humor were promised, but no "personal invective, ribaldry, and immoral writings" would be tolerated. He admitted the merit of foreign works, and the "predelection" of Americans for them; but he urged the point of view that "none of them can be wholly calculated for this country,"[126] and he established as his central policy the program of publishing largely original work. In a subsequent announcement Webster claimed protection of the law of copyright, asserting that several printers had already reprinted several pieces without asking the privilege. He admitted that the absolute meaning of the copyright law had not been determined in this country, but he felt American courts would follow English court rulings, and he stood ready to prosecute infringements. Webster thus be-

---

[125] The issues for Jan.-May inclusive were first advertised in *The New-York Journal* of Feb. 14, March 6, April 3, May 8, and June 12 respectively.

[126] Dec. 1787, p. 2. The subscription price was set at $2.50 a year. An advertisement in *The Connecticut Courant* of Jan. 28, 1788, announced subscription prices of $1.25 for six months and twenty-five cents the single copy. In the first number only New York houses were listed as selling agents, but with the issue for Jan. 1788 agents were listed at Boston, Hartford, New Haven, Hudson, Albany, Philadelphia, and Charleston.

came the first publisher on an American magazine to maintain forcefully that the contents were personal property.[127]

Private letters written during 1788 also reveal some interesting facts regarding the history of the magazine. On February 9, 1788, Webster wrote to Jeremy Belknap at Boston, disclosing a more daring plan of publishing a magazine than any other yet conceived in America. He proposed "to divide the property of the work into ten shares; to have a proprietor in Boston, another in Connecticut, a third in Philadelphia, a fourth in Virginia, a fifth in Charleston, & the Editor with the principal superintendency in New York & four shares. The other share to be disposed of in New Jersey, Maryland, or Georgia, as we can find a suitable person; or perhaps in Connecticut, if all the poets in that State will unite in partnership." He added many details. The distant proprietors would do little else than collect and forward material, such as "deaths, burials, &c., entries at custom-houses, philosophical observations on the weather, the degrees of heat & cold, celestial phenomena, . . . curious anecdotes, &c., &c." The whole collection for each month, he imagined, would fill a hundred pages octavo of pieces "highly beneficial to the States" which "would remove prejudices, & gradually cement our union." He rather audaciously envisioned 3,000 to 5,000 subscribers at three dollars a year, which he estimated would yield a clear profit for a dollar for every subscriber. The shares to be distributed were to be valued at three to five hundred dollars. He further confided to Belknap that he had written to Barlow, Trumbull, Rush, and Ramsay, whom he had considered as possible proprietors, and he now invited Belknap to join the distinguished company. As editor, Webster would "engage to furnish paper, contract for printing, superintend the press, arrange the materials, & dispense the copies to every part of America."[128]

To the invitations thus extended Rush replied on February 13,

[127] Feb. 1788, p. 130. For several years Webster had been aggravated because no definite law of copyright protected his *Spelling Book*.

[128] "The Belknap Papers," *op. cit.*, sixth series, IV, 385-87. Webster's letter of Dec. 31, 1787 to Hudson and Goodwin of Hartford, in which he notified them that he was sending forty copies, is of assistance in measuring the distribution of the magazine. The letter is among the manuscripts of Webster letters at the New York Public Library. Skeel (*op. cit.*, II, 406-07) reprints a letter from Webster to William Young, of Philadelphia, asking him to sell a few copies, promising him "fourteen to a dozen and a quartan or twenty-fifth."

1788. He rejoiced at the establishment of a new magazine, but he declined to become a proprietor on the ground that he wrote "from the impulse of the moment" only, and so could not promise regular contributions. Moreover, he spoke of growing old and of withdrawing himself from public duties and the public eye. But he softened the refusal by promising several essays then in his drawer, and by suggesting that he might make the magazine a "vehicle of some tracts on medicine." Rush probably had no faith in the success of the scheme. The magazines in Philadelphia were not prospering. The doctor wrote Webster that *The Columbian Magazine* was on the decline because of its antifederalist policy, "its deficiency of Matter," and the "impudent conduct" of Dallas, the editor, in "misrepresenting" the proceedings of the Pennsylvania convention; and he furthermore declared that "Carey complains of a want of punctuality in the subscriptions."[129] In answer to this letter Webster wrote to Rush on February 24, 1788, requesting him to submit the essays promised, for he was "confident they are good and deserve universal reading."[130]

Belknap was more wary than Rush. He did not reply to Webster's letter until June 28, 1788, after consultation with friends. Then he declined: "I have as many engagements as I can possibly attend to, & should be loth to form any others lest I should disappoint yᵉ. expectations of my friends," among whom he hoped to rank Webster.[131] Before writing this letter he had inquired of Hazard his opinion of Webster and Hazard had replied on March 5, 1788: "I think the *Monarch* [Webster] a literary puppy. . . . He certainly does not want understanding, and yet there is a mixture of self-sufficiency, all-sufficiency, and at the same time a degree of insufficiency about him, which is (to me) intolerable. I do *not* believe that *he* is fit for a superintendent; that the persons mentioned will be his coadjutors; or that either the *demand* or *profits* will any way near be equal to his expectations. . . . *Considering circumstances*, I would not advise you to engage with him, but I think you may avail yourself of his application with the Columbians."[132] Later, Hazard suggested that Belknap accept the re-

---

[129] Rush's letter is among the Webster manuscripts of letters at the New York Public Library.

[130] Skeel, *op. cit.*, I, 178.

[131] "The Belknap Papers," *op. cit.*, sixth series, IV, 387.

[132] *Ibid.*, fifth series, III, 23.

quest of the publisher of *The Columbian Magazine* for "assistance," and at the same time agree to Webster's proposal. However, he cautioned him not to enter into a proprietorship involving capital: "The Monarch (I think) ought to reign alone."[133] As Webster continued to apply himself to the furthering of his plans for the extension of the magazine, Hazard slightly altered his point of view. In a letter written November 8, 1788, he informed Belknap that under a new proposal Webster was to hold only one share, and that each issue was to be increased to one hundred and four pages—fifty-six to contain the usual material, twenty-four to be devoted to state papers, and the same number to important historical matter still in manuscripts. Under these circumstances Hazard had reluctantly concluded to let Webster print his collection of papers for £500 rather than risk the fortunes of private publication.[134] He was, however, dubious of the ultimate success of the plan.[135] Unlike Hazard, Belknap remained firm. He wrote to his friend that he did not believe he could secure subscribers in Boston for *The American Magazine*, as he had already "exerted all" his "influence" among his friends, "and in many instances without success, to procure subscriptions for the Columbian Magazine." Moreover, Belknap complained that Webster had somewhat spoiled his chances by having "taken care to announce to the world that he has still a hand in it. He is not popular here." Finally, he thought that the coming year would find Thomas's *The Massachusetts Magazine* more popular in the state than any rival.[136]

Webster's plans crumbled; the issue for December 1788 was the last. He attempted further projects, but gave up in despair and turned to Hartford and the law. Thomas had been cold to every proposal; Trenchard had gone his own way. For a brief time, when Webster had spoken enthusiastically of his five hundred subscribers and of the possibility of a thousand upon the announcement of the Hazard papers, Hazard had warmed to the idea and begun to investigate the field. But he had found only two hundred definite subscriptions for the coming year in New York, and lost in-

---

[133] *Ibid.*, III, 26. The letter is dated March 19, 1788. The final quotation is from Hazard's letter to Belknap of May 8, 1788 (*ibid.*, III, 34).

[134] *Ibid.*, III, 71-72.

[135] *Ibid.*, III, 76. The letter is dated Nov. 22, 1788.

[136] *Ibid.*, III, 81-83. The letter is dated Dec. 13, 1788.

terest.[137] No one ventured to publish any successor to the magazine, though a company in New York had not abandoned the idea by February 1, 1789.[138]

There is a unique editorial force in *The American Magazine* not hitherto encountered. This energy emanated from Webster himself, who ranks a peer among those editors of eighteenth-century magazines in America who were most personally dominant within the pages of their periodicals. He did not, like Franklin, hide behind shears. He was not merely a reflection of English classical thought, as was Gridley. Though he was less learned than Prince, his interests found a broader expression within the periodical, and though he was not so trenchant as Livingston, he fought in more than one arena. He did not, like Nicola, conceive of his editorial office as a kind of secretaryship. He was not so full of wisdom as Nevill, but he had more to say and he said it more colorfully. He was inherently an editor and a writer; Thomas was rather a business man and publisher. He could not, like William Smith, gather about him a group of contributors, but he could supply his magazine with well written articles from his own pen. He could ill have filled a chair among the group which edited *The Boston Magazine*, for he was more the gladiator and less the counselor. He was not, like Paine, limited by an Aitken; and he came to his chair less callow (though more lacking in literary power) than Brackenridge. He did not find himself, like Meigs, publishing a virtual newspaper and surrounded by more brilliant writers; nor did he labor under a proprietary system, as did Hopkinson and Dallas.

He followed the general principle of grouping his articles under several topical divisions, including government, antiquities, miscellaneous essays, reviews of new publications, poetry, news, and

---

[137] Hazard to Belknap, Jan. 13, 1789 (*ibid.*, III, 90-96), Belknap to Hazard, Jan. 24. 1789 (*ibid.*, III, 97-100); Hazard to Belknap, Feb. 4, 1789 (*ibid.*, III, 101); Hazard to Belknap, March 7, 1789, (*ibid.*, III, 107). Among the manuscript file of Webster's letters at the New York Public Library is one from Hazard to Webster dated Jan. 13, 1789, which indicated the futility of Webster's attempt to join with the originators of *The Massachusetts Magazine*. Hazard had "consulted Dr. Smith & Mr. Swaine," and they had decided the risk and expense of sending "Materials & Publications backwards & forwards; & the Improbability that the Citizens of New York would be pleased with a Magazine printed in another State" rendered the plan impracticable. The letter also refers to the difficulty of securing subscriptions in New York, which had already been canvassed.

[138] In a letter from Webster to James Greenleaf dated at Boston Feb. 1, 1789, Webster mentioned this company (Skeel, *op. cit.*, II, 408).

occasionally theology and agriculture. Among the original pieces, those by Webster are of chief interest; and among the departments, the "Review of New Publications" is the most noteworthy, for Webster was the first editor of an American magazine to raise the office of literary critic to a plane of intellectual discrimination. On the whole, the literary criticism was overburdened by descriptive matter and by criticism of words and phrases. Still, Webster lucidly presented the essential ideas of the subjects under review, and considered these ideas fairly, without great vaunting of his critical acumen.

The American Magazine was a magazine of ideas. The dominance of Addison and Steele had receded; the light essay and the light poetry of the earlier part of the century were restricted in space. Thought rather than manner counted. Tritely developed general themes were discarded for points of view advanced as distinctive contributions to knowledge or intellectual perspective. Original pieces were favored. Facts were to be learned and principles assayed by inductive processes. There was much to be done in the world, and new methods might be better than old ones. Fiction and memoirs were not banished; indeed, traces of the roisterous comedy of a Fielding and the sentimentalism of a Richardson were present—the first mollified by a public taste less given to the spontaneous and robust, and the second modified by a public attitude tending slightly toward the considered common sense of a Burney. There were gothic and Oriental tales also, well filled with mystery, magic, color, and aphorisms. But fiction in all its forms, including the lurid memoir, was of secondary importance. The primary purpose of the magazine was to instruct and inform, and to this purpose Webster set a diligent hand. He was limited greatly only in verse. He could not write good poetry, though he tried;[139] and the periodical would have lacked good verse if selections by Barlow and Dwight had not been inserted.

Webster's personal contributions to *The American Magazine* may be ascertained by referring to his personally annotated copies at the New York Public Library, to his letters, and especially to his phonetically spelled book, *A Collection of Essays and Fugitiv Writings on Moral, Historical, Political and Literary Subjects*

[139] See, for examples, two poems he wrote for his magazine, "On the New Year" (Dec. 1787, p. 56), and "To the Author" of *The Conquest of Canäan* (March 1788, pp. 265-66).

(1790),[140] in which he reprinted many of his earlier writings, stating in the brief "Preface" that "Most of thoze peeces, which hav appeered before in periodical papers and Magazeens, were published with fictitious signatures."

A definite elevation of editorial energy and a heightened appreciation for dignity of editorial content in American magazines came with the writing of Webster's longer articles. In his essays on "Education"[141] he summarized the more advanced ideas on pedagogy of his time. He became a spokesman for the study of modern languages and grammar; he asked that the philosophy of education entertain, as a fundamental thesis, the principle that educational systems should specifically train students for later activity in occupations, professions, government, and the social duties; theoretically he conceived the ideal school as one located neither amidst the rush of city life nor in the purely sequestered "monkish" spot. Equally important were his several articles on "Government," written over the pseudonym of "Giles Hickory,"[142] which won the admiration of men of similar beliefs as far away as Boston.[143] Some of his ideas in this study have a definite relation to William Paley's *Elements of Moral and Political Philosophy.*[144] Early in the series Webster took the position that "A Bill of Rights against the encroachments of Kings and Barons, or against any power independent of the people, is perfectly intelligible; but a Bill of Rights against the encroachments of an elective Legislature, that is, against our *own* encroachments on *ourselves,* is a curiosity in government."[145] This attitude defined Webster's position as regards the controversy which raged around the original amendments to the Constitution, which he did not favor. His strong federalist opinions were likewise illustrated in the other articles of the series. In the

[140] The copy at the New York Public Library is annotated in Webster's hand.

[141] Dec. 1787-May 1788, pp. 22-26, 80-82, 158-61, 210-16, 311-13, 367-74. Reprinted in *A Collection,* pp. 1-37.

[142] Dec. 1787-March 1788, pp. 13-15, 75-80, 137-45, 204-10. Reprinted in *A Collection,* pp. 45-80.

[143] Royal Flint, in a letter to Webster dated from Boston Feb. 24, 1788, mentioned the first of the Giles Hickory series, "On Bills of Rights" as having been favorably received in that city. "I have shewn it [the article] to several Gentlemen who with me are extremely pleased with your Observations," he wrote. (The letter is among the Webster letters at the New York Public Library.)

[144] In Webster's copy of *A Collection* appears the annotation "Paley, Moral Phil. 342" and "Paley 347" beside passages which appear in the magazine on pp. 79-80.

[145] Dec. 1787, p. 13.

second he asserted that the legislative body should be invested with the whole power of its constituents. In the third he took issue with Jefferson on the constitution of Virginia; he was glad that "It is not shackled with a Bill of Rights."[146] And in the fourth he summarized his views on representative government: that the sovereign power may rest in the people, but that the legislature should be unrestricted in authority save in the right to change the form of government, for the people are not qualified to determine the general good.

Webster was interested, too, in American antiquities, especially in explorations beyond the Alleghanies and the remains of ancient fortifications found in the Middle West. In some letters to Ezra Stiles he advanced opinions as to the origin of certain earthworks in Kentucky and along the Muskingum River, and supported a theory that De Soto may have had a part in the construction of fortifications along the Ohio and Mississippi. These letters, together with two replies by Stiles, who disbelieved Webster's theory, were published in the magazine.[147] The discussion awakened curiosity, and Belknap, who considered Webster to be in the wrong, wrote to Hazard that he was planning to attack the De Soto theory.[148] Webster himself was somewhat doubtful of his ground, and admitted to Stiles that possibly the earthworks along the Muskingum were aboriginal places of worship.[149] Stiles also sent to Webster a copy of Captain John Smith's history of Virginia, together with an abridgment of the book made by Stiles's son which

---

[146] Feb. 1788, p. 137.

[147] The three letters from Webster to Stiles, dated Oct. 22, 1787, Dec. 15, 1787, and Jan. 20, 1788, appear in the issues for Dec. 1787 and Jan. and Feb. 1788 respectively, pp. 15-19, 87-93, 146-56. The two replies by Stiles, dated Feb. 27 and March 18, 1788, appear in the issues for March and April 1788 respectively, pp. 246-47, 291-94. Stiles's letter of Feb. 18 (among the manuscripts at the New York Public Library) acknowledges receipt of two of Webster's letters on the fortifications, and reads in part: "I have only now to say that altho' you have ingeniously & learnedly adduced all that probably can be sd. on the subject, yet it remains in some Measure problematical—I am not satisfied."

[148] In a letter to Hazard ("The Belknap Papers," op. cit., fifth series, III, 52) Belknap wrote on July 24, 1788, that he believed he knew where Webster secured his information for the De Soto theory, and that he could prove him to be in error. Hazard replied in August (ibid., III, 57) that the De Soto theory was one of Webster's "hobyhorses"; but he advised Belknap, in a letter dated Sept. 1788 (ibid., III, 62), not to affix his name to the article Belknap was writing against Webster's theory.

[149] See Webster's letter to Stiles, dated July 4, 1788, and printed in the issue of the magazine for Dec. 1789, pp. 537-41.

the father had "retouched," and Webster printed the condensed narrative in the magazine.[150]

The editor's failure to attract contributors was in some measure compensated by his own versatility. He could present, as well as most men, an analysis of the evils of an inflated currency,[151] and he could speculate entertainingly about the influences of language on opinions and opinions on language.[152] He reprinted, as a text of his own thought, a *Memorial and Remonstrance* against state support of religion presented to the assembly of Virginia in 1785, commenting on the excellent judgment exhibited by the assembly. The teaching of religion, when armed with the sanction of law, was dangerous, in his estimation.[153] He could assume a clear-headed attitude on "Morality," discussing its basis in social customs and noting its natural variations in practice among countries and races.[154] He could interest himself in the project of including music in the curricula of schools, and to a consideration of the relative merits of vocal and instrumental music.[155] He could turn, with the deftness of a Hopkinson, a light essay on city planning, flattering the straight-street patterns of Philadelphia, Charleston, and New Haven without ruffling the pride of those who dwelt in crooked-laned Boston.[156] He could adapt this light essay style to suit the moods of more personal fondnesses and grievances, writing on legal forms, words, Dwight, Ramsay, and the non-support of magazines by the public in a single essay, "The Art

[150] Dec. 1787, Feb. and March 1788, pp. 19-22, 156-58, 216-20. Stiles's letter to Webster introducing the abridgment, dated Feb. 27, 1788 (among the Webster manuscripts at the New York Public Library), reads in part: "I set my son to extract a summary Abridg^t. Afterwards I myself retouched it. I inclose both & from them you will be able to collect all that we can give you. . . . He [Smith] was a very extraord^y enterprising Character. You will not forget the Powhattan & Pocahunta Story, which is well narrated in the Marquis de Chastilling's Travels. It is referred to in Smith, but not fully told. It is of Consequence to be narrated accurately, as an English family in Virginia glory in being descended from Pocahunta to this day."

[151] "Principles of Government and Commerce" (Dec. 1787, pp. 9-12; see also *A Collection*, pp. 38-44).

[152] "A Dissertation concerning the Influence of Language on Opinions and of Opinions on Language" (May 1788, pp. 399-403; see also *A Collection*, pp. 222-28, where the article is reprinted. Webster later made in the book a marginal note, "This Dissertation contains many errors. N. W. 1835," and corrected some of them by hand.

[153] June 1788, pp. 479-84.

[154] July 1788, pp. 526-30; reprinted in *A Collection*, pp. 233-38.

[155] "On Music," June 1788, pp. 448-50 (signed "Orpheus"); reprinted in *A Collection*, pp. 229-32.

[156] Feb. 1788, pp. 164-66; reprinted in *A Collection*, pp. 217-21.

of Pushing into Business," by "Peter Pickpenny."[157] He seemed beyond the bounds of his capacity only when trying to supply material for feminine readers. His inquiries and answers to problems arising amidst the vicissitudes of courtship were patently weak inventions.[158]

Nothing that Webster wrote for the magazine has more significance than his contributions to the "Review of New Publications,"[159] and among these the most stirring is his review of Timothy Dwight's *The Triumph of Infidelity*.[160] It seems certain that before he composed this article he had made the annotations which now appear in his personal copy, preserved in the Connecticut State Historical Society Library at Hartford. These annotations point out the frequent use of the same words and phrases, and abound in humorous and satirical thrusts at some of the theological

[157] Jan.-Feb. 1788, pp. 103-05, 166-70. Although it is not marked in Webster's personal copies of the magazine and does not appear either in *A Collection* or among the manuscripts examined at the New York Public Library, this essay bears internal evidences pointing almost certainly to Webster's authorship. It presents Webster's favorite opinions on legal procedure, speech forms, and words. It suggests that Dwight and Ramsay should look elsewhere than America for their deserved recognition, as prophets were without honor at home—thus complimenting two men whom Webster was trying to secure as proprietors of the contemplated magazine. It grievingly plays with the idea that magazines should exchange their circulations among cities, as support at home seemed always lacking; this attitude could well have sprung from the militant encroachment of the magazines published in Philadelphia on the New York field.

[158] "A Letter from a Lady, with Remarks" (July 1788, pp. 531-34; reprinted in *A Collection*, pp. 239-44); "A Letter to the Author, with Remarks," (July 1788, pp. 582-85; reprinted in *A Collection*, pp. 245-48); "An Address to the Ladies" (March 1788, pp. 241-46; reprinted in *A Collection*, pp. 406-14). There is also in the magazine an untitled essay, written by "Alphonzo," reporting a conversation (April 1788, pp. 333-34), which is not in *A Collection*, but is most probably by Webster, as he had used the girl's name in writing the first letter.

[159] Hitherto the usual policy among editors had been to offer extracts without comment, assuming a neutral stand, or to reprint criticism from British sources.

[160] July 1788, pp. 588-90. This is not *A Collection*, but in his personal copy of the magazine Webster initialed an "N" on the first page of the review and checked the reference to the article in the table of contents of the magazine. This was his usual practice in noting his articles. *The Triumph of Infidelity* (1788), as well as the review, was published anonymously. In his personal copy of *The Triumph of Infidelity* (property of the Hartford Public Library, but now deposited in the Watkinson Library, Hartford), Webster wrote after the line "Now every monk could grunt them from his cell" (p. 16) an ironical "[su]blime"—the *su* is trimmed off in binding. After Dwight's lines satirizing the "Tolands, Tindals, Collinses and Chubbs" as men who "At truth and virtue growl'd, and bark'd at heaven," Webster wrote "thine poor dogs." These examples are illustrative of Webster's comments throughout the volume.

views expressed in the text: they indicate a germinal state of the later devastating review.

This review seems to mark the close of an hitherto happy association between Dwight and Webster. They had known each other since Webster's student days at Yale, where Dwight was a tutor at the time. When Webster launched his magazine, the first number contained two pieces by Dwight, his commencement address to the graduates of Yale, delivered July 25, 1776,[161] and a poem, "The Seasons Moralized."[162] In June 1788 another of his poems appeared, "A Hymn" sung at the public exhibition of the scholars of the academy at Greenfield the previous May.[163] In the meantime the editor had inserted his own poem in praise of Dwight, "To the Author of the *Conquest of Canäan*," written when Webster was nineteen years of age.[164] At about this time Webster conceived the idea of defending Dwight's *The Conquest of Canäan* (1785) against the attacks of British reviewers. In a letter dated June 6, 1788, Dwight replied most gratefully to Webster's proposal.[165] He thanked his young friend for his "obliging Designs to befriend my reputation, as a poet, & vindicate the Conquest of Canäan from those which you esteem illiberal remarks of the Reviewers," and he assured him that the allegorical implications which the British reviewers had seen fit to read into the poem were entirely without foundation, as the poem had been begun in 1771 and was largely written before 1775.[166] Dwight also referred to "A Hymn," which accompanied the letter, as being sent as a contribution to the magazine. He closed the letter with the following paragraph: "I am under obligation to Mr. Carey the publisher of the Museum. Whenever I forward any poetical per-

---

[161] Dec. 1787, Jan. 1788, pp. 42-47, 99-103.

[162] Dec. 1787, pp. 58-59.

[163] Pp. 507-08.

[164] March 1788, pp. 265-66. Webster identified himself as the author in his personal copy of the magazine, writing "N.W." on p. 265. Two lines characterize the whole:

> "Hail, rising genius, whose celestial fire
> Warms the glad soul to tune the sacred lyre."

[165] This letter is in the Webster file of manuscripts at the New York Public Library. Theodore A. Zunder, in a succinct survey of "Noah Webster and *The Conquest of Canäan*" (*American Literature*, May 1929, pp. 200-02), printed the whole of Dwight's letter.

[166] The allegorical structure was interpreted to relate the Egyptians with Great Britain, the Israelites with the Colonists, and Joshua with Washington.

formances hereafter, I will will [*sic*] thank you to copy them, &
to transmit one of the copies to him.   With much esteem & affection I am, dear sir, your very obliged & most obedient servant
Timothy Dwight."   Webster's defense of Dwight's poem appeared
in the issue for July as "The London Reviewers Reviewed," signed
"An American" and dated July 4, 1788.[167]   He called to task the
reviews appearing in *The European Magazine* for February, March,
and April.   He printed part of Dwight's letter and charged the
British reviewers with "national prejudice."

It is worth noting, however, that Webster confined his purpose in the article to an attack on the British reviewers and did
not expand it to "befriend" Dwight's "reputation as a poet."   It
seems more than possible that Webster was considerably irritated
because Dwight had come to terms with Carey and *The American
Museum*.   At a time when Webster was trying to strengthen his
position by uniting with outside interests and by asserting the
intention of prosecuting any infringement of copyright, Dwight's
proposal to serve two magazines must have been most annoying.
No further contributions by Dwight appeared in the magazine, and
Webster treated *The Triumph of Infidelity* with harsh satire,
criticising not only its puerile theology but its lack of literary re-
finement.   It was, he wrote, ill written save where the author had
stolen the lines from other poets.   "In short," Webster's indict-
ment read, "the author appears to be a theological dogmatist, who
has found the right way to heaven, by creeds and systems; and with
more imperiousness than would become infinite wisdom and power,
damns all who cannot swallow his articles of faith.   A man who
can group together such men as *Shaftsbury, Priestly, Chauncey and
Allen* and stigmatize these and many of the first philosophers pro-
miscuously as fools and knaves, can hardly be a candidate for that
heaven of love and benevolence which the scripture informs us is
prepared for good men."   In the next paragraph Webster struck
at Dwight's integrity: "Nor can we think the writer more remarkable for his poetic talents than for his liberality.   He can
indeed borrow lines without giving credit; but he should not borrow
from such a smooth versifier as Pope—the contrast between his own
lines and those borrowed immediately detects the plagiarism."[168]

[167] Pp. 562-66.

[168] P. 590. Rev. N. W. Appleton, of Boston, in a letter to Webster, dated Nov.
30, 1788, (among the manuscript file of Webster letters at the New York Public

What other reviews Webster wrote can probably be inferred only by internal evidence, but his work may be rather easily recognized because of his style, his channeled interests, and his characteristic preoccupation with certain phases of ideas on the subjects of federalism, history, poetry, and language. It seems most likely, for example, that Webster himself began the department of reviews in March 1788 by writing the long discussion of *The Federalist; a Collection of Essays Written in Favor of the New Constitution* (1788), an article which, extending through the issue for June, reiterates the necessity of union among the states and closes with references to the fair and candid reasoning of the author and his correct, smooth, and elegant language marred only by several faults of style which the reviewer illustrated by quotations.[169] The nature of the remarks of the critic of George Richard Minot's *The History of the Insurrections in Massachusetts, in the Year 1786* (1788) suggests Webster's hand with regard both to the content and the phraseology.[170] The tenor of the review of Colonel David Humphreys's *An Essay on the Life of the Honorable Major General Israel Putnam* (1788) is likewise Websterian, and quite· characteristic is the remark that "The style of the author is generally correct and elegant; but sometimes approaches to bombast, or rises considerably above his subject."[171] Surely the subsequent lexicographer, more than any other man at his call, was interested in writing about Jonathan Edward's *Observations on the Language of the . . . Mohegan Indians* (1788).[172] Finally, it seems to me that Webster also wrote the criticism of *The Times* (1788) by Peter Markoe.[173] To criticize this poem might seem at first

Library), possibly refers commendingly to this review, agreeing with Webster's attitude toward "supposed Doctrines."

[169] March-June 1788, pp. 260-61, 337-41, 423-24, 503-07.

[170] Sept. 1788, pp. 739-43.

[171] Sept., Oct. 1788, pp. 743-44, 799-804. Quotation on p. 743.

[172] July 1788, pp. 587-88.

[173] Sept. 1788, pp. 729-30. "We find in this poem a species of that spleen and prejudice which mingle themselves in all party-transactions," the reviewer wrote; and in defense of Barlow, whose republicanism was becoming distasteful to the Federalists, he described Markoe's strictures against the man as "illiberal and unmerited." Other reviews which Webster may have written, as the ideas are in agreement with his principles, include the discussion of the debates of the Pennsylvania Convention on the Constitution (March 1788, p. 262), reviews of two addresses to the people of New York on the Constitution (April 1788, pp. 341-43), letters from a "Federal Farmer" to a Republican (May 1788, pp. 422-23), D. W. Lewis's oration on the death of Eli Kelsey (Sept. 1788, pp. 730-32), Ebenezer Beardsley's history of dysentery in

to be favoring the antifederalists, which Webster would not likely do without just cause; but the review struck at the selfish and contemptible spirit of combativeness between the parties—as evidenced in Markoe's poem—and supported the larger patriotism developed by Barlow in *The Vision of Columbus*, both of which attitudes were congenial to the author's mind.

When Webster's own work has been deducted from the prose of *The American Magazine*, together with contingent material by such men as Dwight and Stiles, there is little of distinction remaining, though the total number of selected pieces is large. Webster was not so astute in his selections from printed sources as were the editors of *The Columbian Magazine*. Moreover, his interest waned during the summer of 1788, and the later numbers are not so fertile as the earlier either in his own or others' writings. Certain classifications can be made of the material which reflect phases of current thought and mode, and these may be quickly summarized and the items they embrace as quickly defined.

From political and patriotic writings the editor chose pieces which would further the cause of federalism, and he followed closely the progress of ratification of the Constitution by the states. Most of the items were essentially news, but some were of more enduring structure. He was eager to support John Adams's *Defence of the American Constitutions* against a review in *The European Magazine*, asserting "The *critic* is lost in the splenic politician."[174] He printed extracts from James Wilson's "Oration" delivered at the famous Fourth of July celebration at Philadelphia in 1788,[175] and also from the junior Thomas Dawes's speech at Boston on the occasion of a similar celebration the year previous.[176]

the 22nd regiment of the Continental Army (Sept. 1788, pp. 732-33), Rev. John Thayer's account of his conversion (Sept. 1788, pp. 738-39), four sermons by Uzal Ogden (Sept. 1788, pp. 736-38), Nicholas Pike's new system of arithmetic (April 1788, p. 343), Dr. Samuel Nesbitt's case of division of the tendon of Achilles (Sept. 1788, pp. 733-35), and thoughts on the political situation by a native of Boston, (Sept., Oct. 1788, pp. 744-47, 804-07).

[174] Dec. 1787, pp. 52-55.

[175] Aug. 1788, pp. 612-16. Wilson was one of the ten men representing the ten states that had ratified the Constitution. A study of the newspapers of the time will best impress the reader with the elaborate fanfare of this celebration, the order of march requiring for presentation a full column in *The Pennsylvania Journal*, which reported the jubilation in the issues of July 5, 9, and 12.

[176] Aug. 1788, pp. 619-23. Mention may also be made of the printing of an extract from Jefferson's *Notes on Virginia* (Jan. 1788, pp. 106-08).

In general, he abetted the cause of national pride and consciousness, and slighted the more unlovely phases of social life, such as slavery.[177]

Pure fiction, mostly selected from the English magazines, assumed an importance nearly commensurate with its status in contemporary miscellanies not given to wholesale pirating, especially in the later and less carefully edited numbers. The correspondents in "Frederick and Felicia," discussing the social patterns of their friends, mixed romance with moral comment and followed in the path of Richardson.[178] Such writers as Francis Walsh, Jr. and George M. Woodward were drawn upon for gothic romances filled with moonlit castles, love, weapons, jousts, and dangers surmounted at the close to bring a happy ending.[179] The Oriental tale was no less a part of the general fare.[180] The novelette, with conversation in dialect, is sometimes encountered, too, as in "The Adventure of the Inn."[181] The spontaneous invention which flowed most richly in Fielding and his major successors was sometimes caught by the writers of such stories as "The Life and Amusements of Isaac Bickerstaffe Junior."[182] In short, Webster's choices mirrored the several trends of mid-eighteenth century fiction.

Important English men of letters fared ill, most of the references to them being brief anecdotes or summary accounts of their lives. Samuel Johnson, possibly by reason of Webster's interest in lexicography, received more space than the others, as not only an account of his "Character"[183] by himself and a few of his letters

---

[177] The two prose items on slavery (May and July 1788, pp. 377-81, 560-62) were reprinted from British sources, and did not apply specifically to the United States.

[178] March-June, Sept.-Nov. 1788, pp. 200, 275-77, 361-63, 463-66, 708-12, 791-95, 836-37. Sentimental fiction mixed with moral instruction is also represented in such stories as "A Series of Original Letters from a Gentlemen to his Friend," published in New York "some time ago" (April-June, Aug., Sept. 1788, pp. 303-06, 382-84, 477-79, 611-12, 691-92) and "Female Gratitude; or the History of Eliza Bentley" (Nov. 1788, pp. 859-63).

[179] "A Gothic Story," by Francis Walsh, Jr. (Oct. 1788, pp. 779-82); "The Castle of Erasmus; or Bertrand and Eliza," by George M. Woodward (Oct. 1788, pp. 782-84).

[180] Extracts from "Solyma and Ossmin. An Oriental Tale" (May, June 1788, pp. 363-67, 435-39); "Hassarack and Selima," by Francis Walsh, Jr. (Oct. 1788, pp. 785-88).

[181] March-May 1788, pp. 229-34, 294-99, 394-98. The story was reprinted from *The Town and Country Magazine.*

[182] March, April, June, Sept.-Nov. 1788, pp. 251-54, 278-80, 460-63, 701-08, 757-62, 831-36.

[183] Aug. 1788, pp. 630-34.

to Piozzi[184] were used, but also his "The Fountains: A Fairy Tale."[185] Pope's letter defending his religious beliefs to the Bishop of Rochester was reprinted.[186] Short accounts of Mrs. Inchbald,[187] Defoe,[188] Gibbon,[189] Sheridan,[190] and Collins[191] were included, apparently to fill space. In one clipped critical selection the current age was lauded with all the gusto of the perennial optimist of the present, for "T.," in "Reflections on the English Drama," placed Shakespeare, Racine, and Vergil below Otway in "one attribute, the mastery of the passions," granted to Nicholas Rowe the highest attainments, and declared of Sheridan that he seemed "not to yield in point of abilities to any comic writer that ever existed."[192]

Webster paid some attention to the world of the spirit. He was not narrow in his attitude toward religious creeds, but he was by no means radical. The four letters by an anonymous "Belzebub," which he selected for the ideas they contained, are satires against the type of argument advanced by Mandeville in his *Fable of the Bees* and by Rousseau in *Émile*.[193] "Clericus," in a department entitled "The Monthly Miscellany," which he planned to conduct for the "*utility* and *amusement*" of subscribers, was cut short by the discontinuance of the magazine, but he had time to include some observations on the translation of the Bible.[194]

Agricultural subjects were foreign to Webster's interests, and were offered only in the hope of attracting readers, being selected often with regard to the authors. Thus Samuel L. Mitchill's account of an insect destructive to wheat,[195] Benjamin Lincoln's letter of November 3, 1780, to James Warren regarding the grafting of

---

[184] May, June, 1788, pp. 355-60, 485-87.

[185] Dec. 1787, pp. 27-36.

[186] Dec. 1787, pp. 47-48.

[187] March, April 1788, pp. 196-99, 281-87.

[188] April 1788, p. 320.

[189] June, July 1788, pp. 466-69, 536-37.

[190] June 1788, pp. 472-73.

[191] Aug. 1788, pp. 626-27.

[192] Aug. 1788, pp. 641-46. For quotations, see pp. 642, 646.

[193] Jan., Feb., April 1788, pp. 82-86, 161-63, 389-90.

[194] Sept.-Nov. 1788, 723-26, 771-75, 837-43. Among selected articles reprinted in the magazine because of their ideas on religion, note should be made of an extract from Jeremy Collier's *Ecclesiastical History* concerning the King James version (Sept. 1788, pp. 692-96).

[195] Feb., March 1788, pp. 173-76, 201-04.

trees and the growing of vegetables,[196] and the description of an "Extraordinary Grass," perennially green and unaffected by cold or heat, by Thomas Walter, of Santee, South Carolina,[197] although wisely chosen, were rather lonesomely ensconced amidst an array of offerings which emphasized them by contrast.

A fairly large number of original contributions came to Webster for the department of poetry, and to this anonymous and amateur group of ephemeral verses he occasionally added selected pieces, the most important (excepting the original work by Dwight already discussed) being excerpts from Trumbull's *The Progress of Dullness*[198] and Barlow's *The Vision of Columbus*, the latter but recently published.[199] One of the original poems, "Utrum Horum Mavis, Elige,"[200] seems to have been later taken from the magazine without date or credit by Elihu H. Smith for his early anthology of American poetry.[201] Among the anonymous writers the most prolific was "Aspasio," most probably of Newark,[202] who followed somewhat the Graveyard School, writing religious verse both lyric and narrative.[203] In "Winter,"[204] his most ambitious effort, he described the interior of a tavern filled with men, contrasting this profligate scene with that of a society met for the purpose of religious instruction. Another contributor, "Alexis," who dated his poems from New York, did lighter moral verse, addressing a favorite Nancy.[205] Some anti-slavery propaganda in verse was inserted by Webster for social reasons, including Ann Yearsley's "On the Inhumanity of the Slave Trade,"[206] Theodore Dwight's

[196] Dec. 1787, Jan. 1788, pp. 4-7, 73-75.

[197] Aug. 1788, pp. 623-25.

[198] Dec. 1787, Jan. 1788, pp. 59-61, 117-19.

[199] March 1788, pp. 263-65. He also printed a review of the poem taken from *The Critical Review* of Jan. 1788 (April 1788, pp. 334-37). The poem had appeared in 1787.

[200] May 1788, pp. 427-28.

[201] *American Poems, Selected and Original* (n.d., 1793, pp. 222-26).

[202] The first contribution was dated from Newark, May 8, 1788.

[203] "An Address to the Deity" (May 1788, pp. 428-29); "Advice from the Tombs" (June 1788, p. 507); and "A Hymn for Redemption" (Nov. 1788, p. 873) are examples.

[204] Nov. 1788, pp. 871-73. According to an accompanying announcement, this poem had been written in 1787.

[205] Two poems addressed to Nancy appeared respectively in issues for March and April 1788, pp. 266, 344.

[206] Aug. 1788, pp. 673-74. It was not taken from her *Poems on Various Subjects* (London, 1787), but is referred to in an editorial note as "her new poem."

"African Distress."[207] and an anonymous piece, "The Negroes [*sic*] Complaint,"[208] a song supposedly sung by a negro rejoicing that his wife has died rather than live in slavery. Pastorals,[209] love laments,[210] and miscellaneous light verse filled most of the pages of the department, but among the offerings seldom may one come across such interesting pieces as Walwyn's "The Village Matron"[211] and the anonymous "A Scene in Rhode Island,"[212] the latter being unusual in form, the author employing feminine verse endings.

In the October number of the magazine Webster took the public into some degree of confidence as regards his publishing venture. He announced to the subscribers that he was leaving the city, and that it was not to his interest or "views in life to devote his whole time to a work of this kind; but he will ever be happy to contribute his share towards the support of a publication, which has public utility for its object."[213] He sailed for New Haven on December 20, "Happy to quit New York,"[214] and arrived at Boston on December 31, where he tried unsuccessfully to merge his plan with Thomas's and busied himself with courtship and the study of law.[215] In October 1789 he was married, and in November he established his home at Hartford, where he practised law, joined the famous literary club of the city, and turned his mind to legal and philological problems until 1793, when he returned to the field of the periodical, commencing an engagement with *The American Minerva* which continued nearly four years.

[207] Aug. 1788, p. 675.

[208] Sept. 1788, p. 751.

[209] See, for example, "Collin's Complaint," by "W. C." July 1788, p. 596.

[210] "On the Departure of a Young Gentleman who Sailed for England a Short Time since," by "Fidelia," dated Jan. 5, 1788 (Feb. 1788, pp. 179-80) is a good example of this type of original ephemeral contribution.

[211] Oct. 1788, pp. 813-14. The extract was introduced with the announcement that the poem was "shortly to be printed."

[212] July 1788, p. 595.

[213] P. 756.

[214] See the Webster manuscript diary under date given, at the New York Public Library.

[215] Webster seems not to have given up hope of reaching some agreement with Thomas until after the beginning of 1789. As late as Feb. 12, 1789, Abiel Holmes, father of Oliver Wendell, wrote from Medway, Ga., stating that he had circulated "a Subscription Paper in this place, and its vicinity, and obtained 16 subscribers," and hoped the magazine would be continued (Skeel, *op. cit.*, I, 194-95).

IV

Since in fashioning his plan for *The American Museum*,[216] Mathew Carey did not contemplate publishing original articles, he did not believe that he required an editor, as he informed Hazard;[217] and it was not until 1789 that he asked Belknap to contribute monthly a few pages of "short scraps, hints and effusions, as constitute the principal part of the Gentleman's Magazine, printed in London."[218] The original plan—never essentially modified—was to make the periodical a museum of American writings worthy of preservation, and to offer about one hundred pages monthly, thus supplying subscribers with the largest magazine that had yet been published at the least relative cost.[219] It was an ambitious program, and it was more successful than any previous venture. The first volume, from January through June 1787, contained a list of 504 subscribers; the issue for July 1788 printed the names of 988 subscribers; a year later the number had reached 1696.[220] To glance over any of the lists is to encounter the names of many of the most influential men of the period,[221] and some of them, including Washington and Dickinson, praised the magazine

[216] See note 4.

[217] Hazard, in a letter to Belknap dated May 5, 1787 ("The Belknap Papers," *op. cit.*, fifth series, II, 476), mentioned receiving a letter from Carey stating that Belknap's work would not be needed for the *Museum*, as ". . . I never expected to receive any original pieces."

[218] Carey's letter of Oct. 16, 1789, inviting Belknap to contribute, is preserved in manuscript among the Belknap Papers (II, 27) at the Massachusetts Historical Society, and from it the quotation in the text above was taken. Carey suggested a wide variety of subjects, asserting a preference for "elucidations of American Antiquities." He promised Belknap a dollar for each piece; he wished four or five pieces a month, the whole not to exceed two or three pages. "For the regular payment of the sum stipulated," he wrote, "I shall appropriate a principal part of the Boston subscriptions."

[219] *The Pennsylvania Gazette* for Feb. 21, 1787 advertised the magazine at 18 shillings a year, or a "Quarter Dollar" a number; outside Pennsylvania the annual price was $2.50.

[220] It was Carey's practice to print the names of subscribers in the issues, perhaps in part as an advertisement.

[221] The first volume includes the names of Washington, Franklin, Dickinson, Hamilton, Jefferson, Madison, Humphreys, Hopkinson, Pinckney, Rush, Webster, Edmund Randolph, Edward Shippen, Robert Yates, Robert Molyneux, Robert Morris, Rufus King, Thomas Willing (president of the Bank of North America), and Phineas Bond (British consul). I have selected the names somewhat at random.

highly.[222] They may well be considered patrons of a project for the "republication of many of the pamphlets which appeared in this country, prior to and during the war."[223] The plan required, however, a wide and generous support by a general public as willing to pay as to receive; this was not forthcoming. Had the subscribers uniformly honored their debts to Carey, the magazine might have prospered, but, as announcements in many of the advertisements show, collections were not easily made. The age of advertising had not yet arrived, and the project was abandoned at the close of 1792.

The first number was advertised in *The Pennsylvania Gazette* of February 21, 1787.[224] The announcement listed sixty articles and poems—seven special features, followed by a long series of departments. Later Carey included only the more celebrated pieces in the announcements[225] and he decreased the number of departments. He dedicated the first volume "To the Patrons of Liberty, Virtue, Art and Science throughout the United States of America," and in a message "To the Reader" expressed some concern lest a magazine "destitute . . . of originality, which in the opinion of many, is indispensable in any periodical,"[226] should not

[222] A lithograph of the letter Washington wrote to Carey under date of June 25, 1788, is preserved in the manuscript department of the New York Public Library in the Carey file. Washington expressed his concern that the magazine was not prospering financially. "A discontinuance of the publication for want of proper support," he wrote, "would, in my judgment, be an impeachment on the Understanding of this Country. For I am of opinion that this work is not only eminently calculated to disseminate [*sic*] political, agricultural, philosophical & other valuable information; but that it has been uniformly conducted with taste, attention, & propriety." Of good magazines in general he expressed his delight: "I consider such easy vehicles of knowledge, more happily calculated than any other, to preserve the liberty, stimulate the industry and meliorate the morals of an enlightened and free People." Carey used this letter for advertising purposes; see especially *The Pennsylvania Gazette*, July 16 and Aug. 20, 1788. The same paper of Aug. 20, 1788, contains commendatory statements to Carey by William Livingston, Benjamin Rush, and John Dickinson, the last writing, "I feverently wish, and firmly trust that a generous and enlightened people will justly estimate the merits of a work carried on with such a variety of exertions, and such fidelity of intentions for the public good."

[223] See prefatory article, "To the Reader," by Mathew Carey, dated Jan. 31, 1787, i, iv.

[224] Carey used newspapers of other cities rather extensively in an effort to gain a national circulation. He also made personal excursions in the interests of circulation. See Bradsher, *op. cit.*, p. 17.

[225] For example, the advertisement in *The Pennsylvania Gazette* of April 4, 1787, announced by name only David Humphreys's "Address to the American Armies" and "A Poem on the Happiness of America."

[226] *The American Museum*, Jan. 1787, pp. iii-iv.

appeal to the public. He was, nevertheless, going to prosecute the plan and publish both American and European work of distinction, and he hoped for a sustaining patronage. In July 1787 Carey went to Lewistown for his health, leaving Henry Rice in charge of the business,[227] and it was from Lewes, Delaware, that the ailing publisher sent his "Preface" to the second volume, citing among the more important selections Paine's *Common Sense* and poetry by Humphreys, Trumbull, and Ladd.[228] He had already begun charily to add original letters and essays, and the subscription list had so increased that a second edition of the first volume, somewhat modified, was soon to be printed to satisfy those who were not subscribers to the original volume.[229] But it should not be inferred that Carey's enterprise was financially lucrative. By his own statement, at no time did he have over $400, and he was at times $3000 to $6000 in debt, and had to exert himself to the utmost to collect dues from subscribers.[230]

As an editor, Carey was both judicious and sincere. He possessed a solid inclination toward decency, morality, and high seriousness. He was apparently unappreciative of light verse and wit for their own sake. He respected the wishes of those who had preferred to write anonymously, and on occasion probably "ascribed" when he could have affirmed authorships. He sometimes added editorial notes when he believed that by doing so he might clarify issues or challenge oppression. He was especially sensitive, as a Roman Catholic in a land prevailingly Protestant, to points of view which might lead to discrimination or restriction of freedom of religious worship. He was diligent in his search for suitable materials to reprint from books, pamphlets, newspapers, and magazines, choosing carefully the more authoritative pieces on

[227] Announcement made in advertisement in *The Pennsylvania Gazette* July 11, 1787.

[228] *The American Museum*, II, 15.

[229] Second edition advertised in *The Pennsylvania Gazette* Nov. 14, 1787 as "This Day Published." By this time Carey had determined that there should be two volumes each year, each volume numbering 624 pages. The original plan considered 576 pages to a volume. The second edition of the first volume was printed in smaller type; the contents, however, were nearly the same, differences arising only in a more complete listing of authors of the selections in the second edition and the insertion of short anecdotes in order to adjust the type pages. The third edition varied from the second somewhat, with inclusion of a little new material. For purposes of reference I have used the first edition.

[230] See Bradsher, *op. cit.*, 8-9, text and note 10.

political, historical, commercial, financial, scientific, agricultural, and literary subjects. He gradually perfected a technique of presentation which became strikingly evident as early as the third volume, printing in each issue an assembled group of articles bearing on some specific subject of moment, and featuring this collection without greatly restricting the broadness of appeal of each number.

As a publisher wishing to preserve a picture of the times, Carey viewed a seaboard nation full of action, hope, experiment, and dissension. There was plenty to do which men hoped might add grace to the sorry scheme of things. Federalism was one problem to solve. Currency, manufactures, trade, and agriculture held tasks challenging the best wits. The minds of a few, especially at Philadelphia, were stirred by a quickening social consciousness to considerations on slavery, crime and punishment, public schools, and spirituous liquors. Others were fumbling with the keys of science at gates separating the known from the unknown in medicine and the physical world. Still others, while engaged in sterner labors, sought also to cultivate their literary proclivities; and if *belles-lettres* were usurped by the world of politics and business, they at least modified the manner in which men's minds phrased thoughts on government and ways of gaining a livelihood. About a third of *The American Museum's* important selections may be classified as literary essays, letters, orations, and poetry.

In an age of clashing debate and disputation, Carey could not hope for complete serenity among the subscribers with regard to the contents of the magazine. Most "thorny" of his editorial problems—to use his adjective—was the discussion of the federal Constitution. Carey had been described as an antifederalist by Rush when the former conducted the *The Columbian Magazine,* but he made *The American Museum* a pro-federalist magazine in spirit, though he gave space to distinguished spokesmen of both sides. On the subject of federalism he had considered omitting the arguments of either side; then he had planned to insert pieces "on the right side of the question, i.e., in favour of the constitution." Finally he had resolved "to insert valuable pieces on each side," but even this principle had cost him "a few subscribers."[231] Among the selected pieces relative to the Constitution were items from the work of Noah Webster, Alexander Hamilton, John Jay, Fisher Ames, Tench Coxe, Francis Hopkinson, John Dickinson, John Hancock, Roger Sherman, Oliver Ellsworth, Benjamin Franklin, Hugh Williamson, David Ramsay, Elbridge Gerry, Richard Henry Lee, Benjamin Rush, George Washington, James Wilson, and Edmund Randolph.[232] It is an indication of Carey's ability that he suc-

[232] Some of the chief articles follow: "Address to All Federalists," by "Curtius," probably Webster (Oct. 1787, pp. 381-84), and his "The Devil Is in You," by "Tom Thoughtful" (Feb. 1787, pp. 116-19; see Skeel, *op. cit.*, II, 526); "The Federalist," letters I-VI, by Hamilton and Jay (Nov., Dec. 1787, pp. 441-46, 523-34); Jay's "Address to the People of . . . New York," by "A Citizen" (June 1788, pp. 554-65); Ames's "Speech" on the convention in Massachusetts, and his "Observations" on the Shays insurrection, by "Camillus" (April 1788, pp. 358-62, Oct. 1787, pp. 315-20); Coxe's "On the Federal Government," being four letters by "An American," his "Address" to the members of the Virginia convention, and his "Thoughts on the Present Situation" (Sept.-Oct. 1787, pp. 300-06, 387-91, May, June 1788, pp. 426-33, 544-48, Nov. 1788, pp. 401-04); Hopkinson's allegorical "The New Roof" (Aug. 1788, pp. 142-46), his satirical "Objections to the Proposed Plan of Government for the United States" (June 1788, pp. 526-28), his possible (Hastings, *op. cit.*, p. 480) letter "To the Freemen of Pennsylvania" (Oct. 1787, pp. 371-75) and his "Account" of (with Rush's "Observations" on) the Grand Federal Procession at Philadelphia, July 4, 1788, (July 1788, pp. 57-78); Dickinson's "Observations on the Constitution Proposed by the Federal Convention," being the nine *Letters of Fabius* (July-Dec. 1788, pp. 55-56, 135-38, 253-56, 357-63, 423-28, 496-501), and his letter regarding the unfortunate Annapolis convention, of which he was chairman (April 1787, pp. 291-94); Hancock's speech of Feb. 27, 1788 to the legislature of Massachusetts (May 1788, pp. 461-63); two speeches by Ellsworth, and his joint letter with Roger Sherman to the governor of Connecticut (April 1788, pp. 334-43, Nov. 1787, pp. 434-35); Franklin's last speech to the federal convention (Dec. 1787, pp. 558-59); Williamson's "Remarks" (June 1788, pp. 548-54); Ramsay's "Address" to the freemen of South Carolina (May 1788, pp. 413-18); Gerry's "Letter" to the assembly of Massachusetts explaining why he did not sign the Constitution (Nov. 1787, pp. 435-36); Lee's comments of Oct. 16, 1787, to Edmund Randolph (Dec. 1787, pp. 553-58); Rush's letter to Ramsay rejoicing at adoption of the Constitution (May 1788, pp. 418-19), his "To the People of the United States" on the defects of the Constitution (Jan. 1787, pp. 9-13); Washington's "A Circular Letter" to the governors of the states on the resignation of his command of the army (May 1787, pp. 387-97), and his "Letter" in favor of the federal Constitution (Jan. 1788, pp. 76-78); Wilson's "Speech" of Oct. 6, 1787 (Oct. 1787, pp. 377-81); and Randolph's explanation of reasons for not signing the Constitution (Jan. 1788, pp. 62-71). In addition to these articles, one might cite, among others, the long account of the ratification of the Constitution by New Jersey, Maryland, South Carolina, New Hampshire, Virginia, and New York. (Aug. 1788, pp. 146-58); the "Address of the Seceding Members of the Assembly of Pennsylvania" (Oct. 1787, pp. 362-66), "The Address, and Reasons of Dissent, of the Minority of the Convention of the State of Pennsylvania" (Dec. 1787, pp. 536-53); "Reply to the Minority of the Convention of Pennsylvania" (Feb.-April 1788, pp. 158-61, 242-45, 365-67); "A View of the Federal Government in America," by "A Bostonian" (April 1787, pp. 294-306); twenty-three "Objections to the New Constitution," with "Answers" (Nov. 1787, pp. 422-32); a draft of the Constitution (Sept. 1787, pp. 276-84); a light essay satirizing those who opposed the Constitution, being "Peter Prejudice's complaint of the taylor, who, instead mending his old breeches

ceeded as well as he did in navigating the pass between Scylla and Charybdis.

Carey's selections on the topics of paper money, agriculture, and manufactures and commerce, stress a conservative, practical out-

---

(Articles of Confederation), made him a new pair" (June 1788, pp. 524-26). Pages 334-65 for April 1788 are given over wholly to a number of speeches in favor of the adoption of the Constitution, and pages 419-26 of the succeeding issue contain an address on the thirteen adopted and fifteen rejected amendments to the Constitution as passed by the Maryland convention.

The account of the federal procession in Philadelphia July 4, 1788 appeared also not only in *The Columbian Magazine* but is the eleventh pamphlet in a volume of pamphlets lettered "Works of Dr. Benjamin Rush" at the Ridgway Branch of the Library Company of Philadelphia, and is also in Hopkinson's *Miscellaneous Essays* (II, 349-402, American Philosophical Society Library), with note by Hopkinson (p. 349) saying he "drew up" the account. To this, Rush appended his own "Observations on the Federal Procession," writing "It was not to celebrate a victory obtained in blood over any part of our fellow-creatures. . . . It was to celebrate a triumph of knowledge over ignorance, of virtue over vice, and of liberty over slavery." (*The American Museum*, July 1788, p. 75.) The account contains one of the best though little known poems on the Revolutionary War ever written, which Hopkinson composed for the occasion. Hopkinson's "Objections to the Proposed Plan of Government for the United States" is one of the best of his light satirical essays. It purports to be an account of a meeting by the "Wheelbarrow Society" in Philadelphia, at which fifty-eight members, with Jem. Doran in the chair, decide they wish very little government of any kind and vote for the author of the "Centinel" papers for President. Rush's "To the People of the United States," on the defects of the Constitution, signed "Nestor," was not credited to him in the magazine until its third edition. He wished a stronger federal government with decisive power over the states, federal control over currency and commerce, and a bicarmeral legislature with fairly long terms of tenure by members.

Dickinson's *The Letters of Fabius* were written because of "an alarming hesitation of some states to ratify the constitution" (*The Political Writings of John Dickinson*, 1801, II, 69), and all in *The American Museum* are dated between April 12 and May 1, 1788. They were not original with the magazine, and were copied extensively in the newspapers of the time. No essayist of the period wrote more distinguished essays. Carey also printed in *The American Museum* the twelve letters of Dickinson's earlier series written in 1767-68, the *Letters from a Farmer in Pennsylvania, to the Inhabitants of the British Colonies* (Sept.-Dec. 1788, pp. 284-86, 371-77, 454-71, 522-47).

Washington's "Circular Letter" listed four principles as "essential to the well-being, I may even venture to say, to the existence of the United States as an independent power." The first was "AN INDISSOLUABLE [sic] UNION OF THE STATES UNDER ONE FEDERAL HEAD" (*The American Museum*, May 1787, p. 390); the others related to the administration of public justice, to a peace establishment, and to the existence of a friendly disposition among the states rising above local prejudices. In his "Letter" in favor of the adoption of the Constitution, he expressed himself as not a "blind admirer" of the draft, but "fully persuaded it is the best that can be obtained at this time" (*The American Museum*, Jan. 1788, pp. 76-77). Coxe's name was not attached by Carey to "On the Federal Government" until the second edition of *The American Museum*. Meigs had published this essay in *The New-Haven Gazette, and the Connecticut Magazine* (Oct. 18, 25, Nov. 1, 8, 15, 1787).

look and emphasize the contributions of the Middle Colonies in founding a well-ordered economic structure on a capitalistic basis. The selections from Franklin's works were probably perfunctorily chosen, but the essays by Rush, Witherspoon, Hugh Williamson and others were definitely inserted to support specie rather than unfunded currency, the coining of money by the national government only, and the redemption of certain issues of outstanding currency according to face rather than market value.[233] The state of trade and manufactures, in the thought of the time as preserved by Carey, demanded the support of a patriotic citizenry and the encouragement of protection by a centralized national government conscious of the assistance foreign governments gave their industrial structures. One of the most active voices of the period was that of Tench Coxe, financier and business man of Philadelphia. His services to the young republic are sometimes overlooked by reason of his neutrality during the Revolution and his failure to attain picturesque leadership in the federal conventions in which he played a part. As a member of the United Company of Philadelphia for Promoting American Manufactures, and later, in the time of *The American Museum*, as the president of the Pennsylvania Society for the Encouragement of Manufactures and the Useful Arts, his articles on trade and manufacturing are especially informative of the efforts of business men to found and extend their enterprises, and they are typically representative of the kind of articles on economics which Carey used. Coxe's "Address to an Assembly of the Friends of American Manufactures, Convened for the Pur-

[233] For Franklin, see "The Way to Make Money Plenty in Every Man's Pocket," and "Remarks and Facts Relative to the American Paper-Money," London, 1764 (July 1787, pp. 87, 17-23); for Rush, see "On the Establishment of a Mint in Rhode Island," and "Thoughts on Paper-Money," both by "Nestor" (April and July 1787, pp. 311-13, 38-43), the latter reprinted in *The New-Haven Gazette, and the Connecticut Magazine* for July 27 and Aug. 3, 1786, and listed as No. 23 of the Rush pamphlets at the Ridgway Branch of the Library Company of Philadelphia; for Witherspoon, see "Essay on Money, as a Medium of Commerce," originally issued as a pamphlet in 1786 and listed in Evans, *op. cit.*, No. 20154 (July 1787, pp. 47-73); for Hugh Williamson, see the seven letters of "Sylvius" entitled "Essay on the Consequences of Emitting Paper-Money" (Aug. 1787, pp. 107-34). There were, besides, many anonymous pieces on paper money and on the funding of currency already in circulation; see, for examples, "A View of the Principles, Operation, and Probable Effects of the Funding System of Pennsylvania" (Feb., March 1788, pp. 180-82, 245-56), and also the several items on paper money in the issue for July 1787, pp. 34-38; the former was originally issued as a pamphlet and is listed in Evans, *op. cit.*, No. 21546.

pose of Establishing a Society" stressed the need of united effort of private enterprise and the government to nurse infant industries.[234] His "An Enquiry into the Principles on which a Commercial System for the United States Should Be Founded," read before the Society for Political Enquiries at the home of Benjamin Franklin, May 11, 1787, asserted that a serious condition was at hand, for the federal government, ineffective and disjointed, could not assist the business structure, which was menaced by importation of goods from foreign nations that had erected barriers along their own shores, preventing importations from the United States.[235] Unless the national government could maintain free trade among the states and a national tariff schedule to combat tariffs from abroad, he saw ruin ahead. Then the clouds lifted. By October 1788 he was more confident of a robust future, for the establishment of the federal government under the Constitution implied in his mind, a strengthening of the United States in foreign trade.[236] Another writer of importance in the world of business was William Barton, who, as secretary of the society over which Coxe presided, occupied a position so distinguished as to render his conservative opinions on trade and industry worthy of preservation.[237] Other writers whose opinions on business Carey made tributary to his magazine included Dickinson, Franklin, Rush, Hamilton, and James M'Henry.[238]

[234] Sept. 1787, pp. 248-55. It was published in pamphlet form also; see Evans, op. cit., No. 20305.

[235] June 1787, pp. 496-514. Carey, in the first edition of the *Museum*, credited the article to "T. C."; in the second edition the name appeared in full.

[236] See "Thoughts on the Present Situation of the United States" (Nov. 1788, pp. 401-04). The content and style of an "Address to the Friends of American Manufactures," by "An American Citizen," dated Philadelphia, Oct. 20, 1788 (Oct. 1788, pp. 341-46) suggest the hand of Coxe also.

[237] Items by Barton include essays on the power of Congress to regulate trade (Jan. 1787, pp. 16-20), the plan of the society of which he was secretary (Aug. 1787, pp. 167-69), the promotion of manufactures (Sept. 1787, pp. 257-58), and two extracts from "The True Interests of the United States . . . Considered" (July 1787, May 1788, pp. 23-33, 442-46).

[238] For Dickinson, see his report of the Annapolis convention on trade and federal regulation (April 1787, pp. 291-94); for M'Henry, see his careful survey of the relative positions of Great Britain and the United States with respect to the economical manufacturing of a long list of items, written in 1784 (April-June 1789, pp. 317-19, 464-67, 550-54); for Franklin, see "Comfort for America" (Jan. 1787, pp. 5-9) and "Of an Open Trade" (Feb. 1787, pp. 113-14); for Hamilton, see his speech to the Assembly of New York, Feb. 18, 1787, respecting the impost (June 1787, pp. 514-26); for Rush, see his speech of March 16, 1775 relative to the production of woolen, cotton, and linen goods in Philadelphia (June 1789, pp. 581-84). Mention

When men's thoughts turned to industry and commerce, they turned almost invariably to government and politics; but when they turned to agriculture, they turned as invariably to the application of scientific knowledge. The pieces on agriculture published in *The American Museum* are related to methods of planting and grafting and cultivating, to the feeding of livestock and the destruction of insects, to experiments and discoveries and inventions. There were organizations that attempted to disseminate knowledge of value to the agrarian, and in an effort to stimulate diversification of crops premiums were sometimes offered by such societies as the Philadelphia Society for Promoting Agriculture and the American Academy of Arts and Sciences.[239] But the faith of the age in processes for development lay in education rather than subsidy and premium, and so Carey's selections were usually so specific as to be of interest only to farmers, and consisted of a multitude of short presentations of fact and experiment.[240]

As a generative locus for expressions of certain aspects of social reform, Philadelphia led Boston in the ninth decade of the eighteenth century. If one were to select a single individual most prominent in urging reforms, one might choose Benjamin Rush, for he touched nearly every issue and was active in the several societies of the city organized to promote better human adjustments. But the spirit was not confined to one man, or to a very few. Carey collected from several sources a number of articles on social reform, and by virtue of these selections showed his interest in the crusading groups. Articles in the magazine against slavery are numerous. Anthony Benezet, whose early pamphlet against slavery (*Observations on the Enslaving, Importing and Purchasing of Negroes*, 1759)

---

should also be made of the three letters "On American Manufactures," by "A Plain, but Real Friend of America" (Jan.-March 1787, pp. 20-24, 120-25, 211-16).

[239] For lists of premiums offered by these societies, see issues for Oct. 1787 and Feb. 1788, pp. 355-56, 173-79.

[240] Among Carey's selections were the following: Jeremy Belknap on drying parsnips (Nov. 1787, p. 455), Crèvecoeur, on the culture of maize (Nov. 1787, pp. 449-50); Cadwallader Ford, on the benefits of salt in agriculture (Jan. 1787, pp. 49-50); Jefferson, on the sale of tobacco and salt in France and on rice growing in South Carolina (March, July 1787, pp. 221-24, 83-84); Joseph Greenleaf, on raising corn on poor land (Jan. 1787, pp. 50-51); Benjamin Lincoln, on grafting fruit trees (Jan. 1788, pp. 39-40); Christopher Gullet, George Morgan, and Decius Wadsworth, on the Hessian fly (Feb., June, Aug., Nov. 1787, pp. 143-46, 529-32, 175-76, 458-59); and many anonymous articles on divers subjects, including cotton planting (Nov. 1787, pp. 454-55), potato planting (Dec. 1787, p. 576), sheep raising (Jan. 1787, pp. 48-49), and silk-worm culture (June 1788, pp. 516-19).

had won for him a distinguished place as a forerunner of the movement for abolition, was celebrated; reports of organizations opposed to slavery were printed, one such being "An Address to the Public, from the Pennsylvania Society for Promoting the Abolition of Slavery," signed by Franklin; extracts on slavery from the works of such men as Crèvecoeur were selected; general essays and state laws against the traffic appeared; poetry pictured brutalities practised; Rush, among others, called science to the aid of the negroes, endeavoring to show the race capable of high mental development; sentimental prose, written or purported to have been written by slaves, lamented their state and asserted their humanity.[241] As a storehouse of anti-slavery propaganda, *The American Museum* is unapproached by any other magazine of the period.

Carey's remembrance of his own prison sentence for political expression may have focused his interest to theories on the punishment of crime which Rush and others were promulgating. The doctor believed that "The punishments should consist of bodily pain, labour, watchfulness, solitude, and silence," but he attacked public punishments on the ground that they lessened a worthy sense of shame without contributing to any change of heart, and he opposed capital punishment as being contrary to both reason and divine law.[242] Though opinion was by no means unanimously in

[241] A selected descriptive list of items follows: Benezet's letter to Queen Charlotte, and some biographical anecdotes (Feb. 1787, Aug. 1788, pp. 128-30, 161); letter by Rev. Robert Boucher Nickolls (May 1788, pp. 404-10); letter signed by Franklin as a member of the Pennsylvania Society (Nov. 1789, pp. 383-84); extract against slavery from *Letters from an American Farmer*, by Crèvecoeur (March 1787, pp. 239-41); constitution of the Pennsylvania Society (May 1787, pp. 460-62); acts of Rhode Island and Massachusetts to prevent slave trade (Nov. 1787, July 1788, pp. 502-03, 86-87); Rush's account of a negro doctor (Jan. 1789, pp. 61-62) and his reference against slavery in a letter to Dr. Price (Feb. 1787, pp. 132-34); Theodore Dwight's poem, "Picture of African in Distress" (Oct. 1789, p. 328); "Petition of Belinda, an African" (June 1787, pp. 538-40); "Letter on Slavery," by a negro (July 1789, pp. 77-80); "Essay on Negro Slavery," by "Othello" (Nov., Dec. 1788, pp. 414-17, 509-12).

[242] "An Enquiry into the Effects of Public Punishments upon Criminals, and upon Society," read before the Society for Promoting Political Enquiries, at the home of Franklin (Aug. 1787, pp. 142-53); reprinted also in pamphlets and *Essays* (1798)," pp. 136-63; "An Enquiry into the Justice and Policy of Punishing Murder by Death (July 1788, pp. 78-81), reprinted by Carey in 1792 in a pamphlet, and by a London firm in 1793, and in *Essays* (1798), pp. 164-82. The quotation is from *The American Museum*, Aug. 1787, p. 149. One of the few original articles in the magazines was a reply to Rush, "Observations on Capital Punishments" (Nov., Dec. 1788, pp. 444-54, 547-53), written by one so aggravated by the personality of the doctor that he characterized him, with some truth, as one who expected "that within a century

Rush's favor, there were some who supported him in whole or in part and made their own contributions of thought to the proper and ideal criminal code. Carey selected a number of items on the subject for his *Museum*. There was at least one voice raised in general opposition to confinement of debtors;[243] another, reviewing the ratio of convictions to the number who were pardoned or broke jail, argued that crimes should not be punished with great severity, but that punishment should be absolute;[244] and one, who signed him-self "Alfred," of Baltimore, wished capital punishment limited to convictions of murder.[245] The management of jails, treatment of convicts, and proper labor for prisoners were among the other phases of the general problem presented in the magazine.[246]

To represent distinguished opinion relative to education, Carey chose Franklin's "Idea of an English School, for the Consideration of the Trustees of the Philadelphia Academy,"[247] Rush's plan for the establishment of free schools and a federal university,[248] and Witherspoon's "Letters on Education,"[249] all hitherto discussed. The editor's collection of articles against the use of spirituous liquors does not present so many celebrated authors but serves to illustrate the activities of Rush, George Logan, John B. Bordley, and some of the members of the Philadelphia Society for Promoting Agriculture in their fight against the use of beverages of high alcoholic content.[250] The articles bearing on religion and morality

hence, all mankind will be of the same opinion with him, and wishes that his performance may live so long, to testify . . . there was at least one man in the year 1788, who was as enlightened and humane as they will be." The author believed capital punishment to be a deterrent to crime, a responsibility under the social contract, and in agreement with the tenets of Christianity.

[243] July, 1788, pp. 37-39.

[244] "Considerations on the Late Law of Pennsylvania, for Mitigating the Severity of the Penal Code," dated May 12, 1788 (June 1788, pp. 509-12). The author was critical of a situation which, out of 98 convictions, pardoned 27, and was not able to prevent 17 from breaking jail.

[245] May 1788, pp. 395-400.

[246] See, for examples, "Utility of Inspecting into the State of Jails" (May 1787, pp. 451-54); constitution of the Philadelphia Society for Alleviating the Miseries of Public Prisons (May 1787, pp. 456-60); "Address" to the friends of humanity on alleviating miseries in public prisons (Oct. 1787, pp. 407-08); "Observations" on management of female convicts (June 1788, p. 512).

[247] May 1789, pp. 473-76.

[248] April, 1787, pp. 326-29; Nov. 1788, pp. 442-44.

[249] July-Nov. 1788, pp. 25-27, 108-11, 217-20, 310-15, 397-401. They had appeared originally in *The Pennsylvania Magazine*.

[250] For Rush, see "Pernicious Effects of the Use of Spiritous [sic] Liquors—Substitutes Proposed," signed "R.," in the issue for July 1788, pp. 39-40; for Logan

can hardly be restrictively classified. They are expressive of an editorial liberalism which selected Livingston's "Thoughts on Deism" and "Remarks on the Origin of Government and on Religious Liberty"[251] on the one hand, and, on the other, pieces on the controversy regarding the second advent stirred up by Jemimah Wilkinson and her followers;[252] and though not many in number, the excerpts were generally taken from the works of prominent men, including John Dickinson[253] and Timothy Dwight.[254] Carey's own interest in morality and religious liberty was vital, and is reflected in his notes to an article original with the magazine, an "Address to the Ministers of the Gospel of Every Denomination in the United States," by "Z."[255] This article condemned spirituous liquors, frequent election with their attendant rowdyism, traveling fairs, the encouragement of lawsuits, scandal in newspapers, horse racing, cock fighting, and amusements on Sundays. Carey departed from his usual editorial practice by annotating this essay. He asked for further contributions by the author, regretted "extremely" that no Sunday schools had been established in Philadelphia, expressed his distress that rowdyism prevailed on the streets on Sundays, and lamented the fact that scandal would probably continue to be broadcast in newspapers, for circulation was thereby increased.

The ruling triumvirate over the thought of post-Revolutionary America were politics, industry and commerce, and science, the last including medicine, treatises upon which were especially popular. In *The American Museum* more selections on medicine and disease were taken from Rush's works than from those of any other man. Rush was interested not only in cancer, fever, tetanus, and

---

and Bordley, both of whose selections were addressed to the Philadelphia Society for Promoting Agriculture, see issues for Sept. 1787 and June 1788, respectively, pp. 295-96, 520-21. See also remarks against spirituous liquors by "Hortensius," of Germantown (Aug. 1788, pp. 123-24) and by "Z.," of New Haven (Sept. 1788, pp. 234-35).

[251] Nov. 1788, pp. 440-42; Dec. 1788, pp. 492-93.

[252] Feb.-May 1787, pp. 165-69, 251-56, 333-38, 462-67.

[253] "Proclamation" exhorting observation of the Sabbath (Nov. 1788, pp. 432-33).

[254] "On the Doctrine of Chance: Containing Remarks on Ethan Allen's Oracles of Reason" (Oct. 1787, pp. 408-10).

[255] July 1788, pp. 30-34. Carey also annotated an article by William Vans Murray (the name of the author appears in the second edition), "Political Sketches" (Sept. 1787, pp. 220-48) which in part maintained that all religions, pagan as well as Christian, should enjoy equal franchise under the government. The author saw no reason for more liberality on the part of the United States, but Carey pointed out (p. 245) that Catholics labored under discriminatory laws in some states.

consumption, but also in exercise and more speculative subjects such as diseases peculiar to negroes and—what is especially worth noting —the influence of physical causes on the moral faculty.[256] Other men represented by their medical speculations include John Morgan, professor of physic at the Philadelphia College of Medicine, William Wright, Hall Jackson, Matthew Wilson (whose article on obstetrics, in Latin, seems to be original with the magazine), and William Turnbull.[257] Comments on natural phenomena— whirlwinds, stars and comets and planets, population, electricity, light, storms, the aurora borealis, steam as power, earthquakes, racial complexions—were taken from the works of Franklin, James Bowdoin, David Rittenhouse, Andrew Oliver, Benjamin West, John Perkins, Jeremy Belknap, John Winthrop the Harvard Professor, Samuel S. Smith, who was professor of moral philosophy at the College of New Jersey, Samuel Dexter, and many others.[258] Phenomena and discoveries pertaining to North America were especially attractive, whether the references were to Indians, springs, adventures and explorations, soil, prehistoric fortifications, mountains, or climate; and among the men whose writings were used by

[256] For the last two, see respectively issues for July 1788, pp. 81-82 and Feb. 1789, pp. 118-21. For other articles by Rush, see issues for Jan., Feb., Nov. 1787, pp. 37-40, 138-43, 461-64; March, April, June, and July 1789, pp. 247-49, 368-70, 559-62, 45-46. See also Rush's "Account of the Life and Death of Edward Drinker," the subject a colleague on the University medical staff (July 1787, pp. 73-75).

[257] Morgan and others, "Medical History of the Cortex Ruber" (July 1789, pp. 50-51), "An Account of the Late Dr. John Morgan" (Nov. 1789, pp. 353-55); Wright, on antiseptic virtues of vegetable and marine salt (Jan. 1787, pp. 42-45); Jackson, on digitalis purpurea in dropsy (Jan. 1788, p. 59); Wilson, "Exemplum Partus Difficillimi" (July 1788, pp. 82-84), on diseases of the air (Nov. 1788, pp. 417-23); Turnbull, on measles (July 1789, pp. 51-53).

[258] Franklin, on meteorology, a whirlwind, north-east storms, varying capacities of colors to absorb heat, increase of mankind, and barometers (June 1787, pp. 552-54 and June 1789, pp. 567-71, July 1787, pp. 75-77, Dec. 1788, pp. 559-60, Feb. 1789, pp. 109-12, 150-51; Bowdoin, on light, and on the existence of an orb surrounding the whole visible material system (March 1788, pp. 206-26); Rittenhouse, on a new method of placing meridian mark, and on a comet (Jan. 1788, pp. 28-29, 36-37); Oliver, on theories of electrical storms and waterspouts (March, April 1788, pp. 226-42, 306-16); West, on the planet Herschel (March 1788, pp. 265-67); Perkins, on waterspouts, tornadoes, hurricanes (Feb. 1788, pp. 113-19); Belknap, on the aurora borealis (Jan. 1788, pp. 29-30); Winthrop, on earthquakes (July 1789, pp. 64-67); Smith, on causes of differentiation among the human species, with a critical review (July-Oct. 1789, pp. 30-35, 123-29, 181-86, 241-49, 272-79); Dexter, on retreat of house swallows in winter (Oct. 1787, pp. 357-59); Professor Williams, of Harvard, on earthquakes in New England (April, June 1788, pp. 291-306, 567-79); John Churchman, surveyor, who published The Magnetic Atlas (1790), "On the Northern and Southern Lights" (Oct. 1788, pp. 351-54).

Carey to store his magazine with such interesting data were Franklin, Benjamin Lincoln, Boone, Lionel Chalmers, Jefferson, Madison, Belknap, Rush, Stiles, Webster, and Brackenridge.[259]

To record the more literary selections in *The American Museum* is to list many writings already treated in this study, as well as many others chosen from other sources than magazines. Among the excerpts from *The New-Haven Gazette, and the Connecticut Magazine* are the first four numbers of "American Antiquities,"[260] by Humphreys, Hopkins, Trumbull, and Barlow, and the first six numbers of "The Friend," edited by Dwight or Meigs under the pseudonym of "James Littlejohn."[261] From Webster's *The American Magazine* Carey chose, among other selections, the lexicographer's "Letter on Marriage" and his "Remarks on the Plans of Boston, Philadelphia, Charleston, and New-Haven,"[262] and Edwards's "Observations on the Language of the Muhhekaneew Indians."[623] From *The Worcester Magazine* were taken some numbers of "The Worcester Speculator,"[264] and from *The Pennsylvania Magazine* Witherspoon's "Letters on Marriage"[265] and many of the selections from the pens of Hopkinson and Paine, including some of "The Old Bachelor" series.[266] Other serial essays, in the

[259] Franklin, on "Information for those who Wish to Remove to America," and "Remarks on the North American Indians" (Sept. 1787, pp. 211-16, April 1789, pp. 343-46); Lincoln, on remarkable springs in Pennsylvania and Virginia (March 1787, pp. 228-29); Boone, on his adventures (Oct. 1787, pp. 321-28); Chalmers, on climate and soil in South Carolina (April 1788, pp. 316-34); Jefferson, on ancient fortifications (Nov. 1787, pp. 492-93); Madison, on sweet springs in Virginia (Jan. 1788, pp. 30-31); Belknap, on the White Mountains (Feb. 1788, pp. 128-32); Rush, on climate of Pennsylvania (July, Sept. 1789, pp. 25-27, 250-54); Stiles and Webster, on ancient fortifications in the West (July-Sept. 1789, pp. 27-30, 136-41, 232-34); see also Brackenridge's "Memoir to the American Philosophical Society" (Aug., Oct. 1788, pp. 133-35, 368-71).

[260] Jan., March 1789, pp. 94-100, 303-05. Carey also chose from Humphreys's pen an account of the life of John Pierce (Oct. 1788, pp. 366-68) and an article on devices and inscriptions of American medals (Nov. 1787, pp. 493-95).

[261] Jan., March, May, June, Aug., Oct. 1789, pp. 69-71, 220-22, 445-47, 564-67, 154-56, 283-86. Carey also reprinted Dwight's "Reflections on Second Marriages of Men" (Dec. 1789, pp. 437-39).

[262] Jan. 1788, pp. 50-51; May 1789, pp. 491-93. Webster's "Essay on the Political Advantages of America" was also reprinted (Nov., Dec. 1789, pp. 389-91, 450-51).

[263] Feb. 1789, pp. 141-44.

[264] Jan., May 1789, pp. 68-69, 441-43; Sept., Nov. 1789, pp. 238-40, 379-81, 385-87.

[265] July-Oct. 1788, pp. 21-25, 105-08, 213-17, 315-16.

[266] Selections by Hopkinson, chosen from whatever sources, comprised essays on whitewashing (Jan. 1787, pp. 62-68); a letter by "Nitidia" (Jan. 1787, pp. 53-55), in third edition of the magazine; the attack on the "Formidable Body of Kegs," with reference to the poem, Jan. 1787, pp. 68-69); "Modern Learning Exemplified by a

general tradition of Addison and Steele, included selections by Carey from the essays of "Atticus," "The Visitant," and Joseph Lathrop's "The Reformer."[267] Some of the more witty essays of Franklin, such as the "Speech of Miss Polly Baker" and "A Prussian Edict,"[268] some of the critical strictures of Joseph Brown Ladd, such as his "Critical Reflections on Style," "Critical Remarks on the Late Dr. Johnson," and "Sketch of the Character of the South Carolinians,"[269] and some of the remarks of the Reverend Jacob Duché on Philadelphia and its institutions, signed "T. Caspipina,"[270]

Specimen of a Collegiate Examination" (Feb. 1787, pp. 154-60); an account of "Dialogues of the Dead" (March 1787, pp. 256-62); "On the Establishment of a High Court of Honour," by "F. H." (May 1787, pp. 433-36); "Plan for the Improvement of the Art of Paper War" (May 1787, pp. 437-44); observations on a means of extinguishing a fire (Nov. 1787, pp. 474-78); an "Address to General Burgoyne," signed "A. B. C. D. E. F." (Nov. 1787, pp. 497-98); the speech of a "Standing Member" against cutting down trees, signed "Silvester" (Feb. 1788, pp. 165-73); "Some Thoughts on the Diseases of the Mind," (Oct. 1788, pp. 327-30); "Speech on the Learned Languages," and "Answer" to the speech (June 1788, pp. 538-44); an account of a horse (June 1788, p. 503); and the probable complaint of "Susannah Trapes" (Nov. 1787, pp. 484-85); the account of a remarkable fish (July 1788, p. 28), and "To the Freemen of Pennsylvania," by "One of the People" (Oct. 1787, pp. 371-75). Of Paine's work, Carey reprinted *Common Sense* (Jan.-March, 1787, pp. 24-37, 99-112, 195-203), and the first two numbers of *The Crisis* (May, Sept. 1788, pp. 476-81, 286-94). Carey also reprinted from "The Old Bachelor" series of *The Pennsylvania Magazine*, to which both Paine and Hopkinson contributed, Nos. I, IV, V, VI, VII, VIII. IX, "Consolation for the Old Bachelor," and "To the Bachelor," by "Aspasia" (Nov. 1787, pp. 498-500, Jan. 1788, pp. 89-91, March 1788, p. 267, June 1788, pp. 565-67, Aug. 1788, p. 126, Dec. 1788, pp. 561-63, 566-68, Feb. 1788, pp. 119-22, Dec. 1788, pp. 563-66).

[267] Only the first five numbers of "Atticus" were used by Carey (Aug.-Nov. 1788, pp. 111-15, 223-24, 317-18, 395-97). The essays, as traditional in their form as *The Spectator* and *The Rambler*, appeared first in sixty numbers in *The Pennsylvania Chronicle* during 1767-69. For "The Visitant," Nos. VIII-XII, see *The American Museum* for Jan., March, June, Aug., Oct. 1789, pp. 65-68, 222-25, 584-87, 147-49, 279-81; the essays first appeared in *The Pennsylvania Chronicle* during 1768, and dealt with "the common incidents of life in a loose unconnected manner, as my humour shall prompt me." For "The Reformer," Nos. I-III, see issues of July, Oct. 1789, pp. 54-55, 269-71.

[268] See issues for March 1787, pp. 243-45, and March 1789, pp. 293-95. For other essays by Franklin, see "Comfort for America" (Jan. 1787, pp. 5-9) and "A Parable against Persecution" (Feb. 1787, p. 125).

[269] See respectively issues for June 1787, pp. 532-36, Aug. 1787, pp. 197-99, Feb. 1789, pp. 130-31. Ladd was an early critic of the pompous style of some eighteenth-century essayists: "The writings of Johnson, Hervey, Akenside, Shaftsbury, and other frothy writers, have introduced this false sublime; have perverted our taste; corrupted our style . . ." (p. 534).

[270] March, May, June 1789, pp. 234-38, 500-01, 562-64. The reflections include a description of the city's college and churches and of the literary activities of local men. He derived his pseudonym, "Tamoc Caspipina," from the first letters of his official title, "the Assistant Minister of Christ's Church and St. Peter's in Phila-

were literary in the spirit of their composition or their application of ideas. Of like nature were William Livingston's "The Impartial Chronicle . . . upon the Plan . . . of the New-York Mercury," a satire printed originally in 1776 striking at pro-British newspaper propaganda,[271] Rush's letter of October 1, 1788, to *The Federal Gazette* against the publication of scandal,[272] and the "Petition in Favour of the Theatre" to the Assembly of Pennsylvania by a group who "humbly trust, that the decision of your honourable house will . . . prove that you think the petitioners in favour of the drama, as capable of judging for their own happiness, as anxious for the prosperity of the state, and as sincere in promoting the welfare of posterity, as those who have testified their opposition. . . ."[273]

Orations which had been delivered on special occasions, especially on the Fourth of July, were frequently inserted, Carey choosing, among others, the efforts of James Wilson, Joseph Ladd, Joel Barlow, Robert Livingston, William Livingston, Col. Morgan Lewis, William Hillhouse, Samuel Magaw, and James Tillary.[274] Barlow's is especially interesting because it combined a love for the Cincinnati and pro-federalism with affection for France and her ideals—a loyalty to which Barlow remained true during the rest of his life, though French and American relations became somewhat strained. Magaw's is equally to be noted because, as vice provost of the University of Pennsylvania, he defended the program of public academical education for girls in the city during an age when "higher education" for the feminine sex was rather unusual. By mixing orations for special occasions with selected

delphia, in North America" (Smyth, *The Philadelphia Magazines and their Contributors*, p. 71).

[271] March, April 1789, pp. 295-98, 371-74.

[272] May 1789, pp. 488-89.

[273] Feb. 1789, pp. 187-90. The quotation is from p. 189.

[274] Wilson's (July 1788, pp. 70-74) and Ladd's (Oct. 1787, pp. 332-36) orations had been delivered on the Fourth of July; Barlow's (Aug. 1787, pp. 135-42), Robert Livingston's (Feb. 1788, pp. 107-12), and Morgan Lewis's (Feb. 1788, pp. 112-13) were special Fourth of July orations delivered before groups of the Cincinnati; Hillhouse's (Oct. 1787, pp. 337-43) was spoken in commemoration of Major-General Greene; William Livingston's (Sept. 1788, pp. 235-40) was directed to the legislature of New Jersey; Magaw's (Jan. 1788, pp. 25-28) had been delivered at a young ladies' seminary; and Tillary's (Feb., June 1789, pp. 126-28, 597-600) was spoken in the interests of Masonry, concerning which society Carey printed articles occasionally, one in especial being "The Influence of Free Masonry" (June 1787, pp. 546-49).

historical data, such as pieces on western expansion[275] or the battles of Lexington and Concord,[276] and by offering intimate glimpses into the minds of important personages, such as Washington and Franklin,[277] Carey showed that he could keep a proper editorial attitude —that he could edit a magazine so that the readers were satisfied both emotionally and intellectually. A comparison of this achievement with a case of adequate purpose but inadequate performance, such as Nevill's manner of editing *The New American Magazine*, illustrates Carey's superior editorial ability, though Nevill was undoubtedly the abler man, as his services clearly indicate in law, in politics, in administrative ability, on the bench, and as a writer.

There is a great deal of distinguished poetry in *The American Museum* written during the second half of the eighteenth century. No other magazine collected so much verse, and with the addition of an appendix of forty-four pages of poetry to the seventh volume in 1790—a policy continued thereafter—the usual amount was augmented much beyond all rivals.[278] The whole file of the magazine becomes the best available anthology of American verse— although limited chiefly to a half-century—before 1793.[279] Certain authors were favored. Carey printed fairly long lists of poems by Freneau, Ladd, Humphreys, and Trumbull; he then represented other such well known or occasional writers of verse as Hopkinson, Dwight, Evans, Livingston, Godfrey, Markoe, Paine, William Moore Smith, Thomas Dawes, Mathew Carey, John Osborn, Samuel Knox, John Swanwick, and Thomas C. James, by more or less popular selections.[280]

[275] May 1788, pp. 433-35.

[276] Jan. 1789, pp. 79-88.

[277] For Washington letters, see issues for Feb., May 1787, pp. 134-35, 387-97; July and Sept. 1788, pp. 51-52, 240-44; for Franklin letters, see issue for Feb. 1787, p. 126.

[278] This study has not taken into consideration specific items after 1789.

[279] Elihu H. Smith's anthology was published in 1793.

[280] Poems selected from the works of Freneau were: "The Prisoner" and "The Death Song of a Cherokee Indian" (Jan. 1787, pp. 86, 90); "The Newsmonger," "On the Emigration [*sic*] to America," "On Prohibiting the Sale of . . . David Ramsay's History of the Revolution of South Carolina, in London," and "The Newsmonger," with additions and alterations (Feb. 1787, pp. 179-80, 185-86, 187, 191); "The Desolate Academy" (June 1787, pp. 567-68); "Verses on the Arrival of General Washington in Philadelphia" and "Verses Written at Sea, in a Heavy Gale" (Aug. 1787, pp. 201-02); "Address to Gen. Washington" (Sept. 1787, pp. 309-10); "The Indian Student" (Oct. 1787, pp. 413-14 of second edition); "To the Memory of the Brave . . . Col. John Laurens," and "Lines Occasioned by a Visit to an Old Indian Burying Ground" (Nov. 1787, pp. 514-16); "The Sea-Faring Bachelor,"

From the evidence of the magazine and other publications, it would appear that following the war Humphreys's poetry, voicing the hopes for the future, was fully as popular as the poetry of Freneau or Trumbull. His association with Washington during

"The Seasons Moralized," and "The Dying Indian" (Feb. 1788, pp. 185-86, 190-91); "The Deserted Farm-House" (Nov. 1788, pp. 478-79).

Poems by Ladd: "Ayder Ali," "Epitaph on an Old Horse," "The Incurable," "The Terribly-Sublime Description of Jehova," and "Remonstrance of Almasa" (Jan. 1787, pp. 86-91), to which may be added "Runic Ode," "The Farewel—To Amanda," and "Ode" (Jan. 1787, pp. 88-92 of third edition); "On the Resignation of . . . Washington," "Retirement," "Charlotte's Soliloquy to the Manes of Werter," "Sweet Polly of Plymouth's Lament," "The Wish," "The War-Horse," "Elegy, Sacred to the Manes of Major Benjamin Huger," "Arouet to Amanda," "Absence," "What Is Happiness" and "Arouet to Amanda," a second poem by this title (Feb. 1787, pp. 178-84, 188-91); "Receipt for a Cough," "Joshua," "Death of Werter," "Werter's Epitaph," and "The Prospect of America" (May 1787, pp. 473-80); "A Night Piece—at Sea," "Epitaph," and "The Dove, A Fragment" (Aug. 1787, pp. 203-04); "Prospect of Carolina" (Nov. 1787, pp. 516-17); "To Amanda, with Emma Corbet," "Sonnet: Humbly Inscribed to the Naiads of Ashley River," "Elegy—Sacred to the Manes of Philander," and "Fragment of an Epistle to a Friend" (April 1788, pp. 383-85); "The Shield of Achilles," translated from the Greek of Homer (May, 1788, pp. 483-86); "The Battle between Swaran and Cuchullin, Translated from Fingal," and "The Happy Man" (June 1788, pp. 584-87).

Poems by Humphreys: "Elegy on the Burning of Fairfield," "Address to the Armies of the United States of America," and "A Poem on the Happiness of America" (March 1787, pp. 265-88); "An Epithalamium," together with Dryden's "Alexander's Feast" to show the close parallelism (June 1787, pp. 568-70); "An Elegy, on Lieutenant De Hart," "Ode—To Laura," "A Song," "An Epitaph Written the Day after the Capitulation of Lord Cornwallis," "Anacreontic," "The Genius of America" and "The Monkey who Saved himself and his Friends" (March 1788, pp. 273-79); "An Ode. Inscribed to General Washington" (May 1788, pp. 482-83).

Poems by Trumbull: "M'Fingal," four cantos (April 1787, pp. 353-81); "The Speech of Proteus to Aristaeus," "The Downfall of Babylon," "The Prophecy of Balaam," "An Elegy on the Death of Mr. Buckingham St. John" (July 1787, pp. 95-103), "Ambition—an Elegy" (Aug. 1787, pp. 206-07).

Poems by Hopkinson; "The Battle of the Kegs" (Jan. 1787, pp. 85-86); "Date Obolum Belisario" (Jan. 1787, pp. 92-94 of the third edition); "A Riddle" (Jan. 1788, p. 96); answer to the riddle (Feb. 1788, p. 192); "The Raising: a Song for Federal Mechanics" (July 1788, p. 95); "Song" (Nov. 1788, p. 483); "Song" (Feb. 1789, p. 204).

Poems by Timothy Dwight: "Address of the Genius of Columbia to the Members of the Continental Convention," and "Columbia: a Song" (June 1787, pp. 563-67). Elihu Smith, in *American Poems* (1793) reprinted the first, pp. 55-62. "The Seasons Moralized" (March 1789, pp. 302-03); "A Song" (April 1789, pp. 408-09); "A Hymn Sung at the Public Exhibition of the Scholars, Belonging to the Academy at Greenfield" (Aug. 1789, pp. 171-72).

Poems by Evans: "The Morning Invitation" (Sept. 1788, pp. 297-98); "Song, Extempore" (Oct. 1789, p. 330).

Poems by Livingston: "A Morning Hymn" (Jan. 1789, pp. 100-01); "Address to his Excellency General Washington" (March 1789, pp. 300-01).

Poem by Godfrey: "A Pindaric Ode on Friendship" (Sept. 1788, pp. 295-97).

the war, and his subsequent power in politics and business, made him a national figure; and he attained international recognition following the publication in London in 1785 of "A Poem, Addressed to the Armies of the United States" by virtue of a free translation into the French by Chastellux and the "Strictures" thereon which appeared in the *Journal de Paris* and was translated into English and reprinted in *The American Museum* and elsewhere.[281]

The devotion of considerable space to the poems of Freneau and Trumbull is to be expected, but Ladd's was a new voice. Several reasons probably induced Carey to print freely from the work of this late young physician of Charleston, South Carolina. The poems had recently appeared in a volume; the author had been known in both Connecticut and South Carolina; and his recent death as the result of a duel was of current interest. But in their own right Ladd's poems deserved the attention accorded them. They probably represent the changing literary manner in England, and the approaching change in America, more clearly than the work of any other writer appearing in the magazine except that of Freneau. His poems bear the marks of unskilled, mannered youth, and they clearly reveal the heritage of his literary loves; but their

Poem by Markoe: "Ode on the Birth-Day of Gen. Washington" (Feb. 1787, pp. 177-78).

Poems by Paine: Verse in "The Bachelor," No. II (Dec. 1787, p. 600); "Liberty Tree" (Oct. 1789, p. 332).

Poems by Smith: "On a Lady's Birthday" (Jan. 1787, p. 87); "Art and Nature" (Feb. 1787, pp. 181-82); "Lampoon" (Aug. 1788, pp. 197-98); "The Man of Sorrow" (Nov. 1787, pp. 517-18).

Poem by Dawes: "Ode on the Opening of the Bridge over the Charles River" (Feb. 1787, pp. 183-84).

Poems by Carey: "On the Entrance of Dr. Franklin into the State-House" (Feb. 1787, p. 191); "The Prayer of an American Citizen" (Oct. 1787, p. 411).

Poem by John Osborn, written in 1735, "An Elegaic Epistle" (Dec. 1789, pp. 486-87).

Poem by Knox: "An Ode," inscribed to Washington (July 1789, pp. 85-86).

Poems by Swanwick: "To the Memory of the Late Tench Tilghman" (Feb. 1787, pp. 184-85); "Poem, on the Prospect of Seeing the Fine Arts Fourish in America" (Dec. 1787, pp. 597-600), the latter full of references to the groups in Philadelphia joined in their several aims in social reform.

Poem by James, of Philadelphia: "The Country Meeting," written under the influence of Shenstone (Jan. 1787, pp. 93-95).

[281] For the "Strictures" see *The American Museum* for May 1787, pp. 467-70. The poem was printed at Hartford in 1786. *The American Museum* contains an original Poem, "The Incantation," by W. P. Carey, of Dublin, Ireland (Oct. 1788, p. 383), who expressed himself in an accompanying note as being pleased in high degree if his poem should appear in a magazine printing Humphreys's poetry.

characteristics are the essence of his young generation. He was greatly influenced by Macpherson's *Ossian*, which he honored as best he could by an "Ode to the Spirit of Ossian" and by several paraphrases; and he quoted from Milton frequently enough to indicate familiarity with his works. Though he reflected Pope's manner and method on occasion, he was not kindly disposed to the prose of Johnson. He modernized the story of Eldred and Isabell from Chatterton, and he was one with Cowper and the more blundering Coleridge in the spirit which evoked an "Epitaph on an Old Horse"—"Let no facetious mortal laugh."[282]

Possibly no special mention need be made of the remaining names among the list of writers of verse; they properly appear as a matter of course in such an anthological scheme as Carey conducted. Biographical and appreciative accounts, generally if not always taken from earlier printed sources, helped to preserve the knowledge of some of the less represented men, such as Osborn, Evans, and Godfrey.[283] Poems by Englishmen were seldom reprinted; names so familiar as Dryden, Chatterton, Gray, and Cowper, when encountered, emphasize the lack rather than the presence of British poetry by reminding the reader how little of it was selected.[284]

The American Museum came at the beginning of a new period of national life, and as a spacious anthology drawing its contents from several decades past, it stands as a valuable storehouse for much eighteenth-century American thought and expression. It was the only magazine of its kind, and it served its period well.

[282] Ladd was born at Newport, R. I., in 1764, but in 1784, having finished his medical studies, he removed to Charleston, S. C., to practise. He was killed in a duel in 1786. There is a brief review of his life by W. B. Chittenden in *The Literary Remains of Joseph Brown Ladd*, collected by his sister, Mrs. Elizabeth Haskins (1832). Ladd's earlier publications were *The Poems of Arouet* (1786), for which there were 195 subscribers, *An Essay, on Primitive, Latent, and Regenerated Light* (1786), and *Select Poems on Various Occasions, Chiefly American, among which Are Several Wrote by the Celebrated Dr. Ladd* (1787).

[283] See "Memoirs of the Poet John Osborn," dated March 21, 1787 (June 1789, pp. 587-90), William Smith's "Sketch of the Life of the Rev. Nathaniel Evans" (Nov. 1789, pp. 405-06), and Nathaniel Evans's account of the life of Thomas Godfrey (Dec. 1789, pp. 471-72).

[284] For selection from the work of Dryden, see "Alexander's Feast" (June 1787, pp. 568-70); for Chatterton, see "Ethelgar, a Saxon Poem" (Feb. 1788, pp. 154-56); for Gray, see "On the Death of his Favorite Cat, Drowned in a Tub of Gold Fishes" (Jan. 1787, pp. 92-93); for Cowper, see "The Rose," and "Tale of the Mahometan Hog" (Jan. 1787, pp. 89-91).

CHAPTER XI

BY THE close of 1788, conditions were more favorable for publishing American magazines. The year 1789 is marked by more activity in the printing of periodicals than had heretofore been known; to describe the ventures of that year is to point the way of a progress so extensive that another volume would be required to trace the history for the next decade and a half. Briefly, the general miscellany was to continue as a dominating factor, but intrepid publishers would venture to appeal to limited interests and specific classes of people by publishing magazines specialized in contents.

When Webster discontinued *The American Magazine* in New York at the close of 1788, the city was to remain without a local magazine until 1790, when *The New-York Magazine; or, Literary Repository* was established. But *The Columbian Magazine* and *The American Museum* persisted in Philadelphia until the end of 1792. Six new magazines were established in 1789. At Hartford, Barzillai Hudson and George Goodwin began *The Children's Magazine* (1789),[1] the first representative of this type of periodical in America; but schoolmasters and parents failed to support the journal, and the publishers issued only four numbers. At Boston, Joseph Nancrède edited and Samuel Hall published the weekly *Courier de Boston* (1789),[2] devoted to the interests of promoting friendly relations between France and America. The journal started with the good wishes of the Gallo-American Society, but survived only half a year. At Philadelphia, William Prichard and Peleg Hall ventured to publish *The Arminian Magazine* (1789-90),[3] edited by Bishops Thomas Coke and Francis Asbury of the Methodist Episcopal Church in America. Methodist societies were becoming numerous, and the magazine helped awaken a sense of

---

[1] See "Bibliography," p. 373.
[2] *Ibid.*, p. 374.
[3] *Ibid.*, p. 373.

unity among the scattered groups. It also assisted Asbury, the more active editor, to preserve his dominant power in the church organization, even against the apparent will of John Wesley. But its greatest service lay in disseminating a great many of the writings and sermons of Wesley at a time when there were scarcely any American imprints of his works. One other dominantly religious magazine was established, *The Christian's, Scholar's, and Farmer's Magazine* (1789-91),[4] published by Shepard Kollock at Elizabeth-Town, and edited by the Reverend David Austin, a Presbyterian clergyman of the city whose interests were sufficiently broad for him to perform his editorial work without reference to creed. As a "Scholar's" magazine, it dutifully conveyed a considerable store of information on history, *belles-lettres,* and classical knowledge. The agricultural section was slight in size, and much of it was taken from the *Encyclopædia Britannica*. The tone of the whole magazine was encyclopedic. At Boston, Nathaniel Coverly tried for two years to compete with Isaiah Thomas by publishing *The Gentlemen and Ladies Town and Country Magazine* (1789-90),[5] as overwhelmingly devoted to sentimentality and sensibility in fiction as was *The Children's Magazine* to information for youthful minds or *The Arminian Magazine* and *The Christian's, Scholar's and Farmer's Magazine* to theological concerns. The greatest magazine to be established in 1789 was *The Massachusetts Magazine* (1789-96),[6] a general miscellany begun by Isaiah Thomas and Company in Boston, which was published by several firms through eight successive years, with only one hiatus of three months within the span. No magazine in the eighteenth century save *The New-York Magazine* can claim so long a life. It was more journalistic in its appeal than *The Columbian*, and edited to amuse popular tastes and excite popular emotions. A great deal of its contents was original with the magazine, however, and, as a glance at the subscription list will show, the more cultured class also supported it.

I

In the same year that William Blake's *Songs of Innocence* and Thomas Day's *The History of Sanford and Merton* were published,

---

[4] *Ibid.*, p. 374.
[5] *Ibid.*
[6] *Ibid.*, p. 373.

Barzillai Hudson and George Goodwin, publishers of *The Connecticut Courant* in a partnership established in 1779, launched *The Children's Magazine*.[7] As early as 1764 Christoph Saur had included catechisms and stories for children in *Ein geistliches Magazien*, but the Hartford publishers were the first to issue a magazine entirely for children. The contents, as may be expected, were congenial to adult eighteenth-century conceptions of material proper for children, close to the spirit of Day and far removed from Blake. One might almost infer that the publishers were seeking to please those who would purchase the periodical—schoolmasters, church teachers, and parents—rather than those for whom the work was edited, though doubtless this remark is more fittingly descriptive of the contents than of the editorial intention. The first number was announced in *The Connecticut Courant* of February 2, 1789. "This work is designed," the publishers stated, "to furnish Children, from seven to twelve years of age, with a variety of lessons on various subjects, written in a plain, neat, familiar style, and proper to lead them from the easy language of the Spelling-Books up to the more difficult style of the best writers. Teachers of Schools have long complained of the want of such a work, and the Publishers are happy that they are now enabled to furnish it at a small expence."[8] This, or a later announcement, caught the eye of Noah Webster, who was then in Boston, and he wrote to the printers an encouraging letter on February 11, 1789: "I see by your paper the Children's Magazine is out. I hope you will forward some to this town, that I may show them to the Schoolmasters & assist in introducing them."[9] But Webster's nor others' probable favors availed, and the venture came to an end with the fourth number.

The editorial principle on which the publishers worked was to supply to their readers, both boys and girls, with offerings of four general kinds. First came articles relating to studies at school, such as "An Easy Introduction to Geography."[10] These, designed as supplementary reading in various branches, were followed by a

---

[7] See note 1.

[8] The advertisement further promised that the magazine would contain forty-eight pages, to be sold at six pence a single number, or four shillings six pence a dozen.

[9] The quotation is from the manuscript volume of Letters at the New York Public Library. Evans, *op. cit.*, VII (1786-89), lists in the classified subject index for the volume (pp. 406-07) 77 titles under juvenile publications, testifying to a fair market for children's books. Isaiah Thomas, of Boston, and William Spotswood, of Philadelphia, were principal publishers of this type of book.

[10] Jan., March, April 1789, pp. 5-11, 97-102, 145-49.

series of "Moral Tales," whereby lessons in reading and illustrations of the better attitudes toward life's circumstances were offered in the interesting form of narrative. As a class these tales are very sentimental, and though some of them, as "The Affectionate Sisters,"[11] may be appropriate for children, others seem to me more fitting preachments for adults. It is doubtful, for example, whether the young readers of the magazine derived much edification from the story of "The Jealous Wife,"[12] in which the chief character, lacking children, fell into a state of jealousy until, taking to her home one of her sister's seven children, she was relieved of her malady the while she lightened the burden of her sister. Tales of this kind were followed by "Familiar Letters on Various Subjects," being such letters as the correspondence of "Phillis Flowerdale" and "Miss Truelove,"[13] which the editors hoped would teach elegant epistolary style and at the same time introduce the readers to the choicest of demure people on earth. Finally, a department of poetry served for instruction in prosody and helpful practical philosophy by printing such poems as "Verses Addressed to a Young Lady with a Nosegay," "The Contented Cottager," and "The Honest Heart."[14] By dealing harshly, time dealt justly with the magazine, granting it barely the duration of a trial. But the student of early American magazines is tempted to regard it more kindly. The stories and articles were often more proper food for adults nourishing pathetic fallacies and eighteenth-century sensibility than for children of any age. The magazine bears unmistakably the aura of editorial minds well-intentioned and age-hardened, unable or unwilling to appreciate childhood's urges and desires. But the aim was sincere, and the program was formulated with some evident care. Its faults are only the faults of its century.

II

The weekly *Courier de Boston*,[15] which received the editorial support of the Gallo-American Society, organized in 1788 at Paris,

[11] April, pp. 168-81.

[12] *Ibid.*, pp. 153-68. Another story of this type is "The Grateful Return" (March, pp. 105-12), in which Edward and Mary-Ann, who are children of wealthy parents, treat a poor boy with respect and kindness and are rewarded, while their arrogant brother, George, is redeemed from snobbery.

[13] Jan.-April 1789, pp. 15-20, (?), 122-26, 181-87.

[14] Jan., April 1789, pp. 98, 191, 192.

[15] See note 2. An earlier French publication had appeared in Philadelphia, the *Courier de l'Amérique*, July 27, 1784-October 26, 1784, the final date being for No.

may perhaps more properly be called a newspaper than a magazine, though in some of its features it bears a resemblance to the latter type of periodical. The pages, of which there were eight rather than the four customary among newspapers, were smaller than those of the typical newspaper, and more closely resemble those of *The Censor* and *The New-Haven Gazette, and the Connecticut Magazine*. Its chief functions were to further understanding and friendship between the French and American people and to print a digest of news both domestic and foreign. Though its interest in European affairs was decidedly localized to France, its point of view toward domestic matters was commendably national rather than regional. Some of its contents were not of the nature of news; and, being printed in the French language, the periodical served the double purpose of a newspaper and of a social and literary journal for its subscribers, of whom, an announcement stated with pride, "trois-quarts . . . sont Américains."[16]

Joseph Nancrède, the editor, was "Le premier 'instructeur' de francais à Harvard College"; his association with the college began in 1787, two years before the *Courier de Boston* made its appearance, and continued through 1800. He engaged himself also as a bookseller in Boston.[17] The periodical did not make its appearance until April, 1789, but for several months previously he had been making efforts to establish the project on a firm basis. He advertized "Proposals" for publishing the weekly journal as early as January 19, 1789, in *The Boston Gazette, and the Country Journal*. "The advantages," he stated, "which must accrue to the

14, probably the last. This newspaper was published semi-weekly in quarto. In addition to the file in the Spanish Archives in Seville, a copy of which is in the Spanish Transcripts in the Ayer Collection at the Newberry Library, Chicago, the Library of Congress has a file containing issues for July 27, 30, August 6, 17, 24, 27, October 5, 19, 22, 1784. The paper was published by Charles Cist, and edited by Daniel Boinod and Alexander Gaillard. It is listed in Brigham, *op. cit.*, new series, XXXII, 102.

[16] No. 1 (April 23, 1789), p. 1.

[17] The quotation in French is from the title of an article regarding Nancrède by Fernand Baldensperger, Professeur à La Sorbonne, in *The Harvard Advocate*, Dec. 5, 1913, pp. 76-79, to which Professor R. H. Haynes, of Harvard, kindly called my attention. Before and during the period of Nancrède's editorship, he advertised that he would conduct evening classes in French, and, as an instructor at Harvard, he praised the encouragement the university was giving to a study of the language. It was his own ambition "to justify the favours of the citizens of this town, by projects of *real utility*." (*The Massachusetts Centinel*, Aug. 18, 1789; *The Boston Gazette, and the Country Journal*, Sept. 22, 29, Oct. 6, 1788).

United States from a periodical publication, calculated to inform foreigners, and above all, merchants, in their own language, of the natural, moral, and political advantages of this country, are obviously of so much importance, and must prove so beneficial to the Commerce of America, that I shall ever view the attempt alone (should it fail of success) as one of the most happy and favorable circumstances that could recommend me to the citizens of the United States." He stated further that it was his ambition to interpret the United States accurately to France. Foreigners, "even the most learned" and friendly travelers in America, such as Raynal Buffon, "have grasped at shadows." Consider for a moment "St. John's Farmer's Letters," he requested; if one book could serve so well, a periodical would be even more valuable in bringing together the virtues of America and Europe. In an announcement made through the public press, printed in *The Massachusetts Centinel* of February 11, 1789, he stated that though the number of subscribers was still "insufficient," the response had been such as to give him "the 'most flattering hopes," and he was elated at the manner in which Boston had greeted the project, hoping only that other cities would evince the same interest. Correspondence with Europe had been established, he informed the public, but was not yet in operation. The Gallo-American Society, some of whose members had "invited him to undertake this paper," had not yet supplied him with correspondence, but the members had promised him that they would send "every information, which may have for its object the advantages of the two countries," and Nancrède was certain some items would shortly come to hand. In the meantime he could not refrain from striking at certain misconceptions concerning the French which he had discovered in America, and which had been inherited from Europe. He was certain that when Americans should truly learn the nature of the French, such prejudices as those which would "not grant the French any solidity of judgment, or principle" would "vanish away."[18]

The publisher, Samuel Hall, had long been engaged in newspaper work. In 1762 he had become associated with *The Newport Mercury* in Rhode Island, and thereafter he had published at Salem *The Essex Gazette* (1768-75), which he moved to Cambridge as

[18] Subject matter and quotations are from *The Massachusetts Centinel* of Feb. 11, 1789, "The Editor of the Courier de Boston to the Publick," the leading article of the number.

The New-England Chronicle (1775-76) and sold in 1776 following its subsequent remove to Boston. During this time he had defended and forwarded the American cause during the early conflicts with the British, and his natural mood was liberal. In 1781 he again entered newspaper work, establishing *The Salem Gazette*, which he moved to Boston in 1785 as *The Massachusetts Gazette*, and from which he withdrew all connections in 1787.[19]

Events in France were approaching a crisis, and the more democratic minds of the time were rejoicing at the trend of affairs, which seemed to be engendering types of democratic structures in Europe as well as America. Americans read in at least one paper: "Every order, every body of men, every individual, has engaged in the contest, concerning rights, pretensions, usages and forms; and in the discussion, all have been obliged to sacrifice more or less to the eternal principles of justice, equity, and reason . . ."; so, adopting Necker's report on the restoration of the States, the new France was in increasing measure federal in its establishment, and half of the thousand deputies were to be representatives of the third estate, leaving to the first and second the remaining half.[20] Altogether, it might seem that the French and Americans could think in somewhat the same terms if not with the same words.

Besides the news reports (the most important of which were sometimes printed in French and English in parallel columns),[21] probably the most interesting pieces in the journal are the articles which an unknown hand has ascribed in the file now at the Library of Congress to "A. Gallatin," later Secretary of the Treasury and an eminent representative of the United States in ministerial capacities in Russia, France, and Great Britain. Albert Gallatin, born in Switzerland in 1761, had arrived as an immigrant in Boston in 1780. He was prepared to make his home in the new country, and engaged in trade, gave instructions in French and taught the language at Harvard for a short time. He soon moved

[19] See Brigham, *op. cit.*, XXXIV, new series, part 1, April 1924, p. 85, XXV, new series, part 2, Oct. 1915, pp. 464, 399, and part 1, April 1915, pp. 258-59; part 2, p. 469, and part 1, p. 253. See also *Publications of the Colonial Society of Massachusetts*, IX, 498-501, "Check-List of Boston Newspapers 1704-1780."

[20] *The Massachusetts Centinel*, April 18, 1789, p. 37.

[21] See especially Washington's address to both houses of congress at New York (May 14, 1789, pp. 25-28) and the seventeen "Articles in Addition to, and Amendments of the Constitution of the United States of America" (Sept. 17, 1789, pp. 170-72), the latter much revised by hand in the copy at the Library of Congress.

to Pennsylvania and Virginia, and in 1789 was married to Sophie Allègre, of Richmond, taking her to Pennsylvania. The articles attributed to him are valiant expressions of the virtues of the United States. But I have not found in them, or in the events of his life during 1789, further evidence of his authorship. The "Lettre, à l'éditeur de cette feuille. A Cambridge, le 10 Mai, 1789,"[22] whether by Gallatin, or Nancrède (whose name never appeared in the imprint), or possibly another person, is an oratorical pean on the state of commerce in the new nation and its prospects as the country rises to its inevitable and glorious destiny. In the second article, "Avis Intéressans aux Personnes qui Cherchent à Émigrer en Amérique,"[23] the author sought to dispel such prevalent European ideas as that the people in the United States are ignorant of sciences and lacking in *belles-lettres* and that immigrants were given land and negroes as an inducement to come to America. The presence of nine colleges and the requirement of a knowledge of the languages and sciences for the professions of law, medicine, and theology were cited as evidence of the presence of culture; and as for the economic establishment, the Europeans were assured that artisans and farmers are welcomed and honored, the climate favorable and the conditions for earning a livelihood excellent, but that one must be willing to work and not count upon a recommendation of previous European social status. The third article, a description of the "Université de Cambridge,"[24] compared Harvard favorably with Oxford and Cambridge, viewing the American institution in a more acceptable light than the English universities because of Harvard's lack of religious restrictions.

With the close of the *Courier de Boston* in October, 1789, no other French periodical of its general type was published in the United States until 1792, when *Le Courier Politique d'l'Univers* was issued for a short time. Definite accounts of this later periodical have been discovered, but no copy located.[25]

[22] May 21, 1789, pp. 36-37.
[23] June 4, 11, pp. 49-51, 57-58.
[24] June 11, 1789, pp. 61-63. In part, it read: "La discipline, le plan d'étude, la distribution des honneurs littéraires sont les mémes que ceux de *Cambridge* et d'*Oxford* en Angleterre; mais, ce qui donne l'avantage à l'institution Américaine, ce qui enchérit sur son éloge, c'est que toutes les sectes quelconques peuvent y être élevées; toute espece de *test* devenant inutile pour y être admis."
[25] Brigham, *op cit.*, XXV, new series, part 1, April 1915, p. 209.

III

The Arminian Magazine (1789-90),[26] the third to be devoted entirely to religion in the territory comprising the United States, was the first magazine of Methodism in America. *The Christian History* (1743-45) had been established to assist the "Great Awakening" and in a broad way to extend the ministrations of Christianity. It had found room for both Calvinists and Episcopalians, for the Friends and for those who, still affiliated in their several denominations, were essentially the future Methodists. But since the fifth decade of the century Methodist or Wesleyan societies had increased in number and importance, and *The Arminian Magazine* was published to promulgate the doctrine of Arminius, to extend the opportunities for reading the works of Wesley, and to combat the doctrines of Calvin, which *The Royal Spiritual Magazine* of 1771 had defended. It was modeled closely on *The Arminian Magazine* (1778-97), published in London and edited for a time by Wesley.

In an announcement "To the Subscribers," dated from North Carolina, April 10, 1789, the editors, Thomas Coke and Francis Asbury, recognized the Calvinistic ascendency in America in the past. They were aware, they wrote, that in the United States the gospel had "chiefly" been interpreted through the "Calvinistic medium," and that the books circulated had "more or less maintained the doctrines of unconditional election and reprobation—that 'GOD is' not 'loving to every man,' . . . that 'Christ did' not 'die for all,' but only for a small select number of mankind." This creed they now challenged through the agency of a magazine, even as they had in other ways been challenging it for a number of years. The Methodist societies were now able to support such a journal, and it would proclaim that " 'GOD willeth all men to be saved,' *by speaking the truth in love. . . .*"[27]

Through its editors, who were the two highest ranking officials in the Wesleyan organization in America, the magazine became at once the authentic organ of Methodism in the United States. In his middle twenties, Francis Asbury had arrived in America in 1771, and the following year he was commissioned by Wesley as

[26] See note 3.
[27] All quotations within the paragraph are from I, III-IV.

the general assistant or superintendent of the Methodist societies in the Colonies.[28] Though officially he had been superseded by Thomas Rankin in 1773, he did not at heart relinquish his leadership, and he had refused to return to England in 1775 at Rankin's request and Wesley's summons. In 1784 Thomas Coke had been sent by Wesley as general superintendent, fully instructed with regard to the establishment of a governing system. Asbury, expressing surprise at the method of personal control by Wesley, had called a conference in Baltimore the same year, which he dominated, though Coke was nominally chairman. There Coke and his assistants ordained Asbury, and the conference elected him a general superintendent, a title which he himself changed to that of bishop. Coke made frequent trips to England, while Asbury kept a strong hand always on affairs in America, and though Asbury was under Coke in rank, he held more actual control. Thus, though Coke's name led Asbury's in the official signatures to the first volume of *The Arminian Magazine,* Asbury seems to have been the chief editor and to have conducted it himself during the waning fortunes of its second year. The publishers, William Prichard and Peleg Hall, had formed a partnership in Philadelphia in 1787, and, being general printers, booksellers, and publishers of books, seem to have had only a commercial interest in the project.[29]

In the decade preceding 1789 few of Wesley's writings were printed in America.[30] But the pages of the new magazine offered an excellent opportunity for reprinting many of his sermons and other works; and as Asbury's interest in editing waned, or as he

---

[28] Asbury and Coke were both young English preachers before coming to America. The former was born in 1745, the latter in 1747. For brief biographies, together with bibliographical references, see *Dictionary of American Biography,* ed. Allen Johnson.

[29] During 1789 they published, as listed in Evans, *op. cit.,* such books as Rush's *An Inquiry into the Natural History of Medicine among the Indians of North America,* John Stirling's *A Compendious System of Rhetoric, for the Use of Schools in America,* John Wesley's *Primitive Physic,* and George Buchanan's *Dissertatio Physiologia Inauguralis, de Causis Respirationis ejusdemque Effectibus.*

[30] Most important seem to have been *A Collection of Psalms and Hymns,* issued by Melchior Steiner at Philadelphia in 1781, and *A Form of Discipline, for the Ministers, Preachers, and Members of the Methodist Episcopal Church in America, Considered and Approved at a Conference Held at Baltimore . . . December, 1784: in which Thomas Coke, and Francis Asbury Presided,* the latter containing Wesley's *The Scripture Doctrine of Predestination, Election, and Reprobation* and *A Plain Account of Christian Perfection, as Believed and Taught by the Rev. Mr. John Wesley,* the fifth edition of which volume appeared in 1789 (Evans, *op. cit.,* Nos. 17427 and 21961).

may have with increasing difficulty found material of importance written in America, he leaned more and more heavily on the printed volumes of Wesley's works, and over half of the second volume of the magazine is devoted to them. Twenty-four "Original Sermons by the Rev. John Wesley" were printed during the two years the magazine was published, each issue save that for September 1789 containing at least one, and the issue for May 1789 containing two.[31] None of these sermons, "lately published in *Europe*," had been printed in America hitherto, according to an editorial announcement. Other offerings from the works of the founder of Methodism include a "Letter" to his brother, "Of Preaching Christ",[32] a long, continued selection entitled "An Extract of the Rev'd Mr. John Wesley's Journal",[33] "Predestination Calmly Considered," which, as a serial occupying the leading space in several issues, sought to confirm the belief that the Scriptures "abundantly prove, that there is not, cannot be, any such things as unconditional Reprobation";[34] and "A Short Account of the Life and Death of the Rev. John Fletcher."[35]

Other selections in the magazine are as fully related to the history and doctrines of Methodism. "The Journal of Francis Asbury, Bishop of the Methodist-Episcopal Church, from August 7, 1771 to February 27, 1772,"[36] and "The Journal of Thomas Coke, Bishop of the Methodist-Episcopal Church, from September 18, 1784 to June 3, 1785,"[37] present historical beginnings of an organ-

[31] Jan.-Aug., Oct.-Dec. 1789, pp. 26-42, 69-79, 119-30, 170-84, 218-37, 273-84, 327-39, 378-91, 477-89, 525-36, 570-82; Jan.-Dec. 1790, pp. 16-26, 57-69, 113-24, 165-75, 216-25, 268-78, 321-34, 373-88, 425-34, 477-86, 529-38, 585-94. The sermons are numbered 1-24 consecutively; No. 21 was misnumbered 22 in the issue for Sept. 1790, but the sequence was rectified in the succeeding number. For editorial announcement of the series, see issue for Jan. 1789, p. V. The Bristol edition of Wesley's *Works*, in thirty-two volumes, had appeared during the years 1771-74.

[32] Oct. 1789, pp. 489-96.

[33] Jan.-May, Nov.-Dec. 1790, pp. 27-36, 69-74, 124-31, 176-83, 225-35, 538-47, 595-600. The series was announced to be continued in the third volume, but the magazine was abandoned.

[34] May-Dec. 1790, pp. 209-16, 261-68, 313-21, 365-72, 417-25, 469-76, 521-29, 573-85. The quotation is taken from p. 268.

[35] Dated from Amsterdam Sept. 12, 1786. The account ran serially, Jan.-Nov. 1790, pp. 37-47, 75-84, 131-41, 183-92, 235-44, 287-96, 340-48, 391-400, 443-53, 495-504, 547-54.

[36] For this series, with the supplemental account from March 26, 1772 to April 14, 1773, see issues of April 1789, pp. 184-98, Feb.-Sept. 1790, pp. 85-90, 141-46, 193-99, 245-51, 297-302, 349-54, 401-07, 453-58.

[37] May-Aug. 1789, pp. 237-44, 286-97, 339-46, 391-98.

ized movement to establish a definite church in America. Asbury's account was later extended from March 1772 to April 1773. Both are particularly valuable for the relation of experiences in New York, Pennsylvania, New Jersey, Virginia, and Maryland, where the societies were active. Excerpts were taken from both old and new founts. An account of the life of Arminius was printed in the first volume—a fitting manner of calling attention to the traditional background of Wesleyan tenets for whatever honor age might bring to them.[38] "A Short Account of the Life and Death of William Adams, a Youth of Virginia,"[39] "The Address of the Bishops of the Methodist-Episcopal Church" to President Washington, with his reply,[40] "An Account of the Synod of Dort,"[41] and "God's Love to Mankind. Manifested by Disproving His Absolute Decree for their Damnation,"[42] are chief among the selections and indicate the nature of the contents. Odd miscellaneous pieces, letters, and accounts of remarkable events were often used; and they served, as did frequently the poetry, to support the theory of "universal redemption."

IV

The Christian's, Scholar's, and Farmer's Magazine[43] was, so far as I know, the first bimonthly published in America and the first magazine of importance since *The New American Magazine* of 1758-60 to be issued in New Jersey. It was serious in import, as its title implies, and not at all weakly sentimental as was its contemporary, *The Gentlemen and Ladies Town and Country Magazine*. Its sympathies lay in the fields of religion, literature, agriculture, history, science, and biography; it was a true miscellany of the general type of *The Columbian Magazine* and *The American Museum*, though it stressed religious subjects more than either of the others, and was more deadly factual and full of instruction.

[38] Jan. 1789, pp. 7-15.
[39] Feb., March 1789, pp. 80-92, 132-39.
[40] June 1789, pp. 284-86.
[41] Jan.-April 1789, pp. 15-25, 51-60, 101-10, 151-60. The account expresses distress in the fact that the synod of Dort "passed over in silence the rigid doctrines of Calvin . . . without condemning them" (p. 160).
[42] Aug.-Dec. 1789, pp. 363-71, 412-20, 463-77, 512-25, 560-69, and Feb.-April 1790, pp. 53-56, 105-12, 157-65.
[43] See note 4.

Shepard Kollock, the publisher and "one of the Proprietors," was a man of good judgment, practical in business, and public spirited. He had been born at Lewes, Delaware, in 1751, and early in life had learned the printer's trade. During the first part of the Revolutionary War he had served as a lieutenant in the militia and the artillery and had taken part in the Battle of Trenton and other engagements. The need for a strong pro-American newspaper in northern New Jersey was real in 1779, and he had established *The New-Jersey Journal* at Chatham in that year. This journal he discontinued in 1783, and he began in the same year *The Political Intelligencer* at New Brunswick. This paper he moved to Elizabeth-Town in 1785, and he changed the title in 1786 to *The New-Jersey Journal*. He continued this enterprise until 1818, meanwhile occasionally publishing books, mainly religious in nature. He became postmaster; and he was a justice of the court of common pleas, an office he held for thirty-five years.[44] Such a pattern of life describes the magazine as well as the man, for Kollock undoubtedly served partially in an editorial capacity, using his shears on printed works extensively. The magazine was designed to be of educational service, and if to the readers it seemed dry, encyclopedic, and lacking in journalistic zest, it definitely served the high aims of its proprietors.

The Reverend David Austin was the editor probably most responsible for the conduct of the magazine, taking as his especial province the religious portion. He had been born at New Haven, and, having been graduated from Yale in 1779, and having studied in Europe, he had been ordained pastor of the Presbyterian church at Elizabeth-Town in 1788. The following year, aged thirty, he was able to indulge his literary and religious interests by undertaking to formulate the editorial policy of the magazine. He was excitable, energetic, and somewhat erratic. Yet while editing the magazine the eccentricities of his later religious convictions had not yet forcibly seized his imagination, but were rather expressed agreeably in a noticeable editorial fervor. His tolerant attitude toward many denominations, which was again to be expressed in his editing

[44] For an account of Kollock, see William Nelson's "Some New Jersey Printers and Printing in the Eighteenth Century," in *Proceedings of the American Antiquarian Society*, XXI, part 1 (1911), pp. 31-33. Edwin Jacquet Sellers's *Genealogy of the Kollock Family* (1897), p. 23, and the alphabetized section of Brigham's "Bibliography of American Newspapers, 1690-1820," in *Proceedings of the American Antiquarian Society*, XXVI, part 2, Oct. 1916, pp. 418, 420, 424, 434.

of *The American Preacher*, a collection of sermons by living divines and chosen without respect to denomination, served him well while conducting a magazine in which the section devoted to religious subjects was given first place in importance.[45] He was on intimate terms with Kollock; they worked agreeably together, and the publisher's religious publications show his support of Austin's labors in metaphysics after the magazine came to an end.[46]

The response of the public to the proposals for printing the new magazine seems to have exceeded the expectations of the editors,[47] who were able to announce in the first number that the price of subscriptions per year, originally set at $2.50, would now be reduced to $2.00 because of the ". . . Encouragement that hath been given." Contributions were requested which would assist the editors in their design "to *subserve* the *interests* of Religion; to *diffuse useful Knowledge*; and to *aid* the Husbandman in his very *necessary* and *important toil*." But Austin was careful not to accept material which might lead to controversy, and on one occasion informed "Orthodox," an anonymous writer whose pen was conceded to be "masterly," that his article was not acceptable "as it is not our Intention to render this Magazine a Vehicle of *religious Controversy*; which is seldom conducted with *Moderation* and *Candor*, and, in general, we apprehend, is productive of more *evil* than *good* Consequences."[48] The decision to issue the magazine bimonthly was probably a wise one, as thus 128 pages could be printed for each number, and the magazine appear in a bulk comparable with *The American Museum*, even though only half as often. For two years it was able to exist without any sign of weakening save in a slight reduction in the number of pages toward the close, and the proprietors gave no other reason for abandoning the periodical than a "want of Leisure."[49]

[45] For a short biographical sketch of Austin, see article by Harris E. Starr in the *Dictionary of American Biography*, ed. Allen Johnson.

[46] While at Elizabeth-Town Kollock published *The American Preacher*, edited by Austin, Bishop Thomas Newton's *Dissertations on the Prophecies*, in which Austin was greatly interested, as well as a *New Testament*, and Friedrich Klopstock's *Messiah*.

[47] In dedicating the first and second volumes respectively to William Livingston, Governor of New Jersey, and George Washington, President of the United States, the formula used was "By the Editors."

[48] For quotations and facts, see issue for April-May 1789, pp. 4-5.

[49] "Two years have elapsed since the Commencement of this Publication. The Editors sincerely regret, that want of Leisure will oblige them (at least for the

From the beginning to the end the editors maintained their plan of dividing the magazine into five major departments, a system other editors had used initially only to relinquish after a few numbers. The departments of theology and literature, arranged in this order, were each accorded about fifty pages an issue; agriculture and poetry followed, the former with approximately a dozen pages and the latter with three to six. At the back was the usual summary of foreign and domestic occurrences extending over two to three pages.

In a "Theological Introduction" addressed to the "Professors of Christianity in These States," Austin pledged his endeavor "to advance the *general interests* of our most holy religion," and, though liberal with respect to creeds, was orthodox enough to define a Christian negatively in these words: "No one . . . can justly be denominated a real Christian, unless he believes the doctrines of the gospel; sincerely and universally, to the utmost of his power, reveres its precepts; trusts in its premises, and fears its threatenings."[50] The selections in the first number are typical of those that followed. Austin began by publishing a series of articles on natural, physico-, astro-, and Christian theology, dividing the last into systematic, moral, homiletic, catechetic, polemic, and casuistic divisions.[51] He followed this type of material with extracts on ecclesiastical and church history, the gospel, errors in translation, and faith in the trinity; and he also included original sermons, and a series of biographies of famous churchmen.[52] He was painstak-

present) to discontinue it.—It affords them very sensible pleasure to reflect, that this Work hath been honored with the Patronage of several of the most eminent literary Characters in these States. . . . As not literary Fame, but the Benefit of Mankind, was the great Object of the Editors in publishing this Miscellany, they beg Leave still to conceal their Names from public View" (II, 743, unnumbered, following table of contents).

[50] April-May 1789, pp. 5-6.

[51] *Ibid.*, pp. 7-13; each division of the series was continued, and the parts considered in order; and the whole ran through the two volumes in about the same amount of space per issue as given in the first.

[52] For "A Concise Ecclesiastical History of the Principal Nations of the Earth" (concluded in the third number cited below) and "A Summary History of the Christian Church, from its Commencement to the Present Century" (which was begun at the same time and placed in juxtaposition with the first article, though continued throughout the life of the magazine), see issues for April 1789-March 1791, pp. 13-17, 139-45, 277-83, 402-05, 538-41, 659-63 (misnumbered 559-63), 7-12, 131-36, 260-66, 387-92, 513-20, 629-36. Among the commentaries on the Gospel is a treatise on St. Matthew (April-Sept. 1789, pp. 19-22, 149-53, 286-88). Special attention was given to "Evidences in Favor of Christianity" (April 1789-March 1791, pp.

ing, and the manner of his editing indicates a fervent desire to instruct his readers. Such a manner would rather have served students in theological seminaries, however. His interest in theology was too academic and specialized for general appeal. He forgot that all his readers were not members of his class, studying theology at Yale.

Something of the same pedantic attitude clung to the literary division, which was philosophically justified on the ground that "though good policy may forbid that any considerable number . . . should receive a *collegiate education*, more than shall be required for the liberal professions, it may, notwithstanding, be of essential service to the community, that our young men, in general, who shall devote themselves to commerce, and to mechanical and agricultural employments, should possess considerable degrees of Literature" for the sake of good breeding, citizenship, and culture.[53] The subjects in this division were not limited to literature, but embraced the usual items in a miscellany, including history, science, and biography.[54]

18-19, 145-48, 285-86, 408-11, 541-44, 663-64 (misnumbered 563-64), 12-13, 136-38, 266-67, 392-93, 520-23, 641-42). Interesting sermons include an ordination sermon by the Rev. John Witherspoon (April-July, Nov. 1789, pp. 38-40, 179-81, 428-30) and a preachment by Provost William Smith of the College and Academy of Philadelphia (Oct.-Nov. 1790, pp. 397-403). For the special benefit of ministers, a series of papers, "The Christian Minister," was printed, designed to instruct divines on their duties and conduct, on the manner to construct a sermon, and other phases of clerical life (April 1789-March 1791, pp. 37-38, 175-78, 303-07, 426-28, 565-67, 683-92, 39-41, 161-66, 279-82, 409-13, 543-45, 654-58). A serial essayist, "The Censor" (whose columns, thus entitled, were open to contributors) introduced his series with the "intention . . . to inculcate *Virtue* and to amuse," to censure "predominate Vices and Follies of men," and point the way of rectitude; the essays ran throughout the two volumes (April 1789-March 1791, pp. 43-45, 182-84, 312-14, 435-36, 571-73, 692-95, 45-49, 166-68, 287-89, 418-20, 548-51, 661-63). The articles on Christian biography in the first volume included, among others, the lives of John Calvin (April-May 1789, pp. 33-35), St. Paul (June-July 1789, pp. 164-68), Martin Luther (*Ibid.*, pp. 170-72), St. Matthew (Aug.-Sept. 1789, pp. 294-98), St. Mark (Oct.-Nov. 1789, pp. 418-20), St. Luke (Dec.-Jan. 1789-90, pp. 556-59), and St. John the Evangelist (Feb.-March 1790, pp. 673-76).

[53] April-May 1789, p. 51.

[54] Indicative of the encyclopedic nature of the contents is the continued article running from the first to the final number of the magazine, "An Analytical Abridgment of the Principal of the Polite Arts, Belles Lettres, and Sciences; particularly Grammar, Rhetoric, Eloquence, Pronunciation, Poetry, Versification, Music, Painting, Engraving, Sculpture, and Plastics, Architecture, Mythology, Chronology, History, ancient and modern, Antiquities, Diplomatics, Statistics, Geography, Genealogy, Blazenry, Philology, Criticism, Jurisprudence, Physic . . . Anatomy, Physiology, Pathology . . . Logic, Metaphysics, Physics . . . Mathematics"; for chief items in

The other two important divisions, agriculture and poetry, were rather perfunctorily edited and without much distinction. Much of the material on agriculture was taken from printed sources, and

this department, other than the historical selections itemized in the succeeding paragraph, see issues for April 1789-March 1791, pp. 56-61, 206-17, 336-42, 454-62, 589-98, 714-22, 72-83, 183-95, 308-18, 440-47, 567-78, 676-84. Biographical accounts include extracts from Humphreys's life of Israel Putnam (April-Nov. 1789, pp. 78-81, 236-39, 361-63, 486-90), Jedediah Morse's account of Major-General Richard Montgomery (April-May 1789, pp. 81-82), Peter Coste's considerations on the life of John Locke (Dec.-March 1789-90, pp. 615-19, 735-38), a "Character of Major General Lee" (Feb.-March 1790, pp. 738-39), "Life of Joseph Addison," "Memoirs of Hogarth," and "Sketch of . . . Dr. Franklin" (April-May, 1790, pp. 102-10), "Memoirs" of Jonathan Belcher and "Character" of William Livingston (Aug.-Sept. 1790, pp. 328-34), "Life of Sir Richard Steele" and "Life of Laurence Sterne" (Dec.-Jan. 1790-91, pp. 593-98).

A great deal of space was given to ancient history, Greek philosophy, Latin authors, and other topics of classical associations. Note particularly "A Dialogue between Demosthenes and Cicero," from Cambray's *Dialogues of the Dead* (April-July 1789, pp. 61, 217-19), "Philosophy of Plato" (June-July 1789, pp. 219-22), "Philosophy of Aristotle" (Aug.-Sept. 1789, pp. 342-44), "A Dialogue between Plato and Aristotle"—with a dissertation on the "Solidity of Plato's Eternal Ideas" (Aug.-Sept., 1789, pp. 344-46), "A Dialogue between Horace and Virgil" (Oct.-Nov. 1789, pp. 465-66), "A Dialogue between Achilles and Homer" (Dec.-Jan. 1789-90, pp. 599-600), "A Dialogue between Romulus and Remus" (April-May 1790, p. 85), "A Dialogue between Octavia, Portia and Arria" (Aug.-Sept. 1790, pp. 359-61). "A Compendium of the History of Greece," "A Concise History of Rome," and "A Concise History of the Origin and Progress, among the most Ancient Nations, of Laws and Government;—of Arts and Manufactures;—of the Sciences;—of Commerce and Navigation . . ." were begun in the first number of the first volume, and continued through the life of the magazine; no other magazine within the range of this study approached such an encyclopedic display of instruction on this period of the world's history. Among offerings in American history were selections from Robertson's *History* of America and Morse's *The American Geography*; both were begun with the initial number, in juxtaposition; the latter was concluded in the issue for Oct.-Nov. 1789, while the former ran throughout the volumes excepting issues for June-Sept. 1790 (April 1789-March 1791, pp. 69-75, 229-34, 354-57, 477-81, 610-11, 731-32, 96-99, 459-61, 588-91, 688-91).

Certain other major writings seem to me worthy of specific mention, especially the dialogue between Fernando Cortez and William Penn, from Lord Littlejohn's *Dialogues of the Dead* (April-July 1789, pp. 82-84, 240-42), "Extracts from an Essay on the Causes of the Variety of Complexion and Figure in the Human Species," by the Rev. Samuel S. Smith, a professor at the College of New Jersey (June 1789-May 1790, pp. 222-24, 346-49, 467-69, 600-603, 724-25, 85-89), "The Spirit of Masonry," reprinted from a book by that title issued in London by William Hutchinson (April-May, Aug.-Jan. 1789-90, Feb.-March, June-July 1790, pp. 84-85, 368-70, 493-95, 621-25, 741-42, 214-16), "The Physical Cause of Love," from Edmund Burke's *Philosophical Inquiry into the Origin of our Ideas of the Sublime and the Beautiful* (June-July, 1790, p. 227), John Locke on the nature of the five senses (June-July 1790, pp. 211-14) and "Thoughts concerning the Reading and Study for a Gentleman" (Oct.-Nov. 1790, pp. 478-82).

there was little of definite instruction by interested correspondents.[55] The poetry was highly serious, often taking virtue as its subject, using the Bible frequently as a source, and being highly partial to odes and paraphrases; but one may find the subjects treated with greater distinction in many other places.[56]

V

Nathaniel Coverly, who had long been a printer in Boston and elsewhere,[57] chose a most unfortunate time to publish *The Gentlemen and Ladies Town and Country Magazine*.[58] He advertised "Proposals" for publishing the periodical earlier than did Thomas for his enterprise, but Thomas's plan materialized more quickly. Under date of January 1788, Coverly set forth his project in *The Boston Gazette, and the Country Journal* of September 1, 1788,

[55] In a note (April-May 1789, p. 99), the editors announced that they would print articles on "History of Agriculture," "Theory of Agriculture," and "Practice of Agriculture" from the *Encyclopædia Britannica*, then being printed in Scotland, of which the editors had received the first volume. The articles, continued monthly, appeared April 1789-March 1790, pp. 99-105, 245-54, 378-83, 501-07, 633-38, 747-50).

[56] For religious poetry, typical examples are some octosyllabic couplets "On Religion," a paraphrase of a section of the first epistle to the Corinthians, done in heroic couplets, entitled "Charity," a paraphrase of part of the sixth chapter of St. Matthew (April-May 1789, pp. 115-16). Social conditions were sometimes viewed definitely, as in the anti-slavery poem, "On Slavery, and the Slave Trade" (April-May 1789, p. 120). Anonymous original poems were liberally sprinkled among these selected from printed sources. At least three contributors should be mentioned. Mrs. "S.," of New Jersey, contributed "An Extemporal Ode in a Sleepless Night" (Oct.-Nov. 1789, pp. 517-18), and "An Ode for Christmas Day" (Dec.-Jan. 1789-90, p. 648). "Aspasio," of Newark, N. J., who had before appeared in the pages of a magazine, wrote "Anniversary Ode for July 4th, 1789" (Oct.-Nov. 1789, pp. 518-19), "The XCVII Psalm Paraphrased," "A Paraphrase on Part of . . . the First Epistle to the Corinthians," and "To Amanda" (Feb.-March 1790, pp. 760-62). Miss "P.D.," of Essex County, N. J., wrote "On the Setting of the Sun" and "In Time of Sickness" (Aug.-Sept. 1789, p. 391), "On the Apostasy and Redemption of Man" (Oct.-Nov. 1789, pp. 521-22) and "On the Day of Judgment" (Oct.-Nov. 1790, pp. 498-99).

[57] Evans, *op. cit.*, IV, 435, lists Coverly as a printer in Boston as early as 1770, and, alone or in combinations of partnerships, his name regularly appears in subsequent volumes. He is mentioned also in *The New England Historical and Genealogical Register*, first (XV, 1861, p. 170) as publisher of the third edition of Robert Cushman's sermons at Plymouth in 1785, and again (XXI, 1867, p. 382) as a publisher in Boston of "many works in Milk Street to as late as 1823." That Thomas did not mention him in *The History of Printing* seems surprising, in view of the long residence in Boston and the rivalry between his and Thomas's magazines.

[58] See note 5.

promising a monthly magazine at a shilling a number, or twelve shillings a year, which would contain the "latest discoveries, progress of Learning, and the most useful improvements in the Arts and Sciences; Husbandry, Gardening, Manufactures and Commerce." The first number, for February 1789, was advertised in one newspaper of January 31, to appear on the first of March, but at the same time Isaiah Thomas and Company were advertising the appearance of the first issue of *The Massachusetts Magazine*.[59] Coverly was no match for Thomas, whose printing business had grown to large proportions, and who had the support of Bostonians interested in publishing a magazine in their city rather than joining Webster in his plan of uniting Boston and New York in one periodical. Besides, Thomas was able to publish a more diversified miscellany than Coverly, whose magazine lacked breadth of interest and could approach Thomas's only in the field of sentimental fiction.

Though the magazine lacked distinction, Coverly was able to keep it alive for a year and a half, winning a local following of women who contributed both prose and poetry. In the twelfth issue—for January 1790—he printed a list of 471 subscribers, over half of whom dwelt in Boston or its suburbs, and nearly all of whom resided at no great distance from that town. He solicited the literary support of women especially, declaring his faith in the presence of mute Anna Sewards in America. Such appeals met with some degree of response, and there are many trivial, anonymous, but original pieces in the magazine.

The half hundred pages of each issue are filled with a motley assortment of ephemeral pieces noteworthy only as emphasizing the popular reign of sentiment and sensibility. Their spirit breathed in the letters, as when Lorenzo, deigning to address Adelaide as "My Amiable Friend," must break into a preliminary apostrophe: "Indulge me the tender, the beloved epithet; the sound of it is sweeter than the music of the valley; it has a charm for the heart of sensibility, which banishes despair."[60] It controlled the mood of the short original and selected essays on such themes as loquacity,

---

[59] *The Massachusetts Centinel*. Thomas continued advertising *The Massachusetts Magazine* in this paper, as well as his own. Coverly advertised the first number of his magazine in the newspaper of March 4, the second number on April 1, and the third on May 2, but thereafter he did not advertise in *The Massachusetts Centinel*.

[60] Feb. 1789, p. 11.

parental severity, riches, marriage, and the ever present libertine lovers. Original essayists who wrote longer articles indulged only the more lengthily in a high comedy of which they, and their readers, were innocent.[61] It permeated the department of questions and answers. Without it there would have been few of the many short love stories,[62] or longer sentimental romances which in pretense exposed the fates of actual patterns in the world,[63] or illustrations from copperplates visualizing scenes in the fiction, or sheets of music,[64] or poetry reposing in the department of "Parnassian Blossoms."[65] There were noble characters in the fiction, but there were also many seducers, ruined females, and virtuous men who trembled lest they should fall. Love was always glorified, but seldom isolated from lust, which was so frequently used for contrast that it became a major theme. Distresses of the heart, bursting bosoms, silent signs, and the "hallowed flood" of tears were the chief resources of the fictionist. All this was in the interests of virtue, which, if one were to believe the evidence in the magazine, was more precious than prevalent. Still, the intent of the editor was sincere. Coverly would occasionally lightly reprove a correspondent for submitting material unsuited to innocent eyes: "We are sorry," he once wrote in his monthly notes to correspondents, "to reject W.Z. An Evening Excursion, as, it appears

---

[61] "Leonidas," for example, wrote "An Inquiry, Whether Love in the Human Heart Has Been the Cause of More Good or Evil in the World" (Feb. 1789, pp. 35-36).

[62] Typical examples are "The Wronged Wife" (March 1789, pp. 59-61) and "Faithful Though at Liberty; or, the History of Claudio and Juliana" (May 1789, pp. 155-156).

[63] See, for example, "The Two Sisters, or Lucinda and Leonora," evidently original with the magazine (Nov. 1789, pp. 510-13, Jan. 1790, pp. 613-615).

[64] Coverly's magazine was ill printed, but he was forced to use some substance of decorative art. Illustrations from copperplate and sheet music with words were by this time necessary accouterments for nearly all general magazines. During 1789 the following plates appeared in the magazine, in main illustrating sentimental love stories: "Conjugal Affection" (Feb.), "The Wronged Wife" (March), "Conjugal Infidelity Detected" (April), "Faithful though at Liberty" (May), "Constantius and Pulchera" (June), "Fidelity" (July), "The Fatal Concealment" (Aug.), "Gray's Elegy" (Sept.), "The Successful Angler" (Oct.), "Lucinda and Leonora" (Nov.), "The Patriotic Lover" (Dec.). John Norman engraved the plates through July 1789, thereafter J. H. Seymour was the engraver. A music plate, "Palaemon to Pastora," being a "new air" by William Selby, appeared in the issue for April 1789.

[65] Besides treating of love both seriously and lightly, the versifiers had recourse to religious and social topics. Riming couplets were very popular, in both octosyllabic and pentameter lines.

rather to corrupt, than to improve the Morals of our young Readers."[66]

One can find pieces in the magazine which are not akin to Richardson and Sterne and Anna Seward. Through most of 1789 "The History of the Conspiracy of the Spaniards, against the Republick of Venice" was serialized,[67] and during about the same period selections from Jonathan Carver's *Travels through the Interior Parts of North-America* appeared.[68] There was a department of foreign and domestic intelligence. Odd biographical and historical anecdotes, notes on medicine, agriculture, and live stock, and other miscellaneous items were scattered through the numbers. But all of these subjects were secondary to the main current of sensibility, which swept through the pages of this journal as it had through the earlier, definitely styled representative of lady's magazines, *The Gentleman and Lady's Town and Country Magazine*, published in Boston in 1784.

VI

Although *The Massachusetts Magazine*[69] was begun in 1789, its proper relation with the history of magazines in America, beyond the facts incident to Thomas's establishment of the periodical, belongs to the years beyond the bounds of this study, for it was continued until the close of 1796. No eighteenth-century magazine in America lived longer, and only one, *The New-York Magazine*, lived as long. Conditions were now propitious for the publication of a major magazine in Boston, which had been barren of important representation since the beginning of pre-Revolutionary hostilities. But by 1788 there was no mistaking the temper of the capital of Massachusetts. Noah Webster, in New York, was then unable to gain consent to his plan for making Boston the spoke and New York the hub for his projected federal magazine.[70] Even a proposal to which both Webster and Thomas agreed— that a register should be published in New York and a companion

---

[66] April 1789, p. 114.

[67] Feb.-Oct. 1789, pp. 26-32, 65-69, 121-26, 177-79, 233-36, 290-92, 363-66, 414-16, 457-61.

[68] May 1789-March 1790, pp. 172-74, 262-64, 287-88, 357-59, 426-28, 461-62, 518-19, 573-75, 630-32, 29-30, 80-82.

[69] See note 6.

[70] See Chapter X relative to *The American Magazine* and *The Columbian Magazine*.

magazine in Boston, with editors in both cities—was abandoned for lack of support.[71] Boston wished a magazine of its own. *The American Museum* and *The Columbian Magazine* were sold to a number of subscribers in the city; but after the ninth issue of *The Massachusetts Magazine*, Belknap, who was acting as an agent in Boston and a contributor for *The Columbian*, recognized that the local publication would drive out most of the magazines coming from Philadelphia.[72] Later this indefatigable contributor to periodicals seems to have become an editor of *The Massachusetts Magazine*.[73]

When Thomas and Company undertook to publish *The Massachusetts Magazine*, its success was at least temporarily assured. Thomas was by this time a foremost newspaper and book publisher; his experience dated back long before the War, and his knowledge of magazines was the greater for his having published *The Royal American Magazine* and *The Worcester Magazine*.[74] Like Franklin, he had made a success of his printing business. His associates, friends, and acquaintances had faith in his practical ability. As

[71] On Jan. 13, 1789, Hazard wrote to Belknap outlining this plan, which was in the form of proposals, signed by Webster and Thomas. Webster, Belknap, or some other able man was to be the editor in Boston ("The Belknap Papers," *op. cit.*, fifth series, III, 92-93).

[72] Belknap wrote to Hazard on Dec. 13, 1788: "Besides, Thomas's Magazine will swallow up all others." On October 13, 1789 Hazard wrote to Belknap: "Do you think Thomas's will *endure?*" Belknap replied on Oct. 22: "Thomas's Magazine, as far as I am able to judge, is likely to continue for some time, at least. It is pretty generally read; and, since it has come out, I have lost near 20 subscriptions for the Columbian." Shortly afterward he wrote of *The Massachusetts Magazine*: "It has so much reputation that I am confident he [Thomas] may venture to continue it another year; but there is room enough for improvement. I expect Trenchard's [*The Columbian Magazine*] will drop, but I shall have a piece in each number till the end of the year." (*Ibid.*, pp. 83, 196, 198, 203). Whether or not Belknap's association with Trenchard came to an end at the close of the year, it is certain that he wrote for Carey's *The American Museum* for some time longer. Carey wrote to Belknap on Dec. 10, 1789: "I accede to *your* proposals; but it appears to me that two dollars per page are rather high for pieces exceeding one page." Further in the letter he became somewhat petulant: "You say your terms are *in addition* to mine, whereas they appear to me to supersede mine altogether" (*Ibid.*, sixth series, IV, 455).

[73] In Vol. XXX, p. 20 of the Benjamin Rush correspondence in manuscript at the Ridgway Branch of the Library Company of Philadelphia is a letter from Belknap to Rush, dated from Boston, May 16, 1791, which states in part: "I am about to reprint your letter on the use of the bible, in Thomas's Magazine for this Month."

[74] For an account of Thomas's life and earlier ventures in publishing magazines, see Chapters VII and IX, which deal respectively with *The Royal American Magazine* and *The Worcester Magazine*.

before, when commencing *The Royal American Magazine*, he advertised the project well, this time even going to the trouble to publish a pretentious twelve-page "Literary Proposal."[75]   He seems to have been determined to make *The Massachusetts Magazine* the equal, in popular appeal, of those published in Philadelphia.   He was primarily a newspaper man, however, and his interest in his newspaper and his general publishing business was greater than in the magazine.[76]

In the "Preface" to the first volume, written in December 1789, the editors requested "assistance" in the form of literary contributions to be paid by "private gratitude" and "publick eulogium." Original material was always sought and printed when available. Instructive articles were desired also, the editors stating that as "their *abiding place* must be the *Temple of Science*," so they did "earnestly entreat her benevolent votaries, to . . . guide them along the paths of knowledge."[77]   It should be noted, however, that *The Massachusetts Magazine* was much less instructive than *The Christian's, Scholar's, and Farmer's Magazine*, which yielded

[75] A copy, dated 1788, is in the American Antiquarian Society Library.   A two-column proposal to publish the magazine, signed by Isaiah Thomas and Company, of Boston, appeared under date of Aug. 1788 in Thomas's *The Massachusetts Spy*, of Worcester, in the issues of Sept. 4, 18, and Oct. 2, 1788.   The reasons set forth for publishing the magazine were that none was being published in the state, that the need for a magazine was great, that friends were urging the project, and that the company was physically equipped for the enterprise and wished to make an honest livelihood.   Sixty-four pages, with an engraving and a sheet of music, were promised monthly, at a price of fifteen shillings a year.   Proposals for publishing the magazine also appeared in *The Boston Gazette, and the Country Journal* (Sept. 15, Nov. 3, 10, 17, Dec. 22, 1788), and the monthly issues were advertised regularly in the newspaper.

[76] In his *The History of Printing*, Thomas wrote with justified pride of his paper, *The Massachusetts Spy*, but of *The Massachusetts Magazine* he made only a slight reference: "Among the books printed by the company in Boston, were, *The Massachusetts Magazine*, published monthly, in numbers, for five years, constituting five octavo volumes"—taking no cognizance of the three years it was published by others (I, 183).   Thaddeus M. Harris, pastor of a Unitarian Church at Dorchester and a contributor to the magazine, became editor in 1795, his name and connection appearing boldly on the title pages.   He was succeeded in June 1796 by William Bigelow, who had contributed over the pseudonym of "Charles Chatterbox" (Mott, *op. cit.*, pp. 110-11).

[77] Unpaged, following title page.   A further reference in the "Preface" mentions the editors' interest in original pieces and commends certain of the contributors: "*Originality* . . . has been their aim.   Many valuable writers . . . have appeared. . . . Such are the *Philanthropist, General Observer, Philo*, and the other periodical writers, &c. in prose; and *Constantia, Septimus, Euphelia, J. L.* &c. in the walks of Parnassus; whose future communications are earnestly requested."

everything else to informative articles, or *The American Museum* under Carey, which strove to preserve the best written thought of its age, or *The Columbian Magazine* under Trenchard, which printed a great deal of factual material and at the same time found space for a considerable body of original literary pieces. With all its pleas for contributions, *The. Massachusetts Magazine* still borrowed constantly from British publications. In general, the editors followed the policy Thomas had used while editing and publishing *The Royal American Magazine*; they appealed to a popular rather than a cultivated taste.

As a magazine conducted to appease the general reader, the periodical was about all one could hope to discover. It was not, nor did it make pretense of being, erudite; it refused to lend its pattern to satisfy some who wished more discussion on matters requiring a considerable background of knowledge. The editorial theory, unlike that which had governed most of the major magazines published in America, was to compile a periodical not only for those whose cultural advantages had been considerable, but for a proletarian class which, until now, had neither supported or found reason for supporting magazines. For it is to be remembered that, as a rule, the subscribers to early American magazines approached the status of patrons, and the contents of the periodicals were selected for their edification. *The Massachusetts Magazine* is the outstanding periodical of its time to appeal to a distinctly journalistic taste, and at the same time enjoy the support of cultured groups. Its engravings on copperplate and its sheets of music were emphasized as being costly features.[78] In sentimental stories

[78] Thomas made a point of advertising these features, often in detail. During 1789, for example, Nos. I-VII and X-XI were advertised in *The Massachusetts Centinel* in some detail in the issues of Jan. 31 and Feb. 7, March 7, April 1, May 13, June 6, July 1, Aug. 8, Sept. 2, Nov. 7, and Dec. 2. Two copperplate engravings were advertised for the May number, two pieces of music for the May and three pieces of music for the October numbers; one each sufficed the other issues. Certain of the illustrations were described, perhaps being considered of more popular interest than others: a "Happy Reconciliation" (Jan.), the Boston lighthouse (Feb.), northeast view of Faneuil Hall (March), death of Prince Leopold of Brunswick (April), north view of Castle William, and a mode of traveling in the East Indies (May), federal edifice in New York (June), head of Necker (Oct.), a view of the Bastile (Nov.). Other engravings for the first volume include a representation of "heaven born" Science (frontispiece for Vol. I), estate of John Hancock (July), south-west view of Baptist Meeting House, Providence (Aug.), Charles River Bridge (Sept.), Thisbe killing herself over the body of Pyramus (Dec.). Samuel Hill, later a pro-

it vied with *The Gentleman and Ladies Town and Country Magazine,* far exceeded the offerings of *The Columbian Magazine* and *The American Museum,* and satisfied popular demand. Thomas had early shown his faith in this kind of literary fare, filling *The Royal American Magazine* with it in 1774-75; and in the very year of the establishment of *The Massachusetts Magazine* he published *The Power of Sympathy,* thus testifying to his assurance that sentimentality in fiction would serve printers well. As Professor Herbert R. Brown has noted, "Of the eleven true, moral, and pathetic tales in the first volume of *The Massachusetts Magazine* in 1789 . . . nine are accounts of seductions and the resultant misery."[79] When villains did not march across the scene, sentiment and sensibility still controlled the mood of the stories, for when the tender feelings lacked the contrast of villainy, they were emphasized by emotional concerns in the manner made popular by Laurence Sterne, from whose letters to Eliza selections were indeed taken.[80]

---

prietor, signed his name as engraver of the plates for the issues of Jan.-April, June, July, Aug., Oct., Nov., Dec., and also the frontispiece, and possibly others.

The songs in the first volume include "The Pursuit," music by a student at Harvard College (Jan. pp. 59-61), "How Cold it Is" (Feb. 122-24), "Bright Dawns the Day," a hunting song, music by a student at Harvard College (March, pp. 188-89), "On Musick," music by William Selby (April pp. 252-53), "The Invitation," written by J. Lathrop, music by a student at Harvard College (May, pp. 323-24), and "Ode on Spring," written by Daniel George, music by Abraham Wood (May, pp. 325-26), "A Hunting Song," by Hans Gram (June, pp. 388-90), "Ode for American Independence," by Daniel George, music by Horatio Garnet (July, pp. 453-54), "Sally," music by S. Holyoke (Aug., pp. 523-26), "Marlborough's Ghost," music by E. Mann of Worcester and "The Pensive Shepherd," written by J. Lathrop, music by S. Holyoke (Sept., pp. 587-89), "The Rural Retreat," music by William Selby, "Ode to Columbia's Favourite Son," and "Ode to the President of the United States," by a lady, music by Hans Gram, organist of the Brattle Street Church (Oct., pp. 657-61), "Song" set to music by a gentleman of Worcester (Nov. 727-28), and "Andre's Ghost," music by E. Mann, of Worcester (Dec., p. 794).

[79] "Elements of Sensibility in the Massachusetts Magazine" (*American Literature,* Nov. 1929, p. 289). Professor Brown included the whole eight volumes within the range of his investigation, and notes that though certain of the essayists, such as "The Speculator" and "The Dreamer" mocked affectation with satire, or attacked it with sane reproach, the critics of the vogue "were always a small minority" (pp. 295-96).

[80] For correspondence between Sterne and Mrs. Draper (Yorick to Eliza and Eliza to Yorick), see issues for Jan.-May 1789, pp. 15, 95-99, 158-60, 208-11, 272-75. Among the stories of sentiment and sensibility printed in the first volume, the following are worthy of special mention: "Story of the Count de Saint Julien," from Keate's *Sketches from Nature* (April, May 1789, pp. 211-16, 267-70), "The Happy Pair: or Virtue and Constancy Rewarded" (May 1789, pp. 290-93), "Innocent Simplicity Betrayed" (Aug., Sept. 1789, pp. 470-73, 539-41), "Amelia: or, the Senti-

Not all the original and selected fare was sentimental. As a true miscellany, the magazine gratified other desires. It was fortunate in attracting a number of serial essayists whose work began in the first volume—several, in fact, writing for the first number. Their essays are not memorable, and are inclined to be merely platitudinous, but this fate has befallen many of the wisest remarks by reason of repetition. "The Dreamer," whose classical background was rather detrimental than helpful to his imagination, organized a club, received contributions occasionally, and wandered hither and thither in dream after dream from considerations on literature to discussions on love, whale bone corsets, and social foibles. "The Reformer" was seriously bent on inculcating the virtue of thrift, and though he considered all follies his legitimate prey, he most frequently wrote of his favorite theme. "The Philanthropist," who tried to keep his eyes on the world to observe how it might be made brighter, looked dutifully about, but saw nothing with a fresh spirit, and could only repeatedly urge the use of one's talents, the fair treatment of colonial possessions by mother nations, and surveillance of human stupidities, ignorance, and follies—all in a manner that had often been better done by others. "The Politician" aimed more definitely; he attacked the slow processes of justice, argued for the abolition of capital punishment, and outlined a plan of prison procedure based on the reform and redemption of criminals rather than on vengeance for antisocial conduct. "The General Observer," like "The Philanthropist," was a generalizing moralizer, but his manner was more engaging. "The Spectator," who likewise moralized despairingly of human follies, debauchees, and poverty, was occasionally fertile in thought, happily directing his attentions to definite points of issue. Both he and "Philo," who came late in the first volume, urged the expansion of feminine activities in the study of liberal arts. "The Babbler," also late in making his appearance, was not original in the magazine, his work having been printed first in Owen's *Weekly Chronicle*, of London.[81]

mental Fair" (Sept. 1789, pp. 579-80), "Amelia; or the Faithless Briton"—"An American Novel"—Oct.-Dec. 1789, pp. 649-51, 675-79 (misnumbered 645-49, 750-54), and "A Pathetick Morceau"—Nov. 1789, pp. 710-12. (misnumbered 680-82).

[81] For "The Dreamer," Nos. I-X, see issues for Jan.-Sept. Nov. 1789, pp. 32-36, 101-04, 152-55, 216-19, 296-300, 370-73, 439-41, 514-16, 534-36, 696-99 (misnumbered 666-68). For "The Reformer," Nos. I-VIII, see issues for Feb., March, May, June, Aug., Sept., Nov., Dec. 1789, pp. 79-80, 141-42, 304-06, 380-81, 508-11, 563-65, 670-72 (misnumbered 640-42), 784-85. For "The Philanthropist," Nos. I-XII, see issues for Jan.-Dec. 1789, pp. 10-11, 75-76, 137-41, 241-43, 294-96,

Some of the miscellaneous pieces, mostly reprints, lend weight to the magazine. Selections from the writings of Noah Webster, Benjamin Rush, Jedediah Morse, Benjamin Franklin, Hugh Williamson, Thomas Jefferson, and William Livingston, though occupying a minor place in the mass of material so far as bulk is concerned, give to the contents elements of enduring interest.[82]   A happily surprising feature is the inclusion through three numbers of William Dunlap's *The Father: or, American Shandyism*, which, having appeared on the stage in New York in September 1789, was begun in the October issue of the magazine.[83]   To the student of early American drama, who must content himself with small reward for his investigations among early magazines, the occasion is particularly bright.   Note also should be taken of two essays by "Socialis" during 1789; however lacking in distinction they may be, they bring to the magazine the name of Joseph Dennie, later a leading essayist.[84]

Finally, there was much original poetry in the magazine even as early as the first volume.   It was contributed by persons who, though lacking creative power and the higher associative qualities of the mind, at least brought to their tasks a cultural background and imitative ability.   In the first volume, translations and imitations of Horace are frequently printed.   Hymns, epitaphs, elegies, fairly elaborate odes, and pastorals are neatly turned.   An elegy by

337-38, 403-05, 476-80, 547-49, 609-10, 691-93 (misnumbered 661-63), 739-40.   For "The Politician," Nos. I-VI, see issues for July-Dec. 1789, pp. 430-32, 499-501, 557-59, 611-13, 700-01 (misnumbered 670-71), 765-67.   For "The General Observer," Nos. I-XI, see issues for Jan.-Sept., Nov., Dec. 1789, pp. 9-10, 73-75, 162-64, 243-46, 306-09, 420-22, 507-08, 576-77, 715-17 (misnumbered 685-87), 736-37.   For "The Speculator," Nos. I-III, see issues for Sept.-Nov. 1789, pp. 565-66, 618-19, 717-18 (misnumbered 687-88).   For "Philo," Nos. I-IV, see issues for Sept.-Dec. 1789, pp. 577-79, 647-48, 672-73 (misnumbered 642-43), 734-36.   For "The Babbler," Nos. I-II, see issues for Oct., Dec. 1789, pp. 613-15, 749-50.

[82] For Webster see "Webster's Criticisms upon Gibbon's History" (July, Aug. 1789, pp. 441-43, 475-76), and "On the Necessity, Advantages, and Practicability of Reforming the Mode of Spelling" (Oct.-Dec. 1789, pp. 605-08, 688-91 misnumbered 658-618, 743-46).   For Rush, see "A Moral and Physical Thermometer" (Feb. 1789, p. 88).   For Morse, see "Memoirs of the Marquis de la Fayette" (Sept. 1789, pp. 573-76).   For Franklin, see "The Way to Wealth" (Aug.-Sept. 1789, pp. 484-86, 545-47).   For Williamson, see "On the Study of Dead Languages" (Dec. 1789, pp. 746-49).   For Jefferson, see excerpts from *Notes on Virginia* (Sept. 1789, pp. 567-69), which dealt with the slave trade.   For Livingston, see "Thoughts on Deism" (Jan. 1789, pp. 25-27).   All are reprints.

[83] Oct.-Dec. 1789, pp. 620-29, 679-85 (misnumbered 649-55), 793.   The last carried the prologue and epilogue in the department of poetry.

[84] "On Friendship" (Sept. 1789, pp. 560-62) and "An Essay on Honour" (Dec. 1789, pp. 764-65).

Daniel George was commended by the editors; and an anecdote introduced an epitaph by Joseph Green. Thomson was awarded a "Panegyrick" in blank verse by a fond admirer. The effusions of the two "Constantias"—Mrs. Sarah Wentworth Morton and Mrs. Judith Murray, wife of John Murray, Universalist divine—were highly praised. Hopkinson and Johnson were represented by selections. Music sheets added to the offerings. One notes in this department—the "Seat of the Muses"—careful workmanship, a fairly wide local interest in verse writing, and the following of traditional patterns.[85] As the volumes progressed, the poetry as well as the essays came to be rather more distinguished, and *The Massachusetts Magazine* must be accorded a place as a peer among the major periodicals of the last decade of the century.

---

[85] For Horatian odes, see issues for Feb., March, May, Sept., Oct., Dec. 1789, pp. 117, 184, 319-20, 585, 656, 792. The translations and imitations are respectively from Book I, Odes I, XII; Book III, Ode I; Book I, Odes XIII, XXIX, XV. The first is by John Adams, A.M., a book of whose poetry, published in Boston in 1745, was elaborately reviewed by "A." in 1789 in an article in the magazine entitled, "Remarks on the Poetical Character of the Rev. John Adams" (April 1789, pp. 232-35). These exercises from the Latin continued to be popular in succeeding volumes, the very first number of the second volume printing a translation of Book IV, Ode II (p. 59), by "J.L.," of Cambridge, who had previously contributed "On Christmas," containing a Vergilian reference (Dec. 1789, pp. 790-91). In the classical tradition, too, is "Ovid's Tristia," Book III, Elegy XII (April 1789, pp. 249-50). The influence of college halls hangs also over an untitled poem in heroic couplets by B. Whitwell, spoken before the overseers of Harvard in 1789 (Nov. 1789, pp. 724-25). For the "Panegyrick on Thomson" and the selections from Joseph Green and Daniel George, see respectively issues for Feb., Sept., and Oct. 1789, pp. 118, 585, 654. An editorial note in "To Correspondents," in the issue for October, requests a Thanksgiving ode from the pen of George, indicating the esteem in which he was held. The poems by Sarah Wentworth Morton ("Constantia") in the first volume include "Invocation to Hope" (July 1789, p. 449), which was highly praised by the editors in "To Correspondents" (p. 468) in the issue for the month following, and "Philander, A Pastoral Elegy," written in May (Sept., 1789, p. 583), which the editors in the same issue ("To Correspondents," p. 532) termed "truly sublime." In 1790 Mrs. Judith Sargent Murray claimed the pseudonym "Constantia" by right of prior use, and the next several poems by Mrs. Morton were designated as by "Constantia*," while Mrs. Murray's work appeared over the same pseudonym without the asterisk. See Vena B. Field, *op. cit.*, pp. 24-25. Excerpts from "Mr. Hopkinson's Songs" (No. VIII) and from Johnson's *The Vanity of Human Wishes* printed in issues for March and Jan. 1789 respectively, pp. 186, 58. It seems to me that "A Pastoral," in dialogue, by "Fidelio" (Aug. 1789, pp. 519-20) and "Ode upon the Arrival of the President of the United States," with recitatives, airs, and a grand chorus, by "G.R.," of Boston (Oct. 1789, pp. 653-54) are deserving of specific mention. The longest poem in the first volume is "Extracts from the Zenith of Glory; a Manuscript Ode" (June, Aug., Oct., Dec. 1789, pp. 384-85, 519, 655-56, 789-90), written in octosyllabics riming *aabccb*, which treats of various phases of the Revolutionary War.

BIBLIOGRAPHY OF AMERICAN MAGAZINES 1741-1789

The following descriptive bibliography is presented as being more nearly complete in detail than any other for the period. It was gathered while I was inspecting files in many libraries in order that I might see every issue of every magazine, and discover whatever annotated copies might be available. It has been checked with such well-known bibliographies as Paul Leicester Ford's *Check-List of American Magazines Printed in the Eighteenth Century* (1889), Charles Evans's *American Bibliography*, Vols. II-VII, William Beer's *Checklist of American Periodicals* 1741-1800 (1923), the *Union List of Serials in Libraries of the United States and Canada* (1927), and on occasion Clarence S. Brigham's *Bibliography of American Newspapers 1690-1820*, printed in *Proceedings of the American Antiquarian Society* beginning with Vol. XXIII, Part 2, 1913, and Joseph Sabin's *Dictionary of Books Relating to America* (1867-). I have added considerable descriptive comment not in these bibliographies, and in some cases I have corrected errors. It is impossible, I believe, to discover "complete" files in the sense that the blue covers have been preserved, and only in the rarest cases are all the copperplate illustrations intact, or all the supplementary items, such as gazetteers, present with the magazine. I have used the word "complete" to indicate files otherwise apparently perfect.

In order to present in one place all available bibliographical detail on American magazines from 1741 through 1789, I have appended, following my own descriptive material, a summary of other facts as given in the *Union List of Serials*, and occasionally by Beer.

In the "Preface" to this work appear a short discussion of resources in libraries and comment explaining the reasons for including several titles which do not come within a rigid definition of the word "magazine."

The several libraries are designated by the following abbreviations: AAS—American Antiquarian Society, Worcester, Mass.; AAAS—American Academy of Arts and Sciences, Boston, Mass.; ABHS—American Baptist Historical Society, Chester, Pa.; AMNH—American Museum of Natural History, New York, N. Y.; ANS—Academy of Natural Sciences of Philadelphia, Philadelphia, Pa.; APS—American Philosophical Society, Philadelphia, Pa.; BA—Boston Athenæum, Boston, Mass.; BC—Bowdoin College, Brunswick, Me.; BCL—Congregational Library, Boston, Mass.; BHC—Burton Historical Collection, Detroit Public Library, Detroit, Mich.; BPL—Public Library of the City of Boston, Boston, Mass.; BroU—Brown University, Providence, R. I.; BrPL—Brooklyn Public Library, Brooklyn, N. Y.; CarLP—Carnegie Library of Pittsburgh, Pittsburgh, Pa.; CaSL—California State Library, Sacramento, Cal.; CHS—Connecticut Historical Society Library, Hartford, Conn.; ChU—University of Chicago, Chicago, Ill.; CoU—Cornell University, Ithaca, N. Y.; CPL—Cleveland Public

Library, Cleveland, O.; CSL—Connecticut State Library, Hartford, Conn.; CU—Columbia University, New York, N. Y.; CUA—Catholic University of America, Washington, D. C.; DC—Dartmouth College, Hanover, N. H.; DPL—Detroit Public Library, Detroit, Mich.; EPFL—Enoch Pratt Free Library, Baltimore, Md.; FLN—Forbes Library, Northampton, Mass.; GrosB—Grosvenor Library, Buffalo, N. Y.; GTS—General Theological Seminary, New York, N. Y.; GU—Georgetown University, Washington, D. C.; HCC—Hamilton College, Clinton, N. Y.; HSP—Historical Society of Pennsylvania, Philadelphia, Pa.; HU—Harvard College, Cambridge, Mass.; ISHS—Iowa State Historical Society, Iowa City, Ia.; ISL—Iowa State Library, Des Moines, Ia.; ISU—University of Iowa, Iowa City, Ia.; JCB—John Carter Brown Library, Providence, R. I.; JCL—John Crerar Library, Chicago, Ill.; KSAC—Kansas State Agricultural College, Manhattan, Kan.; LC—Library of Congress, Washington, D. C.; LCP—Library Company of Philadelphia, Pa.; MHS—Massachusetts Historical Society Library, Boston, Mass.; MiHS—Minnesota Historical Society, St. Paul, Minn.; MSL—State Library of Massachusetts, Boston, Mass.; MU—University of Minnesota, Minneapolis, Minn.; NewPL—Newark, N. J.; NJHS—New Jersey Historical Society, Newark, N. J.; NL—Newberry Library, Chicago, Ill.; NYAM—New York Academy of Medicine, New York, N. Y.; NYHS—New York Historical Society, New York, N. Y.; NYPL—New York Public Library, New York, N. Y.; NYSL—New York Society Library, New York, N. Y.; NYStL—New York State Library, Albany, N. Y.; OC—Oberlin College, Oberlin, O.; PeaI—Peabody Institute Library, Baltimore, Md.; PFL—The Free Library of Philadelphia, Philadelphia, Pa.; PrPL—Providence Public Library, Providence, R. I.; PU—Princeton University, Princeton, N. J.; SL—Gardner A. Sage Library, New Brunswick, N. J.; StanU—Stanford University, Stanford University, Cal.; StLP—Saint Louis Public Library, St. Louis, Mo.; SyU—Syracuse University, Syracuse, N. Y.; TCH—Trinity College, Hartford, Conn.; TxU—University of Texas, Austin, Tex.; UCal—University of California, Berkeley, Cal.; UI—University of Illinois, Urbana, Ill.; UM—University of Michigan, Ann Arbor, Mich.; UMis—University of Missouri, Columbia, Mo.; UNC—University of North Carolina, Chapel Hill, N. C.; UND—University of Notre Dame, Notre Dame, Ind.; UNeb—University of Nebraska, Lincoln, Neb.; UP—University of Pennsylvania, Philadelphia, Pa.; UTS—Union Theological Seminary, New York City; UW—University of Washington, Seattle, Wash.; VC—Vassar College, Poughkeepsie, N. Y.; VSL—Virginia State Library, Richmond, Va.; WRHS—Western Reserve Historical Society, Cleveland, O.; WSHS—State Historical Society of Wisconsin, Madison, Wis.; WU—Wesleyan University, Middletown, Conn.; YU—Yale University, New Haven, Conn.

1. *The American Magazine, or a Monthly View of the Political State of the British Colonies.* Philadelphia. Andrew Bradford, publisher; John Webbe, editor. Jan.-March, 1741, Nos. 1-3. Monthly, 8vo. Pp. I-VIII, 1-120 plus—no complete copy of No. 3 has been located. Listed: Ford, Beer, Evans, *Union List of Serials.* NYHS has a complete file of

numbers, lacking only pages beyond 118; JCB has a perfect copy of No. I, pp. (2), I-VIII, 1-34; LC has issue for March 1741, pp. 81-120.

2. *The General Magazine, and Historical Chronicle, for All the British Plantations in America.* Philadelphia. Printed and sold by Benjamin Franklin. Jan.-June 1741, Nos. 1-6. Monthly, 12mo. Pp. (2), 1-426. Listed: Ford, Beer, Evans, *Union List of Serials.* NYPL has a nearly complete file lacking only pp. 73-76; LCP (Ridgway Branch) a copy of the six issues, lacking pp. 29-32, 61-76, 88-124, 145-158, 171-182, 207-216; HSP has Jan., pp. 1-76; Feb., pp. 77-146; March, pp. 147-216; 159-194; May, pp. 287-354; June, pp. 393-404; YU lacks May; LC has issues for Jan.-March, May; the AAS file of issues for Jan.-March, May is broken; UP has April only. Other files listed: *Union List of Serials*; BPL (1); HU 1.

3. *The Boston Weekly Magazine.* Boston. John Rogers and Daniel Fowles, publishers. March 2, 9, 16, 1743; no other numbers have been found, and probably no others were printed. 8vo. Pp. 1-24. Listed: Ford, Beer, Evans, *Union List of Serials.* MHS possesses the only numbers known.

4. *The Christian History, Containing Accounts of the Revival and Propagation of Religion in Great-Britain & America.* Boston. Printed by Samuel Kneeland and Timothy Green, for Thomas Prince, A.B., editor. March 5, 1743-Feb. 23, 1745, Nos. 1-104. Weekly, 8vo. Vol. 1, pp. (2), VI, 416; Vol. 2, pp. (2), VI, (2), 416. Listed: Ford, Beer, Evans, *Union List of Serials.* AAS, BA, BPL, HU, LC, MHS, NYPL, and YU have complete files, NYPL copy being annotated by Thomas Prince, Sr.; the PU file is complete save for a defective final number; JCB has Vol. I, pp. 5-128, 161-308. Other files listed: *Union List of Serials*—CUA, NYStL, UTS, CSL, 1, CU 1-52, DC 1-52, DPL 1-52, NL 1-52, UI 1-52.

5. *The American Magazine and Historical Chronicle; for All the British Plantations.* Boston. John Rogers and Daniel Fowle, publishers. (In the earlier numbers Samuel Eliot and Joshua Blanchard were also interested as publishers.) Sept. 1743-Dec. 1746. Monthly, 8vo. Vol. 1, Sept. 1743 to Dec. 1744, pp. (4), IV, 704, (8); Vol. 2, Jan. to Dec. 1745, (4), 4, 566, (6), Vol. 3, Jan. to Dec. 1746, pp. (4), 579, (5). Listed: Ford, Beer, Evans, *Union List of Serials.* AAS, HU, MHS, and YU files are complete and the NYPL file is nearly so, lacking only Sept. 1743, Sept.-Oct. 1744, and scattered pages. BA and NYHS lack a few scattered pages only. BPL has Vol. 1 complete, and two copies each (incomplete) of Vols. II and III. The LC file is complete except for scattered pages. Other files listed: Union List of Serials—AAAS, BCL (3), BHC (1-3), CU (1-2), ISL (1746), NYStL (1)-3, UI (1743-44), WSHS (1, 3).

6. *The Independent Reflector: or, Weekly Essays on Sundry Important Subjects.* New York. "Printed (until tyrannically suppressed) in 1753." The quotations are from the volume edition. William Livingston, editor; James Parker, printer. Isaiah Thomas, in *The History of Printing in America* (1810), second ed., 1874, II, p. 125, records that Parker refused to print a supplement vindicating the work, whereupon DeForeest, a rival publisher, issued the defense. The volume was issued with a long prefa-

tory chapter outlining the history of the dispute from one point of view. The separate issues of *The Independent Reflector* bear the imprint of James Parker. Nov. 30, 1752-Nov. 22, 1753. Weekly, 4to. Nos. 1-52. Pp. (4), 31 (preface), 212. Listed: Ford, Beer, Evans, *Union List of Serials*. AAS, JCB, NYHS, NYPL, PU, and LC have complete bound volumes; CU lacks pp. 179-80; WRHS lacks preface; BA lacks No. I; YU lacks Nos. 25, 37; the NJHS has a fairly complete file. Other files listed: *Union List of Serials*—NYStL, UM, WSHS, BPL 7-25, 30-32. At the back of one of the files at the LC is "An Address to his Excellency Sir Charles Hardy, Knt. . . . By the Author of a Weekly Paper entitled, The Watch-Tower." This "address" is ascribed in pencil to William Livingston, and the same hand noted Hugh Gaine as the printer.

7. *The Occasional Reverberator*. New York. J. Parker, printer. Sept. 7-Oct. 5, 1753, Nos. 1-4. Weekly, fol. Pp. 1-16. Listed: Ford, Brigham, "Bibliography of American Newspapers, 1690-1820," *Proceedings of the American Antiquarian Society*, new series, Part 2, XXVII, 472; Beer, Evans. No. 2 was issued Sept. 14; No. 3, Sept. 21. JCB, LC, NYPL, PU and NYHS have complete files; C. S. Brigham, Director of the American Antiquarian Society, has informed me that there is a complete file likewise at SL, while AAS lacks issue of Oct. 5; BA lacks Nos. 3-4. Other file listed: *Union List of Serials*—WSHS.

8. *John Englishman*. New York. James Parker and William Weyman, publishers. April 9-July 5, 1755. Nos. 1-10, fol. Pp. 1-26. First issue entitled *John Englishman's True Notion of Sister-Churches*; other issues entitled *John Englishman, in Defence of the English Constitution*. Issues dated respectively April 9, 18, 25, May 2, 16, 30, June 7, 14, 21, July 5. Listed: Brigham, XXVII, new series, Part 2, p. 445; Beer, *Union List of Serials*. NYPL lacks only No. 9, but has a photostat of this number. YU lacks Nos. 1-3. LC lacks Nos. 1, 7, 10.

9. *The Instructor*. New York. James Parker and William Weyman, editors and publishers. March 6-May 8, 1755. Weekly, 21cm. Nos. 1-10. Pp. 1-40. Listed: Brigham, XXVII, new series, Part 2, p. 444, Evans, Ford, Beer, *Union List of Serials*. LC has the only known copies.

10. *The American Magazine, or Monthly Chronicle for the British Colonies*, Philadelphia. William Bradford, publisher; edited "By a Society of Gentlemen," of whom the Reverend William Smith of Philadelphia was the chief. Oct. 1757-Oct. 1758. Monthly, 8vo. One volume, with "Supplement," pp. (2), 656, (6). After the first number the title was slightly altered to *The American Magazine and Monthly Chronicle for the British Colonies*. Listed: Ford, Beer, Evans, *Union List of Serials*. Complete files are preserved at BPL, HSP, HU, JCB, LC, LCP, NYHS, NYPL, and UP. LC file is slightly annotated; BPL file contains the first seven numbers of Smith's private copy, wherein he annotated "The Hermit" essay series copiously; NYPL has three complete files, and LCP one complete and two incomplete files. AAS lacks Oct. 1757, Jan., March, May, July, Oct. 1758. Other files listed: *Union List of Serials*—APS 4, BHC 2, 11, NYStL 2, 4-7, WSHS 1-11.

11. *The New American Magazine*. Woodbridge, N. J. James Parker,

publisher; Samuel Nevill, editor. Jan. 1758-March 1760. Monthly 8vo. To the magazine proper were added *The Traveller*, by Thomas Gage, separately paged, 1-136, Jan. 1758 through May 1759, and *The History of the Continent of America*, edited by Samuel Nevill, also separately paged, 1-284, Jan. 1758 through March 1760. The magazine proper was continuously paged from Jan. 1758 through Dec. 1759, 1-764, and from Jan. 1760 through March of the same year, 1-120. To these pages must be added two unnumbered pages of "Naval Engagements" running regularly, each month excepting Dec. 1758, when an announcement, "The Author to the Publick" was substituted, and March 1760, when four pages were run. A title page, backed by a table of contents, also unnumbered, was likewise run each month. Listed: Ford, Beer, Evans, *Union List of Serials*. LCP and PU possess complete files; NYPL owns several bound volumes from which a file lacking only Feb. 1759 and other occasional scattered pages may be attained; HSP file is nearly complete, lacking only a few scattered pages. BPL has Jan. 1758 through May 1759, but lacks *The Traveller* and *The History*. MHS lacks Jan. 1758-Feb. 1759 and Dec. 1759; AAS has only March, May, June 1758 and Dec. 1759. LC has issues for Feb.-April, July, Sept., Oct., Nov. 1788, very broken. NJHS owns Jan., March, June, Oct., Nov. 1759, and Feb. 1760. Other files listed: *Union List of Serials*—CU 1758, UP 1 (an error, possessing none).

12. *The New-England Magazine for August 1758*. Boston. Printed and sold by Benjamin Mecom. The title given is the title of the first number. The remaining two numbers bore the title of *The New-England Magazine of Knowledge and Pleasure*. No. 1 was advertised in *The Boston Weekly News-Letter* of Aug. 31, 1758; No. 2 was advertised in the same paper of Oct. 26, 1758; and No. 3 was advertised in *The Boston Gazette* of March 12, 1759. No issue beyond the third is known. Monthly, 12mo. Each number is paged separately, and contains 60 pages. Listed: Ford, Beer, Evans, *Union List of Serials*. The MHS has No. 1 incomplete and No. 3 complete; BPL has Nos. 1 and 2, the latter lacking pp. 33-36; the AAS has No. 3; the LC lacks No. 1.

13. *The North-Carolina Magazine; or, Universal Intelligencer*. New Bern. James Davis, editor and publisher. Weekly, 4to. June 1-8, 1764—(1765?). Listed: Evans. The LC has Vol. I, Nos. 4-18, 20-27, 29, 30 (the last concluding the volume), and Vol. II, Nos. 31-33. The numbers varied from eight and six to four pages an issue.

14. *Ein geistliches Magazien, oder: aus den Schätzen der Schrifftgelehrten zum Himelreich gelehrt, dargereichtes Altes und Neues*. Germantown, Pa. Christopher Saur, editor and publisher. 1764, 1770-72? Vol. I, Nos. 1-50, with index, pp. (6), 406, (8); Vol. II, No. 15 runs to page 160. Vol. I is dated 1764, and as it was complete in 50 numbers, was probably issued weekly, the usual issue containing eight pages. Vol. II, No. 1 is dated 1770 (Lawrence C. Wroth, then Librarian of the Enoch Pratt Free Library, to Clarence S. Brigham, then Librarian of the American Antiquarian Society, in letter dated April 13, 1922). Vol. II, No. 10 is dated 1771 and No. 12 carries the announcement, "Gedruckt mit der

ersten Schrift die jemals in America gegossen worden." William McCulloch, in letters to Isaiah Thomas (*Proceedings of the American Antiquarian Society*, April 1921, pp. 150, 180, 182), notes a No. 12 printed in 1772 which, from his description, corresponds with No. 12 of Vol. II. Listed: Beer, Evans, *Union List of Serials*. HSP possesses Vol. I complete; LC lacks only No. 34 of Vol. I; AAS lacks of Vol. I part of No. 1, and Nos. 13, 16, 34, 41, 44-46, but has Vol. II, Nos. 2-8, 10, 15.

15. *The Penny Post, Containing Fresh News, Advertisements, Useful Hints, &c.* Philadelphia. Benjamin Mecom, editor and publisher. Only nine numbers are known to exist—Jan. 9-27, 1769. Published on Mondays, Wednesdays, Fridays, four pages an issue, each page as small as the usual magazine. Listed: Evans, Brigham, XXXII, new series, Part I, p. 185. LCP possesses the only known original copies.

16. *The American Magazine, or General Repository.* Philadelphia. William and Thomas Bradford, publishers; Lewis Nicola, editor. Jan.-Sept., 1769. Nos. 1-9. Pp. II, 328 plus engravings; to which were subjoined to all issues except the first, *The Transactions of the American Philosophical Society*, sixteen pages an issue, separately paged 1-118. Charles S. R. Hildeburn, *A Century of Printing. The Issues of the Press of Pennsylvania, 1685-1784* (1885-86), II, 86, has noted that p. 38 is followed by p. 44, and p. 67 by p. 69. Isaiah Thomas, *The History of Printing in America*, II, 150, in *Transactions and Collections of the American Antiquarian Society*, Vols. V, VI, (1874), is inaccurate in his reference to the magazine. Monthly, 8vo. Listed: Ford, Beer, Evans, *Union List of Serials*. HSP and LCP have complete files of the magazine proper, the latter possessing also the *Transactions*; NYPL lacks May, and also the *Transactions* pp. 65-80; AAS has issues of June, July, and Sept.; BPL has issues of Jan., Feb., and May. Other files listed: *Union List of Serials*—UM, NYStL 2, 5, 7.

17. *The Royal Spiritual Magazine; or, the Christian's Grand Treasure.* Philadelphia. "By several Divines." Printed by Joseph Crukshank for John M'Gibbons. Jan.-Dec. 1771. Pp. I-VI, 7-72 plus. Listed: Ford, Beer, Evans, *Union List of Serials*. AAS has 72 pages; HSP and LC have the first 24 pages each. Preserved copies carry a volume number (I), but no issue number; however, "Dialogue II" begins on page 37.

18. *The Censor.* Boston. Ezekiel Russell, publisher. Nov. 23, 1771-May 2, 1772. Vol. I, Nos. 1-17 and "Postscript"; Vol. II, Nos. 1-7; continuously paged through both volumes, pp. 1-98. Postscripts were added to Vol. I, Nos. 5, 15, 17, and Vol. II, Nos. 4, 6, 7. Listed: Ford, Beer, Evans, *Union List of Serials*. BPL has a complete file; MHS lacks Vol. II, No. 6, but has postscript for the number; BA has issues from the first number to April 11, 1772, and LC from the first number to Feb. 22, 1772; AAS lacks Vol. II, Nos. 2, 4-7 and some postscripts.

19. *The Royal American Magazine, or Universal Repository of Instruction and Amusement.* Boston. Jan. 1774-March 1775. Monthly, 8 vo. Isaiah Thomas, editor and publisher through June 1774; Joseph Greenleaf, editor and publisher thereafter. Vol. I, pp. 1-480 plus index of 7 pages and 19 full-page engravings; Vol. II, pp. 1-120 plus three full-page engravings.

To the magazine was appended *The History of the Colony of Massachu-setts-Bay,* by Thomas Hutchinson, pp. 1-152, which ran in short install-ments through each monthly issue and comprised also the "Supplement" to the first volume, being incomplete at the termination of the magazine. Listed: Ford, Beer, Evans, *Union List of Serials.* AAS, BA, and LC files are complete; NYPL has one complete file (Spencer Collection) and one file lacking Jan.-March 1775, and some engravings; YU file includes all engravings and lacks only a few scattered pages; BPL file is com-plete except for two engravings; MHS lacks March 1775, and some en-gravings; JCB has April-Nov. 1774, the issue for Aug. incomplete; HU has Jan., April, Oct. 1774, and Feb. 1775 and NYHS Sept. 1774. Other files listed: *Union List of Serials*—NYStL, BHC (1-2), CaSL (2), DC (1-2), WSHS 1 (2), MSL 1. The cover for July 1774 bore an illustration of a lion and a unicorn as a decorative design, but by Jan. 1775 a device representing a state of peace between Indians and the whites had been substituted. The announcement of agents for the magazine printed in the first number shows liberal representation in New England but little strength elsewhere, New York, Pennsylvania, Maryland and South Carolina being the only Colonies outside New England to be included.

20. *The Pennsylvania Magazine; or, American Monthly Museum.* Philadelphia. Jan. 1775-July 1776. Robert Aitken, publisher; Thomas Paine was probably editor, shortly after the magazine was begun. Monthly, 8vo. Vol. I, Jan.-Dec. 1775, with "Supplement," pp. 1-625 plus 5 pages of index and 15 full page engravings; Vol. II, Jan.-July 1776, pp. (5), 344 plus 5 full page engravings. Listed: Ford, Beer, Evans, *Union List of Serials;* see also *A Century of Printing. Issues of the Press of Pennsylvania 1685-1784,* by Charles Hildeburn, II, 229, 263, and *A Dic-tionary of Books Relating to America from its Discovery to the Present Time,* by Joseph Sabin, XIV, 394. LC has two complete and two incom-plete sets, as well as odd numbers, one of the sets containing the annota-tions of Moncure Conway relative to Paine's writing; HSP, JCB, LCP, MHS, NYHS, NYPL, and YU sets are complete; HU lacks only pp. 1-16 of second volume; AAS lacks Feb. and July 1776, but has both the editions of Jan. 1775. PU has Matthew Wilson's marked file, Oct. 1775-July 1776; BA has Jan.-Dec. 1775. Other files listed: *Union List of Serials*—APS, NYStL, UM, ANS (1775), BHC (1-2), BPL (1) BrPL 1, GrosB 1, WSHS 1 (2). The circulation, though concentrated in the Middle Colo-nies, seems to have been fairly widely scattered; an advertisement in *The Pennsylvania Packet* lists agents in the following towns: Charleston, Williamsburgh, Annapolis, Baltimore, Newtown, Chester, Wilmington, New Castle, Trenton, Princeton, Norfolk, Talbot Court House, Carlisle, Burlington, New York, New Haven, Boston, Salem, Portsmouth, Phila-delphia.

21. *The United States Magazine: a Repository of History, Politics and Literature.* Philadelphia. Jan.-Dec. 1779, Francis Bailey, publisher; Hugh Henry Brackenridge, editor. Monthly, 8vo. Pp. 1-504 plus 2 pages of index. Listed: Ford, Beer, Evans, *Union List of Serials;* see also Charles F. Heartman, *A Bibliography of the Writings of Hugh Henry*

Brackenridge Prior to 1825 (1917), p. 17. AAS, HSP, HU, LC, LCP, NYPL (excepting scattered pages) have complete files; LC owns Brackenridge's annotated file, and NYPL a file to which is attached a letter by Mrs. Sarah Bache; NYHS has Feb.-Sept. 1779; MHS has June 1779 only. Other files listed: Beer—WSHS; *Union List of Serials*—MiHS (1), NYStL (1).

22. *The Boston Magazine.* Boston. Oct. 1783-Dec. 1786. John Norman and Joseph White, publishers, Oct. 1783-Jan. 1784; Norman, White, and Edmund Freeman, publishers, Feb.-June 1784; Thomas Greenleaf and Freeman, publishers, July 1784-Aug. 1785; Freeman, publisher, Sept. 1785-Dec. 1786. From Nov. 1783 through Dec. 1784 an editorial board not connected with the publishers edited the magazine; all other issues were edited by the publishers. Monthly (excepting last two issues, which appeared bi-monthly), 8vo. Oct. 1783, pp. IV, 40 plus two engravings and one song. Nov. 1783-Dec. 1784, pp. IV, 630 plus 5 pp. index, 27 engravings, and sections of a *Geographical Gazetteer of the Towns in the Commonwealth of Massachusetts*, likewise embellished by an engraving; this *Gazetteer* was continued as a feature extraneous to the magazine proper, and ran through 96 pages. Jan.-Dec. 1785, pp. 480. Jan.-Dec. 1786, pp. 451. Listed: Ford, Beer, Evans, *Union List of Serials*. BPL and LC have complete files; the excellent YU file lacks issue of Nov.-Dec. 1786 and frontispiece for Oct. 1783; HU lacks Oct. 1783 and odd pages of some other numbers; AAS lacks Aug. 1785, Jan., Nov.-Dec. 1786, and odd pages elsewhere; MHS has Nov. 1783-Dec. 1784, annotated by James Freeman, and the manuscript record of the meetings of the editorial board during this period, and a second file containing issues for Jan., April, May, Nov. 1784, April 1785, and April, Aug.-Oct. 1786; NYPL lacks part of Oct. 1783, Feb., Sept. 1785, and Feb., April 1786; NYSL has two Vols. running through Dec. 1783-Aug. 1785, but lacks a number of pages within this range, especially in Nov. 1784; CU possesses Jan.-March, May, Aug., Nov., Dec. 1785. BA lacks Sept. 1783-April 1784 and scattered pages. Other files listed: *Union List of Serials*—CUA, BC (1784-85), BCL (1783, 86), BHC (1783-1785-86), BroU 3, ChU 1783-84, CoU (1785), GTS 1786, ISL 3, MU 1-2, WSHS 1-(2).

23. *The Gentleman and Lady's Town and Country Magazine; or Repository of Instruction and Entertainment.* Boston. May-Dec. 1784. Job Weedon and William Barrett, publishers and editors, May-Nov. 1784; Barrett, publisher and editor, Dec. 1784. Monthly, 8 vo., forty pages an issue. Pp. 360 and one engraving. Listed: Ford, Beer, Evans, *Union List of Serials*. AAS file is complete; MHS lacks a few scattered pages; LC lacks Dec. 1784; BPL lacks Sept., Nov., Dec.

24. *The American Monitor: or, the Republican Magazine, for October, 1785.* Boston. Ezekiel Russell, editor and publisher. Listed: Beer, Evans, *Union List of Serials*. 8vo. The only issue known to have been printed is at AAS, Beer's listing of NYPL being unfounded.

25. *The New-Haven Gazette, and the Connecticut Magazine.* New Haven. Published by Josiah Meigs and Eleutheros Dana, Dana withdrawing with the issue of Aug. 2, 1787. Feb. 16, 1786-Jan. 1, 1789. Weekly, 8vo., eight pages weekly. Vol. 1 (Feb. 16, 1786-Feb. 15, 1787), pp. 1-399

plus index of five pages exclusive of advertising supplements; Vol. 2 (Feb. 22, 1787-Dec. 27, 1787), pp. 1-358 plus index of two pages; Vol. 3 (Jan. 10, 1788-Jan. 1, 1789), pp. 1-398 plus index of four pages. Listed: Brigham, Beer, Evans. CHS file is complete, and contains two signatory marks by Noah Webster; excellent Yale file is complete except for mutilations of Nos. 23 (Vol. I), 18, 22 (Vol. II), 20, 27 (Vol. III); NYSL has a file from Oct. 5, 1786 through Dec. 27, 1787, presented by N. Meigs, son of the chief publisher, who called attention in an accompanying letter to the "strong abolition articles" in some of the numbers; NYHS has Vols. I and II, and most of the latter part of Vol. III; NYPL has all of Vol. I, Vol. II excepting Nos. 25, 30, 31, 33, and scattered numbers of Vol. III; AAS lacks Vol. III, Nos. 5, 9, 13, 16, 50-52; LC has Vols. I and II complete; MHS lacks Aug. 24, 1786, nearly all of 1787, and scattered numbers of 1788.

26. *The Worcester Magazine . . . Containing Politicks, Miscellanies, Poetry, and News.* Worcester, Mass. Edited and published by Isaiah Thomas from April 1786 to April 1788, during the period of suspension of *The Massachusetts Spy.* Weekly, 8vo., in numbers of twelve to fourteen pages. Vol. I (April 1786-Sept. 1786), pp. 1-314; Vol. II (Oct. 1786-March 1787), pp. 315-652; Vol. III (April 1787-Sept. 1787), pp. 1-352; Vol. IV (Oct. 1787-March 1788), pp. 1-342. Listed: Ford, Brigham, Beer, Evans, *Union List of Serials.* AAS, BA, MHS, and YU have complete files in good condition; NYSL and CHS likewise have good files, the former running from April 1786 through March 1788; BPL lacks fourth week in Aug. through second week in Oct. 1786 and scattered pages; NYPL, HU, and CSL have only a few numbers. Other files listed: *Union List of Serials*—HSP reprint, AAAS 2-4, BC (1786), BHC (2), CUA (3-4), ISL 3-4, LC (1-2)-4, MSL (2), NYStL (3-4), WSHS (1-2)-(4).

27. *The American Musical Magazine. Published in Monthly Numbers; Intended to Contain, a Great Variety of Approved Music; Carefully Selected from the Works of the Best American and Foreign Masters.* New Haven. Published and sold by Amos Doolittle and Daniel Read. Twelve undated numbers were issued during the probable span of time from May 1786 to Sept. 1787. One volume, 50 pp., including title sheet and index. Listed: Beer, Evans, *Union List of Serials.* YU has a complete file in a single binding. Other files listed: *Union List of Serials*—NL, NYPL (1)—an error, possessing none.

28. *The Columbian Magazine; or, a Monthly Miscellany.* Sept. 1786-Feb. 1790. Vols. I-IV. Monthly, 8 vo. In March 1790 the title became *The Universal Asylum, and Columbian Magazine* and continued thus through Dec. 1792, when it ceased publication simultaneously with its competitor, *The American Museum,* and the titles of both magazines were preserved in *The Columbian Museum; or, Universal Asylum,* Jan.-June 1793. From September 1786 through March 1787 the publishers were Thomas Seddon, William Spotswood, Cha·les Cist, James Trenchard, and Mathew Carey, the last named being the printer. Carey withdrew in March 1787 and the remaining four members continued as publishers until Jan. 1789, when only the name of Trenchard appears in the

imprint. From May 1789 through June of the same year Trenchard and Stewart appear as publishers; Trenchard then again carried on alone to Dec. 1789, when the magazine was "Printed for the Proprietors, by W. Spotswood" until March 1790, when William Young was made the printer and continued through Dec. 1792. *The Columbian Museum; or, Universal Asylum,* running from Jan. through June 1793, was published by John Parker, and is listed in the *Union List of Serials* in the NYPL, which has Jan. only. Listed: Ford, Beer, Evans, *Union List of Serials.* AAS has a practically complete set during the years 1786-92, lacking only some illustrations and covers; BPL, HSP, LC, LCP, and NYHS also have nearly complete sets for the same years; BA file is complete save for 1787, pp. 565-68, 719-26, 789-90; JCB has 1786-89, March-July, Sept.-Dec. 1790, 1791, Jan. 1792 complete except for occasional meteorological observations; NYPL file for 1786-93 is complete save for the months of March 1789, Jan., Feb., April-June 1790, May, July, Aug. and Dec. 1791, Nov. 1792, Feb.-May 1793; NYSL has Sept. 1786-Dec. 1789, Vols. I-III, the first incomplete; PU has Sept. 1786-Dec. 1788; YU lacks Jan.-Feb., July-Dec. 1790 and scattered pages; BA file is complete through 1791 save for scattered pages. Other files listed from Sept. 1786 through Dec. 1792: *Union List of Serials*—APS, BC, NL, NYStL, WSHS, ABHS (1790), BroU (1)-9, ChU (1791-92), CUA 3, DC (1791), GrosB (2), HU 1-(7)-9, JCL (1), MHS (1792), NYAM (1), PFL 4-5, StLP 1790-92, TxU (2)-8, UI 3, UM 1-6, UNC 2, UP 1(2-3)7, VC (1), WU 1-2; CoU does not have any copies, contrary to statement. Ford gives the following pagination: I (Sept. 1786-Dec. 1787), (8), 884, (6), 30 plates, 16 tables; II (Jan.-Dec. 1788), (2), IV, 750, (4), 25 plates, 12 tables; III (Jan.-Dec. 1789), (6), 784, (4), 25 plates, 12 tables; IV (Jan.-June 1790), (2), 390, (6), 5 plates; V (July-Dec. 1790), (2), 422, (10), 1 plate; VI (Jan.-June 1791), (2), 430, (10), 2 plates; VII (July-Dec. 1791), (2), 439 (9); VIII (Jan.-June 1792), 383, (I), 50, (6); IX (July-Dec. 1792), 432, (4). Some numbers passed through a second edition, requiring a resetting of the types.

29. *The New-Jersey Magazine, and Monthly Advertiser, Containing a Choice of Curious and Entertaining Pieces in Prose & Verses, with a Collection of the Most Recent Occurrences Received from Europe, the West-Indies & North America, & Several Advertisements.* New Brunswick. Printed and published by Frederick Quequelle and James Prange. Monthly, 8vo. Dec. 1786-Feb. 1787, pp. 1-72, 1-144. Listed: Beer, Evans, *Union List of Serials.* NYHS file is complete; LC has the first two numbers; NJHS and LCP have the issue for Dec. 1786, HSP the issue for Jan. 1787, and NYPL the issue for Feb. 1787. There are copies also at the New Brunswick Public Library and at Rutgers. The magazine was not printed in a uniform size of type, and some pages were set single column widths and others double column.

30. *The American Museum; or Repository of Ancient and Modern Fugitive Pieces &c. Prose and Poetical.* Jan. 1787-Dec. 1789, Vols. I-VI. Monthly, 8 vo. In Jan. 1790 the title became *The American Museum, or, Universal Magazine; Containing Essays on Agriculture—Commerce— Manufactures—Politics, Morals—and Manners. Sketches of National*

Characters—Natural and Civil History—and Biography. Law Information —Public Papers—Proceedings of Congress—Intelligence, Moral Tales— Ancient and Modern Poetry, &c. &c. This title remained until the close of 1792, Vols. VII-XII. Philadelphia. Mathew Carey was editor and publisher until the beginning of 1790, when the firm became Carey, Stewart, & Co. until Jan. 1792, at which time Carey again assumed full ownership. In 1798 Carey attempted to revive the magazine as an annual, *The American Museum: or, Annual Register of Fugitive Pieces, Ancient and Modern,* but only one number was published. Listed: Ford, Beer, Evans, *Union List of Serials.* Some of the earlier volumes passed into more than one edition; I have seen a third edition of some numbers of the first volume, and a second edition of some numbers of the second and third volumes. The files are widely distributed geographically, and complete files are to be found not uncommonly, among the libraries possessing them being BA, BPL, JCB, LC, MHS, NYPL, PU and YU. HSP lacks only Vol. I, Feb., March, July, Aug., Oct., Dec. 1787; NYSL has Vols. 2-6, 8-12. *The Union List of Serials* notes the following other libraries without qualification: AMNH, APS, BC, BroU, BrPL, CaSL, CPL, CoU, CU, DPL, EPFL, GrosB, HU, ISL, ISU, MSL, MU, NewPl, NL, NYStL, PrPL, StanU, StLPL, UCal, UI, UM, UND, UP, UW, UTS, VSL, WSHS, WU; and the following libraries are noted with qualifications: AAAS 2-6, CSL 1-9, CUA (4)-(6)-(9-11)-12, DC 1-10, FLN 1-(10), HCC 3-12, JHU 5-9, MiHS 1792, OC 1-8, 11-12, PeaI 1-8, 11-12, PFL 1-11, SyU 2, UMis 1-10, 12, UNeb 2, 5-7, 9, 12, TxU, 3, 5-8, 11, VC 1-9, 11-12. Vol. I (Jan.-June 1787), pp. XVI, 576; Vol. II (July-Dec. 1787), pp. 600 plus 22 pp. of chronicle and index; Vol. III (Jan.-June 1788), pp. 603; Vol. IV (July-Dec. 1788), pp. 592; Vol. V (Jan.-June 1789), pp. 628 plus two plates; Vol. VI (July-Dec. 1789), pp. 492, 46, 6; Vol. VII (Jan.-June 1790), pp. 344, 44, 44, 40 (misnumbered 44), 40, 4; Vol. VIII (July-Dec. 1790), pp. 288, 40, 80, 52; Vol. IX (Jan.-June 1791), pp. 344, 48, 40, 48; Vol. X (July-Dec. 1791), pp. 308, 36, 48, 44; Vol. XI (Jan.-June 1792), pp. 308, 36, 92, 48, 4; Vol. XII (July-Dec. 1792), pp. IV, 352, 36, 44, 40.

31. *The American Magazine, Containing a Miscellaneous Collection of Original and Other Valuable Essays, in Prose and Verse, and Calculated Both for Instruction and Amusement.* New York. Edited by Noah Webster; published by Samuel Loudon. Dec. 1787-Nov. 1788. Monthly, 8vo. Pp. 1-882 plus 4 plates. Listed: Ford, Beer, Evans, *Union List of Serials.* NYPL has two complete files, one being Webster's private file copiously annotated in his hand. LC has two complete files, and BA, BPL, JCB, NYHS, and YU, one complete file each. HU file lacks only pp. 229-34, 293-98; AAS file lacks Nov. 1788 and plate for June 1788; HSP has Jan., Oct., Nov., 1788. Other files listed: *Union List of Serials*—BC 1788, ISL, NL, NYStL, UM, WSHS, BHC (1787-88), CoU 4, OC 10, TxU 3, 5-6, 8-11. During the year at least four plates embellished the periodical; in Jan. and March respectively appeared an illustration of a new hoisting machine for clearing docks and a drawing of an Indian presenting Congress with gifts of beads, wampum, pipes, etc., both done by Maverick; in June

appeared Cornelius Tiebout's "Plan of the High Court" (British), and in August a map of the Western Territory, the last unsigned.

32. *The Children's Magazine; Calculated for the Use of Families and Schools.* Hartford. "Printed and Sold" by Barzillai Hudson and George Goodwin. Jan.-April 1789. Monthly, 12mo. Pp. 1-192. Listed: Beer, Evans (inaccurate as to date of termination), *Union List of Serials.* See also R. V. Halsey, *Forgotten Books of the American Nursery* (1911), pp. 101-02. BCL has issue for Jan., pp. IV, 5-48; JCB has issue for March, pp. 97-138, and the LC the issue for April, pp. 145-92. I have been unable to discover any issue for Feb. preserved.

33. *The Arminian Magazine: Consisting of Extracts and Original Treatises on General Redemption.* Philadelphia. Jan. 1789-Dec. 1790. Edited by Thomas Coke and Francis Asbury (the second volume by Asbury alone). Published by William Prichard and Peleg Hall, and sold by John Dickins. Monthly, 8vo. Pp. (Vol. I) 600, (Vol. II) 620 plus 4 of index. Listed: Ford, Beer, Evans, *Union List of Serials.* AAS, BA, BPL, HSP, NYHS, NYPL, and LC files are complete; WRHS has Vol. I complete. Other files listed: *Union List of Serials*—SyU, NYStL 1, PFL 2, StLP 1, TCH 2, UTS; Beer—YU (an error, possessing no copy).

34. *The Massachusetts Magazine: or, Monthly Museum of Knowledge and Rational Entertainment. Containing, Poetry, Musick, Biography, History, Physick, Geography, Morality, Criticism, Philosophy, Mathematicks, Agriculture, Architecture, Chymistry, Novels, Tales, Romances, Translations, News, Marriages, Deaths, Meteorological Observations, &c. &c.* Boston. Isaiah Thomas and Company, first publishers. Jan. 1789-Dec. 1796. Thomas and others edited the magazine at first, and until 1795 it is probable the publishers were the responsible editors. From 1795 to June 1796 Thaddeus M. Harris edited the magazine; he was succeeded in June by William Bigelow, who was editor until the close of the year. Eight Vols., 8vo., Monthly. Vols. I (Jan.-Dec. 1789) and II (Jan.-Dec. 1790) contain respectively 802 and 780 pages, with indices. Beginning with the issue for Sept. 1789 the imprint bore the names of Thomas and Ebenezer T. Andrews, and it remained so until Jan. 1794, when Ezra W. Weld, William Greenough, and Samuel Hill published the magazine, Weld dropping out at the end of 1794. The magazine was suspended during the first three months of 1795, but Greenough resumed it in April. Alexander Martin, Benjamin Sweetser, and James Cutler were respectively separate publishers for the periods Oct. 1795-June 1796, July-Oct. 1796, and Nov.-Dec. 1796. The title of Vol. II varies slightly from Vol. I in the secondary portion. Listed: Ford, Beer, Evans, *Union List of Serials.* AAS and LC files are complete. MHS lacks only a few scattered pages. NYHS lacks Dec. 1796 only; NYPL has 1789-93, March-June, Aug., Sept., Nov.-Dec. 1794, July and Dec. 1795, April-Aug., Oct. 1796; YU has only Feb. 1789, March, Aug.-Oct. 1790; JCB has 1789 complete, July-Dec. 1790, 1792-93 complete; BA and HU lack only Jan.-March 1795; BPL lacks Jan.-March 1795 and Jan.-March, Nov.-Dec. 1796. LCP has 1789-93 complete. Other files listed: *Union List of Serials*—AAAS 2, BC 1, 3, (4-7), BCL 1-(8), BHC (1-3, 6-8), BroU (8), ChU 1, CSL (1), DC 2,

5-7, FLN 6, GU 7, HSP fragments, ISHS 1-3, ISL 5-7, JHU (1), KSAC 3-4, MiHS (4-5), MSL 1 (2)-(4-6) 8, NL 1-2, 4-8, NYStL 1-6, OC (1-2, 4-6), TxU (1, 3-4)-(6), UM 1(2), WSHS 1-7.

35. *The Gentlemen and Ladies Town and Country Magazines: Consisting of Literature, History, Politics, Arts, Manners, and Amusements, with Various Other Matter.* Boston. Nathaniel Coverly, editor and publisher. Feb. 1789-Aug. 1790. Monthly, 8vo. During August and September 1789 William Hoyt was in partnership with Coverly. Vol. I, Feb. 1789-Jan. 1790, pp. 1-658; Vol. II, Feb.-Aug. 1790, pp. 1-384. Listed: Ford, Evans, Beer, Union List of Serials. AAS and BPL files are complete; LC has three sets from which a single complete file may nearly be obtained, the first volume lacking only pp. 1-9 and copperplate engravings for Feb. and March, and the second volume lacking No. 11 and some of the plates; MHS lacks Feb. 1789 and Feb.-Aug. 1790; NYPL has May 1789 and part of July 1790. Other files listed: *Union List of Serials*—BC (1790), WSHS (1-2).

36. *Courier de Boston, Affiches, Annonces, et Avis.* Published "A Boston, de l'Imprimerie de Samuel Hall"; edited by Joseph Nancrède. Nos. 1-26, pp. 1-208; April 23-Oct. 15, 1789. Weekly, eight pages, 4to. Priced at five pence a copy. Listed: Beer, Brigham, *Union List of Serials.* LC has two complete files, one annotated by hand; BA, BPL, HU, MHS, and NYHS files are complete also; AAS lacks only issues for Oct. 8 and Sept. 10. Other files listed: Brigham—Essex Institute; *Union List of Serials*—FLN, MSL, WSHS.

37. *The Christian's, Scholar's, and Farmer's Magazine; Calculated, in an Eminent Degree, to Promote Religion; to Disseminate Useful Knowledge; to Afford Literary Pleasure and Amusement, and to Advance the Interests of Agriculture.* "By a Number of Gentlemen." Published bimonthly, 8vo., at Elizabeth-Town, N. J., undated. Printed by Shepard Kollock, "one of the Proprietors" and probably, along with David Austin, an influential editor. Vol. I, April 1789-March 1790, pp. (10), 7-768 plus 7 pages of a table of contents; Vol. II, April 1790-March 1791, pp. 736 plus 6 of a table of contents and 2 pages of remarks "To Subscribers" and "To Correspondents." Listed: Ford, Beer, Evans, *Union List of Serials.* AAS, LC, NYPL, NYSL, and YU have complete files, LC possessing two copies of the first volume; NYHS lacks Feb.-March 1791; NJHS lacks the first sixty-four pages of No. 1, Vol. II; BA and PU have Vol. I complete, and BPL Vol. II complete. Other files listed: *Union List of Serials*—DC, ISL, NYStL, UNH, UTS, BCL 2, GTS 1, HU (2), WSHS 1.

It seems proper, in conclusion, to note two bibliographical errors which have misled some commentators. Ford (*op. cit.*) refers to *The Medical Examiner* of 1788; this is a confused reference to a magazine by the same title, described properly by Joseph Sabin (*A Dictionary of Books Relating to America,* Vol. XI, No. 47316) and others, which was begun at Philadelphia in 1838. Ford (*op. cit.*) and Smyth (*op. cit.*, pp. 73-74) refer to *The Philadelphia Magazine* of 1788-89; this is probably a confused reference on Ford's part to *The Philadelphia Magazine* published in 1788-89 in London by The Philadelphian Society. There were proposals issued in 1789 for *The Philadelphia Magazine, and Universal Asylum,* but the project seems to have been absorbed in the reorganization of the forces behind *The Columbian Magazine,* which became in 1790 *The Universal Asylum, and Columbian Magazine* (see Evans, *op. cit.,* Vol. VII, No. 22068). The original plan must have been fairly extensive, however, for I have noted an advertisement in a distant newspaper, *The Massachusetts Centinel,* for Jan. 16, 1790, p. 147, which stated that *The Philadelphia Magazine* "will be published, as soon as a number of subscribers, sufficient to defray the expense, shall be obtained;—and not on the first day of February, 1790, as was formerly proposed." Evidently the required number was never obtained.

INDEX

THE preface, introduction, and bibliography are not indexed. I have attempted to list all names of persons, and all initials, pseudonyms, and pseudonymous initials. Real names, when known, or residences, when given, are placed in parentheses following entries of initials and pseudonyms, which are entered under the first initial or name. I have tried also to list all titles fully quoted in the book, whether in text or notes, placing surnames of authors, when known, in parentheses. In quoting titles, initial articles have been omitted; the entry begins with the first word succeeding the article. Shortening of titles has been practised, but internal contractions have been indicated. (It should be noted that there are references in the notes to many articles described as to subject matter but not as to title.) Entries of more than one word are alphabetized without regard to separation between words. I have also incorporated a number of references by subject which may be of service to special investigators. The following entries are suggestive of the method: *Canada, Constitution, Currency, Education, Engravings, Federalism, Fiction, French, Germans, Manufactures, Music, Painters, Poetry, Revolutionary War, Science, Slavery.* An *n* following a number refers to a note; if the item is in both text and note on the same page, no *n* is used, since text usually refers to note. An asterisk denotes some doubtfulness in the assignment of a selection to an author, the explanation of which appears in text or note. It is a pleasure to express my appreciation to Mr. George F. Strong, Librarian, Adelbert College Library, Western Reserve University, for counsel graciously given.

377